MW01134891

THE ENGLISH
GENERAL EDITOR: CHRISTOPHER RICKS

Also available in this series

John Skelton

The Complete English Poems

EDITED BY JOHN SCATTERGOOD

NEW HAVEN AND LONDON
YALE UNIVERSITY PRESS

First published 1983 in the United Kingdom in a paperback edition
by Penguin Books Limited in the series Penguin English Poets.
First published 1983 in the United States of America by Yale University Press.

Introductory matter, notes and glossary copyright © 1983 by John Scattergood

Printed in Great Britain

Library of Congress Cataloging in Publication Data

Skelton, John, 1460?–1529.
    John Skelton, the complete English poems.

    (The English poets; 15)
    Bibliography: p.
    I. Scattergood, John, 1940– . II. Title.
III. Title: Complete English poems. IV. Series.
PR2346.S3 1983   821'.2   82–16075
ISBN 0–300–02970–5
ISBN 0–300–02971–3 (pbk.)

10 9 8 7 6 5 4 3 2 1

Contents

Introduction

No editor can be completely certain about what Skelton wrote. Only two of his works are extant in holograph versions – *A Lawde and Prayse Made for Our Sovereigne Lord the Kyng* from Public Record Office MS (TR) E. 36/288, and the dedicatory Latin verses in Corpus Christi College, Cambridge, MS 432 fols. 1v–3v.[1] And the list of Skelton's works given by Occupacyon in the *Garlande of Laurell*, lines 1170–476, creates almost as many problems as it solves. It is true that it helps to confirm Skelton's authorship of some pieces. But it is far from authoritative. It does not aspire to completeness; it seeks to give only 'sum parte of Skeltons bokes and baladis with ditis of plesure'. Moreover, because of its date of compilation, it can provide no evidence for anything written after 1523. Sometimes, as in lines 1188–90 on *Speke Parott*, the description of the poem is not very accurate. Sometimes a disproportionate amount of attention is given to what seem to us comparatively unimportant works and little or no attention to those which seem important: *Collyn Clout* and *Elynour Rummynge*, for example, are treated as 'trifels' (1235). Possibly the most useful part of Occupacyon's list is the information it provides about some thirty 'lost works'. A few items mentioned in it, such as the 'tratyse . . . callid *Speculum Principis*' (1228–9), which were unlocated by Skelton's early editors, have been traced. But its arbitrary incompleteness and the whimsical, playful tone of the list do not inspire confidence that this is a sober record of what Skelton actually wrote: it may, in part, be a parody of this sort of list of works, and some of the pieces which editors (including this one) refer to as 'lost works' may never have existed. In one way at least the list is demonstrably misleading: it refers to certain poems, now lost, by generic titles (such as 'Wofully Arraid' or 'Vexilla Regis') and poems on these subjects which have consequently been attributed to Skelton seem not to be his.

1. On Skelton's handwriting see particularly William Nelson, *John Skelton, Laureate*, 1939, Appendix V (pp. 245–6).

Each of Skelton's early editors contributed both to the establishment of the canon and to its confusion. Henry Tab (for whom Richard Lant printed *Certayne Bokes* in *c*.1545) collected *Ware the Hauke* and three nationalistic outbursts dating from 1513 against the Scots and the French, none of which appears in Occupacyon's list; but he also included several unauthentic poems on religious subjects as well as the elegy for Edward IV. John Stow (who is almost certainly the 'I.S.' for whom Thomas Marshe printed Skelton's *Workes* in 1568)[2] added to what Tab had assembled: among authentic items he included the Northumberland elegy, the lament for the city of Norwich, the eulogies for the tombs of Lady Margaret Beaufort and Henry VII, the mock epitaph for Bedel and *Against Venemous Tongues*, information about the last of which he may have obtained from John Bale's *Catalogus* (1557–9), which mentions it;[3] but Stow also included as Skelton's *The Boke of Three Fooles* which on examination proves to be three chapters of Henry Watson's translation (*c*.1508) of Brant's *Narrenschiff*. It is fairly clear that Skelton's reputation in the latter part of the sixteenth century as a witty and often scurrilous jester was sufficient to ensure that a number of unauthentic pieces were attributed to him: Angel Day, for example, in *The English Secretorie* (1586), preserves five lines expressed in an unfortunately over-elliptic way supposedly written by Skelton in support of the Prioress of Margate, whose mill stream had been dammed up by the Abbot of St Albans:

> Humbly complayneth to your high estate,
> The Lady Prioresse of Margate:
> For that the Abbot of S. Albones did stoppe
> With two stones and a stake her water gappe.
> Helpe, Lord, for God sake.[4]

Marshe's edition of 1568, which was reprinted in 1736 and 1810, became, with all its faults and omissions, the standard text of Skelton. But authentic works, not in Marshe, were coming to light: Bishop Thomas Tanner knew of the *Speculum Principis* in 1748;[5] James Nasmith mentioned the translation of Diodorus Siculus in 1777;[6] and Thomas War-

---

2. See William Ringler, *Studies in Bibliography*, VIII, 1956, 215–16.

3. *Scriptorum Illustrium Maioris Bryttanie Catalogus* . . . Basle 1557, 1559, pp. 651–2.

4. See J.G. McManaway, *Notes and Queries*, CXCVI, 1951, 134–5. 'Margate' must be Markyate, eight miles north-west of St Albans.

5. *Bibliotheca Britannico–Hibernica*, 1748, p. 676.

6. *Catalogus Librorum Manuscriptorum* . . . , 1777, p. 362 (Item CCLVII 1). He also knew and printed the dedicatory Latin verses to the *Chronique de Rains*, p. 400 (Item CCCCXXXII).

ton in the 1780s spoke of *Magnyfycence* and the Garnesche flytings, and claimed to have seen a play called the 'Nigramansir', now 'lost', in a 1504 print by de Worde.[7] Alexander Dyce's two-volume edition of 1843 used Marshe extensively, but augmented the canon with what had been more recently discovered, and added items he had himself located – most notably, the lyrics from *Dyvers Balettys and Dyties Solacyous* and the *Replycacion*. Dyce's, the first critical edition of the poems, became authoritative; in fact it has not yet been replaced. Yet it soon became clear that other authentic poems were extant of which Dyce had no knowledge: while his edition was being printed W.H. Black located the holograph version of *A Lawde and Prayse Made for Our Sovereigne Lord the Kyng*[8] and in 1882 John Ashton found a copy of *A Ballade of the Scottysshe Kynge*. It also emerged, principally through the researches of Friedrich Brie, that several pieces which Dyce had confidently ascribed to Skelton were, at best, of doubtful authenticity.[9] From time to time, other anonymous fifteenth- and sixteenth-century poems have been ascribed to Skelton, usually because they bear a resemblance to a 'lost' work in the *Garlande of Laurell*: the normally sceptical Brie, for example, in 1919 fancied he had identified one of the poems to 'Mistress Anne' and the 'Recule against Gaguyne', but these attributions have not been generally accepted.[10]

The twentieth century's more stringent demands in ascertaining authenticity have somewhat reduced the Skelton canon, which at the moment stands as established in 1967 by Robert Kinsman and Theodore Yonge.[11] It is not impossible that works at present 'lost' or unidentified may be discovered, or that works at present considered authentic may be rejected from the canon.[12] Recently, moreover, Nan C. Carpenter has raised the interesting possibility that Skelton may have occasionally collaborated: she considers a poem by William Cornish, which is included in Marshe's 1568 edition of Skelton, and speculates that 'the style of the poem varies greatly, and some lines sound remarkably like Skelton'.[13] Such a suspicion, however, falls short of proof, and, in the

7. *History of English Poetry*, II 360–63.

8. For an account of the finding of this item and a text see Alexander Dyce, *The Poetical Works of John Skelton*, 1843, I ix–xi.

9. *Englische Studien*, XXXVII, 1907, 1–86.

10. *Archiv*, XXXVIII, 1919, 226–8.

11. *John Skelton: Canon and Census*, Renaissance Society of America: Bibliographies and Indexes No. 4, 1967. I am much indebted to this work.

12. Of the items currently accepted as genuine perhaps the evidence in favour of No. XXII, *A Couplet on Wolsey's Dissolution of the Convocation at St Paul's*, is least secure.

13. *Comparative Literature*, XII, 1970, 157–72.

present edition, only those items considered authentic by Kinsman and Yonge have been accepted. Poems of doubtful authorship, even though once considered to be by Skelton, have not been included.[14]

The poems are arranged chronologically, in so far as it is possible to determine the chronology of Skelton's works. To some poems Skelton himself assigns a date either in conventional form or according to his private chronology, begun probably when he entered the Tudor royal service in October or November 1488; some may be precisely dated on internal evidence; but about some, for example the lyrical pieces collected as *Dyvers Balettys and Dyties Solacyous* and *Agaynste a Comely Coystrowne*, there is little or no evidence apart from style (though these poems are conventionally dated 'c.1495–1500'). Moreover, the chronology of those poems to which a date can with some confidence be assigned may be complicated by other factors. It is clear that Skelton revised and re-used material. Sometimes he re-used material quickly: *Agaynst the Scottes*, composed shortly after 22 September 1513, includes as lines 91–180 a revision of *A Ballade of the Scottysshe Kynge*, hastily composed and published less than a fortnight earlier. On the other hand, the *Garlande of Laurell*, issued as a whole on 3 October 1523 and given its final form shortly before this date, makes use of various lyrics written in the 1490s and of a defence of *Phyllyp Sparowe* written in 1509 or shortly afterwards. What is more, in his topical poems, Skelton follows the development of events: the envoys to *Speke Parott*, for example, seem to have been added separately, at intervals, as the political situation changed. So it is sometimes more appropriate to assign a date to parts of a poem than to the whole.

My aim has been to present an annotated critical text of all of Skelton's English poems. A brief descriptive list of his Latin poems, and references to editions of them, may be found in an Appendix. Since there is no edition of Skelton generally accepted as authoritative – Dyce's misses out some poems Skelton wrote and includes others he did not write; Kinsman's is designedly a selection – I have consulted again the original authorities, and have sought to establish the texts of Skelton's English poems afresh. The earliest text of a poem is usually chosen as the copy-text. If the copy-text is emended the original reading (except where it is a simple mis-spelling) is included in the Notes, where appears also a selection of the more interesting variant readings. Some Latin passages are badly garbled and require extensive emenda-

14. These are listed and discussed by Kinsman and Yonge, op. cit., pp. 16–32, as are Skelton's 'lost works' and those rejected from the canon as spurious.

tion; many passages require minor grammatical adjustments or spelling correction (which are usually not noted). The conventional abbreviations of scribes and printers are expanded without notice. The letters *i/j*, *u/v* have been given their modern values; þ is rendered as *th*, 3 (on the few occasions it occurs) as *gh* or *y*, initial *ff* as *F*. Punctuation and capitalization are editorial; so, in some cases, is the word-division, lineation, stanza-division and paragraphing. In addition to including textual variants, the Notes attempt to explain allusions, difficult passages, word-play and so on, in order to make a remote and often difficult author accessible to the modern reader. The Glossary is selective but, because of the difficulty of Skelton's vocabulary, fairly extensive: it intends to list those words which, in meaning or form, are likely to cause difficulty.

Acknowledgements

I should like to express my gratitude to the librarians and staff of the British Library London, the Bodleian Library Oxford, the University Library Cambridge, Bristol University Library, and the Library of Trinity College Dublin. Much of the work on this edition was done when I taught at Bristol University, and I am grateful to the Trustees of the Winston Churchill Birthday Foundation for various grants. My more personal debts are too numerous to mention fully. But I am particularly grateful to my former colleague Dr Basil Cottle who helped me enormously with Skelton's often intractable Latin; to Dr William G. Glassco who allowed me to make use of his doctoral thesis on Skelton's anti-Wolsey satires; to Ms Janet Wilson who generously made available some of her material on *Phyllyp Sparowe*; and to Professor Christopher Ricks who made valuable suggestions about the organization of the edition and on many scholarly points of detail. My main debts, however, are to those who have previously worked on Skelton, from the Rev. Alexander Dyce (whose magnificent two-volume edition of 1843 this book in some sense tries to replace) to scholars of the present day. I hope my indebtedness to these is sufficiently acknowledged in the notes.

Table of Dates

1460   Perhaps in this year John Skelton is born, probably of a northern, possibly a Yorkshire, family. He is associated with the county early in his career: in 1489 he addresses an affectionate Latin quatrain to Dr William Rukshaw, a distinguished ecclesiastic from York; in the same year he produces an elegy for Henry Percy, fourth Earl of Northumberland, murdered at Topcliffe, Yorkshire; he was perhaps a guest of the Howards at Sheriff Hutton Castle, Yorkshire, in 1495.

1480   On 18 March one 'Skelton', who may be the poet, is recorded as about to take his B.A. at Cambridge. If he was at Cambridge (as he claims to have been) Skelton may have been at Peterhouse, where Rukshaw was a fellow in the 1460s and bursar from 1469 to 1471. Since Skelton is not recorded as having received a B.A. from Cambridge it may be that he left there for Oxford.

1488   The title of 'laureate' (a sort of postgraduate 'degree' in rhetoric) is conferred on him by Oxford University perhaps in this year. At about this time he finishes translating *The Bibliotheca Historica of Diodorus Siculus* into English from Poggio's Latin version. In late October or early November he enters the royal service, and begins his private system of chronology.

1489   After 28 April he writes *Upon the Dolorus Dethe and Muche Lamentable Chaunce of the Mooste Honorable Erle of Northumberlande*.

?1490   In his Preface to *Eneydos* Caxton praises Skelton for his classical learning, his skill in translation and his 'polysshed and ornate termes': 'I suppose he hath dronken of Elycons well.'

1492   According to Robert Whittinton, the title of 'laureate' is conferred on Skelton by Louvain University.

1493   He receives the title of 'laureate' from Cambridge University.

1494   *Epigramma ad tanti principis maiestatem* is written to celebrate Prince Henry's being created Duke of York on 1 November.

1495   Probably at around this time Skelton is living chiefly in London or Westminster: he is recorded as having breakfasted and dined in Fleet Street on two occasions with John Syclyng, Master of Godshouse (now Christ's College), Cambridge. *Manerly Margery Mylk and Ale* and the lyrics in the two collections – *Agaynste a Comely Coystrowne* and *Divers Balettys and Dyties Solacyous* (published in about 1527) – are probably written at around this time. Skelton, in this year, perhaps visits Sheriff Hutton Castle, Yorkshire, and begins to assemble the *Garlande of Laurell*, incorporating some lyrics written earlier.

?1496–1501 During this period, while he is tutor to Prince Henry, Skelton writes several pedagogical works, now lost.

1498   Skelton enters Holy Orders: on 31 March he is ordained sub-deacon, on 14 April deacon, on 9 June priest. He is attached at this time to the Abbey of St Mary of Graces, a 'free chapel royal' near the Tower of London. He is recorded as having celebrated mass on 11 November before Henry VII, who made him an offering of 20 shillings. In the autumn of this year *The Bowge of Courte* is written, and published by de Worde in the following year.

1499   Erasmus praises Skelton as 'that light and glory of English letters'.

1501   Skelton probably lives in London or Westminster still, where he is recorded as having dined twice with John Syclyng again. Peter Ottey, a royal chaplain, makes a complaint against Skelton at the Court of Requests on 14 May. *Speculum Principis*, a book of advice, in ornate Latin prose, for Prince Henry is finished on 28 August.

1502   On 29 April 'the duc of Yorks scolemaster', who is perhaps to be identified with Skelton, receives 40 shillings from Henry VII. On 10 June Skelton is imprisoned as surety for William Guy, Prior of St Bartholomew's, delinquent in a debt.

?1503–12   During this period Skelton resides chiefly in Diss, Norfolk, where he is rector until his death. His first recorded action in Diss is the witnessing, on 10 April 1504, of the will of Margery Cowper, one of his parishioners.

1504–5   Cambridge University grants 'to John Skelton, the laureate poet, that he may stand in the same status here that he has at Oxford, and the right to wear the robe granted to him by the king'. Perhaps this cryptic record means that he was given another honorary degree.

?1505   *Ware the Hauke* and *Phyllyp Sparowe* are perhaps written in this year.

?1506   'Diligo rusticulum cum portat Dis duo quintum . . .' and *Epitaphe* are probably written. The text of the latter is copied out on 5 January 1507 by the parish priest of Trumpington, official copyist of Cambridge University.

1507   *Lamentatio Urbis Norwicen* is written at some time after 25 April, the date of the second disastrous fire in the city.

1509   *A Lawde and Prayse Made for Our Sovereigne Lord the Kyng* is written to celebrate the accession of Henry VIII on 24 June. A copy of *Speculum Principis* is presented to Henry VIII, possibly on 28 June for his birthday. A *palinodium* to it hints that Skelton would like to return to court. On 21 October he is named in the general Pardon Roll, where he is said to be 'late of Diss, Norfolk'. Perhaps he is living in London or Westminster at this time. But he does not stay there. On 3 December he is at the Norwich consistorial court involved in the interrogation of Thomas Pykerell of Diss 'for the welfare of his soul'. The case continues until 4 February 1510. In a 'Brefe addicion' to his *Shyp of Folys*, published in 1509, Alexander Barclay attacks *Phyllyp Sparowe* for its 'wantones'.

?1510   Skelton is mentioned in *The Great Chronicle of London*, with William Cornish and Thomas More as contemporary satiric 'poettes of . . . fame'.

1511   He is in Westminster again on 15 July when he dines with Prior William Mane, but in Norwich on 6 November when he is one of the arbitrators in a dispute between William Dale, rector of Redgrave, Suffolk, and Thomas Revet before the court of Bishop Richard Nykke.

1512   'I, liber, et propera . . .' is written as the dedication to a copy of *Chronique de Rains* presented to Henry VIII perhaps at New Year. *Calliope* and *Eulogium pro suorum temporum conditione* are written sometime after April. *Henrici Septimi . . . epitaphium* is written on 30 November at the suggestion of John Islip, Abbot of Westminster, to hang as a scroll over the tómb of the dead king. Four extra lines are added after September 1513. In this year or the next Skelton assumes the title 'Orator Regius'.

1513   Between 22 and 28 August the *Chorus de Dys contra Gallos* is written to celebrate the French surrender at Thérouanne. Shortly after 9 September but before 22 September Skelton writes *A Ballade of the Scottysshe Kynge*, which is hastily printed by Fakes, to celebrate the English victory at Flodden. From about 22 September comes the *Chorus de Dys contra Scottos*, and from shortly afterwards *Agaynst the Scottes*.

1514   *Agenst Garnesche* is probably written 'By the kynges most noble commandement' before 29 August. In his *Eclogues* Barclay again attacks Skelton as 'voyde of wisedom'.

1515–16   *Against Dundas*, *Against Venemous Tongues* and *Magnyfycence* are all perhaps written in this period. The *Elegia* for Lady Margaret Beaufort dates from 16 August 1516.

1517   Skelton perhaps writes *Elynour Rummynge* in this year; it is printed by de Worde or Pepwell probably in 1521.

1518   On 8 August Skelton is recorded as living within the sanctuary of Westminster in an apartment 'south of the great Belfry'. He writes a satiric *Epitaphium* on William Bedell, Lady Margaret Beaufort's former treasurer and receiver general.

1519   Skelton is involved, on the side of the traditionalists, in the so-called 'Grammarians' War'. William Lily, on whom he had apparently written an attack, describes him as 'neither learned nor a poet'. In a long Latin eulogy, Robert Whittinton, whose position Skelton supported, calls him 'the glory of English poets'.

1521–2   In this period he writes his major satirical attacks on Cardinal Wolsey: *Speke Parott* (Autumn 1521), *Collyn Clout* (late 1521 and early 1522), *Why Come Ye Nat to Courte?* (November 1522).

1523   *A Couplet on Wolsey's Dissolution of the Convocation at St Paul's* is written sometime after late April. The *Garlande of Laurell* is completed, and published on 3 October by Fakes. Shortly after 2–3 November Skelton writes, at the suggestion of Wolsey, to whom he was now reconciled, *Howe the Douty Duke of Albany* to celebrate John Stewart's retreat from the siege of Wark Castle.

1528   On 4 May Skelton is present as a witness at the abjuration of Thomas Bowgas, a fuller of Colchester, accused of heresy at Norwich Inn near Charing Cross, Bishop Nykke's London residence. Skelton probably writes the *Replycacion*, against the Cambridge heretics Thomas Arthur and Thomas Bilney, in this year; it was published almost immediately by Pynson.

1529   On 21 June Skelton dies, and is buried before the high altar in St Margaret's Westminster.

Further Reading

COMPLETE EDITIONS

Dyce, Rev. Alexander, ed., *The Poetical Works of John Skelton*, 2 vols., London: Thomas Rodd 1843, with addenda 1844, reprinted 1965.

Henderson, Philip, ed., *The Complete Poems of John Skelton, Laureate*, London: Dent 1931, 4th edition 1964 (with modernized spelling).

SELECTIONS

Gant, Roland, ed., *Skelton: Poems*, London: Grey Walls Press 1949.

Graves, Robert, ed., *John Skelton, Laureate*, The Augustan Books of English Poetry, Ser. 2 No. 12, London: Benn 1925, reprinted 1970.

Hughes, Richard, ed., *Poems by John Skelton*, London: Heinemann 1924.

Kinsman, Robert S., ed., *John Skelton: Poems*, Oxford: Clarendon Press 1969.

Pinto, Vivian de Sola, ed., *John Skelton: A Selection from his Poems*, London: Sidgwick and Jackson 1950.

Williams, W.H., ed., *A Selection from the Poetical Works of John Skelton*, London: Isbister 1902.

EDITIONS OF SINGLE WORKS

Ashton, John, ed., *The Earliest Known Printed English Ballad: A Ballade of the Scottysshe Kynge*, London: Elliot Stock 1882.

Hammond, Eleanor P., ed., *English Verse Between Chaucer and Surrey*, Durham, North Carolina 1927 (includes the *Garland of Laurel*).

Happé, Peter, ed., *Four Morality Plays*, London: Penguin Books 1979 (includes *Magnyfycence*).

Neuss, Paula, ed., *Magnificence*, Manchester University Press 1980.

Ramsay, R.L., ed., *Magnyfycence*, Early English Text Society, Extra Series XCVIII, 1908, reprinted 1958.

Salter, F.M., ed., 'Skelton's *Speculum Principis*', *Speculum*, IX, 1934, 25–37.

Salter, F.M., and Edwards, H.L.R., eds., *The Bibliotheca Historica of Diodorus Siculus translated by John Skelton*, Early English Text Society, Original Series 233, 239, 1956–7, reprinted 1968, 1971.

BIBLIOGRAPHIES

Fishman, Burton, 'Recent Studies in Skelton', *English Literary Renaissance*, I, 1971, 89–96.

Howarth, R.G., 'Scholarship and Skelton', *Southerly*, VI, 1945, 46–50.

Kinsman, Robert S., and Yonge, Theodore, *John Skelton: Canon and Census*, Renaissance Society of America, Bibliographies and Indexes No. 4, 1967.

Yonge, Theodore, 'John Skelton', in *The New Cambridge Bibliography of English Literature*, ed. George Watson, Vol. I, Cambridge University Press 1974, cols. 1015–19.

STUDIES

Atchity, K.J., 'Skelton's *Collyn Clout*: Visions of Perfectibility', *Philological Quarterly*, LII, 1973, 715–27.

Auden, W.H., 'John Skelton', in *The Great Tudors*, ed. Katherine Garvin, London: Nicholson and Watson 1935.

Berdan, J.M., *Early Tudor Poetry*, New York: Macmillan 1920.

Blunden, Edmund, *Votive Tablets*, London: Cobden Sanderson 1932 (the essay on Skelton first appeared in *The Times Literary Supplement*, 20 June 1929).

Browning, Elizabeth Barrett, *The Greek Christian Poets and the English Poets*, London: Chapman and Hall 1863 (a collection of essays first published in the *Athenaeum* in 1842).

Brownlow, F.W., '*Speke Parrot*: Skelton's Allegorical Denunciation of Cardinal Wolsey', *Studies in Philology*, LXV, 1968, 124–39.

Brownlow, F.W., 'The book compiled by Maister Skelton, Poet Laureate, called *Speake, Parrot*', *English Literary Renaissance*, I, 1971, 3–26.

Brownlow, F.W., '*The book of Phyllyp Sparowe* and the Liturgy,' *English Literary Renaissance*, IX, 1979, 5–20.

Carpenter, Nan C., *John Skelton*, New York: Twayne 1968.

Carpenter, Nan C., 'Skelton's Hand in William Cornish's Musical Parable', *Comparative Literature*, XXII, 1970, 157–72.

Chalker, John, 'The Literary Seriousness of Skelton's *Speke Parrot*', *Neophilologus*, XLIV, 1960, 39–47.

Cook, A.S., 'Skelton's *Garland of Laurel* and Chaucer's *House of Fame*', *Modern Language Review*, XI, 1916, 9–14.

Edwards, H.L.R., 'Skelton: A Genealogical Study', *Review of English Studies*, XI, 1934, 406–20.

Edwards, H.L.R., *Skelton: The Life and Times of an Early Tudor Poet*, London: Cape 1949.

Edwards, H.L.R., and Nelson, William, 'The Dating of Skelton's Later Poems', *Publications of the Modern Language Association of America*, LIII, 1938, 601–22.

Fish, Stanley Eugene, *John Skelton's Poetry*, New Haven and London: Yale University Press 1965.

Forster, E.M., *Two Cheers for Democracy*, London: Arnold 1951, 135–53.

Gingerich, Owen, and Tucker, Melvin J., 'The Astronomical Dating of Skelton's *Garland of Laurel*', *Huntington Library Quarterly*, XXII, 1969, 207–20.

Gordon, Ian A., 'Skelton's *Philip Sparrow* and the Roman Service Book', *Modern Language Review*, XXIX, 1934, 389–96.

Gordon, Ian A., *John Skelton, Poet Laureate*, Melbourne University Press 1943.

Graves, Robert, *Oxford Addresses on Poetry*, London: Cassell 1962 (the essay on Skelton first appeared in *Encounter*, XVII, December 1961, 11–18).

Green, Peter, *John Skelton*, London: Longmans, Green 1960.

Harris, W.O., *Skelton's Magnyfycence and the Cardinal Virtue Tradition*, Chapel Hill: University of North Carolina Press 1965.

Heiserman, A.R., *Skelton and Satire*, Chicago: University of Chicago Press 1961

Holloway, John, *The Charted Mirror: Literary and Critical Essays*, London: Routledge and Kegan Paul 1960 (the essay on Skelton first appeared in *Proceedings of the British Academy*, XLIV, 1959, 83–102).

King, Bruce, 'Skelton's *Phyllyp Sparowe*', *Revue des Langues Vivantes*, XLIV, 1978, 151–63.

Kinsman, Robert S., 'Skelton's *Colyn Cloute*: the Mask of Vox Populi', in *Essays Critical and Historical Dedicated to Lily B. Campbell*, Berkeley: University of California Publications 1950, 17–26.

Kinsman, Robert S., 'The "Buck" and the "Fox" in Skelton's *Why Come Ye Nat to Courte?*', *Philological Quarterly*, XXIX, 1950, 61–4.

Kinsman, Robert S., 'Skelton's "Upponn a deedman's hed": New Light on the Origin of the Skeltonic', *Studies in Philology*, L, 1953, 101–9.

Kinsman, Robert S., 'The Voices of Dissonance: Pattern in Skelton's *Colyn Cloute*', *Huntington Library Quarterly*, XXVI, 1963, 291–313.

Kinsman, Robert S., 'Skelton's *Magnyfycence*: The Strategy of the "Olde Sayde Sawe"', *Studies in Philology*, LXIII, 1966, 99–125.

Larson, Judith S., 'What is the *Bouge of Courte?*', *Journal of English and Germanic Philology*, LXI, 1962, 288–95.

Lloyd, L.J., *John Skelton: A Sketch of his Life and Writings*, Oxford: Blackwell 1938.

Nelson, William, *John Skelton, Laureate*, Columbia University Studies in English and Comparative Literature No. 139, 1939.

Norton-Smith, John, 'On the Origins of Skeltonics', *Essays in Criticism*, XXIII, 1973, 57–72.

Phillips, Norma, 'Observations on the Derivative Method of Skelton's Realism', *Journal of English and Germanic Philology*, LXV, 1966, 19–35.

Pollet, Maurice, *John Skelton: Contribution à l'Histoire de la Prérenaissance Anglaise*, Paris: Libraire Didier 1962. (English translation by John Warrington, London: Dent 1971.)

Pyle, F., 'The Origins of the Skeltonic', *Notes and Queries*, CLXXI, 1936, 362–4.

Sale, Helen Stearns, 'John Skelton and Christopher Garnesche', *Modern Language Notes*, XLIII, 1928, 518–23.

Sale, Helen Stearns, 'The Date of Skelton's *Bowge of Court*', *Modern Language Notes*, LII, 1937, 572–4.

Salter, F.M., 'Skelton's Contribution to the English Language', *Transactions of the Royal Society of Canada*, XXXIX, Section 2, 1946, 119–217.

Schulte, Edvige, *La Poesia di John Skelton*, Naples 1963.

Skelton, Robin, 'The Master Poet: John Skelton as Conscious Craftsman', *Mosaic*, VI, 1973, 67–92.

Southern, Richard, *The Staging of Plays before Shakespeare*, 1973.

Spearing, A.C., *Medieval Dream Poetry*, Cambridge University Press 1976, especially Chapter 4.

Spina, Elaine, 'Skeltonic Meter in *Elynour Rummyng*', *Studies in Philology*, LXIV, 1967, 665–84.

Swallow, Alan, 'The Pentameter Lines in Skelton and Wyatt', *Modern Philology*, XLVIII, 1951, 1–11.

Swallow, Alan, 'John Skelton: The Structure of the Poem', *Philological Quarterly*, XXXII, 1953, 29–42.

Swart, J., 'Skelton's *Philip Sparrow*', *English Studies*, XLV, 1964, 161–4.

Tillemans, Thomas, 'John Skelton, a Conservative', *English Studies*, XXVII, 1946, 141–9.

Tucker, Melvin J., 'Skelton and Sheriff Hutton', *English Language Notes*, IV, 1967, 254–9.

Tucker, Melvin J., 'The Ladies in Skelton's *Garland of Laurel*', *Renaissance Quarterly*, XXII, 1969, 333–45.

Tucker, Melvin J., 'Setting in Skelton's *Bowge of Courte*: A Speculation', *English Language Notes*, VII, 1970, 168–75.

West, Michael, 'Skelton and the Renaissance Theme of Folly', *Philological Quarterly*, L, 1971, 23–35.

Winser, Leigh, 'Skelton's *Magnyfycence*', *Renaissance Quarterly*, XXIII, 1970, 14–25.

Winser, Leigh, '*The Bowge of Courte*: Drama Doubling as Dream', *English Literary Renaissance*, VI, 1976, 3–39.

The Poems

I

Poeta Skelton Laureatus Libéllum Suum Metrice Alloquitur

Ad dominum properato meum, mea pagina, Percy,
Qui Northumbrorum iura paterna gerit;
Ad nutum celebris tu prona repone leonis
Queque suo patri tristia iusta cano.
5   *Ast ubi perlegit, dubiam sub mente volutet*
Fortunam, cuncta que malefida rotat.
Qui leo sit felix, et Nestoris occupet annos;
Ad libitum cuius ipse paratus ero.

Skelton Laureat Upon the Dolorus Dethe and Muche Lamentable Chaunce of the Mooste Honorable Erle of Northumberlande

I wayle, I wepe, I sobbe, I sigh ful sore
The dedely fate, the dolefulle destenny
Of hym that is gone, alas, withoute restore,
Of the blode royall descendinge nobelly;
5   Whos lordshepe doutles was slayne lamentably
Thorow treson, ageyn hym compassyd and wrought,
Trew to his prince in word, in dede, and thought.

Of hevenly poems, O Clyo, calde by name
In the college of musis goddes hystoriall,
10   Adres the to me, whiche am bothe halt and lame,
In elect uteraunce to make memoryall!
To the for succour, to the for helpe I kall,
Myne homely rudnes and drighnes to expelle
With the freshe waters of Elyconys welle.

15   Of noble actis auncyently enrolde
Of famous princis and lordis of astate,
By thy report ar wonte to be extolde
Regestringe trewly every formare date;
Of thy bounte after the usuall rate
20   Kyndle in me suche plente of thy nobles,
Thes sorowfulle ditis that I may shew expres.

In sesons past who hathe harde or sene
Of formar writinge by any presidente
That vilane hastarddis in ther furious tene,
25   Fulfyld with malice of froward entente,
Confeterd togeder of commoun concente
Falsly to slo ther moste singlar goode lorde?
It may be regesterde of shamefull recorde.

So noble a man, so valiaunt lorde and knyght
30   Fulfilled with honour, as all the world dothe ken,
At his commaundement whiche had both day and night
Knyghtis and squyers, at every season when
He calde upon them, as menyall houshold men:
Were not thes commones uncurteis karlis of kynd
35   To slo ther owne lorde? God was not in ther mynde!

And were not thei to blame, I say also,
That were aboute hym, his awne servauntis of trust,
To suffre hym slayn of his mortall fo?
Fled away from hym, let hym ly in the dust,
40   They bode not till the rekenyng were discust.
What, shuld I flatter? What, shulde I glose or paynt?
Fy, fy, for shame, ther hartis wer to faynt.

In Englande and Fraunce which gretly was redouted,
Of whom both Flaunders and Scotland stode in drede,
45   To whome grete astatis obeyde and lowttede,
A maynny of rude villayns made hym for to blede.
Unkindly thei slew hym that help them oft at nede.
He was ther bulwarke, ther paves and ther wall,
Yet shamfully thei slew hym; that sham most them befall.

50   I say, ye commoners, why wer ye so stark mad?
What frantyk frensy fyll in youre brayne?
Where was your wit and reson ye shuld have had?
What willfull foly made you to ryse agayn
Your naturall lord? Alas, I kan not fayne.
55   Ye armed you with wille and left your wit behynd;
Well may ye be cald commons most unkynd.

He was your chyfteyne, your shelde, your chef defens,
Redy to assyst you in every tyme of nede;

Your worship depended of his excellence.
60   Alas, ye madmen, to far ye did excede.
Your hap was unhappy, to ill was your spede.
What movyd you agayn hym to war or to fight?
What aylde you to slo your lord ageyn all right?

The grounde of his quarell was for his sovereyn lord,
65   The welle concernyng of all the hole lande,
Demaundinge soche dutes as nedis most acord
To the right of his prince which shold not be withstand;
For whos causis ye slew hym with your awne hande.
But had his nobillmen donn wel that day
70   Ye had not ben hable to have saide hym nay.

Bot ther was fals packinge or els I am begylde,
Howbeit the mater was evident and playne;
For yf they had occupied ther spere and ther shelde
This noble man doutles had not be slayne.
75   Bot men say thei wer lynked with a double chayn
And held with the commonns under a cloke,
Whiche kyndelde the wyld fyre that made all this smoke.

The commonns renyyd ther taxes to pay
Of them demaunded and asked by the kynge;
80   With one vice importune thei playnly said nay.
They buskt them on a bushment them selfe in baile to bringe
Agayne the kingis plesure to wrastel or to wringe.
Bluntly as bestis withe boste and with cry
They saide they forsede not nor carede not to dy.

85   The nobelnes of the northe, this valyant lorde and knyght,
As man that was innocent of trechery or trayne,
Presed forthe boldly to witstand the myght,
And lyke marciall Hector he faught them agayne
Vigorously upon them with myght and with mayne,
90   Trustinge in noble men that wer with hym there;
Bot all they fled from hym for falshode or fere.

Barons, knightis, squyers, one and alle,
Togeder with servauntis of his famuly,
Turnd ther backis and let ther master fall,
95   Of whos life they countede not a fly.

Take up whos wolde, for ther they let hym ly.
Alas his golde, his fee, his annuall rente,
Upon suche a sort was ille bestowde and spent.

He was envyronde aboute on every syde
100 Withe his enmys that were stark mad and wode;
Yet whils he stode he gave them woundes wyde.
Alas for routhe, what thouthe his mynde wer goode,
His corage manly, yet ther he shed his bloode.
All left alone, alas, he fawte in vayne!
105 For cruelly amonge them ther he was slayne.

Alas for pite that Percy thus was spylt,
The famous Erle of Northumberlande;
Of knightly prowes the sworde, pomel, and hilt,
The myghty lyoun doutted by se and sande.
110 O dolorous chaunce of Fortuns fraward hande!
What man, remembring how shamfully he was slayn,
From bitter wepinge hym self kan restrayne?

O cruell Mars, thou dedly god of war!
O dolorous Teusday, dedicate to thi name,
115 When thou shoke thi sword so noble a man to mar!
O grounde ungracious, unhappy be thy fame,
Whiche wert endiyd with rede blode of the same
Mooste noble Erle! O fowle mysuryd grounde,
Wheron he gat his fynall dedely wounde.

120 O Atropos, of the fatall systers iij,
Goddes mooste cruell unto the lyfe of man,
All merciles in the ys no pite!
O homycide, whiche sleest all that thou kan,
So forcibly upon this Erle thow ran,
125 That with thy sworde enharpid of mortall drede
Thow kit asonder his perfight vitall threde.

Mi wordis unpullysht be nakide and playne,
Of aureat poems they want ellumynynge;
Bot by them to knoulege ye may attayne
130 Of this lordis dethe and of his murdrynge;
Whiche whils he lyvyd had fuyson of every thing,

Of knightis, of squyers, chef lord of toure and toune,
Tyll fykkill Fortune began on hym to frowne.

Paregall to dukis, withe kingis he myght compare,
135   Sourmountinge in honour all erlis he did excede;
To all cuntreis aboute hym reporte me I dare:
Lyke to Eneas benygne in worde and dede,
Valiant as Hector in every marciall nede,
Provydent, discrete, circumspect and wyse,
140   Till the chaunce ran ageyne hym of Fortuns double dyse.

What nedethe me for to extoll his fame
With my rude pen enkankerd all with rust,
Whos noble actis shew worsheply his name,
Transcending far myne homely Muse that must
145   Yet sumwhat wright supprisid with hartly lust,
Truly reportinge his right noble astate,
Immortally whiche is inmaculate?

His noble blode never desteynyd was,
Trew to his prince for to defende his right,
150   Doublenes hatinge fals maters to compas,
Treytory and treson he bannesht ought of sight.
With trowth to medelle was all his hole delight,
As all his kuntrey kan testefy the same:
To slo suche a lord, alas, it was grete shame.

155   If the hole quere of the Musis nyne
In me all onely wer sett and comprisyde,
Enbrethed with the blast of influence dyvyne,
As perfightly as koude be thought or devysyd;
To me also all thouthe yt wer promysyde
160   Of laureat Phebus holy the eloquence
All were to litill for his magnyficence.

O yonge lyon, bot tender yet of age,
Grow and encrese, remembre thyn astate!
God the assyst unto thyne heritage,
165   And geve the grace to be more fortunate!
Agayne rebellyonns arme the to make debate;
And as the lyonne whiche is of bestis kinge
Unto thy subjectis be kurteis and beningne.

I pray God sende the prosperous lyf and long,
170 Stabille thy mynde constant to be and fast,
Right to maynten and to resist all wronge.
All flatringe faytors abhor and from the kast.
Of foule detraccion God kepe the from the blast.
Let double delinge in the have no place,
175 And be not light of credence in no case.

Wythe hevy chere, with dolorous hart and mynd,
Eche man may sorow in his inward thought
This lordis dethe, whos pere is hard to fynd,
All gyf Englond and Fraunce wer thorow sought.
180 All kingis, all princis, all dukis, well thei ought
Bothe temporall and spirituall for to complayne
This noble man that cruelly was slayne.

More specially barons, and thos knightis bold,
And all other gentelmen with hym enterteynd
185 In fee, as menyall men of his houshold,
Whom he as lorde worsheply manteynd,
To soroufull weping thei ought to be constreynd,
As oft as thei call to ther remembrance
Of ther good lord the fate and dedely chaunce.

190 O pereles Prince of hevyn emperyalle
That with one worde formd all thing of nought;
Hevyn, hell and erth obey unto thi kall;
Which to thi resemblance wonderusly has wrought
All mankynd, whom thou ful dere hast boght,
195 With thi blode precious our fenaunce thou dyd pay
And us redemede from the fendys pray.

To the pray we as Prince incomperable,
As thou art of mercy and pite the well,
Thow bringe unto thy joye etermynable
200 The sowle of this lorde from all daunger of hell,
In endles blis with the to byde and dwell
In thy palace above the orient,
Where thow art Lord and God omnipotent.

O Quene of mercy, O lady full of grace,
205 Maiden moste pure, and Goddis moder dere,
To sorowfull harttis chef comfort and solace,

Of all women O floure withouten pere,
Pray to thy son above the starris clere,
He to vouchesaf, by thy mediacioun,
210 To pardon thi servant and brynge to savacioun.

In joy triumphaunt the hevenly yerarchy,
With all the hole sorte of that glorious place,
His soule mot receyve in to ther company,
Thorow bounte of hym that formed all solace,
215 Well of pite, of mercy, and of grace,
The Father, the Son, the Holy Goste,
In Trinitate one God of myghtis moste.

Non sapit humanis qui certam ponere rebus
Spem cupit: est hominum raraque ficta fides.

Tetrasticon Skelton Laureati ad magistrum Rukshaw sacre
theologie egregium professorem

Accipe nunc demum, doctor celeberrime Rukshaw,
Carmina, de calamo que cecidere meo;
Et quamquam placidis non sunt modulata camenis,
Sunt tamen ex nostro pectore prompta pio.

Vale feliciter, virorum laudatissime.

II

Manerly Margery Mylk and Ale

Ay, beshrewe yow! Be my fay
This wanton clarkis be nyse allway.
Avent, avent, my popagay!
'What, will ye do nothyng but play?'
5   Tully, valy, strawe, let be I say!
     Gup, Cristian Clowte, gup, Jak of the Vale,
     With manerly Margery Mylk and Ale.

'Be Gad, ye be a praty pode,
And I love you an hole cart lode.'
10   Strawe, Jamys foder, ye play the fode;
     I am no hakney for your rode;
     Go watch a bole, your bak is brode.

Gup, Cristian Clowte, gup, Jak of the Vale,
With manerly Margery Mylk and Ale.

15 Iwiss, ye dele uncurtesly;
What, wolde ye frompill me now? Fy, fy!
'What, and ye shal be my piggesnye?'
Be Crist, ye shall not! No, no, hardely!
I will not be japed bodely.

20   Gup, Cristian Clowte, gup, Jak of the Vale,
With manerly Margery Mylk and Ale.

'Walke forth your way, ye cost me nought;
Now have I fownd that I have sought,
The best chepe flessh that evyr I bought.'

25 Yet, for his love that all hath wrought,
Wed me or els I dye for thought!
    Gup, Cristian Clowte, your breth is stale,
    With manerly Margery Milk and Ale.
    Gup, Cristian Clowte, gup, Jak of the Vale,

30   With manerly Margery Mylk and Ale.

III

Skelton Laureat

Agaynste a Comely Coystrowne

that curyowsly chawntyd, and curryshly cowntred, and madly
in hys musykkys mokkyshly made agaynste the ix Musys of
polytyke poems and poettys matryculat.

(i)
Of all nacyons under the hevyn,
These frantyke foolys I hate most of all;
For though they stumble in the synnys sevyn,
In pevyshnes yet they snapper and fall,

5 Which men the viii dedly syn call.
This pevysh proud, thys prendergest,
When he is well, yet can he not rest.

A swete suger lofe and sowre bayardys bun
Be sumdele lyke in forme and shap,

10   The one for a duke, the other for dun,
     A maunchet for morell thereon to snap.
     Hys hart is to hy to have any hap;
     But for in his gamut carp that he can,
     Lo, Jak wold be a jentyl man!

15   Wyth, 'Hey, troly-loly-lo, whip here, Jak',
     Alumbek sodyldym syllorym ben!
     Curyowsly he can both counter and knak
     Of Martyn Swart and all hys mery men.
     Lord, how Perkyn is proud of hys Pohen!
20   To ask wher he fyndyth among hys monacordys
     An holy water clarke a ruler of lordys.

     He can not fynd it in rule nor in space:
     He solfyth to haute, hys trybyll is to hy;
     He braggyth of hys byrth, that borne was full bace;
25   Hys musyk withoute mesure, to sharp is hys *my*;
     He trymmyth in hys tenor to counter pyrdewy;
     Hys dyscant is besy, it is withoute a mene;
     To fat is hys fantsy, hys wyt is to lene.

     He lumbryth on a lewde lewte, 'Roty bully joyse',
30   'Rumbyll downe, tumbyll downe, hey, go, now, now!'
     He fumblyth in hys fyngeryng an ugly good noyse;
     It semyth the sobbyng of an old sow!
     He wold be made moch of and he wyst how;
     Wele sped in spyndels and turnyng of tavellys,
35   A bungler, a brawler, a pyker of quarellys!

     Comely he clappyth a payre of clavycordys;
     He whystelyth so swetely he makyth me to swete;
     His descant is dasshed full of dyscordes;
     A red angry man, but easy to intrete.
40   An ussher of the hall fayn wold I get
     To poynte this proude page a place and a rome,
     For Jak wold be a jentylman, that late was a grome.

     Jak wold jet and yet Jyll sayd nay;
     He counteth in his countenaunce to checke with the best:
45   A malaperte medler that pryeth for his pray,
     In a dysh dare he rush at the rypest;
     Dremyng in dumpys to wrangyll and to wrest,

He fyndeth a proporcyon in his prycke songe
To drynk at a draught a larg and a long.

50   Nay, jape not with hym, he is no small fole;
It is a solempne syre and a solayne,
For lordes and ladyes lerne at his scole;
He techyth them so wysely to solf and to fayne
That neyther they synge wel prycke song nor playne.

55   Thys Doctor Deuyas commensyd in a cart;
A master, a mynstrell, a fydler, a farte.

What though ye can cownter *Custodi nos?*
As well it becomyth yow, a parysh towne clarke,
To syng *Sospitati dedit egros.*

60   Yet bere ye not to bold to braule ne to bark
At me, that medeled nothyng with youre wark.
Correct fyrst thy self; walk, and be nought!
Deme what thou lyst, thou knowyst not my thought.

A proverbe of old, 'Say well or be styll':

65   Ye are to unhappy occasyons to fynde
Uppon me to clater or else to say yll.
Now have I shewyd you part of your proud mynde;
Take thys in worth, the best is behynde.
Wryten at Croydon by Crowland in the Clay,

70   On Candelmas evyn, the kalendas of May.

Finis

(ii)

CONTRA ALIUM CANTITANTEM ET ORGANISANTEM ASINUM,
QUI IMPUGNABAT SKELTONIDA PIERIUM, SARCASMOS
Preponenda meis non sunt tua plectra camenis,
Nec quantum nostra fistula clara tua est:
Sepe licet lyricos modularis arundine psalmos,
Et tremulos calamis concinis ipse modos;

5   *Quamvis mille tuus digitus dat carmine plausus,*
Nam tua quam tua vox est mage docta manus;
Quamvis cuncta facis tumida sub mente superbus,
Gratior est Phebo fistula nostra tamen.
Ergo tuum studeas animo deponere fastum,
Et violare sacrum desine, stulte, virum.

Quod Skelton, laureat.

(iii)

Skelton Laureat, uppon a deedmans hed, that was sent to
hym from an honorable Jentyllwoman for a token, Devysyd
this gostly medytacyon in Englysh: Covenable in sentence,
Comendable, Lamentable, Lacrymable, Profytable for the
soule.

Youre ugly tokyn
My mynd hath brokyn
From worldly lust;
For I have dyscust
5   We ar but dust,
And dy we must.
    It is generall
To be mortall:
I have well espyde
10   No man may hym hyde
From deth holow-eyed,
With synnews wyderyd,
With bonys shyderyd,
With hys worme-etyn maw
15   And hys gastly jaw
Gaspyng asyde,
Nakyd of hyde,
Neyther flesh nor fell.
    Then by my councell,
20   Loke that ye spell
Well thys gospell;
For wherso we dwell,
Deth wyll us quell
And with us mell.
25   For all oure pamperde paunchys,
There may no fraunchys
Nor worldly blys
Redeme us from this.
Oure days be datyd
30   To be chekmatyd,
With drawttys of deth
Stoppyng oure breth;
Oure eyen synkyng,
Oure bodys stynkyng,

35   Oure gummys grynnyng,
       Oure soulys brynnyng!
       To whom then shall we sew
       For to have rescew,
       But to swete Jesu
40   On us then for to rew?
          O goodly chyld
       Of Mary mylde,
       Then be oure shylde!
       That we be not exylyd
45   To the dyne dale
       Of boteles bale,
       Nor to the lake
       Of fendys blake.
          But graunt us grace
50   To se thy face,
       And to purchace
       Thyne hevenly place
       And thy palace,
       Full of solace,
55   Above the sky
       That is so hy,
       Eternally
       To beholde and se
       The Trynyte!
              Amen.
       Myrres vous y.

(iv)
Womanhod, wanton, ye want!
Youre medelyng, mastres, is manerles;
Plente of yll, of goodnes skant,
Ye rayll at ryot, recheles.
5   To prayse your porte it is nedeles;
    For all your 'Draffe' yet and your 'Dreggys',
    As well borne as ye full oft tyme beggys.

Why so koy and full of skorne?
'Myne horse is sold, I wene', you say;
10   'My new furryd gowne, when it is worne –
    Put up your purs, ye shall non pay!'

By Crede, I trust to se the day,
As proud a pohen as ye sprede,
Of me and other ye may have nede.

15   Though angelyk be youre smylyng,
Yet is youre tong an adders tayle,
Full lyke a scorpyon styngyng
All those by whom ye have avayle.
Good mastres Anne, there ye do shayle!
20   What prate ye, praty pyggys-ny?
I truste to quyte you or I dy!

Youre key is mete for every lok,
Youre key is commen and hangyth owte;
Youre key is redy, we nede not knok
25   Nor stand long wrestyng there aboute;
Of youre doregate ye have no doute.
But one thyng is: that ye be lewde!
Holde youre tong, now, all beshrewde!

To mastres Anne, that farly swete,
30   That wonnes at the Key in Temmys Strete.

IV

Here folowythe

Dyvers Balettys and Dyties Solacyous

devysyd by Master Skelton Laureat

(i)
With 'Lullay, lullay', lyke a chylde,
Thou slepyst to long, thou art begylde!

'My darlyng dere, my daysy floure,
Let me', quod he, 'ly in your lap.'
'Ly styll', quod she, 'my paramoure,
Ly styll hardely, and take a nap.'
5   Hys hed was hevy, such was his hap,
All drowsy, dremyng, dround in slepe,
That of hys love he toke no kepe,
    With hey, lullay, &c.

With 'Ba, ba, ba', and 'bas, bas, bas',
She cheryshed hym both cheke and chyn
10   That he wyst never where he was;
He had forgoten all dedely syn.
He wantyd wyt her love to wyn:
He trusted her payment and lost all hys pray.
She left hym slepyng and stale away,
    With hey, lullay, &c.

15   The ryvers rowth, the waters wan;
She sparyd not to wete her fete.
She wadyd over, she found a man
That halsyd her hartely and kyst her swete.
Thus after her cold she cought a hete.
20   'My lefe', she sayd, 'rowtyth in hys bed;
I wys he hath an hevy hed,'
    Wyth hey, lullay, &c.

What dremyst thou, drunchard, drousy pate?
Thy lust and lykyng is from the gone;
Thou blynkerd blowboll, thou wakyst to late;
25   Behold, thou lyeste, luggard, alone!
Well may thou sygh, well may thou grone,
To dele wyth her so cowardly;
I wys, powle hachet, she bleryd thyne I!
    Quod Skelton laureate.

(ii)
The auncient acquaintance, madam, betwen us twayn,
The famylyaryte, the formar dalyaunce,
Causyth me that I can not myself refrayne,
But that I must wryte for my plesaunt pastaunce
5   Remembryng your passyng goodly countenaunce,
Your goodly port, your bewteous visage,
Ye may be countyd comfort of all corage.

Of all your feturs favorable to make tru discripcion,
I am insuffycyent to make such enterpryse;
10   For thus dare I say, without tradiccyon,
That Dame Menolope was never half so wyse;
Yet so it is that a rumer begynnyth for to ryse
How in good horsmen ye set your hole delyght,
And have forgoten your old, trew, lovyng knyght.

15 Wyth bound and rebound, bounsyngly take up
    Hys jentyll curtoyl, and set nowght by small naggys!
    Spur up at the hynder gyrth with, 'Gup, morell, gup!'
    With, 'Jayst ye, Jenet of Spayne, for your tayll waggys,'
    Ye cast all your corage uppon such courtly haggys!
20 'Have in sergeaunt ferrour, myne horse behynde is bare.'
    He rydyth well the horse, but he rydyth better the mare.

    Ware, ware, the mare wynsyth wyth her wanton hele!
    She kykyth with her kalkyns and keylyth with a clench;
    She goyth wyde behynde and hewyth never a dele:
25 Ware gallyng in the widders, ware of that wrenche!
    It is perlous for a horseman to dyg in the trenche.
    Thys grevyth your husband, that ryght jentyll knyght,
    And so with your servantys he fersly doth fyght.

    So fersly he fytyth, hys mynde is so fell,
30 That he dryvyth them doune with dyntys on ther day-wach.
    He bresyth theyr braynpannys and makyth them to swell,
    Theyre browys all to-brokyn, such clappys they cach;
    Whose jalawsy malycyous makyth them to lepe the hach!
    By theyr conusaunce knowing how they serve a wily py:
35 Ask all your neybours whether that I ly.

    It can be no counsell that is cryed at the cros.
    For your jentyll husband sorowfull am I;
    Howbeit, he is not furst hath had a los.
    Advertysyng you, madame, to warke more secretly,
40 Let not all the world make an owtcry;
    Play fayre-play, madame, and loke ye play clene,
    Or ells with gret shame your game wylbe sene.
                        Quod Skelton laureat.

    (iii)
    Knolege, aquayntance, resort, favour, with grace;
    Delyte, desyre, respyte, wyth lyberte;
    Corage wyth lust, convenient tyme and space;
    Dysdayns, dystres, exylyd cruelte;
5   Wordys well set with good habylyte;
    Demure demenaunce, womanly of porte;
    Transendyng plesure, surmountyng all dysporte;

Allectuary arrectyd to redres
These feverous axys, the dedely wo and payne
10   Of thoughtfull hertys plungyd in dystres;
Refresshyng myndys the Aprell shoure of rayne;
Condute of comforte and well most soverayne;
Herber enverduryd, contynuall fressh and grene;
Of lusty somer the passyng goodly quene;

15   The topas rych and precyouse in vertew;
Your ruddys wyth ruddy rubys may compare;
Saphyre of sadnes, envayned wyth Indy blew;
The pullyshed perle youre whytenes doth declare;
Dyamand poyntyd to rase oute hartly care
20   Geyne surfetous suspecte the emeraud comendable;
Relucent smaragd, objecte imcomperable;

Encleryd myrroure and perspectyve most bryght,
Illumynyd wyth feturys far passyng my reporte;
Radyent Esperus, star of the clowdy nyght,
25   Lodestar to lyght these lovers to theyr porte,
Gayne dangerous stormys theyr anker of supporte,
Theyr sayll of solace most comfortably clad,
Whych to behold makyth hevy hartys glad;

Remorse have I of youre most goodlyhod,
30   Of youre behavoure curtes and benynge,
Of your bownte and of youre womanhod,
Which makyth my hart oft to lepe and sprynge
And to remember many a praty thynge;
But absens, alas, wyth tremelyng fere and drede,
35   Abashyth me, albeit I have no nede.

You I assure, absens is my fo,
My dedely wo, my paynfull hevynes.
And if ye lyst to know the cause why so,
Open myne hart, beholde my mynde expres.
40   I wold you coud! Then shuld ye se, mastres,
How there nys thynge that I covet so fayne
As to enbrace you in myne armys twayne.

Nothynge yerthly to me more desyrous
Than to beholde youre bewteouse countenaunce:

45   But hatefull absens, to me so envyous,
    Though thou withdraw me from her by long dystaunce,
    Yet shall she never oute of remembraunce,
    For I have gravyd her wythin the secret wall
    Of my trew hart, to love her best of all!
                Quod Skelton laureat.

(iv)
Cuncta licet cecidisse putas discrimina rerum,
Et prius incerta nunc tibi certa manent,
Consiliis usure meis tamen aspice caute,
Subdola non fallat te dea fraude sua:
5   *Sepe solet placido mortales fallere vultu,*
    Et cute sub placida tabida sepe dolent;
    Ut quando secura putas et cuncta serena
    Anguis sub viridi gramine sepe latet.

    Though ye suppose all jeperdys ar paste,
    And all is done ye lokyd for before,
    Ware yet, I rede you, of Fortunes double cast,
    For one fals poynt she is wont to kepe in store,
5   And under the fell oft festerd is the sore:
    That when ye thynke all daunger for to pas,
    Ware of the lesard lyeth lurkyng in the gras.
                Quod Skelton laureat.

(v)
    Go, pytyous hart, rasyd with dedly wo,
    Persyd with payn, bleding with wondes smart,
    Bewayle thy fortune, with vaynys wan and blo.
    O Fortune unfrendly, Fortune unkynde thow art,
5   To be so cruell and so overthwart,
    To suffer me so carefull to endure,
    That wher I love best I dare not dyscure!

    One ther is, and ever one shalbe,
    For whose sake my hart is sore dyseasyd;
10 For whose love, welcom dysease to me!
    I am content so all partys be pleasyd:
    Yet, and God wold, I wold my payne were easyd!

But Fortune enforsyth me so carefully to endure,
That where I love best I dare not dyscure.

Skelton laureat, at the instance of a nobyll lady.

V

Here begynneth a lytell treatyse named

The Bowge of Courte

In autumpne, whan the sonne *in Vyrgyne*
By radyante hete enryped hath our corne;
Whan Luna, full of mutabylyte,
As emperes the dyademe hath worne
5   Of our pole artyke, smylynge halfe in scorne
At our foly and our unstedfastnesse;
The tyme whan Mars to werre hym dyd dres;

I, callynge to mynde the great auctoryte
Of poetes olde, whyche, full craftely,
10   Under as coverte termes as coude be,
Can touche a troughte and cloke it subtylly
Wyth fresshe utteraunce full sentencyously;
Dyverse in style, some spared not vyce to wrythe,
Some of moralyte nobly dyde endyte;

15   Wherby I rede theyr renome and theyr fame
Maye never dye, bute evermore endure.
I was sore moved to aforce the same,
But Ignorance full soone dyde me dyscure
And shewed that in this arte I was not sure;
20   For to illumyne, she sayde, I was to dulle,
Avysynge me my penne awaye to pulle

And not to wrythe, for he so wyll atteyne,
Excedynge ferther than his connynge is,
His hede maye be harde, but feble is his brayne!
25   Yet have I knowen suche er this;
But of reproche surely he maye not mys
That clymmeth hyer than he may fotynge have;
What and he slyde downe, who shall hym save?

Thus up and down my mynde was drawen and cast
30   That I ne wyste what to do was beste;
Soo sore enwered that I was, at the laste,
Enforsed to slepe and for to take some reste,
And to lye downe as soone as I me dreste,
At Harwyche Porte, slumbrynge as I laye,
35   In myne hostes house called Powers Keye,

Me thoughte I sawe a shyppe, goodly of sayle,
Come saylynge forth into that haven brood,
Her takelynge ryche and of hye apparayle;
She kyste an anker, and there she laye at rode,
40   Marchauntes her borded to see what she had lode.
Therein they founde royall marchaundyse,
Fraghted with plesure to what ye coude devyse.

But than I thoughte I wolde not dwell behynde;
Amonge all other I put myselfe in prece.
45   Than there coude I none aquentaunce fynde;
There was moche noyse, anone one cryed, 'Cese!'
Sharpely commaundynge eche man holde hys pece.
'Maysters', he sayde, 'the shyp that ye here see,
The Bowge of Courte it hyghte for certeynte.

50   The awnner therof is lady of estate,
Whoos name to tell is Dame Saunce-Pere.
Her marchaundyse is ryche and fortunate,
But who wyll have it muste paye therfore dere.
This royall chaffre that is shypped here
55   Is called Favore-to-stonde-in-her-good-grace.'
Than sholde ye see there pressynge in a pace

Of one and other that wolde his lady see,
Whiche sat behynde a traves of sylke fyne,
Of golde of tessew the fynest that myghte be,
60   In a trone whiche fer clerer dyde shyne
Than Phebus in his spere celestyne,
Whoos beaute, honoure, goodly porte,
I have to lytyll connynge to reporte.

But of eche thynge there as I toke hede,
65   Amonge all other was wrytten in her trone,

In golde letters, this worde, whiche I dyde rede:
Garder le fortune que est mauelz et bone.
And as I stode redynge this verse myselfe allone,
Her chyef gentylwoman, Daunger by her name,
70   Gave me a taunte, and sayde I was to blame

To be so perte to prese so proudly uppe.
She sayde she trowed that I had eten sause;
She asked yf ever I dranke of saucys cuppe.
And I than softly answered to that clause,
75   That, so to saye, I had gyven her no cause.
Than asked she me, 'Syr, so God the spede,
What is thy name?' and I sayde it was Drede.

'What movyd the,' quod she, 'hydder to come?'
'Forsoth,' quod I, 'to bye some of youre ware.'
80   And with that worde on me she gave a glome
With browes bente, and gan on me to stare
Full daynnously, and fro me she dyde fare,
Levynge me stondynge as a mased man;
To whome there came another gentylwoman.

85   Desyre her name was, and so she me tolde,
Sayenge to me, 'Broder, be of good chere,
Abasshe you not, but hardely be bolde,
Avaunce your selfe to aproche and come nere.
What though our chaffer be never so dere,
90   Yet I avyse you to speke, for ony drede:
Who spareth to speke, in fayth, he spareth to spede.'

'Maystres,' quod I, 'I have none aquentaunce
That wyll for me be medyatoure and mene;
And this an other, I have but smale substaunce.'
95   'Pece,' quod Desyre, 'ye speke not worth a bene!
Yf ye have not, in fayth, I wyll you lene
A precyous jewell, no rycher in this londe:
Bone aventure have here now in your honde.

Shyfte now therwith, let see, as ye can,
100   In Bowge of Courte chevysaunce to make;
For I dare saye that there nys erthly man
But, an he can *Bone aventure* take,
There can no favour nor frendshyp hym forsake.

Bone aventure may brynge you in suche case
105   That ye shall stonde in favoure and in grace.

But of one thynge I werne you er I goo:
She that styreth the shyp, make her your frende.'
'Maystres,' quod I, 'I praye you tell me why soo,
And how I maye that waye and meanes fynde.'
110   'Forsothe,' quod she, 'how ever blowe the wynde,
Fortune gydeth and ruleth all our shyppe.
Whome she hateth shall over the see-boorde skyp.

Whome she loveth, of all plesyre is ryche
Whyles she laugheth and hath luste for to playe.
115   Whome she hateth, she casteth in the dyche,
For whan she frouneth she thynketh to make a fray.
She cheryssheth him, and hym she casseth awaye.'
'Alas,' quod I, 'how myghte I have her sure?'
'In fayth,' quod she, 'by *Bone aventure*.'

120   Thus, in a rowe, of martchauntes a grete route
Suwed to Fortune that she wold be theyre frynde.
They thronge in fast and flocked her aboute,
And I with them prayed her to have in mynde.
She promysed to us all she wolde be kynde;
125   Of Bowge of Court she asketh what we wold have,
And we asked favoure, and favour she us gave.

Thus endeth the prologue, and begynneth the Bowge of Courte
brevely compyled.

DREDE

The sayle is up, Fortune ruleth our helme,
We wante no wynde to passe now over all;
Favoure we have toughther than ony elme,
130   That wyll abyde and never frome us fall.
But under hony ofte tyme lyeth bytter gall,
For, as me thoughte, in our shyppe I dyde see
Full subtyll persones in nombre foure and thre.

The fyrste was Favell, full of flatery,
135   Wyth fables false, that well coude fayne a tale;
The seconde was Suspecte, whiche that dayly

Mysdempte eche man, with face deedly and pale;
And Harvy Hafter that well coude picke a male;
With other foure of theyr affynyte:
140   Dysdayne, Ryotte, Dyssymuler, Subtylte.

Fortune theyr frende, with whome oft she dyde daunce:
They coude not faile, thei thought, they were so sure.
And oftentymes I wolde myselfe avaunce
With them to make solace and pleasure;
145   But my dysporte they could not well endure:
They sayde they hated for to dele with Drede.
Than Favell gan wyth fayre speche me to fede.

FAVELL

'Noo thynge erthely that I wonder so sore
As of your connynge, that is so excellent;
150   Deynte to have with us suche one in store,
So vertuously that hath his dayes spente;
Fortune to you gyftes of grace hath lente:
Loo, what it is a man to have connynge!
All erthely tresoure it is surmountynge.

155   Ye be an apte man, as ony can be founde
To dwell with us and serve my ladyes grace.
Ye be to her, yea, worth a thousande pounde.
I herde her speke of you within shorte space,
Whan there were dyverse that sore dyde you manace.
160   And, though I say it, I was myselfe your frende,
For here be dyverse to you that be unkynde.

But this one thynge ye maye be sure of me,
For by that Lorde that bought dere all mankynde,
I can not flater, I muste be playne to the.
165   And ye nede ought, man, shewe to me your mynde,
For ye have me whome faythfull ye shall fynde;
Whyles I have ought, by God, thou shalt not lacke,
And, yf nede be, a bolde worde I dare cracke.

Nay, naye, be sure, whyles I am on your syde
170   Ye maye not fall; truste me, ye maye not fayle.
Ye stonde in favoure and Fortune is your gyde,
And, as she wyll, so shall our grete shyppe sayle.

Thyse lewde cok wattes shall nevermore prevayle
Ageynste you hardely; therefore be not afrayde.
175 Farewell tyll soone. But no word that I sayde!'

DREDE

Than thanked I hym for his grete gentylnes.
But, as me thoughte, he ware on hym a cloke
That lyned was with doubtfull doublenes.
Me thoughte, of wordes that he had full a poke;
180 His stomak stuffed ofte tymes dyde reboke.
Suspycyon, me thoughte, mette hym at a brayde,
And I drewe nere to herke what they two sayde.

'In fayth,' quod Suspecte, 'spake Drede no worde of me?'
'Why? What than? Wylte thou lete men to speke?
185 He sayth he can not well accorde with the.'
'Twyst,' quod Suspecte, 'goo playe; hym I ne reke!'
'By Cryste,' quod Favell, 'Drede is soleyne freke!
What, lete us holde him up, man, for a whyle.'
'Ye, soo,' quod Suspecte, 'he maye us bothe begyle.'

190 And whan he came walkynge soberly,
Wyth 'Whom' and 'Ha' and with a croked loke,
Me thoughte his hede was full of gelousy,
His eyen rollynge, his hondes faste they quoke;
And to mewarde the strayte waye he toke.
195 'God spede, broder,' to me quod he than,
And thus to talke with me he began.

SUSPYCYON

'Ye remember the gentylman ryghte nowe
That commaunde with you, me thought, a praty space?
Beware of him, for, I make God avowe,
200 He wyll begyle you and speke fayre to your face.
Ye never dwelte in suche an other place,
For here is none that dare well other truste;
But I wolde telle you a thynge, and I durste.

Spake he, a fayth, no worde to you of me?
205 I wote, and he dyde, ye wolde me telle.

I have a favoure to you, wherof it be
That I must shewe you moche of my counselle –
But I wonder what the devyll of helle
He sayde of me, whan he with you dyde talke –
210   By myne avyse use not with him to walke.

The soveraynst thynge that ony man maye have
Is lytyll to saye, and moche to here and see;
For, but I trusted you, so God me save,
I wolde noo thynge so playne be.
215   To you oonly, me thynke, I durste shryve me;
For now am I plenarely dysposed
To shewe you thynges that may not be disclosed.'

DREDE

Than I assured hym my fydelyte,
His counseyle secrete never to dyscure,
220   Yf he coude fynde in herte to truste me.
Els, I prayed hym with all my besy cure,
To kepe it hymselfe; for than he myghte be sure
That noo man erthly coude hym bewreye,
Whyles of his mynde it were lockte with the keye.

225   'By God,' quod he, 'this and thus it is';
And of his mynde he shewed me all and some.
'Fare well,' quod he, 'we wyll talke more of this.'
Soo he departed. There he wolde be come,
I dare not speke; I promysed to be dome.
230   But as I stode musynge in my mynde,
Harvy Hafter came lepynge, lyghte as lynde.

Upon his breste he bare a versynge boxe:
His throte was clere and lustely coude fayne.
Me thoughte his gowne was all furred wyth foxe.
235   And ever he sange, 'Sythe I am no thynge playne'.
To kepe him frome pykynge, it was a grete payne.
He gased on me with his gotyshe berde;
Whan I loked on hym, my purse was half aferde.

HERVY HAFTER

'Syr, God you save, why loke you so sadde?
240   What thynge is that I maye do for you?
A wonder thynge that ye waxe not madde!
For and I studye sholde as ye doo nowe,
My wytte wolde waste, I make God avowe.
Tell me your mynde, me thynke ye make a verse,
245   I coude it skan and ye wolde it reherse.

But to the poynte shortely to procede,
Where hathe your dwellynge ben, er ye cam here?
For, as I trowe, I have sene you in dede
Er this, whan that ye made me royall chere.
250   Holde up the helme, loke up and lete God stere:
I wolde be mery that wynde that ever blowe,
'Heve and how, rombelow, row the bote, Norman, rowe.'

'Prynces of youghte', can ye synge by rote?
Or 'Shall I sayle wyth you' a felashyp assaye?
255   For on the booke I can not synge a note,
Wolde to God it wolde please you some daye
A balade boke before me for to laye,
And lerne me to synge *Re my fa sol*!
And whan I fayle, bobbe me on the noll!

260   Loo, what is to you a pleasure grete
To have that connynge and wayes that ye have!
By Goddis soule, I wonder how ye gete
Soo greate pleasyre, or who to you it gave.
Syr, pardone me, I am an homely knave
265   To be with you thus perte and thus bolde;
But ye be welcome to our housholde.

And I dare saye there is no man hereinne
But wolde be glad of your company.
I wyste never man that so soone coude wynne
270   The favoure that ye have with my lady.
I praye to God that it maye never dy.
It is your fortune for to have that grace;
As I be saved, it is a wonder case.

For, as for me, I served here many a daye,
275   And yet unneth I can have my lyvynge;

But I requyre you no worde that I saye!
For, and I knowe ony erthly thynge
That is agayne you, you shall have wetynge;
And ye be welcome, syr, so God me save,
280   I hope here after a frende of you to have.'

DREDE

Wyth that, as he departed soo fro me,
Anone ther mette with him, as me thoughte,
A man, but wonderly besene was he.
He loked hawte; he sette eche man at noughte;
285   His gawdy garment with Scornnys was all wrought;
With Indygnacyon lyned was his hode;
He frowned as he wolde swere by Cockes blode.

He bote the lyppe; he loked passynge coye;
His face was belymmed as byes had him stounge;
290   It was no tyme with him to jape nor toye.
Envye hathe wasted hys lyver and his lounge;
Hatred by the herte so had hym wrounge
That he loked pale as asshes to my syghte.
Dysdayne, I wene, this comerous carkes hyghte.

295   To Hervy Hafter than he spake of me,
And I drewe nere to harke what they two sayde.
'Now,' quod Dysdayne, 'as I shall saved be,
I have grete scorne and am ryghte evyll apayed.'
'Than,' quod Hervy, 'why arte thou so dysmayde?'
300   'By Cryste,' quod he, 'for it is shame to saye,
To see Johan Dawes, that came but yesterdaye,

How he is now taken in conceyte,
This Doctour Dawcocke, Drede, I wene he hyghte.
By Goddis bones, but yf we have som sleyte,
305   It is lyke he wyll stonde in our lyghte!'
'By God,' quod Hervy, 'and it so happen myghte!
Lete us, therfore, shortely at a worde
Fynde some mene to caste him over the borde.'

'By him that me boughte,' than quod Dysdayne,
310   'I wonder sore he is in such conceyte.'

'Turde,' quod Hafter, 'I wyll the nothynge layne,
There muste for hym be layde some prety beyte.
We tweyne, I trowe, be not withoute dysceyte:
Fyrste pycke a quarell and fall oute with hym then,
315   And soo outface hym with a carde of ten.'

Forthwith, he made on me a prowde assawte,
With scornfull loke mevyd all in moode.
He wente aboute to take me in a fawte:
He frounde, he stared, he stampped where he stoode.
320   I loked on hym, I wende he had be woode.
He set the arme proudly under the syde,
And in this wyse he gan with me to chyde.

DISDAYNE

'Remembrest thou what thou sayd yesternyght?
Wylt thou abyde by the wordes agayne?
325   By God, I have of the now grete dyspyte;
I shall the angre ones in every vayne!
It is greate scorne to see suche a hayne
As thou arte, one that cam but yesterdaye,
With us olde servauntes such maysters to playe.

330   I tell the, I am of countenaunce.
What weneste I were? I trowe thou knowe not me.
By Goddis woundes, but for dysplesaunce,
Of my querell soone wolde I venged be.
But, no force, I shall ones mete with the;
335   Come whan it wyll, oppose the I shall,
Whatsomever aventure therof fall.

Trowest thou, drevyll, I saye, thou gawdy knave,
That I have deynte to see the cherysshed thus?
By Goddis syde, my sworde thy berde shall shave!
340   Well, ones thou shalte be chermed, iwus:
Naye, strawe for tales, thou shalte not rule us;
We be thy betters, and so thou shalte us take,
Or we shall the oute of thy clothes shake!'

DREDE

Wyth that came Ryotte, russhynge all at ones,
345   A rusty gallande, to-ragged and to-rente;
And on the borde he whyrled a payre of bones,
'*Quater treye dews*' he clatered as he wente.
'Nowe have at all, by Saynte Thomas of Kente!'
And ever he threwe, and kyst I wote nere what;
350   His here was growen thorowe oute his hat.

Thenne I behelde how he dysgysed was:
His hede was hevy for watchynge overnyghte,
His eyen blereed, his face shone lyke a glas;
His gowne so shorte that it ne cover myghte
355   His rumpe, he wente so all for somer lyghte;
His hose was garded with a lyste of grene,
Yet at the knee they were broken, I wene.

His cote was checked with patches rede and blewe;
Of Kyrkeby Kendall was his shorte demye;
360   And ay he sange, 'In fayth, Decon, thou crewe.'
His elbowe bare, he ware his gere so nye,
His nose a-droppynge, his lyppes were full drye;
And by his syde his whynarde and his pouche,
The devyll myghte daunce therin for ony crowche.

365   Counter he coude *O lux* upon a potte.
An eestryche fedder of a capons tayle
He set up fresshely upon his hat alofte.
'What, revell route!' quod he, and gan to rayle
How ofte he hadde hit Jenet on the tayle,
370   Of Felyce fetewse and lytell prety Cate,
How ofte he knocked at her klycked gate.

What sholde I tell more of his rebaudrye?
I was ashamed so to here hym prate.
He had no pleasure but in harlotrye.
375   'Ay,' quod he, 'in the devylles date,
What arte thou? I sawe the nowe but late.'
'Forsothe,' quod I, 'in this courte I dwell nowe.'
'Welcome,' quod Ryote, 'I make God avowe.'

RYOTE

'And, syr, in fayth, why comste not us amonge
380 To make the mery, as other felowes done?
Thou muste swere and stare, man, aldaye longe,
And wake all nyghte and slepe tyll it be none.
Thou mayste not studye or muse on the mone.
This worlde is nothynge but ete, drynke and slepe,
385 And thus with us good company to kepe.

Plucke up thyne herte upon a mery pyne,
And lete us laugh a placke or tweyne at nale.
What the devyll, man, myrthe was never one!
What, loo, man, see here of dyce a bale;
390 A brydelynge caste for that is in thy male!
Now have at all that lyeth upon the burde.
Fye on this dyce, they be not worth a turde!

Have at the hasarde or at the dosen browne,
Or els I pas a peny to a pounde!
395 Now wolde to God thou wolde leye money downe!
Lorde, how that I wolde caste it full rounde!
Ay, in my pouche a buckell I have founde;
The armes of Calyce, I have no coyne nor crosse!
I am not happy, I renne ay on the losse!

400 Now renne muste I to the stewys syde
To wete yf Malkyn, my lemman, have gete oughte.
I lete her to hyre that men maye on her ryde;
Her harnes easy ferre and nere is soughte.
By Goddis sydes, syns I her thyder broughte,
405 She hath gote me more money with her tayle
Than hath some shyppe that into Bordews sayle.

Had I as good an hors as she is a mare,
I durse aventure to journey thorugh Fraunce;
Who rydeth on her, he nedeth not to care,
410 For she is trussed for to breke a launce.
It is a curtel that well can wynche and praunce;
To her wyll I nowe all my poverte lege.
And tyll I come, have, here is myne hat to plege.'

DREDE

Gone is this knave, this rybaude foule and leude.
415 He ran as fast as ever that he myghte.
Unthryftynes in hym may well be shewed,
For whome Tyborne groneth both daye and nyghte.
And as I stode and kyste asyde my syghte,
Dysdayne I sawe with Dyssymulacyon,
420 Standynge in sadde communicacion.

But there was poyntynge and noddynge with the hede,
And many wordes sayde in secrete wyse;
They wandred ay and stode styll in no stede.
Me thoughte alwaye Dyscymular dyde devyse;
425 Me, passynge sore, myne herte than gan aryse;
I dempte and drede theyr talkynge was not good.
Anone Dyscymular came where I stode.

Than, in his hode, I sawe there faces tweyne:
That one was lene and lyke a pyned goost,
430 That other loked as he wolde me have slayne.
And to mewarde as he gan for to coost,
Whan that he was even at me almoost,
I saw a knyfe hyd in his one sleve,
Wheron was wryten this worde, *Myscheve*.

435 And in his other sleve, me thought I sawe
A spone of golde, full of hony swete,
To fede a fole, and for to preye a dawe.
And on that sleve these wordes were wrete:
A false abstracte cometh from a fals concrete.
440 His hode was syde, his cope was roset graye;
Thyse were the wordes he to me dyde saye.

DYSSYMULATION

'How do ye, mayster? Ye loke so soberly!
As I be saved at the dredefull daye,
It is a perylous vyce, this envy.
445 Alas, a connynge man ne dwelle maye
In no place well, but foles with hym fraye!
But as for that, connynge hath no foo
Save hym that nought can: scrypture sayth soo.

I knowe your vertu and your lytterkture
450   By that lytel connynge that I have.
Ye be malygned sore, I you ensure,
But ye have crafte your selfe alwaye to save.
It is grete scorne to se a mysproude knave
With a clerke that connynge is to prate.
455   Lete theym go lowse theym, in the devylles date.

For allbeit that this longe not to me,
Yet on my backe I bere suche lewde delynge.
Ryghte now I spake with one, I trowe, I see –
But, what, a strawe! I maye not tell all thynge.
460   By God, I saye, there is a grete herte-brennynge
Betwene the persone ye wote of, you –
Alas, I coude not dele so with a Jew.

I wolde eche man were as playne as I.
It is a worlde, I saye, to here of some –
465   I hate this faynynge, fye upon it, fye!
A man can not wote where to become.
Iwys I coude tell – but humlery, home,
I dare not speke, we be so layde awayte,
For all our courte is full of dysceyte.

470   Now, by Saynte Fraunceys, that holy man and frere,
I hate this wayes agayne you that they take!
Were I as you, I wolde ryde them full nere;
And by my trouthe, but yf an ende they make,
Yet wyll I saye some wordes for your sake
475   That shall them angre, I holde thereon a grote,
For some shall wene be hanged by the throte.

I have a stoppynge oyster in my poke,
Truste me, and yf it come to a nede;
But I am lothe for to reyse a smoke,
480   Yf ye coude be otherwyse agrede;
And so I wolde it were, so God me spede,
For this may brede to a confusyon,
Withoute God make a good conclusyon.

Naye, see where yonder stondeth the teder man!
485   A flaterynge knave and false he is, God wote.
The drevyll stondeth to herken, and he can.

It were more thryft he boughte him a newe cote;
It wyll not be, his purse is not on-flote.
All that he wereth, it is borowed ware;
490   His wytte is thynne, his hode is threde-bare.

More coude I saye, but what this is ynowe.
Adewe tyll soone, we shall speke more of this.
Ye muste be ruled, as I shall tell you howe.
Amendis maye be of that is now amys;
495   And I am your, syr, so have I blys,
In every poynte that I can do or saye.
Gyve me your honde, fare well and have good daye.'

DREDE

Sodaynly, as he departed me fro,
Came pressynge in one in a wonder araye.
500   Er I was ware, behynde me he sayde 'Bo!'
Thenne I, astonyed of that sodeyne fraye,
Sterte all at ones, I lyked no thynge his playe,
For yf I had not quyckely fledde the touche,
He had plucte oute the nobles of my pouche.

505   He was trussed in a garmente strayte –
I have not sene suche anothers page –
For he coude well upon a casket wayte,
His hode all pounsed and garded lyke a cage.
Lyghte lyme-fynger, he toke none other wage.
510   'Harken,' quod he, 'loo here myne honde in thyne;
To us welcome thou arte, by Saynte Quyntyne!'

DISCEYTE

'But by that Lorde that is one, two and thre,
I have an errande to rounde in your ere.
He tolde me so, by God, ye maye truste me.
515   Parde, remembre whan ye were there,
There I wynked on you – wote ye not where?
In A *loco*, I mene *juxta* B:
Woo is hym that is blynde and maye not see!

But to here the subtylte and the crafte,
520   As I shall tell you, yf ye wyll harke agayne:
And whan I sawe the horsons wolde you hafte,
To holde myne honde, by God, I had grete payne;
For forthwyth there I had him slayne,
But that I drede mordre wolde come oute.
525   Who deleth with shrewes hath nede to loke aboute!'

DREDE

And as he rounded thus in myne ere
Of false collusyon confetryd by assente,
Me thoughte I see lewde felawes here and there
Came for to slee me of mortall entente.
530   And as they came, the shypborde faste I hente,
And thoughte to lepe; and even with that woke,
Caughte penne and ynke, and wroth this lytell boke.

I wolde therwith no man were myscontente;
Besechynge you that shall it see or rede,
535   In every poynte to be indyfferente,
Syth all in substaunce of slumbrynge doth procede.
I wyll not saye it is mater in dede,
But yet oftyme suche dremes be founde trewe.
Now constrewe ye what is the resydewe.

Thus endeth the Bowge of Courte.

VI

Here after foloweth the boke entytuled

Ware the Hauke

per Skelton laureat

PROLOGUS SKELTONIDIS LAUREATI SUPER
WARE THE HAWKE

This worke devysed is
For suche as do amys,

And specyally to controule
Such as have cure of soule,
5   That be so far abusyd
They cannot be excusyd
By reason nor by law;
But that they playe the daw
To hawke, or els to hunt
10   From the auter to the funt,
Wyth cry unreverent,
Before the sacrament,
Wythin the holy church bowndis,
That of our fayth the grownd is.
15   That preest that hawkys so,
All grace is far hym fro.
He semeth a sysmatyke
Or els an heretike,
For fayth in hym is faynte.
20   Therefore to make complaynt
Of such mysadvysed
Parsons and dysgysed,
Thys boke we have devysed,
Compendyously comprysed,
25   No good preest to offend,
But suche dawes to amend,
In hope that no man shall
Be myscontent withall.

I shall you make relacyon
30   By way of apostrofacyon
Under supportacyon
Of your pacyent tolleracyon,
How I, Skelton laureat,
Devysed and also wrate
35   Uppon a lewde curate,
A parson benyfyced
But nothynge well advysed.
He shall be as now nameles,
But he shall not be blameles,
40   Nor he shall not be shameles;
For sure he wrought amys
To hawke in my church of Dys.

This fonde frantyke fouconer,
Wyth his polutyd pawtenar,
45   As preest unreverent,
Streyght to the sacrament
He made his hawke to fly,
With hogeous showte and cry.
The hy auter he strypte naked;
50   There on he stode, and craked;
He shoke downe all the clothys,
And sware horryble othes
Before the face of God,
By Moyses and Arons rod,
55   Or that he thens yede,
His hawke shulde pray and fede
Upon a pigeons maw.
The blode ran downe raw
Upon the auter stone.
60   The hawke tyryd on a bone,
And in the holy place
She mutyd there a chase
Upon my corporas face.
Such *sacrificium laudis*
65   He made with suche gambawdis.

OBSERVATE

His seconde hawke wexyd gery
And was with flyenge wery.
She had flowyn so oft,
That on the rode loft
70   She perkyd her to rest.
The fauconer then was prest,
Came runnynge with a dow,
And cryed, 'Stow, stow, stow!'
But she wold not bow.
75   He then, to be sure,
Callyd her with a lure.
Her mete was very crude,
She had not wel endude;
She was not clene ensaymed,
80   She was not wel reclaymed;

But the fawconer unfayned
Was moch more febler brayned.
The hawke had no lyst
To come to his fyst;
85   She loked as she had the frounce;
Wyth that he gave her a bounce
Full upon the gorge.
I wyll not fayne nor forge;
The hawke with that clap
90   Fell downe with evyll hap.
The church dores were sparred,
Fast boltyd and barryd,
Yet wyth a prety gyn
I fortuned to come in,
95   Thys rebell to behold,
Whereof I hym controld;
But he sayde that he wolde
Agaynst my mynde and wyll
In my church hawke styll.

CONSIDERATE

100   On Saynt Johnn decollacyon
He hawked on thys facyon,
Tempore vesperarum,
Sed non secundum Sarum
But lyke a March harum
105   His braynes were so *parum.*
He sayde he wold not let
His houndys for to fet,
To hunte there by lyberte
In the dyspyte of me,
110   And to halow there the fox.
Downe went my offerynge box,
Boke, bell and candyll,
All that he myght handyll;
Cros, staffe, lectryne and banner,
115   Fell downe on thys manner.

DELIBERATE

Wyth, 'Troll, cytrace and trovy,'
They rangyd Hankyn Bovy
My churche all abowte.
Thys fawconer then gan showte,
120 'These be my gospellers,
These be my pystyllers,
These be my querysters
To helpe me to synge,
My hawkes to mattens rynge!'
125 In thys preestly gydynge
His hawke then flew uppon
The rode, with Mary and Johnn.
Delt he not lyke a fon?
Delt he not lyke a daw?
130 Or els is thys Goddis law,
Decrees or decretals,
Or holy sinodals,
Or els provincyals,
Thus within the wals
135 Of holy church to deale,
Thus to ryng a peale
Wyth his hawkys bels?
Dowtles such losels
Make the churche to be
140 In smale auctoryte;
A curate in specyall
To snappar and to fall
Into this opyn cryme;
To loke on this were tyme.

VIGILATE

145 But who so that lokys
In the offycyallys bokys,
There he may se and reed
That thys is matter indeed.
How be it, mayden Meed
150 Made theym to be agreed;
And so the Scrybe was feed,

And the Pharasay
Then durst nothynge say,
But let the matter slyp,
155 And made truth to tryp;
And of the spyrytuall law
They made but a gewgaw,
And toke it oute in drynke,
And this the cause doth shrynke.
160 The church is thus abusyd,
Reproched and pollutyd;
Correctyon hath no place,
And all for lacke of grace.

DEPLORATE

Loke now in *Exodi*,
165 And *de archa Domini*,
With *Regum* by and by;
(The Bybyll wyll not ly)
How the Temple was kept,
How the Temple was swept,
170 Where *sanguis taurorum*,
Aut sanguis vitulorum,
Was offryd within the wallys,
After ceremoniallys;
When it was polutyd
175 Sentence was executyd,
By wey of expyacyon,
For reconcylyacyon.

DIVINITATE

Then moch more, by the rode,
Where Crystis precyous blode
180 Dayly offryd is,
To be polutyd this;
And that he wysshed withall
That the dowves donge downe myght fall
Into my chalys at mas,

185   When consecratyd was
    The blessyd sacrament.
    O pryeest unreverent.
    He sayd that he wold hunt
    From the aulter to the funt.

REFORMATE

190   Of no tyrand I rede,
    That so far dyd excede;
    Neither yet Dyoclesyan,
    Nor yet Domysyan;
    Nother crokyd Cacus,
195   Nor yet dronken Bacus;
    Nother Olybryus,
    Nor Dyonysyus;
    Nother Phalary,
    Rehersyd in Valery,
200   Nor Sardanapall,
    Unhappyest of all;
    Nor Nero the worst,
    Nor Clawdyus the curst;
    Nor yet Egeas,
205   Nor yet Syr Pherumbras;
    Nother Zorobabell,
    Nor cruell Jesabell;
    Nor yet Tarquinius,
    Whom Tytus Lyvyus
210   In wrytynge doth enroll;
    I have red theym poll by poll;
    The story of Arystobell,
    And of Constantynopell,
    Whych cytie myscreantys wan,
215   And slew many a Chrysten man;
    Yet the Sowden, nor the Turke,
    Wrought never such a worke,
    For to let their hawkys fly
    In the church of Saynt Sophy;
220   With moch matter more,
    That I kepe in store.

PENSITATE

>Then in a tabull playne
>I wroute a verse or twayne,
>Whereat he made dysdayne.
>The pekysh parsons brayne
>Cowde not rech nor attayne
>What the sentence ment.
>He sayde, for a crokyd intent,
>The wordis were parvertyd;
>And this he overthwartyd.
>Of the whych proces
>Ye may know more expres,
>If it please you to loke
>In the resydew of thys boke.

225

230

Here after folowyth the tabull.

235

>Loke on this tabull,
>Whether thou art abull
>To rede or to spell
>What these verses tell.

Sicculo lutueris est colo būraarā
240 *Nixphedras uisarum caniuter tūtātes*
Raterplas Natābrian umsudus itnugenus
18. 10. 2. 11. 19. 4. 13. 3. 4. 1 tēūalet.
Cartula stet, precor, hec nullo temeranda petulco:
Hos rapiet numeros non homo, sed mala bos.
Ex parte rem cartae adverte aperte, pone musam
245   *Arethusam hanc.*

>Wherto shuld I rehers
>The sentens of my vers?
>In them be no scolys
>For braynsycke frantycke folys:
>*Construas hoc,*
>*Domine* Daucock!
>   Ware the hauke!

250

>Maister *sophista,*
>Ye *simplex silogista,*

255   Ye develysh dogmatista,
        Your hawke on your fista,
        To hawke when you lista
        In *ecclesia ista,*
        Domine concupisti,
260   With thy hawke on thy fysty?
        Nunquid sic dixisti?
        Nunquid sic fecisti?
        Sed ubi hoc legisti
        Aut unde hoc,
265   Doctor Dawcocke?
          Ware the hawke!

        Doctor *Dialetica,*
        Where fynde you in *Ypotetica,*
        Or in *Cathagoria*
270   *Latina sive Dorica,*
        To use youre hawkys *forica*
        In propitiatorio,
        Tanquam diversorio?
        Unde hoc,
275   *Domine* Dawcocke?
          Ware the hawke!

        Say to me, Jacke Harys,
        Quare accuparis
        Ad sacramentum altaris?
280   For no reverens thou sparys
        To shake my pygyons federis
        Super arcam federis:
        Unde hoc,
        Doctor Dawkocke?
285   Ware the hawke!

        Sir *dominus vobiscum,*
        Per aucupium
        Ye made your hawke to cum
        Desuper candelabrum
290   *Christi crucifixi*
        To fede uppon your fisty;
        Dic, inimice crucis Christi,

Ubi didicisti
Facere hoc,
295   *Domine* Dawcoke?
Ware the hawke!

Apostata Julianus
Nor yet Nestorianus,
Thou shalt no where rede
300   That they dyd such a dede,
To let theyr hawkys fly
Ad ostium tabernaculi
In quo est corpus Domini;
Cave hoc,
305   Doctor Dawcock!
Ware the hawke!

This dowtless ye ravyd,
Dys church ye thus depravyd;
Wherfore, as I be savyd,
310   Ye ar therfore beknavyd.
Quare? Quia evangelia,
Concha et conchelia,
Accipiter et sonalia,
Et bruta animalia,
315   *Cetera quoque talia*
Tibi sunt equalia;
Unde hoc,
Domine Dawkock?
Ware the hawke!

320   *Et relis et ralis*
Et reliqualis,
From Granado to Galys,
From Wynchelsee to Walys,
Non est braynsycke *talys,*
325   *Nec minus racionalis,*
Nec magis bestialis
That synggys with a chalys;
Construas hoc,
Doctor Dawcoke!
330   Ware the hawke!

Masyd, wytles smery smyth,
Hampar with your hammer upon thy styth,
And make hereof a syckyll or a saw,
For though ye lyve a c. yere, ye shal dy a daw.
335   *Vos valete*
        Doctor indiscrete!

SKELTONIS APOSTROPHAT AD DIVUM JOHANNEM
DECOLLATUM IN CUIUS PROFESTO FIEBAT HOC
AUCUPIUM

O memoranda dies, qua, decollate Johannes,
Aucupium facit, haud quondam quod fecerit, intra
Ecclesiam de Dis, violans tua sacra sacrorum!
Rector de Whipstok, doctor cognomine Daucock,
5   *Et dominus Wodcock; probat is, probat hic, probat hec hoc.*

IDEM DE LIBERA DICACITATE POETICA IN EXTOLENDA
PROBITATE, ET IN PERFRICANDA IGNOBILITATE

Libertas veneranda piis concessa poetis
Dicendi est quecunque placent, quecunque juvabunt,
Vel quecunque valent justas defendere causas,
Vel quecunque valent stolidos mordere petulcos.
5   *Ergo dabis veniam.*
                Quod Skelton laureat.

VII

Here after foloweth the boke of

Phyllyp Sparowe

compyled by Mayster Skelton, poete laureate

Pla ce bo,
Who is there, who?
Di le xi,
Dame Margery,
5   *Fa, re, my, my.*

Wherfore and why, why?
For the sowle of Philip Sparowe,
That was late slayn at Carowe
Among the Nones Blake.
10 For that swete soules sake,
And for all sparowes soules
Set in our bede rolles,
Pater noster qui,
With an *Ave Mari*,
15 And with the corner of a Crede,
The more shal be your mede.

Whan I remembre agayn
How mi Philyp was slayn,
Never halfe the payne
20 Was betwene you twayne,
Pyramus and Thesbe,
As than befell to me.
I wept and I wayled,
The tearys downe hayled;
25 But nothynge it avayled
To call Phylyp agayne
Whom Gyb our cat hath slayne.
Gyb, I saye, our cat,
Worrowyd her on that
30 Which I loved best.
It can not be exprest
My sorowfull hevynesse,
But all without redresse;
For within that stounde,
35 Halfe slumbrynge, in a sounde
I fell downe to the grounde.
Unneth I kest myne eyes
Towarde the cloudy skyes;
But whan I dyd beholde
40 My sparow dead and colde,
No creature but that wolde
Have rewed upon me,
To behold and se
What hevynesse dyd me pange:
45 Wherewith my handes I wrange

That my senaws cracked
As though I had ben racked,
So payned and so strayned
That no lyfe well nye remayned.
50   I syghed and I sobbed,
For that I was robbed
Of my sparowes lyfe.
O mayden, wydow, and wyfe,
Of what estate ye be,
55   Of hye or lowe degre,
Great sorowe than ye myght se,
And lerne to wepe at me!
Such paynes dyd me frete
That myne hert dyd bete,
60   My vysage pale and dead,
Wanne, and blewe as lead:
The panges of hatefull death
Well nye had stopped my breath.

Heu, heu, me,
65   That I am wo for the!
Ad dominum, cum tribularer, clamavi.
Of God nothynge els crave I
But Phyllypes soule to kepe
From the marees depe
70   Of Acherontes well,
That is a flode of hell;
And from the great Pluto,
The prynce of endles wo;
And from foule Alecto,
75   With vysage blacke and blo;
And from Medusa, that mare,
That lyke a fende doth stare;
And from Megeras edders,
For rufflynge of Phillips fethers,
80   And from her fyry sparklynges,
For burnynge of his wynges;
And from the smokes sowre
Of Proserpinas bowre;
And from the dennes darke
85   Wher Cerberus doth barke,

Whom Theseus dyd afraye,
Whom Hercules dyd outraye,
As famous poetes say;
From that hell-hounde
90 That lyeth in cheynes bounde,
With gastly hedes thre;
To Jupyter pray we
That Phyllyp preserved may be!
Amen, say ye with me!

95 *Do mi nus,*
Helpe nowe swete Jesus!
Levavi oculos meos in montes:
Wolde God I had Zenophontes,
Or Socrates the wyse,
100 To shew me their devyse
Moderatly to take
This sorow that I make
For Phyllip Sparowes sake!
So fervently I shake,
105 I fele my body quake,
So urgently I am brought
Into carefull thought.
Like Andromach, Hectors wyfe,
Was wery of her lyfe,
110 Whan she had lost her joye,
Noble Hector of Troye;
In lyke maner also
Encreaseth my dedly wo,
For my sparowe is go.
115 It was so prety a fole,
It wold set on a stole,
And lerned after my scole
For to kepe his cut,
With, 'Phyllyp, kepe your cut!'
120 It had a velvet cap,
And wold syt upon my lap,
And seke after small wormes,
And somtyme white bred crommes;
And many tymes and ofte
125 Betwene my brestes softe

It wolde lye and rest –
It was propre and prest.
      Somtyme he wolde gaspe
Whan he sawe a waspe;
130 A fly, or a gnat,
He wolde flye at that;
And prytely he wolde pant
Whan he saw an ant;
Lord, how he wolde pry
135 After the butterfly!
Lorde, how he wolde hop
After the gressop!
And whan I sayd, 'Phyp, Phyp,'
Than he wold lepe and skyp,
140 And take me by the lyp.
Alas, it wyll me slo,
That Phillyp is gone me fro!

Si in i qui ta tes
Alas, I was evyll at ease!
145 *De pro fun dis cla ma vi,*
Whan I sawe my sparowe dye!

Nowe, after my dome,
Dame Sulpicia at Rome,
Whose name regystred was
150 Forever in tables of bras,
Because that she dyd pas
In poesy to endyte
And eloquently to wryte,
Though she wolde pretende
155 My sparowe to commende,
I trowe she coude not amende
Reportynge the vertues all
Of my sparowe royall.
      For it wold come and go,
160 And fly so to and fro;
And on me it wolde lepe
Whan I was aslepe,
And his fethers shake,

Wherewith he wolde make
165   Me often for to wake
And for to take him in
Upon my naked skyn.
God wot, we thought no syn –
What though he crept so lowe?
170   It was no hurt, I trowe.
He dyd nothynge, perde,
But syt upon my kne.
Phyllyp, though he were nyse,
In him it was no vyse;
175   Phyllyp had leve to go
To pyke my lytell too,
Phillip myght be bolde
And do what he wolde;
Phillip wolde seke and take
180   All the flees blake
That he coulde there espye
With his wanton eye.

O pe ra,
La, soll, fa, fa,
185   *Confitebor tibi, Domine, in toto corde meo.*
Alas, I wolde ryde and go
A thousand myle of grounde,
If any such might be found!
It were worth an hundreth pound
190   Of Kynge Cresus golde,
Or of Attalus the olde,
The ryche prynce of Pargame,
Whoso lyst the story to se.
Cadmus, that his syster sought,
195   And he shold be bought
For golde and fee,
He shuld over the see
To wete if he coulde brynge
Any of the ofsprynge
200   Or any of the blode.
But whoso understode
Of Medeas arte,
I wolde I had a parte

Of her crafty magyke!
205   My sparowe than shuld be quycke
With a charme or twayne,
And playe with me agayne.
But all this is in vayne
Thus for to complayne.

210   I toke my sampler ones
Of purpose, for the nones,
To sowe with stytchis of sylke
My sparow whyte as mylke,
That by representacyon
215   Of his image and facyon,
To me it myght importe
Some pleasure and comforte
For my solas and sporte.
But whan I was sowing his beke,
220   Me thought my sparow did spek,
And opened his prety byll,
Saynge, 'Mayd, ye are in wyll
Agayne me for to kyll!
Ye prycke me in the head!'

225   With that my nedle waxed red,
Me thought, of Phyllyps blode.
Myne hear ryght upstode,
And was in suche a fray
My speche was taken away.

230   I kest downe that there was,
And sayd, 'Alas, alas,
How commeth this to pas?'
My fyngers, dead and colde,
Coude not my sampler holde;
235   My nedle and threde
I threwe away for drede.
The best now that I maye
Is for his soule to pray:
    A porta inferi,
240   Good Lorde, have mercy
Upon my sparowes soule,
Wryten in my bede roule!
Au di vi vo cem,
Japhet, Cam, and Sem,

245   *Ma gni fi cat,*
            Shewe me the ryght path
        To the hylles of Armony,
        Wherfore the bordes yet cry
        Of your fathers bote,
250   That was sometyme aflote,
        And nowe they lye and rote;
        Let some poetes wryte
        Deucalyons flode it hyght.
            But as verely as ye be
255   The naturall sonnes thre
        Of Noe the patryarke,
        That made that great arke,
        Wherin he had apes and owles,
        Beestes, byrdes, and foules,
260   That if ye can fynde
        Any of my sparowes kynde,
        (God send the soule good rest!)
        I wolde have yet a nest
        As prety and as prest
265   As my sparowe was.
        But my sparowe dyd pas
        All sparowes of the wode
        That were syns Noes flode;
        Was never none so good;
270   Kynge Phylyp of Macedony
        Had no such Phylyp as I,
        No, no, syr, hardely!
            That vengeaunce I aske and crye,
        By way of exclamacyon,
275   On all the hole nacyon
        Of cattes wylde and tame;
        God send them sorowe and shame!
        That cat specyally,
        That slew so cruelly
280   My lytell prety sparowe
        That I brought up at Carowe.
            O cat of carlyshe kynde,
        The fynde was in thy mynde

Whan thou my byrde untwynde!
285 I wold thou haddest ben blynde!
The leopardes savage,
The lyons in theyr rage,
Myght catche the in theyr pawes,
And gnawe the in theyr jawes!
290 The serpents of Lybany
Myght stynge the venymously!
The dragones with their tonges
Might poyson thy lyver and longes!
The mantycors of the montaynes
295 Myght fede them on thy braynes!
    Melanchates, that hounde
That plucked Acteon to the grounde,
Gave hym his mortall wounde,
Chaunged to a dere,
300 The story doth appere,
Was chaunged to an harte:
So thou, foule cat that thou arte,
The selfe same hounde
Myght the confounde,
305 That his owne lorde bote
Myght byte asondre thy throte!
    Of Inde the gredy grypes
Myght tere out all thy trypes!
Of Arcady the beares
310 Might plucke away thyne eares!
The wylde wolfe Lycaon
Byte asondre thy backe bone!
Of Ethna the brennynge hyll
That day and night brenneth styl,
315 Set in thy tayle a blase
That all the world may gase
And wonder upon the,
From Occyan the great se
Unto the Iles of Orchady,
320 From Tyllbery fery
To the playne of Salysbery!
So trayterously my byrde to kyll
That never ought the evyll wyll!

Was never byrde in cage
325 More gentle of corage
In doynge his homage
Unto his soverayne.
Alas, I say agayne,
Deth hath departed us twayne;
330 The false cat hath the slayne!
Farewell, Phyllyp, adew;
Our Lorde thy soule reskew!
Farewell without restore,
Farewell for evermore!
335   And it were a Jewe,
It wolde make one rew
To se my sorow new.
These vylanous false cattes
Were made for myse and rattes,
340 And not for byrdes smale.
Alas, my face waxeth pale,
Tellynge this pyteyus tale,
How my byrde so fayre,
That was wont to repayre,
345 And go in at my spayre,
And crepe in at my gore
Of my gowne before,
Flyckerynge with his wynges.
Alas, my hert it stynges,
350 Remembrynge prety thynges!
Alas, myne hert it sleth
My Phyllyppes dolefull deth!
Whan I remembre it,
How pretely it wolde syt
355 Many tymes and ofte,
Upon my fynger aloft!
I played with him tytell-tattyll,
And fed him with my spattyl,
With his byll betwene my lippes,
360 It was my prety Phyppes!
Many a prety kusse
Had I of his swete musse;
And now the cause is thus,

That he is slayne me fro,
365   To my great payne and wo.
 Of fortune this the chaunce
Standeth on varyaunce:
Oft tyme after pleasaunce,
Trouble and grevaunce.
370   No man can be sure
All way to have pleasure.
As well perceyve ye maye
How my dysport and play
From me was taken away
375   By Gyb, our cat savage,
That in a furyous rage
Caught Phyllyp by the head,
And slew him there starke dead.
 Kyry, eleyson
380   *Christe, eleyson*
 Kyry, eleson!

For Phylyp Sparowes soule
Set in our bede rolle,
Let us now whysper
385   A *Pater noster.*

 Lauda, anima mea, Dominum!
To wepe with me loke that ye come,
All maner of byrdes in your kynd;
So none be left behynde.
390   To mornynge loke that ye fall
With dolorous songes funerall,
Some to synge, and some to say,
Some to wepe, and some to pray,
Every byrde in his laye:
395   The goldfynche, the wagtayle;
The janglynge jay to rayle,
The fleckyd pye to chatter
Of this dolorous mater.
And Robyn Redbrest
400   He shall be the preest,
The requiem masse to synge,
Softly warbelynge,

With helpe of the red sparow
And the chattrynge swallow,
405 This herse for to halow.
The larke with his longe to;
The spynke and the martynet also;
The shovelar with his brode bek;
The doterell, that folyshe pek;
410 And also the mad coote,
With a balde face to toote;
The feldefare and the snyte;
With feldefare and the synte;
The crowe and the kyte;
The ravyn called Rolfe,
415 His playne songe to solfe;
The partryche, the quayle;
The plover with us to wayle;
The woodhacke, that syngeth 'chur',
Horsly, as he had the mur;
420 The lusty chauntyng nyghtyngale;
The popyngay to tell her tale,
That toteth oft in a glasse,
Shall rede the gospell at masse;
The mavys with her whystell
425 Shall rede there the pystell.
But with a large and a longe
To kepe just playne songe
Our chaunters shalbe the cuckoue,
The culver, the stockedowve,
430 With Puwyt the lapwyng,
The versycles shall syng.
The bitter with his bumpe,
The crane with his trumpe,
The swan of Menander,
435 The gose and the gander,
The ducke and the drake,
Shall watche at this wake;
The pecocke so prowde,
Bycause his voyce is lowde,
440 And hath a glorious tayle,
He shall syng the grayle;
The owle, that is so foule,
Must helpe us to houle;

The heron so gaunce,
445   And the cormoraunce,
With the fesaunte,
And the gaglynge gaunte,
And the churlysshe chowgh;
The knoute and the rowgh;
450   The barnacle, the bussarde,
With the wylde mallarde;
The dyvendop to slepe;
The wather-hen to wepe;
The puffyn and the tele,
455   Money they shall dele
To poore folke at large,
That shall be theyr charge;
The semewe and the tytmose;
The wodcocke with the longe nose;
460   The threstyl with her warblyng;
The starlyng with her brablyng;
The roke, with the ospraye
That putteth fysshes to a fraye;
And the denty curlewe,
465   With the turtyll most trew.

At this *Placebo*
We may not well forgo
The countrynge of the coe;
The storke also,
470   That maketh his nest
In chymneyes to rest;
Within those walles
No broken galles
May there abyde
475   Of cokoldry syde,
Of els phylosophy
Maketh a great lye.
The estryge, that wyll eate
An horshowe so great,
480   In the stede of meate
Such fervent heat
His stomake doth freat;
He can not well fly,
Nor synge tunably;

485 Yet at a brayde
    He hath well assayde
    To solfe above E-la –
    Fa, lorell, *fa, fa* –
    Ne quando
490 *Male cantando*,
    The best that we can,
    To make hym our belman,
    And let hym ryng the bellys;
    He can do nothyng ellys.
495   Chaunteclere, our coke,
    Must tell what is of the clocke
    By the astrology
    That he hath naturally
    Conceyved and cought,
500 And was never tought
    By Albumazer
    The astronomer,
    Nor by Ptholomy,
    Prince of astronomy,
505 Nor yet by Haly;
    And yet he croweth dayly
    And nyghtly the tydes
    That no man abydes,
    With Partlot his hen,
510 Whom now and then
    He plucketh by the hede
    Whan he doth her trede.
    The byrde of Araby,
    That potencyally
515 May never dye
    And yet there is none
    But one alone;
    A phenex it is
    This herse that must blys
520 With armatycke gummes
    That cost great sumes,
    The way of thurifycation
    To make a fumigation
    Swete of reflayre,
525 And redolent of eyre,

This corse for to sence
With greate reverence,
As patryarke or pope
In a blacke cope.
530 Whyles he senseth the herse,
He shall synge the verse
Libe ra me,
In *de*, *la*, *soll*, *re*,
Softly bemole
535 For my sparowes soule.
Plinni sheweth all
In his *Story Naturall*,
What he doth fynde
Of this phenyx kynde;
540 Of whose incyneracyon
There ryseth a new creacyon
Of the same facyon
Without alteracyon,
Savyng that olde age
545 Is turned into corage
Of fresshe youth agayne;
This matter trew and playne,
Playne matter indede,
Whoso lyst to rede
550   But for the egle doth flye
Hyest in the skye,
He shall be the sedeane,
The quere to demeane,
As provost pryncypall,
555 To teach them theyr ordynall;
Also the noble fawcon,
With the gerfawcon,
The tarsell gentyll,
They shall morne soft and styll
560 In theyr amysse of gray;
The sacre with them shall say
Dirige for Phyllyppes soule;
The goshauke shall have a role
The queresters to controll;
565 The lanners and the marlyons
Shall stand in their morning gounes;

The hobby and the muskette
The sensers and the crosse shall fet;
The kestrell in all this warke
570   Shall be holy wather clarke.
   And now the darke cloudy nyght
Chaseth away Phebus bryght,
Taking his course toward the west;
God sende my sparoes sole good rest!
575   *Requiem eternam dona eis, Domine.*
Fa, fa, fa, my, re,
A por ta in fe ri,
Fa, fa, fa, my, my.
Credo vydere bona Domini,
580   I pray God, Phillip to heven may fly.
Domine, exaudi oracionem meam,
To heven he shall, from heven he cam.
Do mi nus vo bis cum,
Of al good praiers God send him sum!
585   *Oremus.*
Deus, cui proprium est miserere et parcere,
On Phillips soule have pyte!

For he was a prety cocke,
And came of a gentyll stocke,
590   And wrapt in a maidenes smocke,
And cherysshed full dayntely,
Tyll cruell fate made him to dy:
Alas, for dolefull desteny!
But whereto shuld I
595   Lenger morne or crye?
To Jupyter I call,
Of heven emperyall,
That Phyllyp may fly
Above the starry sky,
600   To treade the prety wren
That is our Ladyes hen.
Amen, amen, amen!
   Yet one thynge is behynde,
That now commeth to mynde:
605   An epytaphe I wold have
For Phyllyppes grave.

But for I am a mayde,
Tymerous, halfe afrayde,
That never yet asayde
610 Of Elyconys well,
Where the muses dwell:
Though I can rede and spell,
Recounte, reporte, and tell
Of the *Tales of Caunterbury*
615 Some sad storyes, some mery,
As Palamon and Arcet,
Duke Theseus, and Partelet;
And of the Wyfe of Bath,
That worketh moch scath
620 Whan her tale is tolde
Amonge huswyves bolde,
How she controlde
Her husbandes as she wolde,
And them to despyse
625 In the homylyest wyse,
Brynge other wyves in thought
Their husbandes to set at nought:
And though that rede have I
Of Gawen, and Syr Guy,
630 And tell can a great pece
Of the Golden Flece,
How Jason it wan,
Lyke a valyaunt man;
Or Arturs rounde table,
635 With his knightes commendable,
And Dame Gaynour, his quene
Was somwhat wanton I wene;
How Syr Launcelote de Lake
Many a spere brake
640 For his ladyes sake;
Of Trystram, and Kynge Marke,
And all the hole warke
Of Bele Isold his wyfe,
For whom was moch stryfe;
645 Some say she was lyght,
And made her husband knyght
Of the comyne hall,

That cuckoldes men call;
And of Syr Lybius
650 Named Dysconius;
Of *Quater Fylz Amund*,
And how they were sommonde
To Rome, to Charlemayne,
Upon a great payne,
655 And how they rode eche one
On Bayarde Mountalbon;
Men se hym now and than
In the forest of Arden.
What though I can frame
660 The storyes by name
Of Judas Machabeus,
And of Cesar Julious;
And of the love betwene
Paris and Vyene;
665 And of the Duke Hannyball,
That made the Romaynes all
For-drede and to quake;
How Scipion dyd wake
The cytye of Cartage,
670 Which by his mercyfull rage
He bete downe to the grounde:
And though I can expounde
Of Hector of Troye
That was all theyr joye,
675 Whom Achylles slew,
Wherfore all Troy dyd rew;
And of the love so hote
That made Troylus to dote
Upon fayre Cressyde,
680 And what they wrote and sayd,
And of theyr wanton wylles,
Pandaer bare the bylles
From one to the other,
His maisters love to further,
685 Somtyme a presyous thyng,
An ouche or els a ryng,
From her to hym agayn;
Somtyme a pretty chayn,

Or a bracelet of her here,
690 Prayd Troylus for to were
That token for her sake;
How hartely he dyd it take
And moche therof dyd make;
And all that was in vayne,
695 For she dyd but fayne;
The story telleth playne,
He coulde not optayne
Though his father were a kyng;
Yet there was a thyng
700 That made the male to wryng;
She made hym to syng
The song of lovers lay;
Musyng nyght and day,
Mournyng all alone,
705 Comfort had he none
For she was quyte gone;
Thus in conclusyon,
She brought him in abusyon;
In ernest and in game
710 She was moch to blame;
Disparaged is her fame
And blemysshed is her name,
In maner half with shame;
Troylus also hath lost
715 On her moch love and cost,
And now must kys the post;
Pandaer, that went betwene,
Hath won nothing, I wene,
But lyght for somer grene;
720 Yet for a speciall laud
He is named Troylus baud;
Of that name he is sure
Whyles the world shall dure:
    Though I remembre the fable
725 Of Penelope most stable,
To her husband most trew,
Yet long tyme she ne knew
Whether he were onlyve or ded;
Her wyt stood her in sted

730 That she was true and just,
For any bodely lust,
To Ulixes her make,
And never wold him forsake.
   Of Marcus Marcellus
735 A proces I could tell us;
And of Anteocus,
And of Josephus
De Antiquitatibus;
And of Mardocheus,
740 And of great Assuerus,
And of Vesca his queene,
Whom he forsoke with teene,
And of Hester his other wyfe,
With whom he ledd a plesaunt life;
745 Of Kyng Alexander;
And of Kyng Evander
And of Porcena the Great,
That made the Romayns to sweat:
   Though I have enrold
750 A thousand new and old
Of these historious tales,
To fyll bougets and males
With bokes that I have red,
Yet I am nothyng sped,
755 And can but lytell skyll
Of Ovyd or Virgyll,
Or of Plutharke,
Or Frauncys Petrarke,
Alcheus or Sapho,
760 Or such other poetes mo,
As Linus and Homerus,
Euphorion and Theocritus,
Anacreon and Arion,
Sophocles and Philemon,
765 Pyndarus and Symonides,
Philistion and Phorocides;
These poetes of auncyente,
They ar to diffuse for me:
   For as I tofore have sayd,

770 I am but a yong mayd,
  And can not in effect
  My style as yet direct
  With Englysh wordes elect;
  Our naturall tong is rude,
775 And hard to be enneude
  With pullysshed termes lusty;
  Our language is so rusty,
  So cankered and so full
  Of frowardes, and so dull,
780 That if I wolde apply
  To wryte ornatly,
  I wot not where to fynd
  Termes to serve my mynde.
   Gowers Englysh is olde
785 And of no value told;
  His mater is worth gold,
  And worthy to be enrold.
   In Chauser I am sped,
  His tales I have red;
790 His mater is delectable,
  Solacious and commendable;
  His Englysh well alowed,
  So as it is enprowed,
  For as it is enployd,
795 There is no Englysh voyd,
  At those dayes moch commended;
  And now men wold have amended
  His Englyssh whereat they barke
  And mar all they warke;
800 Chaucer, that famus clerke,
  His termes were not darke,
  But plesaunt, easy and playne;
  Ne worde he wrote in vayne.
   Also Johnn Lydgate
805 Wryteth after an hyer rate;
  It is dyffuse to fynde
  The sentence of his mynde,
  Yet wryteth he in his kynd,
  No man that can amend

810   Those maters that he hath pende;
      Yet some men fynde a faute,
      And say he wryteth to haute.
         Wherfore hold me excused
      If I have not well perused
815   Myne Englyssh halfe-abused;
      Though it be refused,
      In worth I shall it take,
      And fewer wordes make.
         But for my sparowes sake,
820   Yet as a woman may,
      My wyt I shall assay
      An epytaphe to wryght
      In Latyne playne and lyght,
      Whereof the elegy
825   Foloweth by and by.

      Flos volucrum formose, vale!
      Philippe, sub isto
      Marmore iam recubas,
      Qui mihi carus eras.
830   *Semper erunt nitido*
      Radiantia sydera celo;
      Impressusque meo
      Pectore semper eris.
         Per me laurigerum
835   *Britanum Skeltonida vatem*
      Hec cecinisse licet
      Ficta sub imagine texta.
      Cuius eris volucris,
      Prestanti corpore virgo:
840   *Candida Nais erat,*
      Formosior ista Joanna est:
      Docta Corinna fuit,
      Sed magis ista sapit.
         Bien men souvient.

      THE COMMENDACIONS

845   *Beati im ma cu la ti in via,*
      O gloriosa femina!

Now myne hole imaginacion
And studyous medytacion
Is to take this commendacyon
850   In this consyderacion;
And under pacyent tolleracyon
Of that most goodly mayd
That *Placebo* hath sayd,
And for her sparow prayd
855   In lamentable wyse.
    Now wyll I enterpryse,
Thorow the grace dyvyne
Of the Muses nyne,
Her beautye to commende,
860   If Arethusa wyll send
Me enfluence to endyte,
And with my pen to wryte;
If Apollo wyll promyse
Melodyously it to devyse
865   His tunable harpe stryngges
With armony that synges
Of princes and of kynges
And of all pleasaunt thynges,
Of lust and of delyght,
870   Thorow his godly myght;
To whom be the laude ascrybed
That my pen hath enbybed
With the aureat droppes,
As verely my hope is,
875   Of Thagus, that golden flod,
That passeth all erthly good;
And as that flode doth pas
Al floodes that ever was
With his golden sandes,
880   Who so that understandes
Cosmography, and the stremys
And the floodes in straunge remes,
Ryght so she doth excede
All other of whom we rede,
885   Whose fame by me shall sprede
Into Perce and Mede,

From Brytons Albion
To the towre of Babilon.
   I trust it is no shame,
890 And no man wyll me blame,
Though I regester her name
In the courte of Fame;
For this most goodly floure,
This blossome of fresshe coulour,
895 So Jupiter me socour,
She floryssheth new and new
In bewte and vertew.
Hac claritate gemina
O gloriosa femina,
900 *Retribue servo tuo, vivifica me!*
Labia mea laudabunt te.
   But enforsed am I
Openly to askry
And to make an outcri
905 Against odyous Envi,
That evermore wil ly
And say cursedly;
With his ledder ey,
And chekes dry;
910 With vysage wan,
As swart as tan;
His bones crake,
Leane as a rake;
His gummes rusty
915 Are full unlusty;
His herte withall
Bytter as gall;
His lyver, his longe
With anger is wronge;
920 His serpentes tonge
That many one hath stonge;
He frowneth ever;
He laugheth never,
Even nor morow;
925 But other mennes sorow
Causeth him to gryn

And rejoyce therin;
   No slepe can him catch,
But ever doth watch,
930 He is so bete
With malyce, and frete
With angre and yre,
His foule desyre
Wyll suffre no slepe
935 In his hed to crepe;
   His foule semblaunt
All displesaunt;
Whan other ar glad,
Than is he sad,
940 Frantyke and mad;
His tong never styll
For to say yll,
Wrythyng and wringyng,
Bytyng and styngyng;
945 And thus this elf
Consumeth himself,
Himself doth slo
With payne and wo.
   This fals Envy
950 Sayth that I
Use great folly
For to endyte,
And for to wryte,
And spend my tyme
955 In prose and ryme,
For to expres
The noblenes
Of my maistres,
That causeth me
960 Studious to be
To make a relation
Of her commendation;
And there agayne
Envy doth complayne,
965 And hath disdayne;
But yet certayne

I wyll be playne,
And my style dres
To this prosses.
970   Now Phebus me ken
To sharpe my pen,
And lede my fyst
As hym best lyst,
That I may say
975 Honour alway
Of womankynd!
Trouth doth me bynd
And loyalte
Ever to be
980 Their true bedell
To wryte and tell
How women excell
In noblenes;
As my maistres,
985 Of whom I thynk
With pen and ynk
For to compyle
Some goodly style;
For this most goodly floure,
990 This blossome of fresh coloure,
So Jupyter me socoure,
She flourissheth new and new
In beaute and vertew:
Hac claritate gemina
995 *O gloriosa femina,*
Legem pone michi, domina, in viam justificationem tuarum!
Quemadmodum desiderat cervus ad fontes aquarum.
    How shall I report
All the goodly sort
1000 Of her fetures clere,
That hath non erthly pere?
Her favour of her face
Ennewed all with grace,
Confort, pleasure, and solace,
1005 Myne hert doth so enbrace,
And so hath ravyshed me

    Her to behold and se,
    That in wordes playne
    I cannot me refrayne
1010 To loke on her agayne.
    Alas, what shuld I fayne?
    It wer a plesaunt payne
    With her aye to remayne.
      Her eyen gray and stepe
1015 Causeth myne hert to lepe;
    With her browes bent
    She may well represent
    Fayre Lucres, as I wene,
    Or els fayre Polexene,
1020 Or els Caliope,
    Or els Penolope;
    For this most goodly floure,
    This blossome of fresshe coloure,
    So Jupiter me socoure,
1025 She florisheth new and new
    In beautye and vertew:
    Hac claritate gemina
    O gloriosa femina,
    Memor esto verbi tui servo tuo!
1030 *Servus tuus sum ego.*
      The Indy saphyre blew
    Her vaynes doth ennew;
    The orient perle so clere,
    The whytnesse of her lere;
1035 The lusty ruby ruddes
    Resemble the rose buddes;
    Her lyppes soft and mery
    Emblomed lyke the chery,
    It were an hevenly blysse
1040 Her sugred mouth to kysse.
      Her beautye to augment
    Dame Nature hath her lent
    A warte upon her cheke,
    Who so lyst to seke
1045 In her vysage a skar
    That semyth from afar

Lyke to the radyant star,
All with favour fret,
So properly it is set:
1050   She is the vyolet,
The daysy delectable,
The columbyn commendable
This jelofer amyable;
For this most goodly floure,
1055   This blossom of fressh colour,
So Jupiter me succour,
She florysheth new and new
In beaute and vertew:
Hac claritate gemina
1060   *O gloriosa femina,*
Bonitatem fecisti cum servo tuo, domina,
Et ex precordiis sonant preconia.
        And whan I perceyved
Her wart and conceyved,
1065   It cannot be denayd
But it was well convayd,
And set so womanly,
And nothynge wantonly,
But ryght convenyently,
1070   And full congruently,
As Nature cold devyse,
In most goodly wyse.
Who so lyst beholde,
It makethe lovers bolde
1075   To her to sewe for grace,
Her favoure to purchase.
        The sker upon her chyn
Enhached on her fayre skyn,
Whyter than the swan,
1080   It wold make any man
To forget deadly syn
Her favour to wyn;
For this most goodly floure,
This blossom of fressh coloure,
1085   So Jupiter me socoure,
She flouryssheth new and new
In beaute and vertew:

Hac claritate gemina
O gloriosa femina,
1090 *Defecit in salutare tuum anima mea;*
Quid petis filio, mater dulcissima? Ba ba!
    Soft, and make no dyn,
For now I wyll begyn
To have in remembraunce
1095 Her goodly dalyaunce,
And her goodly pastaunce:
So sad and so demure,
Behavynge her so sure,
With wordes of pleasure
1100 She wold make to the lure
And any man convert
To gyve her his hole hert.
She made me sore amased
Upon her whan I gased,
1105 Me thought min hert was crased,
My eyne were so dased;
For this most goodly flour,
This blossom of fressh colour,
So Jupyter me socour,
1110 She flouryssheth new and new
In beauty and vertew:
Hac claritate gemina
O gloriosa femina,
Quomodo dilexi legem tuam, domina!
1115 *Recedant vetera, nova sunt omnia.*
    And to amende her tale,
Whan she lyst to avale,
And with her fyngers smale,
And handes soft as sylke,
1120 Whyter than the mylke,
That are so quyckely vayned,
Wherwyth my hand she strayned,
Lorde, how I was payned!
Unneth I me refrayned,
1125 How she me had reclaymed,
And me to her retayned,
Enbrasynge therewithall
Her goodly myddell small

With sydes longe and streyte;
1130 To tell you what conceyte
I had than in a tryce,
The matter were to nyse,
And yet there was no vyce,
Nor yet no vyllany,
1135 But only fantasy;
For this most goodly floure,
This blossom of fressh coloure,
So Jupiter me succoure,
She floryssheth new and new
1140 In beaute and vertew:
Hac claritate gemina
O gloriosa femina,
Iniquos odio habui!
Non calumnientur me superbi.
1145   But whereto shulde I note
How often dyd I tote
Upon her prety fote?
It raysed myne hert rote
To se her treade the grounde
1150 With heles short and rounde.
She is playnly expresse
Egeria, the goddesse,
And lyke to her image,
Emportured with corage,
1155 A lovers pylgrimage.
Ther is no beest savage,
Ne no tyger so wood,
But she wolde chaunge his mood,
Such relucent grace
1160 Is formed in her face;
For this most goodly floure,
This blossome of fressh coloure,
So Jupiter me succour,
She flouryssheth new and new
1165 In beaute and vertew:
Hac claritate gemina
O gloriosa femina,
Mirabilia testimonia tua!
Sicut novelle plantationes in juventute sua.

1170   So goodly as she dresses,
       So properly she presses
       The bryght golden tresses
       Of her heer so fyne,
       Lyke Phebus beames shyne.
1175   Wherto shuld I disclose
       The garterynge of her hose?
       It is for to suppose
       How that she can were
       Gorgiously her gere;
1180   Her fresshe habylementes
       With other implementes
       To serve for all ententes,
       Lyke dame Flora, quene
       Of lusty somer grene;
1185   For this most goodly floure,
       This blossom of fressh coloure,
       So Jupiter me socoure,
       She florisheth new and new
       In beautye and vertew:
1190   *Hac claritate gemina*
       O gloriosa femina,
       Clamavi in toto corde, exaudi me!
       Misericordia tua magna est super me.
           Her kyrtell so goodly lased,
1195   And under that is brased
       Such pleasures that I may
       Neyther wryte nor say;
       Yet though I wryte not with ynke,
       No man can let me thynke,
1200   For thought hath lyberte,
       Thought is franke and fre;
       To thynke a mery thought
       It cost me lytell nor nought.
       Wolde God myne homely style
1205   Were pullysshed with the fyle
       Of Ciceros eloquence,
       To prase her excellence!
       For this most goodly floure,
       This blossome of fressh coloure,
1210   So Jupiter me succoure,

She flouryssheth new and new
In beaute and vertew:
Hac claritate gemina
O gloriosa femina,
1215 *Principes persecuti sunt me gratis!*
Omnibus consideratis,
Paradisus voluptatis
Hec virgo est dulcissima.
My pen it is unable,
1220 My hand it is unstable,
My reson rude and dull
To prayse her at the full;
Goodly maystres Jane,
Sobre, demure Dyane;
1225 Jane this maystres hyght,
The lode stare of delyght,
Dame Venus of all pleasure,
The well of worldly treasure;
She doth excede and pas
1230 In prudence dame Pallas;
For this most goodly floure,
This blossome of fresshe colour,
So Jupiter me socoure,
She florysssheth new and new
1235 In beaute and vertew:
Hac claritate gemina
O gloriosa femina!
Requiem eternam dona eis, Domine!
With this psalme, *Domine, probasti me,*
1240 Shall sayle over the see,
With, *Tibi, Domine, commendamus.*
On pylgrimage to Saynt Jamys,
For shrympes, and for pranys,
And for stalkynge cranys;
1245 And where my pen hath offendyd,
I pray you it may be amendyd
By discrete consyderacyon
Of your wyse reformacyon;
I have not offended, I trust,
1250 If it be sadly dyscust.

It were no gentle gyse
This treatyse to despyse
Because I have wrytten and sayd
Honour to this fayre mayd;
1255 Wherefore shulde I be blamed
That I Jane have named,
And famously proclamed?
She is worthy to be enrolde
With letters of golde.
1260 *Car elle vault.*
Per me laurigerum Britonum Skeltonida vatem
Laudibus eximiis merito hec redimita puella est:
Formosam cecini, qua non formosior ulla est;
Formosam potius quam commendaret Homerus.
1265 *Sic juvat interdum rigidos recreare labores,*
Nec minus hoc titulo tersa Minerva mea est.
 Rien que playsere.

Thus endeth the boke of Philip Sparow, and her foloweth
an addicyon made by Maister Skelton.

The gyse now a dayes
Of some janglynge jayes
1270 Is to discommende
That they cannot amend,
Though they wold spend
All the wyttes they have.
 What ayle them to deprave
1275 Phillip Sparowes grave?
His *Dirige*, her commendacyon
Can be no derogacyon,
But myrth and consolacyon
Made by protestacyon,
1280 No man to myscontent
With Phillyppes enterement.
 Alas, that goodly mayd,
Why shuld she be afrayde?
Why shuld she take shame
1285 That her goodly name,
Honorably reported,
Sholde be set and sorted,

To be matriculate
With ladyes of estate?
1290   I conjure the, Phillip Sparow,
By Hercules that hell dyd harow,
And with a venemous arow
Slew of the Epidaures
One of the Centaures,
1295   Or Onocentaures,
Or Hipocentaures;
By whose myght and mayne
An hart was slayne
With hornes twayne
1300   Of glytteryng gold;
And the appels of gold
Of Hesperides withhold,
And with a dragon kept
That never more slept,
1305   By marcyall strength
He wan at length;
And slew Gerion
With thre bodyes in one;
With myghty corage
1310   Adaunted the rage
Of a lyon savage;
Of Dyomedes stable
He brought out a rable
Of coursers and rounses
1315   With leapes and bounses;
And with myghty luggyng,
Wrestlyng and tuggyng,
He plucked the bull
By the horned skull,
1320   And offred to Cornucopia
And so forth *per cetera*;
Also by Ecates bower
In Plutos gastly tower;
By the ugly Eumenides,
1325   That never have rest nor ease;
By the venemous serpent,
That in hell is never brent,

In Lerna the Grekes fen,
That was engendred then;
1330   By Chemeras flames,
And all the dedly names
Of infernall posty
Where soules frye and rousty;
By the Stygyall flood,
1335   And the streames wood
Of Cocitus botumles well;
By the feryman of hell,
Caron with his beerd hore,
That roweth with a rude ore
1340   And with his frownsid fore top
Gydeth his bote with a prope;
I conjure, Phylyp, and call
In the name of Kyng Saul;
Primo Regum expresse,
1345   He bad the Phitonesse
To wytchcraft her to dresse,
And by her abusyons,
And dampnable illusyons
Of marveylus conclusyons,
1350   And by her supersticyons,
And wonderfull condityons,
She raysed up in that stede
Samuell that was dede;
But whether it were so,
1355   He were *idem in numero*,
The selfe same Samuell,
How be it to Saull dyd he tell
The Philistinis shuld hym ascry,
And the next day he shuld dye,
1360   I wyll my selfe dyscharge
To lettred men at large:
But Phylyp, I conjure the
Now by these names thre,
Diana in the woodes grene,
1365   Luna that so bryght doth shyne,
Procerpina in hell,
That thou shortly tell,

And shew now unto me
What the cause may be
1370 Of this perplexite!

Inferias, Philippe, tuas Scroupe pulchra Joanna
Instanter petiit: cur nostri carminis illam
Nunc pudet? Est sero; minor est infamia vero.

Than suche as have disdayned
1375 And of this worke complayned,
I pray God they be payned
No worse than is contayned
In verses two or thre
That folowe as you may se.

1380 *Luride, cur, livor, volucris pia funera damnas?*
Talia te rapiant rapiunt que fata volucrem!
Est tamen invidia mors tibi continua.

VIII

Epitaphe

This tretise devysed it is
Of two knaves somtyme of Dis.

Though this knaves be deade,
Full of myschiefe and queed,
Yet, where so ever they ly
Theyr names shall never dye.

Compendium de duobus versipellibus, John Jayberd *et* Adam all
a knave, *deque illorum notissima vilitate.*

A DEVOUTE TRENTALE FOR OLD JOHN CLARKE,
SOMETYME THE HOLY PATRIARKE OF DIS.

Sequitur trigentale
Tale quale rationale,
Licet parum curiale,
Tamen satis est formale,
5 *Ioannis Clerc, hominis*
Cuiusdam multinominis,

Ioannes Jayberd *qui vocatur,*
Clerc cleribus nuncupatur.
Obiit sanctus iste pater
10   *Anno domini M.D. sexto.*
In parochia de Dis
Non erat sibi similis;
In malicia vir insignis,
Duplex corde et bilinguis,
15   *Senio confectus,*
Omnibus suspectus,
Nemini dilectus.
Sepultus est amonge the wedes;
God forgeve hym his mysdedes.

Dulce melos
Penetrans celos.

20   *Carmina cum cannis*
Cantemus festa, Ioannis
Clerke obiit vere,
Jayberde *nomenquae dedere;*
Dis populo natus,
25   *Clerke cleribus estquae vocatus.*
Hic vir Caldeus,
Nequam vir ceu Iebuseus,
In Christum domini
Fremuit de more cameli,
30   *Rectori proprio*
Tam verba retorta loquendo
Unde resultando-
Quae Acheronta boando tonaret.
Nunquam sincere
35   *Solitus sua crimina flere;*
Cui male lingua loquax-
Quae dicax mendaxquae fuere,
Et mores tales
Resident in nemine quales;
40   *Carpens vitales*
Auras, turbare sodales
Et cives socios,
Asinus, mulus velut, et bos.
Omne suum studium

45 *Rubium pictum per amictum*
   Discolor; et victum
   Faciens semper maledictum
   Ex intestinis ovium-
   Quae boumquae caprorum;
50 *Tendens adquae forum,*
   Fragmentum colligit horum,
   Dentibus exemptis
   Mastigat cumquae polentis
   Lanigerum caput aut ovis
55 *Aut vacce mugientis.*
   Quid petis, hic sit quis?
   John Jayberd, *incola de Dis;*
   Cui, dum vixerat is,
   Sociantur iurgia, vis, lis.

60 *Iam iacet hic* starke deed,
   Never a toth in his heed.
   Adieu, Jayberd, adue.
   I faith, dikkon, thou crue!
   Fratres, orate,
65 For this knavate,
   By the holy rode,
   Dyd never man good.
   I pray you all,
   And pray shall,
70 At this trentall
   On knees to fall
   To the foteball;
   With, 'Fill the blak bowle
   For Jayberdes sowle.'

75 *Bibite multum:*
   Ecce sepultum
   Sub pede stultum
   Asinum et mulum!
   The devill kis his *culum!*
80 With, 'Hey, howe, rumbelowe,'
   Rumpopulorum,
   Per omnia secula seculorum.
   Amen.

Requiem &c

Per Fredericum Hely
Fratrem de Monte Carmeli,
85 *Qui condunt sine sale*
Hoc devotum trigintale.
Vale, Jayberd, *valde male!*
  Finis.

ADAM UDDERSALE, *ALIAS DICTUS* ADAM ALL A KNAVE,
HIS EPITAPH FOLOWETH DEVOUTLY; HE WAS SOMTIME
THE HOLY BAILLYVE OF DIS.

Of Dis *Adam degebat*:
Dum vixit, falsa gerebat,
Namquae extorquebat
Quicquid nativus habebat,
5 *Aut liber natus; rapidus*
Lupus inde vocatus:
Ecclesiamquae satus
De Belial iste Pilatus
Sub pede calcatus
10 *Violavit nunc violatus:*
Perfidus, iratus,
Numquam fuit ille beatus:
Uddersall *stratus*
Benedictis est spoliatus,
15 *Improbus, inflatus,*
Maledictis iam laceratus:
Dis, tibi baccatus
Ballivus predominatus:
Hic fuit ingratus,
20 *Porcus velut insaciatus,*
Pinguis, crassatus;
Velut Aggag sit reprobatus!
Crudelisquae Cacus
Baratro, peto, sit tumulatus!
25 Belsabub his soule save,
Qui iacet hic, like a knave!
Iam scio mortuus est,
Et iacet hic, like a best!

Anima eius
De male in peius.
30   *Amen.*

De Dis hec semper erit camena,
'Adam Uddersall *sit anathema.*'

Auctore Skelton, rectore de Dis.

Finis &c. Apud Trumpinton scriptum per curatum eiusdem
quinto die Ianuarii, Anno domini secundum computationem
Anglie. M.D. vij.

Adam, Adam ubi es? Genesis. *Re. Ubi nulla requies, ubi nullus*
ordo, sed sempiternus horror inhabitat. Job.

Finis.

IX

A Lawde and Prayse Made for Our Sovereigne Lord the Kyng

The rose both white and rede
In one rose now dothe grow;
Thus thorow every stede
Thereof the fame dothe blow,
5   Grace the sede did sow.
England, now gaddir flowris,
Exclude now all dolowrs.

Noble Henry the eight,
Thy loving sovereine lorde,
10   Of kingis line moost streight,
His titille dothe recorde;
In whome dothe wele acorde
Alexis yonge of age,
Adrastus wise and sage.

15   Astrea, justice hight,
That from the starry sky
Shall now com and do right,

This hunderd yere scantly
A man kowd not aspy
20   That right dwelt us among,
And that was the more wrong.

Right shall the foxis chare,
The wolvis, the beris also,
That wrowght have moche care,
25   And browght Englond in wo;
They shall wirry no mo,
Nor wrote the rosary
By extort trechery.

Of this our noble king
30   The law they shall not breke;
They shall com to rekening,
No man for them wil speke.
The pepil durst not creke
Theire grevis to complaine;
35   They browght them in soche paine.

Therfor no more they shall
The commouns overbace,
That wont wer over all
Both lorde and knight to face;
40   For now the yeris of grace
And welthe ar com agayne,
That maketh England faine.

Adonis of freshe colour,
Of yowthe the godely flour,
45   Our prince of hih honour,
Our paves, our succour,
Our king, our emperour,
Our Priamus of Troy,
Our welth, our worldly joy,

50   Upon us he doth reigne
That makith our hartis glad,
As king moost sovereine
That ever Englond had;
Demure, sober and sad,

55 And Martis lusty knight;
    God save him in his right!

        Amen

    Bien men sovient

    Deo (21) gracias

    Per me laurigerum Britonum Skeltonida vatem

X

Calliope

Why were ye Calliope, embrawdred with letters of golde?
Skelton Laureate, *Orator Regius*, maketh this aunswere etc.

Calliope,
As ye may se,
Regent is she,
    Of poetes al,
5 Whiche gave to me
The high degre
Laureat to be
    Of fame royall;

Whose name enrolde
10 With silke and golde
I dare be bolde
    Thus for to were.
Of her I holde
And her housholde;
15 Though I waxe olde
    And somdele sere,

Yet is she fayne,
Voyde of disdayn,
Me to retayne
20   Her serviture.
With her certayne
I wyll remayne

As my soverayne
  Moost of pleasure.

Maulgre touz malheureux.

  Latinum carmen sequitur.

Cur tibi contexta est aurea Calliope?

  Responsio eiusdem vatis.

Candida Calliope, vatum regina, coronans
Pierios lauro, radiante intexta sub auro!
Hanc ego Pierius Pierius tanto dignabor honore,
Dum mihi vita manet, dum spiritus hos regit artus:
5 *Quamquam conficior senio marcescoque sensim,*
Ipse tamen gestare sua haec pia pignora certo,
Assensuque suo placidis parebo camenis.
Inclita Calliope, et semper mea maxima cura est.

  Haec Pierius omni Spartano liberior.

Calliope, musarum excellentissima, speciosissima, formosissima,
heroicis preest versibus.

XI
A Ballade of the Scottysshe Kynge

Kynge Jamy, Jomy your joye is all go.
Ye summoned our kynge. Why dyde ye so?
To you no thyng it dyde accorde
To sommon our kynge your soverayne lorde.
5 A kynge a somner it is wonder;
Knowe ye not salte and suger asonder?
In your somnynge ye were to malaperte,
And your harolde no thynge experte;
Ye thought ye dyde it full valyauntolye,
10 But not worth thre skyppes of a pye.
Syr squyer-galyarde ye were to swyfte;
Your wyll renne before your wytte.
To be so scornefull to your alye
Your counseyle was not worth a flye.

15   Before the Frensshe kynge, Danes and other
      Ye ought to honour your lorde and brother.
      Trowe ye, Syr James, his noble grace
      For you and your Scottes wolde tourne his face?
      Now ye proude Scottes of Gelawaye
20   For your kynge may synge welawaye.
      Now must ye knowe our kynge for your regent,
      Your soverayne lorde and presedent.
      In hym is figured Melchisedeche,
      And ye be desolate as Armeleche.
25   He is our noble champyon,
      A kynge anoynted, and ye be non.
      Thrugh your counseyle your fader was slayne;
      Wherfore I fere ye wyll suffre payne.
      And ye proude Scottes of Dunbar,
30   Parde ye be his homager
      And suters to his parlyment.
      Ye dyde not your dewty therin,
      Wyerfore ye may it now repent.
      Ye bere yourselfe somwhat to bolde,
35   Therfore ye have lost your copyholde.
      Ye be bounde tenauntes to his estate;
      Gyve up your game, ye playe chek mate;
      For to the castell of Norham
      I understonde to soone ye cam,
40   For a prysoner there now ye be
      Eyther to the devyll or the trinite.
      Thanked be saynte Gorge, our ladyes knythe,
      Your pryd is paste, adwe, good nycht.
      Ye have determyned to make a fraye,
45   Our kynge than beynge out of the waye;
      But by the power and myght of God
      Ye were beten weth your owne rod.
      By your wanton wyll, syr, at a worde,
      Ye have loste spores, cote armure and sworde.
50   Ye had be better to have busked to Huntley Bankes,
      Than in Englonde to playe ony suche prankes;
      But ye had some wyld sede to sowe,
      Therfore ye be layde now full lowe.
      Your power coude no lenger attayne
55   Warre with our kynge to meyntayne.

Of the kynge of Naverne ye may take hede
How unfortunately he doth now spede;
In double walles now he dooth dreme.
That is a kynge without a realme.
60   At hym example ye wolde none take;
Experyence hath brought you in the same brake.
Of the out yles ye rough foted Scottes
We have well eased you of the bottes.
Ye rowe ranke Scottes and dronken Danes
65   Of our Englysshe bowes ye have fette your banes.
It is not syttynge in tour nor towne
A somner to were a kynges crowne.
That noble erle, the Whyte Lyon,
Your pompe and pryde hath layde a downe.
70   His sone the lorde admyrall is full good,
His swerde hath bathed in the Scottes blode.
God save kynge Henry and his lordes all
And sende the Frensshe kynge suche another fall.

Amen, for saynt charyte and God save noble
Kynge Henry the viij.

XII

Skelton laureate

Agaynst the Scottes

Agaynst the prowde Scottys claterynge,
That never wyll leve theyr tratlynge:
Wan they the felde and lost theyr kynge?
They may well say, fye on that wynnynge!

5   Lo, these fond sottes
And tratlyng Skottys,
How they are blynde
In theyr owne mynde,
And wyll not know
10   Theyr overthrow
At Branxton More?
They are so stowre,
So frantyke mad,

      They say they had
15   And wan the felde
      With spere and shelde!
      That is as trew
      As blacke is blew
      And grene is gray.
20   What ever they say,
      Jemmy is ded
      And closyd in led,
      That was theyr owne kynge.
      Fy on that wynnyng!

25   At Floddon hyllys,
      Our bowys, our byllys
      Slew all the floure
      Of theyr honoure.
      Are nat these Scottys
30   Folys and sottys,
      Such boste to make,
      To prate and crake,
      To face, to brace,
      All voyde of grace,
35   So prowde of hart,
      So overthwart,
      So out of frame,
      So voyde of shame,
      As it is enrolde,
40   Wrytten and tolde
      Within this quaire?
      Who lyst repayre
      And therein reed
      Shall fynde indeed
45   A mad rekenynge,
      Consydrynge all thynge,
      That the Scottys may synge,
      'Fy on the wynnynge!'

         When the Scotte lyved
      Joly Jemmy, ye scornefull Scot,
50   Is it come unto your lot
      A solempne sumner for to be?
      It greyth nought for your degre

Our kynge of England for to syght,
Your soverayne lord, our prynce of myght.
55 Ye for to sende suche a cytacyon,
It shameth all your noughty nacyon,
In comparyson but kynge Koppynge
Unto our prince, anoynted kyng.
Ye play Hop Lobbyn of Lowdean;
60 Ye shew ryght well what good ye can;
Ye may be lorde of Locryan –
Chryst sence you with a fryinge pan! –
Of Edyngeborrow and Saynt Jonys towne.
Adieu, syr sumner, cast of your crowne!

When the Scot was slayne
65 Contynually I shall remember
The mery moneth of September,
With the ix day of the same,
For then began our myrth and game.
So that now I have devysed,
70 And in my mynde I have comprised,
Of the prowde Scot, kynge Jemmy,
To write some lytell tragedy,
For no maner consyderacyon
Of any sorowfull lamentacyon,
75 But for the specyall consolacyon
Of all our royall Englysh nacyon.

Melpomone, O muse tragedyall,
Unto your grace for grace now I call,
To guyde my pen and my pen to enbybe!
80 Illumyn me, your poete and your scrybe,
That with myxture of aloes and bytter gall
I may compounde confectures for a cordyall,
To angre the Scottes and Irysh keterynges withall,
That late were discomfect with battayle marcyall.

85 Thalya, my muse, for you also call I,
To touche them with tauntes of your armony,
A medley to make of myrth with sadnes,
The hertes of England to comfort with gladnes.
And now to begyn I wyll me adres,
90 To you rehersyng the somme of my proces.

Kinge Jamy, Jemmy, Jocky my jo,
Ye summond our kyng, why dyd ye so?
To you nothing it dyd accorde
To summon our kyng, your soveraygne lorde.
95 A kyng, a sumner! It was great wonder:
Know ye not suger and salt asonder?
Your sumner to saucy, to malapert;
Your harrold in armes not yet halfe expert.
Ye thought ye dyd yet valyauntly;
100 Not worth thre skyppes of a pye.
Syr skyrgalyard, ye were so skyt,
Your wyll than ran before your wyt.

Your lege ye layd and your aly,
Your frantyck fable not worth a fly,
105 Frenche kyng, or one or other;
Regardyd ye shuld your lord, your brother.
Trowyd ye, Syr Jemy, his nobull grace
From you, Syr Scot, wolde turne his face?
With, 'Gup, Syr Scot of Galaway!'
110 Now is your pryde fall to decay.
Male uryd was your fals entent
For to offend your presydent,
Your soveraygne lorde most reverent,
Your lorde, your brother, and your regent.

115 In him is fygured Melchisedec,
And ye were disloyall Amalec.
He is our noble Scipione;
Anoynted kyng, and ye were none.
Though ye untruly your father have slayne,
120 His tytle is true in Fraunce to raygne;
And ye, proud Scot, Dunde, Dunbar
Pardy, ye were his homager,
And suter to his parlyament.
For your untruth now ar ye shent.
125 Ye bare yourselfe somwhat to bold;
Therfore ye lost your copyehold.
Ye were bonde tenent to his estate;
Lost is your game, ye are checkmate.

Unto the castell of Norram,
130 I understand, to sone ye came.

At Branxton More and Flodden hylles,
Our Englysh bowes, our Englysh bylles,
Agaynst you gave so sharpe a shower,
That of Scotland ye lost the flower.

135   The White Lyon, there rampaunt of moode,
He ragyd and rent out your hart bloode;
He the White, and ye the Red,
The White there slew the Red starke ded.
Thus for your guerdon quyt ar ye,

140   Thankyd be God in trinyte,
And swete Saynt George, our ladyes knyght!
Youre eye is out; adew, good nyght!

Ye were starke mad to make a fray,
His grace beyng out of the way;

145   But, by the power and myght of God,
For youre owne tayle ye made a rod.
Ye wantyd wyt, sir, at a worde;
Ye lost your spurrys, ye lost you sworde.
Ye myght have buskyd you to Huntley Bankys;

150   Your pryde was pevysh to play such prankys:
Youre poverte cowde not attayne
With our kyng royall war to mayntayne.

Of the kynge of Naverne ye might take heed,
Ungraciously how he doth speed.

155   In double delyng so he dyd dreme,
That he is kyng without a reme;
And, for example ye wold none take,
Experiens hath brought you in such a brake.
Your welth, your joy, your sport, your play,

160   Your braggyng bost, your royall aray,
Your beard so brym as bore at bay,
Your Seven Systers, that gun so gay,
All have ye lost and cast away.
Thus fortune hath tourned you, I dare well say,

165   Now from a kyng to a clot of clay.
Out of your robes ye were shaked,
And wretchedly ye lay starke naked.
For lacke of grace hard was your hap;
The Popes curse gave you that clap.

170   Of the out iles the rough-foted Scottes,
       We have well eased them of the bottes.
       The rude ranke Scottes, lyke dronken dranes,
       At Englysh bowes have fetched their banes.
       It is not syttyng in tower and towne
175   A sumner to were a kynges crowne.
       Fortune on you therfore dyd frowne;
       Ye were to hye, ye ar cast downe.
       Syr sumner, now where is your crowne?
       Cast of your crowne, cast up your crowne!
180   Syr sumner, now ye have lost your crowne.

       Quod Skelton laureate, oratour to the kynges most
       royall estate.

       Scotia, redacta in formam provincie,
       Regis parebit nutibus Anglie:
       Alioquin, per desertum Sin, super cherubim,
4   *Cherubin, seraphim, seraphinque, ergo etc.*

       UNTO DYVERS PEOPLE THAT REMORD THIS RYMYNG
       AGAYNST THE SCOT JEMMY

       I am now constrayned,
       With wordes nothing fayned,
       This invectyve to make
       For some peoples sake
5   That lyst for to jangyll
       And waywardly to wrangyll
       Agaynst this my makyng,
       Their males therat shakyng,
       As it reprehendyng,
10   And venemously stingyng,
       Rebukyng and remordyng,
       And nothing accordyng.
           Cause have they none other
       But for that he was brother,
15   Brother unnaturall
       Unto our kyng royall,
       Agaynst whom he dyd fyght
       Falsly agaynst all right,

Lyke that untrue rebell
20   Fals Kayn agaynst Abell.
       Who so therat pyketh mood,
The tokens ar not good
To be true Englysh blood;
For, if they understood
25   His traytourly dispyght,
He was a recrayed knyght,
A subtyll sysmatyke,
Ryght nere an heretyke,
Of grace out of the state
30   And dyed excomunycate.
       And for he was a kyng,
The more shamefull rekenyng
Of him shuld men report,
In ernest and in sport.
35   He skantly loveth our kyng,
That grudgeth at this thing:
That cast such overthwartes
Percase have hollow hartes.

Si veritatem dico, quare non creditis michi?

XIII
Agenst Garnesche

(i)
Skelton Lauriate Defender Agenst Master Garnesche
Chalenger, *et cetera*

Sithe ye have me chalyngyd, Master Garnesche,
Rudely revilyng me in the kynges noble hall,
Soche an odyr chalyngyr cowde me no man wysch,
But yf yt war Syr Tyrmagant that tyrnyd without nall;
5   For Syr Frollo de Franko was never halfe so talle.
But sey me now, Syr Satrapas, what autoryte ye have
In your chalenge, Syr Chystyn, to cale me knave?

What, have ye kythyd yow a knyght, Syr Dugles the dowty,
So curryshly to beknave me in the kynges place?

10   Ye stronge sturdy stalyon, so sterne and stowty,
      Ye bere yow bolde as Barabas, or Syr Terry of Trace.
      Ye gyrne grymly with your gomys and with yor grysly face.
      But sey me yet, Syr Satropas, what auctoryte ye have
      In yor chalenge, Syr Chesten, to calle me a knave?

15   Ye fowle, fers and felle, as Syr Ferumbras the ffreke,
      Syr capten of Catywade, catacumbas of Cayre,
      Thow ye be lusty as Syr Lybyus, launces to breke,
      Yet your contenons oncomly, yor face ys nat fayer.
      For alle your proude prankyng, yor pride may apayere.
20   But sey me yet, Syr Satrapas, wat auctoryte ye have
      In yor chalenge, Syr Chesten, to cal me a knave?

      Of Mantryble the Bryge, Malchus the Murryon,
      Nor blake Baltazar with hys basnet routh as a bere,
      Nor Lycon, that lothly luske, in myn opynyon,
25   Nor no bore so brymly brystlyd ys with here,
      As ye ar brystlyd on the bake for alle your gay gere.
      But sey me yet, Syr Satrapas, what auctoryte ye have
      In yor chalenge, Syr Chesten, to calle me a knave?

      Yor wynde-schakyn shankkes, yor longe lothly legges,
30   Crokyd as a camoke, and as a kowe calfles,
      Bryngges yow out of favyr with alle femall teggys:
      That mastres Punt put yow of, yt was nat alle causeles;
      At Orwelle hyr havyn your anggre was laules.
      But sey me yet, Syr Satrapas, what auctoryte ye have
35   In yor chalenge, Syr Chesten, to calle me a knave?

      I sey, ye solem Sarson, alle blake ys yor ble;
      As a glede glowynge, your ien glyster as glasse,
      Rowlynge in yower holow hede, ugly to see;
      Your tethe teintyd with tawny; your semely snowte doth passe,
40   Howkyd as an hawkys beke, lyke Syr Topyas.
      Boldly bend you to batell, and buske your selfe to save.
      Chalenge yor selfe for a fole, call me no more knave.

      Be the kynges most noble commandement.

      (ii)
      Skelton Lauryate Defender Agenst Master Garnesche
      Chalangar, with Gresy, Gorbelyd Godfrey *et cetera*

How may I your mokery mekely tollerate,
Your gronynge, yor grontynge, yor groinynge lyke a swyne?
Your pride ys alle to peviche, your porte importunate;
You mantycare, ye maltaperte, ye can bothe wins and whyne;
5   Your lothesum lere to loke on, lyke a gresyd bote dothe schyne.
Ye cappyd Cayface copious, your paltoke on your pate,
Thow ye prate lyke prowde Pylate, beware yet of chek mate.

Hole ys your brow that ye brake with Deurandall your awne
      sworde;
Why holde ye on yer cap, syr, then? Yor pardone ys expyryd.
10   Ye hobble very homly before the kynges borde;
Ye countyr umwhyle to capcyously, and ar ye be dysiryd;
Yor moth etyn mokkysh maneres, they be all to-myryd.
Ye cappyd Cayface copyous, your paltoke on your pate,
Thow ye prate lyke prowde Pylate, beware of cheke mate.

15   O Gabionyte of Gabyone, why do ye gane and gaspe?
Huf, a galante, Garnesche, loke on your comly cors!
Lusty Garnysche, lyke a lowse, ye jet full lyke a jaspe;
As wytles as a wylde goos, ye have but small remorrs
Me for to chalenge that of your chalennge makyth so lytyll fors.
20   Ye capyd Cayfas copyous, your paltoke on your pate,
Tho ye prate lyke prowde Pylate, beware of cheke mate.

Syr Gy, Syr Gawen, Syr Cayus, for and Syr Olyvere,
Pyramus, nor Priamus, nor Syr Pyrrus the prowde,
In Arturys auncyent actys nowhere ys provyd your pere;
25   The facyoun of your fysnamy the devyl in a clowde;
Your harte ys to hawte, iwys, yt wyll nat be alowde.
Ye capyd Cayfas copyus, your paltoke on your pate,
Thow ye prate lyke prowde Pylate, beware of cheke mate.

Ye grounde yow upon Godfrey, that grysly gargons face,
30   Your stondarde, Syr Olifranke, agenst me for to splay;
Baile, baile at yow bothe, frantyke folys! Follow on the chase!
Cum Garnyche, cum Godfrey, with as many as ye may!
I advyse yow beware of thys war, rannge yow in aray.
Ye cappyd Cayfas copyous, your paltoke on your pate,
35   Thow ye prate lyke prowde Pylate, beware of cheke mate.

Gup, gorbellyd Godfrey, gup, Garnysche, gaudy fole!
To turney or to tante with me ye ar to fare to seke.

For thes twayne whypslovens calle for a coke stole.
Thow mantycore, ye marmset, garnyshte lyke a Greke,
40 Wranglynge, waywyrde, wytles, wraw, and nothyng meke.
Ye cappyd Cayfas copyous, your paltoke on your pate,
Thow ye prate lyke prowde Pylate, beware of cheke mate.

Mirres vous y,
Loke nat to hy.

By the kynges most noble commaundment.

(iii)
Skelton Lawryate Defender Agenyst Lusty Garnyche
Welle Be Seyn Crysteovyr Chalannger, *et cetera*

I have your lewde letter receyvyd,
And well I have yt perseyved,
And your skrybe I have aspyed,
That your mad mynde contryved.
5 Savynge your usscheres rod,
I caste me nat to be od
With neythyr of yow tewyne:
Wherfore I wryght ageyne
How the favyr of your face
10 Is voyd of all good grace;
For alle your carpet cousshons
Ye have knavyche condycyonns.
Gup, marmeset, jast ye morelle!
I am laureat, I am no lorell.
15 Lewdely your tyme ye spende,
My lyvyng to reprehende;
And wyll never intende
Your awne lewdnes to amende.

Your Englysche lewdly ye sorte,
20 And falsly ye me reporte.
Garnyche, ye gape to wyde:
Yower knavery I wyll nat hyde,
For to aswage your pride.

Whan ye war yonger of age
25 Ye war a kechyn page,
A dyshwasher, a dryvyll,
In the pott your nose dedde snevyll;

Ye fryed and ye broylyd,
Ye rostyd and ye boylyd,
30   Ye rostyd, lyke a fonne,
A gose with the fete upon;
Ye slufferd up sowse
In my lady Brewsys howse.
Wherto xulde I wryght
35   Of soche a gresy knyght?
A bawdy dyscheclowte,
That bryngyth the worlde abowte
With haftynge and with polleynge,
With lyenge and controlleynge.

40   At Gynys when ye ware
But a slendyr spere,
Dekkyd lewdly in your gere,
For when ye dwelt there,
Ye had a knavysche cote
45   Was skantly worthe a grote;
In dud frese ye war schrynyd,
With better frese lynyd;
The outesyde every day,
Ye myght no better a way;
50   The insyde ye ded calle
Your beste gowne festyvalle.
Your drapry ye ded wante
The warde with yow was skante.
When ye kyst a shepys ie,
55   . . . . mastres Audelby,
. . . . gynys upon a gonge,
. . . . sat sumwhat to longe;
. . . . hyr husbandes hed,
. . . . malle of lede,
60   . . . . that ye ther prechyd,
To hyr love ye nowte rechyd.
Ye wolde have bassyd hyr bumme,
So that sche wolde have kum
On to your lowsy den;
65   But sche of all men
Had yow most in despyght;
Ye loste hyr favyr quyt!
Your pyllyd garleke hed

Cowde hocupy ther no stede.
70 She callyd yow Syr Gy of Gaunt,
    Nosyd lyke an olyfaunt,
    A pykes or a twybyll;
    Sche seyd how ye ded brydell,
    Moche lyke a dromadary;
75 Thus with yow sche ded wary,
    With moche mater more
    That I kepe in store.

    Your brethe ys stronge and quike;
    Ye ar an eldyr steke;
80 Ye wot what I thynke;
    At bothe endes ye stynke;
    Gret daunger for the kynge,
    Whan hys grace ys fastynge,
    Hys presens to aproche;
85 Yt ys to your reproche.
    Yt fallyth for no swyne
    Nor sowtters to drynke wyne,
    Nor seche a nody polle
    A pryste for to controlle.

90 Lytyll wyt in your scrybys nolle
    That scrybblyd your fonde scrolle,
    Upon hym for to take
    Agennst me for to make,
    Lyke a doctor dawpate,
95 A lauryate poyete for to rate.
    Yower termys ar to grose,
    To far from the porpose,
    To contaminate
    And to violate
100 The dygnyte lauryate.

    Bolde bayarde, ye are to blynde,
    And grow all oute of kynde,
    To occupy so your mynde;
    For reson can I non fynde
105 Nor good ryme in yower mater.
    I wondyr that ye smatyr,
    So for a knave to clatyr;

Ye wolde be callyd a maker,
And make moche lyke Jake Rakar;
110 Ye ar a comly crakar,
Ye lernyd of sum py-bakar.
Caste up your curyows wrytyng,
And your dyrty endytyng,
And your spyghtfull despyghtyng,
115 For alle ys nat worthe a myteyng,
A makerell nor a wyteyng:
Had ye gonne with me to scole,
And occupyed no better your tole,
Ye xulde have kowththyd me a fole.

120 But now, gawdy, gresy Garnesche,
Your face I wyse to varnyshe
So suerly yt xall nat tarnishe.
Thow a Sarsens hed ye bere,
Row and full of lowsy here,
125 As hevery man wele seethe,
Ful of greet knavys tethe,
In a felde of grene peson
Ye ryme yet owte of reson;
Your wyt ys so geson,
130 Ye rayle all out of seson.

Your skyn scabbyd and scurvy,
Tawny, tannyd, and shurvy;
Now upon thys hete
Rankely whan ye swete,
135 Men sey ye wyll wax lowsy,
Drunkyn, drowpy, drowsy.
Your sworde ye swere, I wene,
So tranchaunt and so kene,
Xall kyt both wyght and grene:
140 Your foly ys to grett
The kynges colours to threte.
Your brethe yt ys so felle
And so puauntely dothe smelle
And so haynnously doth stynke,
145 That naythyr pümp nor synke
Dothe savyr halfe so souer
Ageynst a stormy shouer.

O ladies of bryght colour,
Of bewte that beryth the flower,
150   When Garnyche cummyth yow amonge
With hys brethe so stronge,
Withowte ye have a confectioun
Agenst hys poysond infeccioun,
Els with hys stynkyng jawys
155   He wyl cause yow caste your crawes,
And make youer stomake seke
Ovyr the perke to pryk.

Now Garnyche, garde thy gummys;
My serpentins and my gunnys
160   Agenst ye now I bynde;
Thy selfe therfore defende.
Thou tode, thow scorpyon,
Thow bawdy babyone,
Thow bere, thow brystlyd bore,
165   Thou Moryshe mantycore,
Thou rammysche, stynkyng gote,
Thou fowle, chorlyshe parote,
Thou gresly gargone glaymy,
Thou swety sloven seymy,
170   Thou murrioun, thow mawment,
Thou fals, stynkyng serpent,
Thou mokkyshe marmoset,
I will nat dy in thy det.

Tyburne thou me assynyd
175   Wher thou xulddst have bene shrynyd;
The nexte halter ther xall be
I bequeth yt hole to the.
Soche pelfry thou hast pachchyd,
And so thy selfe hovyr-wachyd
180   That ther thou xuldyst be rachchyd
If thow war metely machchyd.

Ye may wele be bedawyd,
Ye ar a fole owtelauyd;
And for to telle the gronde,
185   Pay Stokys hys fyve pownd.

I say, Syr Dalyrag,
Ye bere yow bold and brag
With othyr menys charge;
Ye kyt your clothe to large,
190   Soche pollyng pajaunttis ye pley,
To poynt yow fresche and gay.

And he that scryblyd your scrolles,
I rekyn yow in my rowllys,
For ij dronken sowllys.
195   Rede and lerne ye may,
How olde proverbys say,
That byrd ys nat honest
That fylythe hys owne nest.
Yf he wyst what sum wotte,
200   The fresche bastyng of hys cote
Was sowyd with slendyr threde.
God sende you wele good spede,
With 'Dominus vobyscum',
God Latyn for Jake a Thrum,
205   Tyll more matyr may cum.

By the kynges most noble commaundment.

(iv)
Donum Laureati Disticon contra Goliardum Garnishe et
Scribam Eius.
Tu, Garnische, fatuus, fatuus tuus est mage scriba:
Qui sapuit puer, insanyt vir, versus in hydram.

(v)
Skelton Laureate Defendar Ageinst Lusty Garnyshe
Well Be Seen Crystofer Chalangar, *et cetera*

Garnyshe, gargone, gastly, gryme,
I have receyvyd your secunde ryme.
Thowthe ye kan skylle of large and longe,
Ye syng allway the kukkowe songe.
5   Ye rayle, ye ryme, with, 'Hay, dog, hay!'
Your chorlyshe chauntyng ys all o lay.
Ye, syr, rayle all in deformite:
Ye have nat red the properte

Of naturys workys, how they be
10   Myxte with sum incommodite,
As provithe well, in hys rethorikys olde,
Cicero with hys tong of golde.
That nature wrowght in yow and me,
Irrevocable ys her decre;
15   Waywardly wrowght she hath in the,
Beholde thi selfe, and thou mayst se.
Thow xalte beholde no wher a warse;
Thy myrrour may be the devyllys ars.
Wyth, 'Knave, syr, knave, and knave agenne',
20   To cal me knave thou takyst gret payne.
The prowdyst knave yet of us tewyne
Within thy skyn he xall remayne.
The starkest knave, and lest good kan,
Thou art callyd of every man.
25   The corte, the contre, wylage, and towne,
Sayth, from thy to unto thi croune,
Of all prowde knavys thow beryst the belle,
Lothsum as Lucifer lowest in helle.
On that syde, on thys syde thou dost gasy,
30   Thou thynkyst thy selfe Syr Pers de Brasy,
Thy caytyvys carkes, cours and crasy;
Moche of thy maneres I can blasy.
Of Lumbardy Gorge Hardyson,
Thow wolde have scoryd hys habarion;
35   That jentyll Jorge the Januay,
Ye wolde have trysyd hys trowle away.
Soche pajantes with your fryndes ye play,
With trechery ye them betray.
Garnyshe, ye gate of Gorge with gaudry
40   Crimsin velvet for your bawdry.
Ye have a fantasy to Fanchyrche strete,
With Lumbardes lemmanns for to mete,
With, 'Bas me, buttyng, praty Cys',
Yower lothesum lypps love well to kyse,
45   Slaveryng lyke a slymy snayle.
I wolde ye had kyst hyr on the tayle!

Also nat fare from Bowgy Row,
Ye pressyd pertely to pluk a crow:

Ye lost your holde, onbende your bow,
50 Ye wan nothyng there but a mow:
Ye wan nothyng there but a skorne;
Sche wolde nat of yt thow had sworne.
Sche seyd ye war coluryd with cole dust;
To daly with yow she had no lust.
55 Sche seyd your brethe stanke lyke a broke;
With, 'Gup, Syr Gy', ye gate a moke.
Sche sware with hyr ye xulde nat dele,
For ye war smery, lyke a sele,
And ye war herey, lyke a calfe;
60 Sche praiid yow walke, on Goddes halfe!
And thus there ye lost yower pray;
Get ye anothyr where ye may.

Dysparage ye myn auncetry?
Ye ar dysposyd for to ly.
65 I sey, thow felle and fowle flessh fly,
In thys debate I the askry.
Thow claimist the jentyll, thou art a curre;
Haroldis they know thy cote-armur;
Thow thou be a jantyll man borne,
70 Yet jentylnes in the ys thred-bare worne.
Haroldes from honor may the devors,
For harlottes hawnte thyn hatefull cors;
Ye bere out brothells lyke a bawde;
Ye get therby a slendyr laude
75 Betweyn the tappett and the walle;
Fusty bawdyas, I sey nat alle.
Of harlottes to use soche an harres,
Yt bredth mothys in clothe of Arres.

What eylythe the, rebawde, on me to rave?
80 A kynge to me myn habyte gave
At Oxforth, the universyte,
Avaunsid I was to that degre;
By hole consent of theyr senate,
I was made poete lawreate.
85 To cal me lorell ye ar to lewde;
Lythe and lystyn, all bechrewde!
Of the Musys nyne, Calliope
Hath pointyd me to rayle on the.

It semyth nat thy pyllyd pate
90   Agenst a poyet lawreat
To take upon the for to scryve;
It cumys the better for to dryve
A dong cart or a tumrell
Than with my poems for to melle.

95   The honor of Englond I lernyd to spelle,
In dygnyte roiall that doth excelle.
Note and mark wyl thys parcele;
I yave hym drynke of the sugryd welle
Of Eliconys waters crystallyne,
100   Aqueintyng hym with the Musys nyne.
Yt commyth the wele me to remorde,
That creaunser was to thy sofreyne lorde;
It plesyth that noble prince roiall
Me as hys master for to calle
105   In hys lernyng primordiall.
Avaunt, rybawde, thi tung reclame!
Me to beknave thow art to blame;
Thy tong untawte, with poyson infecte,
Withowte thou leve thou shalt be chekt,
110   And takyn up in such a frame,
That all the warlde wyll spye your shame.
Avaunt, avaunt, thow slogysh . . . . . .
And sey poetis no dys . . . . . .
It ys for no bawdy knave
115   The dignite lawreat for to have.

Thow callyst me scallyd, thou callydst me mad;
Thow thou be pyllyd, thow ar nat sade.
Thow ar frantyke and lakkyst wyt,
To rayle with me that the can hyt.
120   Thowth it be now ful tyde with the,
Yet ther may falle soche caswelte
Er thow beware, that in a throw
Thow mayst fale downe and ebbe full lowe.
Wherfore, in welthe beware of woo,
125   For welthe wyll sone departe the froo.
To know thy selfe yf thow lake grace,
Lerne or be lewde, I shrow thy face.

Thow seyst I callyd the a pecok;
Thow liist, I callyd the a wodcoke;
For thow hast a long snowte,
A semly nose and a stowte,
Prickyd lyke an unicorne.
I wold sum manys bake ink-horne
Wer thi nose spectacle case;
Yt wold garnyche wyll thy face.

Thow demyst my raylyng ovyrthwarthe;
I rayle to the soche as thow art.
If thow war aquentyd with alle
The famous poettes saturicall,
As Persius and Juvynall,
Horace and noble Marciall,
If they wer lyveyng thys day,
Of the wote I what they wolde say;
They wolde the wryght, all with one stevyn,
The follest sloven ondyr heven,
Prowde, peviche, lyddyr and lewde,
Malapert, medyllar, nothyng well thewde,
Besy, braynles, to bralle and brage,
Wytles, wayward, Syr Wrag-wrag,
Dysdaynous, dowble, ful of dyseyte,
Liing, spying by suttelte and slyght,
Fleriing, flatyryng, fals and fykkelle,
Scornefull and mokkyng over to mykkylle.

My tyme, I trow, I xulde but lese
To wryght to the of tragydese,
It ys nat mete for soche a knave.
But now, my proces for to save,
I have red, and rede I xall,
Inordynate pride wyll have a falle.
Presumptuous pride ys all thyn hope;
God garde the, Garnyche, from the rope!
Stop a tyd, and be welle ware
Ye be nat cawte in an hempen snare.
Harkyn herto, ye Harvy Haftar,
Pride gothe before and schame commyth after.

Thow wrythtyst I xulde let the go pley;
Go pley the, Garnyshe, garnysshed gay!
I care nat what thow wryght or sey;
I cannat let the the knave to play,
170   To dauns the hay or rune the ray;
Thy fonde face can me nat fray.
Take thys for that, bere thys in mynde,
Of thy lewdenes more ys behynde;
A reme of papyr wyll nat holde
175   Of thi lewdenes that may be tolde.
My study myght be better spynt;
But for to serve the kynges entent,
Hys noble pleasure and commandemennt,
Scrybbyl thow, scrybyll thow, rayle or wryght,
180   Wryght what thow wylte, I xall the aquyte.

By the kyngys most noble commandemennt.

XIV

Against Dundas

Vilitissimus Scotus Dundas allegat caudas contra Angligenas.

Caudatos Anglos, spurcissime Scote, quid effers?
Effrons es, quoquae sons, mendax, tua spurcaquae bucca est.

Anglicus a tergo
caudam gerit;
est canis ergo.
Anglice caudate,
5   *cape caudam*
Ne cadat a te.
Ex causa caude
manet Anglica
gens sine laude.

Diffamas patriam, qua non
   est melior usquam.
Cum cauda plaudis dum
   possis, ad ostia pultas

5   *Mendicans; mendicus eris,*
        mendaxquae bilinguis,
    Scabidus, horribilis, quem
        vermes sexquae pedales
    Corrodent misere; miseris
10   *genus est maledictum.*

        Skelton, nobilis poeta.

    Gup Scot,
    Ye blot:
    Laudate
    Caudate,
5   Set in better
    Thy pentameter.
    This Dundas,
    This Scottishe as
    He rymes and railes
10 That Englishmen have tailes.
            Skeltonus laureatus,
    Anglicus natus,
    Provocat Musas
    Contra Dundas
15 *Spurcissimum Scotum,*
    Undiquae notum,
    Rustice fotum,
    Vapide potum.
        Skelton laureat
20 After this rate
    Defendeth with his pen
    All Englysh men
    Agayn Dundas,
    That Scottishe asse.
25 Shake thy tayle, Scot, lyke a cur,
    For thou beggest at every mannes dur.
    Tut, Scot, I sey,
    Go shake the, dog, hey!
    Dundas of Galaway
30 With thy versyfyeng rayles
    How they have tayles.
    By Jesu Christ,
    Fals Scot, thou lyest:

But behynd in our hose
35 We bere there a rose
For thy Scottyshe nose,
A spectacle case
To cover thy face,
With, *tray deux ase.*
40 A tolman to blot,
A rough foted Scot!
Dundas, sir knave,
Why doste thow deprave
This royall reame,
45 Whose radiant beame
And relucent light
Thou hast in despite,
Thou donghyll knyght?
But thou lakest might,
50 Dundas, dronken and drowsy,
Skabed, scurvy and lowsy,
Of unhappy generacion
And most ungracious nacion.
Dundas,
55 That dronke asse,
That ratis and rankis
That prates and prankes
On Huntley bankes,
Take this our thankes;
60 Dunde, Dunbar,
Walke, Scot,
Walke, sot,
Rayle not so far.

XV

Skelton laureate *Oratoris Regis tertio*

Against Venemous Tongues

enpoysoned with sclaunder and false detractions &c.

*Quid detur tibi aut quid apponatur tibi ad linguam dolosam?
Psalm cxlij.*

Deus destruet te, in finem evellet te, et emigrabit te de tabernaculo tuo, et radicem tuam de terra viventium. Psal. lxvii.

Al maters wel pondred and wel to be regarded,
How shuld a fals lying tung then be rewarded?
Such tunges shuld be torne out by the harde rootes,
Hoyning like hogges that groynis and wrotes.

Dilexisti omnia verba precipitationis lingua dolosa. ubi s. &c.

5   For, as I have rede in volumes olde,
A fals lying tunge is harde to withholde;
A sclaunderous tunge, a tunge of a skolde,
Worketh more mischiefe than can be tolde;
That, if I wist not to be controlde,
10   Yet somwhat to say I dare well be bolde,
How some delite for to lye, thycke and threfolde.

Ad sannam hominem redigit comice et graphice.

For ye said, that he said, that I said, wote ye what?
I made, he said, a windmil of an olde mat.
If there be none other mater but that,
15   Than ye may commaunde me to gentil cok wat.

Hic notat purpuraria arte intextas literas Romanas in amictibus post ambulonum ante et retro.

For before on your brest, and behind on your back
In Romaine letters I never founde lack
In your crosse rowe nor Christ crosse you spede,
Your Pater noster, your Ave, nor your Crede.
20   Who soever that tale unto you tolde,
He saith untruly, to say that I would
Controlle the cognisaunce of noble men
Either by language or with my pen.

Pedagogium meum de sublimiori Minerva constat esse: ergo &c.

My scole is more solem and somwhat more haute
25   Than to be founde in any such faute.

Pedagogium meum male sanos maledicos sibilis conplosisque manibus explodit &c.

My scoles are not for unthriftes untaught,
For frantick faitours half mad and half straught;
But my learning is of an other degree
To taunt theim like liddrons, lewde as thei bee.

Laxent ergo antemnan elationis sue inflatam vento vanitatis. li.
ille &c.

30 For though some be lidder, and list for to rayle,
Yet to lie upon me they can not prevayle.
Then let them vale a bonet of their proud sayle,
And of their taunting toies rest with il hayle.

Nobilitati ignobilis cedat vilitas. &c.

There is no noble man wil judge in me
35 Any such foly to rest or to be.
I care muche the lesse what ever they say,
For tunges untayde be renning astray.
But yet I may say safely, so many wel lettred,
Embraudred, enlasid together, and fettred,
40 And so little learning, so lewdly alowed,
What fault find ye herein but may be avowed.
But ye are so full of vertibilite,
And of frenetyke folabilite,
And of melancoly mutabilite,
45 That ye would coarte and enforce me
Nothing to write, but hay the gy of thre,
And I to suffre you lewdly to ly
Of me with your language full of vilany.

Sicut novacula acuta fecisti dolum. Ubi s.

Malicious tunges, though they have no bones,
50 Are sharper then swordes, sturdier then stones.

Lege Philostratum de vita Tyanei Apollonii.

Sharper then raysors, that shave and cut throtes,
More stinging then scorpions that stang Pharaotis.

Venenum aspidum sub labiis eorum. Ps.

More venemous and much more virulent
Then any poysoned tode, or any serpent.

Quid peregrinis egemus exemplis? Ad domestica recurramus, &c.
li. ille.

55 Such tunges unhappy hath made great division
In realmes, in cities, by suche fals abusion.
Of fals fickil tunges suche cloked collusion
Hath brought nobil princes to extreme confusion.

Quicquid loquantur ut effeminantur ita effantur. &c.

Somtime women were put in great blame,
60 Men said they could not their tunges atame;
But men take upon theim nowe all the shame
With skolding and sklaundering make their tungs lame.

Novarum rerum cupidissimi, captatores, delatores, adulatores,
invigilatores, deliratores, &c. id genus. li. ille.

For men be now tratlers and tellers of tales;
What tidings at Totnam, what newis in Wales,
65 What shippis are sailing to Scalis Malis,
And all is not worth a couple of nut shalis.
But lering and lurking here and there like spies,
The devill tere their tunges and pike out their ies!
Then ren they with lesinges, and blow them about,
70 With, 'He wrate suche a bil withouten dout',
With, 'I can tel you what such a man said,
And you knew all ye would be ill apayd'.

De more vulpino, gannientes ad aurem, fictas fabellas fabricant.
li. ille.

In auspicatum, male ominatum, infortunatum se fateatur
habuisse horoscopum, quicunque maledixerit vati Pierio
Skeltonidi Laureato. &c.

But if that I knewe what his name hight,
For clatering of me I would him sone quight;
75 For his false lying, of that I spake never,
I could make him shortly repent him for ever;
Although he made it never so tough,
He might be sure to have shame ynough.

Cerberus horrendo baratri latrando sub antro
Te rodatque voret lingua dolosa precor.

A fals double tunge is more fiers and fell
80 Then Cerberus the cur couching in the kenel of hel;
Wherof hereafter, I thinke for to write,
Of fals double tunges in the dispite.

*Recipit se scripturum opus sanctum, laudabile, acceptabile,
memorabileque, et nimis honorificandum.*

*Disperdat dominus universa labia dolosa et linguam
magniloquam!*

XVI
Magnyfycence

A goodly interlude and a mery devysed and made by
Mayster Skelton, poet laureate late deceasyd.

These be the names of the players:

Felycyte	Courtly Abusyon
Lyberte	Foly
Measure	Adversyte
	Poverte
	Dyspare
Magnyfycence	Myschefe
Fansy	Good Hope
Counterfet Countenaunce	Redresse
Crafty Conveyaunce	Cyrcumspeccyon
Clokyd Colusyon	Perseveraunce

[*Enter* FELYCYTE.]

Fel. Al thyngys contryvyd by mannys reason,
The world envyronn, of hygh and low estate.
Be it erly or late, welth hath a season.
Welth is of wysdome the very trewe probate.
5   A fole is he with welth that fallyth at debate.
But men nowe a dayes so unhappely be uryd,
That nothynge than welth may worse be enduryd.

To tell you the cause me semeth it no nede.
The amense therof is far to call agayne;
10   For, when men by welth, they have lytell drede

Of that may come after; experyence trewe and playne,
Howe after a drought there fallyth a showre of rayne
And after a hete oft cometh a stormy colde.
A man may have welth, but not as he wolde,

15   Ay to contynewe and styll to endure.
But yf prudence be proved with sad cyrcumspeccyon,
Welthe myght be wonne and made to the lure,
Yf noblenesse were aquayntyd with sober dyreccyon.
But wyll hath reason so under subjeccyon,
20   And so dysordereth this worlde over all,
That welthe and felicite is passynge small.

But where wonnys welthe, and a man wolde wyt?
For Welthfull Felicite truly is my name.

[*Enter* LYBERTE.]
Lyb.   Mary, Welthe and I was apoynted to mete,
25   And eyther I am dysseyved, or ye be the same.
Fel.   Syr, as ye say. A have harde of your fame.
Your name is Lyberte, as I understande.
Lyb.   Trewe you say, syr. Gyve me your hande.

Fel.   And from whens come ye, and it myght be askyd?
30   *Lyb.*   To tell you, syr, I dare not, leest I sholde be maskyd
In a payre of fetters or a payre of stockys.
Fel.   Here you not howe this gentylman mockys?
Lyb.   Ye, to knackynge ernyst what and it preve?
Fel.   Why, to say what he wyll, Lyberte hath leve.
35   *Lyb.*   Yet lyberte hath ben lockyd up and kept in the mew.
Fel.   In dede, syr, that lyberte was not worthe a cue.
How be it, lyberte may somtyme be to large,
But yf reason be regent and ruler of your barge.
Lyb.   To that ye say I can well condyssende.
40   Shewe forth, I pray you, here in what you intende.

Fel.   Of that I intende to make demonstracyon
It askyth lesure with good advertence.
Fyrst, I say, we owght to have in consyderacyon
That lyberte be lynkyd with the chayne of countenaunce,
45   Lyberte to let from all maner offence;
For lyberte at large is lothe to be stoppyd,
But with countenaunce your corage must be croppyd.

Lyb. Then thus to you –
Fel.   Nay, suffer me yet ferther to say,
         And peradventure I shall content your mynde.
50   Lyberte, I wote well, forbere no man there may;
         It is so swete in all maner of kynde.
         Howe be it, lyberte makyth many a man blynde;
         By lyberte is done many a great excesse;
         Lyberte at large wyll oft wax reklesse.

55   Perceyve ye this parcell?
Lyb.   Ye, syr, passyng well.
         But and you wolde me permyt
         To shewe parte of my wyt,
         Somwhat I coulde enferre
60   Your consayte to debarre,
         Under supportacyon
         Of pacyent tolleracyon.
Fel.   God forbyd ye sholde be let
         Your reasons forth to fet.
65   Wherfore at lyberte
         Say what ye wyll to me.

Lyb.   Brefly to touche of my purpose the effecte:
         Lyberte is laudable and pryvylegyd from lawe.
         Judycyall rygoure shall not me correcte –
70 Fel. Softe, my frende. Herein your reason is but rawe.
Lyb.   Yet suffer me to say the surpluse of my sawe.
         What wote ye where upon I wyll conclude?
         I say there is no welthe where as lyberte is subdude.

         I trowe ye can not say nay moche to this:
75   To lyve under lawe, it is captyvyte.
         Where drede ledyth the daunce, there is no joy nor
                  blysse.
         Or howe can you prove that there is felycyte,
         And you have not your owne fre lyberte
         To sporte at your pleasure, to ryn, and to ryde?
80   Where lyberte is absent, set welthe asyde.

         Hic intrat MEASURE.
Meas   Cryst you assyste in your altrycacyon!
Fel.   Why, have you harde of our dysputacyon?
Meas. I parceyve well howe eche of you doth reason.

	Lyb.	Mayster Measure, you be come in good season.
85	*Meas.*	And it is wonder that your wylde insolence
		Can be content with Measure presence.

	Fel.	Wolde it please you then –
	Lyb.	Us to informe and ken –
	Meas.	A, ye be wonders men!
90		Your langage is lyke the penne

		Of hym that wryteth to fast.
	Fel.	Syr, yf any worde have past
		Me, other fyrst or last,
		To you I arecte it, and cast

95		Therof the reformacyon.
	Lyb.	And I of the same facyon;
		Howe be it, by protestacyon

		Dyspleasure that you none take
		Some reason we must make.
100	*Meas.*	That wyll not I forsake,

		So it in measure be.
		Come of therfore, let se;
		Shall I begynne or ye?

	Fel.	Nay, ye shall begynne, by my wyll.
105	*Lyb.*	It is reason and skyll
		We your pleasure fulfyll.

	Meas.	Then ye must bothe consent
		You to holde content
		With myne argument;

110		And I muste you requyre
		Me pacyently to here.
	Fel.	Yes, syr, with ryght good chere.
	Lyb.	With all my herte intere.

	Meas.	Oracius to recorde in his volumys olde,
115		With every condycyon measure must be sought.
		Welthe without measure wolde bere hymselfe to bolde;
		Lyberte without measure prove a thynge of nought.
		In ponder, by nomber, by measure all thynge is wrought,
		As at the fyrst orygynall, by godly opynyon;
120		Whych provyth well that measure shold have domynyon.

Where measure is mayster, plenty dothe none offence;
Where measure lackyth, all thynge dysorderyd is;
Where measure is absent, ryot kepeth resydence;
Where measure is ruler, there is nothynge amysse.

125   Measure is treasure. Howe say ye, is it not this?
Fel.   Yes, questyonlesse, in myne opynyon;
Measure is worthy to have domynyon.

Lyb.   Unto that same I am ryght well agrede,
So that lyberte be not lefte behynde.
130 *Meas.*   Ye, lyberte with measure nede never drede.
Lyb.   What, lyberte to measure then wolde ye bynde?
Meas.   What ellys? For otherwyse it were agaynst kynde;
If lyberte sholde lepe and renne where he lyst
It were no vertue, it were a thynge unblyst.

135   It were a myschefe, yf lyberte lacked a reyne
Where with to rule hym with the wrythyng of a rest.
All trebyllys and tenours be rulyd by a meyne.
Lyberte without measure is acountyd for a beste;
There is no surfet where measure rulyth the feste;
140   There is no excesse where measure hath his helthe.
Measure contynwyth prosperyte and welthe.

Fel.   Unto your rule I wyll annex my mynde.
Lyb.   So wolde I, but I wolde be lothe,
That wonte was to be formyst, now to come behynde.
145   It were a shame, to God I make an othe,
Without I myght cut it out of the brode clothe,
As I was wonte ever, at my fre wyll.
Meas.   But have ye not herde say that wyll is no skyll?

Take sad dyreccyon, and leve this wantonnesse.
150 *Lyb.*   It is no maystery.
Fel.   Tushe, let Measure procede,
And after his mynde herdely your selfe adresse,
For, without measure, poverte and nede
Wyll crepe upon us, and us to myschefe lede;
For myschefe wyll mayster us yf measure us forsake.
155 *Lyb.*   Well, I am content your wayes to take.

Meas.   Surely I am joyous that ye be myndyd thus;
Magnyfycence to mayntayne, your promosyon shalbe.

	Fel.	So in his harte he may be glad of us.
	Lyb.	There is no prynce but he hath nede of us thre –
160		Welthe, with Measure and plesaunt Lyberte.
	Meas.	Nowe pleasyth you a lytell whyle to stande;
		Me semeth Magnyfycence is comynge here at hande.

Hic intrat MAGNYFYCENCE.

	Magn.	To assure you of my noble porte and fame,
		Who lyst to knowe, Magnyfycence I hyght.
165		But Measure, my frende, what hyght this mannys name?
	Meas.	Syr, though ye be a noble prynce of myght,
		Yet in this man you must set your delyght.
		And, syr, this other mannys name is Lyberte.
	Magn.	Welcome, frendys, ye are bothe unto me.

170		But nowe let me knowe of your conversacyon.
	Fel.	Pleasyth, your grace, Felycyte they me call.
	Lyb.	And I am Lyberte, made of in every nacyon.
	Magn.	Convenyent persons for any prynce ryall.
		Welthe with Lyberte, with me bothe dwell ye shall,
175		To the gydynge of my measure you bothe commyttynge;
		That Measure be mayster us semeth it is syttynge.

	Meas.	Where as ye have, syr, to me them assygned,
		Suche order I trust with them for to take,
		So that welthe with measure shalbe conbyned,
180		And lyberte his large with measure shall make.
	Fel.	Your ordenaunce, syr, I wyll not forsake.
	Lyb.	And I my selfe hooly to you wyll inclyne.
	Magn.	Then may I say that ye be servauntys myne.

		For by measure I warne you we thynke to be gydyd;
185		Wherin it is necessary my pleasure you knowe:
		Measure and I wyll never be devydyd,
		For no dyscorde that any man can sawe;
		For measure is a meane, nother to hy nor to lawe,
		In whose attemperaunce I have suche delyght,
190		That measure shall nevere departe from my syght.

	Fel.	Laudable your consayte is to be acountyd,
		For welthe without measure sodenly wyll slyde.
	Lyb.	As your grace full nobly hath recountyd,
		Measure with noblenesse sholde be alyde.

195 *Magn.* Then, Lyberte, se that Measure by your gyde,
        For I wyll use you by his advertysment.
     Fel.   Then shall you have with you prosperyte resydent.

     Meas. I trowe good fortune hath annexyd us together,
              To se howe greable we are of one mynde;
200   There is no flaterer nor losyll so lyther,
              This lynkyd chayne of love that can unbynde.
              Nowe that ye have me chefe ruler assyngned,
              I wyll endevour me to order every thynge
              Your noblenesse and honour consernynge.

205 *Lyb.*   In joy and myrthe your mynde shalbe inlargyd
              And not embracyd with pusyllanymyte.
              But plenarly all thought from you must be dyschargyd,
              If ye lyst to lyve after your fre lyberte.
              All delectacyons aquayntyd is with me;
210   By me all persons worke what they lyste.
     Meas. Hem, syr, yet beware of 'Had I wyste!'

              Lyberte in some cause becomyth a gentyll mynde –
              Bycause course of measure – yf I be in the way:
              Who countyth without me is caste to fer behynde
215   Of his rekenynge, as evydently we may
              Se at our eye the worlde day by day.
              For defaute of measure all thynge dothe excede.
     Fel.   All that ye say is as trewe as the crede.

              For howe be it lyberte to welthe is convenyent,
220   And from felycyte may not be forborne,
              Yet measure hath ben so longe from us absent,
              That all men laugh at lyberte to scorne.
              Welth and wyt, I say, be so threde bare worne,
              That all is without measure and fer beyonde the mone.
225 *Magn.* Then noblenesse, I se well, is almoste undone,

              But yf therof the soner amendys be made;
              For dowtlesse I parceyve my magnyfycence
              Without measure lyghtly may fade,
              Of to moche lyberte under the offence;
230   Wherfore, Measure, take Lyberte with you hence,
              And rule hym after the rule of your scole.
     Lyb.   What, syr, wolde ye make me a poppynge fole?

	Meas.	Why, were not your selfe agreed to the same,
		And now wolde ye swarve from your owne ordynaunce?
235	*Lyb.*	I wolde be rulyd and I myght for shame.
	Fel.	A, ye make me laughe at your inconstaunce.
	Magn.	Syr, without any longer delyaunce,
		Take Lyberte to rule, and folowe myne entent.
	Meas.	It shalbe done at your commaundement.

Itaque MEASURE *exeat locum cum* LYBERTATE, *et maneat*
MAGNYFYCENCE *cum* FELICITATE.

240	*Magn.*	It is a wanton thynge, this Lyberte.
		Perceyve you not howe lothe he was to abyde
		The rule of Measure, notwithstandynge we
		Have deputyd Measure hym to gyde?
		By measure eche thynge duly is tryde.
245		Thynke you not thus my frende Felycyte?
	Fel.	God forbede that it other wyse sholde be!

	Magn.	Ye coulde not ellys, I wote, with me endure.
	Fel.	Endure? No, God wote, it were great payne.
		But yf I were orderyd by just measure,
250		It were not possyble me longe to retayne.

Hic intrat FANSY.

	Fan.	Tusche, holde your pece! Your langage is vayne.
		Please it your grace to take no dysdayne,
		To shewe you playnly the trouth as I thynke.
	Magn.	Here is none forsyth whether you flete or synke.

255	*Fel.*	From whens come you, syr, that no man lokyd after?
	Magn.	Or who made you so bolde to interrupe my tale?
	Fan.	Nowe, *benedicite*, ye wene I were some hafter,
		Or ellys some jangelynge Jacke of the Vale.
		Ye wene that I am dronken bycause I loke pale.
260	*Magn.*	Me semeth that ye have dronken more than ye have bled.
	Fan.	Yet amonge noble men I was brought up and bred.

	Fel.	Now leve this jangelynge and to us expounde
		Why that ye sayd our langage was in vayne.
	Fan.	Mary, upon trouth my reason I grounde,
265		That without largesse noblenesse can not rayne.
		And that I sayd ones yet I say agayne:

I say, without largesse worshyp hath no place,
For largesse is a purchaser of pardon and of grace.

Magn. Nowe, I beseche the, tell me what is thy name?
270 *Fan.* Largesse, that all lordes sholde love, syr, I hyght.
Fel. But hyght you, Largesse, encreace of noble fame?
Fan. Ye, syr, undoubted.
Fel.   Then, of very ryght,
With Magnyfycence, this noble prynce of myght,
Sholde be your dwellynge, in my consyderacyon.
275 *Magn.* Yet we wyll therin take good delyberacyon.

Fan. As in that I wyll not be agaynst your pleasure.
Fel. Syr, hardely remembre what may your name avaunce.
Magn. Largesse is laudable so it be in measure.
Fan. Largesse is he that all prynces doth avaunce;
280 I reporte me herein to Kynge Lewes of Fraunce.
Fel. Why have ye hym named and all other refused?
Fan. For, syth he dyed, largesse was lytell used.

Plucke up your mynde, syr, what ayle you to muse?
Have ye not welthe here at your wyll?
285 It is but a maddynge, these wayes that ye use.
What avayleth lordshype, yourselfe for to kyll
With care and with thought howe Jacke shall have Gyl?
Magn. What! I have aspyed ye are a carles page.
Fan. By God, syr, ye se but fewe wyse men of myne age.

290 But covetyse hath blowen you so full of wynde
That *colyca passyo* hath gropyd you by the guttys.
Fel. In fayth, broder Largesse, you have a mery mynde.
Fan. In fayth, I set not by the worlde two Dauncaster cuttys.
Magn. Ye wante but a wylde flyeng bolte to shote at the buttes.
295 Though Largesse ye hyght your langage is to large;
For whiche ende goth forwarde ye take lytell charge.

Fel. Let se this checke yf ye voyde canne.
Fan. In faythe, els had I gone to longe to scole,
But yf I coulde knowe a gose from a swanne.
300 *Magn.* Wel, wyse men may ete the fysshe when ye shal draw the
pole.
Fan. In fayth, I wyll not say that ye shall prove a fole,
But ofte tymes have I sene wyse men do mad dedys.
Magn. Go shake the, dogge, hay, syth ye wyll nedys!

		You are nothynge mete with us for to dwell,
305		That with your lorde and mayster so pertly can prate!
		Gete you hens, I say, by my counsell.
		I wyll not use you to play with me checke mate.
	Fan.	Syr, yf I have offended your noble estate,
		I trow I have brought you suche wrytynge of recorde,
310		That I shall have you agayne my good lorde.

To you recommendeth Sad Cyrcumspeccyon,
And sendeth you this wrytynge closed under sele.

Magn. This wrytynge is welcome with harty affeccyon!
Why kepte you it thus longe? Howe dothe he? Wele?

315 *Fan.* Syr, thanked be God, he hath his hele.

Magn. Welthe, gete you home and commaunde me to Mesure.
Byd hym take good hede of you, my synguler tresure.

Fel. Is there ony thynge elles your grace wyll commaunde me?

Magn. Nothynge but fare you well tyll sone –

320 And that he take good kepe to Lyberte.

Fel. Your pleasure, syr, shortely shall be done.

Magn. I shall come to you myselfe, I trowe, this afternone.

[*Exit* FELYCYTE.]

I pray you, Larges, here to remayne,
Whylest I knowe that this letter dothe contayne.

*Hic faciat tanquam legeret litteras tacite. Interim
superveniat cantando* COUNTERFET
COUNTENAUNCE; *suspenso gradum, qui viso*
MAGNYFYCENCE, *sensim retrocedat; at tempus post
pusillum rursum accedat* COUNTERFET
COUNTENAUNCE *prospectando et vocitando a longe;
et* FANSY *animat silentium cum manu.*

325 *Cou.* What, Fansy! Fansy!

Magn. Who is that that thus dyd cry?
Me thought he called Fansy.

Fan. It was a Flemynge hyght Hansý.

Magn. Me thought he called Fansy me behynde.

330 *Fan.* Nay, syr, it was nothynge but your mynde.
But nowe, syr, as touchynge this letter –

Magn. I shall loke in it at leasure better;
And surely ye are to hym beholde,
And for his sake ryght gladly I wolde

335   Do what I coude to do you good.
 Fan. I pray God kepe you in that mood!
 Magn. This letter was wryten ferre hence.
 Fan. By lakyn, syr, it hathe cost me pence
  And grotes many one or I came to your presence.
340 *Magn.* Where was it delyvered you? Shewe unto me.
 Fan. By God, syr, beyonde the se.
 Magn. At what place, nowe, as you gesse?
 Fan. By my trouthe, syr, at Pountesse.
  This wrytynge was taken me there,
345 But never was I in gretter fere.
 Magn. Howe so?
 Fan.   By God, at the see syde,
  Had I not opened my purse wyde,
  I trowe, by our lady, I had ben slayne,
  Or elles I had lost myne eres twayne.
 Magn. By your soth?
350 *Fan.*   Ye, and there is suche a wache,
  That no man can scape but they hym cache.
  They bare me in hande that I was a spye;
  And another bade put out myne eye;
  Another wolde myne eye were blerde;
355 Another bade shave halfe my berde;
  And boyes to the pylery gan me plucke,
  And wolde have made me Freer Tucke,
  To preche out of the pylery hole
  Without an antetyme or a stole;
360 And some bade, 'Sere hym with a marke.'
  To gete me fro them I had moche warke.
 Magn. Mary, syr, ye were afrayde.
 Fan. By my trouthe, had I not payde and prayde,
  And made largesse, as I hyght,
365 I had not been here with you this nyght.
  But surely largesse saved my lyfe;
  For largesse stynteth all maner of stryfe.
 Magn. It dothe so sure nowe and than.
  But largesse is not mete for every man.
370 *Fan.* No. But for you grete estates
  Largesse stynteth grete debates;
  And he that I came fro to this place
  Sayd I was mete for your grace.

		And in dede, syr, I here men talke –
375		By the way as I ryde and walke –
		Say howe you excede in noblenesse,
		If you had with you largesse.
	Magn.	And say they so in very dede?
	Fan.	With ye, syr, so God me spede.
380	*Magn.*	Yet mesure is a mery mene.
	Fan.	Ye, syr, a blaunched almonde is no bene.
		Measure is mete for a marchauntes hall
		But largesse becometh a state ryall.
		What! Sholde you pynche at a pecke of grotes
385		Ye wolde sone pynche at a pecke of otes.
		Thus is the talkynge of one and of oder,
		As men dare speke it hugger mugger:
		'A lorde a negarde, it is a shame.'
		But largesse may amende your name.
390	*Magn.*	In faythe, Largesse, welcome to me.
	Fan.	I pray you, syr, I may so be;
		And of my servyce you shall not mysse.
	Magn.	Togyder we wyll talke more of this.
		Let us departe from hens home to my place.
395	*Fan.*	I folow even after your noble grace.

Hic discedat MAGNIFICENS *cum* FANSY, *et
intrat* COUNTERFET COUNTENAUNCE. [*He
detains* FANSY *for a moment.*]

	Cou. Cou.	What! I say, herke a worde.
	Fan.	Do away, I say, the devylles torde!
	Cou. Cou.	Ye, but how longe shall I here awayte?
	Fan.	By Goddys body, I come streyte.
400		I hate this blunderyng that thou doste make.
	Cou. Cou.	Nowe to the devyll I the betake,
		For, in fayth, ye be well met.

[Exit FANSY.]

		Fansy hath cachyd in a flye net
		This noble man Magnyfycence,
		Of Largesse under the pretence.
405		They have made me here to put the stone;
		But nowe wyll I, that they be gone,
		In bastarde ryme, after the dogrell gyse,
		Tell you where of my name dothe ryse.

410   For Counterfet Countenaunce knowen am I.
        This worlde is full of my foly.
        I set not by hym a fly
        That can not counterfet a lye,
        Swere and stare, and byde therby,
415   And countenaunce it clenly,
        And defende it manerly.

        A knave wyll counterfet nowe a knyght,
        A lurdayne lyke a lorde to syght,
        A mynstrell lyke a man of myght,
420   A tappyster lyke a lady bryght:
        Thus make I them wyth thryft to fyght.
        Thus at the laste I brynge hym ryght
        To Tyburne, where they hange on hyght.

        To counterfet I can by praty wayes:
425   Of nyghtys to occupy counterfet kayes;
        Clenly to counterfet newe arayes;
        Counterfet eyrnest by way of playes.
        Thus am I occupyed at all assayes.
        What so ever I do, all men me prayse,
430   And mekyll am I made of nowe adays.

        Counterfet maters in the lawe of the lande –
        Wyth golde and grotes they grese my hande,
        In stede of ryght that wronge may stande;
        And counterfet fredome that is bounde;
435   I counterfet suger that is but sande;
        Counterfet capytaynes by me are mande;
        Of all lewdnesse I kyndell the brande.

        Counterfet kyndnesse, and thynke dyscayte;
        Counterfet letters by the way of sleyght;
440   Subtelly usynge counterfet weyght;
        Counterfet langage, *fayty bone geyte*.
        Counterfetynge is a proper bayte.
        A counte to counterfet in a resayte –
        To counterfet well is a good consayte.

445   Counterfet maydenhode may well be borne,
        But counterfet coynes is laughynge to scorne;

It is evyll patchynge of that is torne.
Whan the noppe is rughe, it wolde be shorne.
Counterfet haltynge without a thorne;
450   Yet counterfet chafer is but evyll corne.
All thynge is worse whan it is worne.

What! Wolde ye wyves counterfet
The courtly gyse of the newe jet?
An olde barne wolde be underset.
455   It is moche worthe that is ferre fet.
What! Wanton, wanton, nowe well ymet!
What! Margery Mylke Ducke, mermoset!
It wolde be masked in my net!

It wolde be nyce, thoughe I say nay;
460   By crede, it wolde have fresshe aray,
'And therfore shall my husbande pay'.
To counterfet she wyll assay
All the newe gyse, fresshe and gaye,
And be as praty as she may,
465   And jet it joly as a jay.

Counterfet prechynge, and byleve the contrary;
Counterfet conscyence, pevysshe pope holy;
Counterfet sadnesse, with delynge full madly;
Counterfet holynes is called ypocrysy;
470   Counterfet reason is not worth a flye;
Counterfet wysdome, and workes of foly;
Counterfet Countenaunce every man dothe occupy.

Counterfet worshyp outwarde men may se;
Ryches rydeth out, at home is poverte.
475   Counterfet pleasure is borne out by me;
Coll wolde go clenly, and it wyll not be,
And Annot wolde be nyce, and laughes, 'tehe wehe.'
Your counterfet countenaunce is all of nysyte,
A plummed partrydge all redy to flye.

480   A knokylbonyarde wyll counterfet a clarke;
He wolde trotte gentylly, but he is to starke.
At his cloked counterfetynge dogges dothe barke.
A carter a courtyer, it is a worthy warke,
That with his whyp his mares was wonte to yarke;

485   A custrell to dryve the devyll out of the derke,
                  A counterfet courtyer with a knaves marke.

                  To counterfet this freers have lerned me.
                  This nonnes nowe and then, and it myght be,
                  Wolde take, in the way of counterfet charyte,
490   The grace of God under *benedicite.*
                  To counterfet thyr counsell they gyve me a fee.
                  Chanons can not counterfet but upon thre.
                  Monkys may not for drede that men sholde them se.

                  Hic ingrediatur FANSY *properanter cum* CRAFTY
                  CONVEYAUNCE, *cum famine multo adinvicem*
                  garrulantes; tandem viso COUNTERFET
                  COUNTENAUNCE *dicat* CRAFTY
                  CONVEYAUNCE.

Cra. Con.   What! Counterfet Countenaunce!
495 *Cou. Cou.*   What! Crafty Conveyaunce.
Fan.   What the devyll! Are ye two of aquayntaunce?
                  God gyve you a very myschaunce!
Cra. Con.   Yes, yes, syr. He and I have met.
Cou. Cou.   We have bene togyder bothe erly and late.
500   But Fansy, my frende, where have ye bene so longe?
Fan.   By God, I have bene about a praty pronge –
                  Crafty Conveyaunce, I sholde say, and I.
Cra. Con.   By God, we have made Magnyfycence to ete a flye.
Cou. Cou.   Howe coulde ye do that, and I was away?
505 *Fan.*   By God, man, bothe his pagent and thyne he can
                      play.
Cou. Cou.   Say trouth?
Cra. Con.   Yes, yes, by lakyn, I shall the warent,
                  As longe as I lyve, thou haste an heyre parent.
Fan.   Yet have we pycked out a rome for the.
Cou. Cou.   Why, shall we dwell togyder all thre?
510 *Cra. Con.* Why, man, it were to great a wonder
                  That we thre galauntes sholde be longe asonder.
Cou. Cou.   For Cockys harte, gyve me thy hande.
Fan.   By the masse, for ye are able to dystroy an hole
                      lande.
Cra. Con.   By God, yet it muste begynne moche of the.
515 *Fan.*   Who that is ruled by us, it shalbe longe or he thee.

Cou. Cou.		But I say, kepest thou the olde name styll that thou had?
Cra. Con.		Why, wenyst thou, horson, that I were so mad?
Fan.		Nay, nay. He hath chaunged his, and I have chaunged myne.
Cou. Cou.		Nowe what is his name? And what is thyne?
Fan.	520	In faythe, Largesse I hyght; And I am made a knyght.
Cou. Cou.		A rebellyon agaynst nature – So large a man, and so lytell of stature! But, syr, howe counterfetyd ye?
Cra. Con.	525	Sure Surveyaunce I named me.
Cou. Cou.		Surveyaunce! Where ye survey, Thryfte hathe lost her cofer kay.
Fan.		But is it not well? Howe thynkest thou?
Cou. Cou.		Yes, syr, I gyve God avowe,
	530	Myselfe coude not counterfet it better. But what became of the letter That I counterfeyted you underneth a shrowde?
Fan.		By the masse, odly well alowde.
Cra. Con.		By God, had not I it convayed
	535	Yet Fansy had ben dyscryved.
Cou. Cou.		I wote thou arte false ynoughe for one.
Fan.		By my trouthe, we had ben gone. And yet, in fayth, man, we lacked the For to speke with Lyberte.
Cou. Cou.	540	What! Is Largesse without lyberte?
Cra. Con.		By Mesure mastered yet is he.
Cou. Cou.		What! Is your conveyaunce no better.
Fan.		In faythe, Mesure is lyke a tetter That overgroweth a mannes face,
	545	So he ruleth over all our place.
Cra. Con.		Nowe therfore, whylest we are togyder – Counterfet Countenaunce, nay, come hyder – I say, whylest we are togyder in same –
Cou. Cou.		Tushe, a strawe! It is a shame
	550	That we can no better than so.
Fan.		We wyll remedy it, man, or we go; For lyke as mustarde is sharpe of taste Ryght so a sharp fansy must be founde Wherwith Mesure to confounde.

555	*Cra. Con.*	Can you remedy for a tysyke
		That sheweth yourselfe thus spedde in physyke?
	Cou. Cou.	It is a gentyll reason of a rake.
	Fan.	For all these japes yet that ye make –
	Cra. Con.	Your fansy maketh myne elbowe to ake.
560	*Fan.*	Let se, fynde you a better way.
	Cou. Cou.	Take no dyspleasure of that we say.
	Cra. Con.	Nay, and you be angry and overwharte,
		A man may beshrowe your angry harte.
	Fan.	Tushe, a strawe! I thought none yll.
565	*Cou. Cou.*	What! Shall we jangle thus all the day styll?
	Cra. Con.	Nay. Let us our heddes togyder cast.
	Fan.	Ye, and se howe it may be compast
		That Mesure were cast out of the dores.
	Cou. Cou.	Alasse! Where is my botes and my spores?
570	*Cra. Con.*	In all this hast whether wyll ye ryde?
	Cou. Cou.	I trowe it shall not nede to abyde.
		Cockes woundes! Se, syrs, se, se!

Hic ingrediatur CLOKED COLUSYON *cum elato aspectu, deorsum et sursum ambulando.*

	Fan.	Cockes armes! What is he?
	Cra. Con.	By Cockes harte, he loketh hye.
575		He hawketh, me thynke, for a butterflye.
	Cou. Cou.	Nowe, by Cockes harte, well abyden!
		For had you not come I had ryden.
	Clo. Col.	Thy wordes be but wynde, never they have no wayght.
		Thou hast made me play the *jeu dehayte.*
580	*Cou. Cou.*	And yf ye knewe howe I have mused,
		I am sure ye wolde have me excused.
	Clo. Col.	I say, come hyder. What are these twayne?
	Cou. Cou.	By God, syr, this is Fansy Small-Brayne;
		And Crafty Conveyaunce, knowe you not hym?
585	*Clo. Col.*	Knowe hym, syr, quod he. Yes, by Saynt Sym!
		Here is a leysshe of ratches to renne an hare!
		Woo is that purse that ye shall share!
	Fan.	What call ye him, this?
	Cra. Con.	I trowe that he is –
590	*Cou. Cou.*	Tushe! Holde your pece.
		Se you not howe they prece

		For to knowe your name?
	Clo. Col.	Knowe they not me? They are to blame.
		Knowe you not me, syrs?
	Fan.	No, in dede.
595	*Cra. Con.*	Abyde. Lette me se. Take better hede.
		Cockes harte! It is Cloked Colusyon!
	Clo. Col.	A, syr, I pray God gyve you confusyon!
	Fan.	Cockes armes! Is that your name?
	Cou. Cou.	Ye, by the masse, this is even the same,
600		That all this matter must under grope.
	Cra. Con.	What is this he wereth? A cope?
	Clo. Col.	Cappe, syr. I say you be to bolde.
	Fan.	Se howe he is wrapped for the colde.
		Is it not a vestment?
	Clo. Col.	A, ye wante a rope.
605	*Cou. Cou.*	Tushe! It is Syr Johnn Double-Cope.
	Fan.	Syr, and yf ye wolde not be wrothe –
	Clo. Col.	What sayst?
	Fan.	Here was to lytell clothe.
	Clo. Col.	A, Fansy, Fansy, God sende the brayne!
	Fan.	Ye, for your wyt is cloked for the rayne.
610	*Cra. Con.*	Nay, lette us not clatter thus styll.
	Clo. Col.	Tell me, syrs, what is your wyll?
	Cou. Cou.	Syr, it is so that these twayne
		With Magnyfycence in housholde do remayne;
		And there they wolde have me to dwell.
615		But I wyll be ruled after your counsell.
	Fan.	Mary, so wyll we also.
	Clo. Col.	But tell me where aboute ye go.
	Cou. Cou.	By God, we wolde gete us all thyder,
		Spell the remenaunt, and do togyder.
620	*Clo. Col.*	Hath Magnyfycence ony tresure?
	Cra. Con.	Ye. But he spendeth it all in mesure.
	Clo. Col.	Why, dwelleth Mesure where ye two dwell?
		In faythe, he were better to dwell in hell.
	Fan.	Yet where we wonne, nowe there wonneth he.
625	*Clo. Col.*	And have you not amonge you Lyberte?
	Cou. Cou.	Ye. But he is a captyvyte.
	Clo. Col.	What the devyll! Howe may that be?
	Cou. Cou.	I can not tell you. Why aske you me?

		Aske these two that there dothe dwell.
630	Clo. Col.	Syr, the playnesse you me tell.
	Cra. Con.	There dwelleth a mayster men calleth Mesure –
	Fan.	Ye. And he hath rule of all his tresure.
	Cra. Con.	Nay; eyther let me tell, or elles tell ye.
	Fan.	I care not, I. Tell on for me.
635	Cou. Cou.	I pray God let you never to thee!
	Clo. Col.	What the devyll ayleth you? Can you not agree?
	Cra. Con.	I wyll passe over the cyrcumstaunce
		And shortly shewe you the hole substaunce.
		Fansy and I, we twayne,
640		With Magnyfycence in housholde do remayne;
		And counterfeted our names we have
		Craftely all thynges upryght to save:
		His name Largesse, Surveyaunce myne.
		Magnyfycence to us begynneth to enclyne,
645		Counterfet Countenaunce to have also,
		And wolde that we sholde for hym go –
	Cou. Cou.	But shall I have myne olde name styll?
	Cra. Con.	Pease! I have not yet sayd what I wyll.
	Fan.	Here is a pystell of a postyke!
650	Clo. Col.	Tusshe! Fonnysshe Fansy, thou arte frantyke.
		Tell on, syr. Howe then?
	Cra. Con.	Mary, syr, he told us, when
		We had hym founde, we sholde hym brynge,
		And that we fayled not for nothynge.
655	Clo. Col.	All this ye may easely brynge aboute.
	Fan.	Mary, the better and Mesure were out.
	Clo. Col.	Why, can ye not put out that foule freke?
	Cra. Con.	No. In every corner he wyll peke,
		So that we have no lyberte;
660		Nor no man in courte, but he,
		For Lyberte he hath in gydyng.
	Cou. Cou.	In fayth, and without lyberte there is no
		bydyng.
	Fan.	In fayth, and Lybertyes rome is there but small.
	Clo. Col.	Hem! That lyke I nothynge at all.
665	Cra. Con.	But, Counterfet Countenaunce, go we togyder,
		All thre, I say.
	Cou. Cou.	Shall I go? Whyder?
	Cra. Con.	To Magnyfycence with us twayne.

		And in his servyce the to retayne.
	Cou. Cou.	But then, syr, what shall I hyght?
670	*Cra. Con.*	Ye and I talkyd therof to nyght.
	Fan.	Ye. My fansy was out of owle flyght,
		For it is out of my mynde quyght.
	Cra. Con.	And nowe it cometh to my remembraunce.
		Syr, ye shall hyght Good Demeynaunce.
675	*Cou. Cou.*	By the armes of Calys, well conceyved.
	Cra. Con.	When we have hym thyder convayed,
		What and I frame suche a slyght
		That Fansy with his fonde consayte
		Put Magnyfycence in suche a madnesse
680		That he shall have you in the stede of sadnesse,
		And Sober Sadnesse shalbe your name?
	Clo. Col.	By Cockys body, here begynneth the game!
		For then shall we so craftely cary
		That Mesure shall not there longe tary.
685	*Fan.*	For Cockys harte, tary whylyst that I come agayne.
	Cra. Con.	We wyll se you shortly, one of us twayne.
	Cou. Cou.	Now let us go, and we shall, then.
	Clo. Col.	Nowe let se. Quyte you lyke praty men!

> [*Exeunt* FANSY, CRAFTY CONVEYAUNCE *and*
> COUNTERFET COUNTENAUNCE]

Hic deambulat.

	To passe the tyme and order whyle a man may talke
690	Of one thynge and other to occupy the place,
	Then for the season that I here shall walke,
	As good to be occupyed as up and downe to trace
	And do nothynge. How be it, full lytell grace
	There cometh and groweth of my comynge;
695	For clokyd colusyon is a perylous thynge.

	Double delynge and I be all one;
	Craftynge and haftynge contryved is by me;
	I can dyssemble; I can bothe laughe and grone;
	Playne delynge and I can never agre.
700	But dyvysyon, dyssencyon, dyrysyon – these thre
	And I, am counterfet of one mynde and thought,
	By the menys of myschyef to bryng all thynges to
	nought.

And though I be so odyous a geste,
And every man gladly my company wolde refuse,
705   In faythe, yet am I occupied with the best;
Full fewe that can themselfe of me excuse.
Whan other men laughe, than study I and muse,
Devysynge the meanes and wayes that I can,
Howe I may hurte and hynder every man.

710   Two faces in a hode covertly I bere;
Water in the one hande and fyre in the other.
I can fede forth a fole and lede hym by the eyre;
Falshode in felowshyp is my sworne brother.
By cloked colusyon, I say, and none other,
715   Comberaunce and trouble in Englande fyrst I began.
From that lorde to that lorde I rode and I ran.

And flatered them with fables fayre before theyr
        face,
And tolde all the myschyef I coude behynde theyr
        backe,
And made as I had knowen nothynge of the case –
720   I wolde begyn all myschyef, but I wolde bere no
        lacke.
Thus can I lerne you, syrs, to bere the devyls sacke;
And yet, I trowe, some of you be better sped than I
Frendshyp to fayne and thynke full lytherly.

Paynte to a purpose good countenaunce I can,
725   And craftely can I grope howe every man is mynded.
My purpose is to spy and to poynte every man;
My tonge is with favell forked and tyned.
By Cloked Colusyon thus many one is begyled.
Eche man to hynder I gape and I gaspe;
730   My speche is all pleasure, but I stynge lyke a waspe.

I am never glad but whan I may do yll,
And never am I sory but whan that I se
I can not myne appetyte accomplysshe and fulfyll
In hynderaunce of welthe and prosperyte.
735   I laughe at all shrewdenes, and lye at lyberte.
I muster, I medle amonge these grete estates;
I sowe sedycyous sedes of dyscorde and debates.

To flater and to flery is all my pretence
Amonge all suche persones as I well understonde
740   Be lyght of byleve and hasty of credence;
I make them to startyll and sparkyll lyke a bronde;
I move them, I mase them, I make them so fonde,
That they wyll here no man but the fyrst tale.
And so, by these meanes, I brewe moche bale.

Hic ingrediatur COURTLY ABUSYON *cantando.*

745   *Cou. Ab.*   Huffa, huffa, taunderum, taunderum, tayne, huffa,
            huffa!

  Clo. Col.   This was properly prated, syrs! What sayd a?

  Cou. Ab.   Rutty bully, joly rutterkyn, heyda!

  Clo. Col.   *De que pays este vous?*

        Et faciat tanquam exuat beretum ironice.

  Cou. Ab.   Decke your hofte and cover a lowce.

750   *Clo. Col.*   *Say vous chaunter 'Venter tre dawce'?*

  Cou. Ab.   *Wyda, wyda!*
        Howe sayst thou, man? Am not I a joly rutter?

  Clo. Col.   Gyve this gentylman rome, syrs. Stonde utter!
        By God, syr, what nede all this waste?
755   What is this, a betell or a batowe or a buskyn lacyd?

  Cou. Ab.   What! Wenyst thou that I knowe the not, Clokyd
           Colusyon?

  Clo. Col.   And wenyst thow that I know not the, cankard
           Abusyon?

  Cou. Ab.   Cankard Jacke Hare, loke thou be not rusty;
        For thou shalt well knowe I am nother durty nor
           dusty.

760   *Clo. Col.*   Dusty! Nay, syr, ye be all of the lusty;
        Howe be it of scape thryfte your clokes smelleth
           musty.
        But whether art thou walkynge, in faythe unfaynyd?

  Cou. Ab.   Mary, with Magnyfycence I wolde be retaynyd.

  Clo. Col.   By the masse, for the cowrte thou art a mete man;
765   Thy slyppers they swap it, yet thou fotys it lyke a
           swanne.

  Cou. Ab.   Ye, so I can devyse my gere after the cowrtly maner.

  Clo. Col.   So thou arte personable to bere a prynces baner.
        By Goddes fote, and I dare well fyght, for I wyll not
           start.

	Cou. Ab.	Nay. Thou art a man good inough but for thy false hart.
770	*Clo. Col.*	Well, and I be a coward, there is mo than I.
	Cou. Ab.	Ye, in faythe, a bolde man and a hardy.
	Clo. Col.	A bolde man in a bole of newe ale in cornys.
	Cou. Ab.	Wyll ye se this gentylman is all in his skornys?
	Clo. Col.	But are ye not avysed to dwell where ye spake?
775	*Cou. Ab.*	I am of fewe wordys. I love not to crake.
		Beryst thou any rome? Or cannyst thou do ought?
		Cannyst thou helpe in faver that I myght be brought?
	Clo. Col.	I may do somwhat, and more I thynke shall.

Here cometh in CRAFTY CONVEYAUNCE
poyntyng with his fynger, and sayth,

	Cra. Con.	Hem, Colusyon!
780	*Cou. Ab.*	Cockys harte! Who is yonde that for the dothe call?
	Cra. Con.	Nay, come at ones, for the armes of the dyce.
	Cou. Ab.	Cockys armys! He hath callyd for the twyce.
	Clo. Col.	By Cockys harte, and call shall agayne!
		To come to me I trowe he shalbe fayne.
785	*Cou. Ab.*	What! Is thy harte pryckyd with such a prowde pynne?
	Clo. Col.	Tushe! He that hathe nede, man, let hym rynne.
	Cra. Con.	Nay, come away, man! Thou playst the cayser.
	Clo. Col.	By the masse, thou shalt byde my leyser.
	Cra. Con.	Abyde, syr, quod he! Mary, so I do.
790	*Cou. Ab.*	He wyll come, man, when he may tende to.
	Cra. Con.	What the devyll! Who sent for the?
	Clo. Col.	Here he is nowe, man. Mayst thou not se?
	Cra. Con.	What the devyll, man, what thou menyst?
		Art thou so angry as thou semyst?
795	*Cou. Ab.*	What the devyll! Can ye agre no better?
	Cra. Con.	What the devyll! Where had we this joly jetter?
	Clo. Col.	What sayst thou, man? Why dost thou not supplye,
		And desyre me thy good mayster to be?
	Cou. Ab.	Spekest thou to me?
800	*Clo. Col.*	Ye, so I tell the.
	Cou. Ab.	Cockes bones! I ne tell can
		Whiche of you is the better man,
		Or whiche of you can do most.

	Cra. Con.	In faythe, I rule moche of the rost.
805	*Clo. Col.*	Rule the roste! Thou woldest, ye,
		As skante thou had no nede of me.
	Cra. Con.	Nede? Yes, Mary. I say not nay.
	Cou. Ab.	Cockes harte! I trowe thou wylte make a fray.
	Cra. Con.	Nay, in good faythe. It is but the gyse.
810	*Clo. Col.*	No; for or we stryke, we wyll be advysed twyse.
	Cou. Ab.	What the devyll! Use ye not to drawe no swordes?
	Cra. Con.	No, by my trouthe, but crake grete wordes.
	Cou. Ab.	Why, is this the gyse nowe adays?
	Clo. Col.	Ye, for surety. Ofte peas is taken for frayes.
815		But, syr, I wyll have this man with me.
	Cra. Con.	Convey yourselfe fyrst, let se.
	Clo. Col.	Well, tary here tyll I for you sende.
	Cra. Con.	Why, shall he be of your bende?
	Clo. Col.	Tary here. Wote ye what I say?
820	*Cou. Ab.*	I waraunt you I wyll not go away.
	Cra. Con.	By Saynt Mary, he is a tawle man.
	Clo. Col.	Ye, and do ryght good servyce he can.
		I knowe in hym no defaute
		But that the horson is prowde and hawte.

And so they [CLOKED COLUSYON *and* CRAFTY
CONVEYAUNCE] *go out of the place.*

825	*Cou. Ab.*	Nay. Purchace ye a pardon for the pose,
		For pryde hath plucked the by the nose
		As well as me. I wolde, and I durste –
		But nowe I wyll not say the worste.

COURTLY ABUSYON *alone in the place.*

	What nowe? Let se
830	Who loketh on me
	Well rounde aboute.
	Howe gay and howe stout
	That I can were
	Courtly my gere!

835	My heyre bussheth
	So plesauntly;
	My robe russheth
	So ruttyngly;
	Me seme I flye,

840
I am so lyght
To daunce delyght;

Properly drest
All *poynte devyse*,
My persone prest
845
Beyonde all syse
Of the newe gyse,
To russhe it oute
In every route.

Beyonde measure
850
My sleve is wyde;
Al of pleasure
My hose strayte tyde;
My buskyn wyde,
Ryche to beholde
855
Gletterynge in golde.

Abusyon
Forsothe I hyght;
Confusyon
Shall on hym lyght
860
By day or by nyght
That useth me.
He can not thee.

A very fon,
A very asse
865
Wyll take upon
To compasse
That never was
Abusyd before.
A very pore

870
That so wyll do,
He doth abuse
Hym selfe to to;
He dothe mysse use
Eche man to akuse,
875
To crake and prate.
I befoule his pate.

This newe fonne jet
From out of Fraunce
Fyrst I dyd set;
880   Made purveaunce
And suche ordenaunce,
That all men it founde
Through out Englonde.

All this nacyon
885   I set on fyre;
In my facyon
This theyr desyre,
This newe atyre.
This ladyes have,
890   I it them gave.

Spare for no coste;
And yet in dede
It is coste loste
Moche more than nede
895   For to excede
In suche aray.
Howe be it, I say,

A carlys sonne
Brought up of nought
900   Wyth me wyll wonne
Whylyst he hath ought.
He wyll have wrought
His gowne so wyde
That he may hyde

905   His dame and his syre
Within his slyve;
Spende all his hyre
That men hym gyve.
Wherfore I preve,
910   A Tyborne checke
Shall breke his necke.

Here cometh in FANSY *craynge 'Stow, stow!'*
All is out of harre

		And out of trace,
		Ay warre and warre
915		In every place.
		But what the devyll art thou
		That cryest 'Stow, stow'?
	Fan.	What! Whom have we here, Jenkyn Joly?
		Nowe welcom, by the God holy!
920	*Cou. Ab.*	What! Fansy, my frende! Howe dost thou fare?
	Fan.	By Cryst, as mery as a Marche hare.
	Cou. Ab.	What the devyll hast thou on thy fyste? An owle?
	Fan.	Nay. It is a farly fowle.
	Cou. Ab.	Me thynke she frowneth and lokys sowre.
925	*Fan.*	Torde! Man, it is an hawke of the towre.
		She is made for the malarde fat.
	Cou. Ab.	Methynke she is well becked to catche a rat.
		But nowe what tydynges can you tell? Let se.
	Fan.	Mary, I am come for the.
	Cou. Ab.	For me?
930	*Fan.*	Ye, for the, so I say.
	Cou. Ab.	Howe so? Tell me, I the pray.
	Fan.	Why, harde thou not of the fray
		That fell amonge us this same day?
	Cou. Ab.	No, Mary; not yet.
935	*Fan.*	What the devyll! Never a whyt?
	Cou. Ab.	No, by the masse. What! Sholde I swere?
	Fan.	In faythe, Lyberte is nowe a lusty spere.
	Cou. Ab.	Why, under whom was he abydynge?
	Fan.	Mary, Mesure had hym a whyle in gydynge,
940		Tyll, as the devyll wolde, they fell a chydynge
		With Crafty Convayaunce.
	Cou. Ab.	Ye, dyd they so?
	Fan.	Ye, by Goddes sacrament; and with other mo.
	Cou. Ab.	What neded that, in the dyvyls date?
	Fan.	Yes, yes. He fell with me also at debate.
945	*Cou. Ab.*	With the also? What! He playeth the state?
	Fan.	Ye. But I bade hym pyke out of the gate;
		By Goddes body, so dyd I.
	Cou. Ab.	By the masse, well done and boldely.
	Fan.	Holde thy pease! Measure shall frome us walke.
950	*Cou. Ab.*	Why? Is he crossed than with a chalke?
	Fan.	Crossed? Ye, checked out of consayte.

Cou. Ab.		Howe so?
Fan.		By God, by a praty slyght,
		As here after thou shalte knowe more.
		But I must tary here; go thou before.
955	*Cou. Ab.*	With whom shall I there mete.
	Fan.	Crafty Conveyaunce standeth in the strete
		Even of purpose for the same.
	Cou. Ab.	Ye, but what shall I call my name?
	Fan.	Cockes harte! Tourne the; let me se thyne aray.
960		Cockes bones! This is all of Johnn de Gay.
	Cou. Ab.	So I am poynted after my consayte.
	Fan.	Mary, thou jettes it of hyght.
	Cou. Ab.	Ye, but of my name let us be wyse.
	Fan.	Mary, Lusty Pleasure, by myne advyse,
965		To name thyselfe. Come of, it were done.
	Cou. Ab.	Farewell, my frende.
	Fan.	Adue tyll sone.

[*Exit* COURTLY ABUSYON]

Stowe, byrde, stowe, stowe!
It is best I fede my hawke now.
There is many evyll faveryd, and thou be foule!
970   Eche thynge is fayre when it is yonge; all hayle,
      owle!

Lo, this is
My fansy, iwys;
Nowe Cryst it blysse!
It is, by Jesse,

975   A byrde full swete,
For me full mete.
She is furred for the hete
All to the fete;

Her browys bent,
980   Her eyen glent;
Frome Tyne to Trent,
From Stroude to Kent,

A man shall fynde
Many of her kynde,

985   Howe standeth the wynde
            Before or behynde;

            Barbyd lyke a nonne
            For burnynge of the sonne;
            Her fethers donne;
990   Well faveryd bonne!

            Nowe let me se about
            In all this rowte
            Yf I can fynde out
            So semely a snowte

995   Among this prese –
            Even a hole mese –
            Pease, man, pease!
            I rede we sease.

            So farly fayre as it lokys!
1000   And her becke so comely crokys!
            Her naylys sharpe as tenter-hokys!
            I have not kept her yet thre wokys,

            And howe styll she doth syt!
            Teuyt, teuyt!
1005   Where is my wyt?
            The devyll spede whyt!

            That was before I set behynde;
            Nowe to curteys, forthwith unkynde;
            Somtyme to sober, somtyme to sadde;
1010   Somtyme to mery, somtyme to madde;
            Somtyme I syt as I were solempe prowde;
            Somtyme I laughe over lowde;
            Somtyme I wepe for a gew gaw;
            Somtyme I laughe at waggynge of a straw,
1015   With a pere my love you may wynne,
            And ye may lese it for a pynne.
            I have a thynge for to say,
            And I may tende therto for play;
            But, in faythe, I am so occupyed
1020   On this halfe and on every syde
            That I wote not where I may rest.
            Fyrst to tell you what were best:

Frantyke Fansy-Servyce I hyght;
My wyttys be weke, my braynys are lyght;
1025   For it is I that other whyle
Plucke down lede and theke with tyle;
Nowe I wyll this, and nowe I wyll that –
Make a wyndmyll of a mat –
Nowe I wolde – and I wyst what –
1030   Where is my cappe? I have lost my hat!
And within an houre after,
Plucke downe an house and set up a rafter,
Hyder and thyder, I wote not whyder;
Do and undo, bothe togyder;
1035   Of a spyndell I wyll make a sparre;
All that I make forthwith I marre;
I blunder, I bluster, I blowe, and I blother;
I make on the one day, and I marre on the other.
Bysy, bysy, and ever bysy,
1040   I daunce up and downe tyll I am dyssy.
I can fynde fantasyes where none is;
I wyll not have it so, I wyll have it this.

Hic ingrediatur FOLY *quatiendo crema et*
faciendo multum, feriendo tabulas, et similia.
Fol.   Maysters, Cryst save everychone!
What, Fansy! Arte thou here alone?
1045   Fan.   What, fonnysshe Foly! I befole thy face.
Fol.   What, frantyke Fansy, in a foles case?
What is this, an owle or a glede?
By my trouthe, she hathe a grete hede.
Fan.   Tusshe! Thy lyppes hange in thyne eye;
1050   It is a Frenche butterflye.
Fol.   By my trouthe, I trowe well;
But she is lesse a grete dele
Than a butterflye of our lande.
Fan.   What pylde curre ledest thou in thy hande?
Fol.   A pylde curre?
1055   Fan.   Ye, so I tell the, a pylde curre.
Fol.   Yet I solde his skynne to Mackemurre,
In the stede of a budge furre.
Fan.   What! Fleyest thou his skynne every yere?
Fol.   Yes, in faythe, I thanke God I may here.

1060   *Fan.*   What! Thou wylte coughe me a dawe for forty pens?

     Fol.   Mary, syr, Cokermowthe is a good way hens.

     Fan.   What! Of Cokermowth spake I no worde.

     Fol.   By my faythe, syr, the frubyssher hath my sworde.

     Fan.   A, I trowe ye shall coughe me a fole.

1065   *Fol.*   In faythe, trouthe ye say, we wente togyder to scole.

     Fan.   Ye, but I can somwhat more of the letter.

     Fol.   I wyll not gyve a halfepeny for to chose the better.

     Fan.   But, broder Foly, I wonder moche of one thynge,

           That thou so hye fro me doth sprynge,

1070   And I so lytell alway styll.

     Fol.   By God, I can tell the; and I wyll.

           Thou art so feble-fantastycall,

           And so braynsyke therwithall,

           And thy wyt wanderynge here and there,

1075   That thou cannyst not growe out of thy boyes gere;

           And as for me, I take but one folysshe way,

           And therfore I growe more on one day

           Than thou can in yerys seven.

     Fan.   In faythe, trouth thou sayst nowe, by God of heven!

1080   For so with fantasyes my wyt dothe flete

           That wysdome and I shall seldome mete.

           Nowe, of good felowshyp, let me by thy dogge.

     Fol.   Cockys harte! Thou lyest; I am no hogge.

     Fan.   Here is no man that callyd the hogge nor swyne.

1085   *Fol.*   In faythe, man, my brayne is as good as thyne.

     Fan.   The devyls torde for thy brayne!

     Fol.   By my syers soule, I fele no rayne.

     Fan.   By the masse, I holde the madde.

     Fol.   Mary, I knewe the when thou waste a ladde.

1090   *Fan.*   Cockys bonys! Herde ye ever syke another?

     Fol.   Ye, a fole the tone, and a fole the tother.

     Fan.   Nay, but wotest thou what I do say?

     Fol.   Why, sayst thou that I was here yesterday?

     Fan.   Cockys armys! This is a warke, I trowe.

1095   *Fol.*   What! Callyst thou me a donnyshe crowe?

     Fan.   Nowe, in good faythe, thou art a fonde gest.

     Fol.   Ye, bere me this strawe to a dawys nest.

     Fan.   What! Wenyst thou that I were so folysshe and so

               fonde?

     Fol.   In faythe, ellys is there none in all Englonde.

1100 *Fan.* Yet for my fansy sake, I say,
　　　　Let me have thy dogge, what soever I pay.

　　Fol. Thou shalte have my purse, and I wyll have thyne.

　　Fan. By my trouth, there is myne.

　　Fol. Nowe, by my trouth, man, take, there is my purse;
1105　　And I beshrowe hym that hath the worse.

　　Fan. Torde, I say! What have I do?
　　　　Here is nothynge but the bockyll of a sho,
　　　　And in my purse was twenty marke.

　　Fol. Ha, ha, ha! Herke, syrs, harke!
1110　　For all that my name hyght Foly,
　　　　By the masse, yet art thou more fole than I.

　　Fan. Yet gyve me thy dogge, and I am content;
　　　　And thou shalte have my hauke to a botchment.

　　Fol. That ever thou thryve, God it forfende!
1115　　For, Goddes cope, thou wyll spende!
　　　　Nowe take thou my dogge and gyve me thy fowle.

　　Fan. Hay, chysshe, come hyder!

　　Fol.　　　　　　　Nay, torde! Take hym be tyme.

　　Fan. What callest thou thy dogge?
　　　　　　　　　　　Tusshe! His name is Gryme.

　　Fan. Come, Gryme! Come, Gryme! It is my praty dogges.

1120 *Fol.* In faythe, there is not a better dogge for hogges,
　　　　Not from Anwyke unto Aungey.

　　Fan. Ye. But trowest thou that he be not maungey?

　　Fol. No, by my trouthe. It is but the scurfe and the
　　　　　scabbe.

　　Fan. What! He hathe ben hurte with a stabbe?

1125 *Fol.* Nay, in faythe, it was but a strype
　　　　That the horson had for etynge of a trype.

　　Fan. Where the devyll gate he all these hurtes?

　　Fol. By God, for snatchynge of puddynges and wortes.

　　Fan. What! Then he is some good poore mannes curre?

1130 *Fol.* Ye. But he wyll in at every mannes dore.

　　Fan. Nowe thou hast done me a pleasure grete.

　　Fol. In faythe, I wolde thou had a marmosete.

　　Fan. Cockes harte! I love suche japes.

　　Fol. Ye, for all thy mynde is on owles and apes.
1135　　But I have thy pultre, and thou hast my catell.

　　Fan. Ye. But thryfte and we have made a batell.

　　Fol. Remembrest thou not the japes and the toyes –

	Fan.	What, that we used whan we were boyes?
	Fol.	Ye, by the rode, even the same.
1140	*Fan.*	Yes, yes! I am yet as full of game
		As ever I was, and as full of tryfyls –
		Nil, nichelum, nihil – *anglice* nyfyls.
	Fol.	What! Canest thou all this Latyn yet,
		And hath so mased a wandrynge wyt?
1145	*Fan.*	Tushe, man! I kepe some Latyn in store.
	Fol.	By Cockes harte, I wene thou hast no more.
	Fan.	No? Yes, in faythe; I can versyfy.
	Fol.	Then I pray the hartely,
		Make a verse of my butterfly;
1150		It forseth not of the reason, so it kepe ryme.
	Fan.	But wylte thou make another on Gryme?
	Fol.	Nay, in fayth, fyrst let me here thyne.
	Fan.	Mary, as for that, thou shalte sone here myne.

Versus

	Fan.	*Est suavis vago* with a shrewde face *vilis imago.*
1155	*Fol.*	*Grimbaldus* gredy snatche a puddyng tyl the rost be
		redy.
	Fan.	By the harte of God, well done!
	Fol.	Ye, so redely and so sone!

Here cometh in CRAFTY CONVEYAUNCE.

	Cra. Con.	What, Fansy! Let me se who is the tother.
	Fan.	By God, syr, Foly, myne owne sworne brother.
1160	*Cra. Con.*	Cockys bonys! It is a farle freke.
		Can he play well at the hoddypeke?
	Fan.	Tell by thy trouth what sport can thou make.
	Fol.	A, holde thy peas! I have the tothe ake.
	Cra. Con.	The tothe ake! Lo, a torde ye have.
1165	*Fol.*	Ye, thou haste the four quarters of a knave.
	Cra. Con.	Wotyst thou, I say, to whom thou spekys?
	Fan.	Nay, by Cockys harte, he ne reckys;
		For he wyll speke to Magnyfycence thus.
	Cra. Con.	Cockys armys, a mete man for us!
1170	*Fol.*	What? Wolde ye have mo folys, and are so many?
	Fan.	Nay, offer hym a counter in stede of a peny.
	Cra. Con.	Why, thynkys thou he can no better skyll?
	Fol.	In fayth, I can make you bothe folys, and I wyll.

	Cra. Con.	What hast thou on thy fyst? A kesteryll?
1175	*Fol.*	Nay, iwys, fole. It is a doteryll.
	Cra. Con.	In a cote thou can play well the dyser.
	Fol.	Ye, but thou can play the fole without a vyser.
	Fan.	Howe rode he by you? Howe put he to you?
	Cra. Con.	Mary, as thou sayst, he gave me a blurre.
1180		But where gatte thou that mangey curre?
	Fan.	Mary, it was his, and nowe it is myne.
	Cra. Con.	And was it his, and nowe it is thyne?
		Thou must have thy fansy and thy wyll,
		But yet thou shalt holde me a fole styll.
1185	*Fol.*	Why, wenyst thou that I cannot make the play the fon?
	Fan.	Yes, by my faythe, good Syr Johnn.
	Cra. Con.	For you bothe it were inough.
	Fol.	Why, wenyst thou that I were as moche a fole as thou?
	Fan.	Nay, nay. Thou shalte fynde hym another maner of man.
1190	*Fol.*	In faythe, I can do mastryes, so I can.
	Cra. Con.	What canest thou do but play cocke wat?
	Fan.	Yes, yet he wyll make the ete a gnat.
	Fol.	Yes, yes, by my trouth. I holde the a grote
		That I shall laughe the out of thy cote.
1195	*Cra. Con.*	Than wyll I say that thou haste no pere.
	Fan.	Nowe, by the rode, and he wyll go nere.
	Fol.	Hem, Fansy! *Regardes, voyes vous.*

Here FOLY *maketh semblaunt to take a lowse from* CRAFTY CONVEYAUNCE *showlder.*

	Fan.	What hast thou founde there?
	Fol.	By God, a lowse.
	Cra. Con.	By Cockes harte, I trowe thou lyste.
1200	*Fol.*	By the masse, a Spaynysshe moght with a gray lyste!
	Fan.	Ha, ha, ha, ha, ha, ha!
	Cra. Con.	Cockes armes! It is not so, I trowe.

Here CRAFTY CONVEYAUNCE *putteth of his gowne.*

	Fol.	Put on thy gowne agayne, for thou hast lost nowe.
	Fan.	Lo, Johnn a Bonam, where is thy brayne?
1205		Nowe put on, fole, thy cote agayne.
	Fol.	Gyve me my grote, for thou hast lost.

Here FOLY *maketh semblaunt to take money of* CRAFTY

CONVEYAUNCE, *saynge to hym,*
Shyt thy purse, dawe, and do no cost.

Fan. Nowe hast thou not a prowde mocke and a starke?

Cra. Con. With, yes, by the rode of Wodstocke Parke.

1210 Fan. Nay, I tell the, he maketh no dowtes
To tourne a fole out of his clowtes.

Cra. Con. And for a fole a man wolde hym take.

Fol. Nay, it is I that foles can make;
For be he cayser or be he kynge,

1215 To felowshyp with foly I can hym brynge.

Fan. Nay, wylte thou here nowe of his scoles,
And what maner of people he maketh foles?

Cra. Con. Ye. Let us here a worde or twayne.

Fol. Syr, of my maner I shall tell you the playne:

1220 Fyrst I lay before them my bybyll
And teche them howe they sholde syt ydyll
To pyke theyr fyngers all the day longe;
So in theyr eyre I synge them a songe
And make them so longe to muse

1225 That some of them renneth strayght to the stuse.
To thefte and bryboury I make some fall,
And pyke a locke and clyme a wall.
And where I spy a nysot gay
That wyll syt ydyll all the day

1230 And can not set herselfe to warke,
I kyndell in her suche a lyther sparke
That rubbed she must be on the gall
Bytwene the tappet and the wall.

Cra. Con. What, horson! Arte thou suche a one?

1235 Fan. Nay, beyonde all other set hym alone.

Cra. Con. Hast thou ony more? Let se, procede.

Fol. Ye, by God, syr. For a nede,
I have another maner of sorte
That I laugh at for my dysporte;

1240 And those be they that come up of nought –
As some be not ferre and yf it were well sought –
Suche dawys, what soever they be,
That be set in auctorite.
Anone he waxyth so hy and prowde,

1245 He frownyth fyersly, brymly browde.

The knave wolde make it koy, and he cowde;
All that he dothe muste be alowde;
And, 'This is not well done, syr; take hede';
And maketh hym besy where is no nede.

1250 He dawnsys so long, 'hey, troly, loly',
That every man lawghyth at his foly.

Cra. Con.   By the good Lorde, truthe he sayth.

Fan.   Thynkyst thou not so, by thy fayth?

Cra. Con.   Thynke I not so, quod he. Ellys have I shame,
1255   For I knowe dyverse that useth the same.

Fol.   But nowe, forsothe, man, it maketh no mater;
For they that wyll so bysely smater
So helpe me God, man, ever at the length
I make hym lese moche of theyr strength;
1260   For with foly so do I them lede
That wyt he wantyth when he hath moste nede.

Fan.   Forsothe, tell on. Hast thou any mo?

Fol.   Yes. I shall tell you or I go
Of dyverse mo that hauntyth my scolys.

1265 *Cra. Con.*   All men beware of suche folys!

Fol.   There be two lyther, rude and ranke,
Symkyn Tytyvell and Pers Pykthanke.
Theys lythers I lerne them for to lere,
What he sayth and she sayth to lay good ere,
1270   And tell to his sufferayne every whyt;
And then he is moche made of for his wyt;
And, be the mater yll more or lesse,
He wyll make it mykyll worse than it is;
But all that he dothe, and yf he reken well
1275   It is but foly every dell.

Fan.   Are not his wordys cursydly cowchyd?

Cra. Con.   By God, there be some that be shroudly towchyd.
But, I say, let se and yf thou have any more.

Fol.   I have an hole armory of suche haburdashe in store;
1280   For there be other that foly dothe use
That folowe fonde fantasyes and vertu refuse.

Fan.   Nay, that is my parte that thou spekest of nowe.

Fol.   So is all the remenaunt, I make God avowe;
For thou fourmest suche fantasyes in theyr mynde
1285   That every man almost groweth out of kynde.

	Cra. Con.	By the masse, I am glad that I came hyder
		To here you two rutters dyspute togyder.
	Fan.	Nay, but fansy must be eyther fyrst or last.
	Fol.	And whan foly cometh, all is past.
1290	*Fan.*	I wote not whether it cometh of the or of me,
		But all is foly that I can se.
	Cra. Con.	Mary, syr, ye may swere it on a boke.
	Fol.	Ye, tourne over the lefe, rede there, and loke
		Howe frantyke fansy fyrst of all
1295		Maketh man and woman in foly to fall.
	Cra. Con.	A, syr, a, a! Howe by that?
	Fan.	A peryllous thynge, to cast a cat
		Upon a naked man and yf she scrat.
	Fol.	So how, I say, the hare is squat!
1300		For, frantyke Fansy, thou makyst men madde;
		And I Foly bryngeth them to *qui fuit* gadde;
		With *qui fuit* brayne seke I have them brought;
		From *qui fuit aliquid* to shyre shakynge nought.
	Cra. Con.	Well argued and surely on bothe sydes.
1305		But, for the, Fansy, Magnyfycence abydes.
	Fan.	Why, shall I not have Foly with me also?
	Cra. Con.	Yes, perde, man, whether that ye ryde or go.
		Yet for his name we must fynde a slyght.
	Fan.	By the masse, he shall hyght Consayte.
1310	*Cra. Con.*	Not a better name under the sonne;
		With Magnyfycence thou shalte wonne.
	Fol.	God have mercy, good godfather.
	Cra. Con.	Yet I wolde that ye had gone rather;
		For as sone as you come in Magnyfycence syght
1315		All mesure and good rule is gone quyte.
	Fan.	And shall we have lyberte to do what we wyll?
	Cra. Con.	Ryot at lyberte russheth it out styll.
	Fol.	Ye. But tell me one thynge.
	Cra. Con.	What is that?
	Fol.	Who is mayster of the masshe fat?
1320	*Fan.*	Ye, for he hathe a full drye soule.
	Cra. Con.	Cockes armes! Thou shalte kepe the brewhouse boule.
	Fol.	But may I drynke therof whylest that I stare?
	Cra. Con.	When Mesure is gone, what nedest thou spare?
		Whan Mesure is gone, we may slee care.

1325 *Fol.*   Nowe then goo we hens. Away the mare!

[*Exeunt* FANSY *and* FOLY.]

CRAFTY CONVEYAUNCE *alone in the place.*
Cra. Con.   It is wonder to se the worlde aboute,
To se what foly is used in every place;
Foly hath a rome, I say, in every route;
To put where he lyst, foly hath fre chace;
1330   Foly and fansy all where every man dothe face and
brace.
Foly fotyth it properly, fansy ledyth the dawnce,
And next come I after, Crafty Conveyaunce.

Who so to me gyveth good advertence
Shall se many thyngys donne craftely.
1335   By me conveyed is wanton insolence;
....
Pryvy poyntmentys conveyed so properly;
For many tymes moche kyndnesse is denyed
For drede, that we dare not ofte, lest we be spyed.

1340   By me is conveyed mykyll praty ware –
Somtyme, I say, behynde the dore for nede;
I have an hoby can make larkys to dare;
I knyt togyther many a broken threde.
It is great almesse the hungre to fede,
1345   To clothe the nakyd where is lackynge a smocke –
Trymme at her tayle or a man can turne a socke.

'What howe! Be ye mery! Was it not well conveyed?'
'As oft as ye lyst, so honeste be savyd.
Alas, dere harte, loke that we be not perseyvyd!'
1350   Without crafte nothynge is well behavyd.
'Though I shewe you curtesy, say not that I craved;
Yet convey it craftely, and hardely spare not for
me' –
So that there knowe no man but I and she.

Thefte also and pety brybery
1355   Without me be full ofte aspyed.
My inwyt delynge there can no man dyscry.
Convey it be crafte, lyft and lay asyde.
Full moche flatery and falsehode I hyde;

And by crafty conveyaunce I wyll, and I can,
1360   Save a stronge thefe and hange a trew man.

But some man wolde convey, and can not skyll,
As malypert tavernars that checke with theyr betters,
Theyr conveyaunce weltyth the worke all by wyll;
And some wyll take upon them to conterfet letters,
1365   And therwithall convey hymselfe into a payre of
        fetters;
And some wyll convey by the pretence of sadnesse
Tyll all theyr conveyaunce is turnyd into madnesse.

Crafty conveyaunce is no chyldys game;
By crafty conveyaunce many one is brought up of
        nought;
1370   Crafty Conveyaunce can cloke hymselfe frome
        shame,
For by crafty conveyaunce wonderful thynges are
        wrought.
By convayaunce crafty I have brought
Unto Magnyfycence a full ungracyous sorte,
For all hokes unhappy to me have resorte.

Here cometh in MAGNYFYCENCE *with* LYBERTE *and*
FELYCYTE.

1375   *Magn.*   Trust me, Lyberte, it greveth me ryght sore
                  To se you thus ruled and stande in suche awe.
        Lyb.   Syr, as by my wyll, it shall be so no more.
        Fel.   Yet Lyberte without rule is not worth a strawe.
        Magn.   Tushe! Holde your peas; ye speke lyke a dawe.
- 1380   Ye shall be occupyed, Welthe, at my wyll.
        Cra. Con. All that ye say, syr, is reason and skyll.

        Magn.   Mayster Survayour, where have ye ben so longe?
                  Remembre ye not how my lyberte by mesure ruled
                      was?
        Cra. Con. In good faythe, syr, me semeth he had the more
                      wronge.
1385   *Lyb.*   Mary, syr, so dyd he excede and passe,
                  They drove me to lernynge lyke a dull asse.
        Fel.   It is good yet that lyberte be ruled by reason.
        Magn.   Tushe! Holde your peas; ye speke out of season.

		Yourselfe shall be ruled by lyberte and largesse.
1390	*Fel.*	I am content so it in measure be.
	Lyb.	Must mesure, in the mares name, you furnysshe and dresse?
	Magn.	Nay, nay; not so, my frende Felycyte.
	Cra. Con.	Not and your grace wolde be ruled by me.
	Lyb.	Nay. He shall be ruled even as I lyst.
1395	*Fel.*	Yet it is good to beware of 'had I wyst'.

	Magn.	Syr, by lyberte and largesse I wyll that ye shall
		Be governed and gyded; wote ye what I say?
		Mayster Survayour, Largesse to me call.
	Cra. Con.	It shall be done.
	Magn.	Ye, but byd hym come away
1400		At ones, and let hym not tary all day.

Here goth out CRAFTY CONVAYAUNCE.

	Fel.	Yet it is good wysdome to worke wysely by welth.
	Lyb.	Holde thy tonge, and thou love thy helth.

	Magn.	What! Wyll ye waste wynde and prate thus in vayne?
		Ye have eten sauce I trowe, at the Taylers Hall.
1405	*Lyb.*	Be not to bolde my frende; I counsell you, bere a brayne.
	Magn.	And what so we say, holde you content withall.
	Fel.	Syr, yet without sapyence your substaunce may be smal;
		For where is no mesure, howe may worshyp endure?

Here cometh in FANSY.

	Fan.	Syr, I am here at your pleasure.
1410		Your grace sent for me, I wene. What is your wyll?
	Magn.	Come hyther Largesse; take here Felycyte.
	Fan.	Why, wene you that I can kepe hym longe styll?
	Magn.	To rule as ye lyst, lo, here is Lyberte.
	Lyb.	I am here redy.
	Fan.	What! Shall we
1415		Have welth at our gydynge to rule as we lyst?
		Then fare well thryfte, by hym that crosse kyst!

	Fel.	I truste your grace wyll be agreabyll
		That I shall suffer none impechment
		By theyr demenaunce, nor loss repryvable.

1420	*Magn.*	Syr, ye shall folowe myne appetyte and intent.
	Fel.	So it be by mesure I am ryght well content.
	Fan.	What! All by mesure, good syr, and none excesse?
	Lyb.	Why, welth hath made many a man braynlesse.

	Fel.	That was by the menys of to moche lyberte.
1425	*Magn.*	What! Can ye agree thus and appose?
	Fel.	Syr, as I say, there was no faute in me.
	Lyb.	Ye, of Jacke a Thrommys bybyll can ye make a glose.
	Fan.	Sore sayde, I tell you, and well to the purpose.
		What sholde a man do with you? Loke you under kay?
1430	*Fel.*	I say it is foly to gyve all welth away.

	Lyb.	Whether sholde welth be rulyd by lyberte,
		Or lyberte by welth? Let se, tell me that.
	Fel.	Syr, as me semeth, ye sholde be rulyd be me.
	Magn.	What nede you with hym thus prate and chat?
1435	*Fan.*	Shewe us your mynde then, howe to do and what.
	Magn.	I say that I wyll ye have hym in gydynge.
	Lyb.	Mayster Felycyte, let be your chydynge;

		And so as ye se it wyll be no better,
		Take it in worthe suche as ye fynde.
1440	*Fan.*	What the devyll, man, your name shalbe the greter;
		For welth without largesse is all out of kynde.
	Lyb.	And welth is nought worthe yf lyberte be behynde.
	Magn.	Nowe holde ye content, for there is none other shyfte.
	Fel.	Than waste must be welcome, and fare well thryfte.

1445	*Magn.*	Take of his substaunce a sure inventory,
		And get you home togyther; for Lyberte shall byde
		And wayte upon me.
	Lyb.	And yet for a memory,
		Make indentures how ye and I shal gyde.
	Fan.	I can do nothynge but he stonde besyde.
1450	*Lyb.*	Syr, we can do nothynge the one without the other.
	Magn.	Well, get you hens than and sende me some other.

	Fan.	Whom? Lusty Pleasure or mery Consayte?
	Magn.	Nay, fyrst Lusty Pleasure is my desyre to have;
		And let the other another time awayte.
1455		Howe be it, that fonde felowe is a mery knave.
		But loke that ye occupye the auctoryte that I you gave.
		Here goeth out FELYCYTE, LYBERTE *and* FANSY.

MAGNYFYCENCE *alone in the place.*

For nowe, syrs, I am lyke as a prynce sholde be;
I have welth at wyll, largesse and lyberte.

Fortune to her lawys can not abandune me;
1460 But I shall of Fortune rule the reyne.
I fere nothynge Fortunes perplexyte.
All honour to me must nedys stowpe and lene.
I synge of two partys without a mene.
I have wynde and wether over all to sayle;
1465 No stormy rage agaynst me can pervayle.

Alexander, of Macedony kynge,
That all the oryent had in subjeccyon,
Though al his conquestys were brought to
        rekenynge,
Myght seme ryght wel under my proteccyon
1470 To rayne, for all his marcyall affeccyon;
For I am prynce perlesse, provyd of porte,
Bathyd with blysse, embracyd with comforte.

Syrus, that soleme syar of Babylon,
That Israell releysyd of theyr captyvyte,
1475 For al his pompe, for all his ryall trone,
He may not be comparyd unto me.
I am the dyamounde dowtlesse of dygnyte.
Surely it is I that all may save and spyll,
No man so hardy to worke agaynst my wyll.

1480 Pocenya, the prowde provoste of Turky lande,
That ratyd the Romaynes and made them yll rest,
Nor Cesar July, that no man myght withstande,
Were never halfe so rychely as I am drest.
No, that I assure you; loke who was the best:
1485 I reyne in my robys, I rule as me lyst,
I dryve downe these dastardys with a dynt of my
        fyste.

Of Cato the counte, acountyd the cane,
Daryus, the doughty cheftayn of Perse –
I set not by the prowdest of them a prane,
1490 Ne by non other that any man can rehersse.
I folowe in felycyte without reversse;

I drede no daunger; I dawnce all in delyte:
My name is Magnyfycence, man most of myght.

Hercules the herdy, with his stobburne clobbyd mase,
1495   That made Cerberus to cache, the cur dogge of hell,
And Thesius, that prowde was Pluto to face –
It wolde not become them with me for to mell;
For of all barones bolde I bere the bell;
Of all doughty I am doughtyest duke as I deme;
1500   To me all prynces to lowte man beseme.

Cherlemayne, that mantenyd the nobles of Fraunce,
Arthur of Albyan, for all his brymme berde,
Nor Basyan the bolde, for all his brybaunce,
Nor Alerycus, that rulyd the Gothyaunce by swerd,
1505   Nor no man on molde can make me aferd.
What man is so maysyd with me that dare mete,
I shall flappe hym as a fole to fall at my fete.

Galba, whom his galantys garde for agaspe,
Nor Nero, that nother set by God nor man,
1510   Nor Vespasyan, that bare in his nose a waspe,
Nor Hanyball, agayne Rome gates that ranne,
Nor yet Cypyo, that noble Cartage wanne,
Nor none so hardy of them with me that durste
        crake,
But I shall frounce them on the foretop and gar them
        to quake.

Here cometh in COURTLY ABUSYON, *doynge reverence
and courtesy.*

1515   *Cou. Ab.*   At your commaundement, syr, wyth all dew
                     reverence.
       Magn.   Welcom, Pleasure, to our magnyfycence.
       Cou. Ab.   Plesyth it your grace to shewe what I do shall?
       Magn.   Let us here of your pleasure, to passe the tyme
                     withall.
       Cou. Ab.   Syr, then, with the favour of your benynge
                     sufferaunce,
1520   To shewe you my mynde myselfe I wyll avaunce,
                     If it lyke your grace to take it in degre.
       Magn.   Yes, syr, so good man in you I se,

And in your delynge so good assuraunce,
That we delyte gretly in your dalyaunce.

1525 *Cou. Ab.* A, syr, your grace me dothe extole and rayse;
And ferre beyond my merytys ye me commende and
prayse.
Howe be it, I wolde be ryght gladde, I you assure,
Any thynge to do that myght be to your pleasure.

Magn. As I be saved, with pleasure I am supprysyd
1530 Of your langage, it is so well devysed;
Pullyshyd and fresshe is your ornacy.

Cou. Ab. A, I wolde to God that I were halfe so crafty
Or in electe utteraunce halfe so eloquent,
As that I myght your noble grace content!

1535 *Magn.* Truste me, with you I am hyghly pleasyd;
For in my favour I have you feffyd and seasyd.
He is not lyvynge your maners can amend;
Mary, your speche is as pleasant as though it were
pend,
To here your comon, it is my hygh comforte.
1540 *Poynt devyse*, all pleasure is your porte.

Cou. Ab. Syr, I am the better of your noble reporte;
But of your pacyence under the supporte,
If it wolde lyke you to here my pore mynde –

Magn. Speke, I beseche the. Leve nothynge behynde.

1545 *Cou. Ab.* So as ye be a prynce of great myght,
It is semynge your pleasure ye delyte,
And to aqueynte you with carnall delectacyon;
And to fall in aquayntaunce with every newe facyon,
And quyckely your appetytes to sharpe and adresse;
1550 To fasten your fansy upon a fayre maystresse
That quyckly is envyved with rudyes of the rose,
Inpurtured with fetures after your purpose,
The streynes of her vaynes as asure Inde blewe,
Enbudded with beautye and colour fresshe of hewe,
1555 As lyly whyte to loke upon her leyre,
Her eyen relucent as carbuncle so clere,
Her mouthe enbawmed, dylectable and mery,
Her lusty lyppes ruddy as the chery –
Howe lyke you? Ye lacke, syr, suche a lusty lasse.

1560 *Magn.* A, that were a baby to brace and to basse!

I wolde I had, by hym that hell dyd harowe,
With me in kepynge suche a Phylyp Sparowe.
I wolde hauke whylest my hede dyd warke,
So I myght hobby for suche a lusty larke.

1565   These wordes in myne eyre, they be so lustely
        spoken,
That on suche a female my flesshe wolde be wroken.
They towche me so thorowly and tykyll my
        consayte,
That weryed I wolde be on suche a bayte.
A, Cockes armes! Where myght suche one be
        founde?

Cou. Ab.   Wyll ye spende ony money?
1570 *Magn.*   Ye, a thousande pounde.
Cou. Ab.   Nay, nay; for lesse I waraunt you to be sped,
And brought home and layde in your bed.
Magn.   Wolde money, trowest thou, make suche one to the
        call?

Cou. Ab.   Money maketh marchauntes, I tell you, over all.
1575 *Magn.*   Why, wyl a maystres be wonne for money and for
        golde?

Cou. Ab.   Why, was not for money Troy bothe bought and
        solde?
Full many a stronge cyte and towne hath been
        wonne
By the meanes of money without ony gonne.
A maystres, I tell you, is but a small thynge.
1580   A goodly rybon, or a golde rynge,
May wynne with a sawte the fortresse of the holde.
But one thynge I warne you, prece forth and be
        bolde.

Magn.   Ye, but some be full koy and passynge harde harted.
Cou. Ab.   But, blessyd be our Lorde, they wyll be sone
        converted.
1585 *Magn.*   Why, wyll they then be intreted, the most and the
        lest?

Cou. Ab.   Ye, for *omnis mulier meretrix si celari potest.*
Magn.   A, I have spyed ye can moche broken sorowe.
Cou. Ab.   I coude holde you with suche talke hens tyll to
        morowe.

But yf it lyke your grace more at large
1590   Me to permyt my mynde to dyscharge,
I wolde yet shewe you further of my consayte.
Magn.   Let se what ye say. Shewe it strayte.
Cou. Ab. Wysely let these wordes in your mynde be wayed:
By waywarde wylfulnes let eche thynge be convayed;
1595   What so ever ye do, folowe your owne wyll,
Be it reason or none, it shall not gretely skyll;
Be it ryght or wronge, by the advyse of me,
Take your pleasure and use free lyberte;
And yf you se ony thynge agaynst your mynde,
1600   Then some occacyon or quarell ye must fynde,
And frowne it and face it, as thoughe ye wolde fyght;
Frete yourselfe for anger and for dyspyte;
Here no man what so ever they say
But do as ye lyst and take your owne way.
1605 *Magn.*   Thy wordes and my mynde odly well accorde.
Cou. Ab. What sholde ye do elles? Are not you a lorde?
Let your lust and lykynge stande for a lawe.
Be wrastynge and wrythynge, and away drawe.
And ye se a man that with hym ye be not pleased,
1610   And that your mynde can not well be eased –
As yf a man fortune to touche you on the quyke –
Then feyne yourselfe dyseased, and make yourselfe
          seke.
To styre up your stomake you must you forge,
Call for a caudell and cast up your gorge,
1615   With, 'Cockes armes! Rest shall I none have
Tyll I be revenged on that horson knave.
A, howe my stomake wambleth! I am all in a swete.
Is there no horson that knave that wyll bete?'
Magn.   By Cockes woundes, a wonder felowe thou arte!
1620   For ofte tymes suche a wamblynge goth over my
          harte;
Yet I am not harte seke, but that me lyst.
For myrth I have hym coryed, beten, and blyst,
Hym that I loved not, and made hym to loute;
I am forthwith as hole as a troute.
1625   For suche abusyon I use nowe and than.
Cou. Ab. It is none abusyon, syr, in a noble man.

It is a pryncely pleasure and a lordly mynde.
Suche lustes at large may not be lefte behynde.

Here cometh in CLOKED COLUSYON *with*
MESURE [*to whom he speaks first.*]

Clo. Col.   Stande styll here, and ye shall se
1630   That for your sake I wyll fall on my kne.

[MESURE *waits at the door.*]

Cou. Ab.   Syr, Sober Sadnesse cometh. Wherfore it be?
Magn.   Stand up, syr. Ye are welcom to me.
Clo. Col.   Please it your grace at the contemplacyon
           Of my pore instance and supplycacyon,
1635   Tenderly to consyder in your advertence –
           Of our blessyd Lorde, syr, at the reverence –
           Remembre the good servyce that Mesure hath you
               done,
           And that ye wyll not cast hym away so sone.
Magn.   My frende, as touchynge to this your mocyon,
1640   I may say to you I have but small devocyon.
           Howe be it, at your instaunce I wyll the rather
           Do as moche as for myne owne father.
Clo. Col.   Nay, syr. That affeccyon ought to be reserved,
           For of your grace I have it nought deserved.
1645   But yf it lyke you that I myght rowne in your eyre,
           To shewe you my mynde I wolde have the lesse
               fere.
Magn.   Stande a lytell abacke, syr, and let hym come hyder.
Cou. Ab.   With a good wyll, syr, God spede you bothe togyder.
Clo. Col.   Syr, so it is: this man is here by,
1650   That for hym to laboure he hath prayde me hartely;
           Notwithstandynge to you be it sayde
           To trust in me he is but dyssayved;
           For, so helpe me God, for you he is not mete.
           I speke the softlyer because he sholde not wete.
1655 Magn. Come hyder, Pleasure; you shall here myne entent.
           Mesure, ye knowe wel, with hym I can not be
               content;
           And surely, as I am nowe advysed,
           I wyll have hym rehayted and dyspysed.
           Howe say ye, syrs? Herein what is best?
1660 Cou. Ab. By myne advyse, with you in fayth he shall not rest.

	Clo. Col.	Yet, syr, reserved your better advysement,
		It were better he spake with you or he wente,
		That he knowe not but that I have supplyed
		All that I can his matter for to spede.
1665	*Magn.*	Nowe, by your trouthe, gave he you not a brybe?
	Clo. Col.	Yes. With his hande I made hym to subscrybe
		A byll of recorde for an annuall rent.
	Cou. Ab.	But for all that he is lyke to have a glent.
	Clo. Col.	Ye, by my trouthe, I shall waraunt you for me,
1670		And he go to the devyll, so that I may have my fee,
		What care I?
	Magn.	By the masse, well sayd.
	Cou. Ab.	What force ye, so that ye be payde?
	Clo. Col.	But yet, lo, I wolde, or that he wente,
		Lest that he thought that his money were evyll
		spente,
1675		That he wolde loke on hym, thoughe it were not
		longe.
	Magn.	Well cannest thou helpe a preest to synge a songe.
	Clo. Col.	So it is all the maner nowe a dayes
		For to use suche haftynge and crafty wayes.
	Cou. Ab.	He telleth you trouth, syr, as I you ensure.
1680	*Magn.*	Well, for thy sake the better I may endure
		That he come hyder, and to gyve hym a loke
		That he shall lyke the worse all this woke.
	Clo. Col.	I care not howe sone he be refused,
		So that I may craftely be excused.
	Cou. Ab.	Where is he?
1685	*Clo. Col.*	Mary, I made hym abyde
		Whylest I came to you, a lytell here besyde.
	Magn.	Well, call hym, and let us here hym reason;
		And we wyll be comonynge in the mene season.
	Cou. Ab.	This is a wyse man, syr, where so ever ye hym had.
1690	*Magn.*	An honest person, I tell you, and a sad.
	Cou. Ab.	He can full craftely this matter brynge aboute.
	Magn.	Whylest I have hym, I nede nothynge doute.

Hic introducat COLUSION MESURE,
MAGNYFYCENCE *aspectante vultu elatissimo.*

	Clo. Col.	By the masse, I have done that I can,
		And more than ever I dyd for ony man.

1695		I trowe ye herde yourselfe what I sayd.
	Meas.	Nay, indede, but I sawe howe ye prayed,
		And made instance for me be lykelyhod.
	Clo. Col.	Nay, I tell you, I am not wonte to fode
		Them that dare put theyr truste in me;
1700		And therof ye shall a larger profe se.
	Meas.	Syr, God rewarde you as ye have deserved.
		But thynke you with Magnyfycence I shal be
		reserved?
	Clo. Col.	By my trouth, I can not tell you that.
		But, and I were as ye, I wolde not set a gnat.
1705		By Magnyfycence nor yet none of his;
		For go when ye shall, of you shall he mysse.
	Meas.	Syr, as ye say.
	Clo. Col.	Nay, come on with me.
		Yet ones agayne I shall fall on my kne
		For your sake, what so ever befall;
1710		I set not a flye and all go to all.
	Meas.	The Holy Goost be with your grace.
	Clo. Col.	Syr, I beseche you let pety have some place
		In your brest towardes this gentylman.
	Magn.	I was your good lorde tyll that ye beganne
1715		So masterfully upon you for to take
		With my servauntys, and suche maystryes gan
		make,
		That holly my mynde with you is myscontente;
		Wherfore I wyll that ye be resydent
		With me no longer.
	Clo. Col.	Say somwhat nowe, let se,
		For your selfe.
1720	*Meas.*	Syr, yf I myght permytted be,
		I wolde to you say a worde or twayne.
	Magn.	What! Woldest thou, lurden, with me brawle
		agayne?
		Have hym hens, I say, out of my syght!
		That day I se hym I shall be worse all nyght.

Here MESURE *goth out of the place.*

1725	*Cou. Ab.*	Hens, thou haynyarde, out of dores fast!

[*Exit* COURTLY ABUSYON.]

	Magn.	Alas! My stomake fareth as it wolde cast.

	Clo. Col.	Abyde, syr, abyde. Let me holde your hede.
	Magn.	A bolle or a basyn, I say, for Goddes brede!
		A, my hede! But is the horson gone?
1730		God gyve hym a myscheffe! Nay, nowe let me alone.
	Clo. Col.	A good dryfte, syr, a praty fete!
		By the good Lorde, yet your temples bete.
	Magn.	Nay, so God me helpe, it was no grete vexacyon;
		For I am panged ofte tymes in this same facyon.
1735	*Clo. Col.*	Cockes armes, howe Pleasure plucked hym forth!
	Magn.	Ye, walke he must; it was no better worth.
	Clo. Col.	Syr, nowe me thynke your harte is well eased.
	Magn.	Nowe Measure is gone, I am the better pleased.
	Clo. Col.	So to be ruled by measure, it is a payne.
1740	*Magn.*	Mary, I wene he wolde not be glad to come agayne.
	Clo. Col.	So I wote not what he sholde do here.
		Where mennes belyes is mesured, there is no chere;
		For I here but fewe men that gyve ony prayse
		Unto measure, I say, nowe a days.
1745	*Magn.*	Measure? Tut, what the devyll of hell!
		Scantly one with measure that wyll dwell.
	Clo. Col.	Not amonge noble men, as the worlde gothe.
		It is no wonder, therfore, thoughe ye be wrothe
		With Mesure. Where as all noblenes is, there I have past:
1750		They catche that catche may, kepe and holde fast,
		Out of all measure themselfe to enryche;
		No force what thoughe his neyghbour dye in a dyche.
		With pollynge and pluckynge out of all measure,
		Thus must ye stuffe and store your treasure.
1755	*Magn.*	Yet somtyme, parde, I must use largesse.
	Clo. Col.	Ye, Mary, somtyme – in a messe of vergesse,
		As in a tryfyll or in a thynge of nought,
		As gyvynge a thynge that ye never bought.
		It is the gyse nowe, I say, over all –
1760		Largesse in wordes – for rewardes are but small.
		To make fayre promyse, what are ye the worse?
		Let me have the rule of your purse.
	Magn.	I have taken it to Largesse and Lyberte.
	Clo. Col.	Than is it done as it sholde be;
1765		But use your largesse by the advyse of me,

		And I shall waraunt you welth and lyberte.
	Magn.	Say on; me thynke your reasons be profounde.
	Clo. Col.	Syr, of my counsayle this shall be the grounde:
		To chose out ii., iii., of suche as you love best,
1770		And let all your fansyes upon them rest.
		Spare for no cost to gyve them pounde and peny;
		Better to make iii. ryche than for to make many.
		Gyve them more than ynoughe, and let them not lacke;
		And as for all other, let them trusse and packe;
1775		Plucke from an hundred, and gyve it to thre;
		Let neyther patent scape them nor fee;
		And where soever you wyll fall to a rekenynge,
		Those thre wyll be redy even at your bekenynge;
		For them shall you have at lyberte to lowte.
1780		Let them have all, and the other go without;
		Thus joy without mesure you shall have.
	Magn.	Thou sayst truthe, by the harte that God me gave!
		For as thou sayst, ryght so shall it be,
		And here I make the upon Lyberte
1785		To be supervysour, and on Largesse also;
		For as thou wylte, so shall the game go;
		For in Pleasure and Surveyaunce and also in the,
		I have set my hole felycyte,
		And suche as you wyll shall lacke no promocyon.
1790	*Clo. Col.*	Syr, syth that in me ye have suche devocyon,
		Commyttynge to me and to my felowes twayne
		Your welthe and felycyte, I trust we shall optayne
		To do you servyce after your appetyte.
	Magn.	In faythe, and your servyce ryght well shall I acquyte;
1795		And therfore hye you hens, and take this oversyght.
	Clo. Col.	Nowe Jesu preserve you, syr, prynce most of myght.

Here goth CLOKED COLUSYON *awaye, and leveth*
MAGNYFYCENCE *alone in the place.*

	Magn.	Thus, I say, I am envyronned with solace.
		I drede no dyntes of fatall desteny.
		Well were that lady myght stande in my grace,
1800		Me to enbrace and love moost specyally.
		A, Lorde, so I wolde halse her hartely!
		So I wolde clepe her! So I wolde kys her swete!

Here cometh in FOLY.

Fol.   Mary, Cryst graunt ye catche no colde on your fete!

Magn.   Who is this?
Fol.   Consayte, syr, your owne man.
1805   *Magn.*   What tydynges with you, syr? I befole thy brayne
                    pan.
      Fol.   By our lakyn, syr, I have ben a hawkyng for the
                    wylde swan.
               My hawke is rammysshe, and it happed that she
                    ran —

               Flewe, I sholde say — in to an olde barne
               To reche at a rat — I coude not her warne.
1810   She pynched her pynyon, by God, and catched
                    harme.
               It was a ronner; nay, fole, I warant her blode warme.

Magn.   A, syr, thy jarfawcon and thou be hanged togyder!
Fol.   And, syr as I was comynge to you hyder,
         I saw a foxe sucke on a kowes ydder;
1815   And with a lyme rodde I toke them bothe togyder.
         I trowe it be a frost, for the way is slydder;
         Se, for God avowe, for colde as I chydder.

Magn.   Thy wordes hange togyder as fethers in the wynde.
Fol.   A, syr, tolde I not you howe I dyd fynde
1820   A knave and a carle and all of one kynde?
         I sawe a wethercocke wagge with the wynde!
         Grete mervayle I had, and mused in my mynde.
         The houndes ranne before, and the hare behynde.
         I sawe a losell lede a lurden, and they were bothe
              blynde.
1825   I sawe a sowter go to supper, or ever he had dynde.

Magn.   By Cockes harte, thou arte a fyne mery knave.
Fol.   I make God avowe ye wyll none other men have.
Magn.   What sayst thou?
Fol.   Mary, I pray God your mastershyp to save.
         I shall gyve you a gaude of a goslynge that I gave,
1830   The gander and the gose bothe grasynge on one
              grave.

Than Rowlande the reve ran, and I began to rave,
And wyth a brystell of a bore his berde dyd I shave.

Magn.   If ever I herde syke another, God gyve me shame.
Fol.   Sym Sadylgose was my syer, and Dawcocke my
    dame.
1835   I coude, and I lyst, garre you laughe at a game:
Howe a wodcocke wrastled with a larke that was lame;
The bytter sayd boldly that they were to blame;
The feldfare wolde have fydled, and it wolde not
    frame;
The crane and the curlewe therat gan to grame;
1840   The snyte snyveled in the snowte and smyled at the
    game.

Magn.   Cockes bones! Harde ye ever suche another?
Fol.   Se, syr, I beseche you, Largesse my brother.

Here FANSY *cometh in.*
Magn.   What tydynges with you, syr, that you loke so sad?
Fan.   When ye knowe that I knowe, ye wyll not be glad.
1845 *Fol.*   What, brother braynsyke, how farest thou?
Magn.   Ye, let be thy japes, and tell me howe
The case requyreth.
Fan.   Alasse, alasse, an hevy metynge!
I wolde tell you and yf I myght for wepynge.
Fol.   What! Is all your myrthe nowe tourned to sorowe?
1850   Fare well tyll sone; adue tyll to morowe.
           Here goth FOLY *away.*

Magn.   I pray the, Largesse, let be thy sobbynge.
Fan.   Alasse, syr, ye are undone with stelyng and
    robbynge!
Ye sent us a supervysour for to take hede;
Take hede of your selfe, for nowe ye have nede.
1855 *Magn.*   What! Hath Sadnesse begyled me so?
Fan.   Nay. Madnesse hath begyled you and many mo;
For Lyberte is gone, and also Felycyte.
Magn.   Gone? Alasse, ye have undone me!
Fan.   Nay. He that ye sent us, Clokyd Colusyon,
1860   And your payntyd Pleasure, Courtly Abusyon,
And your demenour with Counterfet Countenaunce,
And your Survayour, Crafty Conveyaunce,

Or ever we were ware, brought us in adversyte,
And had robbyd you quyte from all felycyte.
1865 *Magn.*   Why, is this the largesse that I have usyd?
Fan.   Nay. It was your fondnesse that ye have usyd.
Magn.   And is this the credence that I gave to the letter?
Fan.   Why, coulde not your wyt serve you no better?
Magn.   Why, who wolde have thought in you suche gyle?
1870 *Fan.*   What? Yes, by the rode, syr. It was I all this whyle
That you trustyd, and Fansy is my name;
And Foly, my broder, that made you moche game.

Here cometh in ADVERSYTE.

Magn.   Alas, who is yonder that grymly lokys?
Fan.   Adewe, for I wyll not come in his clokys.

[*Exit* FANSY.]

1875 *Magn.*   Lorde, so my flesshe trymblyth nowe for drede!
Here MAGNYFYCENCE *is beten downe and spoylyd*
from all his goodys and rayment.
Adv.   I am Adversyte, that for thy mysdede
From God am sente to quyte the thy mede.
Vyle velyarde, thou must not nowe my dynt
withstande;
Thou must not abyde the dynt of my hande.
1880   Ly there, losell, for all thy pompe and pryde;
Thy pleasure now with payne and trouble shalbe
tryde.
The stroke of God, Adversyte, I hyght.
I plucke downe kynge, prynce, lorde, and knyght;
I rushe at them rughly and make them ly full lowe;
1885   And in theyr moste truste I make them overthrowe.
Thys losyll was a lorde and lyvyd at his lust;
And nowe lyke a lurden he lyeth in the dust.
He knewe not hymselfe, his harte was so hye;
Nowe is there no man that wyll set by hym a flye.
1890   He was wonte to boste, brage, and to brace;
Nowe dare he not for shame loke one in the face.
All worldly welth for hym to lytell was;
Nowe hath he ryght nought, naked as an asse.
Somtyme without measure he trusted in golde;
1895   And now without measure he shal have hunger and
colde.

Lo, syrs, thus I handell them all
That folowe theyr fansyes in foly to fall.
Man or woman, of what estate they be,
I counsayle them beware of adversyte.

1900   Of sorowfull servauntes I have many scores:
I vysyte them somtyme with blaynes and with sores;
With botches and carbuckyls in care I them knyt;
With the gowte I make them to grone where they
        syt;
Some I make lyppers and lazars full horse;

1905   And from that they love best some I devorse;
Some with the marmoll to halte I them make;
And some to cry out of the bone ake;
And some I vysyte with brennynge of fyre;
Of some I wrynge of the necke lyke a wyre;

1910   And some I make in a rope to totter and walter;
And some for to hange themselfe in an halter;
And some I vysyte with batayle, warre, and murther,
And make eche man to sle other;
To drowne or to sle themselfe with a knyfe –

1915   An all is for theyr ungracyous lyfe.
Yet somtyme I stryke where is none offence,
Bycause I wolde prove men of theyr pacyence.
But nowe a dayes to stryke I have grete cause,
Lydderyns so lytell set by Goddes lawes.

1920   Faders and moders that be neclygent,
And suffre theyr chyldren to have theyr entent,
To gyde them vertuously that wyll not remembre,
Them or theyr chyldren ofte tymes I dysmembre;
Theyr chyldren, bycause that they have no
        mekenesse,

1925   I vysyte theyr faders and moders with sekenesse;
And yf I se therby they wyll not amende,
Then myschefe sodaynly I them sende;
For there is nothynge that more dyspleaseth God
Than from theyr chyldren to spare the rod

1930   Of correccyon, but let them have theyr wyll.
Some I make lame, and some I do kyll,
And some I stryke with a franesy;
Of some of theyr chyldren I stryke out the eye;

And where the fader by wysdom worshyp hath
wonne,

1935   I sende ofte tymes a fole to his sonne.
Wherfore, of adversyte loke ye be ware;
For when I come, comyth sorowe and care;
For I stryke lordys of realmes and landys
That rule not be mesure that they have in theyr
handys,

1940   That sadly rule not theyr howsholde men.
I am Goddys preposytour; I prynt them with a pen;
Because of theyr neglygence and of theyr wanton
vagys,
I vysyte them and stryke them with many sore
plagys.
To take, syrs, example of that I you tell,

1945   And beware of adversyte by my counsell,
Take hede of this captyfe that lyeth here on grounde.
Beholde howe Fortune on hym hath frounde.
For though we shewe you this in game and play,
Yet it proveth eyrnest, ye may se, every day.

1950   For nowe wyll I from this caytyfe go,
And take myscheffe and vengeaunce of other mo
That hath deservyd it as well as he.
Howe, where art thou? Come hether, Poverte.
Take this caytyfe to thy lore.

[*Exit* ADVERSYTE.]

Here cometh in POVERTE.

1955   *Pov.*   A, my bonys ake! My lymmys be sore!
Alasse, I have the cyatyca full evyll in my hyppe!
Alasse, where is youth that was wont for to skyppe?
I am lowsy and unlykynge and full of scurffe;
My colour is tawny, colouryd as a turffe;

1960   I am Poverte that all men doth hate.
I am baytyd with doggys at every mannys gate;
I am raggyd and rent, as ye may se;
Full fewe but they have envy of me.
Nowe must I this carcasse lyft up.

1965   He dynyd with delyte, with poverte he must sup.
Ryse up, syr, and welcom unto me.

Hic accedat ad levandum MAGNYFYCENCE, *et locabit eum super locum stratum.*

	Magn.	Alasse! Where is nowe my golde and fe?
		Alasse, I say, where to am I brought?
		Alasse, alasse, alasse! I dye for thought.
1970	*Pov.*	Syr, all this wolde have bene thought on before.
		He woteth not what welth is that never was sore.
	Magn.	Fy, fy, that ever I sholde be brought in this snare!
		I wenyd ones never to have knowen of care.
	Pov.	Lo, suche is this worlde! I fynde it wryt,
1975		In welth to beware; and that is wyt.
	Magn.	In welth to beware yf I had had grace,
		Never had I bene brought in this case.
	Pov.	Nowe, syth it wyll no nother be,
		All that God sendeth, take it in gre;
1980		For thoughe you were somtyme a noble estate,
		Nowe must you lerne to begge at every mannes gate.
	Magn.	Alasse that ever I sholde be so shamed!
		Alasse that ever I Magnyfycence was named!
		Alasse that ever I was so harde happed
1985		In mysery and wretchydnesse thus to be lapped!
		Alasse that I coude not myselfe no better gyde!
		Alasse in my cradell that I had not dyde!
	Pov.	Ye, syr, ye; leve all this rage,
		And pray to God your sorowes to asswage.
1990		It is foly to grudge agaynst his vysytacyon.
		With harte contryte make your supplycacyon
		Unto your maker that made bothe you and me;
		And whan it pleaseth God, better may be.
	Magn.	Alasse! I wote not what I sholde pray.
1995	*Pov.*	Remembre you better, syr. Beware what ye say,
		For drede ye dysplease the hygh deyte.
		Put your wyll to his wyll, for surely it is he
		That may restore you agayne to felycyte,
		And brynge you agayne out of adversyte.
2000		Therefore poverte loke pacyently ye take,
		And remembre he suffered moche more for your sake;
		Howe be it of all synne he was innocent,
		And ye have deserved this punysshment.

	Magn.	Alasse! With colde my lymmes shall be marde.
2005	*Pov.*	Ye, syr, nowe must ye lerne to lye harde,
		That was wonte to lye on fetherbeddes of downe;
		Nowe must your fete lye hyer than your crowne.
		Where you were wonte to have cawdels for your hede,
		Nowe must you monche mamockes and lumpes of brede;
2010		And where you had chaunges of ryche aray,
		Nowe lap you in a coverlet, full fayne that you may;
		And where that ye were pomped with what that ye wolde,
		Nowe must ye suffre bothe hunger and colde.
		With curteyns of sylke, ye were wonte to be drawe;
2015		Nowe must ye lerne to lye on the strawe.
		Your skynne that was wrapped in shertes of Raynes,
		Nowe must be stormy beten with showres and raynes.
		Your hede that was wonte to be happed moost drowpy and drowsy,
		Now shal ye be scabbed, scurvy, and lowsy.
2020	*Magn.*	Fye on this worlde, full of trechery,
		That ever noblenesse sholde lyve thus wretchydly!
	Pov.	Syr, remembre the tourne of Fortunes whele,
		That wantonly can wynke and wynche with her hele.
		Nowe she wyll laughe, forthwith she wyll frowne;
2025		Sodenly set up and sodenly pluckyd downe;
		She dawnsyth varyaunce with mutabylyte,
		Nowe all in welth, forthwith in poverte;
		In her promyse there is no sykernesse,
		All her delyte is set in doublenesse.
2030	*Magn.*	Alas! Of Fortune I may well complayne.
	Pov.	Ye, syr, yesterday wyll not be callyd agayne.
		But yet, syr, nowe in this case
		Take it mekely, and thanke God of his grace;
		For nowe go I wyll begge for you some mete.
2035		It is foly agaynst God for to plete.
		I wyll walke nowe with my beggers baggys,
		And happe you the whyles with these homly raggys.
		Discedendo dicat ista verba.

A, howe my lymmys be lyther and lame!
Better it is to begge than to be hangyd with shame.
2040   Yet many had lever hangyd to be
Then for to begge theyr mete for charyte.
They thynke it no shame to robbe and stele;
Yet were they better to begge, a great dele;
For by robbynge they rynne to *in manus tuas* quecke;
2045   But beggynge is better medecyne for the necke.
Ye, mary, is it. Ye, so mote I goo.
A, Lord God, how the gowte wryngeth me by the
     too.

                              [*Exit* POVERTE.]

Here MAGNYFYCENCE *dolorously maketh his mone.*
Magn.   O feble fortune, O doulfull destyny!
O hatefull happe, O carefull cruelte!
2050   O syghynge sorowe, O thoughtfull mysere!
O rydlesse rewthe, O paynfull poverte!
O dolorous herte, O harde adversyte!
O odyous dystresse, O dedly payne and woo!
For worldly shame I wax bothe wanne and bloo.

2055   Where is nowe my welth and my noble estate?
Where is nowe my treasure, my landes, and my
     rent?
Where is nowe all my servauntys that I had here a
     late?
Where is nowe my golde upon them that I spent?
Where is nowe all my ryche abylement?
2060   Where is nowe my kynne, my frendys, and my noble
     blood?
Where is nowe all my pleasure and my worldly good?
Alasse my foly! Alasse my wanton wyll!
I may no more speke tyll I have wept my fyll.

     [*Enter* LYBERTE.]
Lyb.   With ye, mary, syrs, thus sholde it be:
2065   I kyst her swete, and she kyssyd me;
I daunsed the darlynge on my kne;
I garde her gaspe, I garde her gle,
With daunce on the le, the le!
I bassed that baby with harte so free;

2070   She is the bote of all my bale.
        A, so! That syghe was farre fet!
        To love that lovesome I wyll not let;
        My harte is holly on her set;
        I plucked her by the patlet;
2075   At my devyse I with her met;
        My fansy fayrly on her I set;
        So merely syngeth the nyghtyngale!

        In lust and lykynge my name is Lyberte.
        I am desyred with hyghest and lowest degre.
2080   I lyve as me lyst, I lepe out at large;
        Of erthely thynge I have no care nor charge.
        I am presydent of prynces; I prycke them with
                pryde.
        What is he lyvynge that lyberte wolde lacke?
        A thousande pounde with lyberte may holde no
                tacke.
2085   At lyberte a man may be bolde for to brake;
        Welthe without lyberte gothe all to wrake.
        But yet, syrs, hardely one thynge lerne of me:
        I warne you beware of to moche lyberte,
        For *totum in toto* is not worth an hawe –
2090   To hardy, or to moche, to free of the dawe,
        To sober, to sad, to subtell, to wyse,
        To mery, to mad, to gyglynge, to nyse,
        To full of fansyes, to lordly, to prowde,
        To homly, to holy, to lewde, or to lowde,
2095   To flatterynge, to smatterynge, to to out of harre,
        To claterynge, to chaterynge, to shorte, and to farre,
        To jettynge, to jaggynge, and to full of japes,
        To mockynge, to mowynge, to lyke a jackenapes –
        Thus *totum in toto* groweth up, as ye may se,
2100   By meanes of madnesse and to moche lyberte.
        For I am a vertue yf I be well used,
        And I am a vyce where I am abused.
Magn.   A, woo worthe the, Lyberte, nowe thou sayst full
                trewe;
        That I used the to moche sore may I rewe.
2105 Lyb.   What, a very vengeaunce, I say! Who is that?
        What brothell, I say, is yonder bounde in a mat?

Magn.   I am Magnyfycence, that somtyme thy mayster was.

Lyb.   What! Is the worlde thus come to passe?

Cockes armes, syrs, wyll ye not se

2110   Howe he is undone by the meanes of me?

For yf Measure had ruled Lyberte as he began,

This lurden that here lyeth had ben a noble man.

But he abused so his free lyberte,

That nowe he hath loste all his felycyte;

2115   Not thorowe largesse of lyberall expence,

But by the way of fansy insolence.

For lyberalyte is most convenyent

A prynce to use with all his hole intent,

Largely rewardynge them that have deservyd;

2120   And so shall a noble man nobly be servyd.

But nowe adayes as huksters they hucke and they stycke,

And pynche at the payment of a poddynge prycke;

A laudable largesse, I tell you, for a lorde,

To prate for the patchynge of a pot sharde!

2125   Spare for the spence of a noble that his honour myght save,

And spende C s. for the pleasure of a knave.

But so longe they rekyn with theyr reasons amysse

That they lose theyr lyberte and all that there is.

Magn.   Alasse, that ever I occupyed suche abusyon!

2130   *Lyb.*   Ye, for nowe it hath brought the to confusyon;

For where I am occupyed and usyd wylfully,

It can not contynew long prosperyously;

As evydently in retchlesse youth ye may se

Howe many come to myschefe for to moche lyberte;

2135   And some in the worlde, theyr brayne is so ydyll

That they set theyr chyldren to rynne on the brydyll,

In youth to be wanton, and let them have theyr wyll –

And they never thryve in theyr age, it shall not gretly skyll.

Some fall to foly, them selfe for to spyll,

2140   And some fall prechynge at the Toure Hyll;

Some hath so moche lyberte of one thynge and other,

That nother they set by father and mother;

Some have so moche lyberte that they fere no synne,

Tyll, as ye se many tymes, they shame all theyr
kynne.

2145   I am so lusty to loke on, so freshe, and so fre,
That nonnes wyl leve theyr holynes and ryn after me;
Freers, with foly I make them so fayne
They cast up theyr obedyence to cache me agayne;
At lyberte to wander and walke over all,

2150   That lustely they lepe somtyme theyr cloyster wall.

Hic aliquis buccat in cornu a retro post populum.

Yonder is a horson for me doth rechate;
Adewe, syrs, for I thynke leyst that I come to late.
                          [*Exit* LYBERTE.]

Magn.   O good Lorde, howe longe shall I indure
This mysery, this carefull wrechydnesse?

2155   Of worldly welthe, alasse, who can be sure?
In Fortunys frendshyppe there is no stedfastnesse;
She hath dyssayvyd me with her doublenesse.
For to be wyse all men may lerne of me,
In welthe to beware of herde adversyte.

Here cometh in CRAFTY CONVEYAUNCE [*and*]
CLOKYD COLUSYON *with a lusty laughter.*

2160 *Cra. Con.*   Ha, ha, ha! For laughter I am lyke to brast.
Clo. Col.   Ha, ha, ha! For sporte I am lyke to spewe and cast.
Cra. Con.   What hast thou gotted, in faythe, to thy share?
Clo. Col.   In faythe, of his cofers the bottoms are bare.
Cra. Con.   As for his plate of sylver and suche trasshe,

2165   I waraunt you I have gyven it a lasshe.
Clo. Col.   What! Then he may drynke out of a stone cruyse.
Cra. Con.   With ye, syr, by Jesu, that slayne was with Jewes!
He may rynse a pycher, for his plate is to wed.
Clo. Col.   In faythe, he may dreme on a daggeswane for ony
fether bed.

2170 *Cra. Con.*   By my trouthe, we have ryfled hym metely well.
Clo. Col.   Ye, but thanke me therof every dele.
Cra. Con.   Thanke the therof, in the devyls date!
Clo. Col.   Leve thy pratynge or els I shall lay the on the pate.
Cra. Con.   Nay, to wrangle, I warant the, it is but a stone-caste.

2175 *Clo. Col.*   By the messe, I shall cleve thy heed to the waste.

	Cra. Con.	Ye, wylte thou clenly cleve me in the clyfte with thy nose?
	Clo. Col.	I shall thrust in the my dagger –
	Cra. Con.	Thorowe the legge in to the hose.
	Clo. Col.	Nay, horson, here is my glove. Take it up and thou dare.
	Cra. Con.	Torde! Thou arte good to be a man of warre.
2180	*Clo. Col.*	I shall skelpe the on the skalpe; lo, seest thou that?
	Cra. Con.	What! Wylte thou skelpe me? Thou dare not loke on a gnat.
	Clo. Col.	By Cockes bones, I shall blysse the and thou be to bolde.
	Cra. Con.	Nay. Then thou wylte dynge the devyll and thou be not holde.
	Clo. Col.	But wottest thou, horson? I rede the to be wyse.
2185	*Cra. Con.*	Nowe I rede the beware. I have warned the twyse.
	Clo. Col.	Why, wenest thou that I forbere the for thyne owne sake?
	Cra. Con.	Peas, or I shall wrynge thy be in a brake.
	Clo. Col.	Holde thy hande, dawe, of thy dagger, and stynt of thy dyn;
		Or I shal fawchyn thy flesshe and scrape the on the skyn.
2190	*Cra. Con.*	Ye, wylte thou, hangman? I say, thou cavell!
	Clo. Col.	Nay, thou rude ravener, rayne beten javell!
	Cra. Con.	What! Thou Colyn Cowarde, knowen and tryde!
	Clo. Col.	Nay, thou false harted dastarde! Thou dare not abyde.
	Cra. Con.	And yf there were none to dysplease but thou and I,
2195		Thou sholde not scape, horson, but thou sholde dye.
	Clo. Col.	Nay, iche shall wrynge the, horson, on the wryst.
	Cra. Con.	Mary, I defye thy best and thy worst.

[*Enter* COUNTERFET COUNTENAUNCE.]

	Cou. Cou.	What a very vengeaunce nede all these wordys?
		Go together by the heddys, and gyve me your swordys.
2200	*Clo. Col.*	So he is the worste brawler that ever was borne.
	Cra. Con.	In fayth, so to suffer the, it is but a skorne.
	Cou. Cou.	Now let us be all one, and let us lyve in rest;
		For we be, syrs, but a fewe of the best.
	Clo. Col.	By the masse, man, thou shall fynde me resonable.

2205	Cra. Con.	In faythe, and I wyll be to reason agreable.
	Cou. Cou.	Then trust I to God and the holy rode,
		Here shalbe not great sheddynge of blode.
	Clo. Col.	By our lakyn, syr, not by my wyll.
	Cra. Con.	By the fayth that I owe to God, and I wyll syt styll.
2210	Cou. Cou.	Well sayd. But, in fayth, what was your quarell?
	Clo. Col.	Mary, syr, this gentylman called me javell.
	Cra. Con.	Nay, by Saynt Mary, it was ye called me knave.
	Clo. Col.	Mary, so ungoodly langage you me gave.
	Cou. Cou.	A, shall we have more of this maters yet?
2215		Me thynke ye are not gretly acomberyd wyth wyt.
	Cra. Con.	Goddys fote! I warant you I am a gentylman borne;
		And thus to be facyd, I thynke it great skorne.
	Cou. Cou.	I can not well tell of your dysposycyons;
		And ye be a gentylman, ye have knavys condycyons.
2220	Clo. Col.	By God, I tell you, I wyll not be out facyd.
	Cra. Con.	By the masse, I warant the, I wyll not be bracyd.
	Cou. Cou.	Tushe, tushe! It is a great defaute;
		The one of you is to proude, the other is to haute.
		Tell me brefly where upon ye began.
2225	Clo. Col.	Mary, syr, he sayd that he was the pratyer man
		Then I was in opynynge of lockys;
		And I tell you, I dysdayne moche of his mockys.
	Cra. Con.	Thou sawe never yet but I dyd my parte,
		The locke of a casket to make to starte.
2230	Cou. Cou.	Nay, I know well inough ye are bothe well handyd
		To grope a gardevyaunce, though it be well bandyd.
	Clo. Col.	I am the better yet in a bowget.
	Cra. Con.	And I the better in a male.
	Cou. Cou.	Tushe! These maters that ye move are but soppys in ale;
		Your trymynge and tramynge by me must be tangyd,
2235		For had I not bene, ye bothe had bene hangyd,
		When we with Magnyfycence goodys made chevysaunce.
	Magn.	And therfore our Lorde sende you a very wengaunce!
	Cou. Cou.	What begger art thou, that thus doth banne and wary?
	Magn.	Ye be the thevys, I say, away my goodys dyd cary.
2240	Clo. Col.	Cockys bonys! Thou begger, what is thy name?

Magn.	Magnyfycence I was, whom ye have brought to shame.
Cou. Cou.	Ye, but trowe you, syrs, that this is he?
Cra. Con.	Go we nere and let us se.
Clo. Col.	By Cockys bonys, it is the same.

2245 *Magn.*   Alasse, alasse, syrs, ye are to blame!
                I was your mayster, though ye thynke it skorne;
                And nowe on me ye gaure and sporne.

Cou. Cou.   Ly styll, ly styll nowe, with yll hayle!

Cra. Con.   Ye, for thy langage can not the avayle.

2250 *Clo. Col.*   Abyde, syr, abyde; I shall make hym to pysse.

Magn.   Nowe gyve me somwhat, for God sake, I crave.

Cra. Con.   In faythe, I gyve the four quarters of a knave.

Cou. Cou.   In faythe, and I bequethe hym the tothe ake.

Clo. Col.   And I bequethe hym the bone ake.

2255 *Cra. Con.*   And I bequethe hym the gowte and the gyn.

Clo. Col.   And I bequethe hym sorowe for his syn.

Cou. Cou.   And I gyve hym Crystys curse
                With never a peny in his purse.

Cra. Con.   And I gyve hym the cowghe, the murre, and the
                pose.

2260 *Clo. Col.*   Ye, for *requiem eternam* groweth forth of his nose.
                But nowe let us make mery and good chere.

Cou. Cou.   And to the taverne let us drawe nere.

Cra. Con.   And from thens to the halfe strete,
                To get us there some freshe mete.

2265 *Clo. Col.*   Why, is there any store of rawe motton?

Cou. Cou.   Ye, in faythe; or ellys thou arte to great a glotton.

Cra. Con.   But they say it is a queysy mete;
                It wyll stryke a man myschevously in a hete.

Clo. Col.   In fay, man, some rybbys of the motton be so ranke
2270   That they wyll fyre one ungracyously in the flanke.

Cou. Cou.   Ye, and when ye come out of the shoppe,
                Ye shall be clappyd with a coloppe
                That wyll make you to halt and to hoppe.

Cra. Con.   Som be wrestyd there that they thynke on it forty
                dayes,
2275   For there be horys there at all assayes.

Clo. Col.   For the passyon of God, let us go thyther.

                   Et cum festinacione discedant a loco.

Magn.		Alas, myn owne servauntys to shew me such reproche!
		Thus to rebuke me and have me in dyspyght!
		So shamfully to me, theyr mayster, to aproche,
2280		That somtyme was a noble prynce of myght!
		Alasse! To lyve longer I have no delyght;
		For to lyve in mysery, it is herder than dethe.
		I am wery of the worlde, for unkyndnesse me sleeth.

Hic intrat DYSPARE.

Dys.		Dyspare is my name, that adversyte dothe folowe;
2285		In tyme of dystresse I am redy at hande;
		I make hevy hertys, with eyen full holowe.
		Of farvent charyte I quenche out the bronde;
		Faythe and good hope I make asyde to stonde.
		In Goddys mercy, I tell them, is but foly to truste;
2290		All grace and pyte I lay in the duste.

What! Lyest thou there lyngrynge, lewdly and lothsome?
It is to late nowe thy synnys to repent.
Thou hast bene so waywarde, so wranglyng, and so
    wrothsome,
And so fer thou arte behynde of thy rent,
2295   And so ungracyously thy dayes thou hast spent,
That thou arte not worthy to loke God in the face.

Magn.   Nay, nay, man. I loke never to have parte of his grace;

For I have so ungracyously my lyfe mysusyd,
Though I aske mercy I must nedys be refusyd.

2300   *Dys.*   No, no; for thy synnys be so excedynge farre,
So innumerable, and so full of dyspyte,
And agayne thy maker thou hast made suche warre,
That thou canst not have never mercy in his syght.

Magn.   Alasse, my wyckydnesse, that may I wyte!
2305   But nowe I se well there is no better rede,
But sygh, and sorowe, and wysshe my selfe dede.

Dys.   Ye, ryd thy selfe rather than this lyfe for to lede.
The worlde waxyth wery of the; thou lyvest to longe.

Hic intrat MYSCHEFE.
Mys.   And I, Myschefe, am comyn at nede,
2310   Out of thy lyfe the for to lede.

And loke that it be not longe
Or that thy selfe thou go honge
With this halter good and stronge;
Or ellys with this knyfe cut out a tonge

2315   Of thy throte bole, and ryd the out of payne.
Thou arte not the fyrst hymselfe hath slayne.
Lo, here is thy knyfe and a halter, and or we go
   ferther,
Spare not thy selfe, but boldly the murder.

Dys. Ye, have done at ones without delay.

2320 *Magn.* Shall I myselfe hange with an halter? Nay,
Nay; rather wyll I chose to ryd me of this lyve
In styckynge my selfe with this fayre knyfe.

Here MAGNYFYCENCE *wolde slee hymselfe with a knyfe.*

Mys. Alarum, alarum! To longe we abyde!

Dys. Out harowe! Hyll burneth! Where shall I me hyde?

Hic intrat GOOD HOPE, *fugientibus* DYSPARE
and MYSCHEFE, *repente* GOOD HOPE *surripiat
illi gladium et dicat:*

2325 *Go. Ho.* Alas, dere sone, sore combred is thy mynde,
Thyselfe that thou wolde sloo agaynst nature and
   kynde.

Magn. A, blessyd may ye be, syr! What shall I you call?

Go. Ho. Good Hope, syr, my name is; remedy pryncypall
Agaynst all sautes of your goostly foo.

2330   Who knoweth me, hymselfe may never sloo.

Magn. Alas, syr! So I am lapped in adversyte
That dyspayre well nyghe had myscheved me;
For had ye not the soner ben my refuge,
Of dampnacyon I had ben drawen in the luge.

2335 *Go. Ho.* Undoubted ye had lost yourselfe eternally.
There is no man may synne more mortally
Than of wanhope thrughe the unhappy wayes,
By myschefe to brevyate and shorten his dayes.
But, my good sonne, lerne from dyspaire to flee;

2340   Wynde you from wanhope and aquaynte you with
   me.
A grete mysadventure, thy maker to dysplease,
Thyselfe myschevynge to thyne endlesse dysease!

              There was never so harde a storme of mysery,
              But thrughe good hope there may come remedy.

2345   *Magn.*   Your wordes be more sweter than ony precyous
                   narde,
              They molefy so easely my harte that was so harde.
              There is no bawme ne gumme of Arabe
              More delectable than your langage to me.

    Go. Ho. Syr, your fesycyan is the grace of God,
2350   That you hath punysshed with his sharpe rod.
              Good Hope, your potecary, assygned am I,
              That Goddes grace hath vexed you sharply
              And payned you with a purgacyon of odyous
                   poverte,
              Myxed with bytter alowes of herde adversyte.
2355   Nowe must I make you a lectuary softe –
              I to mynyster it, you to receyve it ofte –
              With rubarbe of repentaunce in you for to rest;
              With drammes of devocyon your dyet must be drest,
              With gommes goostly of glad herte and mynde,
2360   To thanke God of his sonde; and comforte ye shal
                   fynde.
              Put fro you presumpcyon and admyt humylyte,
              And hartely thanke God of your adversyte;
              And love that Lorde that for your love was dede,
              Wounded from the fote to the crowne of the hede:
2365   For who loveth God can ayle nothynge but good.
              He may helpe you. He may mende your mode.
              Prosperyte by hym is gyven solacyusly to man;
              Adversyte to hym therwith nowe and than;
              Helthe of body his besynesse to acheve;
2370   Dysease and sekenesse his conscyence to dyscryve;
              Afflyccyon and trouble to prove his pacyence;
              Contradyccyon to prove his sapyence;
              Grace of assystence his measure to declare;
              Somtyme to fall, another tyme to beware:
2375   And nowe ye have had, syr, a wonderous fall,
              To lerne you hereafter for to beware withall.
              Howe say you, syr? Can ye these wordys grope?

    Magn.   Ye, syr, now am I armyd with good hope,
              And sore I repent me of my wylfulnesse;
2380   I aske God mercy of my neglygesse,

		Under good hope endurynge ever styll,
		Me humbly commyttynge unto Goddys wyll.
	Go. Ho.	Then shall you be sone delyvered from dystresse,
		For nowe I se comynge to youwarde Redresse.

Hic intrat REDRESSE.

2385	*Redr.*	Cryst be amonge you, and the Holy Goste!
	Go. Ho.	He be your conducte, the Lorde of myghtys moste!
	Redr.	Syr, is your pacyent any thynge amendyd?
	Go. Ho.	Ye, syr, he is sory for that he hath offendyd.
	Redr.	How fele you your selfe, my frend? How is your
		mynde?
2390	*Magn.*	A wrechyd man, syr, to my maker unkynde.
	Redr.	Ye, but have ye repentyd you with harte contryte?
	Magn.	Syr, the repentaunce I have no man can wryte.
	Redr.	And have you banyshed from you all dyspare?
	Magn.	Ye, holly to good hope I have made my repare.
2395	*Go. Ho.*	Questyonlesse he doth me assure
		In good hope alway for to indure.
	Redr.	Than stande up, syr, in Goddys name!
		And I truste to ratyfye and amende your fame.
		Good Hope, I pray you with harty affeccyon
2400		To sende over to me Sad Cyrcumspeccyon.
	Go. Ho.	Syr, your requeste shall not be delayed.

Et exiat.

	Redr.	Now, surely, Magnyfycence, I am ryght well apayed
		Of that I se you nowe in the state of grace.
		Nowe shall ye be renewyd with solace.
2405		Take nowe upon you this abylyment,
		And to that I say gyve good advysement.

MAGNYFYCENCE *accipiat indumentum.*

	Magn.	To your requeste I shall be confyrmable.
	Redr.	Fyrst, I saye, with mynde fyrme and stable
		Determyne to amende all your wanton excesse;
2410		And be ruled by me, whiche am called Redresse.
		Redresse my name is, that lytell am I used
		As the worlde requyreth, but rather I am refused.
		Redresse sholde be at the rekenynge in every
		accompte,
		And specyally to redresse that were out of joynte.

2415   Full many thynges there be that lacketh redresse,
       The whiche were to longe nowe to expresse;
       But redresse is redlesse and may do no correccyon.
       Nowe welcome, forsoth, Sad Cyrcumspeccyon.

       Here cometh in SAD CYRCUMSPECCYON *sayenge.*

Cyrc. Syr, after your message I hyed me hyder streyght,
2420   For to understande your pleasure and also your
              mynde.
Redr. Syr, to accompte you, the contynewe of my consayte
       Is from adversyte Magnyfycence to unbynde.
Cyrc. How fortuned you, Magnyfycence, so far to fal
              behynde?
Magn. Syr, the longe absence of you, Sad Cyrcumspeccyon,
2425   Caused me of adversyte to fall in subjeccyon.

Redr. All that he sayth of trouthe dothe procede;
       For where sad cyrcumspeccyon is longe out of the way,
       Of adversyte it is to stande in drede.
Cyrc. Without fayle, syr, that is no nay:
2430   Cyrcumspeccyon inhateth all rennynge astray,
       But, syr, by me to rule fyrst ye began.
Magn. My wylfulnesse, syr, excuse I ne can.

Cyrc. Then ye of foly in tymes past you repent?
Magn. Sothely to repent me I have grete cause;
2435   Howe be it, from you I receyved a letter sent,
       Whiche conteyned in it a specyall clause
       That I sholde use largesse.
Cyrc.   Nay, syr, there a pause.
Redr. Yet let us se this matter thorowly ingrosed.
Magn. Syr, this letter ye sent to me at Pountes was
              enclosed.

2440 Cyrc. Who brought you that letter? Wote ye what he
              hyght?
Magn. Largesse, syr, by his credence was his name.
Cyrc. This letter ye speke of never dyd I wryte.
Redr. To gyve so hasty credence ye were moche to blame.
Magn. Truth it is, syr; for after he wrought me moch
              shame,
2445   And caused me also to use to moche lyberte,
       And made also mesure to be put fro me.

	Redr.	Then welthe with you myght in no wyse abyde.
	Cyrc.	A ha, fansy and foly met with you, I trowe.
	Redr.	It wolde be founde so yf it were well tryde.
2450	Magn.	Surely my welthe with them was overthrow.
	Cyrc.	Remembre you, therfore, howe late ye were low.
	Redr.	Ye, and beware of unhappy abusyon.
	Cyrc.	And kepe you from counterfaytynge of clokyd colusyon.

	Magn.	Syr, in good hope I am to amende.
2455	Redr.	Use not then your countenaunce for to counterfet.
	Cyrc.	And from crafters and hafters I you forfende.

Hic intrat PERSEVERAUNCE.

	Magn.	Well, syr, after your counsell my mynde I wyll set.
	Redr.	What, brother Perceveraunce, surely well met!
	Cyrc.	Ye com hether as well as can be thought.
2460	Pers.	I herde say that adversyte with Magnyfycence had fought.

	Magn.	Ye, syr, with adversyte I have bene vexyd;
		But good hope and redresse hath mendyd myne estate,
		And sad cyrcumspeccyon to me they have annexyd.
		....

	Redr.	What this man hath sayd, perceyve ye his sentence?
2465	Magn.	Ye, syr. From hym my corage shall never flyt.
		....
		....
		....

	Cyrc.	Accordynge to treuth they be well devysyd.
2470	Magn.	Syrs, I am agreed to abyde your ordenaunce –
		Faythfull assuraunce with good peradvertaunce.
	Pers.	Yf you be so myndyd, we be ryght glad.
	Redr.	And ye shall have more worshyp then ever ye had.

	Magn.	Well, I perceyve in you there is moche sadnesse,
2475		Gravyte of counsell, provydence, and wyt;
		Your comfortable advyse and wyt excedyth all gladnesse;

But frendly I wyll refrayne you ferther, or we
flyt:
Whereto were most metely my corage to knyt?
2480   Your myndys I besche you here in to expresse,
Commensynge this processe at mayster
Redresse.

Redr.   Syth unto me formest this processe is erectyd,
Herein I wyll aforse me to shewe you my
mynde:
Fyrst, from your magnyfycence syn must be
abjectyd;
2485   In all your warkys more grace shall ye fynde;
Be gentyll, then, of corage, and lerne to be
kynde;
For of noblenesse the chefe poynt is to be
lyberall,
So that your largesse be not to prodygall.

Cyrc.   Lyberte to a lorde belongyth of ryght,
2490   But wyfull waywardnesse muste walke out of
the way;
Measure of your lustys must have the oversyght,
And not all the nygarde nor the chyncherde to
play.
Let never negarshyp your noblenesse affray;
In your rewardys use suche moderacyon
2495   That nothynge be gyven without
consyderacyon.

Pers.   To the increse of your honour then arme you
with ryght,
And fumously adresse you with magnanymyte;
And ever let the drede of God be in your syght,
And knowe your selfe mortal for all your
dygnyte;
2500   ....
Set not all your affyaunce in Fortune full of
gyle;
Remember this lyfe lastyth but a whyle.

Magn.   Redresse, in my remembraunce your lesson
shall rest;

And Sad Cyrcumspeccyon I marke in my
        mynde;
2505   But, Perseveraunce, me semyth your probleme
        was best;
I shall it never forget nor leve it behynde,
But hooly to perseveraunce my selfe I wyll
        bynde,
Of that I have mysdone to make a redresse,
And with sad cyrcumspeccyon correcte my
        vantonnesse.

2510 *Redr.* Unto this processe brefly compylyd,
Comprehendynge the worlde casuall and
        transytory,
Who lyst to consyder shall never be begylyd,
Yf it be regystryd well in memory;
A playne example of worldly vaynglory,
2515   Howe in this worlde there is no sekernesse,
But fallyble flatery enmyxyd with bytternesse.

Nowe well, nowe wo, nowe hy, nowe lawe
        degre;
Nowe ryche, nowe pore, nowe hole, now in
        dysease;
Nowe pleasure at large, nowe in captyvyte;
2520   Nowe leve, nowe lothe, nowe please, nowe
        dysplease;
Now ebbe, now flowe, nowe increase, now
        dyscrease;
So in this worlde there is no sykernesse,
But fallyble flatery enmyxyd with bytternesse.

     Cyrc. A myrrour incleryd is this interlude,
2525   This lyfe inconstant for to beholde and se:
Sodenly avaunsyd, and sodenly subdude;
Sodenly ryches, and sodenly poverte;
Sodenly comfort, and sodenly adversyte;
Sodenly thus Fortune can bothe smyle and
        frowne,
2530   Sodenly set up, and sodenly cast downe.

Sodenly promotyd, and sodenly put backe;
Sodenly cherysshyd, and sodenly cast asyde;

Sodenly commendyd, and sodenly fynde a
    lacke;
Sodenly grauntyd, and sodenly denyed;
2535   Sodenly hyd, and sodenly spyed;
Sodenly thus Fortune can bothe smyle and
    frowne,
Sodenly set up, and sodenly cast downe.

Pers.   This treatyse, devysyd to make you dysporte,
Shewyth nowe adayes howe the worlde
    comberyd is,
2540   To the pythe of the mater who lyst to resorte:
Today it is well, tomorowe it is all amysse;
Today in delyte, tomorowe bare of blysse;
Today a lorde, tomorowe ly in the duste:
Thus in this worlde there is no erthly truste.

2545   Today fayre wether, tomorowe a stormy rage;
Today hote, tomorowe outragyous colde;
Today a yoman, tomorowe made of page;
Today in surety, tomorowe bought and solde;
Today maysterfest, tomorowe he hath no holde;
2550   Today a man, tomorowe he lyeth in the duste:
Thus in this worlde there is no erthly truste.

Magn.   This mater we have movyd, you myrthys to
    make,
Precely purposyd under pretence of play,
Shewyth wysdome to them that wysdome can
    take:
2555   Howe sodenly worldly welth dothe dekay;
How wysdom thorowe wantonnesse vanysshyth
    away;
How none estate lyvynge of hymselfe can be
    sure,
For the welthe of this worlde can not indure.

Of the terestre trechery we fall in the flode,
2560   Beten with stormys of many a frowarde blast,
Ensorbyd with the wawys savage and wode;
Without our shyppe be sure, it is lykely to
    brast,
Yet of magnyfycence oft made is the mast:

Thus none estate lyvynge of hymselfe can be
sure,
2565   For the welthe of this worlde can not indure.

Redr.   Nowe semyth us syttynge that ye then resorte
Home to your paleys with joy and ryalte.
Cyrc.   Where every thyng is ordenyd after your noble
porte.
Pers.   There to indeuer with all felycyte.
2570   Magn.   I am content, my frendys, that it so be.
Redr.   And ye that have harde thys dysporte and game,
Jhesus preserve you frome endlesse wo and
shame.

AMEN.

XVII

Here after foloweth the boke called

Elynour Rummynge

The Tunnyng of Elynour Rummyng per Skelton Laureat.

Tell you I chyll,
If that ye wyll
A whyle be styll,
Of a comely gyll
5   That dwelt on a hyll;
But she is not gryll,
For she is somwhat sage
And well worne in age,
For her vysage
10   It woldt aswage
A mannes courage.
   Her lothely lere
Is nothynge clere,
But ugly of chere,
15   Droupy and drowsy,
Scurvy and lowsy;

Her face all bowsy,
Comely crynklyd,
Woundersly wrynklyd,
20 Lyke a rost pygges eare,
Brystled with here.
    Her lewde lyppes twayne,
They slaver, men sayne,
Lyke a ropy rayne,
25 A gummy glayre.
She is ugly fayre:
Her nose somdele hoked
And camously croked,
Never stoppynge
30 But ever droppynge;
Her skynne lose and slacke,
Greuyned lyke a sacke;
With a croked backe.
    Her eyen gowndy
35 Are full unsowndy,
For they are blered;
And she gray-hered;
Jawed lyke a jetty;
A man wolde have pytty
40 To se howe she is gumbed,
Fyngered and thumbed,
Gently joynted,
Gresed and anoynted
Up to the knockles:
45 The bones of her huckels
Lyke as they were with buckels
Togyder made fast.
Her youth is farre past;
Foted lyke a plane,
50 Legged lyke a crane;
And yet she wyll jet,
Lyke a joyly fet
In her furred flocket,
And graye russet rocket,
55 With symper-the-cocket.
Her huke of Lyncole grene,
It had ben hers, I wene,

More then fourty yere;
And so doth it apere,
60 For the grene bare thredes
Loke lyke sere wedes,
Wyddered lyke hay,
The woll worne away.
And yet I dare saye
65 She thynketh her selfe gaye
Upon the holy daye,
Whan she doth her aray,
And gyrdeth in her gytes
Stytched and pranked with pletes;
70 Her kyrtell Brystowe red,
With clothes upon her hed
That wey a sowe of led,
Wrythen in wonder wyse
After the Sarasyns gyse,
75 With a whym-wham
Knyt with a trym-tram
Upon her brayne-pan,
Lyke an Egypcyan
Lapped about.
80 Whan she goeth out
Her selfe for to shewe,
She dryveth downe the dewe
With a payre of heles
As brode as two wheles.
85 She hobles as she gose
With her blanket hose
Over the falowe,
Her shone smered wyth talowe,
Gresed upon dyrt
90 That baudeth her skyrt.

Primus passus

And this comely dame,
I understande, her name
Is Elynour Rummynge,
At home in her wonnynge;
95 And, as men say,

She dwelt in Sothray,
In a certayne stede
Bysyde Lederhede.
She is a tonnysh gyb;
100 The devyll and she be syb.
    But to make up my tale,
She breweth noppy ale,
And maketh thereof port-sale
To travellars, to tynkers,
105 To sweters, to swynkers,
And all good ale drynkers,
That wyll nothynge spare,
But drynke tyll they stare
And brynge them selfe bare,
110 With, 'Now away the mare,
And let us sley care!'
As wyse as an hare!
    Come who so wyll
To Elynoure on the hyll,
115 With, 'Fyll the cup, fyll!'
And syt there by styll,
Erly and late.
Thyther cometh Kate,
Cysly and Sare,
120 With theyr legges bare,
And also theyr fete
Hardely full unswete;
Wyth theyr heles dagged,
Theyr kyrtelles all to-jagged,
125 Theyr smockes all to-ragged,
Wyth tytters and tatters,
Brynge dysshes and platters,
With all theyr myght runnynge
To Elynour Rummynge,
130 To have of her tunnynge.
She leneth them on the same,
And thus begynneth the game.
    Some wenches come unlased,
Some huswyves come unbrased,
135 Wyth theyr naked pappes,
That flyppes and flappes,

It wygges and it wagges
Lyke tawny saffron bagges;
A sorte of foule drabbes
140   All scurvy with scabbes.
Some be flybytten,
Some skewed as a kytten;
Some with a sho clout
Bynde theyr heddes about;
145   Some have no herelace,
Theyr lockes aboute theyr face,
Theyr tresses untrust,
All full of unlust;
Some loke strawry,
150   Some cawry-mawry;
Full untydy tegges,
Lyke rotten egges.
Suche a lewde sorte
To Elynour resorte
155   From tyde to tyde.
Abyde, abyde,
And to you shall be tolde
Howe hyr ale is solde
To mawte and to molde.

Secundus passus

160   Some have no mony
That thyder commy,
For theyr ale to pay;
That is a shreud aray!
Elynour swered, 'Nay,
165   Ye shall not bere awaye
Myne ale for nought,
By hym that me bought!'
      With, 'Hey, dogge, hay,
Have these hogges away!'
170   With, 'Get me a staffe,
The swyne eate my draffe!
Stryke the hogges with a clubbe,
They have dronke up my swyllyng tubbe!'
For, be there never so moche prese,
175   These swyne go to the hye dese,

The sowe with her pygges;
The bore his tayle wrygges,
His rumpe also he frygges
Agaynst the hye benche.

180 With, 'Fo, ther is a stenche!
Gather up, thou wenche.
Seest thou not what is fall?
Take up dyrt and all,
And bere out of the hall.'

185 God gyve it yll prevynge,
Clenly as yvell chevynge!
    But let us turne playne,
There we lefte agayne.
For, as yll a patch as that,

190 The hennes ron in the mashfat;
For they go to roust,
Streyght over the ale-joust,
And donge, whan it commes,
In the ale tunnes.

195 Than Elynour taketh
The mashe bolle, and shaketh
The hennes donge awaye,
And skommeth it into a tray
Where as the yeest is,

200 With her maungy fystis.
And somtyme she blennes
The donge of her hennes
And the ale togyder,
And sayth, 'Gossyp, come hyder,

205 This ale shal be thycker,
And floure the more quycker;
For I may tell you,
I lerned it of a Jewe,
Whan I began to brewe,

210 And I have found it trew.
Drinke now whyle it is new;
And ye may it broke,
It shall make you loke
Yonger than ye be

215 Yeres two or thre,
For ye may prove it by me.'

'Behold,' she sayd, 'and se
How bright I am of ble!
Ich am not cast away,
220   That can my husband say,
Whan we kys and play
In lust and in lykyng.
He calleth me his whytyng,
His mullyng and his mytyng,
225   His nobbes and his conny,
His swetyng and his honny,
With, 'Bas, my prety bonny,
Thou art worth good and monny.'
This make I my falyre fonny,
230   Tyll that he dreme and dronny;
For, after all our sport,
Than wyll he rout and snort;
Than swetely togither we ly,
As two pygges in a sty.'

235   To cease me semeth best,
And of this tale to rest,
And for to leve this letter,
Bicause it is no better;
And bicause it is no swetter,
240   We wyll no farther ryme
Of it at this tyme.
But we wyll turne playne
Where we left agayne.

Tertius passus

In stede of coyne and monny
245   Some brynge her a conny,
And some a pot with honny,
Some a salt, and some a spone,
Some their hose, some their shone;
Some ranne a good trot
250   With a skellet or a pot;
Some fyll theyr pot full
Of good Lemster woll.
An huswyfe of trust
Whan she is athrust,

255   Suche a webbe can spyn,
      Her thryfte is full thyn.
        Some go streyght thyder,
      Be it slaty or slyder;
      They holde the hye waye,
260   They care not what men saye!
      Be that as be maye;
      Some lothe to be espyde,
      Some start in at the backe syde,
      Over the hedge and pale,
265   And all for the good ale.
        Some renne tyll they swete,
      Brynge wyth them malte or whete,
      And Dame Elynour entrete
      To byrle them of the best.
270   Than cometh an other gest;
      She swered by the Rode of Rest,
      Her lyppes are so drye,
      Without drynke she must dye;
      Therefore, 'Fyll it by and by
275   And have here a pecke of ry.'
        Anone cometh another,
      As drye as the other,
      And with her doth brynge
      Mele, salte or other thynge,
280   Her hernest gyrdle, her weddynge rynge,
      To pay for her scot
      As cometh to her lot.
      Some bryngeth her husbandis hood,
      Bycause the ale is good;
285   Another brought her his cap
      To offer to the ale tap,
      With flaxe and with towe;
      And some brought sowre dowe:
      With, 'Hey,' and with, 'Howe,
290   Syt we downe arowe
      And drynke tyll we blowe,
      And pype tyrly-tyrlowe!'
        Some layde to pledge
      Theyr hatchet and theyr wedge,

295   Theyr hekell and theyr rele,
       Theyr rocke, theyr spynnyng whele.
       And some went so narrowe
       They layde to pledge theyr wharrowe,
       Theyr rybskyn and theyr spyndell,
300   Theyr nedell and theyr thymbell:
       Here was scant thyrft
       Whan they made suche shyft.
          Theyr thrust was so great,
       They asked never for mete
305   But, 'Drynke,' styll, 'Drynke,
       And let the cat wynke!
       Let us wasshe our gommes
       From the drye crommes!'

       Quartus passus

       Some for very nede
310   Layde downe a skeyne of threde,
       And some a skeyne of yarne.
       Some brought from the barne
       Both benes and pease;
       Small chaffer doth ease
315   Sometyme, now and than.
       Another there was that ran
       With a good brasse pan –
       Her colour was full wan –
       She ran in all the hast
320   Unbrased and unlast,
       Tawny, swart and sallowe,
       Lyke a cake of tallowe;
       I swere by all hallowe
       It was a stale to take
325   The devyll in a brake.
          And than came haltyng Jone
       And brought a gambone
       Of bakon that was resty;
       But, Lorde, as she was testy,
330   Angry as a waspy!
       She began to yane and gaspy,
       And bad Elynour go bet,
       And fyll in good met;

It was dere that was far fet!
335　　Another brought a spycke
Of a bacon flycke;
Her tonge was very quycke
But she spake somwhat thycke,
Her felowe dyd stammer and stut,
340　But she was a foule slut,
For her mouth fomyd
And her bely groned:
Jone sayde she had eten a fyest.
'By Chryst,' sayde she, 'thou lyest.
345　I have as swete a breth
As thou, wyth shamefull deth!'
　　　Than Elynour sayde, 'Ye calettes,
I shall breke your palettes,
Wythout ye now cease!'
350　And so was made the peace.
　　　Than thydder came dronken Ales
And she was full of tales,
Of tydynges in Wales,
And of Saynte James in Gales,
355　And of the Portyngales;
Wyth, 'Lo, gossyp, iwys,
Thus and thus it is,
There hath ben greate war
Betwene Temple Bar
360　And the Crosse in Chepe,
And thyder came an hepe
Of mylstones in a route.'
She spake thus in her snout,
Snevelyng in her nose,
365　As though she had the pose.
'Lo, here is an olde typpet,
And ye wyll gyve me a syppet
Of your stale ale,
God sende you good sale!'
370　And, as she was drynkynge,
She fyll in a wynkynge
With a barlyhood;
She pyst where she stood.
Than began she to wepe,

375 And forthwith fell on slepe.
Elynour toke her up
And blessed her with a cup
Of newe ale in cornes.
Ales founde therin no thornes,
380 But supped it up at ones,
She founde therein no bones.

Quintus passus

Nowe in cometh another rabell;
First one wyth a ladell,
Another with a cradell,
385 And with a syde-sadell;
And there began a fabell,
A clatterynge and a babell
Of a foles fylly
That had a fole with Wylly,
390 With, 'Jast you, and gup, gylly,
She coulde not lye stylly!'
Then came in a genet,
And sware by Saynt Benet,
'I dranke not this sennet
395 A draught to my pay.
Elynour, I the pray,
Of thyne ale let us assaye,
And have here a pylche of graye;
I were skynnes of conny,
400 That causeth I loke so donny.'
An other than dyd hyche her,
And brought a pottell-pycher,
A tonnell and a bottell,
But she had lost the stoppell.
405 She cut of her sho-sole,
And stopped therewith the hole.
Amonge all the blommer,
Another brought a skommer,
A fryenge pan, and a slyce.
410 Elynour made the pryce
For god ale eche whyt.
Than sterte in made Kyt,

That had lytell wyt;
She semed somdele seke,
415   And brought a peny cheke
To Dame Elynour
For a draught of her lycour.
   Than Margery Mylkeducke
Her kyrtell she dyd uptucke
420   An ynche above her kne,
Her legges that ye myght se;
But they were sturdy and stubbed,
Myghty pestels and clubbed,
As fayre and as whyte
425   As the fote of a kyte.
She was somwhat foule,
Crokenebbed lyke an oule;
And yet she brought her fees,
A cantell of Essex chese
430   Was well a fote thycke,
Full of magottes quycke;
It was huge and greate,
And myghty stronge meate
For the devyll to eate;
435   It was tart and punyete.
Another sorte of sluttes:
Some brought walnuttes,
Some apples, some peres,
Some brought theyr clyppyng sheres,
440   Some brought this and that,
Some brought I wote nere what,
Some brought theyr husbands hat,
Some podynges and lynkes,
Some trypes that stynkes.
445   But of all this thronge
One came them amonge,
She semed halfe a leche,
And began to preche
Of the Tewsday in the weke
450   Whan the mare doth keke;
Of the vertue of an unset leke;
And of her husbandes breke.

With the feders of a quale
She could to Burdeou sayle;
455 And with good ale barme
She could make a charme
To helpe withall a stytch;
She semed to be a wytch.
Another brought two goslynges
460 That were noughty froslynges;
She brought them in a wallet;
She was a cumly callet.
The goslenges were untyde;
Elynor began to chyde,
465 'They be wretchockes thou hast brought,
They are shyre shakyng nought!'

Sextus passus

Maude Ruggy thyther skypped:
She was ugly hypped,
And ugly thycke-lypped
470 Like an onyon syded,
Lyke tan ledder hyded.
She had her so guyded
Betwene the cup and the wall,
That she was therewithall
475 Into a palsey fall;
With that her hed shaked
And her handes quaked.
Ones hed wold have aked
To se her naked.
480 She dranke so of the dregges,
The dropsy was in her legges;
Her face glystryng lyke glas,
All foggy fat she was;
She had also the gout
485 In all her joyntes about;
Her breth was soure and stale
And smelled all of ale.
Such a bedfellaw
Wold make one cast his craw.
490 But yet, for all that,
She dranke on the mash fat.

There came an old rybybe;
She halted of a kybe,
And had broken her shyn
495 At the threshold comyng in,
And fell so wyde open
That one might se her token.
The devyll thereon be wroken!
What nede all this be spoken?
500 She yelled lyke a calfe!
'Ryse up, on Gods halfe,'
Sayd Elynour Rummyng,
'I beshrew the for thy cummyng!'
And as she at her dyd pluck,
505 'Quake, quake,' sayd the duck
In that lampatrams lap.
With, 'Fy, cover thy shap
With sum flyp-flap,
God gyve it yll hap!'
510 Sayd Elynour, 'For shame!'
Lyke an honest dame.
Up she stert, halfe lame,
And skantly could go
For payne and for wo.
515   In came another dant,
With a gose and a gant.
She had a wyde wesant;
She was nothynge plesant;
Necked lyke an olyfant;
520 It was a bullyfant,
A gredy cormerant.
Another brought her garlyke heddes;
Another brought her bedes
Of jet or of cole,
525 To offer to the ale-pole.
Some brought a wymble,
Some brought a thymble,
Some brought a sylke lace,
Some brought a pyncase,
530 Some her husbandes gowne,
Some a pyllowe of downe,
Some of the napery;

And all this shyfte they make
For the good ale sake.
535   'A strawe,' sayde Bele, 'stande utter,
For we have egges and butter,
And of pygeons a payre.'
  Than sterte forth a fysgygge
And she brought a bore pygge.
540 The fleshe thereof was ranke,
And her brethe strongely stanke,
Yet, or she went, she dranke,
And gat her great thanke
Of Elynour for her ware,
545 That she thyder bare
To pay for her share.
Nowe truly, to my thynkynge,
This is a solempne drynkynge.

    Septimus passus

'Soft,' quod one hyght Sybbyll,
550 'And let me with you bybyll.'
She sat downe in the place,
With a sory face
Whey-wormed about;
Garnysshed was her snout
555 With here and there a puscull,
Lyke a scabbyd muscull.
'This ale,' sayd she, 'is noppy;
Let us syppe and soppy,
And not spyll a droppy,
560 For so mote I hoppy,
It coleth well my croppy.'
  'Dame Elynour,' sayde she,
'Have here is for me,
A clout of London pynnes.'
565 And wyth that she begynnes
The pot to her plucke,
And dranke a good lucke.
She swynged up a quarte
At ones for her parte.
570 Her paunche was so puffed

And so with ale stuffed,
Had she not hyed apace,
She had defoyled the place.
    Than began the sporte
575 Amonge that dronken sorte.
'Dame Elynour,' sayde they,
'Lende here a cocke of hey,
To make all thynge cleane;
Ye wote well what we meane.'
    But, syr, amonge all
580 That sate in that hall,
There was a prycke-me-denty,
Sat lyke a seynty,
And began to paynty
585 As though she would faynty.
She made it as koye
As a lege-de-moy;
She was not halfe so wyse
As she was pevysshe nyse.
590 She sayde never a worde,
But rose from the borde
And called for our dame,
Elynour by name.
We supposed, iwys,
595 That she rose to pys;
But the very grounde
Was for to compound
With Elynour in the spence,
To paye for her expence.
600 'I have no penny nor grote
To paye,' sayde she, 'God wote,
For wasshyng of my throte;
But my bedes of amber.
Bere them to your chamber.'
605   Than Elynour dyd them hyde
Within her beddes syde.
But some than sate ryght sad
That nothynge had
There of their awne,
610 Neyther gelt nor pawne.

Suche were there menny
That had not a penny,
But, whan they shoulde walke,
Were fayne with a chalke
615   To score on the balke,
Or score on the tayle.
God gyve it yll hayle,
For my fyngers ytche.
I have wrytten so mytche
620   Of this mad mummynge
Of Elynour Rummynge.
Thus endeth the gest
Of this worthy fest.

Quod Skelton Laureat.

LAUREATI SKELTONIDIS IN DESPECTU MALIGNANTIUM
   DISTICHON

Quamvis insanis, quamvis marcescis inanis,
Invide, cantamus: hec loca plena jocis,
   Bien men souvient.

Omnes feminas, que vel nimis bibule sunt, vel que sordida labe
squaloris, aut qua spurca feditatis macula, aut verbosa
loquacitate notantur, poeta invitat ad audiendum hunc libellum,
& c

Ebria, squalida, sordida femina, prodiga verbis,
   Huc currat, properet, veniat! Sua gesta libellus
Iste volutabit: Pean sua plectra sonando
   Materiam risus cantabit carmine rauco.

Finis

Quod Skelton Laureat

XVIII
Speke Parott

Lectoribus auctor recipit opusculy huius auxesim

Crescet in immensem me vivo pagina presens;
Hinc mea dicetur Skeltonidis aurea fama.

PAROT

My name ys Parott, a byrde of Paradyse,
By Nature devysed of a wonderowus kynde,
Deyntely dyetyd with dyvers delycate spyce,
Tyll Eufrates, that flodde, dryvythe me into Ynde,
5   Where men of that contre by fortune me fynde,
And send me to greate ladyes of estate;
Then Parot moste have an almon or a date.

A cage curyowsly carven, with sylver pynne,
Properly payntyd to be my coverture;
10   A myrrour of glasse, that I may tote therin;
These maydens full meryly with many a dyvers flowur
Fresshely they dresse and make swete my bowur,
With, 'Speke, Parott, I pray yow,' full curteslye they sey,
'Parott ys a goodlye byrde and a pratye popagay.'

15   Wythe my beke bente, and my lytell wanton iye,
My fethyrs fresshe as ys the emerawde grene,
Abowte my necke a cerculett lyke the ryche rubye,
My lytell legges, my fete bothe fete and clene,
I am a mynyon to wayte apon a quene;
20   'My propyr Parott, my lytell pratye fole.'
With ladyes I lerne and goe with them to scole.

'Heghe, ha, ha, Parott, ye can lawghe pratylye!'
'Parott hathe not dyned of all this long day;'
'Lyke owur pus catt Parott can mewte and crye.'
25   Yn Latyn, in Ebrue, and in Caldee,
In Greke tong Parott can bothe speke and sey,
As Percius, that poete, dothe reporte of me,
Quis expeduit psitaco suum Chyre?

Dowche Frenshe of Paris Parot can lerne,
30   Pronownsyng my purpose after my properte,
With, '*Parlez byen, Parott, ow parles ryen.*'
With Dowche, with Spaynyshe, my tonge can agree;
In Englysshe to God Parott can supple:
'Cryste save Kyng Herry the viiith, owur royall kyng,
35   The red rose in honour to flowrysshe and sprynge!'

'With Kateryne incomporabyll, owur royall quene also,
That pereles pomegarnat, Cryste save hyr nobyll grace!'

Parott *saves habeler Castylyano*,
With *fidasso de cosso* in Turke and in Trace;
40 *Vis consilii expers*, as techythe me Orace,
Mole ruit sua, whose dictes ar pregnaunte –
'*Souentez foyz*, Parot, *en sovenaunte*.'

My lady mastres, Dame Phylology,
Gave me a gyfte in my neste when I lay,
45 To lerne all langage and hyt to speke aptlye.
Now *pandes mory*, wax frantycke som men sey;
Phronessys for frenessys may not hold her way.
An almon now for Parott, delycatelye dreste;
In *Salve festa dyes*, *toto* ys the beste.

50 *Moderata juvant* but *toto* dothe exede;
Dyscrecion ys modyr of nobyll vertues all;
Myden agan in Grekys tonge we rede,
But reason and wytte wantythe theyr provynciall,
When wylfulnes ys vicar generall.
55 '*Hec res acu tangitur*, Parrott, *par ma foye* – '
'*Tycez-vous*, Parrott, *tenes-vous coye*.'

Besy, besy, besy, and besynes agayne!
'*Que pensez-voz*, Parrot? What meneth this besynes?'
Vitulus in Oreb troubled Arons brayne;
60 Melchisedeck mercyfull made Moloc mercyles.
To wyse is no vertue, to medlyng, to restles;
In mesure is tresure, *cum sensu maturato*:
Ne tropo sanno, ne tropo mato.

Aram was fyred with Caldies fyer called Ur;
65 Jobab was brought up in the lande of Hus;
The lynage of Lot toke supporte of Assur;
Jereboseth is Ebrue, who lyst the cause dyscus.
'Peace, Parrot, ye prate as ye were *ebrius*!'
Howst the, *lyuer god van hemrik, ic seg*;
70 In Popering grew peres, whan Parrot was an eg.

'What is this to purpose?' Over in a whynnymeg!
Hop Lobyn of Lowdeon wald have e byt of bred;
The Jebet of Baldock was made for Jack Leg;
A narrow unfethered and without an hed,
75 A bagpype without blowynge standeth in no sted:

Some run to far before, some run to far behynde,
Some be to churlysshe, and some be to kynde.

Ic dien serveth for the estrych fether,
Ic dien is the language of the land of Beme;
80   In Affryc tongue *byrsa* is a thonge of lether;
In Palestina there is Jerusalem.
Collustrum now for Parot, whyte bred and swete creme!
Our Thomasen she doth trip, our Jenet she doth shayle;
Parrot hath a blacke beard and a fayre grene tayle.

85   'Moryshe myne owne shelfe,' the costermonger sayth;
'Fate, fate, fate, ye Irysh water-lag.'
In flattryng fables men fynde but lyttyl fayth;
But *moveatur terra*, let the world wag,
Let Syr Wrig-wrag wrastell with Syr Delarag:
90   Every man after his maner of wayes,
Pawbe une aruer, so the Welche man sayes.

Suche shredis of sentence, strowed in the shop
Of auncyent Aristippus and such other mo,
I gader togyther and close in my crop,
95   Of my wanton conseyt, *unde depromo*
Dilemata docta in pedagogio
Sacro vatum, whereof to you I breke;
I pray you, let Parot have lyberte to speke.

'But ware the cat, Parot, ware the fals cat!'
100   With, 'Who is there? A mayd?' Nay, nay, I trow!
Ware, ryat, Parrot, ware ryot, ware that!
'Mete, mete, for Parot, mete I say, how!'
Thus dyvers of language by lernyng I grow:
With, 'Bas me, swete Parrot, bas me, swete swete;'
105   To dwell amonge ladyes, Parrot, is mete.

'Parrot, Parrot, Parrot, praty popigay!'
With my beke I can pyke my lyttel praty too;
My delyght is solas, pleasure, dysporte and pley;
Lyke a wanton, whan I wyll, I rele to and froo.

110   Parot can say, '*Cesar, ave*,' also;
But Parrot hath no favour to Esebon;
Above all other byrdis, set Parrot alone.

Ulula, Esebon, for Jeromy doth wepe!
Sion is in sadness, Rachell ruly doth loke;
115   Madionita Jetro, our Moyses kepyth his shepe;
Gedeon is gon, that Zalmane undertoke,
Oreb *et* Zeb, of *Judicum* rede the boke.
Now Geball, Amon and Amaloch – 'Harke, harke,
Parrot pretendith to be a bybyll clarke!'

120   O Esebon, Esebon, to the is cum agayne
Seon, the regent *Amorreorum*,
And Og, that fat hog of Basan, doth retayne
The crafty *coistronus Cananeorum*;
And *assilum*, whilom *refugium miserorum*,
125   *Non phanum, sed prophanum*, standyth in lytyll sted:
Ulula, Esebon, for Jepte is starke ded!

Esebon, Marybon, Wheston next Barnet;
A trym-tram for an horse-myll it were a nyse thyng,
Deyntes for dammoysels, chaffer far-fet;
130   Bo-ho doth bark wel, Hough-ho he rulyth the ring;
From Scarpary to Tartary renoun therein doth spryng,
With, 'He sayd,' and 'We said.' Ich wot now what ich wot,
Quod magnus est dominus Judas Scarioth.

Tholomye and Haly were cunnyng and wyse
135   In the volvell, in the quadrant and in the astroloby,
To pronostycate truly the chaunce of fortunys dyse;
Som trete of theyr tirykis, som of astrology,
Som *pseudo-propheta* with ciromancy:
Yf fortune be frendly, and grace be the guyde,
140   Honowre with renowne wyll ren on that syde.

140a   'Monon Calon Agaton,'
140b   Quod Parato
140c   *In Greco.*

Let Parrot, I pray you, have lyberte to prate,
For *aurea lyngua Greca* ought to be magnyfyed,
Yf it were cond perfytely, and after the rate,
As *lyngua Latina*, in scole matter occupyed;
145   But our Grekis theyr Greke so well have applyed,
That they cannot say in Greke, rydynge by the way,
'How, hosteler, fetche my hors a botell of hay!'

Neyther frame a silogisme in *phrisesomorum*
Formaliter et Grece, cum medio termino:
150 Our Grekys ye walow in the washbol *Argolycorum*;
For though ye can tell in Greke what is *phormio*,
Yet ye seke out your Greke in *Capricornio*;
For ye scrape out good scrypture, and set in a gall:
Ye go about to amende, and ye mare all.

155 Some argue *secundum quid ad simpliciter*,
And yet he wolde be rekenyd *pro Ariopagita*;
And some make distinctions *multipliciter*,
Whether *ita* were before *non*, or *non* before *ita*,
Nether wise nor wel lernid, but like *hermaphradita*:
160 Set *Sophia* asyde, for every Jack Raker
And every mad medler must now be a maker.

In *Achademia* Parrot dare no probleme kepe,
For *Greci fari* so occupyeth the chayre,
That *Latinum fari* may fall to rest and slepe,
165 And *silogisari* was drowned at Sturbrydge Fayre;
Tryvyals and quatryvyals so sore now they appayre,
That Parrot the popagay hath pytye to beholde
How the rest of good lernyng is roufled up and trold.

Albertus *De modo significandi*
170 And Donatus be dryven out of scole;
Prisians hed broken now, handy-dandy,
And *Inter didascolos* is rekened for a fole;
Alexander, a gander of Menanders pole,
With, 'Da causales,' is cast out of the gate,
175 And 'Da racionales' dare not shew his pate.

Plautus in his comedies a chyld shall now reherse,
And medyll with Quintylyan in his *Declamacyons*,
That *Pety Caton* can scantly construe a verse,
With, 'Aveto' in *Greco*, and such solempne salutacyons,
180 Can skantly the tensis of his conjugacyons;
Settyng theyr myndys so moche of eloquens,
That of theyr scole maters lost is the hole sentens.

Now a nutmeg, a nutmeg, *cum gariopholo*,
For Parrot to pyke upon, his brayne for to stable,
185 Swete synamum styckis and *pleris cum musco*!

In Paradyce, that place of pleasure perdurable,
The progeny of Parrottis were fayre and favorable;
Nowe *in valle* Ebron Parrot is fayne to fede:
'Cristecrosse and Saynt Nycholas, Parrot, be your good spede!'

190   The myrrour that I tote in, *quasi diaphonum,*
Vel quasi speculum, in enigmate,
Elencticum, or ells *enthimematicum,*
For logicions to loke on, somwhat *sophistice*;
Retoricyons and oratours in freshe humanyte,
195   Support Parrot, I pray you, with your suffrage ornate,
Of *confuse tantum* avoydynge the chekmate.

But of that supposicyon that callyd is arte,
Confuse distrybutyve, as Parrot hath devysed,
Let every man after his merit take his parte;
200   For in this processe, Parrot nothing hath surmysed,
No matter pretendyd, nor nothyng enterprysed,
But that *metaphora, alegoria* withall,
Shall be his protectyon, his pavys and his wall.

For Parot is no churlish chowgh, nor no flekyd pye,
205   Parrot is no pendugum, that men call a carlyng,
Parrot is no woodecocke, nor no butterfly,
Parrot is no stameryng stare, that men call a starlyng;
But Parot is my owne dere harte, and my dere derling.
Melpomene, that fayre mayde, she burneshed his beke:
210   I pray you, let Parrot have lyberte to speke.

Parrot is a fayre byrd for a lady;
God of his goodnes him framed and wrought;
When Parrot is ded, he dothe not putrefy;
Ye, all thyng mortall shall torne unto nought
215   Except mannes soule, that Chryst so dere bought;
That never may dye, nor never dye shall:
Make moche of Parrot, the pogegay ryall.

For that pereles prynce that Parrot dyd create,
He made you of nothynge by his magistye;
220   Poynt well this probleme that Parrot doth prate,
And remembre amonge how Parrot and ye
Shall lepe from this lyfe, as mery as we be.
Pompe, pryde, honour, ryches and worldly lust,
Parrot sayth playnly, shall tourne all to dust.

225   Thus Parott dothe pray yow,
     With herte moste tendyr,
     To rekyn with thys recule now
     And hyt to remembyr.

     Psitacius, ecce, cano, nec sunt mea carmina Phebo
230 *Digna scio, tamen est plena camena deo.*

     Secondum Skeltonida famigeratum,
     In Piereorum cathalogo numeratum.

232a *Itaque consolamyni invicem in verbis istis, etc.*
232b *Candidi lectores, callide callete, vestrum fovete Psitacum, etc.*

GALATHEA

     Speke, Parotte, I pray yow, for Maryes saake,
     Whate mone he made when Pamphylus loste hys make.

PARROTTE

235   My propir Besse,
     My praty Besse,
     Turne ons agayne to me;
     For slepyste thou, Besse,
     Or wakeste thow, Besse,
240   Myne herte hyt ys with the.

     My deysy delectabyll,
     My prymerose commendabyll,
     My vyolet amyabyll,
     My joye inexplicabill,
245   Nowe torne agayne to me.

     I wyl be ferme and stabyll,
     And to yow servyceabyll,
     And also prophytabyll,
     Yf ye be agreabyll,
250   My propyr Besse,
     To turne agayne to me.

     Alas, I am dysdayned,
     And as a man halfe-maymed,
     My harte is so sore payned,

255   I pray the, Besse, unfayned,
       Yet com agayne to me!

       Be love I am constreyned
       To be with yow retayned,
       Hyt wyll not be refrayned:
260   I pray yow be reclaymed,
       My propyr Besse,
       And torne agayne to me!

262a   Quod Parot, thy popagay royall.

       Marcialis cecinit carmen; fit michi scutum:
       Est michi lasciva pagina, vita proba.

       GALATHEA

265   Now kusse me, Parot, kus me, kus, kus;
       Goddes blissyng lyght on thy lytell swete musse!

       Vita et Anima
       Zoe ke psiche.

       Concumbunt Grece. Non est hic sermo pudicus.

269a   *Ergo*
270   *Attica dictamina*
       Sunt plumbi lamina,
       Vel spurea vitulamina:
       Avertat hec Urania.

273a   *Amen*
       Amen, Amen,
       Amen, Amen,
275   And sette to a D,
       And then hyt ys 'Amend',
       Owur new-founde A. B. C.

277a   *Candidi lectores calide callete; vestrum fovete Psitacum.*

                    Lenvoy primere

       Go, litelle quayre, namyd the Popagay,
       Home to resorte Jerobesethe perswade;
280   For the cliffes of Scaloppe they rore wellaway,

And the sandes of Cefas begyn to waste and fade,
For replicacion restles that he of late ther made;
Now Neptune and Eolus ar agreed of lyclyhod,
For Tytus at Dover abydythe in the rode;

285 Lucina she wadythe among the watry floddes,
And the cokkes begyn to crowe agayne the day;
Le tonsan de Jason is lodgid among the shrowdes;
Of Argus revengyd, recover when he may,
Lyacon of Libyk and Lydy hathe cawghte hys pray:
290 Goe, lytyll quayre, pray them that yow beholde,
In there remembraunce ye may be inrolde.

Yet some folys say ye arre furnysshyd with knakkes,
That hang togedyr as fethyrs in the wynde;
But lewdlye ar they lettyrd that your lernyng lackys,
295 Barkyng and whyning lyke churlysshe currys of kynde,
For whoo lokythe wyselye in your warkys may fynde
Muche frutefull mater. But now for your defence,
Agayne all remordes arme yow with paciens.

Monosticon

Ipse sagax eque ceu verax nuncius ito.
300 *Merda! puros mal desires!*

300a *Penultimo die Octobris, 33°*

Secunde Lenvoy

Passe forthe, Parotte, towardes some passengere;
Require hym to convey yow ovyr the salte fome;
Addressyng your selfe, lyke a sadde messengere,
To owur soleyne Seigneour Sadoke, desire hym to cum home,
305 Makyng hys pylgrimage by *Nostre Dame de Crome*:
For Jerico and Jerssey shall mete togethyr as sone
As he to exployte the man owte of the mone.

With porpose and graundepose he may fede hym fatte,
Thowghe he pampyr not hys paunche with the grete seall;
310 We have longyd and lokyd long tyme for that,
Whyche cawsythe pore suters have many a hongry mele;
As presydent and regente he rulythe every deall.
Now pas furthe, good Parott, Owur Lorde be your stede,
In this your journey to prospere and spede.

315 And thowe sum dysdayne yow and sey how ye prate,
    And howe your poemys arre barayne of polyshed eloquens,
    There is none that your name woll abbrogate
    Then nodypollys and gramatolys of smalle intellygens:
    To rude ys there reason to reche to your sentence;
320 Suche malyncoly mastyvys and mangye curre dogges
    Ar mete for a swyne herde to hunte after hogges.

Monosticon
Psitace, perge volans, fatuorum tela retundas.
Merda! puros mall desers!
323a *In diebus Novembris*
323b   34.

Le dereyn lenveoy

    Prepayre yow, Parrot, brevely your passage to take,
325 Of Mercury undyr the trynall aspecte,
    And sadlye salute owur solen Syre Sydrake,
    And shewe hym that all the world dothe conjecte,
    How the maters he mellis in com to small effecte;
    For he wantythe of hys wyttes that all wold rule alone;
330 Hyt ys no lytyll bordon to bere a grete mylle stone.

    To bryng all the see into a cheryston pytte,
    To nombyr all the sterrys in the fyrmament,
    To rule ix realmes by one mannes wytte,
    To suche thynges ympossybyll, reason cannot consente;
335 Muche money, men sey, there madly he hathe spente;
    Parott, ye may prate thys undyr protestacion,
    Was nevyr suche a senatour syn Crystes Incarnacion.

    Wherfor he may now come agayne as he wente,
    Non sine postica sanna, as I trowe,
340 From Calys to Dovyr, to Caunterbury in Kente,
    To make reconyng in the resseyte how Robyn loste hys bowe,
    To sowe corne in the see-sande, ther wyll no crope growe.
    Thow ye be tauntyd, Parotte, with tonges attayntyd,
    Yet your problemes ar preignaunte and with loyalte acquayntyd.

Monasticon
345 *I, properans, Parrote, malas sic coripe linguas.*
346 *Merda! puros mall desires!*
346a *15 Kalendis Decembris*

34.

Dysticon miserabill

347   *Altior, heu, cedro, crudelior, heu, leopardo;*
    Heu, vitulus bubali fit dominus Priami!

Tetrasticon

    Non annis licet et Priamus sed honore voceris:
350   *Dum foveas vitulum, rex, regeris, Britonum;*
    Rex, regeris, non ipse regis, rex inclite, calle;
    Subde tibi vitulum ne fatuet nimium.

    God amend all,
    That all amend may!
355   Amen, quod Parott,
    The royall popagay.

356a   *Kalendis Decembris*
356b   34·

Lenvoy royall

    Go, propyr Parotte, my popagay,
    That lordes and ladies thys pamflett may behold,
    With notable clerkes; supply to them, I pray,
360   Your rudeness to pardon and also that they wolde
    Vouchesafe to defend yow agayne the brawlyng scolde
    Callyd Detraxion, encankryd with envye,
    Whose tong ys attayntyd with slaundrys obliqui.

    For trowthe in parabyll ye wantonlye pronounce,
365   Langagys divers; yet undyr that dothe reste
    Maters more precious than the ryche jacounce,
    Diamounde, or rubye, or balas of the beste,
    Or eyndye sapher with oryente perlys dreste:
    Wherfor your remorders ar madde or else starke blynde,
370   Yow to remorde erste or they know your mynde.

Disticon

    I, volitans, Parrotte, tuam moderare Minervam:
    Vix tua percipient, qui tua teque legent.

Hyperbaton

    Psitacus heu notus seu Percius est, puto, notus,

Nec, reor, est nec erit, licet est erit undique notus.
375 *Maledite soyte bouche malheurewse!*

375a   34.

Laucture de Parott

O My Parrot, *O unice dilecte, votorum meorum*
omnis lapis, lapis preciosus operimentum tuum!

PARROTT

Sicut Aron populumque,
Sic bubali vitulus,
Sic bubali vitulus,
380 *Sic bubali vitulus.*

Thus myche Parott hathe opynlye expreste;
Let se who dare make up the reste.

382a   *Le Popagay sen va complayndre*

Helas! I lamente the dull abusyd brayne,
The enfatuate fantasies, the wytles wylfulnes
385 Of on and hothyr at me that have dysdayne.
Som sey they cannot my parables expresse;
Som sey I rayle att ryott recheles;
Some say but lityll and thynke more in there thowghte,
How thys prosses I prate of, hyt ys not all for nowghte.

390 O causeles cowardes, O hartles hardynes,
O manles manhod, enfayntyd all with fere,
O connyng clergye, where ys your redynes
To practise or postyll thys prosses here and there?
For drede ye darre not medyll with suche gere,
395 Or elles ye pynche curtesy, trulye as I trowe,
Whyche of yow fyrste dare boldlye plucke the crowe.

The skye is clowdy, the coste is nothyng clere;
Tytan hathe truste up hys tressys of fyne golde;
Jupyter for Saturne darre make no royall chere;
400 Lyacon lawghyth thereatt and berythe hym more bolde;
Racell, rulye ragged, she is like to cache colde;

Moloc, that mawmett, there darre no man withsay;
The reste of suche reconyng may make a fowle fraye.

Dixit, quod Parrott, the royall popagay.

PARROTTE

405   *Jupiter ut nitido deus est veneratus Olimpo;*
    Hic coliturque deus.
    Sunt data thura Jovi, rutilo solio residenti;
    Cum Jove thura capit.
    Jupiter astrorum rector dominusque polorum;
410   *Anglica sceptra regit.*

GALATHEA

I compas the conveyaunce unto the capitall
Of owur clerke Cleros. Whythyr, thydyr and why not hethyr?
For passe-a-Pase apase ys gone to cache a molle,
Over Scarpary *mala vy*, Monsyre Cy-and-sliddyr.
415   Whate sequele shall folow when pendugims mete togethyr?
Speke, Parotte, my swete byrde, and ye shall have a date,
Of frantycknes and folysshnes whyche ys the grett state?

PAROTTE

Difficille hit ys to ansswere thys demaunde;
Yet, aftyr the sagacite of a popagay,
420   Frantiknes dothe rule and all thyng commaunde;
Wylfulnes and Braynles now rule all the raye.
Agayne Frentike Frenesy there dar no man sey nay,
For Frantiknes and Wylfulnes and Braynles ensembyll,
The nebbis of a lyon they make to trete and trembyll,

425   To jumbyll, to stombyll, to tumbyll down lyke folys;
To lowre, to droupe, to knele, to stowpe and to play
      cowche-quale;
To fysshe afore the nette and to drawe polys.
He maketh them to bere babylles, and to bere a lowe sayle;
He caryeth a kyng in hys sleve, yf all the worlde fayle;
430   He facithe owte at a flusshe with, 'Shewe, take all!'
Of Pope Julius cardys, he ys chefe Cardynall.

He tryhumfythe, he trumpythe, he turnythe all up and downe,
With, 'Skyre-galyard, prowde palyard, vaunte-parler, ye prate!'
Hys wolvys hede, wanne, bloo as lede, gapythe over the crowne:
435   Hyt ys to fere leste he wolde were the garland on hys pate,
Paregall with all prynces, farre passyng hys estate;
For of owur regente the regiment he hathe, *ex qua vi,*
Patet per versus quod ex vi bolte harvi.

Now, Galathea, lett Parrot, I pray yow, have hys date –
440   Yett dates now are deynte, and wax verye scante,
For grocers were grugyd at and groynyd at but late;
Grete reysons with resons be now reprobitante,
For reysons ar no resons but resons currant –
Ryn God, rynne Devyll! Yet the date of Owur Lord
445   And the date of the Devyll dothe shurewlye accord.

Dixit, quod Parrott, the popagay royall.

GALATHEA

Nowe, Parott, my swete byrde, speke owte yet ons agayn,
Sette asyde all sophysms, and speke now trew and playne.

PAROTTE

So many morall maters, and so lytell usyd;
450   So myche newe makyng, and so madd tyme spente;
So myche translacion into Englyshe confused;
So myche nobyll prechyng, and so lytell amendment;
So myche consultacion, almoste to none entente;
So myche provision, and so lytell wytte at nede –
455   Syns Dewcalyons flodde there can no clerkes rede.

So lytyll dyscressyon, and so myche reasonyng;
So myche hardy-dardy, and so lytell manlynes;
So prodigall expence, and so shamfull reconyng;
So gorgyous garmentes, and so myche wrechydnese,
460   So myche portlye pride, with pursys penyles;
So myche spente before, and so myche unpayd behynde –
Syns Dewcalyons flodde there can no clerkes fynde.

So myche forcastyng, and so farre an after-dele;
So myche poletyke pratyng, and so lytell stondythe in stede;

465 So lytell secretnese, and so myche grete councell;
     So manye bolde barons, there hertes as dull as lede;
     So many nobyll bodyes, undyr on dawys hedd;
     So royall a kyng, as reynythe uppon us all –
     Syns Dewcalions flodde, was nevyr sene nor shall.

470 So many complayntes, and so smalle redresse;
     So myche callyng on, and so smalle takyng hede;
     So myche losse of merchaundyse, and so remedyles;
     So lytell care for the comynweall, and so myche nede;
     So myche dowghtfull daunger, and so lytell drede;
475 So myche pride of prelattes, so cruell and so kene –
     Syns Dewcalyons flodde, I trowe, was nevyr sene.

     So many thevys hangyd, and thevys neverthelesse;
     So myche presonment, for matyrs not worth a hawe;
     So myche papers weryng for ryghte a smalle exesse;
480 So myche pelory pajauntes undyr colowur of good lawe;
     So myche towrnyng on the cooke-stole for every guy-gaw;
     So myche mokkyshe makyng of statutes of array –
     Syns Dewcalyons flodde was nevyr, I dar sey.

     So braynles calvys hedes, so many shepis taylys;
485 So bolde a braggyng bocher, and flesshe sold so dere;
     So many plucte partryches, and so fatte quaylles;
     So mangye a mastyfe curre, the grete greyhoundes pere;
     So bygge a bulke of brow-auntleres cabagyd that yere;
     So many swannes dede, and so small revell –
490 Syns Dewcalyons flodde, I trow, no man can tell.

     So many trusys takyn, and so lytyll perfyte trowthe;
     So myche bely-joye, and so wastefull banketyng;
     So pynchyng and sparyng, and so lytell profyte growth;
     So many howgye howsys byldyng, and so small howse-holdyng;
495 Suche statutes apon diettes, suche pyllyng and pollyng –
     So ys all thyng wrowghte wylfully withowte reson and skylle.
     Syns Dewcalyons flodde the world was never so yll.

     So many vacabondes, so many beggers bolde,
     So myche decay of monesteries and relygious places;
500 So hote hatered agaynste the Chyrche, and cheryte so colde;
     So myche of my lordes grace, and in hym no grace ys;
     So many holow hartes, and so dowbyll faces;

So myche sayntuary brekyng, and prevylegidde barryd –
Syns Dewcalyons flodde was nevyr sene nor lyerd.

505   So myche raggyd ryghte of a rammes horne;
So rygorous revelyng, in a prelate specially;
So bold and so braggyng, and was so baselye borne;
So lordlye of hys lokes, and so dysdayneslye;
So fatte a magott, bred of a flesshe-flye;
510   Was nevyr suche a fylty gorgon, nor suche an epycure,
Syn Dewcalyons flodde, I make the faste and sure.

So myche prevye wachyng in cold wynters nyghtes;
So myche serchyng of loselles, and ys hym selfe so lewde;
So myche conjuracions for elvyshe myday sprettes;
515   So many bullys of pardon publysshed and shewyd;
So myche crossyng and blyssyng and hym all be shrewde;
Suche pollaxis and pyllers, suche mulys trapte with gold –
Sens Dewcalyons flodde, in no cronycle ys told.

       Dixit, quod   Parrot

     Crescet in immensem me vivo Psitacus iste;
520   *Hinc mea dicetur Skeltonidis inclita fama.*
520a   Quod Skelton Lawryat
520b   *Orator Regius*
520c   34.

XIX

Here after foloweth a lytell boke called

Collyn Clout

compyled by Mayster Skelton, Poete Laureate

*Quis consurget mihi adversus malignantes, aut quis stabit
mecum adversus operantes iniquitatem? Nemo, Domine!*

What can it avayle
To dryve forth a snayle,
Or to make a sayle
Of a herynges tayle?
5   To ryme or to rayle,

To wryte or to indyte,
Other for delyte
Or elles for despyte?
Or bokes to compyle
10   Of dyvers maner style,
Vyce to revyle
And synne to exyle?
To teche or to preche
As reason wyll reche?
15   Sey this and sey that:
'His heed is so fat
He wottyth never what
Ne whereof he speketh.'
'He cryeth and he creketh,
20   He pryeth and he preketh,
He chydeth and he chatters,
He prayeth and he patters;
He clyttreth and he clatters,
He medleth and he smatters,
25   He gloseth and he flatters.'
Or yf he speke playne,
Than he lacketh brayne:
'He is but a foole;
Let hym go to scole!
30   A thre-foted stole
That he may downe sytte,
For he lacketh wytte.'
And yf that he hytte
The nayle on the hede
35   It standeth in no stede:
'The devyll,' they say, 'is dede,
The devyll is dede.'
     It may well so be,
Or elles they wolde se
40   Otherwyse, and fle
From worldly vanyte
And foule covytousnesse
And other wretchednesse,
Fyckell falsenesse,
45   Varyablenesse,
With unstablenesse.

And yf ye stande in doute
Who brought this ryme aboute,
My name is Collyn Cloute.
50 I purpose to shake oute
All my connynge bagge,
Lyke a clerkely hagge.
For though my ryme be ragged,
Tattered and jagged,
55 Rudely rayne-beaten,
Rusty and mothe-eaten,
Yf ye take well therwith
It hath in it some pyth.
For, as farre as I can se,
60 It is wronge with eche degre;
For the temporalte
Accuseth the spirytualte;
The spirytualte agayne
Dothe grudge and complayne
65 Upon the temporall men.
Thus eche of other blother
The tone against the tother.
Alas, they make me shoder,
For in hoder-moder
70 The churche is put in faute.
The prelates ben so haute
They say, and loke so hye
As though they wolde flye
Aboute the sterry skye.

75   Laye men say, in dede,
Howe they take no hede
Theyr sely shepe to fede,
But plucke away and pull
Theyr fleces of wull.
80 Unneth they leve a locke
Of wolle amongest theyr flocke.
And as for theyr connynge,
A glommynge and a mommynge,
And make therof a jape!
85 They gaspe and they gape
All to have promocyon:
There is theyr hole devocyon,

With money, yf it wyll happe
To catche the forked cappe.
90 For sothe, they are to lewde
To say so, all beshrewde!

What trowe ye they say more
Of the bysshoppes lore?
Howe in matters they ben rawe,
95 They lumber forth the lawe
To herken Jacke and Gyll
Whan they put up a byll;
And judge it as they wyll,
For other mens skyll,
100 Expoundynge out theyr clauses,
And leve theyr owne causes.
In theyr pryncypall cure
They make but lytell sure,
And meddels very lyght
105 In the churches ryght.
But *ire* and *venyre*,
And *sol fa* so *alamyre*
That the premenyre
Is lyke to be set afyre
110 In theyr jurysdictyons,
Through temporall afflictyons.
Men say they have prescrypcyons
Agaynst the spirytual contradictyons,
Accomptynge them as fictyons.
115 And whyles the heedes do this,
The remenaunt is amys
Of the clergye all,
Bothe great and small.
I wote never howe they warke,
120 But thus the people carke,
And surely thus they sey:
'Bysshoppes, yf they may,
Small housholdes woll kepe,
But slombre forth and slepe,
125 And assay to crepe
Within the noble walles
Of the kynges halles,

To fatte theyr bodyes full,
Theyr soules lame and dull;
130 And have full lytell care
Howe evyll theyr shepe fare.'

The temporalte say playne
Howe bysshoppes dysdayne
Sermons for to make,
135 Or suche laboure to take.
And, for to say trouth,
A great parte is for slouth;
But the greatest parte
Is for they have but small arte
140 And ryght slender connynge
Within theyr heedes wonnynge.
But this reason they take:
Howe they are able to make
With theyr golde and treasure
145 Clerkes out of measure,
And yet that is a pleasure.
Howebeit, some there be,
Almoost two or three,
Of that dygnyte,
150 Full worshypfull clerkes,
As appereth by theyr werkes,
Lyke Aron and Ure,
The wolfe from the dore
To wary and to kepe
155 From theyr goostly shepe,
And theyr spirytuall lambes
Sequestred from rambes
And from the berded gotes
With theyr heery cotes;
160 Set nought by golde ne grotes,
Theyr names yf I durst tell.

But they are lothe to mell,
And lothe to hange the bell
Aboute the cattes necke,
165 For drede to have a checke.
They are fayne to play deuz decke.

Howebeit they are good men,
Moche herted lyke an hen.
Theyr lessons forgoten they have
170 That Saynt Thomas of Canterbury gave.
Thomas *manum mittit ad forcia,*
Spernit dampna, spernit opprobria,
Nulla Thomam frangit iniuria.
But nowe every spirytuall father,
175 Men say, they had rather
Spende moche of theyr share
Than to be combred with care.

Spende? Nay, but spare!
For let se who that dare
180 Shoo the mockyssh mare;
They make her wynche and kycke,
But it is not worth a leke.
Boldenes is to seke
The churche for to defende;
185 Take me as I entende,
For lothe I am to offende
In this that I have pende.
I tell you as men say.
Amende whan ye may,
190 For, *usque ad montem Sare,*
Men say, ye can nat appare;
For some say ye hunte in parkes
And hauke on hobby larkes
And other wanton warkes
195 Whan the nyght darkes.

What have laye men to do
The gray goos for to sho?
Lyke houndes of hell,
They crye and they yell
200 Howe that ye sell
The grace of the Holy Goost.
Thus they make theyr boost
Through every coost,
Howe some of you dothe eate
205 In lenton season flesshe meate,

Fesauntes, partryche and cranes;
Men call you therfore prophanes.
Ye pyke no shrympes nor pranes,
Saltfysshe, stockfyssh nor herynge,
210 It is nat for your werynge,
Nor in holy lenton season
Ye wyll neyther beanes ne peason.
But ye loke to be let lose
To a pygge or to a goose,
215 Your gorge nat endued
Without a capon stued,
Or a stewed cocke
Under her surfled smocke
And her wanton wodicocke.
220   And howe whan ye gyve orders
In your provyncyall borders,
As at *Sicientes*,
Some are *insufficientes*,
Some *parum sapientes*,
225 Some *nichil intelligentes*,
Some *valde negligentes*,
Some *nullum sensum habentes*,
Some bestyall and untaught.
But whan they have ones caught
230 *Dominus vobiscum* by the hede,
Then renne they in every stede,
God wote, with dronken nolles.
Yet take they cure of soules,
And wotteth never what thei rede,
235 Paternoster nor crede;
Construe nat worth a whystell
Neyther gospell nor pystell,
Theyr matyns madly sayde,
Nothynge devoutly prayde,
240 Theyr lernynge is so small,
Theyr prymes and houres fall
And lepe out of theyr lyppes
Lyke sawdust or drye chyppes.
I speke nat nowe of all,
245 But the moost parte in generall.
Of suche *vacabundus*

Speketh *totus mundus*:
Howe some synge *letabundus*
At every ale stake,
250 With, 'Welcome, hake and make!'
By the breed that God brake,
I am sory for your sake!
I speke nat of the good wyfe,
But of her apostels lyfe.
255 *Cum ipsis vel illis*
Qui manent in villis
Est uxor vel ancilla.
'Welcom Jacke and Gylla!'
'My prety Petronylla,
260 And you wyll be stylla,
You shall have your wylla!'
Of suche paternoster pekes
All the worlde spekes.

In you the faute is supposed
265 For that they are nat apposed
By juste examynacyon
In connynge and conversacyon.
They have none instructyon
To make a trewe constructyon.
270 A preest without a letter,
Without his vertue be greatter,
Doutlesse were moche better
Uppon hym for to take
A mattocke or a rake.
275 Alas, for very shame,
Some can nat declyne theyr name!
Some can nat scarsly rede,
And yet he wyll nat drede
For to kepe a cure,
280 And in nothynge is sure.
This *dominus vobiscum*
As wyse as Jacke-a-Thrum,
A chaplayne of trust,
Layth all in the dust.
285 Thus I, Collyn Cloute,
As I go aboute,

And wandrynge as I walke,
I here the people talke.
   Men say, for sylver and golde,
290 Myters are bought and solde;
Theyr shall no clergye appose
A myter nor a crose,
But a full purse.
A strawe for Goddes curse!
295 What are they the worse?
For a symoniake
Is but a hermoniake;
And no more ye make
Of symony, men say,
300 But a chyldes play.

Over this, the foresayd lay
Reporte howe the pope may
An holy anker call
Out of the stony wall,
305 And hym a bysshop make,
Yf he on hym dare take
To kepe so harde a rule,
To ryde upon a mule
With golde all betrapped,
310 In purple and paule belapped;
Some hatted and some capped,
Rychly bewrapped,
God wotte, to theyr great paynes,
In rotchettes of fyne raynes,
315 Whyte as mares mylke;
Theyr tabertes of fyne sylke;
Theyr styrops of myxt golde begared,
There may no cost be spared;
Theyr moyles golde dothe eate,
320 Theyr neyghbours dye for meate.

What care they thoughe Gyll swete,
Or Jacke of the Nocke?
The poore people they yoke
With sommons and citacyons
325 And excommunycacyons

Aboute churches and market.
The bysshop on his carpet
At home full softe dothe sytte.
This is a farly fytte
330   To here the people jangle.
Howe warely they wrangle!
Alas, why do ye nat handle
And them all to-mangle?
Full falsely on you they lye,
335   And shamfully you ascrye,
And say as untrewly
As the butterfly,
A man myght say in mocke,
Ware the wether cocke
340   Of the steple of Poules.
And thus they hurte theyr soules,
In sclaundrynge you for truthe.
Alas, it is great ruthe!
    Some say ye sytte in trones,
345   Lyke *princeps aquilonis*,
And shryne your rotten bonys
With perles and precyous stonys.
But howe the commons gronys,
And the people monys,
350   For prestes and for lonys
Lent and never payde,
But from daye to daye delayde,
The communewelth decayde.
Men say ye are tonge-tayde,
355   And therof speke nothynge
But dyssymulynge and glosynge,
Wherfore men be supposynge
That ye gyve shrewed counsell
Agaynst the communewell,
360   By pollynge and pyllage
In cytes and vyllage;
By taxynge and tollage,
Ye make monkes to have the colerage
For coverynge of an olde cottage
365   That commytted is a collage
In the charter of dottage

Tenure par service de sottage,
And nat *par service de socage,*
After olde seygnours,
370   And the lernynge of Lytelton *Tenours*
Ye have so overthwarted,
That good lawes are subverted
And good reason perverted.

Relygyous men are fayne
375   For to tourne agayne
In secula seculorum,
And to forsake theyr *corum*
And *vacabundare per forum,*
And take a fyne *meritorum,*
380   *Contra regulam morum,*
Aut blacke *monacorum,*
Aut canonicorum,
Aut Bernardinorum,
Aut Crucifixorum,
385   And to synge from place to place,
Lyke apostataas.
      And the selfe same game
Begon, and now with shame,
Amongest the sely nonnes.
390   My lady nowe she ronnes,
Dame Sybly our abbesse,
Dame Dorothe and Lady Besse,
Dame Sare our pryoresse,
Out of theyr cloyster and quere
395   With an hevy chere,
Must cast up theyr blacke vayles
And set up theyr fucke sayles
To catche wynde with theyr ventayles.
What, Collyn, there thou shayles!
400   Yet thus with yll hayles
The lay fee people rayles.

And all the faute they lay
In you prelates, and say
Ye do them wronge and no ryght
405   To put them thus to flyght;
No matyns at mydnyght,

Boke and chalys gone quyte;
Plucke away the leedes
Over theyr heedes,
410 And sell away theyr belles
And all that they have elles.
Thus the people telles,
Rayles lyke rebelles,
Redes shrewdly and spelles,
415 And with foundacyons melles,
And talkes lyke tytyvylles
Howe ye breke the dedes wylles,
Turne monasteries into water mylles,
Of an abbey ye make a graunge –
420 Your workes, they say, are straunge –
So that theyr founders soules
Have lost theyr bedde roules;
The money for theyr masses
Spent among wanton lasses;
425 Theyr dyriges are forgotten,
Theyr founders lye there rotten;
But where theyr soules dwell,
Therwith I wyll nat mell.
What coude the Turke do more
430 With all his false lore –
Turke, Sarazyn or Jewe?
I reporte me to you.

O mercyfull Jesu,
You supporte and rescue,
435 My style for to dyrecte,
It may take some effecte!
For I abhorre to wryte
Howe the lay fee despyte
You prelates, that of ryght
440 Shulde be lanternes of lyght.
Ye lyve, they say, in delyte,
Drowned *in deliciis,*
In gloria et deviciis,
In o admirabili honore
445 *In gloria et splendore*
Fulgurantes haste,
Viventes parum caste.

Yet swete meate hath soure sauce,
For after *gloria, laus,*
450   Chryst by cruelte
Was nayled upon a tre;
He payed a bitter pencyon
For mans redempcyon,
He dranke eysell and gall
455   To redeme us with all.
But swete ypocras ye drynke,
With, 'Let the catte wynke!
Iche wotte what yche do thynke!'
    Howebeit, *per assimile,*
460   Some men thynke that ye
Shall have penalte
For your iniquite.
Nota what I say
And bere it well away.
465   Yf it please nat theologys
It is good for astrologys,
For Tholome tolde me
The sonne somtyme to be
In Ariete
470   Ascendent a degre.
Whan Scorpyon descendynge,
Was so then pretendynge
A fatall fall for one
That shall sytte in a trone
475   And rule all thynges alone.
Your teth whett on this bone
Amongest you everychone
And let Collyn Clout have none
Maner of cause to mone.
480   Lay salve to your owne sore,
For elles, as I sayd before,
After *gloria, laus,*
May come a soure sauce.
Sory therfore am I,
485   But trouth can never lye.

With language thus poluted
Holy churche is bruted
And shamfully confuted.

My penne nowe wyll I sharpe,
490 And wrest up my harpe
With sharp twynkyng trebelles
Agayne all suche rebelles
That laboure to confounde
And brynge the churche to the grounde.
495 As ye may dayly se
Howe the lay fee
Of one affynyte
Consent and agre
Agaynst the churche to be,
500 And the dygnyte
Of the bysshoppes see.
    And eyther ye be to badde,
Or elles they are madde
Of this to reporte.
505 But under your supporte,
Tyll my dyenge day
I shall bothe wryte and say,
And ye shall do the same,
Howe they are to blame
510 You thus to dyffame.
For it maketh me sad
Howe the people are glad
The churche to deprave.
And some there are that rave,
515 Presumyng on theyr owne wytte,
Whan there is never a whytte,
To maynteyne argumentes
Agaynst the sacramentes.

Some make epylogacyon
520 Of hygh predestynacyon;
And of resydevacyon
They make enterpretacyon
Of auquarde facyon,
And of the prescyence
525 Of divyne assence
And what ipostacis
Of Chrystes manhode is.
Suche logyke men woll choppe,
And in theyr fury hoppe,

530 Whan the good ale soppe
     Dothe daunce in theyr foretoppe;
     Bothe women and men,
     Suche ye may well knowe and ken
     That agaynst preesthode
535 Theyr malyce sprede abrode,
     Raylynge haynously
     And dysdaynously
     Of preestly dygnytes
     By theyr malygnytes.
540 And some have a smacke
     Of Luthers sacke,
     And a brennynge sparke
     Of Luthers warke,
     And are somewhat suspecte
545 In Luthers secte.
     And some of them barke,
     Clatter and carpe
     Of that heresy arte
     Called Wytclyftista,
550 The devylyshe dagmatista.
     And some be Hussians,
     And some be Arryans,
     And some be Pollegyans,
     And make moche varyans
555 Bytwene the clergye
     And the temporaltye:

     How the churche hath to mykell
     And they have to lytell,
     And brynge in materyalytes
560 And qualyfyed qualytes
     Of pluralytes,
     Of tryalytes,
     And of tot quottes;
     They commune lyke sottes,
565 As cometh to theyr lottes,
     Of prebendaries and deanes,
     Howe some of them glenes
     And gathereth up in store
     For to catche more and more:

570 Of parsons and vycaryes
      They make many outcryes:
      'They can nat kepe theyr wyves
      From them for theyr lyves!'
      And thus the loselles stryves,
575 And lewdely sayes by Chryst
      Agaynst the sely preest.
      Alas, and wellaway,
      What eyles them thus to say?
      They mought be better advysed
580 Then to be so dysgysed.
      But they have enterprysed
      And shamfully surmysed
      How prelacye is solde and bought
      And come up of nought;
585 And where the prelates be
      Come of lowe degre
      And set in majeste
      And spirytuall dygnyte,
      Farewell benygnyte,
590 Farewell symplycyte,
      Farewell humylyte,
      Farewell good charyte!

      Ye are so puffed with pryde,
      That no man may abyde
595 Your hygh and lordely lokes.
      Ye caste up then your bokes
      And vertue is forgotten,
      For then ye wyll be wroken
      Of every lyght quarell,
600 And call a lorde a javell.
      A knyght a knave ye make.
      Ye boost, ye face, ye crake,
      And upon you take
      To rule kynge and kayser.
605 And yf ye may have layser,
      Ye wyll brynge all to nought,
      And that is all your thought.
      For the lordes temporall,
      Theyr rule is very small,
610 Almoost nothynge at all.

Men say howe ye appalle
The noble bloode royall
In ernest and in game.
Ye are the lesse to blame,
615 For lordes of noble bloode,
Yf they well understode
Howe connynge myght them avaunce,
They wolde pype you another daunce.
But noble men borne,
620 To lerne they have scorne,
But hunte and blowe an horne,
Lepe over lakes and dykes,
Set nothynge by polytykes.
Therfore ye kepe them base,
625 And mocke them to theyr face.
This is a pyteous case:
To you that over the whele
Lordes must crouche and knele,
And breke theyr hose at the kne,
630 As dayly men may se,
And to remembraunce call;
Fortune so tourneth the ball
And ruleth so over all
That honoure hath a great fall.
635   Shall I tell you more? Ye, shall.
I am lothe to tell all;
But the communalte ye call
Ydolles of Babylon,
De terra Zabulon,
640 *De terra* Neptalym;
For you love to go trym,
Brought up of poore estate,
With pryde inordynate,
Sodaynly upstarte
645 From the donge carte,
The mattocke and the shovll
To reygne and to rule;
And have no grace to thynke
Howe ye were wonte to drynke
650 Of a lether bottell
With a knavysshe stoppell,

Whan mammockes was your meate,
With moulde brede to eate –
Ye coude none other gette
655 To chewe and to gnawe
To fyll therwith your mawe –
Lodged in the strawe,
Couchynge your drousy heddes
Somtyme in lousy beddes.
660   All this is out of mynde.
Ye growe nowe out of kynde.
Many one ye have untwynde
And make the commons blynde.
But *qui se existimat stare*,
665 Let hym well beware
Leste that his fote slyppe,
And have suche a tryppe,
And fall in suche decay,
That all the worlde myght say,
670 'Come downe, on the devyll way.'

Yet over all that,
Of bysshoppes they chat,
That though ye rounde your heere
An ynche above your eere,
675 And have *aures patentes*
And *parum intendentes*,
And your tonsors be croppyd,
Your eeres they be stopped!
For Mayster *Adulator*,
680 And Doctour *Assentator*,
And *Blandior Blandiris*,
With *Mentior Mentiris*,
They folowe your desyris,
And so they blere your eye
685 That ye can nat espye
Howe the male dothe wrye.
    Alas, for Goddes wyll,
Why syt ye prelates styll
And suffre all this yll?
690 Ye bysshoppes of estates
Shulde open the brode gates

For your spirytuall charge,
And com forthe at large,
Lyke lanternes of lyght,
695 In the peoples syght,
In pulpyttes autentyke,
For the wele publyke
Of preesthode in this case;
And all wayes to chase
700 Suche maner of sysmatykes
And halfe heretykes,
That wolde intoxicate,
That wolde conquinate,
That wolde contemminate,
705 And that wolde vyolate,
And that wolde derogate,
And that wolde abrogate
The churche hygh estates,
After this maner rates;
710 The whiche shulde be
Bothe franke and free,
And have theyr lyberte,
As of antyquyte
It was ratyfyed,
715 And also gratyfyed
By holy synodalles
And bulles papalles,
As it is *res certa*
Conteyned in *Magna Carta*.

720 But mayster Damyan,
Or some other man
That clerkely is, and can
Well scrypture expounde
And hys textes grounde –
725 His benefyce worth ten pounde,
Or scante worth twenty marke,
And yet a noble clerke –
He must do this werke;
As I know aparte
730 Some maysters of arte,
Some doctours of lawe,
Some lerned in other sawe,

As in divynyte,
That hath no dygnyte
735 But the poore degre
Of the universyte;
Or elles frere Frederyk,
Or elles frere Dominyk,
Or frere Hugulinus,
740 Or frere Augustinus,
Or frere Carmellus,
That goostly can heale us;
Or elles yf we may
Gette a frere gray,
745 Or elles of the order
Upon Grenewytche border
Called Observaunce,
And a frere of Fraunce,
Or elles the poore Scot,
750 It must come to his lot
To shote forthe his shot;
Or of Babvell besyde Bery
To postell upon a kyry,
That wolde it shulde be noted
755 How scrypture shulde be coted,
And so clerkely promoted,
And yet the frere doted!

But men say your auctoryte
And your noble se
760 And your dygnyte
Shulde be imprynted better
Then all the freres letter.
But yf ye wolde take payne
To preche a worde or twayne,
765 Though it were never so playne,
With clauses two or thre,
So as they myght be
Compendyously conveyed,
These words shuld be more weyed,
770 And better perceyved,
And thankefullyer receyved,
And better shulde remayne
Amonge the people playne,

That wolde your wordes retayne
775   And reherse them agayne,
Than a thousande thousande other
That blaber, barke, and blother,
And make a Welchmans hose
Of the texte and the glose.

780   For protestacyon made
That I wyll nat wade
Farther in this broke,
Nor farther for to loke
In devysynge of this boke,
785   But answere that I may,
For myselfe alway
Eyther *analogice*,
Or elles *cathagorice*,
So that in divynyte
790   Doctours that lerned be
Nor bachelers of that faculte
That hath taken degre
In the unyversyte
Shall nat be objected by me.
795   But doctour *Bullatus*
Parum litteratus,
Dominus doctoratus
At the Brode *gatus*,
Doctour *Daupatus*,
800   And bacheler *Bacheleratus*,
Dronken as a mouse
At the ale house,
Taketh his pyllyon and his cappe
At the good ale tappe,
805   For lacke of good wyne;
As wyse as Robyn Swyne,
Under a notaries sygne
Was made a divyne;
As wyse as Waltoms calfe,
810   Must preche a Goddes halfe
In the pulpyt solempnely –
More mete in a pyllory –
For, by saynt Hyllary,

He can nothynge smatter
815 Of logyke nor scole matter,
Neyther *sylogysare*,
Nor of *enthymemare*;
Nor knoweth not his elenkes,
Nor his predicamentes;
820 And yet he wyll melle
To amende the gospell,
And wyll preche and tell
What they do in hell.
And he dare nat well neven
825 What they do in heven;
Nor how farre Temple Barre is
From the seven sterrys!

Nowe wyll I go
And tell of other mo,
830 *Semper protestando*
De non impugnando
The foure ordres of freres,
Though some of them by lyres.
As limyters at large
835 Wyll charge and dyscharge,
As many a frere, God wote,
Preches for his grote,
Flatterynge for a newe cote
And for to have his fees,
840 Some to gather chese.
Lothe they are to lese
Eyther corne or malte,
Somtyme meale and salte,
Somtyme a bacon flycke
845 That is thre fyngers thycke
Of larde and of grece,
Theyr covent to encrease.

I put you out of dout,
This can nat be brought about
850 But they theyr tonges fyle,
And make a pleasaunt style
To Margery and to Maude
Howe they have no fraude.

And somtyme they provoke
855 Bothe Gyll and Jacke at Noke
Theyr dewtyes to withdrawe,
That they ought by the lawe
Theyr curates to content
In open tyde and in lent.
860 God wotte, they take great payne
To flatter and to fayne,
But it is an olde sayd sawe
That nede hath no lawe.
Some walke about in melottes,
865 In gray russet and heery cotes;
Some wyl neyther golde ne grotes;
Some plucke a partryche in remotes,
And by the barres of her tayle
Wyll knowe a raven from a rayle,
870 A quayle, the rayle, the olde raven.
Sed libera nos a malo. Amen.
And by *Dudum*, theyr Clementyne,
Agaynst curates, they repyne,
And say properly thei are sacerdotes
875 To shryve, assoyle, and to reles
Dame Margeres soule out of hell.
But whan the frere fell in the well
He coude nat synge hymselfe therout
But by the helpe of Christen Clout.
880 Another Clementyne also:
Howe frere Fabian with other mo
'*Exivit de paradiso . . .*'
When thei agayn thyder shal come,
De hoc petimus consilium.
885 And through all the worlde thei go
With *Diryge* and *Placebo*.

But now my mynde ye understande,
For they must take in hande
To preche, and withstande
890 All maner of abjections;
For bysshoppes have protections,
They say, to do corrections,
But they have no affections
To take sadde dyrections.

895 In suche maner of cases,
   Men say, they bere no faces
   To occupye suche places,
   To sowe the sede of graces.
   Theyr hertes are so faynted,
900 And they be so attaynted
   With covytous ambycyon
   And other superstycyon,
   That they be deefe and dum,
   And play scylence and glum,
905 Can say nothynge but 'mum'.
   They occupy them so
   With syngynge *Placebo*,
   They wyll no farder go.
   They had lever to please
910 And take theyr worldly ease
   Than to take on hande
   Worshypfully to withstande
   Suche temporall warre and bate
   As now is made of late
915 Agaynst holy churche estate,
   Or to maynteyne good quarelles.
   The lay men call them barelles
   Full of glotony
   And of ypocrysy,
920 That counterfeytes and payntes
   As they were very sayntes.

   In matters that them lyke
   They shewe them polytyke,
   Pretendynge gravyte
925 And seygnyoryte,
   With all solempnyte,
   For theyr indempnyte;
   For they wyll have no losse
   Of a peny nor of a crosse
930 Of theyr predyall landes,
   That cometh to theyr handes;
   And as farre as they dare set,
   All is fysshe that cometh to the net:
   Buyldynge royally
935 Theyr mancyons curyously,

With turrettes and with toures,
With halles and with boures,
Stretchynge to the sterres,
With glasse wyndowes and barres;
940   Hangynge about the walles
Clothes of golde and paules,
Arayse of ryche aray,
Fresshe as flours in May;
With Dame Dyana naked;
945   Howe lusty Venus quaked,
And howe Cupyde shaked
His dart, and bent his bowe
For to shote a crowe
At her tyrly tyrlowe;
950   And howe Parys of Troy
Daunced a lege moy,
Made lusty sporte and joy
With Dame Helyn the quene.
With suche storyes bydene
955   Theyr chambres well sene,
With tryumphes of Cesar
And of his Pompeyus warre,
Of renowne and of fame
By them to gette a name.
960   Howe all the worlde stares
Howe they ryde in goodly chares,
Conveyde by olyfauntes
With lauryat garlantes,
And by unycornes
965   With theyr semely hornes;
Upon these beestes rydynge,
Naked boyes strydynge,
With wanton wenches wynkyng!

Nowe trewely, to my thynkyng,
970   That is a speculacyon
And a mete meditacyon
For prelates of estate,
Theyr courage to abate
From worldly wantones,
975   Theyr chambre thus to dresse

With suche perfytenesse
And all suche holynesse.
Howebeit they let downe fall
Theyr churches cathedrall.

980 Squyre, knyght and lorde
Thus the churche remorde.
With all temporall people
They renne agaynst the steple,
Thus talkynge and tellynge
985 Howe some of you are mellynge.
Yet softe and fayre for swellynge,
Beware of a quenes yellynge!
It is a besy thynge
For one man to rule a kynge
990 Alone, and make rekenynge
To governe over all
And rule a realme royall
By one mannes wytte.
Fortune may chaunce to flytte,
995 And whan he weneth to sytte
Yet may he mysse the quysshon!
For I rede a preposycyon:
Cum regibus amicare
Et omnibus dominare
1000 *Et supra te gravare*;
Wherfore he hath good ure
That can hymselfe assure
How fortune wyll endure.
Than lette reason you supporte,
1005 For the communalte reporte
That they have great wonder
That ye kepe them so under;
Yet they mervayle so moche lesse,
For ye play so at the chesse,
1010 As they suppose and gesse,
That some of you but late
Hath played so checkmate
With lordes of great estate
After suche a rate,
1015 That they shall mell nor make,

Nor upon them take,
For kynge nor kayser sake,
But at the pleasure of one
That ruleth the rest alone.

1020 Helas, I say, helas!
Howe may this come to pas,
That a man shall here a masse,
And nat so hardy on his hede
To loke on God in fourme of brede,
1025 But that the parysshe clerke
Therupon must herke,
And graunte hym at his askynge
For to se the sacrynge?
And howe may this accorde,
1030 No man to our sovereygne lorde
So hardy to make suete,
Nor to execute
His commaundement,
Without the assent
1035 Of your presydent;
Nor to expresse to his parson,
Without . . .
Graunte hym his lycence
To prease to his presence;
1040 Nor to speke to hym secretly,
Openly nor prevyly,
Without his presydent be by,
Or elles his substytute
Whome he wyll depute?
1045 Neyther erle ne duke
Permytted? By saynt Luke,
And by swete saynt Marke,
This is a wonderous warke!
That the people talke this,
1050 Somwhat there is amysse!
The devyll can nat stop their mouthes
But they wyl talke of suche uncouthes,
All that ever they ken
Agaynst all spirytuall men.

1055 Whether it be wronge or ryght
Or elles for despyght,

Or howeever it hap,
Theyr tonges thus do clap;
And through suche detractyon
1060 They put you to your actyon.
And whether they say trewly
As they may byde therby,
Or elles that they do lye,
Ye knowe better than I.
1065   But nowe *debetis scire*
And groundly *audire*
In your *convenire*
Of this premenyre,
Or elles in the myre
1070 They say they wyll you cast.
Therfore stande sure and fast.
        Stande sure and take good fotyng,
And let be all your motynge,
Your gasynge and your totynge
1075 And your parcyall promotynge
Of those that stande in your grace.
But olde servauntes ye chase
And put them out of theyr place.
Make ye no murmuracyon
1080 Though I wryte after this facyon;
Though I, Collyn Clout,
Amongest the hole rout
Of you that clerkes be,
Take upon me
1085 Thus copyously to wryte,
I do it nat for no despyte.
Wherfore, take no dysdayne
At my style rude and playne,
For I rebuke no man
1090 That vertuous is. Why than
Wreke ye your anger on me?
For those that vertuous be
Have no cause to say
That I speke out of the way.

1095 Of no good bysshop speke I,
Nor good preest I escrye,
Good frere, nor good chanon,

Good nonne, nor good canon,
Good monke, nor good clerke,
1100 Nor of no good werke;
But my recountynge is
Of them that do amys
In spekynge and rebellynge
In hyndrynge and dysavaylynge
1105 Holy churche our mother,
One agayne another.
To use suche despytynge
Is all my hole wrytynge;
To hynder no man
1110 As nere as I can,
For no man have I named.
Wherfore shulde I be blamed?
Ye ought to be ashamed
Agaynst me to be gramed,
1115 And can nat tell no cause why
But that I wryte trewly.

Then yf any there be
Of hygh or lowe degre
Of the spyrytualte
1120 Or of the temporalte,
That doth thynke or wene
That his conscyence be nat clene,
And feleth hymselfe sycke,
Or touched on the quycke,
1125 Suche grace God them sende
Themselfe to amende;
For I wyll nat pretende
Any man to offende.

Wherfore, as thynketh me,
1130 Great ydeottes they be,
And lytell grace they have
This treatyse to deprave;
Nor wyll here no prechynge,
Nor no vertuous techynge,
1135 Nor wyll have no resytynge
Of any vertuous wrytynge;

Wyll knowe none intellygence
To refourme theyr neglygence,
But lyve styll out of facyon,
1140   To theyr owne dampnacyon.
To do shame, they have no shame;
But they wolde no man shuld them blame.
They have an evyll name,
But yet they wyll occupye the same.

1145   With them the worde of God
Is counted for no rod;
They counte it for a raylynge
That nothynge is avaylynge;
The prechers with evyll haylynge:
1150   'Shall they taunt us prelates,
That be theyr prymates?
Nat so hardy on theyr pates!
Harke, howe the losell prates
With a wyde wesaunt!

1155   Avaunt, Syr Gye of Gaunt!
Avaunt, lewde preest, avaunt!
Avaunt, syr doctour Deuyas!
Prate of thy matens and thy mas,
And let our matters pas!
1160   How darest thou, daucocke, mell?
Howe darest thou, losell,
Allygate the gospell
Agaynst us of the counsell?
Avaunt to the devyll of hell!

1165   Take him, wardeyn of the Flete,
Set hym fast by the fete!
I say, lieutenaunt of the Toure,
Make this lurdeyne for to loure;
Lodge hym in Lytell Ease,
1170   Fede hym with beanes and pease!
The Kynges Benche or Marshalsy,
Have hym thyder by and by!
The vyllayne precheth openly
And declareth our vyllany;
1175   And of our fee symplenes
He sayes that we are recheles,

And full of wylfulnes,
Shameles, and mercyles,
Incorrigible and insaciate;
1180 And after this rate
Agaynst us dothe prate.
At Poules Crosse, or elswhere,
Openly at Westmynstere
And Saynt Mary Spytell
1185 They set nat by us a shyttell;
And at the Austen Fryars
They counte us for lyars;
And at Saynt Thomas of Akers
They carpe of us lyke crakers;
1190 Howe we wyll rule all at wyll
Without good reason or skyll;
And say howe that we be
Full of parcyallyte;
And howe at a pronge
1195 We tourne ryght into wronge,
Delay causes so longe
That ryght no man can fonge.
They say many matters be borne
By the ryght of a rambes horne.
1200 Is nat this a shamfull scorne
To be tered thus and torne?

Howe may we thus endure?
Wherfore we make you sure,
Ye prechers shall be yawde:
1205 Some shall be sawde,
As noble Isaias,
The holy prophet, was;
And some of you shall dye
Lyke holy Jeremy;
1210 Some hanged, some slayne,
Some beaten to the brayne;
And we wyll rule and rayne,
And our matters mayntayne,
Who dare say there agayne,
1215 Or who dare dysdayne,
At our pleasure and wyll.
For, be it good, be it yll,

As it is, it shall be styll,
For all maister Doctour of Cyvyll
1220   Or of Divynyte, or Doctour Dryvyll,
Let him cough, rough or snevyll!
Renne god, renne devyll,
Renne who may renne best,
And let take all the rest!
1225   We set nat a nutte shell
The way to heven or to hell!'

Lo, this is the gyse noweadayes!
It is to drede, men sayes,
Lest they be Seduces,
1230   As they be sad sayne,
Whiche determyne playne
We shulde nat ryse agayne
At dredfull Domesday.
And so it semeth they play,
1235   Whiche hate to be corrected
Whan they be infected,
Nor wyll suffre this boke
By hoke ne by croke
Prynted for to be,
1240   For that no man shulde se
Nor rede in any scrolles,
Of theyr dronken nolles,
Nor of theyr noddy polles,
Nor of theyr sely soules,
1245   Nor of some wytles pates
Of dyvers great estates,
As well as other men.
Nowe to withdrawe my pen,
And now a whyle to rest,
1250   Me semeth it for the best.

The forecastell of my shyppe
Shall glyde and smothely slyppe
Out of the wawes wodde
Of the stormy flodde,
1255   Shote anker, and lye at rode,
And sayle nat farre abrode,
Tyll the coost be clere

That the lodesterre appere.
My shyp nowe wyll I stere
1260   Towarde the porte salue
Of our Savyoure Jesu,
Suche grace that he us sende
To rectyfye and amende
Thynges that are amys,
1265   Whan that his pleasure is.

Amen

1266   *In opere imperfecto,*
In opere semper perfecto,
Et in opere plusquam perfecto.

Colinus Cloutus, 'Quanquam mea carmina multis
Sordescunt stulte, sed pneumata sunt rara cultis,
Pneumatis altisoni divino flamine flatis.
Unde mea refert tanto minus, invida quamvis
5   *Lingua nocere parat, quia, quanquam rustica canto,*
Undique cantabor tamen et celebrabor ubique,
Inclita dum maneat gens Anglica. Laurus honoris,
Quondam regnorum regina et gloria regum,
Heu, modo marcescit, tabescit, languida torpet!
10   *Ah, pudet! Ah miseret! Vetor hic ego pandere plura*
Pro gemitu et lacrimis; prestet peto premia pena.'

XX

Here after foloweth a lytell boke, whiche hath to name
Why Come Ye Nat to Courte?

compyled by Mayster Skelton, Poete Laureate

All noble men of this take hede,
And beleve it as your crede.

To hasty of sentence,
To ferce for none offence,
5   To scarce of your expence,
To large in neglygence,

    To slacke in recompence,
    To haute in excellence,
    To lyght intellegence,
10 And to lyght in credence;
    Where these kepe resydence,
    Reson is banysshed thence,
    And also dame Prudence,
    With sober Sapyence.

15 All noble men of this take hede,
    And beleve it as your crede.

    Than, without collusyon,
    Marke well this conclusyon:
    Through suche abusyon,
20 And by suche illusyon,
    Unto great confusyon
    A noble man may fall,
    And his honour appall.
    And yf ye thynke this shall
25 Not rubbe you on the gall,
    Than the devyll take all!

    All noble men of this take hede,
    And beleve it as your crede.

    Hec vates ille
30 *De quo loquntur mille.*

        Why come ye nat to court?

    For age is a page
    For the courte full unmete;
    For age can nat rage,
35 Nor basse her swete swete.
        But whan age seeth that rage
    Dothe aswage and refrayne,
    Than wyll age have a corage
    To come to court agayne.

40 But
    Helas! sage overage
    So madly decayes,
    That age for dottage

Is reconed nowadayes.
45   Thus age, (a *graunt domage*),
Is nothynge set by,
And rage in arerage
Dothe rynne lamentably.

So
50   That rage must make pyllage
To catche that catche may,
And with suche forage
Hunte the boskage,
That hartes wyll ronne away,
55   Bothe hartes and hyndes
With all good myndes.
Farewell, than, have good day!

Than have good daye. Adewe!
For defaute of rescew,
60   Some men may happely rew,
And some theyr hedes mew.
The tyme dothe fast ensew
That bales begynne to brew.
I drede, by swete Jesu,
65   This tale will be to trew:
'In faythe, Dycken, thou krew,
In fayth, Dicken, thou krew, etc.'

Dicken, thou krew doutlesse!
For trewly to expresse,
70   There hath ben moche excesse:
With banketynge braynlesse,
With ryotynge rechelesse,
With gambaudynge thryftlesse,
With, 'Spende,' and wast witlesse,
75   Treatinge of trewse restlesse,
Pratynge for peace peaslesse.
The countrynge at Cales
Wrang us on the males!
Chefe counselour was carlesse,
80   Gronynge, grouchyng, gracelesse,
And to none entente,

Our talwod is all brent,
Our fagottes are all spent.
We may blowe at the cole!
85   Our mare hath cast her fole,
And, 'Mocke hath lost her sho;
What may she do therto?'
An ende of an olde song:
'Do ryght and do no wronge.'
90   As ryght as a rammes horne!
For thrifte is threde bare worn,
Our shepe are shrewdly shorn,
And trouthe is all to-torne;
Wysdom is laught to skorne,
95   Favell is false forsworne,
Javell is nobly borne;
Havell and Harvy Hafter,
Jack Travell and Cole Crafter,
We shall here more herafter!
100   With pollynge and shavynge,
With borowynge and cravynge,
With revynge and ravynge,
With swerynge and starynge,
There vayleth no resonynge;
105   For Wyll dothe rule all thynge,
Wyll, Wyll, Wyll, Wyll, Wyll!
He ruleth alway styll.
Good Reason and good Skyll,
They may garlycke pyll,
110   Cary sackes to the myll,
Or pescoddes they may shyll,
Or elles go rost a stone!
There is no man but one
That hathe the strokes alone;
115   Be it blacke or whight
All that he dothe is ryght.
As right as a cammocke croked!
This byll well over loked,
Clerely percevye we may
120   There went the hare away;
The hare, the fox, the gray,

The harte, the hynde, the buck.
God sende us better luck!
God sende us better lucke, etc.

125   Twit, Andrewe! Twit, Scot!
Ge heme! ge scour thy pot,
For we have spente our shot!
We shall have a *tot quot*
From the Pope of Rome
130   To weve all in one lome
A webbe of lylse wulse,
Opus male dulce!
The devyll kysse his cule!
For whyles he doth rule,
135   All is warse and warse.
The devyll kysse his arse!
For whether he blesse or curse,
It can not be moche worse.
From Baumberow to Bothombar
140   We have cast up our war,
And mad a worthy trewse.
With, 'Gup, levell suse!'
Our mony madly lent,
And mor madly spent.
145   From Croydon into Kent
Wote ye whyther they went?
From Wynchelsey to Rye
And all nat worth a flye,
From Wentbridge to Hull,
150   Our armye waxeth dull,
With, 'Tourne all home agayne!'
And never a Scot slayne!
Yet the good Erle of Surray,
The Frenche men he doth fray,
155   And vexeth them day by day
With all the power he may.
The French men he hath faynted,
And mad theyr hertes attaynted.
Of chevalry he is the floure;
160   Our lorde be his soccoure!
The French men he hathe so mated,

And theyr courage abated,
That they are but halfe men;
Lyke foxes in theyr denne,
165   Lyke cankerd cowardes all,
Lyke urcheons in a stone wall,
They kepe them in theyr holdes
Lyke hen-herted cokoldes.

But yet they over-shote us
170   Wyth crownes and wyth scutus;
Wyth scutis and crownes of golde
I drede we are bought and solde.
It is a wonders warke.
They shote all at one marke:
175   At the Cardynals hat.
They shote all at that!
Oute of theyr stronge townes
They shote at him with crownes.
With crownes of golde enblased
180   They make him so amased,
And his eyen so dased,
That he ne se can
To know God nor man.
He is set so hye
185   In his ierarchy
Of frantycke frenesy
And folysshe fantasy,
That in the Chambre of Sterres
All maters there he marres,
190   Clappyng his rod on the borde.
No man dare speke a worde,
For he hathe all the sayenge
Without any renayenge.
He rolleth in his recordes,
195   He sayth, 'How saye ye, my lordes?
Is nat my reason good?'
Good evyn, good Robyn Hode!
Some say 'yes', and some
Syt styll as they were dom.
200   Thus thwartyng over thom,
He ruleth all the roste

With braggynge and with bost,
Borne up on every syde
With pompe and with pryde,
205   With, 'Trompe up!' 'Alleluya!'
For Dame Philargerya
Hathe so his herte in holde,
He loveth nothyng but golde;
And Asmodeus of hell
210   Maketh his membres swell
With Dalyda to mell,
That wanton damosell.

Adew Philosophia,
Adew Theologia.
215   Welcome dame Simonia,
With dame Castrimergia,
To drynke and for to eate
Swete ypocrus and swete meate.
To kepe his flesshe chast
220   In lent, for a repast,
He eateth capons stewed,
Fesaunt and partriche mewed,
Hennes, checkynges, and pygges.
He foynes and he frygges;
225   Spareth neither mayde ne wyfe.
This is a postels lyfe.
      Helas, my herte is sory
To tell of vayne glory;
But now upon this story
230   I wyll no further ryme
Tyll another tyme;
Tyll another tyme etc.

      What newes? What news?

Small newes that true is
235   That be worth ii kues.
But at the naked stewes
I understande how that
The Sygne of the Cardynall Hat,
That inne, is now shyt up,
240   With, 'Gup, hore, gup! Now gup,

Gup, Guilliam Travillian!'
With, 'Jast you, I say, Jullian!
Wyll ye bere no coles?'
A mayny of marefoles
245   That occupy theyr holys;
Full of pocky molys.

What here ye of Lancashyre?

They were nat payde their hyre.
They are fel as any fyre!

250   What here ye of Chesshyre?

They have layde all in the myre.
They grugyd and sayde
Theyr wages were nat payde.
Some sayde they were afrayde
255   Of the Scottysshe hoost.
For all theyr crack and bost,
Wylde fyre and thonder;
For all this worldly wonder,
A hundred myle asonder
260   They were, whan they were next.
This is a trew text!

What here ye of the Scottes?

They make us all sottes,
Poppynge folysshe dawes.
265   They make us to pyll strawes;
They play their olde pranckes
After Huntley Bankes.
At the streme of Banockesburne
They dyd us a shrewde turne,
270   Whan Edwarde of Karnarvan
Lost all his father wan.

What here ye of the lorde Dakers?

He maketh us Jack Rakers;
He sayes we ar but crakers;
275   He calleth us England men
Stronge-herted lyke an hen.

For the Scottes and he,
To well they do agre,
With, 'Do thou for me,
280   And I shall do for the.'
Whyles the red hat doth endure,
He maketh himselfe cock sure.
The red hat with his lure
Bryngeth all thynges under cure.

285   But as the worlde now gose,
What here ye of the lord Rose?

Nothynge to purpose
Nat worth a cockly fose!
Their hertes be in thyr hose!
290   The Erle of Northumberlande
Dare take nothynge on hande.
Our barons be so bolde,
Into a mouse hole they wolde
Rynne away and crepe;
295   Lyke a mayny of shepe
Dare nat loke out at dur
For drede of the mastyve cur,
For drede of the bochers dogge
Wold wyrry them lyke an hogge.
300   For and this curre do gnar,
They must stande all afar
To holde up their hande at the bar.
For all their noble blode,
He pluckes them by the hode,
305   And shakes them by the eare,
And brynges them in suche feare.
He bayteth them lyke a bere,
Lyke an oxe or a bull;
Theyr wyttes, he saith, are dull;
310   He sayth they have no brayne
Theyr astate to mayntayne;
And maketh them to bow theyr kne
Before his majeste.

Juges of the kynges lawes,
315   He countys them foles and dawes;

Sergyantes of the Coyfe eke,
He sayth, they are to seke
In pletynge of theyr case
At the Commune Place,
320   Or at the Kynges Benche.
He wryngeth them suche a wrenche,
That all our lerned men
Dare nat set theyr penne
To plete a trew tryall
325   Within Westmynster Hall.
In the Chauncery where he syttes,
But suche as he admyttes,
None so hardy to speke.
      He sayth, 'Thou huddy peke!
330   Thy lernynge is to lewde,
Thy tonge is nat well thewde,
To seke before our grace.'
And openly in that place
He rages and he raves,
335   And cals them cankerd knaves.
Thus royally he dothe deale
Under the kynges brode seale;
And in the Checker he them cheks,
In the Ster Chambre he noddis and beks,
340   And bereth him there so stowte
That no man dare rowte;
Duke, erle, baron, nor lorde,
But to his sentence must accorde.
Whether he be kynght or squyre,
345   All men must folow his desyre.

      What say ye of the Scottysh kynge?
That is another thyng.
He is but an yonglyng,
A stalworthy stryplyng.
350   There is a whyspring and a whipling
He shulde be hyder brought;
But and it were well sought,
I trow all wyll be nought,
Nat worth a shyttel-cocke,
355   Nor worth a sowre calstocke.

There goth many a lye
Of the Duke of Albany,
That of shulde go his hede,
And brought in quycke or dede,
360 And all Scotlande owers
The mountenaunce of two houres.
    But, as some men sayne,
I drede of some false trayne
Subtelly wrought shall be
365 Under a fayned treatee.
But within monethes thre
Men may happely se
The trechery and the prankes
Of the Scottysshe Bankes.

370   What here ye of Burgonyons
    And the Spainyardes onyons?

They have slain our Englisshmen
Above threscore and ten.
For all youre amyte,
375 No better they agre!
God save my Lorde Admyrell!

    What here ye of Mutrell?

Therewith I dare nat mell.

    Yet what here ye tell
380   Of our graunde counsell?

I coulde say some what,
But speke ye no more of that,
For drede of the red hat
Take peper in the nose;
385 For than thyne heed of gose.
Of! by the harde arse!
But there is some travarse
Bytwene some and some
That makys our syre to glum.
390 It is somewhat wronge
That his berde is so longe.
He morneth in blacke clothynge.

I pray God save the kynge.
Where ever he go or ryde
395   I pray God be his gyde.
Thus wyll I conclude my style,
And fall to rest a whyle;
And so to rest a whyle etc.

Ones yet agayne
400   Of you I wolde frayne
Why come ye nat to court?

To whyche court?
To the kynges courte?
Or to Hampton Court?

405   Nay, to the kynges court!
The kynges courte
Shulde have the excellence;
But Hampton Court
Hath the preemynence!
410   And Yorkes Place,
With, 'My lordes grace',
To whose magnifycence
Is all the conflewence,
Sutys, and supplycacyons,
415   Embassades of all nacyons.
Strawe for lawe canon,
Or for lawe common,
Or for lawe cyvyll;
It shall be as he wyll.
420   Stop at lawe tancrete,
An abstract or a concrete,
Be it soure, be it swete!
His wysdome is so dyscrete
That in a fume or an hete,
425   'Wardeyn of the Flete,
Set hym fast by the fete!'
And of his royall powre
Whan him lyst to lowre,
Than, 'Have him to the Towre
430   Saunz aulter remedy!
Have hym forthe by and by

To the Marshalsy,
Or to the Kynges Benche!'
He dyggeth so in the trenche
435 Of the court royall
That he ruleth them all.
So he dothe undermynde,
And suche sleyghtes dothe fynde,
That the kynges mynde
440 By him is subverted;
And so streatly coarted
In credensynge his tales,
That all is but nutshales
That any other sayth,
445 He hath in him suche fayth.

Now yet all this myght be
Suffred and taken *in gre*
If that that he wrought
To any good ende were brought.
450 But all he bringeth to nought,
By God that me dere bought!
    He bereth the kyng on hand
That he must pyll his lande
To make his cofers ryche;
455 But he laythe all in the dyche,
And useth suche abusyoun,
That in the conclusyoun
All commeth to confusyon.
Perceyve the cause why:
460 To tell the trouth playnly,
He is so ambicyous,
So shamles and so vicyous,
And so supersticyous,
And so moche oblivyous
465 From whens that he came,
That he falleth into *Acidiam*,
Whiche, truly to expresse,
Is a forgetfulnesse,
Or wylfull blyndnesse,
470 Wherwith the Sodomites

Lost theyr inward syghtes.
  The Gommoryans also
Were brought to deedly wo,
As scrypture recordis
475 *A cecitate cordis,*
In the Latyne synge we,
Lybera nos domine!
  But this madde Amalecke,
Lyke to a Mamelek,
480 He regardeth lordes
No more than potshordes.
He is in suche elacyon
Of his exaltacyon,
And the supportacyon
485 Of our soverayne lorde,
That, God to recorde,
He ruleth all at wyll
Without reason or skyll.
How be it the primordyall
490 Of his wretched originall,
And his base progeny,
And his gresy genealogy,
He came of the sank royall
That was cast out of a bochers stall!

495 But, however he was borne,
Men wolde have the lesse scorne
If he coulde consyder
His byrth and rowme togeder,
And call to his mynde
500 How noble and how kynde
To him he hathe founde
Our sovereyne lord, chyfe grounde
Of all this prelacy,
And set hym nobly
505 In great auctoryte
Out from a low degre,
Whiche he can nat se.
For he was, parde,
No doctor of devinyte,

510   Nor doctor of the law,
      Nor of none other saw;
      But a poore maister of arte!
      God wot, had lytell parte
      Of the quatrivials,
515   Or yet of trivials;
      Nor of philosophy,
      Nor of philology,
      Nor of good pollycy,
      Nor of astronomy;
520   Nor acquaynted worth a fly
      With honorable Haly,
      Nor with royall Ptholomy,
      Nor with Albumasar,
      To treate of any star
525   Fyxt or els mobyll.
      His Latyne tonge dothe hobbyll,
      He doth but cloute and cobbill
      In Tullis faculte
      Called humanyte.
530   Yet proudly he dare pretende
      How no man can him amende!
      But have ye nat harde this,
      How an one-eyed man is
      Well-syghted when
535   He is amonge blynde men?

      Than, our processe for to stable,
      This man was full unable
      To reche to suche degre,
      Had nat our prynce be
540   Royall Henry the eyght,
      Take him in suche conceyght
      That he set him on heyght,
      In exemplyfyenge
      Great Alexander the kynge,
545   In writynge as we fynde
      Whiche, of his royall mynde
      And of his noble pleasure
      Transcendynge out of mesure,
      Thought to do a thynge

550   That perteyneth to a kynge,
      To make up one of nought,
      And made to him be brought
      A wretched poore man
      Whiche his lyvenge wan
555   With plantyng of lekes
      By the dayes and by the wekes.
      And of this poore vassall
      He made a kynge royall,
      And gave him a realme to rule
560   That occupyed a showell,
      A mattoke and a spade,
      Before that he was made
      A kynge, as I have tolde,
      And ruled as he wolde.
565   Suche is a kynges power
      To make within an hower,
      And worke suche a myracle,
      That shall be a spectacle
      Of renowme and worldly fame.
570   In lykewyse now the same
      Cardynall is promoted,
      Yet with lewde condicyons cotyd
      As herafter ben notyd:
          Presumcyon and vayne glory,
575   Envy, wrath, and lechery,
      Covetys and glotony;
      Slouthfull to do good,
      Now frantick, now starke wode!
          Shulde this man of suche mode
580   Rule the swerde of myght?
      How can he do ryght?
      For he wyll as sone smyght
      His frende as his fo!
      (A proverbe longe ago.)

585   Set up a wretche on hye,
      In a trone triumphantlye,
      Make him a great astate,
      And he wyll play checke mate
      With ryall majeste

590 Counte himselfe as good as he;
A prelate potencyall
To rule under Bellyall,
As ferce and as cruell
As the fynd of hell!
595 His servauntes menyall
He dothe revyle and brall
Lyke Mahounde in a play.
No man dare him withsay.
He hath dispyght and scorne
600 At them that be well borne;
He rebukes them and rayles,
'Ye horsons, ye vassayles,
Ye knaves, ye churles sonnys,
Ye rebads nat worth two plummis!
605 Ye raynbetyn beggers rejagged,
Ye recrayed ruffyns all ragged!'
With, 'Stowpe, thou havell!
Rynne, thou javell!
Thou pevysshe pye pecked,
610 Thou losell longe necked!'
Thus dayly they be decked,
Taunted and checked,
That they are so wo
They wot not whether to go.
615   No man dare come to the speche
Of this gentell Jacke Breche,
Of what estate he be
Of spirituall dygnyte;
Nor duke of hye degre,
620 Nor marques, erle nor lorde;
Whiche shrewdly doth accorde!
    Thus he, borne so base,
All noble men shulde outface,
His countynaunce lyke a kayser.
625 'My lorde is nat at layser.
Syr, ye must tary a stounde,
Tyll better layser be founde;
And syr, ye must daunce attendaunce,
And take pacient sufferaunce,
630 For my lordes grace

Hath nowe no tyme nor space
To speke with you as yet.'
   And thus they shall syt –
Chuse them syt or flyt,
635 Stande, walke, or ryde –
And his layser abyde,
Parchaunce halfe a yere;
And yet never the nere!

   This daungerous dowsypere
640 Lyke a kynges pere!
And within this xvi yere
He wolde have ben ryght fayne
To have been a chapleyne,
And have taken ryght gret payne
645 With a poore knyght,
Whatsoever he hyght!
The chefe of his owne counsell,
They can nat well tell
Whan they with hym shulde mell,
650 He is so fyers and fell.
He rayles and he ratis,
He calleth them doddy patis;
He grynnes and he gapis
As it were Jack Napis!
655 Suche a madde bedleme
For to rewle this reame,
It is a wonders case:
That the kynges grace
Is toward hym so mynded,
660 And so farre blynded,
That he can nat parceyve
How he doth hym disceyve.
I dought, lest by sorsery
Or suche other loselry
665 As wychecraft or charmyng;
For he is the kynges derlyng
And his swete hart rote,
And is governed by this mad kote!

670 For what is a man the better
For the kynges letter?

For he wyll tere it asonder!
Wherat moche I wonder
Now suche a hoddy poule
So boldely dare controule
675   And so malapertly withstande
The kynges owne hande,
And settys nat by it a myte!
He sayth the kynge doth wryte,
And writeth he wottith nat what.
680   And yet, for all that,
The kynge his clemency
Despensyth with his demensy.

But what his grace doth thinke,
I have no pen nor inke
685   That therwith can mell.
But wele I can tell
How Frauncis Petrarke,
That moche noble clerke,
Wryteth how Charlemayn
690   Coude nat himselfe refrayne,
But was ravysht with a rage
Of a lyke dotage.
But how that came aboute,
Rede ye the story oute,
695   And ye shall fynde surely
It was by nycromansy,
By carectes and conjuracyon
Under a certayne constellacion,
And a certayne fumygacion
700   Under a stone on a golde ryng
Wrought to Charlemayn the king,
Whiche constrayned him forcebly
For to love a certayne body
Above all other inordinatly.
705   This is no fable nor no lye;
In Acon it was brought to pas,
As by myne auctor tried it was.
But let mi masters mathematical
Tell you the rest; for me they shal.

710   They have the full intellygence,
     And dare use the experyens
     In there absolute consciens
     To practique suche abolete sciens.
       For I abhore to smatter
715   Of one so devyllysshe a matter.
     But I wyll make further relacion
     Of this isagogicall colation,
     How maister Gaguine, the crownycler
     Of the feytis of war
720   That were done in Fraunce,
     Maketh remembraunce
     How Kynge Lewes of late
     Made up a great astate
     Of a poore wretchid man,
725   Wherof moche care began.
       Johannes Balua was his name
     (Myne auctor writeth the same);
     Promoted was he
     To a cardynalles dygnyte
730   By Lewes the kyng aforesayd,
     With hym so wele apayd
     That he made him his chauncelar
     To make all or to mar,
     And to rule as hym lyst;
735   Tyll he cheked at the fyst,
     And agayne all reason
     Commyted open trayson
     And against his lorde soverayn!
     Wherfore he suffred payn,
740   Was hedyd, drawen, and quarterd,
     And dyed stynkingly marterd.
       Lo, yet for all that
     He ware a cardynals hat;
     In hym was small fayth,
745   As myne auctor sayth.
     Nat for that I mene
     Suche a casuelte shulde be sene
     Or suche chaunce shulde fall
     Unto our cardynall!

750   Allmyghty God, I trust,
        Hath for him dyscust
        That of force he must
        Be faythfull, trew and just
        To our most royall kynge,
755   Chefe rote of his makynge.
        Yet it is a wyly mouse
        That can bylde his dwellinge house
        Within the cattes eare
        Withouten drede or feare!
760   It is a nyce reconynge
        To put all the governynge,
        All the rule of this lande,
        Into one mannys hande;
        One wyse mannys hede
765   May stande somwhat in stede.
        But the wyttys of many wyse
        Moche better can devyse
        By theyr cyrcumspection,
        And theyr sad dyrection,
770   To cause the commune weale
        Longe to endure in heale.
        Christ kepe King Henry the Eyght
        From trechery and dysceyght,
        And graunt him grace to know
775   The faucon from the crow,
        The wolfe from the lam;
        From whens that mastyfe cam.
        Let him never confounde
        The gentyll greyhownde.
780   Of this matter the grownde
        Is easy to expounde,
        And soone may be perceyvid
        How the warlde is conveyed.

        But harke, my frende, one worde
785   In ernest of in borde:
        Tell me nowe in this stede,
        Is maister Mewtas dede,
        The kynges Frenshe secretary
        And his untrew adversary?

790   For he sent in writynge
    To Fraunces the French kyng
    Of our maisters counsel in everithing.
    That was a peryllous rekenyng!

    Nay, nay, he is nat dede.
795   But he was so payned in the hede
    That he shall never ete more bred.
    Now he is gone to another stede
    With a bull under lead,
    By way of commissyon
800   To a straunge jurisdictyon
    Called Dymingis Dale,
    Farre by yonde Portyngale,
    And hathe his pasport to pas
    Ultra Sauromatas
805   To the devyll Syr Sathanas,
    To Pluto and Syr Bellyall,
    The devyls vycare generall,
    And to his college conventuall,
    As well calodemonyall
810   As to cacademonyall,
    To purvey for our cardynall
    A palace pontifycall
    To kepe his court provyncyall
    Upon artycles judicyall,
815   To contende and to stryve
    For his prerogatyve,
    Within that consystory
    To make sommons peremtory
    Before some prothonotory,
820   Imperyall or papall.
    Upon this matter mistycall
    I have told you part, but nat all.
    Herafter perchaunce I shall
    Make a larger memoryall
825   And a further rehersall
    And more paper I thinke to blot
    To the court why I cam not,
    Desyring you above all thynge
    To kepe you from laughynge

830 Whan ye fall to redynge
    Of this wanton scrowle.
    And pray for Mewtas sowle;
    For he is well past and gone.
    That wolde God everychone
835 Of his affynyte
    Were gone as well as he!
    Amen, amen, say ye
    Of your inward charyte;
    Amen,
840 Of your inward charyte.

    It were great rewth
    For wrytynge of trewth
    Any man shulde be
    In perplexyte
845 Of dyspleasure;
    For I make you sure,
    Where trouth is abhorde,
    It is a playne recorde
    That there wantys grace
850 In whose place
    Dothe occupy,
    Full ungracyously,
    Fals flatery,
    Fals trechery,
855 Fals brybery,
    Subtyle Sym Sly
    With madde foly.
    For who can best lye,
    He is best set by!
860 Than farewell to the,
    Welthfull Felycite;
    For prosperyte
    Away than wyll fle.
    Than must we agre
865 With poverte;
    For mysery
    With penury
    Myserably
    And wretchydly

870   Hath made askrye
      And outcry
      Folowynge the chase
      To dryve away grace.
      Yet sayst thou, per case
875   We can lacke no grace,
      For, 'my Lordes grace',
      And, 'my ladies grace',
      With, '*trey duse ase*',
      And, 'ase in the face'.
880   Some haute and some base.
      Some daunce the trace
      Ever in one case.
      Marke me that chase
      In the tennys play,
885   For, '*Synke quater trey*'
      Is a tall man.
      He rod, but we ran.
      Hay the gye and the gan!
      The gray gose is no swan;
890   The waters wax wan,
      And beggers they ban,
      And they cursed Datan
      De tribu Dan
      That this warke began
895   *Palam et clam*
      With Balak and Balam,
      The golden ram
      Of flemmyng dam,
      Sem, Japheth, or Cam.
900   But howe comme to pas
      Your cupbord that was
      Is tourned to glasse,
      From sylver to brasse,
      From golde to pewter
905   Or els to a newter,
      To copper, to tyn,
      To lede, or alcumyn?
      A goldsmyth youre mayre:
      But the chefe of your fayre
910   Myght stande now by potters,

And such as sell trotters,
Pytchars, potshordis.
This shrewdly accordis
To be a copborde for lordys!
915   My lorde now and syr knyght,
Good evyn and good nyght!
For now, Syr Trestram,
Ye must weare bukram,
Or canves of Cane,
920   For sylkes are wane.
Our royals that shone,
Our nobles are gone
Amonge the Burgonyons
And Spanyardes onyons,
925   And the Flanderkyns.
Gyll swetis and Cate spynnys!
They are happy that wynnys,
But Englande may well say
Fye on this wynnyng allway!
930   Now nothynge but 'pay, pay!'
With, 'laughe and lay downe,
Borowgh, cyte, and towne!'
Good Sprynge of Lanam
Must counte what became
935   Of his clothe makynge.
He is at suche takynge,
Though his purs wax dull,
He must tax for his wull
By nature of a newe writ.
940   My lordys grace nameth it
A 'quia non satisfacit!'
In the spyght of his tethe
He must pay agayn
A thousande or twayne
945   Of his golde in store.
And yet he payde before
An hunderd pounde and more,
Whiche pyncheth him sore!
My lordis grace wyll brynge
950   Downe this hye sprynge;

And brynge it so lowe
It shall nat ever flowe.

Suche a prelate, I trowe,
Were worthy to rowe
955 Thorow the streytes of Marock
To the gybbet of Baldock.
He wolde dry up the stremys
Of ix kinges realmys,
All ryvers and wellys,
960 All waters that swellys;
For with us he so mellys
That within Englande dwellys.
I wolde he were somwhere ellys;
For els by and by
965 He wyll drynke us so drye,
And suck us so nye,
That men shall scantly
Have peny or halpeny.
God save his noble grace,
970 And graunt him a place
Endlesse to dwell
With the devyll of hell!
For and he were there,
We nede never feere
975 Of the fendys blake;
For I undertake
He wolde so brag and crake
That he wolde than make
The devyls to quake,
980 To shudder and to shake
Lyke a fyer drake,
And with a cole rake
Brose them on a brake,
And bynde them to a stake,
985 And set hell on fyer
At his owne desyer.
He is suche a grym syer,
And suche a potestolate,
And suche a potestate,

990   That he wolde breke the braynes
      Of Lucyfer in his chaynes,
      And rule them echone
      In Lucyfers trone.
      I wolde he were gone;
995   For amonge us is none
      That ruleth but he alone,
      Without all good reason.
      And all out of season!
      For Folam peason
1000 With him be nat geson;
      They growwe very ranke
      Upon every banke
      Of his herbers grene,
      With, 'my lady bryght and shene'.
1005 Of theyr game it is sene
      They play nat all clene,
      And it be as I wene.

      But as touchynge dystrectyon,
      With sober dyrectyon
1010 He kepeth them in subjectyon.
      Non can have protectyon
      To rule nor to guyde,
      But all must be tryde,
      And abyde the correctyon
1015 Of his wylfull affectyon.
      For as for wytte,
      The devyll spede whitte!
      But braynsyk and braynlesse,
      Wytles and rechelesse,
1020 Careles and shamlesse,
      Thriftles and gracelesse
      Together are bended,
      And so condyscended,
      That the commune welth
1025 Shall never have good helth;
      But tatterd and tuggyd,
      Raggyd and ruggyd,
      Shavyn and shorne,
      And all threde bare worne!

1030 Suche gredynesse,
     Suche nedynesse,
     Myserablenesse,
     With wretchydnesse,
     Hath brought in dystresse,
1035 And moche hevynesse,
     And great dolowre
     Englande the flowre
     Of relucent honowre,
     In olde commemoracion
1040 Most royall Englyssh nacion.
     Now all is out of facion,
     Almost in desolation.
     I speke by protestacion:
     God of his miseracyon
1045 Send better reformacyon!
         Lo, for to do shamfully
     He jugeth it no foly;
     But to wryte of his shame
     He sayth we ar to blame!
1050 What a frensy is this,
     No shame to do amys;
     And yet he is ashamed
     To be shamfully named!
     And ofte prechours be blamed
1055 Bycause they have proclamed
     His madnesse by writynge,
     His symplenesse resytynge,
     Remordynge and bytynge,
     With chydyng and with flytynge,
1060 Shewynge him Goddis lawis.
     He calleth the prechours dawis.

     And of holy scriptures sawis,
     He counteth them for gygawis;
     And putteth them to sylence
1065 And with wordis of vyolence,
     Lyke Pharao, voyde of grace,
     Dyd Moyses sore manase
     And Aron sore he thret,
     The worde of God to let.

1070   This maumet in lyke wyse
        Against the churche doth ryse.
        The prechour he dothe dyspyse
        With crakynge in suche wyse,
        So braggynge all with bost
1075   That no prechour almost
        Dare speke for his lyfe
        Of my lordis grace nor his wyfe!
        For he hath suche a bull,
        He may take whom he wull,
1080   And as many as him lykys,
        May ete pigges in lent for pikys
        After the sectes of heretykis!
        For in lent he wyll ete
        All maner of flesshe mete
1085   That he can onywhere gete,
        With other abusyons grete;
        Wherof for to trete
        It wolde make the devyll to swete!
        For all privileged places
1090   He brekes and defaces,
        All placis of relygion
        He hathe them in derisyon,
        And makith suche provisyon
        To dryve them at divisyon,
1095   And fynally, in conclusyon,
        To bringe them to confusyon –
        Saint Albons, to recorde,
        Wherof this ungracyous lorde
        Hathe made himselfe abbot
1100   Against their wylles, God wot.
        All this he dothe deale
        Under strength of the great seale,
        And by his legacy,
        Whiche madly he dothe apply
1105   Unto an extravagancy,
        Pyked out of all good lawe,
        With reasons that ben rawe.
        Yet whan he toke first his hat,
        He said he knew what was what.

1110 All justyce he pretended:
      All thynges sholde be amended,
      All wronges he wolde redresse,
      All injuris he wolde represse,
      All perjuris he wolde oppresse.
1115 And yet, this gracelesse elfe,
      He is perjured himselfe.
      As playnly it dothe appere,
      Who lyst to enquere,
      In the regstry
1120 Of my lorde of Cantorbury,
      To whom he was professed
      In thre poyntes expressed:
      The fyrst, to do him reverence,
      The seconde, to owe hym obedyence,
1125 The thirde, with hole affectyon
      To be under his subjectyon.
      But now he maketh objectyon,
      Under the protectyon
      Of the kynges great seale,
1130 That he setteth never a deale
      By his former othe,
      Whether God be pleased or wroth.
      He makith so proude pretens,
      That in his equipolens
1135 He jugyth him equivalent
      With God omnipotent.
      But yet beware the rod
      And the stroke of God!
          The apostyll Peter
1140 Had but on pore myter
      And a poore cope
      Whan he was creat pope
      First in Antioche.
      He dyd never approche
1145 Of Rome to the see
      Weth suche dygnyte.
          Saynt Dunstane, what was he?
      'Nothynge,' he sayth, 'lyke to We.
      There is a dyversyte

1150 Bytwene him and me;
     We passe hym in degre
     As *legatus a latere.*'
          Ecce sacerdos magnus
     That wyll hed us and hange us,
1155 And streitly strangle us
     And he may fange us.
     Decre and decretall,
     Constytucyon provincyall,
     Nor no lawe canonicall
1160 Shall let the preest pontyficall
     To syt in *causa sanguinis.*
     Nowe God amende that is amys;
     For I suppose that he is
     Of Jeremy the whyskynge rod,
1165 The flayle, the scourge of Almighty God.
          This Naman Sirus,
     So fell and so irous,
     So full of malencoly,
     With a flap afore his eye,
1170 Men wene that he is pocky,
     Or els his surgions they lye;
     For as far as they can spy
     By the craft of surgery,
     It is *manus Domini.*
1175 And yet this proude Antiochus,
     He is so ambicious,
     So elate and so vicious,
     And so cruell hertyd,
     That he wyll nat be convertyd;
1180 For he setteth God apart.
     He is nowe so overthwart,
     And so payned with pangis,
     That all his trust hangis
     In Balthasor, whiche heled
1185 Domingos nose that was wheled.
     That Lumberdes nose meane I
     That standeth yet awrye;
     It was nat heled alderbest,
     It standeth somwhat on the west;
1190 I meane Domyngo Lomelyn

That was wont to wyn
Moche money of the kynge
At the cardys and haserdynge.
Balthasor, that helyd Domingos nose
1195 From the puskylde pocky pose,
Now with his gummys of Araby
Hath promised to hele our cardinals eye.
Yet sum surgions put a dout
Lest he wyll put it clene out,
1200 And make him lame of his neder limmes.
God sende him sorowe for his sinnes!
   Some men myght aske a question,
By whose suggestyon
I toke on hand this warke,
1205 Thus boldly for to barke?
And men lyst to harke,
And my wordes marke,
I wyll answere lyke a clerke:
For trewly and unfayned,
1210 I am forcebly constrayned
At Juvynals request
To wryght of this glorious gest,
Of this vayne gloryous best,
His fame to be encrest
1215 At every solempne feest,
Quia difficile est
Satiram non scribere.

   Contra quendam doctorem
   Suum calumpniatorem.

Now mayster doctor, howe say ye,
Whatsoever your name be?
What though ye be namelesse,
Ye shall nat escape blamelesse,
5 Nor yet shall scape shamlesse.
   Mayster doctor, in your degre,
Yourselfe madly ye overse!
Blame Juvinall, and blame nat me.
   Maister doctor *decretorum*,
10 'Omne animi vicium . . .'

As Juvinall dothe recorde,
A small defaute in a great lorde,
A lytell cryme in a great astate,
Is moche more inordinate,
15   And more horyble to beholde
Than any other a thousand folde.
Ye put to blame ye wot nere whom.
Ye may weare a cockes come,
Your fonde hed in your furred hode!
20   Holde ye your tong, ye can no goode.
And at more convenyent tyme
I may fortune for to ryme
Somwhat of your madnesse;
For small is your sadnesse
25   To put any man in lack
And say yll behynde his back,
And, my wordes marke truly,
That ye can nat byde thereby.
For *smigma non est sinamomum*
30   But *de absentibus nil nisi bonum.*
Complayne or do what ye wyll,
Of your complaynt it shall nat skyl.
This is the tenor of my byl,
A daucock ye be, and so shal be styll!

> *Sequitur epitoma*
> *De morbilloso Thoma.*
> *Nec non obsceno*
> *De Poliphemo, etc.*

Porro perbelle dissimmulatum
Illud Pandulphum, tantum legatum,
Tam formidatum nuper prelatum,
Ceu Naman Sirum nunc elongatum,
5   *In solitudine iam commoratum,*
Neapolitano morbo gravatum,
Malagmate cataplasmate stratum,
Pharmacopole ferro foratum,
Nihilo magis alleviatum,
10   *Nihilo melius aut medicatum,*
Relictis famulis ad famultatum,
Quo tollatur infamia.
Sed major patet insania.

A modo ergo ganea
15 *Abhoreat ille ganeus,*
    Dominus male creticus,
    Aptius dictus tetricus,
    Phanaticus freneticus,
    Graphicus sicut metricus
20   *Autumat.*
    Hoc genus dictaminis
    Non eget examinis
    In centiloquio,
    Nec centimetro
25 *Honorati*
    Grammatici
    Mauri.

        Decastichon virulentum
        In galeratum
        Licaonta marinum, etc.

    Progh dolor, ecce maris lupus et nequissimus ursus,
    Carnificis vitulus, Britonumque bubulcus iniquus,
    Conflatus vitulus, vel Oreb, vel Salmane, vel Zeb,
    Carduus, et crudelis Asaphque Datan reprobatus,
5   *Blandus et Acchitiphel regis, scelus omne Britannum;*
    Ecclesias qui namque Thomas confundit ubique,
    Non sacer iste Thomas, sed duro corde Goleas,
    Quem gestat mulus. Sathane, cacet, obsecro, culus
    Fundens aspaltum! Precor, hunc versum lege cautum;
10 *Asperius nichil est misero quum surget in altum.*

    Apostropha ad Londini cives, (citante mulum asino aureo
    galerato), in occursum aselli, etc.

1   *Excitat, en, asinus mulum, mirabile visu,*
    Calcibus! O vestro cives occurite aselo
    Qui regnum regemque regit, qui vestra gubernat
    Predia, divitias, nummos, gasas, spoliando!

    Dixit alludens, immo illudens, parodoxam de asino aureo
    galerato.

                    xxxiiii.

    Hec vates ille
    De quo loquntur mille.

XXI

A ryght delectable tratyse upon a goodly

Garlande or Chapelet of Laurell

by Mayster Skelton, Poete Laureat, studyously dyvysed at
Sheryfhotten Castell, in the foreste of Galtres, wherein ar
comprysyde many and dyvers solacyous and ryght
pregnant allectyues of syngular pleasure, as more at large it
doth apere in the proces folowynge.

> *Eterno mansura die dum sidera fulgent,*
> *Equora dumque tument, hec laurea nostra virebit:*
> *Hinc nostrum celebre et nomen referetur ad astra,*
> *Undique Skeltonis memorabitur alter Adonis.*

Arectyng my syght toward the zodyake,
The sygnes xii for to beholde a farre,
When Mars retrogradant reversed his bak,
Lorde of the yere in his orbicular,
5   Put up his sworde, for he cowde make no warre,
And whan Lucina plenarly did shyne,
Scorpione ascendynge degrees twyse nyne;

In place alone then musynge in my thought
How all thynge passyth as doth the somer flower,
10 On every halfe my reasons forthe I sought,
How oftyn fortune varyeth in an howre,
Now clere wether, forthwith a stormy showre;
All thynge compassyd, no perpetuyte,
But now in welthe, now in adversyte.

15 So depely drownyd I was in this dumpe,
Encraumpysshed so sore was my conceyte,
That, me to rest, I lent me to a stumpe
Of an oke, that somtyme grew full streyghte,
A myghty tre and of a noble heyght,
20 Whose bewte blastyd was with the boystors wynde,
His levis loste, the sappe was frome the rynde.

Thus stode I in the frytthy forest of Galtres,
Ensowkid with sylt of the myry wose,
Where hartis belluyng, embosyd with distres,

25   Ran on the raunge so longe, that I suppose
     Few men can tell where the hynde calfe gose.
     Faire fall that forster that so well can bate his hownde!
     But of my purpose now turne we to the grownde.

     Whylis I stode musynge in this medytatyon,
30   In slumbrynge I fell and halfe in a slepe;
     And whether it were of ymagynacyon,
     Or of humors superflue, that often wyll crepe
     Into the brayne by drynkyng over depe,
     Or it procedyd of fatall persuacyon,
35   I can not tell you what was the occasyon.

     But sodeynly at ones, as I me advysed,
     As one in a trans or in an extasy,
     I sawe a pavylyon wondersly disgysede,
     Garnysshed fresshe after my fantasy,
40   Enhachyde with perle and stones preciously,
     The grounde engrosyd and bet with bourne golde,
     That passynge goodly it was to beholde:

     Within that, a prynces excellente of porte;
     But to recounte her ryche abylyment,
45   And what estates to her did resorte,
     Therto am I full insuffycyent;
     A goddesse inmortall she dyd represente;
     As I harde say, Dame Pallas was her name,
     To whome supplyed the royall Quene of Fame.

     The Quene of Fame to Dame Pallas

50   'Prynces moost pusant, of hygh preemynence,
     Renownyd lady above the sterry hevyn,
     All other transcendyng, of very congruence
     Madame regent of the scyence sevyn
     To whos astate all noblenes most leven,
55   My supplycacyon to you I arrect,
     Whereof I beseche you to tender the effecte.

     Not unremembered it is unto your grace,
     How you gave me a ryall commaundement
     That in my courte Skelton shulde have a place,

60   Bycause that he his tyme studyously hath spent
     In your servyce; and, to the accomplysshement
     Of your request, regestred is his name
     With laureate tryumphe in the courte of Fame.

     But, good madame, the accustome and usage
65   Of auncient poetis, ye wote full wele, hath bene
     Them selfe to embesy with all there holl corage,
     So that there workis myght famously be sene,
     In figure wherof they were the laurell grene.
     But, how it is, Skelton is wonder slake,
70   And, as we dare, we fynde in hym grete lake:

     For, ne were onely he hath your promocyon,
     Out of my bokis full sone I shulde hym rase;
     But sith he hath tastid of the sugred pocioun
     Of Elyconis well, refresshid with your grace,
75   And wyll not endevour hymselfe to purchase
     The favour of ladys with wordis electe,
     It is sittynge that ye must hym correct.'

Dame Pallas to the Quene of Fame

     'The sum of your purpose, as we ar advysid,
     Is that our servaunt is sum what to dull;
80   Wherin this answere for hym we have comprisid,
     How ryvers rin not tyll the spryng be full;
     Bete a dum mouthe than a brainles scull;
     For if he gloryously publisshe his matter,
     Then men wyll say how he doth but flatter.

85   And if so hym fortune to wryte true and plaine,
     As sumtyme he must vyces remorde,
     Then sum wyll say he hath but lyttil brayne,
     And how his wordes with reason wyll not accorde.
     Beware, for wrytyng remayneth of recorde!
90   Displease not an hundreth for one mannes pleasure.
     Who wryteth wysely hath a grete treasure.

     Also, to furnisshe better his excuse,
     Ovyde was bannisshed for suche a skyll,
     And many mo whome I cowde enduce;

95　Juvenall was thret, parde, for to kyll
　　For certayne envectyfys, yet wrote he none ill,
　　Savynge he rubbid sum on the gall.
　　It was not for hym to abyde the tryall.

　　In generrall wordes, I say not gretely nay,
100　A poete somtyme may for his pleasure taunt,
　　Spekyng in paroblis, how the fox, the grey,
　　The gander, the gose, and the hudge oliphaunt,
　　Went with the pecok ageyne the fesaunt;
　　The lesarde came lepyng, and sayd that he must,
105　With helpe of the ram, ley all in the dust.

　　Yet dyverse ther be, industryous of reason,
　　Sum what wolde gadder in there conjecture
　　Of suche an endarkid chapiter sum season.
　　How be it, it were harde to construe this lecture;
110　Sophisticatid craftely is many a confecture;
　　Another manes mynde diffuse is to expounde;
　　Yet harde is to make but sum fawt be founde.'

The Quene of Fame to Dame Pallas

　　'Madame, with favour of your benynge sufferaunce,
　　Unto your grace then make I this motyve:
115　Whereto made ye me hym to avaunce
　　Unto the rowme of laureat promotyve?
　　Or wherto shulde he have the prerogatyve,
　　But if he had made sum memoryall,
　　Wherby he myght have a name inmortall?

120　To pas the tyme in slowthfull ydelnes,
　　Of your royall palace it is not the gyse,
　　But to do sumwhat iche man doth hym dres
　　For how shulde Cato els be callyd wyse,
　　But that his bokis, whiche he did devyse,
125　Recorde the same? Or why is had in mynde
　　Plato, but for that he left wrytynge behynde,

　　For men to loke on? Aristotille also,
　　Of phylosophers callid the princypall,
　　Olde Diogenes, with other many mo,

130   Dymostenes, that oratour royall,
      That gave Eschines suche a cordyall,
      That banisshed was he by his proposicyoun,
      Ageyne whom he cowde make no contradiccyoun?'

Dame Pallas to the Quene of Fame

      'Soft, my good syster, and make there a pawse.
135   And was Eschines rebukid as ye say?
      Remembre you wele, poynt wele that clause,
      Wherfore then rasid ye not away
      His name? Or why is it, I you praye,
      That he to your courte is goyng and commynge,
140   Sith he is slaundred for defaut of konnyng?'

The Quene of Fame to Dame Pallas

      'Madame, your apposelle is wele inferrid,
      And at your avauntage quikly it is
      Towchid, and hard for to be barrid.
      Yet shall I answere your grace as in this,
145   With your reformacion, if I say amis,
      For, but if your bounte did me assure,
      Myne argument els koude not longe endure.

      As towchyng that Eschines is remembred,
      That he so sholde be, me semith it sittyng,
150   All be it grete parte he hath surrendred
      Of his onour, whos dissuasyve in wrytyng
      To corage Demostenes was moche excitynge,
      In settyng out fresshely his crafty persuacyon,
      From whiche Eschines had none evacyon.

155   The cause why Demostenes so famously is brutid
      Onely procedid for that he did outray
      Eschines, whiche was not shamefully confutid
      But of that famous oratour, I say,
      Whiche passid all other; wherfore I may
160   Among my recordes suffer hym namyd,
      For though he were venquesshid, yet was he not shamyd:

      As Jerome, in his preamble *Frater Ambrosius*,
      Frome that I have sayde in no poynt doth vary,

Wherein he reporteth of the coragius
165 Wordes that were moch consolatory
By Eschines rehersed to the grete glory
Of Demostenes, that was his utter foo.
Few shall ye fynde or none that wyll do so.'

Dame Pallas to the Quene of Fame

'A thanke to have, ye have well deservyd,
170 Your mynde that can maynteyne so apparently;
But a grete parte yet ye have reservyd
Of that most folow then consequently,
Or els ye demeane you inordinatly;
For if ye laude hym whome honour hath opprest,
175 Then he that doth worste is as good as the best.

But whome that ye favoure, I se well, hath a name,
Be he never so lytell of substaunce,
And whome ye love not ye wyll put to shame.
Ye counterway not evynly your balaunce;
180 As wele foly as wysdome oft ye do avaunce,
For reporte ryseth many deverse wayes.
Sume be moche spokyn of for makynge of frays;

Some have a name for thefte and brybery;
Some be called crafty that can pyke a purse;
185 Some men be made of for the mokery;
Some carefull cokwoldes, some have theyr wyves curs;
Some famous wetewoldis, and they be moche wurs;
Some lidderons, some losels, some noughty packis;
Some facers, some bracers, some make great crackis;

190 Some dronken dastardis with their dry soules;
Some sluggysh slovyns, that slepe day and nyght;
Ryot and Revell be in your courte rowlis;
Maintenaunce and Mischefe, theis be men of myght;
Extorcyon is counted with you for a knyght;
195 Theis people by me have none assignement,
Yet they ryde and rinne from Carlyll to Kent.

But lytell or nothynge ye shall here tell
Of them that have vertue by reason of cunnyng,
Whiche soverenly in honoure shulde excell;

200   Men of suche maters make but mummynge,
      For wysdome and sadnesse be out a sunnyng;
      And suche of my servauntes as I have promotyd,
      One faute or other in them shalbe notyd.

      Eyther they wyll say he is to wyse,
205   Or elles he can nought bot whan he is at scole;
      "Prove his wytt", sayth he, "at cardes or dyce,
      And ye shall well fynde he is a very fole;
      Twyse! set hym a chare, or reche hym a stol
      To syt hym upon, and rede Jacke a thrummis bybille,
210   For truly it were a pyte that he sat ydle."

The Quene of Fame to Dame Pallas

      'To make repugnaunce agayne that ye have sayde,
      Of very dwte it may not well accorde,
      But your benynge sufferaunce for my discharge I laid,
      For that I wolde not with you fall at discorde.
215   But yet I beseche your grace that good recorde
      May be brought forth, such as can be founde,
      With laureat tryumphe why Skelton sholde be crownde.

      For elles it were to great a derogacyon
      Unto your palas, our noble courte of Fame,
220   That any man under supportacyon
      Withoute deservynge shulde have the best game.
      If he to the ample encrease of his name
      Can lay any werkis that he hath compylyd,
      I am content that he be not exylide

225   Frome the laureat senate by force of proscripcyon.
      Or elles, ye know well, I can do no lesse
      But I most bannysshe hym frome my jurydiccyon,
      As he that aquentyth hym with ydilnes.
      But if that he purpose to make a redresse,
230   What he hath done, let it be brought to syght.
      Graunt my petycyon, I aske you but ryght.'

Dame Pallas to the Quene of Fame

      'To your request we be well condiscendid;
      Call forthe, let se where is your clarionar,

To blowe a blaste with his long breth extendid;
235 Eolus, your trumpet, that knowne is so farre,
That *bararag* blowyth in every mercyall warre,
Let hym blowe now, that we may take a vewe
What poetis we have at our retenewe.

To se if Skelton wyll put hymselfe in prease
240 Amonge the thickeste of all the hole rowte,
Make noyse enoughe; for claterars love no peas.
Let se, my syster, now spede you, go aboute.
Anone, I sey, this trumpet were founde out,
And for no man hardely let hym spare
245 To blowe *bararag* tyll bothe his eyne stare.'

Skelton Poeta

Forthwith there rose amonge the thronge
A wonderfull noyse, and on every syde
They presid in faste; some thought they were to longe;
Sume were to hasty and wold no man byde;
250 Some whispred, some rownyd, some spake, and some cryde,
With hevynge and shovynge, 'have in' and 'have oute';
Some ranne the nexte way, sume ranne abowte.

There was suyng to the Quene of Fame;
He plucked hym backe, and he went afore.
255 'Nay, holde thy tunge,' quod another, 'let me have the name.'
'Make rowme,' sayd another, 'ye prese all to sore.'
Sume sayd, 'Holde thy peas, thou getest here no more.'
A thowsande thowsande I sawe on a plumpe.
With that I harde the noyse of a trumpe,

260 That longe tyme blewe a full timorous blaste,
Lyke to the boryall wyndes whan they blowe,
That towres and townes and trees downe caste,
Drove clowdes together lyke dryftis of snowe.
The dredefull dinne drove all the rowte on a rowe;
265 Some tremblid, some girned, some gaspid, some gasid,
As people halfe pevysshe, or men that were masyd.

Anone all was whyste, as it were for the nonys,
And iche man stode gasyng and staryng upon other.
With that there come in wonderly at ones

270 A murmer of mynstrels, that suche another
     Had I never sene, some softer, some lowder;
     Orpheus, the Traciane, herped meledyously
     Weth Amphion, and other musis of Archady

     Whos hevenly armony was so passynge sure,
275 So truely proporsionyd, and so well did gree,
     So duly entunyd with every mesure,
     That in the forest was none so great a tre
     But that he daunced for joye of that gle.
     The huge myghty okes them selfe dyd avaunce,
280 And lepe frome the hylles to lerne for to daunce;

     In so moche the stumpe, whereto I me lente
     Sterte all at ones an hundrethe fote backe.
     With that I sprange up towarde the tent
     Of noble Dame Pallas, wherof I spake;
285 Where I sawe come after, I wote, full lytell lake
     Of a thousande poetes assembled togeder.
     But Phebus was formest of all that cam theder;

     Of laurell levis a cronell on his hede,
     With heris encrisped yalowe as the golde,
290 Lamentyng Daphnes, whome with the darte of lede
     Cupyde hath stryken so that she ne wolde
     Concente to Phebus to have his herte in holde,
     But, for to preserve her maidenhode clene,
     Transformyd was she into the laurell grene.

295 Meddelyd with murnynge the moost parte of his muse,
     'O thoughtfull herte,' was evermore his songe!
     'Daphnes, my derlynge, why do you me refuse?
     Yet loke on me, that lovyd you have so longe,
     Yet have compassyon upon my paynes stronge.'
300 He sange also how, the tre as he did take
     Betwene his armes, he felt her body quake.

     Then he assurded into his exclamacyon
     Unto Diana, the goddes inmortall,
     'O mercyles madame, hard is your constellacyon,
305 So close to kepe your cloyster virgynall,
     Enhardid adyment the sement of your wall!
     Alas, what ayle you to be so overthwhart,
     To banysshe pyte out of a maydens harte?

Why have the goddes shewyd me this cruelte,
310   Sith I contryvyd first princyples medycynable?
I helpe all other of there infirmite,
But now to helpe myselfe I am not able.
That profyteth all other is nothynge profytable
Unto me; alas, that herbe nor gresse
315   The fervent axes of love can not represse!

O fatall Fortune, what have I offendid?
Odious Disdayne, why raist thou me on this facyon?
But sith I have lost now that I entended,
And may not atteyne it by no medyacyon,
320   Yet, in remembraunce of Daphnes transformacyon,
All famous poetis ensuynge after me
Shall were a garlande of the laurell tre.'

This sayd, a great nowmber folowyd by and by
Of poetis laureat of many dyverse nacyons;
325   Parte of there names I thynke to specefye:
Fyrst, olde Quintiliane with his Declamacyons;
Theocritus with his bucolycall relacyons;
Esiodus, the iconomicar,
And Homerus, the fresshe historiar;

330   Prynce of eloquence, Tullius Cicero,
With Salusty ageinst Lucius Catelyne,
That wrote the history of Jugurta also;
Ovyde, enshryned with the musis nyne;
But blessed Bacchus, the pleasant god of wyne,
335   Of closters engrosyd with his ruddy flotis
These orators and poetes refresshed there throtis.

Lucan, with Stacius in Achilliedos;
Percius presed forth with problemes diffuse;
Virgill the Mantuan, with his Eneidos;
340   Juvenall satirray, that men makythe to muse;
But blessed Bacchus, the pleasant god of wyne,
Of clusters engrosed with his ruddy flotes
These orators and poetes refreshed their throtes.

There Titus Lyvius hymselfe dyd avaunce
345   With decadis historious, whiche that he mengith
With maters that amount the Romayns in substaunce;
Enyus that wrate of mercyall war at lengthe;

But blessyd Bachus, potenciall god of strengthe,
Of clusters engrosid with his ruddy flotis
350   Theis orators and poetis refresshed there throtis.

Aulus Gelius, that noble historiar;
Orace also with his new poetry;
Mayster Terence, the famous comicar,
With Plautus, that wrote full many a comody;
355   But blessyd Bachus was in there company,
Of clusters engrosyd with his ruddy flotis
Their orators and poetis refresshed there throtis.

Senek full soberly with his tragediis;
Boyce recounfortyd with his philosophy;
360   And Maxymyane, with his madde ditiis,
How dotynge age wolde jape with yonge foly;
But blessyd Bachus most reverent and holy,
Of clusters engrosid with his ruddy flotis
Theis orators and poetis refresshed there throtis.

365   There came Johnn Bochas with his volumys grete;
Quintus Cursius, full craftely that wrate
Of Alexander; and Macrobius that did trete
Of Scipions dreme what was the treu probate;
But blessyd Bachus that never man forgate,
370   Of clusters engrosed with his ruddy flotis
These orators and poetis refresshid ther throtis.

Poggeus also, that famous Florentine,
Mustred ther amonge them with many a mad tale;
With a frere of Fraunce men call Sir Gagwyne,
375   That frownyd on me full angerly and pale;
But blessyd Bachus, that bote is of all bale,
Of clusters engrosyd with his ruddy flotis
Theis orators and poetis refresshid there throtis.

Plutarke and Petrarke, two famous clarkis;
380   Lucilius and Valerius Maximus by name;
With Vincencius *in Speculo*, that wrote noble warkis;
Propercius and Pisandros, poetis of noble fame;
But blissed Bachus, that mastris oft doth frame,
Of clusters engrosed with his ruddy flotis
385   Theis notable poetis refresshid there throtis.

And as I thus sadly amonge them avysid,
I saw Gower, that first garnisshed our Englysshe rude,
And maister Chaucer, that nobly enterprysyd
How that our Englysshe myght fresshely be ennewed;
390   The monke of Bury then after them ensuyd,
Dane Johnn Lydgate. Theis Englysshe poetis thre,
As I ymagenyd, repayrid unto me,

Togeder in armes, as brethern, enbrasid;
There apparell farre passynge beyonde that I can tell;
395   With diamauntis and rubis there tabers were trasid,
None so ryche stones in Turkey to sell;
Thei wantid nothynge but the laurell;
And of there bounte they made me godely chere
In maner and forme as ye shall after here.

Mayster Gower to Skelton

400   'Brother Skelton, your endevorment
So have ye done, that meretoryously
Ye have deservyd to have an enplement
In our collage above the sterry sky,
Bycause that ye encrese and amplyfy
405   The brutid Britons of Brutus Albion,
That welny was loste when that we were gone.'

Poeta Skelton to Maister Gower

'Maister Gower, I have nothyng deserved
To have so laudabyle a commendacion:
To yow thre this honor shalbe reserved
410   Arrectinge unto your wyse examinacion
How all that I do is under refformation,
For only the substance of that I entend,
Is glad to please, and loth to offend.'

Mayster Chaucer to Skelton

'Counterwayng your besy delygence
415   Or that we beganne in the supplement,
Enforcid ar we you to recompence,

Of all our hooll collage by the agreament,
That we shall brynge you personally present
Of noble Fame before the Quenes grace,
420 In whose court poynted is your place.'

Poeta Skelton answeryth

'O noble Chaucer, whos pullisshyd eloquence
Oure Englysshe rude so fresshely hath set out,
That bounde ar we with all deu reverence,
With all our strength that we can brynge about,
425 To owe to yow our servyce, and more if we mowte!
But what sholde I say? Ye wote what I entende,
Whiche glad am to please, and loth to offende'

Mayster Lydgate to Skelton

'So am I preventid of my brethern tweyne
In rendrynge to you thankkis meritory,
430 That welny nothynge there doth remayne
Wherwith to geve you my regraciatory,
But that I poynt you to be prothonotary
Of Fames court, by all our holl assent
Avaunced by Pallas to laurell preferment.'

Poeta Skelton answeryth

435 'So have ye me far passynge my meretis extollyd,
Mayster Lidgate, of your accustomable
Bownte, and so gloryously ye have enrollyd
My name, I know well, beyonde that I am able,
That but if my warkes therto be agreable,
440 I am elles rebukyd of that I intende,
Which glad am to please, and lothe to offende.'

So finally, when they had shewyd there devyse,
Under the forme as I sayd tofore,
I made it straunge, and drew bak ones or twyse,
445 And ever they presed on me more and more,
Tyll at the last they forcyd me sore,
That with them I went where they wolde me brynge,
Unto the pavylyon where Pallas was syttyng.

Dame Pallas commaundid that they shold me convay
450   Into the ryche palace of the Quene of Fame:
'There shal he here what she wyl to hym say
When he is callid to answere to his name.'
A cry anone forthwith she made proclame,
All orators and poetis shulde thider go before,
455   With all the prese that there was lesse and more.

Forthwith, I say, thus wandrynge in my thought,
How far it was, or ellis within what howris,
I can nat tell you, but that I was brought
Into a palace with turrettis and towris,
460   Engolerid goodly with hallis and bowris,
So curiously, so craftely, so connyngly wrowght,
That all the worde, I trowe, and it were sought,

Suche an other there coude no man fynde;
Wherof partely I purpose to expounde,
465   Whyles it remanyth fresshe in my mynde.
With turkis and grossolitis enpavyd was the grounde;
Of birrall enbosid wer the pyllers rownde;
Of elephantis tethe were the palace gatis,
Enlosenged with many goodly platis

470   Of golde, entachid with many a precyous stone;
An hundred steppis mountyng to the halle,
One of jasper, another of whalis bone;
Of dyamauntis pointed was the wall;
The carpettis within and tappettis of pall;
475   The chambres hangid with clothes of arace;
Envawtyd with rubies the vawte was of this place.

Thus passid we forth walkynge unto the pretory
Where the postis wer enbulyoned with saphiris indy blew,
Englasid glittering with many a clere story;
480   Jacinctis and smaragdis out of the florthe they grew.
Unto this place all poetis there did sue,
Wherin was set of Fame the noble Quene,
All other transcendynge, the most rychely besene,

Under a gloryous cloth of astate,
485   Fret all with orient perlys of garnate,
Encrownyd as empresse of all this wordly fate,
So ryally, so rychely, so passyngly ornate,

It was excedyng byyonde the commowne rate.
This hous envyrowne was a myle about;
490   If xii were let in, xii hundreth stode without.

Then to this lady and soverayne of this palace
Of pursevantis ther presid in with many a dyverse tale:
Some were of Poyle, and sum were of Trace,
Of Lymerik, of Loreine, of Spayne, of Portyngale,
495   Frome Napuls, from Navern, and from Rouncevall,
Some from Flaunders, sum from the se coste,
Some from the mayne lande, some fro the Frensche hoste;

With, 'How doth the north?' 'What tydingis in the sowth?'
'The west is wyndy.' 'The est is metely wele.'
500   It is harde to tell of every mannes mouthe:
'A slipper holde the taile is of an ele'
And 'He haltith often that hath a kyby hele.'
Some shewid his salfe cundight, some shewid his charter,
Some lokyd full smothely, and had a fals quarter,

505   With, 'Sir, I pray you, a lytyll tyme stande backe,
And lette me come to delyver my lettre.'
Another tolde how shyppes wente to wrak.
There were many wordes smaller and gretter,
With, 'I as good as thou, ifayth, and no better.'
510   Some came to tell treuth, some came to lye,
Some came to flater, some came to spye.

There were, I say, of all maner of sortis,
Of Dertmouth, of Plummouth, of Portismouth also;
The burgeis and the ballyvis of the v portis,
515   With, 'Now let me come', and 'Now let me go.'
And all tyme wandred I thus to and fro,
Tyll at the last theis noble poetis thre
Unto me sayd, 'Lo, syr, now ye may se

Of this high courte the daylÿ besines;
520   From you most we, but not longe to tary.
Lo, hither commyth a goodly maystres,
Occupacyon, Famys regestary,
Whiche shall be to you a sufferayne accessary,
With syngular pleasurs to dryve away the tyme,
525   And we shall se you ageyne or it be pryme.'

When they were past and wente forth on there way,
This gentilwoman, that callyd was by name
Occupacyon, in ryght goodly aray,
Came towarde me, and smylid halfe in game;
530 I sawe hir smyle, and I then did the same.
With that on me she kest her goodly loke.
Under her arme, me thought, she hade a boke.

Occupacyoun to Skelton

'Lyke as the larke, upon the somers day,
Whan Titan radiant burnisshith his bemis bryght,
535 Mountith on hy with her melodious lay,
Of the soneshyne engladid with the lyght,
So am I supprysyd with pleasure and delyght
To se this howre now, that I may say,
How ye ar welcome to this court of aray.

540 Of your acqueintaunce I was in tymes past,
Of studyous doctryne when at the port salu
Ye fyrste aryvyd; whan broken was your mast
Of worldly trust, then did I you rescu;
Your storme dryven shyppe I repared new,
545 So well entakeled, what wynde that ever blowe,
No stormy tempeste your barge shall overthrow.

Welcome to me as hertely as herte can thynke!
Welcome to me with all my hole desyre!
And for my sake spare neyther pen nor ynke;
550 Be well assurid I shall aquyte your hyre,
Your name recountynge beyonde the lande of Tyre,
From Sydony to the mount Olympyan,
Frome Babill towre to the hillis Caspian.'

Skelton Poeta answeryth

I thanked her moche of her most noble offer,
555 Affyaunsynge her myne hole assuraunce
For her pleasure to make a large profer,
Enpryntyng her wordes in my remembraunce,
To owe her my servyce with true perseveraunce.

'Come on with me,' she sayd, 'let us not stonde';
560 And with that worde she toke me by the honde.

So passyd we forthe into the forsayd place,
With suche communycacyon as came to our mynde;
And then she sayd, 'Whylis we have tyme and space
To walke where we lyst, let us somwhat fynde
565 To pas the tyme with, but let us wast no wynde,
For ydle jangelers have but lytill braine;
Wordes be swordes, and hard to call ageine.'

Into a felde she brought me wyde and large,
Enwallyd aboute with the stony flint,
570 Strongly enbateld, moche costious of charge.
To walke on this walle she bed I sholde not stint;
'Go softly,' she sayd, 'the stones be full glint.'
She went before, and bad me take good holde;
I sawe a thowsande yatis new and olde.

575 Then questionyd I her what thos yatis ment;
Wherto she answeryd, and brevely me tolde
How from the est unto the occident,
And from the sowth unto the north so colde,
'Theis yatis,' she sayd, 'which that ye beholde,
580 Be issuis and portis from all maner of nacyons';
And seryously she shewyd me ther denominacyons.

They had wrytyng, sum Greke, sum Ebrew,
Some Romaine letters, as I understode;
Some were olde wryten, sum were writen new,
585 Some carectis of Caldy, sum Frensshe was full good;
But one gate specyally, where as I stode,
Had gravin in it of calcydony a capytall A.
'What yate call ye this?' And she sayd, 'Anglea'.

The beldynge therof was passynge commendable;
590 Wheron stode a lybbard, crownyd with golde and stones,
Terrible of countenaunce and passynge formydable,
As quikly towchyd as it were flesshe and bones,
As gastly that glaris, as grimly that gronis,
As fersly frownynge as he had ben fyghtyng,
595 And with his forme foote he shoke forthe this wrytyng:

Formidanda nimis Jovis ultima fulmina tollis:
Unguibus ire parat loca singula livida curvis
Quam modo per Phebas nummos raptura Celeno;
Arma, lues, luctus, fel, vis, fraus, barbara tellus;
600 *Mille modis erras odium tibi querere Martis;*
Spreto spineto cedat saliunca roseto.

Then I me lent, and loked over the wall:
Innumerable people presed to every gate.
Shet were the gatis; thei might wel knock and cal,
605 And turne home ageyne, for they cam al to late.
I her demaunded of them and ther astate.
'Forsothe,' quod she, 'theys be haskardis and rebawdis,
Dysers, carders, tumblars with gambawdis,

Furdrers of love, with baudry aqueinted,
610 Brainles blenkardis that blow at the cole,
Fals forgers of mony, for kownnage atteintid,
Pope holy ypocrytis, as they were golde and hole,
Powle hatchettis, that prate wyll at every ale pole,
Ryot, reveler, railer, brybery, theft,
615 With other condycyons that well myght be left.

Sume fayne themselfe folys, and wolde be callyd wyse,
Sum medelynge spyes, by craft to grope thy mynde,
Sum dysdanous dawcokkis that all men dispyse,
Fals flaterers that fawne the, and kurris of kynde
620 That speke fayre before the and shrewdly behynde.
Hither they come crowdyng to get them a name,
But hailid they be homwarde with sorow and shame.

With that I herd gunnis russhe out at ones,
Bowns, bowns, bowns! that all they out cryde.
625 It made sum lympe-legged and broisid there bones;
Sum were made pevysshe, porisshly pynk iyde,
That ever more after by it they were aspyid;
And one ther was there, I wondred of his hap,
For a gun stone, I say, had all to-jaggid his cap,

630 Raggid, and daggid, and cunnyngly cut;
The blaste of the brynston blew away his brayne;
Masid as a Marche hare, he ran lyke a scut.
And, sir, amonge all me thought I saw twaine,

The one was a tumblar, that afterwarde againe
635 Of a dysour, a devyl way, grew a jentilman,
Pers Prater, the secund, that quarillis beganne;

With a pellit of pevisshenes they had suche a stroke,
That all the dayes of ther lyfe shall styck by ther rybbis.
Foo, foisty bawdias, sum smellid of the smoke.
640 I saw dyvers that were cariid away thens in cribbis,
Dasyng after dotrellis, lyke drunkardis that dribbis;
Theis titivyllis with taumpinnis wer towchid and tappid;
Moche mischefe, I hyght you, amonge theem ther happid.

Sometyme, as it semyth, when the mone light
645 By meanys of a grosely endarkyd clowde
Sodenly is eclipsid in the wynter night,
In lyke maner of wyse a myst did us shrowde;
But wele may ye thynk I was no thyng prowde
Of that aventuris, whiche made me sore agast.
650 In derkenes thus dwelt we, tyll at the last

The clowdis gan to clere, the myst was rarifiid;
In an herber I saw, brought where I was,
There birdis on the brere sange on every syde,
With alys ensandid about in compas,
655 The bankis enturfid with singular solas,
Enrailid with rosers, and vinis engrapid;
It was a new comfort of sorowis escapid.

In the middis a coundight, that coryously was cast,
With pypes of golde engusshing out stremes;
660 Of cristall the clerenes theis waters far past,
Enswymmyng with rochis, barbellis and bremis,
Whose skales ensilvred again the son beames
Englisterd, that joyous it was to beholde.
Then furthermore aboute me my syght I revolde,

665 Where I saw growyng a goodly laurell tre,
Enverdurid with levis contynually grene;
Above, in the top, a byrde of Araby,
Men call a phenix; her wynges bytwene
She bet up a fyre with the sparkis full kene
670 With braunches and bowghis of the swete olyve,
Whos flagraunt flower was chefe preservatyve

Ageynst all infeccyons with cancour enflamyd,
Ageynst all baratows broisiours of olde,
It passid all bawmys that ever were namyd,
675 Or gummis of Saby so derely that be solde.
There blew in that gardynge a soft piplyng colde
Enbrethyng of Zepherus with his pleasant wynde;
All frutis and flowris grew there in there kynde.

Dryades there daunsid upon that goodly soile,
680 With the nyne Muses, Pierides by name;
Phillis and Testalis, ther tressis with oyle
Were newly enbybid; and rownd about the same
Grene tre of laurell moche solacyous game
They made, with chapellettes and garlandes grene;
685 And formest of all dame Flora, the quene

Of somer, so formally she fotid the daunce.
There Cintheus sat twynklyng upon his harpe stringis;
And Iopas his instrument did avaunce,
The poemis and storis auncient inbryngis
690 Of Athlas astrology, and many noble thyngis,
Of wandryng of the mone, the course of the sun,
Of men and of bestis, and whereof they begone,

What thynge occasionyd the showris of rayne,
Of fyre elementar in his supreme spere,
695 And of that pole artike whiche doth remayne
Behynde the taile of Ursa so clere;
Of Pliades he prechid with ther drowsy chere,
Immoysturid with mislyng and ay droppyng dry,
And where the two Trions a man shold aspy,

700 And of the winter days that hy them so fast,
And of the wynter nyghtes that tary so longe,
And of the somer days so longe that doth last,
And of their shorte nyghtes; he browght in his songe
How wronge was no ryght, and ryght was no wronge;
705 There was counteryng of carollis in meter and verse
So many, that longe it were to reherse.

Occupacyon to Skelton

'How say ye? Is this after your appetite?

May this contente you and your mirry mynde?
Here dwellith pleasure, with lust and delyte;
710 Contynuall comfort here ye may fynde,
Of welth and solace no thynge left behynde;
All thynge convenable here is contryvyd
Wherewith your spiritis may be revyvid.'

Poeta Skelton answeryth

'Questionles no dowte of that ye say;
715 Jupiter hymselfe this lyfe myght endure;
This joy excedith all wordly sport and play,
Paradyce this place is of syngular pleasure.
O wele were hym that herof myght be sure,
And here to inhabite and ay for to dwell!
720 But, goodly maystres, one thynge ye me tell.'

Occupacyon to Skelton

'Of your demawnd shew me the content,
What it is, and where upon it standis;
And if there be in it any thyng ment,
Wherof the answere restyth in my handis,
725 It shall be losyd ful sone out of the bandis
Of scrupulus dout. Wherfore, your mynde discharge,
And of your wyll the plainnes shew at large.'

Poeta Skelton answeryth

'I thanke you, goodly maystres, to me most benynge,
That of your bounte so well have me assurid;
730 But my request is not so great a thynge,
That I ne force what though it be discurid.
I am not woundid but that I may be cured.
I am not ladyn of liddyrnes with lumpis,
As dasid doterdis that dreme in their dumpis.'

Occupacyon to Skelton

735 'Now what ye mene, I trow I conject.
Gog gyve you good yere, ye make me to smyle.

Now, by your faith, is not this theffect
Of your questyon ye make all this whyle
To understande who dwellyth in yone pile,
740 And what blunderar is yonder that playth didil diddil?
He fyndith fals mesuris out of his fonde fiddill.'

Interpolata, que industriosum postulat interpretem, satira in
vatis adversarium.

Tressis agasonis species prior, altera Davi:
Aucupium culicis, limis dum torquet ocellum,
Concipit, aligeras rapit, appetit, aspice, muscas!
745 *Maia queque fovet, fovet aut que Juppiter, aut que*
Frigida Saturnus, Sol, Mars, Venus, algida Luna,
Si tibi contingat verbo aut committere scripto,
Quam sibi mox tacita sudant precordia culpa!
Hinc ruit in flammas, stimulans hunc urget et illum,
750 *Invocat ad rixas, vanos tamen excitat ignes,*
Labra movens tacitus, rumpantur ut ilia Codro.

    17. 4. 7. 2. 17. 5. 18.
    18. 19. 1. 19. 8. 5. 12.

His name for to know if that ye lyst,
Envyous Rancour truely he hight.
Beware of hym, I warne you; for and ye wist
755 How daungerous it were to stande in his lyght,
Ye wolde not dele with hym, thowgh that ye myght,
For by his devellysshe drift and graceles provision
An hole reame he is able to set at devysion:

For when he spekyth fayrest, then thynketh he moost yll;
760 Full gloryously can he glose, thy mynde for to fele;
He wyll set men a feightynge and syt hymselfe styll,
And smerke, lyke a smythy kur, at sperkes of steile;
He can never leve warke whylis it is wele.
To tell all his towchis it were to grete wonder;
765 The devyll of hell and he be seldome asonder.'

Thus talkyng we went forth in at a postern gate.
Turnyng on the ryght hande, by a windyng stayre,
She brought me to a goodly chaumber of astate,
Where the noble Cowntes of Surrey in a chayre

770 Sat honorably, to whome did repaire
  Of ladys a beve with all dew reverence:
  'Syt downe, fayre ladys, and do your diligence!

  Come forth, jentylwomen, I pray you,' she sayd,
  'I have contryvyd for you a goodly warke,
775 And who can worke beste now shall be asayde;
  A cronell of lawrell with verduris light and darke
  I have devysyd for Skelton, my clerke;
  For to his servyce I have suche regarde,
  That of our bownte we wyll hym rewarde:

780 For of all ladyes he hath the library,
  Ther names recountyng in the court of Fame;
  Of all gentylwomen he hath the scruteny,
  In Fames court reportyng the same;
  For yet of women he never sayd shame,
785 But if they were counterfettes that women them call,
  That list of there lewdnesse with hym for to brall.'

  With that the tappettis and carpettis were layd,
  Whereon theis ladys softly myght rest,
  The saumpler to sow on, the lacis to enbraid;
790 To weve in the stoule sume were full preste,
  With slaiis, with tavellis, with hedellis well drest;
  The frame was browght forth with his wevyng pin.
  God geve them good spede there warke to begin!

  Sume to enbrowder put them in prese,
795 Well gydyng ther glowtonn to kepe streit theyr sylk,
  Sum pirlyng of goldde theyr worke to encrese
  With fingers smale, and handis whyte as mylk;
  With, 'Reche me that skane of tewly sylk';
  And, 'Wynde me that botowme of such an hew',
800 Grene, rede, tawny, whyte, purpill, and blew.

  Of broken warkis wrought many a goodly thyng,
  In castyng, in turnynge, in florisshyng of flowris,
  With burris rowth and bottons surffillyng,
  In nedill wark raysyng byrdis in bowris,
805 With vertu enbesid all tymes and howris;
  And truly of theyr bownte thus were they bent
  To worke me this chapelet by goode advysemente.

Occupacyon to Skelton

'Beholde and se in your advertysement
How theis ladys and gentylwomen all
810 For your pleasure do there endevourment,
And for your sake how fast to warke they fall:
To your remembraunce wherfore ye must call
In goodly wordes plesauntly comprysid,
That for them some goodly conseyt be devysid,

815 With proper captacyons of benevolence,
Ornatly pullysshid after your faculte,
Sith ye must nedis afforce it by pretence
Of your professyoun unto umanyte,
Commensyng your proces after there degre,
820 To iche of them rendryng thankis commendable,
With sentence fructuous and termes convenable.'

Poeta Skelton answeryth

Avaunsynge my selfe sum thanke to deserve,
I me determynyd for to sharpe my pen,
Devoutly arrectyng my prayer to Mynerve,
825 She to vowchesafe me to informe and ken;
To Mercury also hertely prayed I then,
Me to supporte, to helpe, and to assist,
To gyde and to governe my dredfull tremlyng fist.

As a mariner that amasid is in a stormy rage,
830 Hardly bestad and driven is to hope
Of that the tempestous wynde wyll aswage
In trust wherof comforte his hart doth grope,
From the anker he kuttyth the gabyll rope,
Committyth all to God, and lettyth his shyp ryde;
835 So I beseke Jhesu now to be my gyde.

To the ryght noble Countes of Surrey

After all duly ordred obeisaunce,
In humble wyse as lowly as I may,
Unto you, madame, I make reconusaunce,
My lyfe endurynge I shall both wryte and say,

840 Recount, reporte, reherse without delay
The passynge bounte of your noble astate,
Of honour and worshyp which hath the formar date:

Lyke to Argyva by just resemblaunce,
The noble wyfe of Polimites kynge;
845 Prudent Rebecca, of whome remembraunce
The Byble makith; with whos chast lyvynge
Your noble demenour is counterwayng,
Whos passynge bounte, and ryght noble astate,
Of honour and worship it hath the formar date.

850 The noble Pamphila, quene of the Grekis londe,
Habillimentis royall founde out industriously;
Thamar also wrought with her goodly honde
Many divisis passynge curyously;
Whome ye represent and exemplify,
855 Whos passynge bounte, and ryght noble astate,
Of honour and worship it hath the formar date.

As dame Thamarys, whiche toke the kyng of Perce,
Cirus by name, as wrytith the story;
Dame Agrippina also I may reherse
860 Of jentyll corage the perfight memory;
So shall your name endure perpetually,
Whos passyng bounte, and ryght noble astate,
Of honour and worship it hath the formar date.

To my Lady Elisabeth Howarde

To be your remembrauncer, madame, I am bounde,
865 Lyke to Aryna, maydenly of porte,
Of vertu and konnyng the well and perfight grounde;
Whome dame Nature, as wele I may reporte,
Hath fresshely enbewtid with many a goodly sorte
Of womanly feturis, whos florysshyng tender age
870 Is lusty to loke on, plesaunte, demure, and sage:

Goodly Creisseid, fayrer than Polexene,
For to envyve Pandarus appetite;
Troilus, I trowe, if that he had you sene,
In you he wolde have set his hole delight.
875 Of all your bewte I suffyce not to wryght:

But, as I sayd, your florisshinge tender age
Is lusty to loke on, plesaunt, demure, and sage.

To my Lady Mirriell Howarde

Mi litell lady I may not leve behinde,
But to do you servyce nedis now I must;
880   Beninge, curteyse, of jentyll harte and mynde,
Whom fortune and fate playnly have discust
Longe to enjoy plesure, delyght, and lust:
The enbuddid blossoms of roses rede of hew
With lillis whyte your bewte doth renewe.

885   Compare you I may to Cidippes, the mayd,
That of Aconcyus whan she founde the byll
In her bosome, lorde, how she was afrayd!
The ruddy shamefastnes in her vysage fyll,
Whiche maner of abasshement became her not yll;
890   Right so, madame, the roses redde of hew
With lillys whyte your bewte dothe rei. we.

To my Lady Anne Dakers of the Sowth

Zeuxes, that enpicturid fare Elene the quene,
You to devyse his crafte were to seke;
And if Apelles your countenaunce had sene,
895   Of porturature which was the famous Greke,
He coude not devyse the lest poynt of your cheke;
Princes of yowth, and flowre of goodly porte,
Vertu, conyng, solace, pleasure, comforte.

Paregall in honour unto Penolepe,
900   That for her trowth is in remembraunce had;
Fayre Diianira surmowntynge in bewte;
Demure Diana womanly and sad,
Whos lusty lokis make hevy hartis glad;
Princes of youth, and flowre of goodly porte,
905   Vertu, connyng, solace, pleasure, comforte.

To mastres Margery Wentworthe

With margerain jentyll,
The flowre of goodlyhede,

Enbrowdred the mantill
Is of your maydenhede.

910   Plainly, I can not glose,
Ye be, as I devyne,
The praty primrose,
The goodly columbyne.

With margerain jantill,
915   The flowre of goodlyhede,
Enbrawderyd the mantyll
Is of yowre maydenhede.

Benynge, corteise, and meke,
With wordes well devysid;
920   In you, who list to seke,
Be vertus well comprysid.

With margerain jantill,
The flowre of goodlyhede,
Enbrawderid the mantill
925   Is of yowr maydenhede.

To mastres Margaret Tylney

I you assure,
Ful wel I know
My besy cure
To yow I owe;
930   Humbly and low
Commendynge me
To yowre bownte.

As Machareus
Fayre Canace,
935   So I, iwus,
Endevoure me
Yowr name to se
It be enrolde,
Writtin with golde.

940   Phedra ye may
Wele represent;
Intentyfe ay

And dylygent,
No tyme myspent;
945 Wherfore delyght
I have to whryght.

Of Margarite,
Perle orient,
Lodesterre of lyght,
950 Moche relucent;
Madame regent
I may you call
Of vertuows all.

To maystres Jane Blenner-Haiset

What though my penne wax faynt,
955 And hath smale lust to paint?
Yet shall there no restraynt
Cause me to cese,
Amonge this prese,
For to encrese
960 Yowre goodly name.

I wyll my selfe applye,
Trust me, ententifly,
Yow for to stellyfye;
And so observe
965 That ye ne swarve
For to deserve
Inmortall fame.

Sith mistres Jane Haiset
Smale flowres helpt to sett
970 In my goodly chapelet,
Therfore I render of her the memory
Unto the legend of fare Laodomi.

To maystres Isabell Pennell

By saynt Mary, my Lady,
Your mammy and your dady
975 Brought forth a godely babi!

340 XXI GARLANDE OR CHAPELET OF LAURELL

My mayden Isabell,
Reflaring rosabell,
The flagrant camamell;

The ruddy rosary,
980 The soverayne rosemary,
The praty strawbery;

The columbyne, the nepte,
The jeloffer well set,
The propre vyolet;

985 Enuwyd your colowre
Is lyke the dasy flowre
After the Aprill showre;

Sterre of the morow gray,
The blossom on the spray,
990 The fresshest flowre of May;

Maydenly demure,
Of womanhode the lure;
Wherfore, I make you sure,

It were an hevenly helth,
995 It were an endeles welth,
A lyfe for God hymselfe

To here this nightingale,
Amonge the byrdes smale,
Warbelynge in the vale

1000 Dug, dug,
Jug, jug,
Good yere and good luk,
With chuk, chuk, chuk, chuk.

To maystres Margaret Hussey

Mirry Margaret,
1005 As mydsomer flowre,
Jentill as fawcoun
Or hawke of the towre;

With solace and gladnes,
Moche mirthe and no madnes,

1010 All good and no badnes,
So joyously,
So maydenly,
So womanly
Her demenyng
1015 In every thynge,
Far, far passynge
That I can endyght,
Or suffice to wryght
Of mirry Margarete,
1020 As mydsomer flowre,
Jentyll as fawcoun
Or hawke of the towre,

As pacient and as styll,
And as full of good wyll,
1025 As fayre Isaphill;
Colyaunder,
Swete pomaunder,
Good Cassaunder;
Stedfast of thought,
1030 Wele made, wele wrought;
Far may be sought
Erst that ye can fynde
So corteise, so kynde
As mirry Margarete,
1035 This midsomer flowre,
Jentyll as fawcoun
Or hawke of the towre.

To mastres Geretrude Statham

Though ye wer hard hertyd,
And I with you thwartid
1040 With wordes that smartid,
Yet nowe doutles ye geve me cause
To wryte of you this goodli clause,
Maistres Geretrude,
With womanhode endude,
1045 With vertu well renwde.

I wyll that ye shall be
In all benyngnyte

Lyke to Dame Pasiphe;
For nowe dowtles ye geve me cause
1050 To wryte of yow this goodly clause,
Maistres Geretrude,
With womanhode endude,
With vertu well renude.

Partly by your councell,
1055 Garnisshed with lawrell
Was my fresshe coronell;
Wherfore doutles ye geve me cause
To wryte of you this goodly clause,
Maistres Geretrude
1060 With womanhode endude,
With vertu well renude.

To maystres Isabell Knyght

But if I sholde aquyte your kyndnes,
Els saye ye myght
That in me were grete blyndnes,
1065 I for to be so myndles,
And cowde not wryght
Of Isabell Knyght.

It is not my custome nor my gyse
To leve behynde
1070 Her that is bothe womanly and wyse,
And specyally which glad was to devyse
The menes to fynde
To please my mynde,

In helpyng to warke my laurell grene
1075 With sylke and golde.
Galathea, the made well besene,
Was never halfe so fayre, as I wene,
Whiche was extolde
A thowsande folde

1080 By Maro, the Mantuan prudent,
Who list to rede.
But, and I had leyser competent,
I coude shew you suche a presedent

In very dede
1085   How ye excede.

Occupacyon to Skelton

'Withdrawe your hande, the tyme passis fast.
Set on your hede this laurell whiche is wrought.
Here you not Eolus for you blowyth a blaste?
I dare wele saye that ye and I be sought.
1090   Make no delay, for now ye must be brought
Before my ladys grace, the Quene of Fame,
Where ye must brevely answere to your name.'

Skelton Poeta

Castyng my syght the chambre aboute,
To se how duly ich thyng in ordre was,
1095   Towarde the dore, as he were comyng oute,
I sawe maister Newton sit with his compas,
His plummet, his pensell, his spectacles of glas,
Dyvysynge in pycture, by his industrious wit,
Of my laurell the proces every whitte.

1100   Forthwith upon this, as it were in a thought,
Gower, Chawcer, Lydgate, theis thre
Before remembred, me curteisly brought
Into that place where as they left me,
Where all the sayd poetis sat in there degre.
1105   But when they sawe my lawrell rychely wrought,
All other besyde were counterfete they thought

In comparyson of that whiche I ware.
Sume praysed the perle, some the stones bryght.
Wele was hym that thereupon myght stare.
1110   Of this warke they had so great delyght,
The silke, the golde, the flowris fresshe to syght,
They seyd my lawrell was the goodlyest
That ever they saw, and wrought it was the best.

In her astate there sat the noble Quene
1115   Of Fame. Perceyvynge how that I was cum,
She wonderyd, me thought, at my laurell grene;

She loked hawtly, and gave on me a glum.
There was amonge them no worde then but mum,
For eche man herkynde what she wolde to me say;
1120   Wherof in substaunce I brought this away.

The Quene of Fame to Skelton

'My frende, sith ye ar before us here present
To answere unto this noble audyence,
Of that shalbe resonde you ye must be content;
And for as moche as, by the hy pretence
1125   That ye have now by the preemynence
Of laureat triumphe, your place is here reservyd,
We wyll understande how ye have it deservyd.'

Skelton Poeta to the Quene of Fame

'Ryght high and myghty princes of astate,
In famous glory all other transcendyng,
1130   Of your bounte the accustomable rate
Hath bene full often and yet is entendyng
To all that to reason is condiscendyng,
But if hastyve credence by mayntenance of myght
Fortune to stande betwene you and the lyght.

1135   But suche evydence I thynke for to enduce,
And so largely to lay for myne indempnite,
That I trust to make myne excuse
Of what charge so ever ye lay ageinst me;
For of my bokis parte ye shall se,
1140   Whiche in your recordes, I know well, be enrolde,
And so Occupacyon, your regester, me told.'

Forthwith she commaundid I shulde take my place.
Caliope poynted me where I shulde sit.
With that, Occupacioun presid in a pace;
1145   'Be mirry,' she sayd, 'be not afferde a whit,
Your discharge here under myne arme is it.'
So then commaundid she was upon this
To shew her boke; and she sayd, 'Here it is.'

The Quene of Fame to Occupacioun

'Yowre boke of remembrauns we will now that ye rede;
1150 If ony recordis in noumbyr can be founde,
What Skelton hath compilid and wryton in dede,
Rehersyng by ordre, and what is the grownde,
Let se now for hym how ye can expounde;
For in owr courte, ye wote wele, his name can not ryse
1155 But if he wryte oftenner than ones or twyse.'

Skelton Poeta

With that, of the boke losende were the claspis.
The margent was illumynid all with golden railles
And byse, enpicturid with gressoppes and waspis,
With butterfllyis and fresshe pecoke taylis,
1160 Enflorid with flowris and slymy snaylis,
Envyvid picturis well towchid and quikly.
It wolde have made a man hole that had be ryght sekely,

To beholde how it was garnysshyd and bounde,
Encoverde over with golde of tissew fyne;
1165 The claspis and bullyons were worth a thousande pounde;
Witn balassis and charbuncles the borders did shyne;
With *aurum musicum* every other lyne
Was wrytin; and so she did her spede,
Occupacyon, immediatly to rede.

> *Occupacyoun redith and expoundyth sum parte of Skeltons*
> *bokes and baladis with ditis of plesure, in as moche as it were*
> *to longe a proces to reherse all by name that he hath*
> *compylyd, &c.*

1170 'Of your oratour and poete laureate
Of Englande, his workis here they begynne:
In primis the Boke of Honorous Astate;
Item the Boke how Men Shulde Fle Synne;
Item Royall Demenaunce Worshyp to Wynne;
1175 Item the Boke to Speke Well or be Styll;
Item to Lerne You to Dye When ye Wyll;

Of Vertu also the soverayne enterlude;
The Boke of the Rosiar; Prince Arturis Creacyoun;

The False Fayth that Now Goth, which dayly is renude;
1180 Item his Diologgis of Ymagynacyoun;
Item Automedon of Loves Meditacyoun;
Item New Gramer in Englysshe compylyd;
Item Bowche of Courte, where Drede was begyled;

His commedy, Achademios callyd by name;
1185 Of Tullis Familiars the translacyoun;
Item Good Advysement, that brainles doth blame;
The Recule ageinst Gaguyne of the Frenshe nacyoun;
Item the Popingay, that hath in commendacyoun
Ladyes and gentylwomen suche as deservyd,
1190 And suche as be counterfettis they be reservyd;

And of Soveraynte a noble pamphelet;
And of Magnyfycence a notable mater,
How Cownterfet Cowntenaunce of the new get
With Crafty Conveyaunce dothe smater and flater,
1195 And Cloked Collucyoun is brought in to clater
With Courtely Abusyoun; who pryntith it wele in mynde
Moche dowblenes of the worlde therin he may fynde.

Of Manerly Margery Maystres Mylke and Ale;
To her he wrote many maters of myrthe;
1200 Yet, thoughe I say it, therby lyith a tale,
For Margery wynshed, and breke her hinder girth;
Lorde, how she made moche of her gentyll birth!
With, 'Gingirly, go gingerly!' Her tayle was made of hay;
Go she never so gingirly, her honesty is gone away.

1205 Harde to make ought of that is nakid nought;
This fustiane maistres and this giggisse gase
Wonder is to wryte what wrenchis she wrowght,
To face out her foly with a midsomer mase;
With pitche she patchid her pitcher shuld not crase;
1210 It may wele ryme, but shroudly it doth accorde,
To pyke out honesty of suche a potshorde.

Patet per versus

Hinc puer hic natus; vir conjugis hinc spoliatus
Jure thori; est fetus Deli de sanguine cretus;
Hinc magis extollo, quod erit puer alter Apollo;
1215 *Si queris qualis? meretrix castissima talis;*
   Et relis, et ralis, et reliqualis.

A good herynge of thes olde talis;
Fynde no mo suche fro Wanflete to Walis.

Et reliqua omelia de diversis tractatibus.

Of my ladys grace at the contemplacyoun,
1220   Owt of Frenshe into Englysshe prose,
Of Mannes Lyfe the Peregrynacioun,
He did translate, enterprete, and disclose;
The Tratyse of the Triumphis of the Rede Rose,
Wherein many storis ar brevely contayned
1225   That unremembred longe tyme remayned.

The Duke of Yorkis creauncer whan Skelton was,
Now Henry the viij, Kyng of Englonde,
A tratyse he devysid and browght it to pas,
Callid *Speculum Principis*, to bere in his honde,
1230   Therin to rede, and to understande
All the demenour of princely astate,
To be our kyng, of God preordinate.

Also the Tunnynge of Elinour Rummyng,
With Colyn Clowt, Johnn Ive, with Joforth Jack;
1235   To make suche trifels it asketh sum konnyng,
In honest myrth, parde, requyreth no lack;
The whyte apperyth the better for the black,
And after conveyauns as the world goos,
It is no foly to use the Walshemannys hoos.

1240   The umblis of venyson, the botell of wyne,
To fayre maistres Anne that shuld have be sent,
He wrate therof many a praty lyne,
Where it became, and whether it went,
And how that it was wantonly spent;
1245   The Balade also of the Mustarde Tarte.
Suche problemis to paynt it longyth to his arte.

Of one Adame all a knave, late dede and gone –
Dormiat in pace, lyke a dormows –
He wrate an Epitaph for his grave stone,
1250   With wordes devoute and sentence agerdows,
For he was ever ageynst Goddis hows;
All his delight was to braule and to barke
Ageynst Holy Chyrche, the preste, and the clarke.

Of Phillip Sparow the lamentable fate,
1255   The dolefull desteny, and the carefull chaunce,
Dyvysed by Skelton after the funerall rate;
Yet sum there be therewith that take grevaunce
And grudge therat with frownyng countenaunce;
But what of that? Hard it is to please all men;
1260   Who list amende it, let hym set to his penne.

For the gyse nowadays
Of sum jangelyng jays
Is to discommende
That they can not amende,
1265   Though they wolde spende
All the wittis they have.
    What ayle them to deprave
Phillippe Sparows grave?
His *dirige*, her commendacioun
1270   Can be no derogacyoun;
But myrth and consolacyoun,
Made by protestacyoun,
No man to myscontent
With Phillippis enterement.
1275   Alas, that goodly mayd,
Why shulde she be afrayd?
Why shulde she take shame
That her goodly name,
Honorably reportid,
1280   Shulde be set and sortyd,
To be matriculate
With ladyes of astate?
    I conjure the, Phillip Sparow,
By Hercules that hell did harow,
1285   And with a venomows arow
Slew of the Epidawris
One of the Centawris,
Or Onocentauris,
Or Hippocentauris;
1290   By whos myght and maine
An hart was slayne
With hornnis twayne
Of glitteryng golde;

And the apples of golde
1295 Of Hesperides withholde,
And with a dragon kepte
That never more slepte ˙
By merciall strength
He wan at length;
1300 And slew Gerione
With thre bodys in one;
With myghty corrage
Adauntid the rage
Of a lyon savage;
1305 Of Diomedis stabyll
He brought out a rabyll
Of coursers and rounsis
With lepes and bounsis;
And with myghty luggyng,
1310 Wrastelynge and tuggyng,
He pluckid the bull
By the hornid scull,
And offred to Cornucopia;
As so forthe *per cetera*;
1315 Also by Hecates powre
In Plutos gastly towre;
By the ugly Eumenides,
That never have rest nor ease;
By the venemows serpent
1320 That in hell is never brente,
In Lerna the Grekis fen
That was engendred then;
By Chemeras flamys,
And all the dedely namys
1325 Of infernall posty,
Where soulis fry and rosty;
By the Stigiall flode,
And the stremes wode
Of Cochitos bottumles well;
1330 By the feryman of hell,
Caron with his berde hore,
That rowyth with a rude ore,
And with his frownsid fortop
Gydith his bote with a prop.

1335   I conjure, Phillippe, and call,
In the name of Kyng Saull;
Primo Regum expres,
He bad the Phitones
To witchecraft her to dres,
1340 And by her abusiouns,
And damnable illusiouns
Of mervelous conclusiouns,
And by her supersticiouns
Of wonderfull condiciouns
1345 She raysed up in that stede
Samuell that was dede.
    But whether it were so,
He were *idem in numero*,
The selfe same Samuell,
1350 How be it to Saull he did tell
The Phillistinis shulde hym askry,
And the next day he shulde dye,
I wyll myselfe discharge
To letterd men at large.
1355   But, Phillip, I conjure the
Now by theys names thre,
Diana in the woddis grene,
Luna that so bryght doth shene,
Proserpina in hell,
1360 That thou shortely tell,
And shew now unto me
What the cause may be
Of this perplexyte.

Inferias, Philippe, tuas Scroupe pulchra Johanna
1365 *Instanter petiit: cur nostri carminis illam*
Nunc pudet? Est sero; minor est infamia vero.

Then such that have disdaynyd
And of this worke complaynyd,
I pray God they be paynyd
1370 No wors than is contaynyd
In verses two or thre
That folowe as ye may se:
Luride, cur, livor, volucris pia funera damnas?
Talia te rapiant rapiunt que fata volucrem!
1375 *Est tamen invidia mors tibi continua.*

The Gruntyng and the Groynninge of the Gronnyng Swyne;
Also the Murnyng of the Mapely Rote;
How the grene coverlet sufferd grete pine,
Whan the flye net was set for to catche a cote,
1380   Strake one with a birdbolt to the hart rote;
Also a Devoute Prayer to Moyses Hornis,
Metrifyde merely, medelyd with scornis;

Of Pajauntis that were played in Joyows Garde;
He wrate of a muse throw a mud wall;
1385   How a do cam trippyng in at the rerewarde,
But, lorde, how the parker was wroth with all.
And of Castell Aungell the fenestrall,
Glittryng and glistryng and gloryously glasid,
It made sum mens eye dasild and dasid;

1390   The Repete of the Recule of Rosamundis bowre,
Of his pleasaunt paine there and his glad distres
In plantynge and pluckynge a propre jeloffer flowre;
But how it was, sum were to recheles,
Notwithstandynge it is remedeles;
1395   What myght she say? What myght he do therto?
Though Jak sayd nay, yet Mok there loste her sho;

How than lyke a man he wan the barbican
With a sawte of solace at the longe last;
The colour dedely, swarte, blo and wan
1400   Of Exione, his limbis dede and past,
The cheke and the nek but a shorte cast;
In fortunis favour ever to endure,
No man lyvyng, he sayth, can be sure;

How Dame Minerva first found the Olyve Tre, *she red*
1405   And plantid it there where never before was none, *unshred*
An hynde unhurt hit by casuelte, *not bled*
Recoverd whan the forster was gone, *and sped*
The hertis of the herd began for to grone, *and fled*
The howndes began to yerne and to quest; *and dred*
1410   With litell besynes standith moche rest; *in bed*

His Epitomis of the Myller and his joly Make;
How her ble was bryght as blossom on the spray,
A wanton wenche and wele coude bake a cake;
The myllar was loth to be out of the way,

1415 But yet for all that, be as be may,
   Whether he rode to Swaffhamm or to Some,
   The millar durst not leve his wyfe at home.

   With Wofully Arayd and Shamefully Betrayd;
   Of his makyng devoute medytacyons;
1420 *Vexilla regis* he devysid to be displayd;
   With *Sacris Solempniis*, and other contemplacyons,
   That in them comprisid consyderacyons;
   Thus passyth he the tyme both nyght and day,
   Sumtyme with sadnes, sumtyme with play.

1425 Though Galiene and Diascorides,
   With Ipocras and mayster Avycen,
   By there phesik doth many a man ease,
   And though Albumasar can the enforme and ken
   What constellacions ar good or bad for men,
1430 Yet whan the rayne rayneth and the gose wynkith,
   Lytill wotith the goslyng what the gose thynkith.

   He is not wyse ageyne the streme that stryvith.
   Dun is in the myre, dame, reche me my spur.
   Nedes must he rin that the devyll dryvith.
1435 When the stede is stolyn, spar the stable dur.
   A jentyll hownde shulde never play the kur.
   It is sone aspyed where the thorne prikkith.
   And wele wotith the cat whos berde she likkith.

   With Marione Clarione, sol, lucerne,
1440 *Graund juir*, of this Frenshe proverbe olde,
   How men were wonte for to discerne
   By Candelmes day what wedder shuld holde;
   But Marione Clarione was caught with a colde colde,
   And all overcast with cloudis unkynde,
1445 This goodly flowre with stormis was untwynde.

   This jeloffer jentyll, this rose, this lylly flowre,
   This primerose pereles, this propre vyolet,
   This columbyne clere and fresshest of coloure,
   This delycate dasy, this strawbery pretely set,
1450 With frowarde frostis, alas, was all to-fret!
   But who may have a more ungracyous lyfe
   Than a chyldis birde and a knavis wyfe?

Thynke what ye wyll
Of this wanton byll;
1455   By Mary Gipcy,
Quod scripsi, scripsi;
Uxor tua, sicut vitis,
Habetis in custodiam,
Custodite sicut scitis,
1460   *Secundum Lucam &c*

Of the Bonehoms of Ashrige besyde Barkamstede,
That goodly place to Skelton moost kynde,
Where the sank royall is, Crystes blode so rede,
Whereupon he metrefyde after his mynde;
1465   A pleasaunter place than Ashrige is, harde were to fynde,
As Skelton rehersith, with wordes few and playne,
In his distichon made on verses twaine.

Fraxinus in clivo frondetque viret sine rivo,
Non est sub divo similis sine flumine vivo.

1470   The Nacyoun of Folys he left not behynde.
Item Apollo that whirllid up his chare,
That made sum to snurre and snuf in the wynde;
It made them to skip, to stampe, and to stare,
Whiche, if they be happy, have cause to beware
1475   In ryming and raylyng with hym for to mell,
For drede and he lerne them there A B C to spell.'

Poeta Skelton

With that I stode up, halfe sodenly afrayd,
Suppleyng to Fame, I besought her grace,
And that it wolde please her, full tenderly I prayd,
1480   Owt of her bokis Apollo to rase.
'Nay, sir,' she sayd, 'what so in this place
Of our noble courte is ones spoken owte,
It must nedes after rin all the worlde aboute.'

God wote, theis wordes made me full sad;
1485   And when that I sawe it wolde no better be,
But that my peticyon wolde not be had,
What shuld I do but take it in gre?
For, by Juppiter and his high mageste,

I did what I cowde to scrape out the scrollis,
1490 Apollo to rase out of her ragman rollis.

Now hereof it erkith me lenger to wryte.
To Occupacyon I wyll agayne resorte,
Whiche redde on still, as it cam to her syght,
Rendrynge my devisis I made in disporte
1495 Of the Mayden of Kent callid Counforte,
Of Lovers Testamentis and of There Wanton Wyllis,
And how Iollas lovyd goodly Phillis;

Diodorus Siculus of my translacyon
Out of fresshe Latine into owre Englysshe playne,
1500 Recountyng commoditis of many a straunge nacyon;
Who redyth it ones wolde rede it agayne;
Sex volumis engrosid together it doth containe.
But when of the laurell she made rehersall,
All orators and poetis, with other grete and smale,

1505 A thowsande, thowsande, I trow, to my dome,
'Triumpha, triumpha!' they cryid all aboute.
Of trumpettis and clariouns the noyse went to Rome;
The starry hevyn, me thought, shoke with the showte;
The grownde gronid and tremblid, the noyse was so stowte.
1510 The Quene of Fame commaundid shett fast the boke,
And therwith, sodenly, out of my dreme I woke.

My mynde of the grete din was somdele amasid.
I wypid myne eyne for to make them clere.
Then to the hevyn sperycall upwarde I gasid,
1515 Where I saw Janus, with his double chere,
Makynge his almanak for the new yere;
He turnyd his tirikkis, his volvell ran fast,
Good luk this new yere, the olde yere is past.

Mens tibi sit consulta, petis? Sic consule menti;
1520 *Emula sit Jani, retro speculetur et ante.*

Skeltonis alloquitur librum suum

Ite, Britannorum lux O radiosa, Britannum
Carmina nostra pium vestrum celebrate Catullum!
Dicite, Skeltonis vester Adonis erat;

Dicite, Skeltonis vester Homerus erat.

1525 *Barbara cum Latio pariter jam currite versu;*
Et licet est verbo pars maxima texta Britanno,
Non magis incompta nostra Thalya patet,
Est magis inculta nec mea Caliope.
Nec vos peniteat livoris tela subire,

1530 *Nec vos peniteat rabiem tolerare caninam,*
Nam Maro dissimiles non tulit ille minas,
Immunis nec enim Musa Nasonis erat.

Lenvoy

Go, litill quaire,
Demene you faire.

1535 Take no dispare,
Though I you wrate
After this rate
In Englysshe letter.
    So moche the better

1540 Welcome shall ye
To sum men be;
For Latin warkis
Be good for clerkis,
Yet now and then

1545 Sum Latin men
May happely loke
Upon your boke,
And so procede
In you to rede,

1550 That so indede
Your fame may sprede
In length and brede.
    But then I drede
Ye shall have nede

1555 You for to spede
To harnnes bryght,
By force of myght,
Ageyne envy,
And obloquy.

1560 And wote ye why?
    Not for to fyght

Ageyne dispyght,
Nor to derayne
Batayle agayne
1565 Scornfull disdayne,
Nor for to chyde,
Nor for to hyde
You cowardly;
    But curteisly
1570 That I have pende
For to deffend,
Under the banner
Of all good manner,
Under proteccyon
1575 Of sad correccyon,
With toleracyon
And supportacyon
Of reformacyon,
If they can spy
1580 Circumspectly
Any worde defacid
That myght be rasid,
    Els ye shall pray
Them that ye may
1585 Contynew still
With there good wyll.

*Ad serenissimam Majestatem Regiam, pariter cum Domino
Cardinali, Legato a latere honorificatissimo &c*

    Lautre Envoy

*Perge, liber, celebrem pronus regem venerare
Henricum octavum, resonans sua praemia laudis.
Cardineum dominum pariter venerando salutes,*
1590 *Legatum a latere, et fiat memor ipse precare
Prebendae, quam promisit mihi credere quondam,
Meque suum referas pignus sperare salutis.
Inter spemque metum.*

    Twene hope and drede
1595 My lyfe I lede,
But of my spede
Small sekernes;

Howe be it I rede
Both worde and dede
1600 Should be agrede
In noblenes:
Or els &c

ADMONET SKELTONIS OMNES ARBORES DARE LOCUM VIRIDI LAURO JUXTA GENUS SUUM

Fraxinus in silvis, altis in montibus ornus,
Populus in fluviis, abies, patulissima fagus,
Lenta salix, platanus, pinguis ficulnea ficus,
Glandifera et quercus, pirus, esculus, ardua pinus,
5 Balsamus exudans, oleaster, oliva Minerve,
Juniperus, buxus, lentiscus cuspide lenta,
Botrigera et domino vitis gratissima Baccho,
Ilex et sterilis labrusca perosa colonis,
Mollibus exudans fragrancia thura Sabeis
10 Thus, redolens Arabis pariter notissima mirrha,
Et vos, O corili fragiles, humilesque miricae,
Et vos, O cedri redolentes, vos quoque mirti,
Arboris omne genus viridi concedite lauro!

Prennees en gre The Laurelle.

EN PARLEMENT A PARIS

Justice est morte,
Et Veryte sommielle;
Droit et Raison
Sont alez aux pardons.
5 Lez deux premiers
Nul ne les resuelle;
Et lez derniers
Sount corrumpus par dons.

OUT OF FRENSHE INTO LATYN

Abstulit atra dies Astraeam; cana Fides sed
Sompno pressa iacet; Jus iter arripuit,
Et secum Racio proficiscens limite longo:
Nemo duas primas evigilare parat;

5 *Atque duo postrema absunt, et munera tantum*
  Impediunt, nequiunt quod remeare domum.

OWT OF LATYNE INTO ENGLYSSHE

Justyce now is dede;
Trowth with a drowsy hede,
As hevy as the lede,
Is layd down to slepe,
5 And takith no kepe;
And Ryght is over the fallows
Gone to seke hallows,
With Reason together,
No man can tell whether.
10 No man wyll undertake
The first twayne to wake;
And the twayne last
Be withholde so fast
With mony, as men sayne,
15 They can not come agayne.

A grant tort
Foy dort.

Here endith a ryght delectable tratyse upon a goodly
Garlonde or Chapelet of Laurell, dyvysed by Mayster
Skelton, Poete Laureat.

XXII

A Couplet on Wolsey's Dissolution
of the Convocation at St Paul's

Gentle Paule laie doune thy sweard,
For Peter of Westminster hath shaven thy beard.

XXIII

Skelton Laureate etc

Howe the Douty Duke of Albany

lyke a cowarde knyght, ran awaye shamfully with an
hundred thousande tratlande Scottes and faint harted
Frenchemen: beside the water of Twede, etc

Rejoyse, Englande,
And understande
These tidinges newe,
Whiche be as trewe
5   As the gospell:
This Duke so fell
Of Albany,
So cowardly,
With all his hoost
10 Of the Scottyshe coost,
For all theyr boost,
Fledde lyke a beest.
Wherfore to jeste
Is my delyght
15 Of this cowarde knyght,
And for to wright
In the dispyght
Of the Scottes ranke
Of Huntley banke,
20 Of Lowdyan,
Of Locryan,
And the ragged ray
Of Galaway.

Dunbar, Dunde,
25 Ye shall trowe me,
False Scottes are ye.
Your hartes sore faynted,
And so attaynted,
Lyke cowardes starke,
30 At the castell of Warke,
By the water of Twede,
Ye had evill spede.

Lyke cankerd curres
Ye loste your spurres;
35 For in that fraye
Ye ranne awaye
With, 'hey, dogge, hay.'
    For Sir William Lyle
Within shorte whyle,
40 That valiaunt knyght,
Putte you to flyght
By his valyaunce.
Two thousande of Fraunce
There he putte backe
45 To your great lacke
And utter shame
Of your Scottysshe name.
    Your chefe cheftayne,
Voyde of all brayne,
50 Duke of Albany,
Than shamefuly
He reculed backe,
To his great lacke,
Whan he herde tell
55 That my Lorde Amrell
Was comyng downe
To make hym frowne
And to make hym lowre,
With the noble powre
60 Of my Lorde Cardynall,
As an hoost royall
After the auncient manner
With Sainct Cutberdes banner
And Sainct Williams also.
65 Your capitayne ranne to go,
To go, to go, to go,
And brake up all his hoost.
For all his crake and bost,
Lyke a cowarde knyght
70 He fledde and durst nat fyght;
He ran awaye by night.

But now must I
Your Duke ascry

Of Albany
75 With a worde or twayne
In sentence playne.
   Ye Duke so doutty,
So sterne, so stoutty,
In shorte sentens,
80 Of your pretens
What is the grounde
Brevely and rounde
To me expounde.
   Or els wyll I
85 Evydently
Shewe as it is:
For the cause is this,
Howe ye pretende
For to defende
90 The yonge Scottyshe kyng,
But ye meane a thyng
And ye coude bryng
The matter about
To putte his eyes out
95 And put hym downe,
And set hys crowne
On your owne heed
Whan he were deed.
   Suche trechery
100 And traytory
Is all your cast.
Thus ye have compast
With the Frenche kyng
A fals rekenyng
105 To envade Englande,
As I understande.
But our kyng royall
Whose name over all
Noble Henry the Eyght
110 Shall cast a beyght,
And sette suche a snare
That shall cast you in care,
Bothe Kyng Fraunces and the,
That knowen ye shall be

115 For the moost recrayd
    Cowardes afrayd,
    And falsest forsworne
    That ever were borne.

    O ye wretched Scottes,
120 Ye puaunt pyspottes,
    It shalbe your lottes
    To be knytte up with knottes
    Of halters and ropes
    About your traytours throtes.
125   O Scottes parjured,
    Unhaply ured,
    Ye may be assured
    Your falshod discured
    It is, and shal be
130 From the Scottish se
    Unto Gabione.
    For ye be false echone,
    False and false agayne,
    Never true nor playne,
135 But flery, flatter and fayne;
    And ever to remayne
    In wretched beggary
    And maungy misery,
    In lousy lothsumnesse,
140 And scabbed scorffynesse,
    And in abhominacion
    Of all maner of nacion,
    Nacion moost in hate,
    Proude and poore of state.

145 Twyt, Scot, go kepe thy den.
    Mell nat wyth Englyshe men.
    Thou dyd nothyng but barke
    At the castell of Warke.
    Twyt, Scot, yet agayne ones,
150 We shall breke thy bones
    And hang you upon polles
    And byrne you all to colles,
    With, 'twyt Scot, twyt Scot, twyt.'
    Walke, Scot, go begge a byt

155 Of brede at ylke mannes hecke.
The fynde, Scot, breke thy necke.
'Twyt, Scot,' agayne I saye,
'Twyt, Scot, of Galaway.
Twyt, Scot, shake the dogge, hay.
160 Twyt, Scot, thou ran away.'
      We set nat a flye
By your Duke of Albany.
We set nat a prane
By suche a dronken drane.
165 We set nat a myght
By suche a cowarde knyght,
Suche a proude palyarde,
Suche a skyrgaliarde,
Suche a starke cowarde,
170 Suche a proude pultrowne,
Suche a foule coystrowne,
Suche a doutty dagswayne.
Sende him to Fraunce agayne
To bring with hym more brayne
175 From Kynge Fraunces of Frauns.
God sende them bothe myschauns!
      Ye Scottes all the rable,
Ye shall never be hable,
With us for to compare.
180 What though ye stampe and stare?
God sende you sorow and care!
      With us, whan ever ye mell
Yet we bear away the bell,
Whan ye cankerd knaves
185 Must crepe in to your caves
Your heedes for to hyde
For ye dare nat abyde.
      Sir Duke of Albany,
Right inconvenyently
190 Ye rage and ye rave,
And your worshyp deprave:
Nat lyke Duke Hamylcar
With the Romayns that made war,
Nor lyke his sonne Hanyball,
195 Nor lyke Duke Hasdruball

Of Cartage in Aphrike;
Yet somwhat ye be lyke
In some of their condicions,
And their false sedycions,
200 And their dealyng double,
And their weywarde trouble.
But yet they were bolde
And manly manyfolde,
Their enemyes to assayle
205 In playn felde and battayle.
　　But ye and your hoost,
Full of bragge and boost,
And full of waste wynde,
Howe ye wyll beres bynde
210 And the devill downe dynge,
Yet ye dare do nothynge
But lepe away lyke frogges
And hyde you under logges,
Lyke pygges and lyke hogges
215 And lyke maungy dogges.
What an army were ye?
Or what actyvyte
Is in you, beggars braules,
Full of scabbes and scaules,
220 Of vermyne and of lyce
And of all maner vyce?
　　Syr Duke, nay, syr ducke,
Syr drake of the lake, sir ducke
Of the donghyll, for small lucke
225 Ye have in feates of warre.
Ye make nought but ye marre.
Ye are a fals entrusar,
And a fals abusar,
And an untrewe knyght.
230 Thou hast to lytell myght
Agaynst Englande to fyght.
Thou art a graceles wyght
To put thy selfe to flyght.
A vengeaunce and dispight
235 On the must nedes lyght
That durst nat byde the sight

Of my Lorde Amrell,
Of chivalry the well,
Of knighthode the floure
240 In every marciall shoure,
The noble Erle of Surrey,
That put the in suche fray.
Thou durst no felde derayne,
Nor no batayle mayntayne,
245 Against our stronge captaine;
But thou ran home agayne
For feare thou shoulde be slayne
Lyke a Scottyshe keteryng
That durst abyde no reknyng;
250 Thy herte wolde nat serve the.
The fynde of hell mot sterve the!
    No man hath harde
Of suche a cowarde,
And such a mad ymage
255 Caried in a cage,
As it were a cotage,
Or of suche a mawment
Caryed in a tent.
In a tent? Nay. Nay.
260 But in a mountayne gay,
Lyke a great hill,
For a wyndmil
Therin to couche styll
That no man hym kyll;
265 As it were a gote
In a shepe cote,
About hym a parke
Of a madde warke,
Men call it a toyle.
270 Therin, like a royle,
Sir Dunkan, ye dared.
And thus ye prepared
Youre carkas to kepe,
Lyke a sely shepe,
275 A shepe of Cottyswolde,
From rayne and from colde,

And from raynning of rappes,
And such after-clappes.
Thus in your cowardly castell
280 Ye decte you to dwell;
Suche a captayne of hors
It made no great fors
If that ye had tane
Your last deedly bane
285 With a gon stone,
To make you to grone.
But hyde the, Sir Topias,
Nowe into the castell of Bas,
And lurke there lyke an as
290 With some Scotyshe las,
With dugges, dugges, dugges.
I shrewe thy Scottishe lugges,
Thy munpynnys, and thy crag,
For thou can not but brag,
295 Lyke a Scottyshe hag.
Adue, nowe, Sir Wrig-wrag!
Adue, Sir Dalyrag!
    Thy mellyng is but mockyng.
Thou mayst give up thy cocking.
300 Gyve it up, and cry, 'creke',
Lyke an huddy peke.
    Wherto shuld I more speke
Of suche a farly freke,
Of suche an horne keke,
305 Of suche an bolde captayne
That dare nat turne agayne,
Nor durst nat crak a worde,
Nor durst nat drawe his swerde
Agaynst the lyon white,
310 But ran away quyte?
He ran away by nyght
In the owle flyght
Lyke a cowarde knyght.
Adue, cowarde, adue!
315 Fals knight and mooste untrue,
I render the fals rebelle
To the flingande fende of helle.

Harke yet, Sir Duke, a worde
In ernest or in borde.
320 What have ye, villayn, forged,
And virulently dysgorged
As though ye wolde parbrake
Your avauns to make,
With wordes enbosed,
325 Ungraciously engrosed,
Howe ye wyll undertake
Our royall kyng to make
His owne realme to forsake?
Suche lewde langage ye spake.

330   Sir Dunkan, in the devill waye,
Be well ware what ye say.
Ye saye that he and ye –
Whyche he and ye? Let se;
Ye meane Fraunces, French kyng,
335 Shulde bring about that thing.
I say, thou lewde lurdayne,
That neyther of you twayne
So hardy nor so bolde
His countenaunce to beholde.

340 If our moost royall Harry
Lyst with you to varry
Full soone ye should miscary,
For ye durst nat tarry
With hym to stryve a stownde.
345 If he on you but frounde
Nat for a thousande pounde
Ye durst byde on the grounde.
Ye wolde ryn away rounde
And cowardly tourne your backes
350 For all your comly crackes.
And for feare *par case*
To loke hym in the face
Ye wolde defoyle the place
And ryn your way apace.

355 Thoughe I trym you thys trace
With Englyshe somwhat base,
Yet, *save voster grace*,
Therby I shall purchace

No displesaunt rewarde,
360   If ye wele can regarde
Your cankarde cowardnesse
And your shamfull doublenesse.

Are ye nat frantyke madde,
And wretchedly bestadde,
365   To rayle agaynst his grace
That shall bring you full bace
And set you in suche case
That bytwene you twayne
There shalbe drawen a trayne
370   That shalbe to your payne?
To flye ye shalbe fayne
And never tourne agayne.
        What, wold Fraunces, our friar,
Be suche a false lyar,
375   So madde a cordylar,
So madde a murmurar?
Ye muse somwhat to far;
All out of joynt ye jar.
God let you never thrive!
380   Wene ye, daucockes, to drive
Our kyng out of his reme?
Go heme, ranke Scot, ge heme,
With fonde Fraunces, French kyng.
Our mayster shall you brynge,
385   I trust, to lowe estate
And mate you with chek mate.
        Your braynes are ydell;
It is time for you to brydell
And pype in a quibyble,
390   For it is impossible
For you to bring about
Our kyng for to dryve out
Of this, his realme royall
And lande imperiall,
395   So noble a prince as he
In all actyvite
Of hardy merciall actes,
Fortunate in all his fayctes.

And nowe I wyll me dresse
400 His valiaunce to expresse,
Though insufficient am I
His grace to magnify
And laude equivalently.
Howe be it, loyally
405 After myne allegyaunce
My pen I will avaunce
To extoll his noble grace
In spyght of thy cowardes face,
In spyght of kyng Fraunces,
410 Devoyde of all nobles,
Devoyde of good corage,
Devoyde of wysdome sage,
Mad, frantyke and savage.
Thus he dothe disparage
415 His blode with fonde dotage.
   A prince to play the page
It is a rechelesse rage,
And a lunatyke overage.
What though my stile be rude?
420 With trouthe it is ennewde.
Trouth ought to be rescude;
Trouthe should nat be subdude.

But nowe will I expounde
What noblenesse dothe abounde,
425 And what honour is founde
And what vertues be resydent
In our royall regent,
Our perelesse president,
Our kyng most excellent.
430   In merciall prowes
Lyke unto Hercules,
In prudence and wysdom
Lyke unto Salamon,
In his goodly person
435 Lyke unto Absolon,
In loyalte and foy
Lyke to Ector of Troy,
And his glory to incres

Lyke to Scipiades,
440   In royal mageste
Lyke unto Ptholome,
Lyke to Duke Josue
And the valiaunt Machube,
    That if I wolde reporte
445   All the roiall sorte
Of his nobilyte,
His magnanymyte,
His animosite,
His frugalite,
450   His lyberalite,
His affabilite,
His humanyte,
His stabilite,
His humilite,
455   His benignite
His royall dignyte,
My lernyng is to small
For to recount them all.
    What losels than are ye
460   Lyke cowardes as ye be
To rayle on his astate
With wordes inordinate?

He rules his cominalte
With all benignite.
465   His noble baronage
He putteth them in corage
To exployte dedes of armys
To the domage and harmys
Of suche as be his foos
470   Where ever he rydes or goos.
His subjectes he dothe supporte,
Maintayne them with comforte
Of his moste princely porte,
As all men can reporte.
475   Than ye be a knappishe sorte
Et faitez a luy grant torte,
With your enbosed jawes

To rayle on hym lyke dawes.
The fende scrache out your mawes!
480   All his subjectes and he
Moost lovyngly agre
With hole hart and true mynde,
They fynde his grace so kynde;
Wherwith he dothe them bynde
485 At all houres to be redy
With hym to lyve and dye,
And to spende their hart blode,
Their bodyes and their gode,
With hym in all dystresse,
490 Alway in redynesse
To assyst his noble grace,
In spyght of thy cowardes face,
Moost false attaynted traytour,
And false forsworne faytour.
495   Avaunt, cowarde recrayed!
Thy pride shalbe alayd,
With Sir Fraunces of Fraunce
We shall pype ȝou a daunce
Shall tourne you to myschauns.
500   I rede you, loke about;
For you shalbe driven out
Of your lande in shorte space.
We will so folowe in the chace
That ye shall have no grace
505 For to tourne your face;
And thus, Sainct George to borowe,
Ye shall have shame and sorowe.

Lenvoy

Go, lytell quayre, quickly.
Shew them that shall you rede
510 How that ye are lykely
Over all the worlde to sprede.
The fals Scottes for dred,
With the Duke of Albany,
Beside the water of Twede
515 They fledde full cowardly.

Though your Englishe be rude,
Barreyne of eloquence,
Yet, brevely to conclude,
Grounded is your sentence
520 On trouthe under defence
Of all trewe Englyshemen,
This mater to credence
That I wrate with my pen.

Skelton Laureat: *obsequious et loyall.*

To my Lorde Cardynals right noble grace etc

Lenvoy

Go, lytell quayre, apace,
In moost humble wyse,
525 Before his noble grace
That caused you to devise
This lytel enterprise;
And hym moost lowly pray,
In his mynde to comprise,
530 Those wordes his grace dyd saye
Of an ammas gray.

Je foy enterment en sa bone grace.

XXIV

*Honorificatissimo, amplissimo, longeque reverendissimo in Christo
patri, ac domino, domino Thome, etc. tituli sancte Cecilie,
sacrosancte Romane ecclesie presbytero, Cardinali meritissimo,
et apostolice sedis legato, a latereque legato superillustri, etc.
Skeltonis laureatus, orator regius, humillimum dicit obsequium
cum omni debita reverentia, tanto tamque magnifico digna
principe sacerdotum, totiusque justitie equabilissimo
moderatore, necnon presentis opusculi fautore excellentissimo,
etc., ad cuius auspicatissimam contemplationem, sub
memorabili prelo gloriose immortalitatis, presens pagella
felicitatur, etc.*

A Replycacion Agaynst Certayne Yong Scolers Abjured of Late, Etc.

Argumentum

Crassantes nimium, nimium sterilesque labruscas,
Vinea quas Domini Sabaot non sustinet ultra
Laxius expandi, nostra est resecare voluntas.

> *Cum privilegio a rege indulto.*

Protestacion alway canonically prepensed, professed, and
with good delyberacion made, that this lytell pamphilet,
called the Replicacion of Skelton laureate, *orator regius*,
remordyng dyvers recrayed and moche unresonable
errours of certayne sophystycate scolers and rechelesse
yonge heretykes lately abjured, etc. shall evermore be, with
all obsequious redynesse, humbly submytted unto the ryght
discrete reformacyon of the reverende prelates and moche
noble doctours of our mother Holy Churche, etc.

Ad almam Universitatem Cantabrigensem, etc.

Eulogium consolationis

Alma parens O Cantabrigensis
Cur lacrimaris? Esto tui sint
Degeneres hi filioli, sed
Non ob inertes, O pia mater,
5 *Insciolos vel decolor esto.*
Progenies non nobilis omnis,
Quam tua forsan mamma fovebat.
Tu tamen esto Palladis alme
Gloria pollens plena Minerve,
10 *Dum radiabunt astra polorum:*
Iamque valeto, meque foveto,
Namque tibi quondam carus alumnus eram.

Howe yong scolers nowe a dayes enbolned with the
flyblowen blast of the moche vayne glorious pipplyng
wynde, whan they have delectably lycked a lytell of the
lycorous electuary of lusty lernyng, in the moche studious
scolehous of scrupulous philology, countyng them selfe

clerkes exellently enformed and transcendingly sped in
moche high connyng, and whan they have ones
superciliusly caught

A lytell ragge of rethorike,
A lesse lumpe of logyke,
A pece or a patche of philosophy,
Than forthwith by and by
5   They tumble so in theology,
Drowned in dregges of divinite,
That they juge them selfe able to be
Doctours of the chayre in the Vyntre
At the Thre Cranes,
10   To magnifye their names.
But madly it frames,
For all that they preche and teche
Is farther than their wytte wyll reche.
Thus by demeryttes of their abusyon,
15   Finally they fall to carefull confusyon,
To beare a fagot, or to be enflamed.
Thus are they undone and utterly shamed.

> *Ergo*
> *Licet non enclitice,*
> *Tamen enthymematice,*
> *Notandum in primis,*
> *Ut ne quid nimis.*
> *Tantum pro primo.*

Over this, for a more ample processe to be farther delated
and contynued, and of every true Christen man laudably to
be enployed, justifyed, and constantly mainteyned; as
touchyng the tetrycall theologisacion of these demy divines,
and stoicall studiantes, and friscajoly yonkerkyns, moche
better bayned than brayned, basked and baththed in their
wylde burblyng and boyling blode, fervently reboyled with
the infatuate flames of their rechelesse youthe and wytlesse
wontonnese, enbrased and enterlased with a moche
fantasticall frenesy of their insensate sensualyte, surmysed
unsurely in their perihermeniall principles, to prate and to
preche proudly and leudly, and loudly to lye; and yet they
were but febly enformed in maister Porphiris problemes,
and have waded but weakly in his thre maner of clerkly

workes, analeticall, topicall, and logycall: howbeit they were
puffed so full of vaynglorious pompe and surcudant
elacyon, that popholy and pevysshe presumpcion provoked
them to publysshe and to preche to people imprudent
perilously, howe it was idolatry to offre to ymages of our
blessed lady, or to pray and go on pylgrimages, or to make
oblacions to any ymages of sayntes in churches or
elswhere.

    Agaynst whiche erronyous errours, odyous, orgulyous,
and flyblowen opynions, etc.,

In the honour of our blessed lady,
And her most blessed baby,
20   I purpose for to reply
Agaynst this horryble heresy
Of these yong heretikes, that stynke unbrent,
Whom I nowe sommon and convent,
That leudly have their tyme spent,

25   In their study abhomynable,
Our glorious lady to disable,
And heynously on her to bable
With langage detestable;
With your lyppes polluted
30   Agaynst her grace disputed,
Whiche is the most clere christall
Of all pure clennesse virgynall,
That our Savyour bare,
Whiche us redemed from care.

35   I saye, thou madde Marche hare,
I wondre howe ye dare
Open your janglyng jawes,
To preche in any clawes,
Lyke pratynge poppyng dawes,
40   Agaynst her excellence,
Agaynst her reverence,
Agaynst her preemynence,
Agaynst her magnifycence,
That never dyde offence.

45   Ye heretykes recrayed,
Wotte ye what ye sayed

Of Mary, mother and mayed?
With baudrie at her ye brayed;
With baudy wordes unmete
50   Your tonges were to flete;
Your sermon was nat swete;
Ye were nothyng discrete;
Ye were in a dronken hete.
Lyke heretykes confettred,
55   Ye count your selfe wele lettred:
Your lernyng is starke nought,
For shamefully ye have wrought,
And to shame your selfe have brought.

Bycause ye her mysnamed,
60   And wolde have her defamed,
Your madnesse she attamed;
For ye were worldly shamed,
At Poules Crosse openly,
All men can testifye.
65   There, lyke a sorte of sottes,
Ye were fayne to beare fagottes;
At the feest of her concepcion
Ye suffred suche correction.

Sive per equivocum,
70   *Sive per univocum,*
Sive sic, sive nat so,
Ye are brought to, 'Lo, Lo, Lo!
Se where the heretykes go,
Wytlesse wandring to and fro!'
75   With, 'Te he, ta ha, bo ho, bo ho!'
And suche wondringes many mo.
Helas, ye wreches, ye may be wo!
     Ye may syng weleaway
And curse bothe nyght and day,
80   Whan ye were bredde and borne,
And whan ye were preestes shorne,
Thus to be laughed to skorne,
Thus tattred and thus torne,
Thorowe your owne foly,
85   To be blowen with the flye
Of horryble heresy.

Fayne ye were to reny,
And mercy for to crye,
Or be brende by and by,
90 Confessyng howe ye dyde lye
In prechyng shamefully.

Your selfe thus ye discured
As clerkes unassured,
With ignorance obscured:
95 Ye are unhappely ured.
In your dialeticall
And principles silogisticall,
If ye to remembrance call
Howe *syllogisari*
100 *Non est ex particulari,*
Neque negativis,
Recte concludere si vis,
Et cetera id genus,
Ye coude nat *corde tenus,*
105 Nor answere *verbo tenus,*
Whan prelacy you opposed.
Your hertes than were hosed,
Your relacions reposed;
And yet ye supposed
110 *Respondere ad quantum,*
But ye were *confuse tantum,*
Surrendring your supposycions,
For there ye myst your quosshons.

Wolde God, for your owne ease,
115 That wyse Harpocrates
Had your mouthes stopped,
And your tonges cropped,
Whan ye logyke chopped,
And in the pulpete hopped,
120 And folysshly there fopped,
And porisshly forthe popped
Your sysmaticate sawes
Agaynst Goddes lawes,
And shewed your selfe dawes!
125 Ye argued argumentes,
As it were upon the elenkes,

De rebus apparentibus
Et non existentibus.
And ye wolde appere wyse
130 But ye were folysshe nyse.
Yet be meanes of that vyse
Ye dyde provoke and tyse,
Oftnar than ones or twyse,
Many a good man
135 And many a good woman,
By way of their devocion
To helpe you to promocion,
Whose charite wele regarded
Can nat be unrewarded.

140 I saye it for no sedicion,
But under pacient tuicyon,
It is halfe a supersticyon
To gyve you exhibycion
To mainteyne with your skoles,
145 And to prove your selfe suche foles.
    Some of you had ten pounde,
Therwith for to be founde
At the unyversyte,
Employed whiche myght have be
150 Moche better other wayes.
But, as the man sayes,
The blynde eteth many a flye.
What may be ment hereby,
Ye may soone make construction
155 With right lytell instruction;
For it is an auncyent brute,
Suche apple tre, suche frute.
What shulde I prosecute,
Or more of this to clatter?
160 Retourne we to our matter.

Ye soored over hye
In the ierarchy
Of Jovenyans heresy,
Your names to magnifye,
165 Among the scabbed skyes
Of Wycliffes flesshe flyes.

Ye strynged so Luthers lute
That ye dawns all in a sute
The heritykes ragged ray,
170   That bringes you out of the way
Of Holy Churches lay.
Ye shayle *inter enigmata*
And *inter paradigmata*,
Marked in your cradels
175   To beare fagottes for babyls.
     And yet some men say,
Howe ye are this day,
And be nowe as yll,
And so ye wyll be styll,
180   As ye were before.
What shulde I recken more?

Men have you in suspicion
Howe ye have small contrycion
Of that ye have myswrought;
185   For, if it were well sought,
One of you there was
That laughed whan he dyd pas
With his fagot in processyon.
He counted it for no correction,
190   But with scornefull affection
Toke it for a sporte,
His heresy to supporte;
Whereat a thousande gased,
As people halfe amased,
195   And thought in hym smale grace
His foly so to face.

Some juged in this case
Your penaunce toke no place,
Your penaunce was to lyght;
200   And thought, if ye had right,
Ye shulde take further payne
To resorte agayne
To places where ye have preched,
And your lollardy lernyng teched,
205   And there to make relacion
In open predycacion,

And knowlege your offence
Before open audyence,
Howe falsely ye had surmysed,
210   And devyllysshely devysed
The people to seduce,
And chase them thorowe the muse
Of your noughty counsell,
To hunt them into hell,
215   With blowyng out your hornes,
Full of mockysshe scornes,
With chatyng and rechatyng,
And your busy pratyng.
Of the gospell and the pystels
220   Ye pyke out many thystels,
And bremely with your bristels
Ye cobble and ye clout
Holy scripture so about,
That people are in great dout
225   And feare leest they be out
Of all good Christen order.
Thus all thyng ye disorder
Thorowe out every border.

It had ben moche better
230   Ye had never lerned letter,
For your ignorance is gretter,
I make you fast and sure,
Than all your lytterature.
    Ye are but lydder *logici*,
235   But moche worse *isagogici*,
For ye have enduced a secte
With heresy all infecte.
Wherfore ye are well checte,
And by Holy Churche correcte,
240   And in maner as abjecte,
For evermore suspecte,
And banysshed in effect
From all honest company,
Bycause ye have eaten a flye,
245   To your great vyllony,
That never more may dye.

Come forthe, ye pope holy,
Full of melancoly!
Your madde ipocrisy,
250   And your idiosy,
And your vayne glorie
Have made you eate the flye,
Pufte full of heresy,
To preche it idolatry,
255   Who so dothe magnifye
That glorious mayde Mary;
That glorious mayde and mother,
So was there never another,
But that princesse alone,
260   To whom we are bounde echone
The ymage of her grace
To reverence in every place.

I saye, ye braynlesse beestes,
Why jangle you suche jestes,
265   In your divynite
Of Luthers affynite,
To the people of lay fee,
Raylyng in your rages
To worshyppe none ymages,
270   Nor do pylgrymages?
      I saye, ye devyllysshe pages
Full of suche dottages,
Count ye your selfe good clerkes,
And snapper in suche werkes?

275   Saynt Gregorie and saynt Ambrose,
Ye have reed them, I suppose,
Saynt Jerome and saynt Austen,
With other many holy men,
Saynt Thomas de Aquyno,
280   With other doctours many mo,
Whiche *de latria* do trete.
They saye howe *latria* is an honour grete,
Belongyng to the Deite.
To this ye nedes must agre.
285   But, I trowe, your selfe ye overse
What longeth to Christes humanyte.

If ye have reed *de hyperdulia*,
Than ye know what betokeneth *dulia*:
Than shall ye fynde it fyrme and stable,
290   And to our faithe moche agreable,
To worshyppe ymages of sayntes.
Wherfore make ye no mo restrayntes,
But mende your myndes that are mased;
Or els doutlesse ye shalbe blased,
295   And be brent at a stake,
If further busynesse that ye make.
Therfore I vyse you to forsake
Of heresy the devyllysshe scoles,
And crye God mercy, lyke frantyke foles.

Tantum pro secundo.

Peroratio ad nuper abjuratos quosdam hipothiticos hereticos, etc.

Audite, viri Ismelite, non dico Isrelite;
Audite, inquam, viri Madianite, Ascolonite;
Ammonite, Gabionite, audite verba que loquar.

Opus evangelii est cibus perfectorum;
Sed quia non estis de genere bonorum,
Qui catechisatis categorias cacodemoniorum,

   Ergo
Et reliqua vestra problemata, schemata,
Dilemata, sinto anathemata!
Ineluctabile argumentum est.

A confutacion responsyve, or an inevytably prepensed
answere to all waywarde or frowarde altercacyons that can
or may be made or objected agaynst Skelton laureate,
devyser of this Replycacyon, etc.

300   Why fall ye at debate
With Skelton laureate,
Reputyng hym unable
To gainsay replycable
Opinyons detestable
305   Of heresy execrable?
      Ye saye that poetry
Maye nat flye so hye

In theology,
Nor analogy,
310 Nor philology,
Nor philosophy,
To answere or reply
Agaynst suche heresy.
    Wherfore by and by
315 Nowe consequently
I call to this rekenyng
Davyd, that royall kyng,
Whom Hieronymus,
That doctour glorious,
320 Dothe bothe write and call
Poete of poetes all,
And prophete princypall.
    This may nat be remorded
For it is wele recorded
325 In his pystell *ad Paulinum,*
Presbyterum divinum,
Where worde for worde ye may
Rede what Jerome there dothe say.

David, inquit, Simonides noster, Pindarus, et Alceus, Flaccus
quoque, Catullus, atque Serenus, Christum lyra personat, et in
decachordo psalterio ab inferis excitat resurgentem. Hec
Hieronymus.

The Englysshe
Kyng David the prophete, of prophetes principall,
330 Of poetes chefe poete, saint Jerome dothe wright,
Resembled to Symonides, that poete lyricall
Among the Grekes most relucent of lyght,
In that faculte whiche shyned as Phebus bright;
Lyke to Pyndarus in glorious poetry,
335 Lyke unto Alcheus, he dothe hym magnify.

Flaccus nor Catullus with hym may nat compare,
Nor solempne Serenus, for all his armony
In metricall muses, his harpyng we may spare;
For Davyd, our poete, harped so meloudiously
340 Of our savyour Christ in his decacorde psautry,
That at his resurrection he harped out of hell
Olde patriarkes and prophetes in heven with him to dwell.

Returne we to our former processe.

Than, if this noble kyng,
Thus can harpe and syng
345   With his harpe of prophecy
And spyrituall poetry,
And saynt Jerome saythe,
To whom we must gyve faythe,
Warblynge with his strynges
350   Of suche theologicall thynges,
Why have ye than disdayne
At poetes, and complayne
Howe poetes do but fayne?
Ye do moche great outrage,
355   For to disparage
And to discorage
The fame matryculate
Of poetes laureate.
For if ye sadly loke,
360   And wesely rede the Boke
Of Good Advertysement,
With me ye must consent
And infallibly agre
Of necessyte,
365   Howe there is a spyrituall,
And a mysteriall,
And a mysticall
Effecte energiall,
As Grekes do it call,
370   Of suche an industry
And suche a pregnacy,
Of hevenly inspyracion
In laureate creacyon,
Of poetes commendacion,
375   That of divyne myseracion
God maketh his habytacion
In poetes whiche excelles,
And sojourns with them and dwelles.

By whose inflammacion
380   Of spyrituall instygacion
And divyne inspyracion

We are kyndled in suche facyon
With hete of the Holy Gost,
Which is God of myghtes most,
385   That he our penne dothe lede,
And maketh in us suche spede
That forthwith we must nede
With penne and ynke procede,
Somtyme for affection,
390   Sometyme for sadde dyrection,
Somtyme for correction,
Somtyme under protection
Of pacient sufferance,
With sobre cyrcumstance,
395   Our myndes to avaunce
To no mannes anoyance.
Therfore no grevance,
I pray you, for to take,
In this that I do make
400   Agaynst these frenetykes,
Agaynst these lunatykes,
Agaynst these sysmatykes,
Agaynst these heretykes,
Now of late abjured,
405   Most unhappely ured;
For be ye wele assured,
That frensy nor jelousy
Nor heresy wyll never dye.

Dixi

*iniquis, Nolite inique agere; et delinquentibus, Nolite exaltare
cornu.*

Tantum pro tertio.

*De raritate poetarum, deque gimnosophistarum, philosophorum,
theologorum, ceterorumque eruditorum infinita numerositate,
Skeltonidis Laureati epitoma*

*Sunt infiniti, sunt innumerique sophiste,
Sunt infiniti, sunt innumerique logiste,
Innumeri sunt philosophi, sunt theologique,*

Sunt infiniti doctores, suntque magistri
5 *Innumeri; sed sunt pauci rarique poete.*
Hinc omne est rarum carum: reor ergo poetas
Ante alios omnes divine flamine flatos.
Sic Plato divinat, divinat sicque Socrates;
Sic magnus Macedo, sic Caesar, maximus heros
10 *Romanus, celebres semper coluere poetas.*

Thus endeth the Replicacyon of Skelton Laureate, etc.

Notes

The headnote to each poem seeks to establish, where possible, the date and occasion of that poem, and to supply brief details about the sources of the edited text. The other notes are primarily intended to elucidate difficult passages, to explain allusions, and to identify the sources of Skelton's ideas or phrasing. A selection of the more important textual variants is given. The following abbreviations are used:

Archiv: Archiv für das Studium der Neueren Sprachen und Literaturen

BL: British Library

Brewer: J.S. Brewer, *The Reign of Henry VIII from his Accession to the Death of Wolsey*, 2 vols., London: John Murray 1884

Carpenter: Nan C. Carpenter, *John Skelton*, New York: Twayne 1968

Dyce: Rev. Alexander Dyce, ed., *The Poetical Works of John Skelton*, 2 vols., London: Thomas Rodd 1843, reprinted 1965

Edwards: H.L.R. Edwards, *Skelton: The Life and Times of an Early Tudor Poet*, London: Cape 1949

EETS OS; EETS ES: Early English Text Society, Original Series; Early English Text Society, Extra Series

EHR: English Historical Review

ELN: English Language Notes

Fish: Stanley Eugene Fish, *John Skelton's Poetry*, New Haven and London: Yale University Press 1965

Hammond: Eleanor P. Hammond, ed., *English Verse between Chaucer and Surrey*, Durham: North Carolina 1927

Harris: W.O. Harris, *Skelton's Magnyfycence and the Cardinal Virtue Tradition*, Chapel Hill: University of North Carolina Press 1965

Heiserman: A.R. Heiserman, *Skelton and Satire*, Chicago: University of Chicago Press 1961

Henderson: Philip Henderson, ed., *The Complete Works of John Skelton, Laureate*, London: Dent 1931, 4th edition 1964

HLQ: Huntington Library Quarterly

Index: C.F. Brown and R.H. Robbins, eds., *The Index of Middle English Verse*, New York: Columbia University Press 1943

Kinsman: Robert S. Kinsman, ed., *John Skelton: Poems*, Oxford: Clarendon Press 1969

L & P: Letters and Papers, Foreign and Domestic of the Reign of Henry VIII, eds. J.S. Brewer, J. Gairdner, and R.H. Brodie, 22 vols., London: HMSO 1862–1932

MED: Middle English Dictionary, eds. Hans Kurath, Sherman M. Kuhn, John Reidy, Ann Arbor: University of Michigan Press 1954–

MLN: Modern Language Notes

MLR: Modern Language Review

N & Q: Notes and Queries

Nelson: William Nelson, *John Skelton, Laureate*, Columbia University Studies in English and Comparative Literature No. 139, 1939

Neuss: Paula Neuss, ed., *Magnificence*, Manchester University Press 1980

ODEP: Oxford Dictionary of English Proverbs, eds. W.G. Smith and Janet E. Heseltine, 2nd edition by Sir Paul Harvey, Oxford: Clarendon Press 1948

OED: Oxford English Dictionary

PMLA: Publications of the Modern Language Association of America

Pollet: Maurice Pollet, *John Skelton: Contribution à l'Histoire de la Prérenaissance Anglaise*, Paris: Libraire Didier 1962 (English translation by John Warrington, London: Dent 1971)

PQ: Philological Quarterly

PRO: Public Record Office

Ramsay: R.L. Ramsay, ed., *Magnyfycence*, EETS ES 98, 1908, reprinted 1958

RES: Review of English Studies

RQ: Renaissance Quarterly

Scattergood: V.J. Scattergood, *Politics and Poetry in the Fifteenth Century*, London: Blandford Press 1971

SP: Studies in Philology

STC: A.W. Pollard and G.R. Redgrave, *A Short-Title Catalogue of Books Printed in England, Scotland and Ireland . . . 1475–1640*, London: Bibliographical Society 1926, reissued 1950

Stevens: John Stevens, *Music and Poetry in the Early Tudor Court*, London: Methuen 1961

STS: Scottish Text Society

Tilley: Morris Palmer Tilley, *A Dictionary of the Proverbs in England in the Sixteenth and Seventeenth Centuries*, Ann Arbor: University of Michigan Press 1950

TLS: Times Literary Supplement

Whiting: B.J. and H.W. Whiting, *Proverbs, Sentences and Proverbial Phrases*, Cambridge, Mass.: The Belknap Press 1968

Williams: W.H. Williams, ed., *A Selection from the Poetical Works of John Skelton*, London: Isbister 1902

I   UPON THE DOLORUS DETHE AND MUCHE LAMENTABLE CHAUNCE OF THE
MOOSTE HONORABLE ERLE OF NORTHUMBERLANDE

In the spring of 1489 Henry VII, in order to raise money for his war in Brittany,
levied high taxes which caused considerable popular unrest (78–82). A York-
shire mob, led by one John a Chambre, rebelled and refused to pay their taxes;
and on Tuesday (114), 28 April, at Topcliffe near Thirsk, killed Henry Percy,
fourth Earl of Northumberland, who, as sheriff, had gone there to restore order.
The rebellion was put down by Thomas Howard, Earl of Surrey, and John a
Chambre was executed at York.

The text is taken from British Library MS Royal 18 Dii ff. 165r–166v (*R*),
which formerly belonged to the boy mentioned here (162–75) who became fifth
earl; collated with the copy in Marshe's 1568 edition of Skelton's *Workes* (*M*).
Bishop Percy printed a text of this poem from *R* in his *Reliques of Ancient
English Poetry* (1765), I, 95.

Poeta . . . paratus ero: 'Skelton, the laureate poet, addresses his little book in
verse. My page hastily to my lord, Percy, who bears the ancestral rights of the
Northumbrians: that which has fallen put back into the sway of the celebrated
lion, for whose father I sing the sad obsequies. But when he reads this through
may he turn over in his mind doubtful Fortune, who, untrustworthy, turns
everything round. Wherefore, may the lion be fortunate, may he live as long as
Nestor: I shall myself be prepared to please him.'

3   leonis: An allusion to the heraldic lion in the Percy crest; compare 109,
162, 167.

4   cano] *not M*.

7   Nestor was, according to *Iliad* i 250, more than two generations old; accord-
ing to Ovid's *Metamorphoses* xii 187 he was over 200 years old.

4   What Skelton has in mind here is not precisely clear; but the important Percy
family can be shown to have among their ancestors Charlemagne and the ancient
kings of France, Henry III and Edward III of England.

8–14   Properly Helicon was a range of mountains in Boeotia, sacred to Apollo
and the Muses. The celebrated fountains of the Muses, Aganippe and Hippo-
crene, were there. Clio was the muse of history. See also 155–61.

34   not] no *R*.

48   As military governor of the central and eastern Marches of Scotland the Earl
of Northumberland was the protector of those who killed him against the Scots.

52   your] ys *R*.

55   Perhaps based on the proverbial opposition of *wit* and *will* (compare Whit-
ing W 268). See also *Agaynst the Scottes* 102.

88   Hector was the son of Priam, king of Troy, famous for his valour. Compare
138.

89   with myght and with mayne: Proverbial (Whiting M 537).

92   one] *not M*.

95   life] *Percy's emendation, not RM. countede not a fly*: Proverbial (Whiting
F 341).

105   cruelly] cruell *RM*.

109   sande] lande *M*.

113–14   Tuesday is called after the Teutonic deity Tiw, equivalent to the

Roman god of war, Mars, who likewise gives his name to the third day of the week (*dies Martis*).

120–26 The *Parcae* or Fates, the sisters Clotho, Lachesis and Atropos, were supposed to preside respectively over the birth, life and death of all men. The name *Atropos* means inexorable (compare *merciles* 122). She was traditionally supposed to cut the thread of a man's life (*vitall threde* 126) not with a *sworde* (125), as here, but with scissors.

137 The reputation of Aeneas, the Trojan hero, for pious gentleness appears in Homer (*Iliad* xx 298) and this virtue is an important characteristic of Virgil's *pius Aeneas*.

139 Provydent] Prudent *M*.

144 far] for *R*.

184–5 with hym enterteynd/In fee: 'kept by him in his service'.

190 O] not *M*.

199 Thow] how *R*.

211 yerarchy] gerarchy *RM*.

217 In Trinitate: 'In Trinity'.

Non sapit...fides: 'He who wishes to have certain hope in things does not know of human affairs: the faith of men is rare and deceptive.'

Tetrasticon.....laudatissime: 'Four lines by the laureate Skelton to Master Rukshaw, an eminent professor in holy theology. Famous Doctor Rukshaw, receive now at last the songs which fall from my pen, and although they are not made musical in sweet poetry they nonetheless come from our affectionate breast. Farewell happily, most excellent of men.'

Skelton] Shelton *R*.

1 Rukshaw: William Rukshaw, of Peterhouse Cambridge, became M.A. in 1460–61 and Doctor of Theology in 1480. In this same year he entered the service of the Earl of Northumberland, and was installed as succentor at York. See Pollet, p. 10.

2 cecidere] Dyce's emendation, *occidere R*.

3 quamquam] *quaqua RM*; *camenis*] *carmenis M*.

II MANERLY MARGERY MYLK AND ALE

This is presumably one of the verses referred to in the *Garlande of Laurell*, 1198–211, and perhaps dates from the 1490s. Though it seems clearly to be Skelton's version of a clerk and serving maid ballad, it is difficult to be precise about who is meant to be speaking some of the lines. Fish's explanation (pp. 42–6) of the movement of the poem seems to me to be convincing, and I follow him in attributing the lines in inverted commas to the clerk.

The text is taken from British Library MS Additional 5465 (Fayrfax MS) fols. 96v–99r, where it appears as a song for three voices with music by William Cornish.

3 popagay: 'vain fellow', because the parrot was proverbial for its vanity (Whiting P 305).

6 A contemptuous line. *Gup* is a word usually applied to horses. For *Cristian Clowte* compare *Collyn Clout* 879, and for *Jak of the Vale* compare *Magnyfycence* 258 and Whiting J 4.

8 pode: 'toad', but here a term of endearment. Compare 'A littell, pratye, foolyshe poade' from *Rede Me and Be Nott Wrothe* (quoted by Dyce II 104).

10 'Nonsense, rubbish, you are playing the deceiver.' *Jamys foder* is jamesweed or ragwort.

11 *hakney*: 1. a horse for ordinary riding; 2. a prostitute.

12 If *bole* means 'bull' perhaps the line may be rendered 'Go, look after farm animals; you are capable enough.' The phrase *your bak is brode* appears to be proverbial (Whiting B 4).

17 *piggesnye*: The name of a flower, but also a term of endearment. Compare *The Canterbury Tales* I 3268.

19 *japed bodely*: 'seduced'.

III   AGAYNSTE A COMELY COYSTROWNE

The text is taken from what is probably the unique surviving copy of John Rastell's print of about 1527 (*R*) collated with the text in Marshe's works of Skelton of 1568 (*M*). The poems appear to date, however, from the period 1495–1500. See R.S. Kinsman, *HLQ* XVI, 1953, 203–10.

(i) *'Agaynste a comely coystrowne'*

The subject of this, the title poem of the miscellany, is sometimes supposed to be Lambert Simnel, the Yorkist impostor, captured by Henry VII after the Battle of Stoke (1487) and made a turnspit in the royal kitchens. But the *coystrowne* ('kitchen boy') in question was obviously a musician of sorts, and, from the references to Martin Swart (see lines 16–18 and note), to a Flemish *basse dance* (line 29 note) and to clothmaking for which the Flemish were renowned (line 34 note), it seems he was a foreigner, perhaps Flemish. If the references in 19 to *Perkyn* and his *Pohen* are to another Yorkish impostor Perkin Warbeck and his wife, Lady Catherine Gordon, the poem must have been composed between November 1495, when they married, and late September 1497, when Warbeck was captured and imprisoned.

4 they] the *R*.

5 syn] sins *M*.

14 Compare Whiting J 9, and see also line 42.

15 A song refrain, see John Stevens, *Music at the Court of Henry VIII*, in *Musica Britannica* xviii, Nos. 37, 75, 109.

16–18 Dyce (II 93) compares lines from William Wager's *The Longer Thou Livest*, *c.*1568, Sig. A3:

   Martin Swart and his man, sodledum, sodledum,
   Martin Swart and his man, sodledum bell.

Martin Swart, or Schwarz, was the brave and skilful leader of two thousand German mercenaries sent by the Duchess of Burgundy to assist Lambert Simnel. He died at the Battle of Stoke on 16 June 1487.

21 *holy water clarke*: The position of *aquae bajulus clericus* was a humble one; the only musical skill such a clerk needed was to enable him to assist in singing parts of the Mass.

26 *pyrdewy*: Probably a popular love song, mentioned in *Hickescorner* 207 and *Colkelbie Sow* 302.

29 'Roty bully joyse': 'fine roast boiled', a *basse danse* which originated in Brabant, but which seems to have been popular elsewhere, here mentioned probably because it was old-fashioned and vulgar. See Nan C. Carpenter, *RES* VI, 1955, 279–84.

34   spyndels . . . tavellys: Instruments used in clothmaking, for which the Flemish were famous. The *spyndel* was a rounded piece of wood used for twisting the wool fibres into thread, and the *tavell* was a bobbin on which the thread was wound.

47   A punning line. *dumpys* may mean either a melancholy reverie or a lamenting song for someone dead (see *OED dump* sb 1); *wrest* may mean either to contend or to tune a lute or clavichord by turning its pins (see *OED wrest* v).

49   Another punning line: it accuses the *coystrowne* of haunting taverns (compare 35), and also suggests he cannot read music well. The *larg* and the *long* were the two longest note values of the period and should have been sustained not swallowed in a breath.

55   Deuyas] dellias *M*. For *Doctor Deuyas* compare *Collyn Clout* 1157 and note.

57   Custodi nos: The opening of a versicle sung after the hymn at Compline, except on double feasts.

58–9   In the larger churches where there were many altars and a lot of chantry services, there were many clerks in minor orders, one of whom was designated Parish Clerk. Kinsman (p. 136) points out that the patron saint of the Guild of Master Parish Clerks of London was St Nicholas, at whose feast at Matins was sung the prose *Sospitati dedit egros*.

59   Sospitati] Dyce's emendation, suspitati *R*, supitati *M*.

62   Walk, and be nought: 'Clear off, and be damned.'

64   Proverbial (Whiting S 77).

65   occasyons] occasion *M*.

68   the best is behynde: Compare Whiting B 265. This embodies a threat for the usual form of the proverb is 'The best is behind, the worst is before'.

69–70   A deliberately nonsensical ending: Croydon (Surrey) is not 'by' Crowland (Lincolnshire); and Candlemas (2 February) does not fall on the Kalends of May (1 May). Compare *Mankind* 687–93.

(ii) '*Contra alium cantitantem et organisantem asinum*'

This is evidently on the same subject as the previous poem, and was probably written at about the same time.

'A sarcastic poem against another singer and doltish musician who criticized the muse-like Skelton. The tunes you play on your lute are not to be preferred to my songs, nor is your pipe as clear as ours: though often you play lyric psalms on a reed and also harmonize tremulous melodies on pipes; though your finger gives a thousand accompaniments to your song, yet how much more clever is your hand than your voice; though, proud man, you set all things below your pompous mind, yet our pipe is more pleasing to Phoebus. Therefore you should study in your mind to set aside your pride, and, foolish man, cease to dishonour a holy man. Said Skelton Laureate.'

8   Phebo: Apollo, in Greek mythology the god of poetry and song.

Quod Skelton laureat] not *M*.

(iii) '*Uppon a deedmans hed*'

Though the 'honorable Jentyllwoman' who sent the skull to Skelton has not been identified, Kinsman has suggested that the poem was written after Skelton was ordained (June 1498) but before he left the court for Diss (1504). See *S P L*, 1953, 101–9.

11–18   These lines recall medieval pictures of Death, as, for example, in B L M S Additional 37049 f. 20r or Bodleian Douce 322 f. 19v.

18   nor] not *M*.

30–31   An allusion to the commonplace idea of Death playing chess with man for his life; see, for example, *Roman de la Rose* 6620ff. and Chaucer's *Book of the Duchess* 618ff.

33–6   These lines recall the popular medieval 'signs of death' poems, for which see Rosemary Woolf, *The English Religious Lyric in the Middle Ages*, 1968, pp. 68–72.

46   boteles] botemles *M*.

Myrres vous y: 'Look upon yourself herein'. Kinsman (p. 137) points out that Skelton possibly took this colophon from the opening of a 'mirover des dames' poem by Jean Castel (written about 1470):

Mirez vous cy, dames et damoiselles,
Mirez vous cy et regardes ma face.

Compare the colophon to *Agenst Garnesche* ii.

(iv) 'Womanhod, wanton, ye want'

In the *Garlande of Laurell* 1241–2, Skelton mentions 'many a praty lyne' he wrote to 'fayre maistres Anne', yet this seems to be the only poem which has survived. It was almost certainly written before 1504, while he was still in London. Fish (pp. 40–42) suggests the poem may be for two voices.

4   Compare *Speke Parott* 387.

13   *proud as pohen*: A variant of the proverbial 'as proud as a peacock'. Compare Whiting P 71, P 73.

15–17   Based loosely on the proverb 'The scorpion flatters with its head when it will sting with its tail' (Whiting S 96).

22–30   Kinsman (p. 137) points out the quadruple pun on the word *key*: 1. the metal instrument for opening locks; 2. the emblem of St Zita, patron saint of serving maids; 3. a slang term for the female pudend; 4. the name of an inn at which 'mastres Anne' lives or perhaps serves. In the Thames Street area in the time of Henry VI there was a house called the Key.

IV   DYVERS BALETTYS AND DYTIES SOLACYOUS

Dyce (p. xcii) attributes the unique surviving text of these poems to Pynson, but Edward Hodnett, on the basis of their illustrations, argues for John Rastell (*English Woodcuts 1480–1535*, 1935, pp. 56–7). The four leaves which survive, and from which the texts are taken, were probably printed by Rastell in about 1527 (*R*), but the poems themselves probably date from as early as 1495–1500. See also R.S. Kinsman, *HLQ* XVI, 1953, 203–10.

(i) 'My darlyng dere, my daysy floure'

The general situation of the man deceived by a tavern prostitute recalls Lydgate's 'Ballade on an Ale-Seller' (*Minor Poems* II No. 9), though there are no close verbal correspondences. The refrain is a parody of the fairly popular lullaby

poems of Mary and the Christ child. Compare R.L. Greene, *Early English Carols*
Nos. 142–155.

2   ly in your lap: Compare *Hamlet* III ii 108–14, where there is a similar sexual
innuendo.

19   Probably based on the proverb 'After great cold comes great heat' (Whiting
C 365, and compare also H 305); but here *cought a hete* also means 'became sex-
ually aroused'.

28   powle hachet: 'a soldier who uses a pole-axe' (see R.L. Greene, *N & Q*
CCXIX, 1974, 128–30).

(ii) *'The auncient acquaintance'*

11   Dame Menolope: According to Diodorus Siculus iv 16, 'Menalyppe' was
queen of the Amazons for whom Hercules took a girdle 'rychely embullyond'.
(Usually in this story the Amazonian queen is called Hippolyta.) A 'Menalip' is
spoken of as having 'marcial power' enough to defeat Theseus in a ballade of
'The ix Ladies Worthie' attributed to Chaucer in his *Works* (1602) f. 324.

13–25   For another passage in which Skelton exploits equestrian imagery with a
sexual innuendo compare *The Bowge of Courte* 407–12.

16   curtoyl] *Dyce's emendation*, curtoyt *R*. The line is full of puns: *curtoyl* means
both 'a horse with a docked tail' and 'a tunic'; *naggys* both 'small horses' and
(in slang) 'the human testicles'.

17–18   Gup and *Jayst* are words frequently applied to horses; compare *Agenst
Garnesche* iii 13, *Elynour Rummynge* 390. *Jenet of Spayne*: A jennet (from French
genet or Spanish *ginete* or *jinete*) was originally a Spanish light horseman who rode
with short stirrups (*a la gineta*). In English and French the word was transferred
from the rider to the horse. Perhaps if the lady the poem is addressed to had an
actual existence her name was Janet and is referred to punningly here. See also
The Bowge of Courte 369 and note.

20   'Send in the officer in charge of horses; my horse has lost the shoes on its
hind legs.' But there is a pun on 'horse' and 'whore's' too.

23   keylyth with a clench: This means both 'she (as a mare) kills by means of a
kick' (the *clench* was that part of a nail turned back to keep a horseshoe in place,
OED clinch sb 1), and also 'she (as a woman) grows cooler after having been
closely embraced'.

24   'She walks with her legs spread apart, not with her feet closely together',
that is, like a heavily used horse.

36   Proverbial (compare Whiting C 469).

38   Howbeit] Howbeis *R.*

(iii) *'Knolege, aquayntance, resort'*

An acrostic, using the first letter of each stanza, spells out KATERYN, to whom
the poem evidently refers. To speak of the lady as a medicine (8–10), to compare
her beauty and personal qualities to those supposedly possessed by precious
stones (15–21), and to compare her to stars (24–5) were devices frequently used
in love poetry.

10   Compare Lydgate's *Life of Our Lady* i: 'O thoughtfull herte, plunged in dis-
tresse', and the *Garlande of Laurell* 296.

12–13 Kinsman (p. 134) points out that the Virgin Mary was frequently referred to, in medieval religious symbolism, as the well of living waters and the enclosed garden.

24 Esperus: Hesperus, the evening star.

(iv) *'Though ye suppose'*

The Latin and the English versions are closely equivalent except that the English has *lesard* for *anguis* ('snake'), presumably in order to provide alliteration in line 7, thus giving a unique variant of the common proverbial phrase 'The serpent in the grass' (Whiting S 153).

3 Compare Whiting F 516: 'Fortune has a double face'.
5 Perhaps some variant of the proverb 'When one looks on the outer skin he knows little what is within' (Whiting S 365).

(v) *'Go, pytyous hart'*

The 'nobyll lady' at whose instance this poem was written has not been identified.

V   THE BOWGE OF COURTE

From lines 1–7 it appears that the poem was written in the late autumn, perhaps of 1498, as suggested by Helen Stearns Sale on the basis of the dates of the early printed editions (*MLN* LII, 1937, 572–4). However, Melvin J. Tucker (*ELN* VII, 1970, 168–75) argues for '1480 or thereabouts', because 'On September 11, 1480 a close conjunction between Mars and the quarter moon took place three days before the autumn equinox', because in September 1480 the Scots invaded England (perhaps the implication of 7), and because Lord John Howard (who favoured Skelton) owned a house on the quay at Harwich in 1481 and that a certain John Power was in charge of it (34–5). If this is correct the poem is very early indeed.

The idea of a 'ship of fools' may have been taken from Brant's *Narrenschiff* (1494) or from Locher's Latin version *Stultifera Navis* (1497). A ship of vices had, however, already appeared in Jacquemart Gielé's *Renard le Nouvel* (1288) lines 4949ff.

The text is taken from the unique copy of Wynkyn de Worde's 1499 printing in Advocate's Library Edinburgh (*A*), collated with the second edition of this (*c.* 1510) in the University Library Cambridge (*C*) and with Marshe's edition of 1568 (*M*).

Title: Derives from 'bouche de court', the free rations provided in the royal household.
1   the sonne in Vyrgyne: The sun is in the sign of Virgo from about 22 August to 22 September. Poems with an autumn opening often have a sombre tone (see Heiserman, pp. 21, 32–3).
2–6 In these lines the *dyademe...Of our pole artyke* refers to the Corona Borealis or Ariadne's crown. From mid-April until early December it is visible after sunset in the north-eastern sky. Kinsman suggests that 'the harvest moon which had dominated the north easterly skies with the Corona Borealis (4), is now on the wane (3), and just enough of her surface shows to suggest a scornful smile' (p. 138).

11 it] *not M.*

14 moralyte] mortalyte *A M.*

18 dyscure] dysture *A C.*

19 I] *not A C.*

24 his] *not M.*

27–8 Proverbial (compare Tilley F 131).

29–33 Heiserman thinks that the narrator's anxious and agitated frame of mind when he goes to sleep, and the frightening nature of his dream, would suggest 'to the learned reader' that this was an ambiguous *somnium animale* (p. 33). According to Vincent of Beauvais autumn dreams were particularly confused and disordered (see W.C. Curry, *Chaucer and the Medieval Sciences*, 1926, p. 211).

33 me] my *A C M.*

35 *Powers Keye*: Kinsman identifies a John Power who lived in Harwich during the reign of Richard III: 'It is likely that Powers Key bears his name or that of a member of his family' (p. 138). See also introductory note above.

40 lode] *not M.*

49 certeynte] certeynet *A* certayne *C.*

51 *Dame Saunce-Pere*: 'Lady Peerless'.

52 Her] Here *A.*

58 traves] tranes *A C M.*

60 clerer] clere *M.*

61 '. . . than the sun in its heavenly sphere.'

67 *Garder*] Garde *M.* The line is deliberately ambiguous: 1. 'Preserve fortune which is both bad and good.' 2. 'Beware of fortune which is both bad and good.'

72 had] *not A C.* The whole line is based on a proverb meaning 'to be bold'. See Whiting S 67.

91 Compare Whiting S 554.

94 And] But *M.*

98 *Bone aventure*: 'good luck'.

102 an] and *C M.*

111–17 The description of Fortune in these lines takes up again the phrase *mauelz et bone* (67) and elaborates it through a series of antithetical statements. Fortune was frequently treated in this way; see, for example, *The Book of the Duchess* 620–49. On the concept of Fortune in general see H.R. Patch, *The Goddess Fortuna in Medieval Literature*, 1927.

112 see-boorde] shyp borde *M.*

114 laugheth] laughed *A.*

117 cheryssheth] cherysshed *A C M*; casseth] casteth *C* chasseth *M.*

120 *martchauntes*; Because they put themselves and their property at risk merchants were thought to be especially dependent on Fortune. Compare *The Canterbury Tales* VIII 946–50:

> Us moste putte oure good in aventure.
> A marchant, pardee, may nat ay endure,
> Trusteth me wel, in his prosperitee.
> Somtyme his good is drowned in the see,
> And somtyme comth it sauf unto the londe.

In fact, merchants justified the 'fortunes' they sometimes made on the grounds that they took great risks. On this whole subject see R.H. Tawney, *Religion and the Rise of Capitalism*, 1926, Chapter 1.

Thus endeth . . . compyled] Thus endeth the Prologue *M.*

127–8   For the concept of Fortune as a favourable wind compare Gower's *Confessio Amantis* V 7554–7, and Lydgate's *Troy Book* I 1234–6.
131   Compare Whiting H 433.
134   *Favell* was frequently used as the type-name of the flatterer. Compare, for example, *Piers Plowman* B II 6, 41, and Hoccleve's *Minor Poems* III 209–88. See also *Magnyfycence* 727.
138   Hafter] Haster *A C M*. The reading in the editions looks like the result of confusion between *f* and *long s*; the emendation seems justified by reference to *Why Come Ye Nat to Courte?* 97 and *Magnyfycence* 257, 697, 1678, 2456. A 'hafter' is a sharper or a trickster.
152   In this line Favell is alluding to the traditional distinction between the gifts of Fortune and the gifts of Grace, *connynge* being of the second category. Compare *The Canterbury Tales* X 454 ff.:
   'Goodes of fortune been richesse, hyghe degrees of lordshipes, preisynges of the peple. Goodes of grace been science, power to suffre spiritueel travaille, benignitee, vertuous contemplacioun, withstondynge of temptacioun, and semblable thynges.'
At ibid. X 450 the Parson also distinguishes a category 'the goodes of nature'. For another passage on the gifts of Fortune and Nature see ibid. VI 294ff. See also Whiting G 71.
158   shorte] a shorte *C*.
173   wattes] witts *M*.
186   Twyst] Whist *C* Twysshe *M*.
190–93   These lines, and also 288–94, seem to owe something to medieval descriptions of the deadly sin of Envy, who is characteristically pale (293), thin (294), wasted by disease (290), sometimes fever (193), sometimes leprosy (289), his eyes are emphasized (191, 193) and he sometimes bites his lip in suppressed anger (288). Compare the portrait in *Piers Plowman* B V 78 ff.

   He was as pale as a pelet   in the palsye he semed,
   And clothed in a caurimaury   I couthe it noughte discreve;
   In kirtel and kourteby   and a knyf bi his side,
   Of a freres frokke   were the forsleves.
   And as a leke hadde yleye   longe in the sonne,
   So loked he with lene chekes   lourynge foule.
   His body was to-bolle for wratthe   that he bote his lippes…

See further M.W. Bloomfield, *The Seven Deadly Sins*, 1952, pp. 172, 195, 221, 231, 242, 355.
198   commaunde] commened *C*; a praty space] *Dyce's emendation*, a party spake *A M* a party space *C*.
212   Compare Whiting H 264.
219   dyscure] dysture *A C*.
223   man] wan *A*.
231   Hafter] Haster *A C M*.
234   Me] My *A*.
235   '*Sythe I am nothynge playne*' was apparently the first line of a song now lost. For mentions of other songs see 252, 253, 254 and 360.
238   my] me *M*.
   HAFTER] HASTER *A C M*.
245   skan] stan *A C*; it (2nd)] *not M*.
252   Compare C.L. Kingsford, *Chronicles of London*, 1905, p. 164: '… and this

yere (1453–4), upon the morne after Symound and Jude, John Norman befor-named, beyng chosyn Mair for that present yere, was rowed by water to West-mynster wt the Aldermen; and alle the chief of the Comoners of the Cite went also thedir by barges; which of tymes owte of mynde were used before season by the Mairs to ride allwey by land to take their charge. Wherfore the watermen of Themmys made a song of this John Norman, whereof the begynnyng was, "Rowe thy bote Norman"; whiche newe custume was welle allowed, & hathe contynued from his daies to this season.'

Fabyan's *Chronicle*, ed. H. Ellis, 1811, p. 628 gives what may have been the first two lines, 'Rowe the bote Norman, rowe to thy lemman', and Skelton's snatch may be the refrain. The phrase 'Heve and how, rombelow', or some variation on it, is frequently used in sailors' songs (see Dyce II 110–11 for examples).

253–4 'Prynces of youghte' is the opening of an early fifteenth-century song (*Index* No. 2782). See Lydgate's *Temple of Glass* 970. 'Shall I sayle with you' seems to be another song, now lost.

255 I] *not A*.

284 hawte] hawtie *M*.

285 Scornnys] storunys *A C* scornes *M*.

288 the] his *C*.

293 Compare Whiting A 205.

294 carkes] *Kinsman's emendation*, carbes *A C* crabes *M*.

295 Hafter] Haster *A C M*.

305 our] your *M*.

311 Hafter] Haster *A C M*; layne] sayne *A M*.

315 Compare Whiting C 36, meaning 'play confidently on not a very high card, bluff'.

344–71 Kinsman (p. 140) compares 350ff. with the description of Covetise in *Piers Plowman* B V 195–7. But Ryotte is called initially *a rusty gallande* and it seems to me the portrait owes much to the tradition of poems which satirize 'gal-lants'. With some of Skelton's ideas here compare the late-fifteenth-century 'Huff! A Galaunt', ed. R.H. Robbins, *Historical Poems* No. 52. With Ryotte's dicing and lack of money compare:

Galaunt, by thy gyrdyl ther hangyth a purss;

Ther-in ys neyther peny ner crosse,

But iij dysse, and crystys curse. (33–5)

With his short garments (354–5) compare:

Theyre gownys be sett with plytys fele,

To schortt yt ys theyre kneys to hele. (18–19)

With his broken hose and patched garments (357–8) compare:

Galawntt, with thy curtesy,

Thow brekyst thy hose at kne,

And with a pacche thou clowtyst Aye. (5–7)

With Ryotte's dagger and pouche (363) compare:

Galaunt, with thy daggar a-crosse

And thyn hanggyng pouche upon thy narse. (37–8)

Like Ryotte (417) this 'gallant' has criminal tendencies: 'Thow art ful abyl to stele a horse' (39). For an account of other poems in this tradition see Scatter-good, pp. 340–47, and *N & Q* CCXIX, 1974, 83–5.

346 *payre of bones*: 'a set of dice', evidently three, as was usual, for Ryotte throws 'four three two' in the next line.

399   V THE BOWGE OF COURTE

348   Saynte Thomas of Kente: St Thomas Becket (murdered 1170).
350   A proverbial way of describing a poor man or a spendthrift (compare Whiting H 22).
355   all for somer lyght: Compare *The Canterbury Tales* VIII 568, and *Phyllyp Sparowe* 719.
358   checked] checkered *M*.
359   Kyrkeby Kendall: A place in Westmorland, where was produced a low-grade green woollen cloth.
360   Evidently the refrain or opening line of a song. Compare *Why Come Ye Nat to Courte?* 66–7 and *A Devoute Trentale* 63.
362   a-droppynge] droppynge *M*.
364   Compare Whiting D 191. Many coins were marked with a cross on one side. The gallants New Gyse, Nowadays and Nought in *Mankind* have purses but no money (479–89) and this same proverb is used at line 488.
365   O lux beata Trinitas is a phrase from the hymn sung at Vespers on Saturday.
366   An] And *M*.
366–7   Hats with long feathered decorations were fashionable in the reign of Henry VII; see F.W. Fairholt, *Costume in England*, rev. H.A. Dillon, 1896, I, pp. 220–21.
368   Compare *Ralph Roister Doister* I i 20.
369   hadde] *not M*. A punning line. A 'jennet' is a small horse (OF *genet*) and in this reading *tayle* can have its normal meaning 'tail'. But the line also means 'how often he had had sexual intercourse with Janet'. For *tayle* meaning the female sexual organs see *The Canterbury Tales* VII 416, 434, where this meaning is punned on. For the phrase 'Ionete-of-the-stewis' meaning prostitute see *Piers Plowman* A VII 64 and *The Towneley Plays* XXX 350.
371   Compare 'Womanhod, wanton, ye want' (26) for a similar sexual innuendo.
375   Compare Whiting D 200. See also 455; *Magnyfycence* 943, 2172; *Speke Parott* 445.
386   a mery pyne: Proverbial for being in a happy mood (see Whiting P 215).
387   placke] plucke *M*. *placke* is difficult; perhaps it should be 'pluck' and the whole line may mean 'let us laugh while we drink a draught or two of ale'.
388   was never one] is here within *M*.
389   of dyce a bale: 'A set of dice', but *bale* also means 'torment' usually of hell and Skelton may intend that meaning also, since gambling was commonly regarded as sinful.
390   brydelynge caste: Probably, as Dunbabin suggested (*MLR* XII, 1917, 251), 'a final throw', that is, a roll of the dice while the horses are being harnessed.
394   I] *not C*. Kinsman (p. 141) translates the line 'Or else let us play "passage" and I'll give you odds,' 'passage' being a dice game. But to 'pass' can also mean to 'leave the game' or 'forgo one's opportunity to throw' (*OED pass* v XI 26).
397   Compare *Magnyfycence* 1108.
398   armes of Calyce: Here it looks like an oath; but until the middle of the fifteenth century some English coins were minted at Calais. Compare *Magnyfycence* 675.
399   happy: Used here in its original sense 'lucky' (ON *happ*).
403   harnes] *Kinsman's emendation*, harmes *A C* armes *M*. For the sexual implications of the riding metaphor see 'The auncient acquaintance' 13–25, and for the pun on *tayle* see 369 and note.
408   Fraunce: Twice previously Ryotte has mentioned things connected with

France (398, 406). In some anti-gallant verses it is suggested that the fashions satirized are French. See 'Treatyse of this Galaunt' 43–56, ed. F.J. Furnivall, *Ballads from Manuscripts*, 1868, I, pp. 445–53.

411   curtel] curtet *A C*.

413   is] *not M*.

416   Unthryftynes] Unthryftnes *A C*.

417   whome] home *A*; *Tyborne*: Tyburn, until 1783 a place of public execution.

428   Compare Whiting F 13.

430   me have] have me *C*.

433–7   Perhaps, as Kinsman suggests (p. 142), based on a proverb (Tilley H 547): 'He has honey in his mouth and a razor at his girdle.' But compare the Chaucerian *Romaunt of the Rose*, which says of Fals-Semblant:

> . . . in his sleve he gan to thringe
> A rasour sharp and wel bytynge. (7417–18)

Also *The Canterbury Tales* I 1999: 'The smylere with the knyf under the cloke.'

437   preye] preve *C*.

441   he] that he *M*.

446   hym] *not A M*.

448   *scrypture sayth soo*: Perhaps the previous lines on fools and wisemen were suggested by Proverbs xxvi 1–12.

449   lytterkture] lytterature *C*.

461   you] Iou *A M*.

462   Jew] yew *A M*. The line is proverbial (Whiting J 41).

464   to] te *A*.

467   tell] not tell *C*.

471   this] these *C*.

477   'I have in my pouch an answer which will silence your enemies.' Based on a proverb (see Whiting O 93).

479   *to reyse a smoke*: Proverbial (Whiting S 413).

496   In] To *M*.

508   hode] body *M*.

509   *lyme-fynger*: Compare Whiting L 293.

511   *Saynte Quyntyne*: It is not certain to whom this refers. For possible identifications see *The Catholic Encyclopaedia* under 'Quinctianus'. Compare *Mankind* 271.

515   Parde] Parte *A C M*.

524   *mordre wolde come oute*: Compare Whiting M 806.

526   rounded] roynded *A*.

538   Probably based on the proverb 'Dreams are true' (Whiting D 388).

VI   WARE THE HAUKE

The poem obviously dates from the period 1503–12 when Skelton was mainly resident at Diss. Much the same sort of date is also suggested if the hawking priest who violated his church there is to be identified with John Smith, who was rector of East Wretham from 1503 to 1517 (see note to line 331). It is difficult to be much more precise than this, though Kinsman and Yonge suggest 'perhaps before 29 August 1505' (*Canon and Census*, p. 13). The hunting or hawking cleric, however, was a traditional target for satirists: compare *The Canterbury Tales* I 165–207 and *Pires Plowman* B V 400–428.

The text is taken from Richard Lant's edition (*L*) of *Certayne Bokes* (*c*.1545) collated with the editions of John Kynge and Thomas Marche (*c*.1554) (*K*), John Day (*c*.1560) (*D*) and Thomas Marshe's edition of Skelton's *Workes* of 1568 (*M*).

8   playe the daw: 'play the fool'. The *daw* or 'crow' was proverbial for its foolishness. Compare Whiting D 27, D 28, D 29. Skelton picks up this idea again in the 'Daucock' refrain in line 246ff.

28   Be] By *K*.

54   For Moses see Exodus iiff., and for Aaron's rod which budded see Numbers xvii 8.

60–65   'The hawk tugged on a bone and in the holy place she dunged on my communion cloth. Such a sacrifice of praise he made with such pranks.' *tyryd* is a technical falconry term meaning 'tore with the beak' (see *OED tire* v 3 II). *chase* here seems to mean 'spot' and properly is a technical term in tennis meaning 'the second impact on the floor of a ball which the opponent has not returned' (see *OED chase* sb 1 7). The *corporas* is the square of cloth on which is set the host and chalice during Mass.

60   bone] bonne *L*.

OBSERVATE: 'Observe.'

69   rode loft: A loft or gallery which in medieval churches formed the top of the rood screen, a partition usually of elaborately carved wood which divided the chancel from the nave. On the top of the screen was usually a carved cross showing Christ crucified, with the figures of the Virgin Mary and John on either side. Compare line 127.

71   prest] priest *KD*.

73   Stow, stow, stow!: A call used by falconers to make their birds come to hand. 'Make them come from it to your fist, eyther much or little, with calling and chirping to them, saying: Towe, Towe or Stowe, Stowe, as Falconers use' (Turbervile, *Booke of Falconrie*, 1611, p. 182). Compare *Magnyfycence* 917.

85   frounce: An illness causing soreness around the hawk's mouth. 'The Frounce proceedeth of moist and cold humours, which descend from the hawk's head to their palate and the roote of the tongue. And of that cold is engendred in the tongue the Frownce...' (Turbervile's *Booke of Falconrie*, 1611, p. 303).

93   prety gyn: Nelson suggested an explanation based on the unusual structure of St Mary's Diss: 'The western tower stands apart from the rest of the edifice, and is connected with it only by a hollow arch. From the space beneath this arch one door leads into the church and another into the tower. In Skelton's day, if the church door were bolted one might have entered and climbed the tower, passed through the arch, and descended by a small door (now blocked up) into the nave of the church' (p. 105, note 10).

96   I hym] him I *KDM*.

CONSIDERATE: 'Regard carefully.'

100   Saynt Johnn decollacyon: 29 August.

102–3   'At the time of vespers, but not according to Sarum use.' *Sarum* is the ecclesiastical name for Salisbury, and 'Sarum use' was the order of divine service established there in the eleventh century and, until the Reformation, adopted in all parts of the country.

104–5   Based on the proverb, 'As mad as a March hare' (Whiting H 116). *parum* 'small'.

112   Again proverbial (compare Whiting B 456).

DELIBERATE: 'Consider.'

116–17 Hankyn Bovy is a kind of rustic dance, and *Troll, cytrace* and *trovy* are the sorts of words likely to be sung in accompaniment.

119 then] *not DM*.

124 rynge: The falconer is cynically comparing the bells on his hawk's feet to the matins bell. See also 136–7.

125 In] Is *L*.

VIGILATE: 'Be vigilant.'

145–54 The implication of this passage is that Skelton reported this matter to the ecclesiastical court (*In the offycyallys bokys*), but there is no evidence of such an action. The mention of *mayden Meed* ('lady Bribery') implies that his opponent bribed the officials (compare *Piers Plowman* B II 7ff.). The Pharisees were an ancient Jewish sect who held a strict observance of the traditional and written Law; the Scribes were a class of professional interpreters of the Law. For their dispute with Christ see Mark vii, Luke v 21ff. Here Skelton applies the terms to his ecclesiastical superiors with the implication that they are hypocritical, and excessively formal.

147 he] her *M*.

DEPLORATE: 'Lament.'

164–72 Skelton has in mind Exodus xxv–xxvi, xxxv–xl, and I Kings vi–viii. For 'the ark of the Lord' see Exodus xxv 10–16, and for 'the blood of bulls and the blood of calves' see Exodus xxix 10–14.

177 not D M.

DIVINITATE: 'Prophesy.'

188–9 Compare 9–10, of which these lines are practically a repeat.

REFORMATE: 'Reform.'

192 Dyoclesyan: Valerius Diocletianus, Roman Emperor 284–305, notable for his fierce persecutions of the Christians in 303.

193 Domysyan: Titus Flavius Domitianus, Roman Emperor 81–96, who behaved cruelly and tyrannously in the last years of his reign.

194 Nother] Nor yet *KDM. Cacus* was the son of Vulcan, a terrible giant who lived in a cave on Mount Aventine and plundered the surrounding countryside. He stole some of the oxen of Geryon from Hercules, who, because of this, killed him.

195 Bacus: Bacchus, in Greek and Roman mythology, was the god of wine but is usually associated with peace and civilization. Perhaps Skelton has in mind the incident in which Pentheus, king of Thebes, who forbade the worship of the god, was first driven mad then torn to pieces by his mother and sisters, who in their Bacchic fury believed him to be a wild beast. In Argos also the people refused to worship Bacchus at first, but consented after he had punished all the women with frenzy.

196 Olybryus: The 'provost' who first tortured, then beheaded St Margaret at Antioch.

197 Dyonysyus the Elder (430–367 BC), the tyrant of Syracuse, who subjugated the rest of Sicily, Carthage and annexed part of southern Italy. He is described as having been suspicious and cruel. He built the terrible prison Lautumiae carved out of solid rock at Epipolae in Syracuse.

198–9 Phalaris, another Sicilian tyrant, reigned in Agrigentum from *c.*570 to *c.*564 BC. The most infamous example of his inhumanity was the brazen bull in which he is said to have burnt people alive so that their groans simulated the bellowing of a real bull. Perillus, who built the bull, was its first victim. The story appears in Valerius Maximus, *De Factis Dictisque Memorabilibus* III iii.

200 Sardanapalus, king of Assyria from 668 BC, conquered many of the surrounding countries, most notably Babylon. Classical historians depicted him, probably wrongly, as an effeminate, voluptuous and cruel despot.

202 *Nero* was Roman Emperor from 54 to 68. Soon after his succession he had put to death Britannicus, son of the Emperor Claudius, Agrippina his mother, and Octavia his wife so that he could marry his mistress, Poppaea Sabina.' A conspiracy against his tyranny led by Piso was crushed in 65, and among those put to death for their part in it were Lucan and Seneca. Nero committed suicide in 68 when he was overthrown by Galba.

203 Claudius I was Roman Emperor from 41 to 54. He was unfortunate in his choice of wives and associates, who led him to commit acts of tyranny. He was poisoned by Agrippina in 54.

204 *Egeas*: Probably a reference to Aegeus, king of Athens, and father of Theseus. Why he should be listed among tyrants is not immediately clear. Perhaps Skelton has in mind Aegeus's declaration that Theseus was to be his successor, thus excluding the fifty sons of Pallas.

205 Ferumbras was the tyrannous giant heathen king of Alexandria who defied Charlemagne and his douzepeers. He was overcome by Oliver and converted to Christianity. Compare *Agenst Garnesche* i 15.

206 Why Zerubbabel appears here is not clear. He was entrusted by Cyrus with the rebuilding of the temple in Jerusalem in c.536 BC. Skelton may have in mind Haggai i 4–6, where Zerubbabel is criticized for not getting on with the work.

207 Jezebel was the cruel and infamous wife of Ahab (see I Kings xvi 31 ff.).

208–10 The reference is probably to Lucius Tarquinius Superbus, who, on becoming king of Rome, abolished the rights conferred on the plebeians by his predecessor Servius, and had all those senators and patricians whom he distrusted put to death or exiled. Or alternatively his son, Sextus, may be meant. He ruled tyrannously over the Gabii and his rape of Lucretia, his cousin's wife, was the cause of the Tarquins' banishment from Rome in 510 BC. See Titus Livius I xlix–lix.

212 Probably Aristobulus, ruler of Judea, who starved his mother to death in prison and had his brother Antigonus killed, is referred to here.

213–21 Constantinople was taken by Sultan Mehmet and the Turks on 29 May 1453. The Christian dead, including civilians, were said to number four thousand. The cathedral of St Sophia was plundered immediately the Turks entered the city. See Steven Runciman, *The Fall of Constantinople*, Cambridge 1965, Chapters X and XI.

PENSITATE: 'Ponder.'

239–45 The first four lines of the Latin puzzle may be solved if certain superfluous letters are omitted, if the contractions are expanded and if then the syllables are inverted. The numbers correspond to the letters of the alphabet, taking i/j as one letter; vowels are numbered 1 to 5. The last but one number is 3 in the prints but has to be emended to 4. This gives:

Sic velut est arabu(m)
Phenix avis unica tantum
Terra Britan(n)a suum genuit
SKELTONIDA vate(m).
Just like the phoenix of Arabia,

A bird not like any other,
The Land of Britain has produced
Its own poet Skelton.

For a similar number puzzle see the *Garlande of Laurell* 742ff., and Henry Bradley, *The Academy*, 1 August 1896, p. 83, who first suggested the solution.

The rest of the Latin is more straightforward: 'I pray that this little paper may remain, to be violated by no wanton person: not a man, only an evil ox may destroy these numbers. Perceive openly the matter of this paper in part, behind this Arethusan muse.'

243   nullo] *uello DM*.

250–51   'Work this out, Master Dawcock.'

253–5   'Master sophist, you simpleminded logician, you devilish philosopher ...'

255   Ye] *Dyce's emendation*, The *LKDM*.

257   you] *your LKDM*.

258–9   'In this church, Master, you have been desirous ...'; *concupisti*] *Dyce's emendation, cacapisti L*.

261–4   'Did you never speak thus? Did you never behave thus? But where did you read that or whence this?'

267–75   'Doctor Logician, where do you find it conditionally proposed or categorically asserted, in Latin or Greek, that your hawk may use the mercy seat as a lavatory as if it were in an inn. Whence this, Master Dawcock?' In logic the 'hypothetical' and the 'categorical' denoted different types of proposition.

277   Jacke Harys: Jack Hare became a proverbial name for an idle layabout. Compare Lydgate's *Ballade of Jak Hare*:

A ffroward knave pleynly to descryve,
And a sloggard shortly to declare;
A precious knave that castith hym never to thryve,
His mouth weel weet, his slevis riht thredbare ...

(1–4) and so on for eighty lines (*Minor Poems* II No. 14). See also Whiting J 10, J 12, and *Magnyfycence* 758.

278–9   'Why do you hawk for birds by the sacrament of the altar.'

280   reverens] revens *KDM*.

282–3   '... over the ark of the covenant: whence this ...'

285   Ware] Whare *L*.

286–95   'Sir, ignorant priest, through your hunting for birds you made your hawk come over the candlesticks of Christ crucified to feed on your hand; tell me, enemy of the cross of Christ, where did you learn to do this, Master Dawcock?' The phrase *dominus vobiscum*, 'the lord be with you', is a priest's salutation to the congregation. Skelton here, and elsewhere (e.g. *Collyn Clout* 230, 281), implies that this is about all the divine service many ignorant priests know.

287   per] par *L M D M*.

297   Apostata Julianus: Flavius Claudius Julianus, usually called the Apostate. He was born in Constantinople in 331 and brought up as a Christian; but on becoming Roman Emperor in 361 he declared himself a pagan. He died in 363 fighting against the Persians.

298   Nestorianus: Nestorius, patriarch of Constantinople, argued that distinct human and divine persons were to be attributed to Christ. He was deposed in 431.

302–4   '... to the entrance of the tabernacle, in which is the body of the Lord; beware of this ...'

311–18 'Why? Because the Gospels, vessels and vestments, a hawk with its bells and unreasoning animals and other such things are all the same to you; where do you get this from, Master Dawcock?' *conchelia* perhaps means 'purple' or 'purple garments' here (compare Juvenal, *Satires* iii 81, viii 101).

313   *Accipiter*] *Dyce's emendation, Ancipiter L K D M.*

314   *not D M.*

319   Ware] *Whare L.*

320–21   I can make no sense of this phrase, though Skelton uses it again in the *Garlande of Laurell* 1216.

322   'From Granada to Galicia.'

324–8   '. . . there is not such a one as brainsick nor less rational nor more bestial who sings with a chalice; work this out . . .'

326   *bestialis*] *bestia D, bestis M.*

331   *smyth*: Though in line 38 Skelton has said that the falconer should be 'nameles' these concluding lines may refer to his name – Smith. Nelson suggested a John Smyth of Diss as the culprit (p. 104 note), but Edwards's candidate, John Smith, Rector of East Wretham (about fifteen miles from Diss) from 1503 to 1517, looks more likely (pp. 91–2).

335–6   'Farewell to you, undistinguished doctor.'

Skeltonis . . . hec hoc: 'Skelton apostrophizes the decollation of St John, on whose day this bird-catching took place. O memorable day, O beheaded John, on which he made this bird-catching, which he will not have done before, inside the church of Diss, violating your holy of holies. Rector of Whipstock, doctor called Dawcock, and master Woodcock; this, this, and this prove it.'

1   *decollate*] *decolare L K D M.*

2   *haud*] *hod L K D M; intra*] *infra L K D M.*

3   *tua*] *sua L K D M.*

5   *Wodcock*: Like 'Daucock' (see note to line 8), the woodcock was proverbial for its foolishness (Whiting W 565).

Idem de . . . dabis veniam: 'The same about the freedom of poetical satire in praising honesty and attacking meanness. An ancient privilege is given to pious poets, that of saying what they wish in a way which will delight, either whatever is effective in defending just causes, or whatever is necessary for stinging obtuse wantons. Therefore you will comply.'

3   *valent*] *volent L K D M.*

VII   PHYLLYP SPAROWE

Lines 1–844 of *Phyllyp Sparowe* comprise a mock elegy for the death of a pet sparrow belonging to Jane Scrope. After the death of her husband Richard Scrope in 1485 Jane's mother married Sir John Wyndham; but she was widowed for a second time in 1502 when he was executed. After this, Lady Eleanor and her unmarried daughters, including Jane, went to live at Carrow Abbey, a Benedictine house near Norwich, where Jane was when her sparrow was killed (8–9). Lady Eleanor died in 1505 and it is likely that lines 1–844 were written before this. These lines, it is argued, make use of various services for the dead, and throughout phrases from these services are interspersed in Jane's lament: lines 1–386 follow the *Officium Defunctorum*, 387–512 the *Missa pro Defunctis*, 513–70 the *Absolutio super Tumulum*, 571–602 the *Officium Defunctorum* again and 845–1260 the *Ordo Commendationis Animae* (see I.A. Gordon, *MLR* XXIX, 1934,

389–96). Janet Wilson (University of Auckland) suggests, in an unpublished article, that many of the Latin quotations in the poem may derive from the *Vigile Mortuorum* as it appears in the Sarum Primer. Primers were traditionally dedicated to the Blessed Virgin: Caxton, in fact, entitled a primer published in 1490 as *'O Gloriosa Femina...'* (*STC* 15872), a phrase with which Skelton makes great play in 845ff. See also F.W. Brownlow, *English Literary Renaissance* IX, 1980, 5–20. The 'commendations', however, do not praise the soul of the departed but Jane herself; and, more than this, the lines deify her, *domina* being substituted for *domine* in the quotations at lines 996, 1061, 1114 (see Edwards, pp. 110–11). Kinsman suggests that the 'commendations' 'may have been added after Lady Wyndham's death as a way of flattering Jane out of a double shock' (p. 143) but there is no evidence of this.

The 'addicyon' (1268–1382) seems to have been a reply to Alexander Barclay's criticism of Skelton in his 'Brefe addicion of the syngularyte of some newe folys' with which he ended his *Shyp of Folys* (1509):

Wyse men love vertue, wylde people wantones;
It longeth nat to my scyence nor cunnynge
For Phylyp the Sparowe the *Dirige* to synge.

Lines 1282–9 seem to indicate that Jane herself had misgivings about the poem too. This 'adicyon' must have been written later than 1509; and it makes its earliest extant appearance as lines 1261–1375 of the *Garlande of Laurell*, printed 3 October 1523.

Phyllyp Sparowe is based on no one source. Edwards suggests it may have been prompted by the account in Caxton's *Reynard the Fox*, Chapter xvi, of the killing of Cop, Chantekler's daughter, by Reynard and the funeral obsequies said for her (pp. 106–7). Something is certainly owed to Catullus's *'Lugete, O Veneres Cupidinesque...'*, the lament for Lesbia's dead sparrow (iii), and to his previous poem on the same bird *'Passer, deliciae meae puellae...'* (ii). And perhaps Skelton also took hints from other classical poems on the deaths of pets: Corinna's lament for her parrot in Ovid's *Amores* II vi; Martial's epigram on Publius's lap dog (I cix); and Statius's *Silvae* II iv.

The text of *Phyllyp Sparowe* is taken from Kele's print of *c*.1545 (*K*) collated with the prints of Wyght *c*.1553 (*W*), Kitson *c*.1560 (*Kit*), and the copy in Marshe's *Workes* of 1568 (*M*). Occasionally *K* can be corrected in lines 1268–1382 from the version of these lines in the *Garlande of Laurell* (1310, 1340, 1345, 1371).

1   Pla ce bo: Vulgate Psalm cxiv 9, the opening antiphon of the Vespers of the Office for the Dead. The spacing between the syllables in this and other phrases from the Office is probably to suggest the plainsong background.

3   Di le xi: Vulgate Psalm cxiv 1, the opening psalm of the Vespers of the Office for the Dead. Lines 23–4 may be loosely based on verse 8 and 31–2 on verse 4.

4–9 St Mary's Carrow was a small Benedictine house founded in 1146. The Visitation Rolls indicate that it had thirteen nuns in 1492 and ten in 1514. Dame Margery probably refers to the senior nun, who had been there in 1492 and was still there in 1514.

7–12 R.S. Kinsman suggests that the phrasing of these lines recalls the *titulus* or memorial verse (see *SP* XLVII, 1950, 473–84).

13 'Our Father which...'

14   Ave Mari: 'Hail Mary.'

15   the corner of a crede: Janet Wilson points out that the first page of most primers contained in full the Pater Noster, the Ave Maria and part of the Credo, which was then continued overleaf, and that Skelton here has in mind this layout.

21   The story of Pyramus and Thisbe comes from Ovid's *Metamorphoses* iv 55–166; but was familiar in English through its inclusion in Chaucer's *Legend of Good Women* 706–923, and Gower's *Confessio Amantis* iii 1331–1494.

26–7   Phillip or Phip was a traditional name for a sparrow, and Gib (short for Gilbert) for a cat, usually a tom-cat, though evidently this one was a she-cat. See Chaucer's *Romaunt* 6204 'Gibbe oure cat'.

53–7   The lines recall a Marian lament in Carleton Brown, *Religious Lyrics of the Fifteenth Century*, 1939, No. 9.

61   Based on two proverbs 'As wan as lead' (Whiting L 129) and 'As blue as lead' (Whiting L 118). Compare *Speke Parott* 434.

63   had] *not W Kit M.*

64, 66   The second antiphon of the Vespers, Vulgate Psalm cxix 5: 'Woe, woe is me'; followed by the second psalm of the Vespers, Vulgate Psalm cxix 1: 'In my distress, I cried unto the Lord.'

68–91   Compare, in general terms, Catullus iii 11–12, in which Lesbia's sparrow faces the terrors of Hades. Acheron (70) was one of the rivers of the underworld. Pluto (72) was the king of Hades and Proserpina (83) his queen. Alecto (74) and Megaera (78) were two of the snake-haired Furies. Medusa (76) was one of the Gorgons; her *stare* (77) turned to stone those who looked upon it. Theseus (86) went to Hades to rescue Proserpina but was himself captured and had to be freed by Hercules (87), one of whose 'labours' was to capture Cerberus (85), the three-headed dog (91) which guarded the entrance to the underworld.

79   For] From *W Kit M.*

89   From] *Dyce's emendation*, For *K W Kit M.*

95, 97   The third antiphon of the Vespers, Vulgate Psalm cxx 5, 7; followed by the third psalm of the Vespers, Vulgate Psalm cxx, 1: 'I lifted up my eyes to the hills.'

98   Zenophontes: Xenophon (*c.*428/7–*c.*354 BC), a Greek philosopher and follower of Socrates (469–399 BC).

108–11   For Andromache's lament for Hector see *Iliad* xxiv 725–45.

118   'In order to know his place'. Proverbial (Whiting C 656).

125–6   Compare Catullus ii 1–2:

Passer, deliciae meae puellae,
quicum ludere, quem in sinu tenere . . .

('Sparrow, my lady's pet, with whom she often plays when she holds you on her breast . . .'.) See also Song of Solomon i 13.

143, 145   The fourth antiphon of the Vespers, Vulgate Psalm cxxix 3: 'If iniquities . . .'; followed by the fourth psalm of the Vespers, Vulgate Psalm cxxix 1: 'Out of the depths have I cried . . .'.

148   Sulpicia] Sulspicia *K*. Perhaps Skelton has in mind the daughter of Servius Sulpicius Rufus, authoress of six short poems expressing her love for Cerinthus. Or he may be thinking of the wife of Calenus who is praised by Martial (*Epigrams* X xxxv, xxxviii) as the authoress of poems of honourable love.

151   that] *not M.*

163   fethers] fether *K.*

169   though] thought *K.*

183–5   An allusion to the fifth antiphon of the Vespers, Vulgate Psalm cxxxvii

8: '*Opera manuum tuarum, Domine, ne despias*' ('O lord, forsake not the works of thine own hands'); followed by the fifth psalm of the Vespers, Vulgate Psalm cxxxvii 1: 'I will praise thee, Lord, with my whole heart.' Perhaps the phrase *omnes reges terrae* (v.5) suggests the passage on kings at 190ff.

185 in] *not Kit M.*

190 Croesus, the last king of Lydia (reigned c.560–546 BC) was proverbially wealthy (see Whiting C 556).

191 Attalus] *Dyce's emendation*, Artalus *K W Kit M*. Perhaps an allusion to Attalus I (269–197 BC) king of Pergamum, a notable patron of literature, philosophy and the arts; though perhaps Attalus III who left his kingdom to the Romans in 134 BC may be meant. More likely than either, however, is Attalus II who once gave 100 talents (cf. 189) for a single picture (see Pliny, *Naturalis Historia* vii 39).

194–200 Cadmus was ordered by his father Agenor, king of Tyre, to seek his sister Europa who had been abducted by Zeus and taken to Crete (see Ovid's *Metamorphoses* iii 1–9).

199 ofsprynge] sprynge *Kit M*.

201–7 Medea, through her magical arts, renewed the youth of Aeson, Jason's father (see Ovid's *Metamorphoses* vii 162ff.).

210ff. Compare the painting of Publius's lap dog in Martial's *Epigrams* I cix.

213 *Whyte as mylke*: Proverbial (Whiting M 545); compare line 1120.

225 waxed] ware *M*.

239 'From the gates of hell'. Compare Isaiah xxxviii 10, Matthew xvi 18. This is followed at 240 with a parody of the response to the versicle *Erne, domine animam eius.*

243 'I heard a voice', Revelation xiv 13, is properly followed in the Vespers by the Magnificat (245).

244 The sons of Noah (Genesis v 32) are invoked to lead Jane to the Ark on Mount Ararat, now in Turkey but then in Armenia (*Armony*), where she can look for another such bird as her sparrow (260–61).

248 bordes] byrdes *W Kit M*.

253 For Deucalion's flood, which is in many ways similar to that survived by Noah, see Ovid's *Metamorphoses* i 274ff. See also Juvenal's *Satires* i 81ff.

263 have yet] yet have *W Kit M*.

270 Probably Skelton has in mind Philip II, king of Macedon from 359 to 336 BC.

282 carlyshe] churlyshe *Kit M*.

290 The] *Dyce's emendation*, These *K W Kit M*; *Lybany*: Libya.

294 *mantycors*: A legendary beast, according to Pliny (*Naturalis Historia* viii 30), having a man's face, a lion's body and a scorpion's tail. See Caxton's account in *The Mirror of the World* (1480) Chapter vi.

296–306 According to Ovid's *Metamorphoses* iii 232, Melanchates was the first of Actaeon's hounds to bite his master, who had been transformed by Diana into a stag because he saw her bathing.

307 *Inde*: India.

309 *Arcady*: Arcadia, Greece.

311 Lycaon, king of Arcadia, offered a sacrifice of human flesh to Jupiter, who, for this crime, transformed him into a wolf (Ovid's *Metamorphoses* i 163ff.).

313 *Ethna*: The volcanic Mount Etna, Sicily.

318   Occyan the great se: According to medieval cosmography the great outer sea encircling the lands of the earth.

319   the Iles of Orchady: The Orkneys; used proverbially to indicate great distance (Whiting O 52).

320-21   Tilbury lies on the Thames about twenty-five miles downstream from London; Salisbury Plain is about eighty miles south-west: hence the lines mean roughly 'from east to west'.

323   'Who never bore you any ill-will'.

335   were] where *K*. The line is proverbial (Whiting J 40).

345-6   And often at my spayre
          And gape in at my gore *Kit*.

362   his] this *KW*.

376   a] *not M*.

379-85   'Lord, have mercy. Christ have mercy. Lord have mercy.' This formula properly follows the Magnificat (245), and is itself properly followed by a *Pater noster* (385) and an *Ave*, recited *secreto* (in a *whysper*).

382   Phylyp] Phyyp *K*.

386   'Praise the Lord, O my soul' (Vulgate Psalm cxlv 1). Here Skelton breaks off the Vespers of the Office for the Dead and does not resume it in detail until 575. He interrupts it with his elaborate version of a fairly common convention in medieval poetry – a service sung by birds: see particularly 'The Bird's Matins', ed. H.N. MacCracken, *Archiv* CXXX, 1913; and *The Court of Love* 1352-428.

387-94   Compare the opening lines of Ovid's *Amores* II vi.

402   Softly] Loftly *M*.

403   *red sparow*: Reed-bunting; not sedge warbler as glossed by Kinsman.

405   It was the duty of the deacon (*red sparow*) and the sub-deacon (*swallow*) at a Requiem Mass to sprinkle the coffin with lustral water.

408   *shovelar*: The spoonbill (*Platalea leucorodia*), known as 'shovelars' until the seventeenth century; not what is now called the shoveler (*Spatula clypeata*).

410-11   Based on two proverbs: 'As bald as a coot' (Whiting C 419) and 'A mad coot' (Whiting C 421).

418   Dyce (II 129) glossed *woodhacke* as 'woodpecker' on the basis of the *Promptorium Parvulorum* 'Wodehac or nothac byrde: *Picus*'. But woodpeckers do not sing 'chur'; perhaps the nightjar is meant.

426-7   Compare *Midsummer Night's Dream* III i 120: 'The plain-song cuckoo grey.'

428-9   The *cuckoue*, *culver* and *stockedowve* are conceived as the three clerics who sing over the body when it is present.

430   The peewit (imitative of its song) is a name often given to the lapwing (*Vanellus vanellus*).

432   bitter] better *K*. 'The bittern with its booming voice.'

434   See *Speke Parott* 173 and note.

436   the] *not KW*.

438   The peacock is proverbially proud (Whiting P 73).

442   is] *not Kit M*.

449   The route and the kowgh *K W Kit M*. The correct reading was suggested to Dyce (II 131) by the Rev. J. Mitford. The birds referred to are the knot (*Calidris canutus*), which is not (as Kinsman says) the same as the red-breasted sandpiper; and the ruff (*Philomachus pugnax*).

451   wylde] wynde *K*.

454 puffyn] pussyn *K*.

455–6 After the burial service alms were customarily distributed.

462 The osprey (*Pandion haliaetus*) is not the same (as Kinsman says) as the sea-eagle. For the fairly common notion that the osprey subdued its prey before it touched it compared *Coriolanus* IV vii 33–5.

465 Proverbial, Whiting T 542.

469–77 Probably Skelton's version of the belief that the stork kills or leaves his female if he finds her unfaithful. See e.g. Bartholomaeus Anglicus, *De Proprietatibus Rerum* xii 8 (where he cites Aristotle) and Chaucer's *Parliament of Fowls* 361.

473 No] Nor *Kit*.

478–82 According to Bartholomaeus Anglicus's *De Proprietatibus Rerum* xii 33, the ostrich is 'so hot that he swalloweth and defieth and wasteth yron'.

482 doth freat] so great *K W Kit*.

486–7 *E-la* is the highest note in the Guidonian scale; the lines are based on the proverbial phrase 'To assay above Ela' (Whiting E 58), meaning to try to do things of which one is scarcely capable.

488 Fa] Ga *K W Kit*. This and the next two lines seem to mean 'Content yourself with lower notes like Fa, lest by singing badly...' *Ne quando*, however, is from the Office of the Dead (Vulgate Psalm vii 3) so lines 489–90 may mean '... singing *Ne quando* badly...'

491–4 Dyce (II 132) quotes the Latin proverb, '*Sit campanista, qui non vult esse sophista*, Let him be a bellringer that will be no good singer.'

495–9 The cock is described by Chaucer as 'commune astrologer' in *Troilus and Criseyde* iii 1415. In the *Nun's Priest's Tale* Chaunteclere is the name of the cock, and Pertelote is his favourite hen (VII 2849, 2870).

501–5 *Albumazer* was a ninth-century Arab astrologer, *Ptholomy* a second-century Arab astronomer and Haly Aben Raghel (early twelfth century) an Arab astrologer. All three are mentioned in *Why Come Ye Nat to Courte?* 521–3. See also *Speke Parott* 134.

507–8 Proverbial (Whiting T 318).

513–70 This passage is based on the Absolution over the Tomb. Thus, following the directions of this office, the celebrant wears *a blacke cope* (529), the sub-deacon comes first facing him at the head of the coffin (552), the acolytes who carry the *sensers and the crosse* (568) are present and the *holy wather clarke* properly brings up the rear (570). Line 533 contains the plainsong notes actually used for the responsory *Libera me* ('Deliver me').

513ff. The *byrde of Araby* is the legendary phoenix which was supposed, after a cycle of years, to prepare a funeral pyre of sweet-smelling spices on which it burnt itself, to emerge from the ashes with renewed youth in order to live through another cycle of years. In Christian symbolism it is associated with Christ and the Resurrection. Because of its association with sweet-smelling spices the phoenix is aptly given the task of thurification (522). For Pliny's account see *Naturalis Historia* x ii (536–7). In this passage the *phenex* is seen as the celebrant of the mass: he properly dons a *blacke cope* (529), and, assisted by his acolytes (the *hobby* and the *muskette* 567–8), he hallows the body (522ff.) and sings the responsory (531); all the time the choir, led by the eagle (553), continue singing.

523 a] *not W Kit M*.

526 to] *not M*.

530 the herse] *Dyce's emendation, not K W Kit M*.

552 the] thye *K*, thy *W Kit M*.
557 gerfawcon] grefawcon *K*.
565 the] not *W Kit M*.
566 *morning gounes*: 'mourning garments'. The predominantly staid grey and blue plumage of these hawks is seen by Skelton as appropriate for the sad occasion. Compare 560.
571 As the sun (*Phebus* 572) goes down the Absolution over the Tomb is brought to an end by Skelton and the Vespers of the Office of the Dead are picked up again where they were interrupted. Thus the *Lauda anima mea* (386) is properly followed (575) by the *Requiem eternam dona eis, Domine* ('Lord, give them eternal rest').
576 re] re re *Kit*.
577 'From the gates of hell . . .' Compare 239.
579 'I had thought to see the goodness of the Lord . . .' (Vulgate Psalm xxvi 13).
581 'Lord, hear my prayer' (Vulgate Psalm ci 2).
585 'Let us pray.'
586 'Lord, whose nature it is to be merciful and to spare . . .', a prayer.
599 Janet Wilson suggests that this translates '*Excelsis supra sidera*' from the '*O gloriosa femina*' hymn.
600–601 According to Whiting W 710, a proverb.
604 to mynde] to mi mynde *W Kit*.
610–11 Helicon was a range of mountains in Boeotia, sacred to Apollo and the Muses. The fountains of the Muses, Aganippe and Hippocrene, were there.
614 By 1505 *The Canterbury Tales* had been printed four times: by Caxton (*c*.1478 and *c*.1484), by Pynson (*c*.1492) and by de Worde (1498).
619 That] Thay *K W Kit*.
629 *Gawen*: Gawain, though it is impossible to know which of the many stories about him Skelton has in mind. *Syr Guy*: Guy of Warwick, one of the most popular heroes of romance. Both Pynson and de Worde had printed romances about him around 1500.
630–33 Caxton had printed the *History of Jason*, a translation of Raoul le Fèvre's French version, in about 1477. But information about this hero could have been derived from many sources.
634–48 Malory's *Morte Darthur* had been printed by Caxton in 1485.
649–50 A reference to the fairly popular romance of *Lybeaus Desconus*, 'The Fair Unknown', or Guingelain, the son of Gawain.
651–8 To judge from the title Skelton has in mind a French version of the *Quater Fylz Amund*, perhaps that printed at Lyons in 1480. But it was translated into English by Caxton in 1489, and a second edition was printed by de Worde in 1504. The horse of the four sons was called Bayard (656), and because Reynawde, one of the sons, had a castle called Montawbon Skelton adds *Mountalbon* to the name. In one incident in the romance Charlemagne had Bayard thrown into the river Meuse with a millstone round his neck. But the horse escaped drowning and fled into the Ardennes forest (658) '. . . and wit it for very certayn that the folke of the country saien, that he is yet alyve within the wood of Ardeyn'.
651 Amund] Emund *K*.
659 though] thought *K*.
661–2 The stories of Judas Maccabeus and Julius Caesar were widely known. They appear together in lists of the 'Nine Worthies'.

664 The romance of *Parys and Vyenne* was translated from the French by Caxton in 1485, issued in Antwerp in 1492 by Gherard Leeu, and by de Worde in 1502. Caxton's title mentions that the hero and heroine 'suffred many adversytees bycause of theyr true love'.

665 Hannyball] of Hannyball *W Kit M*. The suggestion for this and the next two lines may have come from Caxton's *Fayttes of Armes*, translated in 1489 from Christine de Pisan's French, Chapter xxvii, in which the 'romayns were ... affrayed [of Hannibal] and ... full of sorowe for theyre grate losse'.

666 That] What *K W*.

668–71 A paraphrase of the example illustrating the figure of *circuitu* in the *Rhetorica Ad Herennium* IV xxii 43. The phrase '*Scipoionis providentia*' lends support to the reading *mercyfull* (*W Kit M* read 'unmercifull'), which must be ironic. Scipio Aemilianus Africanus Numantinus destroyed Carthage in 146 BC.

672–6 The story of the fall of Troy was well known. Caxton's translation *Recuyell of the Histories of Troy* was printed in 1475.

677–723 A summary of Chaucer's *Troilus and Criseyde*, first printed by Caxton in 1483. What lines 685–7 refer to is not clear. On one occasion Criseyde asks Pandarus to bear a 'blewe ryng' to Troilus (iii 885), and Skelton seems to have confused this with the occasion on which the lovers 'entrechaungeden hire rynges' and Criseyde gave Troilus a brooch of gold and azure (iii 1366–72).

700 the] tha *K*. Compare *Collyn Clout* 686 and *Why Come Ye Nat to Courte?* 78 and note.

709 Proverbial (Whiting E 18).

716 *kys the post*: A proverbial expression (Whiting P 315) meaning 'to have the door slammed in one's face', hence 'to fail'.

717 Pandaer] Pandara *K W Kit M*.

719 Compare *The Bowge of Courte* 355 and note.

724–33 Penelope, the faithful wife of Ulysses, resisted her suitors by persuading them she could not marry until she had finished weaving a shroud for Laertes, Ulysses' father. What she wove by day she unravelled at night.

734 Marcus Claudius Marcellus, the Roman general, was killed fighting against Hannibal in about 208 BC.

736 Presumably Antiochus III of Syria (241–187 BC), to whose court Hannibal fled in 195 BC.

737–8 A Latin translation of Josephus's *Jewish Antiquities*, originally written in Greek in AD 93 or 94, was printed in 1470, and reissued in 1486 and 1499.

739–44 Mordecai brought up his uncle's daughter Esther (Esther ii 7), who married King Ahasuerus and supplanted his unsatisfactory queen Vashti (ii 17).

746 *Kyng Evander*, son of Hermes and Themis, had left Arcadia and settled in Italy, founding Pallanteum on the left bank of the Tiber. He welcomed Aeneas and supplied him with food (*Aeneid* vii 126ff.). Caxton's *Eneydos*, a translation of a French prose version of Virgil, had appeared in 1490.

747 Lars Porsena, king of Clusium, who supported the banished Tarquins against Rome, is mentioned in *Aeneid* viii 646–52. See also Titus Livius II ix.

748 sweat] *Dyce's emendation*, smart *K W Kit M*.

749–68 Kinsman (p. 151) is probably right in suggesting that Skelton took this list from a rhetorical handbook. Eight of the Greek poets here mentioned appear in Quintilian's *Institutio Oratoria* X 46ff.

756 Publius Ovidius Naso (43 BC–AD 17) and Publius Vergilius Maro (70–19 BC).

757   Lucius? Mestrius Plutarchus (?50–?120).

758   Or] Or of *Kit M*. Francesco Petrarca (1304–74).

759   Alcaeus (born *c*.620 BC) and Sappho (born *c*.612 BC) were both from Mytilene in Lesbos.

761   Linus was the supposed inventor of a mournful-sounding type of song (*Iliad* xviii 570). Homer is the probable author of the *Iliad* and *Odyssey*.

762   Euphorion (died 187 BC) wrote epigrams and poems on mythological subjects. Theocritus (*c*.300–260 BC) is most notable for his pastorals.

763   Anacreon (born *c*.570 BC) was a lyric poet; Arion (seventh century BC) is said to have invented the dithyramb.

764   Sophocles (*c*.496–406 BC) was one of the most famous of Greek tragic writers; Philemon (*c*.368/60–*c*.267/63 BC) was a writer of New Comedy.

765   Symonides Dymonides *K W Kit M*. The lyric and elegiac poet Simonides (*c*.556–468 BC) appears to have been confused by the printers with Diomedes. Pindar (518–438 BC) was his more famous, younger contemporary lyric poet.

766   According to Martial (II xli 15) Philistion was a Greek writer of mimes. Pherecydes (fifth century) wrote mythologies and genealogies.

773   elect] clere *K*.

774–83   Complaints, such as this, about the uneloquent nature of the English language were fairly common at this time. See R.F. Jones, *The Triumph of the English Language*, 1953, Chapter 1.

781   ornatly] ordinately *Kit M*.

784–812   To refer together to Gower, Chaucer and Lydgate as the founders of English poetry was conventional. See, for example, Hawes, *The Pastyme of Pleasure* 1317–407; and the *Garlande of Laurell* 386–441. Kinsman (pp. 151–2) suggests that 795 may be derived from Caxton's epilogue to *The Book of Fame* (*c*. 1483) where, speaking of Chaucer, he says: '... he wrytteth no voyde wordes but alle hys mater is ful of hye and quycke sentence ...'.

785   told] is tolde *W Kit M*.

809–10   Compare Hawes, *Pastyme of Pleasure* 1368: 'whose famous draughtes no man can amende.'

826–43   'Best of birds, beautiful one, farewell. Phyllyp, beneath that marble now you rest, who were dear to me. Always there will be shining stars in the clear sky; and you will always be stamped in my heart. Through me, Skelton the laureate poet of Britain, these compositions could be sung under a feigned likeness. She whose bird you were is a maiden of surpassing physical beauty: the naiad was fair, but Jane is more beautiful; Corinna was learned, but Jane knows more.' For Corinna's lament for her dead parrot see Ovid's *Amores* II vi.

844   'I recall it well.' Compare the colophons to *Elynour Rummynge* and *A Lawde and Prayse Made for our Sovereigne Lord the Kyng*. Pollet suggests that the phrase may be taken from Henri Baudé's 'Supplique au Roy faicte en Rondeau' (pp. 209–10).

845–6   'Blessed are the undefiled in the way, O glorious woman.' The first line is from Vulgate Psalm cxviii 1, the psalm used in the Commendations of the Soul.

852   goodly] godly *W Kit M*.

860   The nymph Arethusa, according to Ovid's *Metamorphoses* v 573, was turned into a river by Diana to enable her to escape the advances of Alpheus. Virgil invokes her as a Muse in *Eclogue* x 1.

863   Apollo was the Greek god of music and poetry, often depicted playing instruments, invoked again as Phoebus at 970.

875 *Thagus*: Tagus, a river in Portugal, the sands of which were supposed to contain gold (see Ovid's *Amores* I xv 34).

876 all] all the *W Kit M*.

886 'Into Persia and Media.'

900–901 'Deal bountifully with thy servant, that I may live. My lips shall praise thee.' From Vulgate Psalms cxviii 17 and lxii 4.

904 an] a *K*.

905–48 This description of Envy appears to be loosely based on Ovid's *Metamorphoses* ii 775–82. See also *Piers Plowman* B V 76ff.

911 swart] wart *K W Kit*. The line is apparently proverbial (see Whiting T 38).

913 Proverbial (Whiting R 23).

917 A very common proverbial comparison (see Whiting G 8).

918 longe] longes *W Kit M*.

936 foule] feule *K W*.

937 displesaunt] displseaunt *K*.

967 be] me *K*.

988 goodly] godly *K*.

989 goodly] gooly *K*.

996 'Teach me, Lady, to justify thy ways.' Based on Vulgate Psalm cxviii 33. I follow Dyce in reading *domina*, as at lines 1061, 1114, though *K W Kit M* read 'domine' here as in the Vulgate passage.

997 'As the hart panteth after the water brooks.' Vulgate Psalm xli 1.

1003 all with] with all *W Kit M*.

1010 on] to *M*.

1014–21 *gray* eyes and *bent* brows were two of the conventional attributes of beautiful women, as are the *myddell small* and the *sydes longe* of lines 1128–9 (see D.S. Brewer, *MLR* L, 1955, 257–69). Lucrece, after being raped by Sextus, son of Tarquin the Proud, took her own life; Polyxena, daughter of Priam, was, according to some stories, beloved of Achilles; Penelope was the faithful wife of Ulysses (see 724–33 and note). All three were renowned for their beauty and modesty. Calliope was the muse of epic poetry.

1029–30 'Remember thy word unto thy servant. I am thy servant.' Vulgate Psalm cxviii 49, 125.

1031–40 Compare *Magnyfycence* 1550–59 and note.

1047–53 Compare the *Garlande of Laurell* 982–8.

1054 For] Not *K W Kit M*.

1061 'Thou hast dealt bountifully with thy servant, lady.' Based on Vulgate Psalm cxviii 65.

1062 'And from his heart your praises ring out.'

1079 Proverbial (Whiting S 930).

1083 goodly] godly *K*.

1090 'My soul fainteth for thy salvation.' Vulgate Psalm cxviii 81.

1091 'What seek you for your son, sweetest mother?'

1094 have] heve *K*.

1108 This] The *Kit M*.

1114 'O how I love thy law, lady.' Based on Vulgate Psalm cxviii 97.

1115 'Old things are passed away, all things are become new.' Based on Vulgate II Corinthians v 17.

1116–17 Dyce (II 147) suggests that these lines may be defective; but perhaps they mean 'And in order to enhance what she was saying when she wanted to accomplish her purpose...' It seems Jane Scrope had pressed the poet's hand to give emphasis to something she said.

1119   *soft as sylke*: A common proverbial comparison (Whiting S 313).

1120   the] *not Kit M.*

1128   goodly] godly *K.*

1136   goodly] gooly *K.*

1137   This] The *K W Kit M.*

1143–4   'I hate vain thoughts. Let not the proud oppress me.' Vulgate Psalm cxviii 113, 122.

1152   Egeria, according to Ovid (*Metamorphoses* xv 547), gave counsel to her husband Numa. At his death she became so disconsolate and wept so much that Diana changed her into a fountain.

1168   'Wonderful are thy testimonies.' Vulgate Psalm cxviii 129.

1169   'As plants grow up in their youth.' Vulgate Psalm cxliii 12.

1170–76   Dyce (II 148) compares a passage from Hawes' *Pastyme of Pleasure* 3851ff.

1183   *Flora* was the Roman goddess of flowers and gardens.

1185   For] *not Kit M.*

1192   'I have cried with my whole heart, hear me!' Based on Vulgate Psalm cxviii 145.

1193   'Great is thy mercy towards me.' Vulgate Psalm lxxxv 13.

1200–1201   Both lines are proverbial (see Whiting T 238).

1203   nor] or *W Kit M.*

1205   pullysshed] publysshed *K.*

1206   Marcus Tullius Cicero (106–43 BC), the most famous of Roman orators.

1208   For this] The *Kit M.*

1209   This] Thus *K.*

1215   'Princes have persecuted me without cause.' Vulgate Psalm cxviii 161.

1216–18   'All things considered, this sweetest of all girls is a paradise of delights.'

1223–30   Diana and Venus were the Roman goddesses of chastity and love. Pallas was the Greek goddess of wisdom.

1231   For] *not K W Kit M*; this] the *W Kit M.*

1238   'Give them eternal rest, O Lord.'

1239   *Domine, probasti me*: 'O Lord, thou hast searched me.' Vulgate Psalm cxxxviii 1.

1241   'We commend ourselves to thee, O Lord.' The final oration from the Commendations of the Soul.

1242   *Saynt Jamys*: The shrine of St James of Compostella, a famous place of pilgrimage. Compare *Elynour Rummynge* 354. His emblem was a cockle-shell; hence perhaps 1243.

1244   stalkynge] stalke *K.*

1256   have] *not M.*

1260   'Because she is worthy.'

1261–7   'Through me, Skelton, the laureate poet of Britain, this girl is deservedly crowned with choice praises. I have sung of the beautiful girl than whom there is no one more beautiful; a beautiful girl preferable to any Homer might commend. Thus, it is pleasant occasionally to refresh hard labours; nor is my wisdom any less brief than this inscription. Only to please.' *Minerva* was the Roman goddess of wisdom.

1261 vatem] *Dyce's emendation,* latem *K W Kit M.*

1263 cecini] pocecini *K W Kit M.*

1269 janglynge jayes means 'chatterers' and is based on the proverbial phrase 'To jangle like a jay' (Whiting J 21).

1290–321 An allusive account of some of the labours supposed to have been performed by Hercules for Eurystheus. Line 1291 refers to his carrying of Cerberus, the three-headed dog who guarded Hades, to the upper world. 1292–6 refer to his battle with the centaurs at the house of Chiron; the poisoned arrows of 1292 obtained after his fight with the Hydra. 1297–300 allude to his capture of the Arcadian stag which had golden antlers and brazen feet. 1301–6 refer to the golden apples of the Hesperides which were guarded by the dragon Ladon on Mount Atlas; Atlas himself obtained them for Hercules while Hercules took his place, temporarily, holding up the heavens on his shoulders. 1307–8 allude to the slaying of the three-bodied monster Geryones and 1309–11 either to Hercules's victorious fight against the Nemean lion or to his killing of the lion which haunted Mount Cithaeron and ate the animals of Amphitryon and Thespius. Lines 1312–15 are on the capture of the mares of Diomedes, king of the Bistones in Thrace. 1316–21 refer to Hercules's fight with the river god Achelous for Deianira; when defeated Achelous took the form of a bull and fought again, but was again overcome. In the fight, one of his horns was broken off and, according to Ovid (*Metamorphoses* ix 87), the Naiads changed this into the horn of plenty.

1293 Epidaures: Dyce (II 150) suspects textual corruption here. The line seems to refer to Epidaurus, a town on the Saronic Gulf, but this is a place not usually connected with the Centaurs. Perhaps Epirus is meant, a country in north-west Greece to the borders of which the Centaurs were banished after their fight with the Lapiths at the wedding of Pirithous and Hippodamia. Eleanor Hammond suggested Skelton may have had in mind Virgil's *Georgics* iii 44: '*domitrix Epidaurus equorum*' (p. 523). Williams (p. 203) refers to Horace's *Satires* I iii 27: '*serpens Epidaurius*'. These lines, however, seem to refer specifically to the death of *one* (1294) Centaur, Chiron, who was fatally wounded with a poisoned arrow (cf. 1292) by Hercules; and Chiron can be associated with Epidaurus because he was responsible for the upbringing of the great healer Aesculapius, whose principal shrine was at Epidaurus.

1296 Hipocentaures] Hipocentaurius *K W Kit M.*

1310 Adaunted] *Dyce's emendation on the basis of the* Garlande of Laurell *1303,* Avaunted *K W Kit M.*

1322–3 Hecate, one of the Titans, took an active part in the search for Proserpina who was taken to Hades by Pluto. When she was found there Hecate stayed with her as an attendant and companion.

1323 Plutos] Plutus *K W Kit M.*

1324 Eumenides: Three goddesses from Tartarus who punished the crimes of men.

1326–9 These lines refer to the nine-headed Hydra, overcome by Hercules, which dwelt in a swamp in Lerna.

1330 Chemeras flames: Here Skelton has in mind the Chimaera, a fire-breathing monster, part-lion, part-goat, part-dragon, which was killed by Bellerophon, and probably not the volcano of this name near Phaselis in Lycia.

1334–41 Styx was the principal river of Hades and Cocytus one of its tributaries. The Greek gods swore their most sacred oaths by Styx. Charon, who is always represented as an aged man in mean dress, ferried the souls of the dead over the rivers of Hades; the description of him may owe something to *Aeneid* vi 298–315.

1340 frownsid] *Dyce's emendation on the basis of the Garlande of Laurell* 1333, not *K W Kit M*. For the meaning see *Magnyfycence* 1514 and note.

1342–61 The story of Saul and the Witch of Endor is from I Samuel xxviii, which used to be called the First Book of Kings (1337).

1345 bad] *Dyce's emendation on the basis of the Garlande of Laurell* 1338, had *K W Kit M*.

1355 *idem in numero*: 'one and the same'. It was a matter of theological dispute whether Samuel was actually raised or whether an evil spirit was impersonating him. See R.H. Robbins, *Encyclopaedia of Witchcraft and Demonology*, 1959, pp. 159–60.

1364–6 Diana was the goddess of the chase; Luna of the Moon; and Proserpina, as wife of Pluto, was queen of Hades. These were the three forms, earthly, heavenly and infernal, of Diana.

1371–3 'Phyllyp, the beautiful Jane Scrope urgently asked for your obsequies. Why now is she ashamed of our song? It is too late; shame is less than truth.'

1371 Inferias] *Dyce's emendation on the basis of the Garlande of Laurell* 1364, *Infera K W Kit, Inferia M*; tuas] *Dyce's emendation on the basis of the Garlande of Laurell* 1364, not *K W Kit M*.

1372 petiit] *persit W Kit M*.

1380–82 'Why, green envy, do you condemn the pious obsequies of a bird? May the same fate which seized the bird also seize you! Yet death is continuous for you through envy.'

VIII   EPITAPHE

The will of John Clarke was proved on 14 April 1506 (see line 10). It is not known when Adam Uddersall died (see Edwards, p. 93, for an attempt at identification), but it must have been at around this date. It appears from the colophon that the poems were copied out on 5 January 1507 by the parish priest of Trumpington, official copyist of the University of Cambridge. To this man is probably owed the attribution to Skelton, though the epitaph for Uddersall is listed among Skelton's poems in the *Garlande of Laurell* 1247–53.

The text is taken from Marshe's 1568 edition of Skelton's *Workes* (*M*).

Compendium de . . . vilitate: 'A collection about two hypocrites, John Jaybeard and Adam All a Knave, and about their most infamous vileness.'

Perhaps Clarke is called 'Jaybeard' because he wore his beard in a particular style (see Edwards, p. 92), or perhaps to associate him with the jay (*garrulus glaudarius*) which, like Clarke, had a reputation for ostentatious display (44–6), and noisy chatter (28–33, 36–7, 40–42). For proverbial associations see Whiting J 17–J 21.

1–18 'Here follows a trental of a reasonable enough kind, though it has little to do with the court yet it is sufficiently formal, for John Clarke, a certain man of many names, who is called John Jaybeard, though named Clarke by the clergy. This holy father died in 1506. In the parish of Diss there was nobody like him; a man noted for his malice, treacherous of heart, and double-tongued, consumed by old age, mistrusted by everybody, beloved by nobody. He is buried . . .'

Dulce melos penetrans celos: 'a sweet melody, penetrating the skies'.

20–59 'Let us sing, to the accompaniment of pipes, sacred songs; John Clarke, who they called Jaybeard, is truly dead; born among the people of Diss, he is called Clarke by the clergy. This Chaldean man, a worthless man like a Jebusite, roared in the manner of a camel against the Lord's Christ, and spoke such words back at his own rector that Acheron thundered with his bellowing. Never sincerely accustomed to weep for his crimes, he had an evil tongue, garrulous, sarcastic and lying, and such habits as exist in nobody else; he sniffed the living air to stir up comrades and fellow citizens; he was just like an ass, a mule or an ox. All his fondness was for being dressed in a variegated cloak dyed red, and he made always his cursed food out of the stomachs of sheep and oxen and goats; went to market to collect his scraps; without teeth he chewed the woolly head of either a sheep or a lowing cow cooked with barley. What are you asking? Who this is? John Jaybeard, inhabitant of Diss; with whom, while he lived here, were associated quarrels, violence and litigation.'

26–7 The Chaldeans and the Jebusites were among the most persistent enemies of the Israelites.

33 Acheronta: Acheron, originally a river in Epirus, whose name was applied by Homer to one of the rivers of Hades. Sometimes, as here perhaps, the word is applied to Hades itself.

53–5 Presumably a sort of stew. According to *The Chester Plays*, ed. H. Deimling, EETS ES 62, 1892, VII 121, 'a sheepes head soused in ale' was a shepherd's delicacy.

54 caput aut ovis] Dyce's emendation based on a conjecture by the Rev. J. Mitford, *caput caput M*.

57 incola] Dyce's emendation, Nicolas M.

60 Iam iacet hic: 'Now he lies here.' Compare the *Epitaph to Uddersall* 26, 28, which also alludes to this characteristic tombstone inscription.

63 Evidently the refrain or the opening of a song. Compare *The Bowge of Courte* 360 and *Why Come Ye Nat to Courte?* 66–7.

64 Fratres, orate: 'Brothers, pray.'

75–9 'Drink deeply. Behold, buried under foot, a foolish ass and a mule. May the devil kiss his arse.' The allusion in the last line is to the *osculum infame* ('the kiss of shame') by means of which the devil's followers worshipped him. Skelton's implication is that Clarke is so evil that the devil ought to worship him.

80 With] Wit *M. Hey, howe, rumbelowe*: A refrain often used in sailors' songs. Compare *The Bowge of Courte* 252, and see Dyce (II 110–11) for examples.

82 'For ever and ever. Amen.'

83–7 'By Fredericus Hely, brother of the Carmelites, who celebrate without sarcasm this devout trental. Goodbye, Jaybeard, do very badly.' The Carmelite friar referred to here has not been identified. It may be that 'Fredericus Hely' is an invented name, by means of which Skelton, in a not very convincing fashion, attempts to disguise his authorship of this poem. An unidentified (and probably non-existent) 'Frere Frederyk' is referred to in *Collyn Clout* 737. 'Hely' is the usual late medieval form of Elijah; for Elijah on Mount Carmel see I Kings xviii. Alternatively 'Hely' may mean 'of Ely'.

ALIAS DICTUS: 'Otherwise known as'.

1–28 'Adam of Diss used to be alive; while he lived he cherished fraud, indeed he extorted whatever the resident or the free man possessed; because of that he was called a swift wolf. This seed of Belial, this Pilate, having trodden the church underfoot, violated it and is now himself violated. Treacherous, wrathful, he was never blessed. Uddersall is stretched out, deprived of blessings, wicked, pompous, now torn with curses. Diss, to you he was a drunken, overbearing bailiff. He was ungrateful; like an insatiate pig, greasy, fat. May he be condemned like Agag. And I pray that this cruel Cacus be buried in hell. May Beelzebub save the soul of the man who lies here like a knave! Now I know he is dead, and he lies here like a beast.'

8   In the Old Testament the phrase 'son of Belial' or 'man of Belial' indicates someone worthless; Pontius Pilate was the Roman procurator of Judea from 26–36 who condemned Christ.

14   Benedictis] *Benedictus M.*

16   Maledictis] *Maledictus M.*

17   Dis] *Sis M.*

18   Ballivus] *Balians M.*

22   sit] *fit M.* Agag was the wicked king of the Amalekites slain by Samuel (I Samuel xv 8–33).

23   Cacus, son of Vulcan and Medusa, a robber who stole Hercules's cattle and was killed because of this (*Aeneid* viii 194ff.).

25   Beelzebub, a heathen deity originally, but a name more usually applied to a devil.

29–30   '. . . his soul from bad to worse . . .'

31–2   'From Diss this will always be the song, "May Adam Uddersall be cursed".'

computationem] *computat M.*

Adam, Adam, ubi es: 'Adam, Adam, where are you?' Vulgate Genesis iii 9.

Ubi nulla . . . inhabitat: 'Where there is no rest, no order but everlasting horror.' Based on Vulgate Job x 22.

IX   A LAWDE AND PRAYSE MADE FOR OUR SOVEREIGNE LORD THE KYNG

These verses were probably written shortly after 24 June 1509, when Henry VIII was crowned. Perhaps this poem is 'The Boke of the Rosiar' mentioned in the *Garlande of Laurell* 1178.

   The text is taken from PRO Records of the Treasury of the Receipt of the Exchequer MS E 36–228, which may be Skelton's autograph copy. The title, which is written in a different hand, appears on the back of the two leaves containing the poem.

1–2   The marriage of Henry VII, who used the Tudor red rose badge, and Elizabeth (daughter of Edward IV), who used the Yorkist white rose, was frequently referred to in early Tudor propaganda as a joining of the two roses (see Scattergood, pp. 215–16). Henry VIII, their son, could thus be said symbolically to embody roses of both colours. Compare Hawes, *A Ioyfull Medytacyon* 36–42.

10–11   The early Tudors were understandably nervous about their claims to the English throne. Henry VIII was the lineal descendant of Henry VII; but Henry VII's claim by lineage was meagre – his father was a half-brother of Henry VI.

13   Alexis: Perhaps the youth mentioned in Virgil's *Eclogue* ii is referred to here.

14   Adrastus: Perhaps the aged king of Argos who survived the war of the seven against Thebes. Lydgate describes him as 'riche and wonder sage' (*Siege of Thebes* 1193).

15 Astrea was the daughter of Zeus and Themis; she was goddess of justice on earth during the golden age, but when the wickedness of mankind increased she withdrew to heaven, and, under the name of Virgo, was placed among the stars.

22ff. These lines allude to Henry VIII's public promise of a redress of grievances. Richard Empson and Edmund Dudley, two of his father's most hated financial agents, were sent to the Tower and executed on 17 August 1510. Compare Hawes, *A Ioyfull Medytacyon* 92–8.

43 Adonis, a beautiful youth beloved of Aphrodite; Henry VIII was young (nearly eighteen when he succeeded to the throne) and very handsome.

48 Priamus of Troy, the son of Laomedon and king of Troy during its siege and destruction by Agamemnon. He was the father of fifty sons, some by Hecuba, some by his concubines. Perhaps he is alluded to here because it was hoped that Henry VIII (who had married Catherine of Aragon on 11 June 1509, a fortnight before his coronation) would soon produce an heir to secure the succession.

55 Martis lusty knight: Henry VIII in his youth had shown great aptitude in jousting and tilting.

Bien men . . . Skeltonida vatem: 'I recall it well. To God (21) be thanks. Written by me, Skelton, Laureate poet of the Britons.'

Bien men sovient, Skelton's *impresa*, also appears following a Latin distich at the end of *Elynour Rummynge* and in *Phyllyp Sparowe* 844 and note. The line *Per me laurigerum Britonum Skeltonida vatem* also appears in *Phyllyp Sparowe* 834–5. The figure '21' refers to 1509 in Skelton's own system of chronology; it indicates 21 years after he first entered the Tudor service in October or November 1488. Compare also *Speke Parott* 300a, 323a–b, 356a–b, 375a, and *Why Come Ye Nat to Courte?* Apostrophe.

X CALLIOPE

On the evidence of a patent, dated in the fifth year of Henry VIII's reign, in which Skelton was granted the title of royal poet, this poem may be dated after April 1512. The patent itself is now lost, but an account of it remains (see Dyce I xv).

The text is taken from Marshe's 1568 edition of Skelton's *Workes* (*M*), where it is untitled; the present title 'Calliope' is editorial. The Latin verses which follow the English are a free version of the English.

1 Calliope: The Muse of heroic poetry.

Maulgre touz malheureux: 'despite all misfortunes'.

XI A BALLADE OF THE SCOTTYSSHE KYNGE

On 30 June 1513 Henry VIII arrived in France, and by 4 August he was besieging Thérouanne. On 11 August a message arrived from James IV of Scotland threatening to invade England in Henry's absence unless he gave up his attempt to conquer France, with which Scotland had treaties (see 15–16 and note). Before Henry's defiant reply could reach him James had crossed the border, but had been defeated and killed at Flodden Field on 9 September by an English force under Thomas Howard I, Earl of Surrey (see 68–70 and note). Skelton's poem shows such a precise knowledge of the interchange between Henry and James (see 2, 8, 56–9 and notes) that some scholars have argued he must have been in France at the time (Nelson, pp. 125–33, Pollet, pp. 68–73, but see Edwards, pp. 139–41 for another view). This poem must have been written after 9 September but before 22 September (the date of the highly informed *Chorus de Dys contra Scottos*), for Skelton has no precise facts about Flodden (38–41 and note). A revised version of this 'ballade' makes up *Agaynst the Scottes* 91–180.

The unique copy (*F*) of *A Ballade of the Scottysshe Kynge* was found lining one cover of the French romance *Huon of Bordeaulx* (Paris, Michel le Noir 1513), with two leaves of *The Trewe Encounter*, printed by Fakes in 1513 lining the other. Similarities between the two printings indicate Fakes printed the 'ballade' as well. The many mistakes it contains may mean it was done hurriedly.

2–7   Compare the account in BL MS Harley 2252 f.41 (printed by Nelson, Appendix IV) of the meeting at Thérouanne between the Scottish herald and Henry VIII:

'The kyng [Henry VIII] stondyng stylle wythe sobyr contenaunce havyng hys hand on hys swerde sayd, "Have ye now your tale at an ende?" The herawld of armes seyd, "Nay". "Sey forthe then," sayd the kyng. "Syr, he [James IV] somonyth your grace to be at home in your realme in the defence of hys alye." Then the kyng answeryd, "Ye have well don your message. Neverthelesse, hyt becommyth yll a Scotte to somon a kyng of Yngelond . . . and tell your master that I mystruste not so the ream of ynglond, but he shall have enowghe to do whan so evyr he begynnythe. And also I trustyd not hym so well but that I provyded for hym ryghte well, and that shall he well knowe. And he to somon me now beyng here for my ryght and enherytaunce, hyt wold mych better agreed with hys honowr to have somonyd me being at home, for he knewe well before my comyng hether that hether wold I come, and now to send me somons . . .'

Perhaps Skelton also has in mind the stigma attached to the name of a summoner in Chaucer:

He durst nat, for verray filthe and shame,
Seye he was a somoner, for the name.

(*The Canterbury Tales* III 1393–4.)

6   Based on a proverb (Whiting S 871).

8   Compare Hall's *Chronicle*: 'Then the kyng [Henry VIII] commaunded Garter [the English herald] to take hym [Sir David Lindsay, the Scottish herald] to his tente, & make him good chere, which so dyd, and cherished him wel for he was sore appalled' (p. 545).

10   The line is proverbial (Whitting S 366).

12   Based on the common proverbial collocation between 'wit' and 'will' (see Whiting W 408, W 419).

14   *not worth a flye*: Proverbial (Whiting F 345).

15–16   The 'auld alliance' between France and Scotland, renewed on 16 March 1512 on the usual terms, was re-negotiated and after 10 July was widely interpreted (particularly in France) to mean that Scotland was at war with England. The alliance between Scotland and Denmark was originally made between James IV and his uncle Haakon I, but after 20 February 1513 was with Haakon's successor, Christian II. The English claim to overlordship in Scotland was an old one; but hardly ever amounted to much in practice. James IV was married to Henry VIII's sister Margaret, and was therefore his brother-in-law.

18   Compare the MS Harley 2252 account: 'Tell hym [James IV] there shalle nevyr Scotte cawse me to retorne my fase.'

19   *Gelawaye*: Galloway.

23–4 Melchizedek (see Genesis xiv 18ff.) was the priestly king of Salem with whom Skelton elsewhere compared Henry VIII (*Speke Parott* 60). The Amalekites were enemies of Israel, frequently defeated (see, for example, Genesis xiv 7, I Chronicles iv 43) with whom Skelton elsewhere identifies the enemies of England (*Speke Parott* 118).

38–41 These lines seem to reflect early uncertainty about the Battle of Flodden (Skelton does not seem to know precisely where it was fought) and about the fate of James IV. A Venetian writing from London on 14 September says: 'As yet nothing certain was known of the King; he was supposed to be either dead or a prisoner' (*Calendar of State Papers* [Venetian] II Nos. 331, 337). In fact James IV's body was not found until the day after the battle (10 September), when it was taken to Norham Castle.

50 be] bet *F*; *Huntley Bankes*: For this place, frequently mentioned by Skelton in anti-Scottish verses, see *Why Come Ye Nat to Courte?* 267 and note.

52 wyld] wyle *F*.

56–9 Based on Henry VIII's reply to James IV dated 12 August: 'And yf the example of the kyng of Navarre beynge excluded from his royalme for assistence gyven to the Frenche king cannot restrayne you from this unnaturall dealynge, we suppose ye shall have like assistence of the sayde Frenche kynge as the kyng of Navarre hath now: Who is a kynge withoute a realme...' (Hall's *Chronicle*, p. 547). Jean d'Albret, who lost his throne in 1512, had like James IV supported Louis XII of France.

58 walles] welles *F*.

62 'You rough-footed Scots from the Hebrides'; 'rough-footed' because they wore shoes of undressed deerskin with the fur outwards.

64 *dronken Danes*: Compare Prince Hamlet on the reputation of Danes:
  This heavy headed revel east and west
  Makes us traduc'd and tax'd of other nations;
  They clepe us drunkards... (I iv 17–19)

68–70 The *Whyte Lyon* was the badge of Thomas Howard I, Earl of Surrey, later second Duke of Norfolk, commander of the English forces at Flodden; his son Thomas Howard II was made *lorde admyrall* on 4 May 1513.

XII AGAYNST THE SCOTTES

This poem is a revised and augmented version of *A Ballade of the Scottysshe Kynge* (for a convenient reprinting of the two texts parallel see Pollet, pp. 251–3). It probably dates from 22 September 1513 or slightly later, when the details about the Battle of Flodden were fully known. Certainly Skelton's alterations and additions are in the direction of greater precision: he knew the battle took place on Branxton Moor and Flodden Edge (11, 25, 131), he knew about the death of James IV and about the fate of his body (22, 166 and notes).

The text is taken from Lant's edition of *Certayne Bokes* (c.1545) (*L*), collated with the later editions of Kynge and Marshe (c.1554) (*K*), Day (c.1560) (*D*) and Marshe's 1568 edition of Skelton's *Workes* (*M*).

3 *wan they the felde*: A sardonic allusion to the early uninformed rumours which circulated, especially in France and Italy, to the effect that the Scots had won a great victory at Flodden. (See *L & P* I, 2254, 2307.) Compare lines 14–16, 24, 48.

18–19 Proverbial according to Whiting (B 326), but the only instance given.
22 *closyd in led*: Compare John Stow's *Survey of London*, ed. C.L. Kingsford, 1908, I, p. 298, on St Michael's Woodstreet:
'There is also (but without any outward monument) the head of James, the fourth king of Scots of that name, slayne at Flodden Field, and buried here by this occasion. After the battell the body of the saide king being founde, was closed in lead, and conveyed from thence to London, and so to the monastery of Sheyne in Surrey, where it remained for a time, in what order I am not certain . . .'
47 synge] sin *M*.
51 Compare 91–6 and *A Ballade of the Scottysshe Kynge* 2–7 and note.
53 syght: 'cite' (see 55). *DM* read 'fyght'.
57 *kynge Koppynge*: Compare *The Towneley Plays* XXI 167, 'kyng copyn in oure game', where 'copyn' is sometimes glossed 'empty-skein' (see *English Dialect Dictionary* under *coppin*). However, A.C. Cawley, *The Wakefield Pageants in the Towneley Cycle*, 1958, p. 120, suggests it may be better to relate the word to *cop* meaning 'a crest on the head of a bird' (*OED cop* sb 2 1d) and to render it 'coxcomb' in that context.
59 Compare *Speke Parott* 72.
61 *Locryan*: Loch Ryan, a bay in Wigtonshire. Compare *Howe the Douty Duke of Albany* 21.
62 sence] fence *L*.
63 'Of Edinburgh and Perth'.
67 ix] xi *LKDM*.
72 Skelton's poem is a 'tragedy' in the sense defined by Chaucer's Monk:
Tragedie is to seyn a certeyn storie,
As olde bokes maken us memorie,
Of hym that stood in greet prosperitee,
And is yfallen out of heigh degree
Into myserie, and endeth wrecchedly.
(*The Canterbury Tales* VII 1973–7.)
83 *Irysh keterynges*: 'marauders from the Highlands and Isles'.
85 *Thalya*: The muse of comedy.
91–180 For explanatory notes on those lines taken over directly from *A Ballade of the Scottysshe Kynge* see the notes to that poem.
92 Ye] *not KDM*.
117 *Scipione*: Probably Publius Cornelius Scipio Africanus Major (216–184/183 BC) is meant.
146 owne] *not DM*.
157 ye] he *LKLM*.
161 According to Leland's *Collectanea* (1770 ed.) IV 285, James IV wore 'his beerde somethynge longe'. Stow mentions that this beard was 'redde' (*Survey* I 298).
162 Among James IV's preparations for his invasion of England was the obtaining of:
'. . . sewin cannonis that he tuik fourtht of the castell of Edinburgh, quhik was callit the sewin sisteris, cassin be Robert Borthik the maister gounar witht wther small qrtaillze, bullat, powder and all maner of order as the maister gounar could devyse.'

Robert Lindesay of Pitscottie, *The Historie and Cronicles of Scotland*, ed. A.J.G. MacKay, STS (First Series 42) I 259–60.

166 your] not *KDM*. On 16 September Queen Katherine received from the Earl of Surrey James IV's gauntlet and a piece of his plaid coat as proof of his death (see *L & P* I, 2268). They reached Henry VIII in France on 20 September 1513.

167 starke naked] starke your naked *KD*, starke all naked *M*.

169 curse] cures *LKDM*. James IV had died under the sentence of excommunication for having broken the peace with England.

    Scotia . . . ergo etc. 'Scotland, reduced to the condition of a province, will be obedient to the commands of the King of England; otherwise, through the wilderness of Sin . . .' followed by fragments from the *Te Deum*.

1 Scotia] *Scotica LKDM*.

3 desertum Sin: See Exodus xvi 1.

THIS] HIS *LK*.

8 Compare *Collyn Clout* 50–51.

13 have they] they have *DM*.

14 brother] hys brother *DM*.

20 For Cain's murder of his brother see Genesis iv 8.

21 Who so] but who so *DM*. *pyketh mood*: 'grows angry'.

27–30 Compare Henry VIII's letter of 12 August 1513 accusing James IV of being one of a group of '. . . scysmatyques and their adherentes beynge by the generall counsayll expressely excommunicate and interdicted' (Hall's *Chronicle*, p. 547).

    Si veritatem . . . michi: 'If I speak the truth why do you not believe me?'

XIII AGENST GARNESCHE

Sir Christopher Garnesche, the object of Skelton's vituperation in these poems, was born into a prosperous East Anglian family. After service in France he became in 1509 one of Henry VIII's gentlemen ushers. For his services at court he was rewarded lavishly with money and manors in Norfolk, Suffolk, Sussex and Shropshire. When Henry VIII invaded France in 1513 Garnesche was made Sergeant of the King's Tents, and on 25 September of that year he was knighted at Tournai. As Helen Stearns pointed out (*MLN* XLIII, 1928, 518–23), Skelton's frequent jeers at Garnesche's title make it fairly likely that his poems are to be dated shortly after this honour was conferred. Edwards argued further that the lines

    Now upon thys hete

    Rankely whan ye swete (iii 133–4)

make the poems appropriate to the summer of 1514, which was apparently a hot one (p. 151). They must have been composed before 29 August 1514, when Garnesche again went to Europe.

    The text is taken from BL MS Harley 367 fol. 101r–109r(*H*), a manuscript badly stained and in places difficult to read. The MS once belonged to John Stow. Garnesche's contributions have, so far as is known, not survived. According to Skelton, Garnesche began the quarrel by referring to him as a 'knave' (i 9) and Henry VIII encouraged Skelton to reply. 'Flytyngs' of this sort were common in the courts of Italy and France, but Skelton's chief debt seems to be to *The Flytyng of Dunbar and Kennedy* (published 1508) which F. Brie argues that Skelton knew (*Englische Studien* XXXVII, 1907, 1–86).

i 4   nall] *Originally 'alle' but crossed through and corrected. Tyrmagant*: Probably a reference to Termagant, a supposed heathen deity worshipped by the Saracens; in medieval drama represented as a violent, blustering bully.

i 5   *Syr Frollo de Franko*: According to Geoffrey of Monmouth's *History of the Kings of Britain* I ix 2, he was a Roman governor of Gaul, killed by King Arthur.

i 6–7   *Syr Satrapas* and *Syr Chystyn* (or *Chesten*) do not seem to be figures of romance, but names invented by Skelton. The first looks to be based on the word 'satrap', originally the governor of a province under the ancient Persian monarchy, but usually a subordinate chieftain with a reputation for cruelty and ostentation (see *OED satrap*). The second is probably based on 'chesteine' or 'chesten', meaning 'chestnut-tree' or 'chestnut' and referring either to Garnesche's height (compare 5, 29) or to his swarthy complexion (compare 18, 36).

i 8   *Syr Dugles the dowty*: James Douglas, second Earl of Douglas, celebrated in ballads as one of the heroes of the battle of Otterburn of 19 August 1388 in which he was killed.

i 11   Trace] Tracy *H. Barabas* may be the man offered by Pilate to the Jews, described in Luke xxiii 19 as guilty of sedition and murder, and in John xviii 40 as a robber: or perhaps Barbas, Admiral of Persia, a great enemy of the Christians against whom he attempts to hold Jerusalem in the *Four Sons of Aymon*. *Syr Terry of Trace* looks like a romance hero, but neither Sir Tyrry of Gormoyse (*Guy of Warwick*) nor Thierry, Emperor of Germany (*Huon of Bordeaux*), nor Terry, son of Saber (*Beves of Hamtoun*), nor Thierry the douzepeer seems to be meant. The most obvious Thracian is Tereus, husband of Procne and ravisher of Philomela, her sister (see Ovid, *Metamorphoses* vi 424ff.).

i 15   *Syr Ferumbras* was the giant heathen king of Alexandria who challenged the douzepeers of Charlemagne; he was vanquished by Oliver and converted to Christianity. Compare *Ware the Hauke* 205.

i 16   *catacumbas of Cayre* refers to the Mausoleum, the huge sepulchral monument built at Halicarnassus in about 350 BC by Artemisia for her husband, Mausolus, Prince of Caria. It is referred to here as an ironic contrast to the remote Suffolk hamlet Cattawade (*Catywade*) where there was a shrine (see H.L.R. Edwards and B. Redstone, *TLS* 9, 16, 30 August 1934).

i 17   *Syr Lybyus*: Lybeaus Desconus, 'the fair unknown', hero of the Arthurian romance of this title.

i 22   The massive bridge at Mantrible and its fearsome giant guardian figure in several Charlemagne romances, but the giant's name is usually Agolafre or Golafre, not 'Malchus the Moor' as Skelton indicates here.

i 23   *blake Baltazar*: Probably, as Dyce suggested (II 179), one of the Magi or the Three Kings of Cologne, as they were sometimes called in the Middle Ages. The third, Balthasar, was sometimes depicted as a Moor.

i 24   *Lycon*: Lycaon, king of Arcadia, who served to Zeus a dish of human flesh. According to some traditions, he and his sons were turned into wolves as a punishment.

i 27–8   *not H.*

i 29   lothly] lothy *H.*

i 30   *Crokyd as a camoke*: Compare Whiting C 17.

i 32–3   The *mastres Punt* of Orwell referred to here has not been identified.

i 34–5   not H.

i 37   Based on two proverbs: 'To glow like a gleed' (Whiting G 152) and 'To glister like glass' (Whiting G 122). Compare *Elynour Rummynge* 482.

i 40   Howkyd as an hawkys beke: According to Whiting H 196 a proverb, but this is the only instance. Compare, however, 'As hook-nebbed as a hawk' (H 197). *Syr Topyas*: The hero of Chaucer's satirical romance of the same name. The *semely snowte* may have been suggested by Chaucer's line 'He hadde a semely nose' (*The Canterbury Tales* VII 729).

ii   Gresy, Gorbelyd Godfrey: There has been some speculation about the identity of Garnesche's helper in his quarrel with Skelton. He is somewhat similar to a character mentioned in Alexander Barclay's *Eclogues* I 838ff.:

Godfrey Gormand lately did me blame.
And as for him selfe, though he be gay and stoute,
He hath nought but foly within and eke without.
To blowe in a bowle, and for to pill a platter,
To girne, to braule, to counterfayte, to flatter,
He hath no felowe...

He is also similar to Godfrey Gobelive, the abusive dwarf companion of Grand Amour in Stephen Hawes's *Pastyme of Pleasure* (1508) who, like Gorbelyd Godfrey, is 'boln in the waist' (line 3502). Ian Gordon suggested that Skelton's character was meant to represent Hawes himself and that he was the assistant of Garnesche (*TLS* 15 November 1934, 795). Pollet suggests that the reference may not be specific, and that Gorbelyd Godfrey may simply be an invented character, as are Frippelippe and Matthieu de Bontigny in the flyting between Marot and Sagan (p. 78).

ii 2–5   The first word in each of these lines is supplied, since *H* is torn here.

ii 2   Compare the *Garlande of Laurell* 1376, *Against Venemous Tongues* 4.

ii 4   mantycare] mantyca *H*. Compare Caxton's *Mirror of the World* (1480): 'Another maner of bestes ther is in ynde that ben callyd *manticora*, and hath visage of a man, and thre huge grete teeth in his throte, he hath eyen lyke a ghoot and body of a lyon, tayll of a scorpyon and voys of a serpente in suche wyse that by his swete songe he draweth to hym the peple and devoureth them and is more delyverer to goo than is a fowle to flee.' Compare also XIII iii 165.

ii 6–7   Caiaphas was the Jewish high priest and Pilate the Roman governor who condemned Christ.

ii 8   Hole] *Originally 'Thow hole' but corrected*; Deurandall] Deundall *H*; the famous sword of Roland the douzepeer.

ii 15   Gabionyte of Gabyone: For the deceit of the Gibeonites because of their fear of Israel see Joshua ix 3ff.

ii 16   loke] *Originally 'kloke' but corrected. Huf, a galante*: 'Huff' is frequently an expression attributed to swaggerers. Compare *Digby Mysteries* iii 491: 'Her xal entyr a galaunt thus sayying: Hof, hof, hof, a frysche new galawnt!'; and also the refrain of a poem on gallants:

Huff! a galawnt, vylabele!
Thus syngyth galawntys in here revele.

(See Robbins, *Historical Poems* No. 52.) Compare *Magnyfycence* 745.

ii 17   jet full lyke a jaspe: According to Whiting J 16, a proverb, but this is the only instance given.

ii 18   As wytles as a wylde goos: Compare Tilley G 348.

ii 22–4   These lists of heroes appear to be constructed principally with an eye to the alliteration, and to have little in common with each other. Sir Gawain and Sir Kay were two of Arthur's knights. Priamus is more likely to refer to the pagan prince, who, in Malory's *Morte Darthur* v 10, fought with Gawain, than to the King of Troy. *Pyramus* is probably the Babylonian lover of Thisbe; but *Pyrrus* could be the historical king of Epirus (318–272 BC) who fought against Rome or Pyrrhus, the son of Achilles, who killed Priam at the sack of Troy. The others referred to are Guy of Warwick, the romance hero, and Oliver, the douzepeer.

ii 25   devyl in a clowde: Proverbial, according to Whiting B 216.

ii 30   Syr Olifranke: Perhaps Skelton has in mind the 'greet geaunt' called 'sire Olifaunt' against whom Chaucer's Sir Thopas fought (*The Canterbury Tales* VII 808).

ii 34   your paltoke . . . 35] *not H.*

ii 41   Cayfas copyous . . . 42] *not H.*

Colophon: *Mirres vous y*: 'Look upon yourself herein.' Compare the colophon to 'Uppon a deedmans hed'.

iii 3   your skrybe: Presumably Gorbelyd Godfrey of the previous poem.

iii 16   Added in a different hand.

iii 19   lewdly] *Dyce's emendation*, lewly *H.*

iii 33   my lady Brewsys howse: Hasketon Hall, Suffolk, the home of Lady Elizabeth Brews, grandmother of Thomas Brews who became the husband of Jane Scrope, the heroine of *Phyllyp Sparowe*.

iii 40   Gynys: The garrison town of Guisnes, near Calais, where Garnesche had apparently served as a soldier.

iii 54   kyst a shepys ie: 'looked lovingly at', a proverbial expression (see Whiting S 231).

iii 55–60   In *H* the beginnings of these lines are torn away.

iii 68   pyllyd garleke hed: 'bald head'; according to Dyce (II 184) '*Pilled-garlick* was a term applied to a person whose hair had fallen off by disease'.

iii 70   Syr Gy of Gaunt: Compare *Collyn Clout* 1155 and note.

iii 79   Probably an allusion to the proverb 'As sweet as the elder' (i.e. not sweet) in Whiting E 63. The proverbial phrase is applied to breath in 'The Lover's Mocking Reply':

> Of alle feturys so ungodly for to se,
>   with brethe as swete as ys the Elder tre.

(Robbins, *Secular Lyrics* No. 209, 34–5.)

iii 101   Based on the very common proverb 'As bold as blind Bayard' (Whiting B 71). 'Bayard' (OF baiard) was originally a bay-coloured horse, and the name of the horse Charlemagne gave to Reynawde. But by the sixteenth century it had come to be used as a satiric name for any horse, or as denoting blindness or blind recklessness. Compare *Phyllyp Sparowe* 651–8 and note.

iii 104–5   Based on a common proverbial phrase (compare Whiting R 103). See also line 128.

iii 109   Jake Rakar: A term of abuse perhaps from 'raker', meaning 'scavenger'. Compare *Speke Parott* 160, *Why Come Ye Nat to Courte?* 273.

iii 115–16   Compare *Elynour Rummynge* 223–4.

iii 131   Your] *Added in a different hand in H.*

iii 139   both wyght and grene: Dyce (II 187) suggests that this refers to the dress which Skelton wore as laureate.

iii 152 confection: An allusion to the use of mixtures of sweet smelling herbs and spices as a way of purifying the air in times of plague.

iii 168 gargone: The Gorgons were originally three mythical sisters who had serpents for hair, wings, brazen claws and enormous teeth. All who looked upon them were turned into stone.

iii 173 thy] they *H*.

iii 174 Tyburne: Until 1783 the place of public execution for Middlesex.

iii 178 Perhaps 'You have fraudulently collected so much plunder', though *pelfry* here may mean 'trumpery, rubbish, trash' (*OED pelfry* 2).

iii 185 Stokys, to whom Garnesche evidently owed money, has not been identified.

iii 186 Syr Dalyrag, a contemptuous name (see *OED rag* sb 1 3b). Compare also *Speke Parott* 89, *Howe the Douty Duke of Albany* 297.

iii 189 Perhaps based on the proverb 'To cut one's coat after one's cloth' (Whiting C 342), meaning 'to live within one's income', something Skelton says Garnesche conspicuously fails to do.

iii 190 'You get up to such thievish tricks.' See *OED pageant* sb 1b and Dyce's note (II 189).

iii 197–8 Compare Tilley B 377.

iii 200 fresche] flesche *H*.

iii 201 threde] *Dyce's emendation*, thre *H*.

iii 203 'With "The Lord be with you".'

iii 204 Jake a Thrum: Compare also *Magnyfycence* 1427, *Garlande of Laurell* 209 and *Collyn Clout* 282 and note.

iv 'The laureate's offering of a couplet against Goliardic Garnesche and his scribe. You, Garnesche are a fool, and your scribe is a greater fool: he who was wise as a boy as a man goes mad, changed into a hydra.'

    Goliardum: The group of twelfth- and thirteenth-century Latin poets known as the 'goliards' were educated men, sometimes clerics, who wrote verses, often ribald and comic, celebrating the physical life. Perhaps Skelton applies the term to Garnesche here, however, because of the Old French meaning 'glutton'.

    hydram: Originally the Hydra was the many-headed snake of the marshes of Lerna, killed by Hercules. Here it simply means 'monster'.

v 2 your secunde ryme: Edwards (p. 153) takes this to mean that Garnesche's poem to which Skelton was replying was written, like Garnesche's first poem, without the help of 'Godfrey'.

v 4–6 According to Whiting C 603, line 4 is based on the common proverbial connection between cuckoos and cuckolds. But line 6 makes it clear that the proverb 'The cuckoo can sing but one lay (song)' (Whiting C 600) underlies these lines.

v 8–12 A sidenote in *H* refers the reader to '*prologus libri 2 in vetery rhetorica ciceronis*,' that is, to *De Inventione* II i, where the idea that Nature deliberately refrains from creating perfection appears. Line 10 is a fairly direct version of Cicero's *aliquo adiuncto incommodo muneratur*.

v 18 Thy] They *H*.

v 26 *Added in a different hand*. Compare Whiting C 575.

v 27 beryst the belle: 'have the pre-eminence'. Compare Whiting B 230.

v 30 Syr Pers de Brasy: The famous French soldier, Pierre de Brézé, grand-seneschal of Anjou, Poitou and Normandy, killed at Montlhéry in 1465.

v 32 can] cam *H*.

v 33–6 These lines appear to refer to men with whom Garnesche had quarrelled. Dyce (II 190–91) identifies the Lombard *Gorge Hardyson* with a 'George Ardeson' mentioned in *Bokis of Kyngis Paymentis Temp. Hen. vii and viii*; but *Jorge from Genoa* has not been identified.

v 36 trysyd: See *OED* trice v, 'To pull; pluck, snatch; rarely, to carry off (as plunder)'.

v 37 Compare iii 190 and note.

v 41–2 Fenchurch Street, like Budge Row (47), was part of the city of London. The Lombards there were principally merchants and bankers.

v 48 pluk a crow: Proverbial for 'engage in a dispute'. Compare Whiting C 572 and *Speke Parott* 396.

v 49 holde] *Dyce's emendation*, bolde *H*. onbende your bow: Compare Whiting B 483.

v 56 Syr Gy: Compare iii 70 and *Collyn Clout* 1155 and note.

v 75 'Between the hangings and the wall'. Compare *Magnyfycence* 1233 where the same expression is used in a similar context.

v 76 Fusty bawdyas: Compare the *Garlande of Laurell* 639.

v 78 Arres: Arras, Artois, famous for the manufacture of tapestries.

v 80–84 Skelton was made *poete lawreate* by the University of Oxford probably in 1488, by Louvain in 1492 and by Cambridge in 1493. The distinction, which could be held by several people at the same time, was awarded for particular skill in rhetoric.

v 87 Calliope: The muse of epic poetry.

v 98–100 The nine Muses, supposedly the daughters of Zeus and Mnemosyne, were born in Pieria, at the foot of Mount Olympus. Helicon is a range of mountains in Boeotia, sacred to Apollo and the Muses, in which were the fountains of the Muses, Aganippe and Hippocrene.

v 102 sofreyne] *Dyce's emendation*, sofre *H*. creaunser: Precisely when Skelton was appointed tutor to the young prince who became Henry VIII is not known. Henry VIII was born on 28 June 1491, and since Skelton says he taught him spelling (95) it may be assumed he supervised the prince's education from the first. Children learned their alphabet and the rudiments of writing at about the age of 4, so perhaps Skelton was a royal tutor as early as 1495 or 1496.

v 112–13 *The ends of these two lines are illegible because of staining on the MS.*

v 117 'Though you are bald you are not wise.'

v 133–4 Compare *Against Dundas* 34–8.

v 140–41 Aulus Persius Flaccus (34–62), Decimus Junius Juvenalis (c.55–c.138), Quintus Horatius Flaccus (65–8 BC), Marcus Valerius Martialis (c.40–c.104), four famous Latin satirists.

v 149 Syr Wrag-wrag: Compare *Speke Parott* 89, *Howe the Douty Duke of Albany* 296.

v 159 A very common proverb (Whiting P 393).

v 164 Haftar] Hastar *H*. Compare *Why Come Ye Nat to Courte?* 97, *Magnyfycence* 257, 697, 1678, 2456, *The Bowge of Courte* 138 and note.

v 165 Proverbial (Whiting P 385).

XIV   AGAINST DUNDAS

The object of these vituperative verses is perhaps George Dundas, knight of Rhodes, who was involved in a dispute with the secretary of James V, Patrick

Paniter, in 1513–15 over his right to the preceptory of Torphichen – a dispute in which both James V and Henry VIII were somewhat involved (see *L & P* I, 843, 1077–8, 1230, 1263–4, 1720; II, 87–8, 2800). Perhaps this poem was written around 1515.

The story of the 'tailed Englishmen' was well known in the Middle Ages. One of the most influential versions appeared in the life of St Augustine in *The Golden Legend*:

'After this Saynt Austyn entryd in to Dorsetshyre, and came in to a towne where as were wycked peple & refused his doctryne and prechyng utterly & droof hym out of the towne castyng on hym the tayles of thornback or like fisshes, wherfore he besought almyghty God to shewe his jugement on them, and God sente to them a shameful token, for the chyldren that were borne after in that place had tayles as it is sayd, tyl they had repented them. It is sayd comynly that thys fyl at Strode in Kente, but blessyd be God at this day is no suche deformyte.' (Caxton's translation, 1483)

Indeed, Scots earlier than Dundas appear to have used this jibe. According to the historian Walter Bower, the Scots sang songs about 'tailed Englishmen' before the battle of Dupplin in 1332 (see R.M. Wilson, *Lost Literature of Medieval England*, 1952, p. 214).

The text is taken from Marshe's 1568 edition of Skelton's *Workes* (*M*). The title is editorially supplied.

Vilitissimus ... Angligenas: 'The most vile Scot Dundas mentions that Englishmen have tails.'

Caudatos ... bucca est: 'Most base Scot, what things do you proclaim about Englishmen with tails? You are shameless, and a guilty man, a liar, and foul-mouthed.'

Spurcaquae] spureaquae *M*.

Anglicus a tergo ... sine laude: 'The Englishman carries a tail behind him; he is, therefore, a dog. Tailed Englishman, hold on to your tail so that it may not fall from you. Because of their tails the English people are without praise.' These three internally rhyming (see 9) hexameters are presumably by Dundas. Skelton calls them pentameters at line 6.

Diffamas patriam ... maledictum: 'You malign this country, than which there is not a better one anywhere. You wag your tail when you can; begging you beat at the doors. You will be a beggar, and a double-tongued liar, scabby, horrible you whom worms and six feet of earth will destroy wretchedly; for miserable men, their stock is cursed.'

Skelton nobilis poeta: 'Skelton the noble poet.'

11–18 'Skelton, the laureate poet, born an Englishman, calls forth the Muses against Dundas, the filthy Scot, everywhere infamous, reared as a boor, wretchedly drunk.'

15 *Spurcissimum*] Dyce's emendation, *Norpacissimum M*.

25 the] thy *M*. Compare *Magnyfycence* 303, *Howe the Douty Duke of Albany* 159.

29 *Galaway*: Galloway. Compare *Agaynst the Scottes* 109, *Howe the Douty Duke of Albany* 23.

34–8 Compare *Agenst Garnesche v* 133–4.

39 'With three, two, one', which literally looks like a throw at dice (compare *The Bowge of Courte* 347; *Why Come Ye Nat to Courte?* 878); but, in view of the context, perhaps also a bilingual punning phrase meaning 'very soft arse'.

40 tolman: Dyce (II 226) interprets as 'penman', and compares *Agenst Garnesche* ii 117. This makes adequate sense. But compare *Why Come Ye Nat to Courte?* 885–6, where 'tall man' means 'a loaded dice', which Skelton may also have had in mind here.

41 rough foted: Compare *A Ballade of the Scottysshe Kynge* 62 and note. This was a jibe used by earlier versifiers, e.g. *The Poems of Laurence Minot*, ed. J. Hall, 2nd edition 1897, ii 19.

58 Huntley bankes: Frequently mentioned by Skelton in his anti-Scottish verses; see *Why Come Ye Nat to Courte?* 267 and note.

60 Dunde Dunbar] Dunde bar *M*. Compare *Agaynst the Scottes* 121, *Howe the Douty Duke of Albany* 24.

XV   AGAINST VENEMOUS TONGUES

If Edwards's emendation (pp. 276–7) is right, the phrase *Oratoris Regis tertio*, which he interprets as meaning 'in the third year as orator royal', may provide evidence for dating the poem. Skelton was apparently granted a patent making him orator royal in 1512 or 1513 (see Nelson, pp. 122–4) which would indicate a date of 1515 or 1516 for the poem. This squares well with its similarities to *Magnyfycence* (see 13, 55–8 and notes) which was probably written in 1515, and also with the possible allusion in 64 (see note) which would indicate some time after early May 1516.

The poem is of a very conventional sort – an attack on back-biters (see Heiserman, pp. 281–2) – and it is difficult to be sure about its occasion. Pollet (pp. 82–3) argues that the concern with liveries makes it plain that the poem is about Wolsey's anger at certain lords 'because they had so many men in a livery at the meeting of the Scotch Queen' (*L & P* II, 2018).

The text is taken from Marshe's 1568 printing of Skelton's *Workes* (*M*).

tertio] *Edwards's emendation, tertius M.*

Quid detur . . . dolosam: 'What shall be given unto thee? or what shall be done unto thee, thou false tongue?' Vulgate Psalm cxix 3.

Deus destruet . . . viventium: 'God shall likewise destroy thee for ever, he shall take thee away, and pluck thee out of thy dwelling place, and root thee out of the land of the living.' Vulgate Psalm li 7.

4 'Making noises like hogs which grunt and root about.' Compare *Agenst Garnesche* ii 2, *Garlande of Laurell* 1376.

Dilexisti omnia . . . dolosa: 'Thou lovest all devouring words, O thou deceitful tongue.' Vulgate Psalm li 6.

Ad sannam . . . graphice: 'He turns a man to mockery in a derisive and pointed way.'

13 Compare *Magnyfycence* 1. 28.

Hic notat . . . retro: 'Here he refers to Roman letters woven in bright colours on the front and back of liveries of followers.' Edwards refers to a passage in Cavendish's *Life of Wolsey* describing his retinue as he left London in 1527: 'And all his yeomen, with noblemen's and gentlemen's servants, following him in French tawny livery coats; having embroidered upon the backs and breasts of the said coats these letters: T and C, under the cardinal's hat.' (The letters stood for 'Thomas Cardinalis'.) He points out that Wolsey was created cardinal on 10 September 1515 (p. 165); but there is no evidence to show that Wolsey's servants wore such liveries in this year.

Pedagogium meum de . . . esse: 'My learning is from the more sublime Minerva.' Minerva was the Roman goddess of wisdom.

Pedagogium meum male . . . explodit: 'My learning drives off stage with hissing and applause the mad and the scurrilous.'

Laxent ergo . . . vanitatis: 'Let them therefore lower the sail of their arrogance, filled by the wind of their vanity.'

32   *vale a bonet*: Here *vale* means 'lower' (see *OED vail* v 2) and *bonet* means 'a piece of canvas laced to the foot of a sail to catch more wind' (see *OED bonnet* sb 2), but this line also alludes to the phrase 'vale the bonnet' meaning 'take off the hat' as a sign of respect or submission.

Nobilitati . . . vilitas: 'Let obscure baseness give place to nobility.'

46   *hay the gy of thre*: Probably the 'haydeguise', a kind of country dance.

Sicut novacula . . . dolum: 'Like a sharp razor working deceitfully.' Vulgate Psalm li 4. *novacula*] *nouocla* M.

49–50   Based on the proverb 'The tongue breaks bone though itself has none' (Whiting T 384).

Lege Philostratum . . . Apollonii: 'Read Philostratus on the life of Apollonius of Tyana.' Apollonius was a philosophizing mystic of the first century; Flavius Philostratus (*c*.170–*c*.244/249) was an Athenian philosopher.

52   *Pharaotis*: Pharaoh.

Venenum aspidum . . . eorum: 'Adders' poison is under their lips.' Vulgate Psalm cxxxix 4.

Quid peregrinis . . . recurramus: 'Why do we need examples from abroad? Let us revert to our own land.'

55–8   Ramsay (p. cxviii) compares these lines with *Magnyfycence* 1629–1725, in which Courtly Abusyon and Cloked Colusyon plot to remove Measure from the prince's favour.

Quicquid loquantur . . . effantur: 'Whatever they are saying they chatter as if they were turning into women.'

Novarum rerum . . . deliratores: 'Greedy for new things, legacy hunters, informers, flatterers, spies, fools.'

64   *Totnam*] *Totman* M. Perhaps this refers to the meeting in early May 1516 at Tottenham between Henry VIII and his sister Margaret, widow of James IV (killed at Flodden in 1513), who had married Archibald Douglas, sixth Earl of Angus, in August 1514, and who, with her husband, had been ejected from Scotland in September 1515. With the phrase *what newis in Wales* compare *Elynóur Rummynge* 353, where it similarly seems to indicate inconsequential chatter.

65   *Scalis Malis*: Cadiz.

66   Proverbial (Whiting N 195).

De more . . . fabricant: 'In the manner of foxes, snarling in the ear, they make up their false fables.'

Inauspicatum, male . . . Laureato: 'Whoever has slandered the muse-like poet Skelton laureate, let him admit that he has an inauspicious, ill-omened, unlucky horoscope.' *Skeltonidi Laureato*] *S.L. M.*

77   Based on the common proverbial phrase 'To make it tough' (Whiting T 431), meaning to make something difficult.

Cerberus horrendo . . . precor: 'I pray that Cerberus, with terrible baying, beneath the cave of the abyss, may bite and devour you, deceitful tongue.' *Cerberus* was the three-headed dog supposed to guard Hades.

Recipit se . . . honorificandum: 'He undertakes to write a work holy, praiseworthy, acceptable, and memorable, and altogether honourable.'
Disperdat dominus . . . magniloquam: 'May the Lord destroy all deceitful lips and boasting tongues.' Vulgate Psalm xi 4.

XVI   MAGNYFYCENCE

The play is usually assumed to have been written in 1515–16. The reference in 280–82 (see note) is usually thought to be to Louis XII, who died on 1 January 1515, and the *wache* of 350–52 (see note) to refer to the tense situation which existed between England and France at this time. Leigh Winser, however, has recently argued that the similarity with *The Bowge of Courte* indicates that Skelton wrote *Magnyfycence* '. . . if not before he reached Diss in 1504 then perhaps shortly thereafter'. The *wache* that resulted in Fansy's capture he takes to be a reference to the border patrols set up by Henry VII during Perkin Warbeck's rebellion, and the *Kynge Lewes of Fraunce* to Louis XI (*RQ* XXIII, 1970, 14–25). Neuss, on the other hand, argues for 'between 1520 and 1522'(17).

Interpretations of the play have also varied. R.L. Ramsay in the introduction to his edition (EETS ES 98, 1908) argues that the philosophical allegory is based on the concept of liberality found in Aristotle's *Nichomachean Ethics* (pp. xxxii–xliv, lxxii–lxxviii); and that on a political level it refers to the power struggle around Henry VIII between the party of Thomas Howard, Duke of Norfolk (Measure), and that of Wolsey (the six vices) (pp. cvi–cxxviii). But evidence has recently been brought forward to show that anti-Wolseyan satires did not appear before the 1520s, and that the play is unlikely to have had this precise political significance, though it is agreed that it offers advice to the king. Heiserman suggests that the proper use of wealth is the play's principal issue (p. 69), and Harris produces evidence to show that Skelton's conception of 'magnyfycence' is compatible with *magnificentia*, a sub-virtue of Fortitude, a virtue traditionally held to consist of a measured self-control through which one could withstand the temptations of both prosperity and adversity.

The play is based directly on no one source. It owes something in structure and characterization to previous morality plays; the set of moral ideas it embodies Skelton could have found in a number of places, for example Hoccleve's *Regement of Princes* or Lydgate and Burgh's *Secrees of Old Philisoffres* (see Ramsay, pp. lxxiii–lxxvi); the passages of satire on the court vices may owe something to Barclay's version of *The Shyp of Folys* (see Ramsay, pp. lxxviii–lxxxix). But the play relies greatly on conventional elements which could be infinitely paralleled in medieval literature; in fact, R.S. Kinsman has argued that it is through a rigorous deployment of *sententiae* and proverbs that Skelton works out his theme (*SP* LXIII, 1966, 99–125).

The surviving texts give little indication of how *Magnyfycence* was meant to be performed. The stage directions, though occasionally elaborate, are too sporadic to be adequate and many (indicated by square brackets) have had to be supplied editorially. Some idea of how the play was meant to be staged can be deduced. It was probably meant to be played at night (see 365), probably indoors. There were evidently two exits (called *dores*, 1725); this would have allowed for characters to enter by one door as other characters left by the other (see 395ff., 2324ff.). The stage could have been small since there are never more than four characters on stage at any one time, and Ramsay argues plausibly that *Magnyfycence* could have been performed adequately with only five actors (see pp. xlviii–1). The action is evidently meant to be continuous since the stage is never empty and since there is no indication of act or scene divisions. Nor does the scene alter; the action was evidently meant to take place a short distance from Magnyfycence's palace (see 2567) in London (see 423, 910, 1404, 2263).

A little may be deduced about costume. Magnyfycence is a prince and is probably meant to be dressed as such until he is ruined by Adversyte (1875ff.), after which he becomes like a beggar (2238) until covered by the *abylyment* of Redresse (2405). The courtly vices are evidently gallants (see 511), Courtly Abusyon being dressed in a particularly extravagant manner (see 829ff.). Clokyd Colusyon appears in disguise (594), dressed in a priest's cope (601) which is apparently too small for him (see 607). Fansy and Foly are both 'fools'. Fansy is perhaps meant to be a 'naturall' fool: he is 'feble-fantastycall' and 'braynsyke' (1072–3). He is small, perhaps a dwarf (see 288–9, 522–3, 1068–78) and was probably played by a boy. He appears to have been dressed in the costume of a professional fool (see 1046). Foly was probably an 'artificial' or 'allowed' fool, expert at practical jokes and twisting words: he wears a fool's coat and mask (1176–7), and carries a bauble (1042ff.). Both Fansy and Foly bear large purses which were standard parts of the fool's equipment (1102ff.). Fansy has an owl (1047) on his wrist and Foly leads a mangy dog (1054). Of the other characters little can be deduced. Poverte is arthritic and dressed in rags (1962). Good Hope describes himself as a *potecary* (2351), uses medical terms (2353–8) and is asked about his *pacyent* (2387); perhaps he was also dressed appropriately.

The text is taken from the Cambridge University Library copy (*C*) of the *c.*1530 printing by Rastell and Treveris; collated with the imperfect British Library copy (*B*) which differs in a few places only, the most important being at 2014 where it reads 'courtely silkes' for *curteyns of sylke*; and with the two pages from Bodleian Library Oxford Douce Fragments d.7 (*D*) which preserve lines 2198–364.

The lineation of the present edition differs from that of Dyce, who counts single lines divided between two speakers as two lines; and also from that of Ramsay, who counts as line 912 what appears to be part of a stage direction, and who (like Dyce) does not include in the line-count lines obviously omitted in the printing (1336, 2464, 2467–9, 2500). The text at 2464–9 is very fragmentary, and it is possible that passages of some length have been omitted there.

These be the names...Perseveraunce: In *CB* this list is placed after the play. The characters are listed in order of appearance, and grouped according to function: the three virtues originally possessed by the hero; then the hero; then the ten vices who cause his fall and almost cause his death; and finally the four virtues who save him.

Felycyte: prosperous happiness (see line 23)

Lyberte: the power to act as one pleases, whether for good or ill (see lines 2001–2)

Measure: restraint, moderation, temperance

Magnyfycence: a composite term involving, amongst other things, magnanimity or greatness of soul, princely authority and judgement, dignity, glory, liberality

Fansy: capricious whimsicality, erratic self-centredness

Counterfet Countenaunce: both false appearance and simulated restraint

Crafty Conveyaunce: both crafty behaviour and the ability to steal without detection

Clokyd Collusyon: underhand plotting

Courtly Abusyon: perversion of fashionable, high-style, noble behaviour

Myschefe: suicide

Redresse: reparation, reform

Cyrcumspeccyon: intelligent carefulness

Counterfet Countenaunce] Counterfet Counte *CB*

1–3 Perhaps 'when all things are directed by man's reason, throughout the whole world, by men of high or low rank, wealth comes sooner or later.' *envyronn* is Neuss's emendation; *CB* reads 'envyronnyd'. According to Whiting (W 149) line 3 is proverbial, but this is the only instance given.

4 'The possession of wealth is very reliable evidence of wisdom.'

5 Based on the proverb 'A fool and his money are soon parted' (Tilley F 452).

6 unhappely be uryd] Compare *Replycacion* 95, 405; *Howe the Douty Duke of Albany* 126.

7 '. . . so that they find nothing harder to sustain than wealth'.

12 Proverbial (compare Whiting D 417).

13 Perhaps a version of the proverb 'After great heat comes cold . . .' (Whiting H 305), or a reversal of Whiting C 365.

36 not worthe a cue: Proverbial (compare Whiting C 606). A *cue* was half a farthing (*OED cue* sb 2).

37 Proverbial (Whiting L 225).

38 your barge: This image of the hero's moral well-being is taken up again in 2559–63.

42 advertence] *Ramsay's emendation*, advertysment *CB*.

44, 47 countenaunce] Ramsay emends to 'continence', but the *CB* reading 'countenaunce' can carry the meaning 'self-restraint' as well as retain an association with Counterfet Countenaunce.

52 Proverbial (Whiting L 224).

67 'To touch briefly on the direction of my argument . . .'

Hic intrat MEASURE: 'Here enters MEASURE.'

97–9 'However, on condition that you take no offence, we must have some argument.'

114 Oracius: The reference is almost certainly to Horace's *Odes* II x 5 on the golden mean ('*auream . . . mediocritatem*'), though the opening of II iii deals with the same topic. Perhaps alternatively from *Satires* I 100. Harris demonstrates that these passages from Horace were sometimes used as illustrations of Fortitude in medieval treatments of the cardinal virtues (pp. 139–44). Measure's speech is a collection of commonplaces such as may be found, for example, in Lydgate's 'Song of Just Mesure' and 'Mesure is Tresour' (*Minor Poems*, ed. H.N. MacCracken, EETS OS 192, 1934, Nos. 61, 62).

118 In] Neuss's emendation, I *CB*. The 'godly opynyon' is that of Solomon and the line depends on Wisdom xi 21: 'omnia mensura et numero et pondere disposuisti' ('all things by measure and number and weight you have arranged').

125 Measure is treasure: A common proverb (Whiting M 461).

137 The middle voice ('meyne') ensures that the treble does not go too low or the tenor too high; hence it regulates or 'rules' them. Compare 1463.

139 Proverbial (Whiting S 917), but the only instance given.

144 An allusion to the common notion that the first shall be last (Matthew xix 30).

146   cut it out of the brode clothe: Proverbial (Whiting C 309).

148   wyll is no skyll: Proverbial (Whiting W 273).

150   is] it *CB*.

Hic intrat MAGNYFYCENCE: 'Here enters MAGNYFYCENCE.'

188   measure is a meane: Proverbial (compare Whiting M 454). The more usual form of this proverb appears at 380.

201   This lynkyd chayne of love: The phrase recalls 'the faire cheyne of love' of *The Canterbury Tales* I 2988, though the philosophical ideas present in Chaucer, and deriving ultimately from Homer (*Iliad* viii 19), do not seem to be important in this context.

211   beware of 'Had I wyste!': 'beware of regret', one of the most common proverbial phrases (Whiting H 9). See also 1395.

214   countyth] Dyce's emendation, countyd *CB*.

216   Se] So *CB*.

218   as trewe as the crede: Proverbial (Whiting C 541).

*222   Perhaps 'All men laugh derisively when they wish.'

224   fer beyonde the mone: Proverbial (Whiting M 657).

Itaque MEASURE ... cum FELICITATE: 'And so let MEASURE leave the place with LIBERTY, and let MAGNYFYCENCE remain with FELICITY.'

Hic intrat FANSY: 'Here enters FANSY.'

*254   'There is nobody here who cares whether you sink or swim.' Based on a proverb (Tilley S 485).

257   benedicite: 'bless you'.

258   Jacke of the Vale: A contemptuous name; compare *Manerly Margery Mylk and Ale* 6, and see Whiting J 4.

259   dronken bycause I loke pale: The collocation between 'dronken' and 'pale' was a common one; compare *The Canterbury Tales* I 3120, 4150, IX 20, 30.

*260   Proverbial (Tilley D 608).

278   be in measure] in measure be *CB*.

280–82   Kynge Lewes of Fraunce: Louis XII, who died on 1 January 1515. Skelton's impression of his 'largesse' is probably based on the elaborate and costly festivities with which Louis had celebrated his marriage to Mary, Henry VIII's sister, in 1514, and on the gifts of diamonds and jewels he gave to her (see Brewer I 84). On Mary's marriage to Charles Brandon, Duke of Suffolk in early 1515, Louis's successor, Francis I, sought to recover these presents.

287   Jacke shall have Gyl: The proverb is usually 'All is well: Jack shall have Gill' (Whiting J 7); perhaps, therefore, this line means '... with care and with thought how to make things turn out right'.

291   colyca passyo: 'colic'.

293   Dauncaster cuttys: 'Doncaster horses'. A 'cut' was a common or labouring horse, or possibly a 'cut-tail' horse, or a gelding (*OED cut* sb 2 VI 28). Proverbial (Whiting C 654).

294   bolte to shote at the buttes: Perhaps based on the proverb 'To bring one's bolt to stand in the butt' (Whiting B 435).

*296   Based on the proverb 'To care which end goes before' (Whiting E 88).

299   knowe a gose from a swanne: Proverbial (Whiting G 387).

*300   Based on the proverb 'Fools lade pools, wise men eat the fish' (Whiting F 418).

303   Go shake the, dogge, hay: Compare *Against Dundas* 28, *Howe the Douty Duke of Albany* 159.

Hic ficiat . . . cum manu: 'Let him act as if he were reading the letter silently. Meanwhile let COUNTERFET COUNTENAUNCE come in singing; with a gentle step, on seeing MAGNYFYCENCE, let him withdraw gradually; but after a short time let him come back looking about and calling repeatedly from a distance; and FANSY motions him, with his hand, to be quiet.'

sensim] *sensum C*; *at*] *ad CB*.

343   Pountesse: Pontoise, France.

350   Magn.] *Fansy C*; *Fan*] *not C*.

350–52   suche a wache . . . a spye: Though the two nations were officially at peace, there was, especially on the French coast, tension between England and France in early 1515. Anthony Spinelly writes to England on 14 April 1515 that he had been accused (rightly) of spying by the French (*L & P* II, 321).

357   Freer Tucke: Friar Tuck is mentioned in two early ballads of Robin Hood (F.J. Child, *English and Scottish Popular Ballads* Nos. 145, 147) and in two early fragmentary plays. But no incident such as that mentioned here when he preached 'out of the pylery hole' appears in them. He was, however, a character in May games, as some lines from 1586 indicate:

At Paske began our Morris, and ere Penticost our May;
   Tho Robin Hood, Liell John, Frier Tucke and Marian deftly play.
(Child, III, 45)
Perhaps such a pillory incident occurred in a May game.

367   Proverbial (Whiting L 82).

381   Proverbial, according to Whiting A 112, but this is the only instance given.

384   grotes] *Dyce's emendation*, *otes CB*. The word, as elsewhere in Skelton, refers primarily to coins, but here may bear the secondary meaning 'hulled or crushed grain' (*OED groats* sb pl 1).

385   otes] *Dyce's emendation*, *grotes CB*.

387   hugger mugger: 'secretly' (Whiting H 628).

   Hic discedat . . . COUNTERFET COUNTENAUNCE: 'Here let MAGNIFICENS depart with FANSY, and COUNTERFET COUNTENAUNCE enters.'

*403–6   The central image of this passage appears to be from hunting: Fancy has caught Magnyfycence in a net and Counterfet Countenaunce is to weight the net with a stone so that he shall not escape.

408   bastarde ryme, after the dogrell gyse: Compare *Collyn Clout* 53–8. John Norton-Smith (*Essays in Criticism*, XXIII, 1973, 57–62) thinks that this line 'may be taken to refer to Skelton's own characterization of his measure', the Skeltonic. Doggerel rhyme (the first reference to it is *The Canterbury Tales* VII 925) was according to George Puttenham that which observed 'no rules at all' (*Arte of English Poesie*, 1589, II iii iv); it appears to have been a demotic, subliterary form. Norton-Smith suggests that the Skeltonic has its origins in a type of verse epistle practised in East Anglia (particularly Norfolk), examples of which may be found among the *Paston Letters*. Skelton came into contact with this form when he moved to Diss in 1504.

   For the opinion that the Skeltonic originated in an adaptation of medieval mono-rhyming measure used in poems on death see R.S. Kinsman, *SP* L, 1953, 101–9; and for a summary of other opinions see Nelson, pp. 82–101.

*412   Proverbial (Whiting F 344). See also 1710, 1889.

418   Syght] *fyght CB*.

423   Tyburne: The place of public execution for Middlesex until 1783.

432 Based on the proverb 'To grease a man in the fist' (Tilley M 397) meaning 'to bribe'.

435 sande] *Ramsay's emendation,* founde *CB.*

441 *fayty bone geyte:* Dyce (II 242) suggests this may be a corruption of the French phrase *fait à bon get* or *geste* meaning 'elegant' or 'finely fashioned'.

443 'To give a false account of what has been received . . .'

447 Proverbial (Whiting P 47), but the only instance given.

448 Proverbial (Whiting N 22), but the only instance given. The line means 'It is difficult to patch up that which is torn.'

451 Proverbial (Whiting T 91).

455 A variant of the proverbial phrase 'Far-fetched and dear bought' (Whiting F 58).

457 Compare *Elynour Rummynge* 418.

465 *joly as a jay:* Proverbial (Whiting J 17).

470 *not worth a flye:* Proverbial (Whiting F 345).

477 *tehe wehe:* Though Annot wishes to be refined (*nyce*) her laughter connotes a crude sexual excitement; compare Alison in Chaucer's *Miller's Tale* (I 3740), the students' horse in *The Reeve's Tale* (I 4066), and also *Winner and Waster* 282 and *Piers Plowman* B VII 91–2.

Hic ingrediatur . . . CRAFTY CONVEYAUNCE: 'Here let FANSY enter quickly with CRAFTY CONVEYAUNCE, talking a lot, chattering by turns; at last, having noticed COUNTERFET COUNTENAUNCE, let CRAFTY CONVEYAUNCE say.'

503 *ete a flye:* 'be deceived', because the whole proverb is 'The blind eat many a fly' (Tilley B 451). Compare the proverbial phrase 'ete a gnat' (1192) (Whiting G 176).

504 I] *not CB.*

505 'By God, man, he can play both his part and yours'; based on a proverb (Whiting P 5).

525 Cra. Con.] *Dyce's emendation,* Cou. Cou. *CB.*

526 Cou. Cou.] *Dyce's emendation,* Cra. Con. *CB.*

535 dyscryved] *Dyce's emendation,* dysceyved *CB.*

552 Compare the proverb 'As strong as mustard' (Tilley M 1332). But the whole passage with its allusions to medicine (543–5, 555–6) suggests that the use of mustard for medicinal purposes was in Skelton's mind.

557 'That is the sort of opinion one would expect from a rake.'

558 ye] *Dyce's emendation,* we *CB.*

566 Proverbial (Whiting H 236).

Hic ingrediatur . . . sursum ambulando: 'Here let CLOKED COLUSYON enter with a lofty look, walking up and down.'

575 Proverbial (Whiting B 627), but the only instance given.

578 *Thy wordes be but wynde:* Proverbial (Whiting W 643).

579 *play the jeu dehayte:* jurde hayte *C B.* A baffling phrase, but perhaps a corruption of the French *jeu dehait* ('joyous game'). See Edmond Huguet's *Dictionnaire de la Langue Française du Seisième Siècle* under *dehait,* especially the quotation from de Collerye: '*Or après le lendit Jourrez vos jeux dehet, à la friscade.*'

586 A 'rache' is a dog which hunts by scent and according to Henderson (p. 183) not appropriate for hunting hares. A 'leash' of hounds is a set of three (*OED leash* sb 2). Cloked Colusyon is implying, if Henderson is right, that the other three are not likely to be very effective plotters. But see Robbins, *Secular Lyrics* No. 119 line 17 where 'rochis' hunt a hare.

605 Cope] *Ramsay's emendation*, cloke CB. The idea is reminiscent of *The Bowge of Courte* 177–8 where Favell's 'cloke' is lined 'with doubtfull doubleness'.

609 An allusion to the proverb 'To have a cloak for the rain' (Tilley C 417) meaning 'to have an expedient or excuse in a time of difficulty'.

626 *a captyvyte*: 'in captivity' (see *OED a* prep I 4).

630 *Clo. Col.*] *Dyce's emendation Cra. Con. CB*; you me tell] you tell me *CB*.

631 *Cra. Con.*] *not CB*.

642 '. . . with guile to give things an appearance of honesty'.

649 Perhaps 'Here is an epistle with a postscript' as glossed by Ramsay. But *postyke* may derive from Latin *posticus* (= hinder, posterior, back) which *OED* has in an adjectival form *postic*, first used in 1638. If Skelton's word is a noun from the same root the line may mean 'Here is a letter with something written on the back'.

665 *Cra. Con.*] *not CB*.

667 *Cra. Con.*] *Dyce's emendation, Clo. Col. CB*.

675 *By the armes of Calys*: Compare *The Bowge of Courte* 398 and note.

Hic deambulat CLOKED COLUSYON: 'Here CLOKED COLUSYON walks about.'

710 *Two faces in a hode*: A proverbial expression signifying duplicity (Whiting F 13).

711 Perhaps a variant of the proverb 'Water and fire are contrarious' (Whiting W 83).

712 *lede hym by the eyre*: 'lead him by the ear', i.e. deceive him by words. Based on a proverb (Whiting E 9). The phrase 'fede forth' means 'to beguile' (*OED feed* v 2 b); see *The Bowge of Courte* 437.

721 *to bere the devyls sacke*: Proverbial (Whiting D 204).

730 *stynge lyke a waspe*: Proverbial (Whiting W 53), but the only instance given.

741 *to startyll and sparkyll lyke a bronde*: Proverbial (Whiting B 510), but the only instance given.

743 Proverbial (Whiting T 32).

Hic ingrediatur . . . cantando: 'Here let COURTLY ABUSYON enter, singing.'

745 Since he is a fashionable gallant Courtly Abusyon enters singing appropriately 'Huffa'. Compare *The Digby Plays*, ed. F.J. Furnivall, EETS ES 70, 1896, III 491: 'Her xal entyr a galavnt thus seyying: Hof, hof, hof, a frysche new galavnt'; and the refrain of Robbins, *Historical Poems* No. 52:

Huff! a galawnt, vylabele!

Thus syngyth galawntys in here revele.

Compare *Agenst Garnesche* ii 16. The rest of the line may be a garbled version of the Flemish tune 'Taunder naken . . .' (Stevens, Index No. 292).

747 Two songs seem to be alluded to here. *Rutty bully* ('roast boiled') probably refers to a *basse danse* which originated in Brabant; compare 'Agaynst a Comely Coystrowne' 29 and note and see Nan C. Carpenter, *RES* VI, 1955, 279–84. *joly rutterkyn* ('fine gallant') (see also 752) seems to refer to a song such as that in Fayrfax MS f.101v–104r which has the refrain:

Hoyda, hoyda, joly rutterkin!

Like a rutterkin, hoyda!

It appears to be a satire on the drinking habits of the Flemings (see further John Stevens, *Music and Poetry in the Early Tudor Court*, 1961, p. 380).

748 'From what country are you?' – an ironic question since Cloked Colusyon

recognizes Courtly Abusyon (757). But the question is given point because Courtly Abusyon sings snatches of songs from the Low Countries (747), though his manner of dress is French (876–83) – hence the language of the question.

Et faciat . . . ironice: 'And ironically let him make as if to doff his hat'. *exuat beretum ironice*] Dyce's *suggestion modified by Ramsay, exiat beretrum cronice* CB.

749 *Decke your hofte*: 'Adorn your head', i.e. put on your hat.

750 'Do you know how to sing "Venter tre dawce"?' Ramsay suggests '*Ventre très douce*', perhaps meaning 'very soft stomach'. But presumably it is the opening of a French song, perhaps *Votre très douce . . .* by Gilles Binchois (died 1460) as suggested by Carpenter, p. 117.

751 'Yes, yes'; *Wyda* for *Oui-da!*

755 A difficult line. A *buskyn* is a half-boot, and *batowe* here may mean 'a short boot' (see *OED botew*). *betell* perhaps means 'mallet, hammer, bat or club' (see *MED betel*).

758 *Jacke Hare*: The implication of this is derogatory, but in precisely what way is difficult to decide. Whiting cites two proverbs: 'No more power than Jack Hare' (J 10) which implies weakness, and 'To play Jack the hare' (J 12) which implies foolishness. Either could be in Skelton's mind here, or he may be thinking of Lydgate's *Ballade of Jak Hare* where the man is foolish and lazy (*Minor Poems* II 445–8).

760–61 'Dusty? No sir, you are very gaily dressed, although because you are a spendthrift your clothes smell stale.'

765 *thou fotys it lyke a swanne*: Proverbial (Whiting 936). In this line *swap* probably means 'strike the ground noisily' (*OED swap, swop* v I).

775 crake] *Ramsay's emendation*, barke CB.

781 *Cra. Con.*] *Dyce's emendation*, *Clo. Col.* CB.

786 Proverbial (Whiting N 45) and compare N 57.

788 *Clo. Col.*] *Dyce's emendation*, *Cou. Ab.* CB.

804 *I rule moche of the rost*: Proverbial (Whiting R 152).

805 Thou woldest, ye] ye thou woldest CB.

808 harte] hate CB.

826 *plucked the by the nose*: Proverbial (Whiting N 126), but the only instance cited.

829–911 Courtly Abusyon declares himself to be a fashionably dressed gallant, and he has many of the features of this type of character: long hair (835–6), wide sleeves and narrow hose (850–52); everything is 'Of the newe gyse' (846) and comes from France (877–88). He resembles Skelton's 'Ryotte' (see *The Bowge of Courte* 344–71 and note) and such characters as Pride in Henry Medwall's *Nature* (ed. J.S. Farmer, '*Lost*' *Tudor Plays*, 1907, pp. 76–7) who says of himself:

  And when he is in such array –
  'There goeth a rutter' men will say;
  'A rutter, huffa gallant.'

Compare 745–52.

837–8 Perhaps 'My robe rustles in such a way as befits a gallant.'

843 *poynte devyse*: 'perfectly exact'. See also 1540.

869–76 'A very insignificant person who wishes to do this abuses himself too much; he misuses everyone, accusing, boasting, and chattering; I make a fool of him.'

874 akuse] *Ramsay's emendation*, take a fe CB.

910 A proverbial phrase (Whiting T 551) meaning 'to be hanged'.

912–15 'All is out of joint and out of order, always worse and worse every-where.' *harre* means 'hinge', and *trace* may mean 'course, road' or, more likely, 'harness' (*OED trace* sb 2).

917 '*Stow, stow*': Compare *Ware the Hauke* 73 and note.

921 as mery as a Marche hare: Proverbial (Whiting H 114), but the only instance given.

925 an hawke of the towre: 'a hawk which towers high in the air'.

943 in the dyvyls date: Proverbial (Whiting D 200). See also 2172.

946 pyke out of the gate: 'be off out of the way'.

950 Is he crossed than with a chalke?: 'Is he cancelled out?'

970 Eche thynge is fayre when it is yonge: Proverbial (Whiting T 117), but the only instance given.

981–2 'From the river Tyne to the river Trent, and from Stroud (Gloucester-shire) to Kent'; i.e., roughly, from north to south, and from east to west.

1006 'May the devil prosper not a jot'. Compare *Why Come Ye Nat to Courte?* 1016–17.

1014 Proverbial (Whiting W 4), indicating Fansy's capacity for being amused by trifles.

1015–16 Both a pear (*pere*) and a pin (*pynne*) are proverbially trifling objects, see Whiting P 79–P 85, and P 209–P 213.

1028 Compare *Against Venemous Tongues* 13.

1035 Proverbial (Whiting S 551).

1036 Proverbial (Whiting M 24).

Hic ingrediatur . . . et similia: 'Here let FOLY enter shaking his bauble and doing many things, rattling clappers and such things.' *quatiendo*] Dyce's emendation, *quesiendo C B*.

1049 eye] eyen *CB*. The line is proverbial (Whiting L 377). Here it means 'you are blind'.

1056 Mackemurre: An Irish name; perhaps the line is as Kinsman suggests, 'a thrust at Irish poverty and gullibility' (p. 159), but the MacMurroughs were kings of Leinster in the fifteenth century.

1060 coughe me a dawe: 'make a fool of me'. Proverbial (Whiting D 28); for another version see 1064.

1061 Cokermowthe: Cockermouth (Cumberland); Foly's deliberate misunder-standing of 'coughe me' above.

1067 Perhaps a version of the proverb 'Not the better of a halfpenny' (Whiting H 43).

1082 dogge] Dyce's emendation, hogge *CB*.

1083 hogge] Dyce's emendation, dogge *CB*.

1102 purse: A large purse or wallet worn at the girdle was a standard piece of the fool's equipment.

1104 my purse] Ramsay's emendation, myne *CB*.

1107 Compare *The Bowge of Courte* 397.

1113 to a botchment: 'as a make-weight'.

1115 Perhaps alluding to the proverb 'He would spend God's cope if he had it' (Tilley G 271) meaning he would spend a great deal.

1121 from Anwyke unto Aungey: It is generally agreed that *Anwyke* is Anwick, a village in south Lincolnshire; but Aungey was taken by Dyce (II 254) to be Angers or Anjou (followed by Ramsay and Whiting A 135). Kinsman suggests

442 NOTES

Skelton may have written 'Aunbey' for Aunby, another south Lincolnshire village, because 'The context clearly suggests that Gryme's reputation is deservedly local' (p. 159).

1134 Compare Chaucer: 'Men dreme alday of owles and apes' (*The Canterbury Tales* VII 3092).

1142 'Nothing, nothing, nothing – in English worthless things.'

1150 Proverbial (Whiting R 103).

Versus] In *CB* it appears between the two macaronic hexameters 1154–5.

1154 *C B* read *Est snaui snago*, which makes no sense, and Neuss's emendation looks convincing. She translates, 'It is a sweet wag' – *vago* being a coined Latin word based on English 'wag'. *vilis imago* translates the preceding English phrase. Mock Latin of this sort is found elsewhere in moralities: see, for example, *Mankind* 57 'Corn seruit bredibus, chaffe horsibus, straw fyrybusque' and 60, 398–9.

1155 *Grimbaldus*: The word appears to have been made up of the dog's name 'Grim' (for *Gryme* 1118), 'bald' (for *pylde* 1053) and the Latin masculine termination '-us'.

1165 Proverbial (Whiting Q 13). See also line 2252. The implication is that he is a villain who ought to be hung, drawn, and quartered.

1174 kesteryll] besteryll *CB*.

1175 *doteryll*: Perhaps a pun here, for the word can mean both the dotterel, a kind of plover (*Endromias marinellus*), and a silly person or simpleton.

1176 *dyser*: 'fool, professional jester'. (See *OED disour* and *dizzard*.)

1177 *play the fole without a vyser*: 'play the fool without a mask', i.e. behave like a fool without trying to. Proverbial (Whiting F 457).

1178–9 Neuss (p. 138) argues that these lines are to be understood in terms of jousting (suggested by *vyser* in the previous line). She thinks that 'Howe put he to you' means 'Did he thrust home?' and that *blurre* means 'smear', a scratch but not a home thrust.

1191 Proverbial (Whiting C 359).

1192 Yes, yet] Yet yes *CB*.

1197 *Regardes, voyes vous*: 'Look, see.' *vous*] Ramsay's emendation, not *CB*.

1200 *a Spaynysshe moght with a gray lyste*: 'a Spanish moth with a gray stripe'.

1203 thou hast lost nowe] nowe thou hast lost *CB*.

1204 *Johnn a Bonam*: Perhaps the 'Jac of Bonam' who appears in *The Hunttyng of the Hare* (see Weber, *Metrical Romances* iii, 279).

1209 *Wodstocke Parke*: Situated about eight miles north of Oxford, Woodstock Park was first enclosed by Henry I who had a royal residence there.

1214 A variant of the proverbial collocation 'King or kaiser' (Whiting K 46).

1226 *thefte and bryboury*: 'theft and pilfering'. See also 1354.

1232–3 'She must have her sexual lust (the *lyther sparke* of 1231) satisfied between the tapestry hangings and the wall.' For the proverb on which 1232 is based see Whiting G 7; and for another appearance, in a similar context, of 1233 see *Agenst Garnesche* v 75.

1233 tappet] Dyce's emendation, tap *CB*.

1250 *hey, troly, loly*: Perhaps a reference to the specific contemporary dance song in Henry VIII's MS (see Stevens, Index No. 111); but songs using this refrain had been current since the fourteenth century (see *Piers Plowman* B VI 118–19).

1261 Compare Chaucer's 'good conseil wanteth whan it is moost nede' (*The Canterbury Tales* VII 1048) which is evidently a proverb (Whiting C 458).

1262 mo] more *CB*.

1267 'Simkin the tell-tale and Piers the sycophant.' Compare *Collyn Clout* 416 and note.

1271 wyt] whyt *CB*.

1292 The *boke* of which a *lefe* (1293) is turned over may be the fool's *bybyll* (1220). If so, perhaps 1295 is Folly's allusion to the Fall of Adam and Eve.

1299 *the hare is squat*: Proverbial (Whiting H 117), but the only instance given. It appears to mean 'The prey is cornered.'

1301-3 'And I, Foly, bring them into the state of someone who rushed about frenziedly; I have brought them into the condition of someone who was brainsick; from someone who was something to absolutely nothing.' With the phrase *shyre shakynge nought* compare *Elynour Rummynge* 466.

1308 slyght] *Dyce's emendation*, shyfte *CB*.

1325 *Away the mare!*: Proverbial (Whiting M 375), meaning 'Away with melancholy.' Compare *Elynour Rummynge* 110.

1330 *face and brace*: Neuss (p. 147) suggests 'confront and embrace' (as in a dance) because of 1331, but Skelton's usual meaning 'bluster and threaten' cannot be excluded (compare *Agaynst the Scottes* 33).

1342 'I have a small hawk that can make larks cower.' Dyce notes that 'To *dare larks* was an expression applied to the catching of larks by terrifying them ... When the hobby ... was employed for that purpose, the larks lay still in terror till a net was thrown over them' (II 258). But from its occurrence here, at 1564, and in *Collyn Clout* 193 (see note) it looks as though the phrase for Skelton had sexual implications.

1344 hungre] hunger *CB*.

1344-5 Feeding the hungry and clothing the naked were two of the Seven Bodily Works of Mercy. See Matthew xxv 35-6.

1346 'Copulate with her instantly.' For *trymme* in this sense, see *Titus Andronicus* V i 93-6. For *tayle* as the female pudendum see *The Canterbury Tales* VII 416, 434. The second half of the line is proverbial (Whiting S 455).

1348-50 'As often as you wish, if our reputations can be preserved. Alas, sweetheart, see to it that we are not found out. Without cunning nothing is well-managed.'

1351 craved] crave *CB*.

1378 *not worth a strawe*: Proverbial (Whiting S 815). So too is the whole line, according to Whiting L 226.

1379 *speke lyke a dawe*: Proverbial (Whiting D 29).

1386 *lyke a dull asse*: A version of the proverb 'As dull as an asse' (Whiting A 218).

1391 'Must measure, in the name of misery, provide for you and organise you?'

1404 *Ye have eten sauce*: Proverbial (Whiting S 67), meaning 'to be bold'. *at the Taylers Hall*: The hall of the Merchant Taylors' Company, off Threadneedle Street in the City of London, in its day one of the most sumptuous of guild halls.

1427 *Jacke a Thrommys bybyll*: Proverbial (Whiting J 1). See *Collyn Clout* 282 and note.

1429 kay] bay *CB*.

1446 you] thou *CB*.

1454 time] *Ramsay's emendation, not CB.*

1457 *Magn.*] Fansy *C B.* Magnyfycence's long boasting speech recalls those typically made by Herod in the mystery plays: compare *The Towneley Plays* XVI 8off.; *The York Plays* XVI 1ff.; *Ludus Coventriae* XVIII 1ff.; *The Chester Plays* X 1ff.

1466 Alexander the Great (356–323 BC) succeeded to the Macedonian throne in 336 BC. He secured Macedonia and Greece, conquered the Persians, occupied Phoenicia, Palestine and Egypt, and overran north-west India. Though he did not have 'all the oryent . . . in subjeccyon' he had a good part of it.

1473 Cyrus (559–529 BC), the founder of the Persian empire, one of the major cities of which was Babylon (conquered 539 BC). He allowed Hebrew captives to return to Jerusalem and rebuild their temple (II Chronicles xxxvi 22–3).

1480–81 According to one version of the story the Etruscan Lars Porsena, in order to restore the banished Tarquins, laid siege to Rome, but was foiled by the bravery of Horatius Cocles. According to another version he conquered the Capitol and ruled Rome, imposing harsh laws on her citizens. Either way he could be said to have made the Romans 'yll rest'.

1483 Julius Caesar (100–44 BC).

1487 Marcus Porcius Cato Uticensis (95–46 BC), according to Dyce (II 260) and Ramsay (p. 90). But Pollet (p. 248) suggests that Cato the Censor (234–149 BC) is meant and that the second half of this line means '. . . who counted the tax'.

1489 Whiting (P 364) takes this to be a variant of the proverb 'Not set a preen (= pin)'. But *prane* in Skelton means 'prawn'.

1494–5 Hercules, who was frequently depicted with a club, had, as one of his labours, to carry Cerberus, the dog who guarded hell, to the upper world. Compare the *Garlande of Laurell* 1284–314 and note.

1496 that] the *CB.* According to legend Theseus helped Pirithous to invade the lower world in an attempt to carry off Persephone. He was rescued by Hercules, though Pirithous remained below.

1498 *bere the bell*: 'am pre-eminent'. Proverbial (Whiting B 230).

1500 beseme] be sene *CB.*

1501–2 Charlemagne (774–814), king of the Franks, was like Arthur regarded as among the mightiest of medieval rulers.

1503 *Basyan*: Dyce (II 260) suggested Antoninus Bassianus Caracalla (who is called by Robert of Gloucester, *Chronicle*, ed. W.A. Wright, 1887, 1716ff. 'Basian'), Emperor from 211 to 217 and renowned for his wickedness.

1504 Alaric, king of the Goths, who in 395 plundered Rome.

1508 The Emperor Servius Sulpicius Galba, killed by a praetorian conspiracy, organized by Otho, on 15 January 69.

1509 The Emperor Nero (37–68), infamous for his reckless vanity and extravagant cruelty.

1510 The Emperor Flavius Vespasian (9–79). For the detail of the second half of Skelton's line compa   when he was bore, he had waspus in his nos, and therfor men callyd hyme Waspassyon' (*The Siege of Jerusalem in Prose*, ed. Auvo Kurvinen, Helsinki 1969, lines 97–8).

1511 The Carthaginian general Hannibal marched on Rome in 211 BC.

1512 Cypyo] Typyo *CB.* This line may refer to Scipio Africanus Major (236–184/3 BC) who, by defeating Hannibal at Zama (202 BC), virtually broke Carthaginian power in the Mediterranean; or, alternatively, to Scipio Aemilianus

Africanus Numantinus (185/4–129 BC) who, in the spring of 146 BC, took and destroyed Carthage.

1514   frounce them on the foretop: Perhaps 'make their hair curl' as glossed by Ramsay; or maybe 'make them wrinkle their foreheads' (see *OED frounce* v). Compare *Phyllyp Sparowe* 1340.

1540   'To perfection, your behaviour is entirely to my pleasure.'

1550–59   In its itemizing technique and in its aureate diction Courtly Abusyon's description of the 'fayre maystresse' has much in common with descriptions found in fifteenth-century courtly love lyrics (see, for example, Robbins, *Secular Lyrics* No. 130).

1555   leyre] *Dyce's emendation*, heyre *CB*. The phrase *lyly whyte* is proverbial (Whiting L 279a) and forms a frequent collocation with *leyre* (i.e. cheeks).

1556   as carbuncle so clere: Proverbial (Whiting C 35).

1558   ruddy as the chery: Proverbial (Whiting C 181). The earlier phrase *rudyes of the rose* is probably also proverbial. See Whiting R 200.

1562   suche a Phylyp Sparowe: The phrase must mean here something like 'such a darling'.

1568   'That I would be satiated on such an allurement', though it may be that *weryed* means 'choked' (*OED worry* v 2b).

1573   make . . . to the call: 'cause to be obedient to the summons', a metaphor from falconry.

1574   Money maketh marchauntes: Proverbial (Whiting M 629).

1576   bought and solde is a common proverbial expression (Whiting B 637) meaning 'to be betrayed'. According to classical myth, Laomedon's failure to pay the wages of Apollo and Poseidon (who had helped him build the city) caused them to devastate Troy.

1586   'Yes, for every woman is a whore if she can conceal the fact.'

1587   broken sorowe: 'petty misery' perhaps, but an uncertain phrase. Compare Chaucer's 'broken harm' (*The Canterbury Tales* IV 1425).

1596   'Whether it is reasonable or not, it will not greatly matter.'

1611   to touche you on the quyke: Proverbial (Whiting Q 15).

1614   caudell] candell *CB*.

1624   as hole as a troute: Proverbial (Whiting T 485).

1661   'Yet, sir, with all respect to your superior judgement . . .'

1666–7   'Yes, with his hand I made him sign a legal document for an annual income . . .'

1672   ye] he *CB*.

1675   he] There is no need here to emend to 'ye' as in Dyce and Ramsay. Courtly Abusyon is probably speaking to Collusyon here, who replies to him in the next speech. The *he* of 1673 is Measure, and that of 1675 is Magnyfycence.

Hic introducat . . . . elatissimo: Here let COLUSION bring forward MESURE to MAGNYFYCENCE who looks on him with a lofty face.

1704   not set a gnat: Proverbial (Whiting G 172).

1710   set not a flye: Proverbial (Whiting F 344), meaning 'care not a jot'. This is reinforced by the second half of the line which means 'whatever happens'.

1714–17   'I was your generous lord until you began to take it upon yourself to deal so masterfully with my servants, and began to dominate so that I am dissatisfied with you . . .'

1736   'Yes, he had to go; there was no other way . . .'

1742 'Where there is restraint in what one is allowed to eat there is no enjoyment . . .'

1750 They catche that catche may: Proverbial (Whiting C 112) meaning, 'They get what they can.'

1779 them] then *CB*.

1807 rammyshe: 'ramage', i.e. wild, shy. Dyce (II 265) quotes Latham's *Faulconry*, 1658: 'Ramage is when a hawk is wilde, coy, or disdainfull to the man, and contrary to be reclamed.'

1808–11 '. . . flew, I ought to say, into an old barn to get at a rat – I could not stop her. She injured her wing, by God, and came to harm. It (the rat) ran. No, fool, I am sure she is alive . . .'

1818 'What you say does not make sense.' Proverbial (Whiting F 101). Foly is deliberately talking nonsense in this passage.

1823–4 The first line looks like a reversal of the proverb 'To chase (follow) as hound does the hare' (Whiting H 577, 582), and the second to be on the analogy of 'If the blind lead the blind they both fall into the ditch' (Whiting B 350).

1829–30 Two proverbs run together: 'Goose and gander and gosling are three sounds but one thing' (Tilley G 351) and 'To eat of the goose that grazes on one's grave' (Whiting G 383).

1862 Survayour] *Dyce's emendation*, supervysour *CB*. The 'supervysour' was Clokyd Collusyon (see *1785*).

1873 who] why *CB*.

1885 'And in their moment of greatest confidence I cause them to fall down . . .'

1893 naked as an asse: Proverbial (Whiting A 221, but the only instance given).

1902 'With boils and inflammations I entangle them in pain . . .'

1906 'Some I make limp with an ulcer.' Compare *The Canterbury Tales* I 386 '. . . on his shyne a mormal hadde he'.

1907 bone ake: J.C. Maxwell suggests that this means 'syphilis' (*N & Q* CCVIII, 1963, 13–14) as in *Troilus and Cressida* II iii 20, but this is questioned by Beryl Rowland (*N & Q* CCIX, 1964, 211). Perhaps *cyatyca* ('sciatica') which makes Poverte's 'bonys ake' at 1955 is meant. Compare also 2254.

1909 'And some I strangle as with a wire . . .'

1912 with] to *CB*.

1929 to spare the rod: Proverbial (Tilley R 155). See also Proverbs xxiii 13–14: 'Withhold not correction from the child, for if thou beatest him with the rod he shall not die. Thou shalt beat him with the rod, and shalt deliver his soul from hell.'

1947 on] of *CB*.

1948–9 For the proverbial collocation of 'earnest' and 'game' see Whiting E 18.

1965 Proverbial (Whiting D 158), but the only instance given.
    Hic accedat . . . locum stratum: Perhaps, 'Here let him approach MAGNYFYCENCE to raise him up, and he shall put him on a level place' or perhaps '. . . on a bed.'

1971 Proverbial (Whiting W 144), but the only instance given.

1975 Proverbial (Whiting W 145). See also 2158–9.

2014 curteyns of sylke] courtely sylkes *B*.

2016 Raynes: Rennes, Brittany; a place famous for the manufacture of delicate linen.

2022–9 The notion of Fortune's variableness and duplicity was commonplace (see H.R. Patch, *The Goddess Fortune in Mediaeval Literature*, 1927). Lines 2022 and 2024 are based on proverbs (Whiting F 506, 508).

2031 Proverbial (Whiting Y 15).

Discedendo dicat ista verba: 'As he departs let him say these words.'

Discedendo] Dyce's emendation, *Difidendo CB*.

2044 'for through robbery they quickly get themselves hanged', i.e. they say 'into your hands (O Lord, I commend my spirit)' (Psalm xxx 6, Luke xxiii 46), the opening of a prayer said for the dying. *quecke* is a word used to represent the sound of choking; compare *Mankind* 516 'For drede of in manus tuas quecke.'

2046 *So mote I goo*: 'if only I could walk'.

2089 *totum in toto*: 'all in all', 'unlimited'. See 2099. *not worth an hawe*: 'worthless'. Proverbial (Whiting H 193).

2122 'And be mean over the payment of something of small value.' Proverbial (Whiting P 434). A *poddynge prycke* is a skewer with which the pudding-bag is secured.

2127 they] theyr *CB*.

2136 *to rynne on the brydyll*: Proverbial (Whiting B 539), meaning 'to run freely'.

2140 'and some end up by being executed'. The phrase *prechynge at the Toure Hyll* is similar to 'preach at Tyburn Cross' meaning 'to be hanged' (see Eric Partridge, *A Dictionary of Slang and Unconventional English*, 1961), since Tower Hill was a place of public execution.

Hic aliquis . . . post populum: 'Here someone blows a horn behind the audience.'

2156–7 Based on the proverbial uncertainty of Fortune (see Whiting F 523).

2165 Perhaps, 'I assure you I have used it to pay a debt' (see *OED lash* sb 1 4) but alternatively *lasshe* may simply mean 'blow'.

2174 *a stone-caste*: 'a stone's throw', i.e. a short distance.

2176 cleve] clene *CB*.

2183 'No. Then you will strike the devil if nobody holds you back.'

2187 *wrynge thy be in a brake*: Bright suggested that *be* is used as a quibbling echo of the *be* used in the preceding dialogue ('and thou *be* to bolde', 'I rede the to *be* wyse', 'I rede the *be*ware') so that the line would mean 'I'll put thy "be" (i.e. thy injunction) on the rack' (quoted by Ramsay, p. 88). Neuss (p. 196) thinks 'thy be' means 'thy behind'.

2198 *Cou. Cou.*] not *CBD*.

2199 'Come to an agreement and give me your swords.' Probably loosely based on the proverbial saying 'to cast heads together' (Whiting H 236). Compare line 566.

2230–31 'No, I know well enough that you are both skilled with your hands at getting inside a treasure chest even though it had strong bands.'

2233 *soppys in ale*: 'worthless things'. Proverbial (Whiting S 497).

2234 *trymynge and tramynge*: 'insignificant efforts'.

2236 'When we negotiated a loan with Magnyfycence's goods.' According to 2168 they used his plate as security. For the phrase 'make chevysaunce' see Chaucer's *Canterbury Tales* VII 329, 347.

2260 *requiem eternam*: 'eternal rest'. The second half line seems to allude to the proverb 'Hunger drops out of his nose' (Whiting H 639). Since the Latin phrase is from the Office of the Dead (see *Phyllyp Sparowe* 575) the implication is that Magnyfycence is consigned to death.

2263–76 A passage full of sexual allusions. *the halfe strete* was on the Bank-side, Southwark, where the stews were. Dyce (II 273) quotes a long passage from *Cocke Lorelles Bote* which mentions it. *mete* and *motton* are terms for whores or prostitutes (compare *2 Henry IV* II iv 123–4, *Measure for Measure* III ii 183–6). *glotton* probably means 'having a strong sexual appetite'. The phrases *stryke...in a hete* and *fyre...in the flanke* may mean 'arouse sexually', or perhaps 'cause one to get a venereal disease'. Line 2272 certainly seems to mean 'You will get gonorrhoea from a whore', but *OED* gives no example of *clap* as verb before 1658, and none as noun before 1587. Alternatively *clappyd* may mean 'struck sharply together', hence 'copulated' (Eric Partridge, *Shakespeare's Bawdy*, revised and enlarged edition 1968, s.v. *clap*). Lines 2265–6 seem additionally to be based on the proverb 'Mutton is good meat for a glutton' (Whiting M 813).

Et cum...a loco: 'And with haste let them leave the place.'

Hic intrat DYSPARE: 'Here enters DYSPARE.'

2284 folowe] felowe *CBD*.

2294–5 '...and you are so far in arrears with what you owe God, and you have spent your time so wickedly...' But 'ungracyously' also suggests 'lacking God's grace' (2297–8). Despair is the most serious sin against the Holy Ghost, when one gives up hope of obtaining God's mercy (2299–2304).

Hic intrat MYSCHEFE: 'Here enters MYSCHEFE.'

2313–22 Compare Despair's offer of halter and knife to the Redcrosse Knight in Spenser's *Faerie Queene* I ix 50; and see F.I. Carpenter, *MLN* XVI, 1897, 257–73 for further instances. Myschief is the name given to suicide in *Mankind*.

2323 Mys.] Magn. *CBD*.

Hic intrat...et dicat: 'Here enters GOOD HOPE, DYSPARE and MYSCHEFE fleeing; quickly let GOOD HOPE snatch away the knife from him and say:' *gladium*] Dyce's emendation, *gladio CBD*.

2329 sautes] fautes *CBD*.

2334 'I would have been dragged to the prison of damnation', i.e. I would have gone to hell for committing suicide.

2341–2 'It would be a great misfortune to offend your creator by killing yourself, to your eternal misery.'

2345–8 Spikenard (*narde*), balm (*bawme*) and gum-arabic (*gumme of Arabe*) were all used for aromatic and soothing ointments.

2354 bytter alowes: A bitter but gentle purgative (see 2353) drug made from the inspissated juice of the leaves of various species of aloe. *rubarbe* (2357) was also used as a purgative, but here Skelton may have in mind its supposed efficacy in purifying the blood (see Gerard's *Herball*, 1597, under 'rubarb').

2358–60 '...your diet must be prepared with measures of devotion, with the spiritual gums of a glad heart and mind, so that you thank God for what he sends, and you shall find comfort...'

2367 by] Ramsay's emendation, to *CB*.

2380 neglygesse] Ramsay's emendation, neglygence *CB*.

Hic intrat REDRESSE: 'Here enters REDRESSE.'

Et exiat: 'And let him go out.'

MAGNYFYCENCE accipiat indumentum: 'Let MAGNYFYCENCE receive the garment.

2408 Redr.] not *CB*.

2433 Suggested by a reviewer in The Gentleman's Magazine *(see Dyce II 487) and adopted by Ramsay.* Then ye repent you of foly in tymes past *CB.*

2435 sent] *not CB. Emendation suggested by a reviewer in* The Gentleman's Magazine *(see Dyce II 487) and adopted by Ramsay.*

Hic intrat PERSEVERAUNCE: 'Here enters PERSEVERAUNCE.'

2459 'Your arrival here was opportune.'

2472 Faythfull] Faythfully *CB.*

2479 'On what would it be most fitting that I should fix my heart?'

2515 sekernesse] sekenesse *CB.*

2529 Proverbial (Whiting F 508). See also 2536.

2540 'If anyone wants to get to the heart of the matter.'

2547 made of page: 'considered as a page'.

2552–4 'This material which we have treated in order to amuse you, which we have set out particularly in the form of a play, shows wisdom to those who can apprehend wisdom . . .'

2559 trechery] rechery *CB.*

2561 ensorbyd] ensordyd *CB.* The image is of a shipwreck, and Dyce's emendation is preferable to the less specific reading of the prints. *ensorbyd* must mean something like 'swallowed up' or 'sucked in' (from Latin *sorbeo*). 'ensordyd' seems to be from Latin *sordeo* and means 'made grimy'.

2564 hymselfe] hym *CB.*

XVII   ELYNOUR RUMMYNGE

The poem is difficult to date, but the existence of a real 'Alianora Romyng' living in Leatherhead in 1525 (see 93 and note) and the date of *X* (*c.*1521) provide some indication. Lines 355–62 contain what appears to be a reference to the Evil May Day riots of 1517 (see note) and it is likely that the poem dates from around this time.

Elynour Rummynge is in the tradition of 'good gossips' or 'ale wives' poem (see R.H. Robbins, *RES* XX, 1969, 182–9 for references to others) but seems to owe little directly to any previous poem. Pollet's identification of a particular 'source' (pp. 254–7) is not convincing.

The text is taken from Richard Lant's edition (*L*) of *Certayne Bokes* (*c.*1545), the earliest and best complete text, collated with the editions of John Kynge and Thomas Marche (*c.*1554) (*K*), John Day (*c.*1560) (*D*), and Thomas Marshe's edition of Skelton's works of 1568 (*M*). Fragments of an edition of *c.*1521 perhaps by Wynkyn de Worde or Henry Pepwell (*X*) provide some readings. For details of these fragments see R.S. Kinsman, *HLQ* XVIII, 1955, 315–27.

1–3 The opening of the poem, many of the transitions and the conclusion are marked by this mocking imitation of the minstrel intrusions of medieval oral verse. Compare lines 156–9, 187–8, 235–43, 619–23.

12–90 A parody of rhetorical descriptions of beautiful ladies; compare H. Person, *Cambridge Middle English Lyrics*, 1953, pp. 38–40, R.H. Robbins, *Secular Lyrics of the XIVth and XVth Centuries*, 1952, Nos. 209, 210.

45 of] *Dyce's emendation, not LKDM;* huckels] buckels *DM.*

46 not DM.

50 Legged] *Dyce's emendation following Rand's edition of 1624,* Legges *LKDM.*

52 fet] set *M.*

55   Compare Whiting S 332. The phrase means 'with affectation'.

56   *Lyncole grene*: A type of green cloth made at Lincoln. Compare *Brystowe red* (70), another local cloth.

59   doth it] it dothe *DM*.

60   For] And *DM*.

71–2   Compare Chaucer's portrait of the Wife of Bath, *The Canterbury Tales* I 453–5.

72   That wey] That they wey *KDM*.

73   in] in a *DM*.

78   *Lyke an Egypcyan*: Kinsman (p. 153) refers to the account of a mumming in 1509–10 where it is stated that the court ladies' heads were 'rouled in pleasauntes and typpets like the Egipcians' (*Hall's Chronicle*, ed. George Whibley, 1904, I 17).

79   Lapped] Capped *KDM*.

85   as she gose] as a gose *DM*.

86   *blanket hose*: Stockings made from blanket, a kind of woollen cloth, usually undyed, but sometimes dyed white.

87   not *DM*.

93   *Elynour Rummynge*: Records for 1525 relating to Leatherhead, Surrey, show that one 'Alianora Romyng' a 'common tippellar of ale' was fined 2d for selling ale 'at excessive price by small measures' (J. Harvey, *TLS* 26 October 1946, 521).

102   *noppy ale* was a fermented drink made from malted barley. It was frothy, sweet and heavy.

103   port-sale] pore sale *KD*. *port-sale* usually meant public sale to the highest bidder, sale by auction; but here it simply means that Elynour got as high a price as she could for her ale.

110–12   These lines are based on proverbs; compare Whiting M 375, C 38, and H 116, the last of which is a reversal of 'As wood as any hare'.

131   on] of *DM*.

133   unlased] unbrased *DM*.

134   not *DM*.

142   Kinsman (p. 155) suggests 'some walk with the peculiar sideways, sudden-starting lope of a kitten', but *skewed* here is probably an adjective meaning 'irregularly marked in colour' usually applied to horses but also to other animals (*OED skewed* a 1).

150   *cawry-mawry*: A kind of coarse cloth; thus the line means 'some appear coarse skinned'.

159   Dyce (I 100) takes *mawte* and *molde* as proper names, but Kinsman (p. 155) is probably right in taking them to mean 'malt' and 'mould': 'Eleanor's mash is green and still needs to "malt" . . . and may even mould from the careless and hasty treatment of the grain.'

168   Compare *Howe the Douty Duke of Albany* 37.

169   hogges] dogges *DM*.

178   not *DM*.

190   *mashfat*: The vat or tun in which the malt mixture is 'mashed', i.e. mixed with hot water.

198   into] in *DM*.

224   mytyng] *Dyce's emendation on the basis of Rand's edition of 1624*, mittine;

nytyng LKDM. Evidently a term of endearment as are several words in lines 223–7. Compare its use in *Agenst Garnesche* iii 115.

232   X begins.

233   Than swetely] Thus swete *X.*

234   Proverbial according to Whiting P 188, but this is the only instance given. Perhaps a variant of P 190: 'To wallow (turn) like two pigs in a poke.'

240–41   For a similar concluding formula compare *Why Come Ye Nat to Courte?* 230–32.

252   Lemster woll: A fine wool of short staple produced by the Ryeland or Herefordshire breed of sheep, called after Leominster in Herefordshire.

265   ale] all *L.*

280   hernest] haruest *DX*; the meaning is 'harnessed, ornamented'.

292   tyrly-tyrlowe: Perhaps the refrain of a song. Compare *Collyn Clout* 949, where, however, the phrase seems to have sexual connotations (see note).

303–4   Compare the proverb 'The cup abyes the default of supper' (Whiting C 622) for a similar idea.

306   Let the cat wynke: Half of a proverb 'Let the cat wink and let the mouse run' (Whiting C 96). Compare also *Collyn Clout* 457.

312   not *DM.*

321   sallowe] swallowe *KDM.*

324   stale] *Dyce's emendation confirmed by X,* stare *LKDM.* 324–5 mean 'She was a likely sort of bait to take the devil in a trap.'

330   Compare Whiting W 50.

331   began] gan *X.*

334   Based on the proverbial phrase 'Far-fetched and dear bought' (Whiting F 58).

350   the peace] *Dyce's emendation,* the drunken peace *LKDM.*

353   Compare *Against Venemous Tongues* 64.

354   Saynte James in Gales: The shrine of St James at Compostella in Galicia, a famous place of pilgrimage.

355–62   Probably a reference to the Evil May Day uprising of 1517 when a London mob attacked foreigners in the city whom they blamed for the depressed state of the economy. The Portuguese ambassador and his attendants had arrived in London on the day the trouble started (*Calendar of State Papers* II 382).

361   thyder] there *LKDM.*

363   spake thus] speketh this *LKDM.*

381   bones] bornes *D.* The line is a mixture of two proverbs: 'Beef has bones, eggs have shells, but ale has nothing else' (Whiting B 178), and 'To find no bones in something' (Whiting B 448).

387   babell] batell *X.*

388   a] *not LKDM;* fylly] silly *M.* The *foles fylly* is either 'foal's filly' or 'foolish young girl'. For a similar sexual innuendo in equestrian terms see 'The auncient acquaintaunce...' (13–26).

393   Saynt Benet: Saint Benedict.

401   hyche] hye *X.*

415   brought] brought up *DM.*

417   her] *not LKDM.*

421   ye] he *X.*

422   stubbed] stubbled *KDM.*

424–5 An ironic variation of 'As yellow as a kite's feet' (Whiting K 74), though the comparison as made by Skelton is cited by Whiting K 73 as a separate proverb.

427 Crokenebbed] *Kinsman's reading from X,* Croke necked *LKDM.* Whiting O 67 cites 'As crooknecked as an owl' as proverbial, but this is the only instance given.

429–35 The thick, strong-tasting Essex cheeses were made of ewes' milk. Heywood (*Epigrammes* No. 24) says:

I never saw Banbury chese thicke enough,

But I have oft seene Essex cheese quicke enough.

444 stynkes] stynges *K.*

451 Dyce (II 173) quotes Horman's *Vulgaria:* 'Unsette lekes be of more vertue than they that be sette...'

452 And] *not LKDM.*

453–4 A similar boast to that of the First Witch:

Her husband's to Aleppo gone, master o' th' Tiger:

But in a sieve I'll thither sail...(*Macbeth* I iii 7–8)

454 Burdeou] *Dyce's emendation,* burde on *LKDM.*

461 She] Some *DM.*

465 They] The *D.* 465–6 mean 'Those that you have brought are the smallest of the brood; they are utterly worthless.' With 466 compare *Magnyfycence* 1303.

Sextus] Secundus *LKD.*

480 dregges] dragges *LKD.*

482 glystryng lyke glas: A proverbial comparison (see Whiting G 121, 122, 123).

504 And] *not DM*; pluck] pulck *L.*

507 thy] the *KDM.*

517 wyde] wyse *K.* For the phrase *wyde wesant* compare *Collyn Clout* 1154.

521 *gredy cormerant:* Compare Chaucer's *Parliament of Fowls* 362: 'The hote cormeraunt of glotenye'.

532, 537 These lines are unrhymed; presumably the lines which rhymed with them have been lost in all surviving editions.

549 hyght] high *DM.*

561 croppy] coppy *DM.*

587 lege-de-moy] lege moy *LK.* Compare *Collyn Clout* 951 and note.

613–16 'But when they had to go marked their indebtedness to Elynour up on a beam with chalk, or notched it on a stick.'

Colophon: 'A couplet in contempt of the wicked by Skelton the laureate poet. Jealous man, however mad you are and however you waste away in your vanity, we sing; these places are full of jests. I recall it well. All women who are either very fond of drinking, or who bear the dirty stain of filth, or who have the sordid blemish of squalor, or who are marked out by garrulous loquacity, the poet invites to listen to this little satire. Drunken, filthy, sordid, gossiping woman, let her run here, let her hasten, let her come; this little satire will willingly record her deeds: Apollo, sounding his lyre, will sing the theme of laughter in a hoarse song.'

jocis] *Dyce's emendation, locis LKDM.*

Bien men souvient: Compare *Phyllyp Sparowe* 844 and note, and the colophon of *A Lawde and Prayse Made for our Sovereigne Lord the Kyng.*

qua spurca] quam spuria *DM.*

Sua gesta libellus] Sua libellus *D,* Sua facta libellus *M.*

XVIII   SPEKE PAROTT

Internal evidence provides a fairly reliable basis on which to date the poem. Allu-sions to Wolsey's attempt to get the laws of sanctuary changed (lines 124–5 and note) indicate a date after November 1519, and the lines on the Grammarians' War (141ff. and note, 169–82) suggest 1519 or later. The envoys, however, indi-cate a date towards the end of 1521 since they follow pretty closely Wolsey's manoeuvrings at the Calais Conference of 2 August to 24 November (lines 280, 281, 283–4, 288, 308–9, 398–9 and notes). Early in 1521 armed conflict had broken out between Francis I of France and the Emperor Charles V; Wolsey, on Henry VIII's behalf, was supposed to mediate. Though he made a show of impartiality and gave Francis I assurances, Wolsey was determined to procrastinate but eventually support Charles V, with whom he had plotted in Bruges in August 1521 (287 and note) and by whom he had been promised the papacy (70 and note). Pope Leo X died on 2 December 1521 and there is reference to English attempts to influence the choice of his successor (411–14 and note). These indications are confirmed by the successive dates based on Skelton's pri-vate chronology begun when he entered the Tudor royal service in October or November 1488: the numbers 33 and 34 (lines 300a, 323a–b, 356a–b, 375a, 520c) denote the number of years after this date. *Speke Parott* is alluded to in *Garlande of Laurell* 1189–90, printed 3 October 1523.

Speke Parott owes something to several sources. Parott has some of the charac-teristics – his colours, his loyalty to his mistress, his loquacity – of Corinna's pet Psittacus, whose death was lamented by Ovid (*Amores* II vi). In his wisdom, however, he resembles Psyttacus, the son of Deucalion and Pyrrha, who, when he had grown old, was transformed by the gods, at his own request, into a parrot (Boccaccio, *De Genealogia Deorum* IV xlix). This gives extra point to Parott's mention of 'Dewcalyons flodde' (455ff.) which Jupiter loosed on the world because of the wickedness of men, particularly Lycaon (Ovid, *Metamorphoses* i 177 ff.), with whom Skelton, by a pun, identifies Wolsey (293 and note). Parott also has some of the characteristics of the 'green lover' of Jean Lemaire de Belges's 'Première Épitre de l'Amant Vert' (ed. Paul Spaak, Paris 1926, pp. 206–17), written in 1505 and known in England (see Heiserman, pp. 174–7); and the character of Galathea derives from the twelfth-century pseudo-Ovidian *Pamphi-lus* (see lines 233–4 and note).

No completely satisfactory text has survived. The poem is here edited from British Library MS Harley 2252 fols. 133v–140r (*H*), the commonplace book (*c*.1525–35) of the London grocer John Colyns, which provides lines 1–57, 225–end; and from Lant's *Certayne Bokes* (*c*.1545) (*L*) which supplies lines 58–224 (missing in *H*); collated with the editions of Kynge and Marche (*c*.1554) (*K*), Day (*c*.1560) (*D*), and the text in Marshe's *Workes* (1568) (*M*). The printed texts preserve 1–232 entire, but then become hopelessly confused with the introduc-tion of Galathea. Only lines 265–9, 274–7 of the subsequent material appear. It is not impossible that some lines have been lost, but Dyce's combination (II 1–25) of the surviving material (followed by subsequent editors) makes convincing textual sense.

Title: THE BOKE COMPILED BY MAISTER SKELTON, POET LAUREAT, CALLED SPEAKE PARROT *M*.

Epigraphs: 'By his readers an author receives an amplification of his short poem.' *Auxesis* is a rhetorical figure of amplification. 'The present book will grow greatly while I am alive; thence will the golden reputation of Skelton be proclaimed.'

1   a byrde of Paradyse: Compare Lydgate, *Minor Poems* II No. 70 line 89: 'Popyngayes froo Paradys comyn al grene.'

4   Eufrates: According to Genesis ii 14 the fourth river of Paradise.

6   to greate ladyes] to grece to lordys *H*.

8–9   Compare the splendid cage of Melior's parrot in Statius, *Silvae* II iv 11–13.

11   a] *not H*.

13   Speke, Parott: An expression which became proverbial (compare Whiting 33).

14   and] *not LKDM*.

15   and] *not LKDM*.

16   Compare Ovid *Amores* II vi 21: '*Tu poteras virides pennis hebetare smargados*' ('You will be able, with your feathers, to dim the green emeralds') of Corinna's parrot.

17   Perhaps based on Reuchlin's *Breviloquus* under 'Psitacus': '*torquem... puniceum circa collum*' ('a collar... of purple around your neck), or Lemaire's '*collier vermeil et purpurin*' (p. 208).

19   a (2nd)] the *LKDM*.

24   owur] your *LKDM*.

25   and] Araby and *LKDM*.

25–6   More than simply a list of languages, this is an indication that Parott is a pretender to the 'new learning'. Compare Rabelais '. . . now the mindes of men are qualified with all manner of discipline, and the old sciences revived, which for many ages were extinct: now it is that the learned languages are to their pristine purity restored, *viz*. Greek (without which a man may be ashamed to account himself a scholar), Hebrew, Arabick, Chaldaean and Latine' (*Gargantua and Pantagruel*, translated by Sir Thomas Urquhart and Peter le Motteux, ed. W.E. Henley, Tudor Translations XIV, 1900, I 230).

27   Percius] precius *H*.

28   'Who made it easy for the parrot to say his "hello"?' Persius, *Choliambi* 8.

29ff.   Compare the languages in which Lemaire's parrot is skilled (p. 213).

31   'Speak well, Parrot, or speak nothing.' Perhaps Skelton's version in French of some English proverb such as 'Speak fitly or be silent wisely' (Tilley S 721).

33   supple] shewe propyrlye *H*.

37   pereles pomegarnat: The pomegranate was one of the heraldic badges of Katherine of Aragon.

38   'Parrot, can you speak Spanish?'

39   fidasso de cosso: A marginal note in *H* reads: 'Fidasso de cosso; i.e. habeto fidem in temet ipso', so Skelton apparently meant the phrase to be lingua franca for 'Have faith in yourself.'

40–41   expers] *not H*. 'Brute force without a plan, as Horace teaches whose poems are full of wisdom, falls by its own weight.' Horace, *Odes* III iv 65.

42   'Many times, Parrot, in memory' *not KDM*. Souentez] Souentem *H*.

44   I] he *H*.

46   mory] mery *H*; men] mad *H*. *pandes mory*: French *pandez morie* or *prenez folie*, 'grow mad'.

47 Phronessys: Greek *phronesis*, 'understanding'; *frenessys*: Greek *phrenesis*, 'madness' or 'frenzy'.

48 An almon now for Parott: A phrase which has become proverbial (see Whiting A 111).

49 ys the] theyr doth *LKDM*. 'On holiday to have everything is best.' *Salve festa dies* was the Easter processional hymn.

50 'Moderation gratifies, but everything is too much.'

51 Proverbial (compare Whiting D 254).

52 Myden agan: 'Nothing in excess.'

55–6 '"You have hit the nail on the head, Parrot, truly." "Be quiet, Parrot, keep still."'

58–224 not H.

58 '*Que pensez-voz*': 'What do you think?'

59 On Mt Horeb Aaron took the people's gold and made with it a calf, which angered God and Moses and impoverished the people (Exodus xxxii 1–24). *Vitulus* ('bull-calf') applies also to Wolsey, the butcher's son from Ipswich. See also lines 348–52, 377–80, and in the *Decastichon Virulentum* 2–3 of *Why Come Ye Nat to Courte?* where 'vitulus' is again used.

60 Melchizedek was a priestly king of Salem (Genesis xiv 18–20) with whom Skelton compares Henry VIII in *Agaynst the Scottes* 115. Moloch was the bull-god of the Midianites (I Kings xi 5, II Kings xxiii 13). Here, as at 402, Skelton refers to Wolsey; the implication being that he will prosper if Henry VIII is too kind and indulgent.

62 In mesure is tresure: A popular proverb (see Whiting M 461). *cum sensu maturato*: 'with mature judgement'.

63 'Neither too sane nor too mad.'

64–7 An obscure set of biblical references perhaps forming a generalized comment on the contemporary political situation. Haran, son of Terah, died in Ur of the Chaldees (Genesis xi 27–8). According to medieval commentary on these verses *Ur* meant 'fire', therefore 'Caldies fyer called Ur' was what Haran was burnt to death with for refusing to bow to the false god (Migne, *Patrologia Latina* cxv 168). Job lived in the land of Uz (Job i 1). Lot's children, the Moabites and the Ammonites, joined with the Assyrians to threaten the Israelites (Psalm lxxxiii 8–9). Jerubbesheth, another name for Gideon, appeared in the Venice Bible of 1519 at II Samuel xi 21; the name was construed as meaning 'judging the shameful'. Kinsman (p. 164) interprets 67 to mean 'like Israel, England and the Church need a doughty defender and a return to the heroic strength of an earlier time and remoter ancestors'. Edwards (pp. 186–8) takes Jerubbesheth to refer to Wolsey (compare 279), who is the 'worst foe of all' and 'no alien but the very leader of her people'.

65 Jobab] Iob *DM*.

67 cause] law *DM*.

68 ebrius: A pun on 'Hebrew' recalling 67 and its Latin meaning 'drunken'. The Flemish were notorious for their drunkenness.

69 'Hush, dear God of Heaven, I say' – aptly in Dutch.

70 In Popering grew peres: This half line appears to have a multiplicity of reference. Poperinghe was a town in West Flanders, famous for its pears. A 'poperin pear' was also a slang expression for a penis (compare *Romeo and Juliet* II i 37–8). The reference to Flanders in 69–70 is meant also to draw the reader's attention to Wolsey's activities. He was at Bruges negotiating with Emperor Charles V in August 1521 where he obtained the pledge that the Emperor would support his ambition to be elected Pope ('popering'). The French had made him similar promises in 1520 (see Pollard, *Wolsey*, p. 126). *peres* may also allude to Wolsey's ambition to become Henry VIII's equal ('the grete greyhoundes pere', 487).

71   *Over in a whynnymeg*: Probably means 'Over in an instant'. The phrase seems to have been the title or opening of a ballad; one such was apparently among the repertoire of Captain Cox who helped to entertain Elizabeth I at Kenilworth Castle on 17 July 1575 (see *Captain Cox: His Ballads and Books*, ed. F.J. Furnivall, 1871, p. cxxxi).

72   'Hob-Lobbin of Lothian would have a bit of bread.' Skelton seems to have intended this as Scottish dialect. The implication of the line seems to be that the Scots would help their old ally France by invading England. Compare *Agaynst the Scottes* 59.

73   Compare *Why Come Ye Nat to Courte?* 956 and note.

75   bagpype] bagbyte *LK*.

78–9   *Ic dien*: 'I serve'. This was both a royal motto of Henry VIII ('the estrych fether' was a royal badge) and a phrase used in the Empire ('Beme' = Bohemia), the interests of whose Emperor, Charles V, Wolsey at this time seemed to be serving.

80   Another line of complex reference. In the gloss to '*byrsam*' in Landino's edition of the *Aeneid* (1487) i 367 the point is made that the word meant 'hide' in both Greek and Punic ('Affryc tongue'), though properly the earliest part of Carthage to be built was called, in Punic, *Bosra* (= 'castle'). Dido, its mythical founder, was said to have contracted to buy as much land as could be enclosed by a bull's hide; by cutting the hide into thin thongs she then acquired a lot of ground. Edwards (p. 189) suggests that *byrsa* also refers to Wolsey's power over the *burse* in which the Great Seal of England was kept (see 309), something not rightfully his but which he exploited. Hence the reference to the proverb 'To take broad thongs of unbought (other men's) leather' (Whiting T 217). The line may also refer back to Flemish affairs (see 69–70 and notes), for the original 'Burse' was the money exchange at Bruges.

81   Probably a reminder that in October 1518 Wolsey had been involved in negotiating a treaty, still to be honoured, whereby the kings of England, France and Spain would together attack the Turks for the recovery of the Holy Land.

82   *Collustrum*: 'Beestings', the first milk from a cow after parturition.

84   *grene tayle*: A phrase connoting lechery. Compare *The Canterbury Tales* I 3878: 'To have an hoor heed and a grene tayle.' See also Whiting H 240.

85–6   Obviously an attempt at Irish dialect, but what the lines mean is difficult to say. The first half of 85 may mean 'I, Morris, am for my own self'; and the thrice-repeated 'fate' may be a version of 'water'.

88   The second half of the line, a proverb (see Whiting W 659) meaning 'let things slide', translates the Latin phrase. F.W. Brownlow, however, suggests the Latin phrase may be from Psalms xcix 1 and may have an eschatological significance (*SP* LXV, 1968, 124–39).

89   Compare *Agenst Garnesche* iii 186 and note, and *Howe the Douty Duke of Albany* 297.

90–91   With 90 compare Whiting M 70; Dyce (II 341) points out that the old Welsh proverb could take two forms, *Paub un arver* (Every one his manner) or *Paub yn ei arver* (Every one in his manner).

93 Aristippus (c.435–356 BC), a friend of Socrates, a professional teacher of
rhetoric with a reputation for hedonism.

95–7 '... whence I bring forth learned arguments in a sacred school of poets'.

110 Cesar ave: 'Hail Caesar.' From Martial, *Epigrams* XIV lxxiii 2; but com-
pare Statius, *Silvae* II iv 29–30.

111 Esebon: Heshbon, ruled over by Sihon, king of the Amorites (see 121). He
refused passage through his territories to the Israelites but was defeated by them
and lost his city (Numbers xxi 21–35). In medieval exegesis two Heshbons were
distinguished: the sinful heathen city (as here) and the city restored to truth
under the Israelite occupation and equated with Holy Church as in 113 (see
Migne, *Patrologia Latina* cxii 917). For an allegorical interpretation of lines 111–
26 see F.W. Brownlow, *SP* LXV, 1968, 124–39.

113 'Weep, Heshbon', Jeremiah il 3.

114 Rachell: Jeremiah xxxi 15, here another type of Holy Church.

115 Jetro: A Midianite priest whose sheep were kept by his son-in-law Moses
(Exodus iii 1).

116–17 Zalmunna was a Midianite king killed by Gideon (Judges viii 10–21);
Oreb and Zeb, also Midianites, were killed by the Ephraimites who sent their
heads to Gideon (Judges vii 24–5).

118 Gebal, Ammon and Amalek, three enemies of Israel in Psalm lxxxiii 7,
which in verse 11 also mentions Oreb, Zeb and Zalmunna.

122 of] or *KDM*. Og, king of Bashan, is mentioned along with Sihon, king of
the Amonites, in Psalm cxxxv 11: the last part of this verse 'all the kingdoms
of Canaan' appears to have suggested the phrase *coistronus Cananeorum,* 'the kitchen
boy of the Canaanites' (123). *LKDM* read here 'Canaueorum'. Og, who is 'fat',
is meant to represent Wolsey; compare *Why Come Ye Nat to Courte?, Decastichon* 3.

124–5 'And asylum, formerly the refuge of wretches, is not a sanctuary but is
to be made secular.' In November 1519 Wolsey attempted, but failed, to get the
laws of sanctuary changed. Abbot Islip succeeded in defending the old privileges
of the perpetual sanctuary at Westminster, where Skelton lived. Compare 489,
and *Why Come Ye Nat to Courte?* 1089–90.

126 Jepte: Jephthah died after judging Israel for six years (Judges xii 7).

127–8 These lines shift the scene momentarily from the capital via Marylebone
to Whetstone, near which was situated the abbey of Bromhall, which had a
water-mill. This abbey was dissolved by Wolsey in September 1521. Compare
Collyn Clout 387–428 and note.

129 Based on the proverb 'Far-fetched and dear bought is good for ladies'
(Whiting F 58).

131 Scarpary: Mt Scarpario in Tuscany; see also 414.

133 '... that Judas Iscariot is a great lord'.

134 Tholomye and Haly: See *Phyllyp Sparowe* 501–5 and *Why Come Ye Nat to
Courte?* 521–3 and notes.

140 on] of *KDM*.

140a–c Skelton's latinization of the Greek saying which can be translated either
'Only the good is beautiful' or 'Only the beautiful is good'.

141ff. Greek was only just beginning to be taught at Oxford and Cambridge. In
1516 Bishop Richard Fox, when founding Corpus Christi College Oxford, made
provision for a course in Greek as well as in Latin. In 1518 Richard Croke was
appointed under Henry VIII's auspices to teach Greek at Cambridge. In 1520

Wolsey appointed Matthew Colphurne to be Greek reader at Oxford. In 1518 and 1519 there were various quarrels between the adherents of the Old Learning (nicknamed 'Trojans') and those who supported the New ('Greeks'). Skelton is typically conservative, though it seems to have been the way in which the 'golden Greek language' was taught which disturbed him as much as anything.

148 phrisesomorum: In medieval logic one of the five moods of the fourth figure of categorical syllogism.

149 'Formally and in Greek with the middle term of the syllogism.'

150 'You wallow in the washbowl of the Greeks.'

151 phormio: 'a fool who talks about things he does not understand'; after the Ephesian philosopher who lectured to Hannibal on the duties of military commanders. See Cicero, *De Oratore* II xviii 75. Also a parasite whose name forms the title of one of Terence's plays.

152 in Capricornio: 'in the dark', since the sun enters Capricorn at the winter solstice.

153 ye] *Dyce's emendation*, they *LKDM*. This line and the next seem to refer to Erasmus's translation of the New Testament (1516). The second edition of 1518 in particular aroused controversy: Edward Lee, dean of Colchester, and John Batmanson, later prior of Hinton, wrote attacks on it; in July 1520 Henry Standish, bishop of St Asaph, preached against it at Paul's Cross.

155 Probably as Kinsman suggests (p. 169): 'Some argue fallaciously, assuming that what is true in a qualified sense is true absolutely.'

156 pro Ariopagita: 'as a learned man'. The Areopagus was a hill in Athens where the highest judicial court held its sittings.

157–9 'And some make manifold distinctions, whether "thus" should be before "not" or "not" before "thus", neither wise nor greatly learned, neither one thing nor the other . . .'

160 Sophia: 'Wisdom'; *Jack Raker*: Compare *Why Come Ye Nat to Courte?* 273, *Agenst Garnesche* iii 109 and note.

162–8 The Academy (*Achademia*) was originally a grove near Athens where Plato taught, but Skelton here probably has in mind the appointments in Greek at Cambridge (see 141ff. and note), hence the mention of the annual fair at Sturbridge near Cambridge. He feels that the teaching of the Greek tongue (*Greci fari*) may take attention away from the Latin (*Latinum fari*) and scholastic methods of argument (*silogisari*) so that the seven liberal arts ('Tryvyals and quatryvyals') will be destroyed.

168 roufled] roulled *DM*.

169–82 These stanzas refer to the so-called Grammarians' War of 1519–21. It concerned two different methods of teaching Latin. Robert Whittinton's *Vulgaria*, printed in 1519 by de Worde, was conservative and traditional: it sought to teach spoken Latin by rule and precept. William Horman's *Vulgaria*, printed in the same year by Pynson, invites the learner to imitate good classical authors and to give less attention to the rules of the language. Skelton was a supporter of the traditionalists.

169 The *Liber Modorum Significandi*, first printed in England in 1480, and the *Questiones de Modis Significandi* (1496) were both mistakenly ascribed to Albertus Magnus.

170 The *Ars Grammatica* of the fourth-century grammarian Aelius Donatus was so popular that a form of his name *donet* came to mean 'an elementary school book'.

171 Popular also were the eighteen books called *Institutiones Grammaticae* by the Spaniard Priscian (fl. 500). 'To break Priscian's head' was proverbial for 'to speak bad Latin' (Whiting P 404).

172 *Inter didascolos*: Apparently a grammar book, but one which has not been identified.

173 A difficult line. It refers probably to Alexander of Ville Dieu who synthesized Priscian's grammatical system in his *Doctrinale* (1199) in leonine verse. The phrase *a gander of Menanders pole* seems to be a variation of Ovid's *Heroides* vii 2: '*Ad vada Maeandri concinit albus olor*' ('The white swan sings by the shallows of Maeander'). The *Maeander* was a twisting Greek river; Reuchlin's *Breviloquus* under '*Olor*' mistakenly reads *Menandri*, presumably a confusion with the comic writer Menander (*c*.342–*c*.293 BC), whence Skelton's form here and in *Phyllyp Sparowe* 434.

The substitution of *gander* for swan rests probably on the proverbial association of this bird (and the goose) with foolishness (see Whiting G 27, G 377), and the association of 'goose' and 'swan' in another proverb (Whiting G 387). Skelton seems to be wishing to say that the supporters of the New Learning do not regard Alexander's verses as sounding sweet like a swan's song, but as being foolish like a gander.

174 *Da causales*: 'Give the causal conjunctions.'

175 *Da racionales*: 'Give the conjunctions which mark inferences.'

176 *Plautus*: Titus Maccius Plautus (died *c*.184 BC), the Roman comic dramatist.

177 *Declamacyons*] *Declaracyons LKDM*. See the *Garlande of Laurell* 326 and note.

178 *Pety Caton*: A brief prolegomenon to the *Distichs* ascribed to Dionysius Cato, written probably in the third or fourth centuries. See the *Garlande of Laurell* 123–9 and note.

179 '*Aveto' in Greco*: '"Hail", in Greek,' though *Aveto* is Latin.

183–5 Kinsman (p. 171) refers to John of Garland's *Morale Scolarium Cap* xxxi which says that nutmeg with cloves (*cum gariopholo*) expels gas from the stomach and eases the cerebellum. The phrase *pleris cum musco* seems to mean 'an electuary with musk', since John of Garland's gloss for *pliris* is *electuarium* (line 594).

188 *in valle Ebron*: 'in the vale of Hebron'. F.W. Brownlow points out that Hebron was one of the 'cities of refuge' (Joshua xxi 13), hence a sanctuary (*SP* LXV, 1968, 124–39).

189 *Saynt Nycholas*: Here invoked as the patron saint of travellers.

190–91 The mirror 'almost transparent' into which Parott looks is the 'glass' through which man sees 'darkly' (I Corinthians xiii 12). The phrase *in enigmate* means literally 'in a riddle', and lines 190–203 are a defence of the deliberately puzzling indirectness of Parott's way of speaking.

192 *Elencticum*] *Dyce's* emendation, *Elencum LKDM*. '. . . in the form of an elenchus or an enthymeme'. An elenchus is a syllogistic refutation; an enthymeme is an argument based on probable premisses as distinct from a demonstration. Logicians might react somewhat 'quibblingly' (*sophistice*) to an elenchus, and might suspect the enthymeme, in which one of the premisses was suppressed. But rhetoricians might value them, particularly the enthymeme which Aristotle said was one of the most persuasive of figures (*Rhetorica* I ii).

196 *confuse tantum*: 'so confusedly'.

198 *Confuse distrybutyve*: 'ordered confusion'.

202 metaphora, alegoria: 'metaphor, allegory', i.e. indirect ways of speaking.
208 dere (2nd)] *not DM*.
209 Melpomene: The muse of tragedy.
213 he] she *LKDM*.
227 now] *not H*.
229–32 'Behold, I, a parrot, sing; nor, I know, are my songs suitable to Phoebus; all the same, my poem is full of the god. According to the famous Skelton, numbered in the catalogue of the Muses.'
232 Piereorum cathalogo] periorum thalago H.
232a Itaque consolamyni in verbis istibus H, not DM; before this line LK have 'Galathea'. 'Wherefore comfort one another with these words' (I Thessalonians iv 18).
232b not H here, at 277a only, reading 'callige' for 'callete' and omitting 'etc.'. 'Fair readers, understand skilfully, cherish your Parrot etc.'
233–4 The marginal note in *H* makes the allusion here plain: '*Hic occurrat memorie Phamphilus de Amore Galathee*', 'Let here be remembered *Pamphilus de Amore Galathea*.' The pseudo-Ovidian poem called *Pamphilus* or *de arte amandi* or *liber de amore*, written in the late twelfth century, was apparently very popular (it survives in twenty-five manuscripts) and gave rise to the word 'pamphlet'. See line 358 for Skelton's knowing pun.
235–262a Skelton's version of a popular song which itself had an amorous and a moralistic form. For the amorous version in Ritson's M S see John Stevens, *Music and Poetry in the Early Tudor Court*, 1961, Appendix A No. R 15, beginning:
>   In wyldernes
>   Ther founde I Besse...

The moralistic version R 16 is as follows:
>   Come over the burne, Besse,
>   Thou lytyll, pretty Besse,
>   Come over the burne, Besse, to me.

>   The burne ys this worlde blynde
>   And Besse ys mankynde;
>   So propyr I can none fynde as she;
>   She daunces and she lepys,
>   And Crist stondes and clepys;
>   Cum over the burne, Besse, to me.

Skelton makes the song into the 'mone' of Pamphilus (the 'all-lover') for Galathea. Edwards (p. 193) suggests that 'Pamphilus, like the singer in the ballad, can be no other than Christ, the God of Love. What the age would call a wanton trifle turns out to be a pious allegory – Christ's lament over the fickleness of humanity.' He also feels that Besse, as well as representing mankind, stands for Skelton's patroness Elizabeth Countess of Surrey (p. 198).
262a Quod] Quid *H*.
263–4 R.L. Dunbabin suggests the insertion of *quod* before *fit* to make the line scan better (*MLR* XII, 1917, 265). The lines are perhaps meant to read 'Martial made a song (which) provides a shield for me. My page is lascivious, my life upright.' 264 is a version of Martial's '*Lasciva est nobis pagina, vita proba*' (*Epigrams* I iv 8).
267–8 Both phrases mean 'Life and Soul'; the Greek suggested by its appearance in Juvenal, *Satires* vi 195, appropriately an attack on the lascivious Greek fashions newly assumed by his Roman contemporaries.

269 'They lie together in the Greek manner. This is not a modest way of speaking.' Again from Juvenal, *Satires* vi 191, 193.

269a   *not H.*

269a–273 'Therefore, Greek poems are plates of lead, or false shoots: may Urania remove them.' For *plumbi lamina* see Job xix 24; lead plate, according to Pliny's *Naturalis Historia* xxxiv 18(50), was also used as an aphrodisiac. For *spurea vitulamina* see Wisdom of Solomon iv 3, where the passage relates to the temporary triumph but ultimate punishment of the ungodly.

271   *Sunt] suus LKDM.*

272   *Vel] Ve H.*

275   *to] not H.*

277a   See note to 232b.

280   *cliffes of Scaloppe*: Scales or Escalles (French for 'scallop') is a village on Cap Blanc-Nez, near Calais, where Wolsey was negotiating from 2 August to 24 November 1521.

281   Cefas] Tefas *H.* The sands of Cephas or St Peter's, Dampierre-lez-Dunes, again near Calais.

283–4 These lines are difficult. Probably Skelton intended Neptune, god of the sea, to represent Henry VIII who ruled an island kingdom, and Eolus to represent Charles V who ruled parts of Italy off whose coast lay the cave of Aeolus the god of the winds. One of the agreements reached in Calais on 24 November 1521 was that the English should keep open the Channel and see that the Emperor, who was to land at Dover, had access to Spain. So perhaps *Tytus* refers to the Roman Emperor from 79–81, hence the current Emperor Charles V.

285   *Lucina*: The moon.

287   *Le tonsan de Jason*: 'The Order of the Golden Fleece' instituted by Philip the Good, Duke of Burgundy at Bruges in 1430. It was in Bruges that Wolsey had negotiated with Charles V in August 1521 (see note to line 70). The implication here seems to be that Wolsey, like Jason the Argonaut, has come back with what he set out for.

288   *Argus*: H.L.R. Edwards (*PMLA* LIII, 1938, 608) argues that this refers to 'the ruthless dandy Francis', on the grounds that Argus had one hundred eyes, as does the tail of the peacock, which is a dandified bird.

289   *Lyacon*: Lycaon, king of Arcadia, turned into a wolf by Zeus for serving to him a dish of human flesh. Here the reference is to Wolsey (compare also 400, 434, and the *Decastichon virulentum* following *Why Come Ye Nat to Courte?*). *Libyk*: Libya. *Lydy*: Lydia.

293   Proverbial; compare *Magnyfycence* 1818, and see Whiting F 101.

299   'Go as a wise or true speaking messenger of what is seemly.'

300   'Excrement! Sheer slanders!' See also 323, 346.

304   *Seigneour Sadoke*: Zadok, an Israelite priest, desired by David to return to Jerusalem as a seer (II Samuel xv 27); hence an ironic reference to Wolsey bidding him return to England.

305   *Nostre Dame de Crome*: The church of St Mary Hill Croome, Worcestershire. Wolsey is asked to return by an obscure way.

306–7 These lines seem to mean that Wolsey's attempted feat to reconcile Charles V and Francis I is as impossible as it would be to make Jericho and Jersey meet, or to bring down the man from the moon.

308–9 These lines allude to Wolsey's love of fish and also to his tactics – deceit and delay – at the Calais conference: *porpose* is a pun on 'porpoise' and 'purpose'; *graundepose* is a pun on 'grampus' and (probably) on 'graunde pause' (= long delay) and 'graunde pose' (= great pretence). *the grete sealle* refers both to the 'great seal' (*Phoca barbata*) and the Chancellor's Great Seal, which Wolsey took with him to Calais. As lines 310–12 indicate, this caused great administrative inconvenience. Compare Hall's *Chronicle*: 'Duryng the continuance of the Cardinall in Calayce all writtes and patentes wer there by hym sealed and no shyriffes chosen for lacke of his presence' (p. 627).

313 stede] *Dyce's emendation*, spede H.

322 *Psitace, perge*] *Psitage perage H*. 'Parrot, go quickly, to blunt the weapons of fools.'

325 *Mercury* was the messenger of the gods, and the god of roads and travel.

326 *Syre Sydrake*: In the story of *Kyng Boccus and Sydracke* he was the adviser to the king; hence another ironic reference to Wolsey.

330 Perhaps Skelton has in mind a proverb: 'To lay a millstone on one's neck' (Whiting M 565) or 'To weigh heavier than a millstone' (Whiting M 567).

331 *cheryston pytte*: 'Cherry pit' is a children's game in which cherry stones are thrown into a small hole in the ground.

339 *Non sine postica sanna*: 'Not without a grimace behind his back'. Probably based on Persius, *Satire* i 62: '*posticae occurrite sannae*', 'turn round and face the gibes behind you.'

341 *how Robyn loste hys bowe*: Perhaps Skelton is recalling the proverb 'Many men speak of Robin Hood that never bent his bow' (Whiting R 156).

342 Compare the proverbial phrase 'He sows the sand' (Tilley S 87).

345 *Parrote*] *Parrot H*. 'Go hastening, Parrot, thus reprove all evil tongues.'

347–8 'Higher, alas, than the cedar, more cruel, alas, than the leopard. Alas, the bull-calf of the ox has become the master of Priam'; i.e. Wolsey had become master of Henry VIII.

349–52 'Granted that it is not because of your age but because of your rank that you (Henry VIII) are called Priam, as long as you cherish the bull-calf, king of Britain, you are ruled; king, you are ruled, you do not yourself rule; celebrated king, learn by experience; make the bull-calf subservient to you, lest he become too foolish.'

369 remorders] remordes H.

371 *volitans*] *Dyce's emendation*, vtilans H.

371–2 'Go, flying, Parrot, restrain your wisdom. They shall scarcely understand your poem, who read you and your poem.' *Minerva* was the Roman goddess of wisdom. *Hyperbaton* is a figure of speech in which the natural order of words and phrases is reversed.

373–4 'The Parrot, alas, is known as Persius is, I think, known. Nor, I believe, is he (i.e. the Parrot) nor will he be everywhere known, though he (i.e. Persius) is and will be everywhere known.' Kinsman adds the phrase *undique notus* in 374.

375 'Cursed be a wicked mouth.'

376–376a 'O my Parrot, O only loved one, the whole jewel of my prayers, a precious jewel is your covering.' Based on Proverbs xxxi 2 and Ezekial xxviii 13. *operimentum*] opermentum H.

377–80 'Like Aaron and the people, so the ox's calf, so the ox's calf, so the ox's calf.' See line 59 note.

382a 'The Parrot begins to complain.'

387 Compare 'Womanhod, wanton, ye want...' (4).

396   plucke the crowe: 'dispute, make protest'. Based on the proverb 'to have a crow to pluck' (Whiting C 572).

397   the coste is nothyng clere: Compare *Collyn Clout* 1257 and see Whiting C 339.

398–9   These lines do more than refer to cloudy weather conditions in which the sun (*Tytan*) is behind clouds and the planets do not shine. *Tytan* is probably to be identified with Charles V (see 284 note); *Jupyter* with Henry VIII (see 405–10); and *Saturne* with Francis I. Skelton seems to be saying the only one to gain from the negotiations has been *Lyacon*, i.e. Wolsey (see 289 note).

401   Racell: A type of Holy Church (see 114 note).

402   Moloc that mawmett: Molech or Moloch was a Semite diety, worship of whom was strictly prohibited by Hebrew law (see Leviticus xviii 21, xx 1–5). The reference here is probably to Sultan Soleiman, the Turk, whose armies were invading Hungary (see *Calendar of State Papers* [Venetian] III Nos. 350, 351).

405–10   'On bright Olympus Jupiter is venerated as a god; and here a god is honoured. Incense is given to Jupiter sitting on his golden throne; with Jupiter he (i.e. the god on earth) takes incense. Jupiter is ruler of the stars and lord of the heavens; he (i.e. the god on earth) rules the English realm.' The 'god on earth' is presumably Henry VIII.

409   polorum] Dyce's emendation, *populorum H*.

411–14   After the news of Pope Leo X's death (2 December 1521) Richard Pace (*c.*1482–1536) (*passe-a-Pase*), First Secretary to Henry VIII, was sent to obtain Venetian support for Wolsey's bid for the papacy. Thomas Clark (*Cleros*) was sent ahead with letters from Henry VIII and Wolsey to the cardinals assembled at Rome (see *L & P* III, 1981). *Over Scarpary* means 'into Italy' (see 131 note). *mala vy*: 'with ill hail'.

421   now] no *H*.

427–8   Based on proverbs 'To fish before the net' (Whiting N 91), 'To bear a bauble' (Whiting B 70), 'To bear a low sail' (Whiting S 14).

428   maketh] make *H*.

431   In 1511 Wolsey had tried to persuade Henry VIII to join the Holy League of Julius II against Louis XII.

434   wolvys hede: A pun on Wolsey ('Wolf of the sea') as in the *Decastichon virulentum* following *Why Come Ye Nat to Courte?*, and wolf's head ('outlaw'). *wanne, bloo as lede* appears to be a combination of two proverbial phrases 'As blo as lead' (Whiting L 117) and 'As wan as lead' (Whiting L 129).

435   garlande: The papal tiara.

437–8   '... from which power, it is plain from my verse that from strength ...' but the end of the Latin has never been satisfactorily explained.

439–45   A stanza full of puns: *date* refers to the fruit and also means 'appointed time'; 442 plays on 'large raisins' and 'great reasons' (= 'matters of political importance'); 443 recalls the puns of the previous line and adds another, *resons currant*, meaning both 'current matters of political importance' and 'raisins of Corinth' (French '*raisins de Corinthe*'), the small seedless raisin normally used in cookery. 'The Devil's date' is proverbial (Whiting D 200) and see also *The Bowge of Courte* 375, 455; *Magnyfycence* 943, 2172.

445   shurewlye: An unusual form, perhaps a pun on 'surely' and 'shrewdly'.

449–518   The generalized sentiments and the repetitious antithetical manner recall other poems on 'the abuses of the age', particularly 'Now is England Perished' (Robbins, *Historical Poems* No. 62):

Nowe is England perisshed in fight,
With moche people & consciens light,
Many knyghtes & lytyll myght,
Many lawys & lityll right... (1-4)

and Dunbar's *General Satyre*. (On the tradition see Heiserman, pp. 168-89, and Scattergood, pp. 298-306.)

449 many] many many *H*.

451 *translacion into Englyshe*: Perhaps Skelton is thinking of Barclay's translation of Sallust's *Jugurtha* or Rastell's of Lucian's *Menippus* and Terence's *Andria* – all dating from 1520.

454 *provision*: Wolsey, as legate *a latere*, used the long-abandoned practice of 'providing' candidates for vacant benefices (see Pollard, pp. 204-5) without consulting the bishops.

467 *on dawys hede*: A pun on *daw* (= fool) and a reference to Wolsey's badge the Cornish chough, a type of crow.

479-80 In 1516 Wolsey made criminals wear notes on their backs indicating their offences. He also used Star Chamber for passing judgment on forgery, libel, slander and perjury, for which the pillory was used as punishment (see Pollard, p. 71).

482 *statutes of array*: A reference to the Act of Apparel passed with difficulty by Wolsey in 1515 (see Pollard, p. 71), and the royal proclamation on apparel, vagabonds and labourers of 19 February 1517. Compare 498.

484-5 An allusion to the fact that Wolsey was the son of an Ipswich butcher. Compare *Why Come Ye Nat to Courte?* 297-8, 494.

486 The *plucte partryches* and *fatte quaylles* perhaps allude to Wolsey's sexual improprieties. Compare *Collyn Clout* 213-19 and note, 867-70.

487 Based on the proverb 'The mastiff never loves the greyhound' (Tilley M 743). Since a 'white greyhound courant' was one of Henry VIII's badges, it refers to Wolsey's aspirations to be the equal of the king. Compare *Why Come Ye Nat to Courte?* 777-9 and note.

489 *So many swannes dede*: Perhaps an allusion to the execution of Edward Stafford, third Duke of Buckingham (whose badge was a swan), in May 1521. Compare also *Collyn Clout* 612, 1011-19 and *Why Come Ye Nat to Courte?* 1-28, 874-87 and notes.

491 perfyte] profyte *H*.

494 Perhaps a reference to Wolsey's palaces at Hampton Court and York Place. Compare *Collyn Clout* 934-9, *Why Come Ye Nat to Courte?* 408-10.

495 *statutes apon diettes*: On 31 May 1517 it was proclaimed 'by the Kynges highnes and his counsayle for puttynge aparte thecessyve fare and redusynge the same to...moderacion' (R. Steele, ed., *Tudor and Stuart Proclamations 1485-1714*, 1910, No. 75).

497 the world] the world the world *H*.

499-500 Compare *Collyn Clout* 406-11 and note.

503 Compare lines 124-5 and note.

505 *ryghte of a rammes horne*: Proverbial (compare Whiting R 27).

510 Compare *Collyn Clout* 204-19 and note and *Why Come Ye Nat to Courte?* 219-23, 1081-5 and notes.

514 *myday sprettes*: Compare Vulgate Psalm xc 6: 'Daemonium meridianum.'

517 Compare Cavendish's *Life and Death of Cardinal Wolsey*, pp. 23-4 (the description of Wolsey's journey daily to Westminster): '...wt ij great pillers of sylver... And when he came to the hall doore there was attendaunt for hym his mewle trapped all to gether in Crymmosym velvett and gylt Stirroppes.' He was guarded by 'iiij or footmen wt gylt pollaxes in ther handes'. See also *Why Come Ye Nat to Courte?*, *Decastichon* and *Apostrophe*.

519–20   A version of the second part of the epigraph with which the poem begins: *Psitacus* ('Parrot') is substituted for *pagina* and *inclita* ('renowned') for *aurea*.

XIX   COLLYN CLOUT

Since *Collyn Clout* is mentioned at line 1234 of the *Garlande of Laurell*, printed 3 October 1523, its composition must pre-date this. Various references to events of 1521–2 appear: 153–9 seem to allude to Bishop Fisher's sermon against Luther preached at Paul's Cross on 12 May 1521; 612 and 1011–19 may be on the fall of Edward Stafford, third Duke of Buckingham, in 1521; 387–428 seem to refer to the suppression of the nunneries Higham, Lillechurch and Bromhall in 1521–2; and 348–61 may refer to the forced loans of June 1522 to June 1523 (see P.E. McLane, *ELN* X, 1972, 85–9).

The text here is taken from Thomas Godfray's edition of *c.*1530 (*G*) collated with that of Kele (*c.*1545) (*K*) and Marshe's edition of Skelton's *Workes* of 1568 (*M*). Also used are the version in British Library MS Harley 2252, fols. 147r–154v (*H*) and, for lines 460–78, the extract entitled 'The profecy of Skelton' from British Library MS Lansdowne 762 fol. 71r (*L*). The version in MS Harley 2252 probably pre-dates Godfray's edition, but it is in many ways defective; in particular several long passages are omitted: 431–58, 479–556. Yet it does include the Epilogue, which the editions lack, and provides the correct reading in several lines.

The lineation here differs slightly from that in the editions by Dyce and Kinsman. Like previous editors, I have included 1138, which is not in Godfray, but, unlike Dyce, I exclude those lines from MS Harley 2252 which follow 166 and 216. Kinsman, in his selection, presumably follows the editions at 758 where I follow MS Harley 2252, and this makes his text a line longer. I have also omitted a name at 1037, following Godfray, because I think it was Skelton's intention to omit it.

Epigraph   From Vulgate Psalm xciii 16 and John viii 11: 'Who will rise up for me against the evil doers? or who will stand up for me against the workers of iniquity? No man, Lord!'

consurget] resurgat *H*; *adversus* (1st)] ad *H*.

mihi] mecum *K M*, not *H*.

1–2   Compare Whiting S 420. Dyce (II 277–8) quotes similar lines from *Gentylnes and Nobylyte*:

In effect it shall no more avayle

Than with a whyp to dryfe a snayle.

7   for delyte] for to endyte *H*.

8   despyte] to desyte *G*.

14   reche] reherse *H*.

17   And saythe he wott not whate *H*.

19   not *H*.

20   preketh] peketh *K M*.

22   prayeth] prates *KM*, pratythe *H*.

30 A] On a *H*. Compare the *Garlande of Laurell* 207–8.

33–4 Proverbial (Whiting N 9).

36 Proverbial (Whiting D 187).

37 *not H*.

46 unstablenesse] unstedfastnes *H*.

49 *Collyn Cloute*: 'Collyn' derives from Latin *colonus* 'farmer' and was used as early as the reign of Edward II to indicate a person of humble birth. 'Cloute' seems to mean 'rag' or 'patch' and further emphasizes his poverty. See R.S. Kinsman in *Essays Critical and Historical Dedicated to Lily B. Campbell*, Berkeley 1950, pp. 17–27.

51–3 Compare *Mum and the Sothsegger M* 1343–6 where the protagonist has a bagful of poems complaining about the evils of contemporary society:

Now forto conseille the king unknytte I a bagge
Where many a pryve poyse is preyntid withynne
Yn bokes unbredid in balade-wise made,
Of vice and of vertue fulle to the margyn.

56 mothe] moche *G*, moughte *K*.

57 And yf thow take well that wythe *H*; take] talke *K M*.

66 Thys eche with hothyr blen *H*; blothier] bloder *G K*.

74 Aboute] Above *K M*.

80 Unneth] Scantly *H*.

89 *the forked cappe*: 'the bishop's mitre'.

95 They labor forthe so in the lawe *H*.

102 pryncypall] provynciall *H*.

106 *ire and venyre*: 'coming and going', probably a reference to those bishops who spent a lot of time at court, and away from their sees; but also puns on the English versions of the words *ire* meaning 'wrath' and *'venyre'* meaning (1) 'the practice of hunting', (2) 'the pursuit of sexual pleasure'.

107 *sol fa*] so fa *G*, solfe *H*. *alamyre*: From the musical notes *la mi re*, the lowest note but one on the scale of Guido di Arezzo.

108 *premenyre*: 'praemunire', originally a writ summoning a person accused of prosecuting in a foreign court a suit cognizable by the laws of England. Sometimes it involved attempts to assert papal jurisdiction in England. Perhaps here Skelton is alluding to Wolsey's attempts to use his legatine authority to influence Archbishop Warham's consistorial courts (*L & P* III, 77, 127).

114 fictyons] affeccions *H*.

120 carke] barke *H*.

129 lame] lene *H*.

132–41 When this poem was written there were few bishops who preached – John Fisher (Rochester), Richard Fitzjames (London), John Longland (Lincoln) and Dr Henry Standish (St Asaph). Skelton is correct in attributing the silence of the other bishops to ignorance of theology, for most of them had risen through the civil service. See P. Hughes, *The Reformation in England*, 1950, I, 81.

137 for] full *G*.

139 Ys they have lytell arte *H*.

142–6 Perhaps a slighting reference to Wolsey who, in 1519, founded, at his own expense, six lectureships at Oxford; or to Richard Fox (Bishop of Winchester) who, in 1517, founded Corpus Christi College, Oxford.

152 Aaron and Hur, the two chief priests of the Israelites, who supported Moses' raised hands in the battle with Amalek (Exodus xvii 10–12) and who were left to guard the Israelites when Moses went up Mount Sinai (Exodus xxiv 14).

153–9   The *wolfe* and the *rambes* are perhaps meant to indicate heretics. Bishop Fisher, who was doubtless one of the 'two or three . . . worshypfull clerkes' Skelton had in mind, had preached against heretics and particularly Luther at Paul's Cross on 12 May 1521. The phrase 'heery cotes' appears again at 865 and refers to the dress of the friars, so perhaps here they are indicated as *gotes*. 153 is proverbial (see Whiting W 468).

163–4   Compare Whiting B 232, a proverb which alludes to the fable of the mice who planned to put a bell around the cat's neck. The fable is sometimes used, as in *Piers Plowman* B Prologue 146–207, about those who fear a higher authority. Here it probably refers to the way in which the bishops fail to stand up to Wolsey.

166   deuz decke]˙decke *H*, and *H* follows this line with 'They ar made for the becke'. *deuz decke* appears to be either some sort of card game played with two packs, or perhaps the line means 'They are eager to play a low card'.

170   That becket them gave *K M*.

171–3   'Thomas puts forth his hand to bold deeds, he spurns misfortune and opprobrium, no injury destroys Thomas.' The contrast between Thomas Becket, martyred in 1170 for his loyalty to the Church, and Thomas Wolsey was pointed out elsewhere. Compare the lines from 'The Impeachment of Wolsey':

> Then Thomas was & nowe Thomas ys:
> Where he dyd well, thow does amys.

(*Ballads from Manuscripts*, ed. F.J. Furnivall, 1868, I, 32.)

178   The collocation *spende* and *spare* appears in several proverbs (see Whiting S 553, 626).

179–80   For the proverb on which these lines appear to be based see Tilley M 655: 'To ride (shoe) the wild mare'. Of the nine examples given Skelton's is the earliest and his application of the phrase is unique. Most later examples refer to a children's Christmas game (see *ODEP*, p. 583). For *mockyssh* in this context *OED* gives 'wild', though it usually means 'derisive'.

182   not *H*.

186   not *H*.

190   Sare] *Fare M, sciire H*. The whole line means 'For as far as Mount Seir'. Mount Seir was on the northern boundary of Judah (Joshua xv 10).

192   ye] they *G*; in parkes] partrykes *G*.

193   'and hawk at larks with a hobby', which was a small, swift hawk. Compare also *Magnyfycence* 1342, 1564. From its occurrences in Skelton it seems the phrase meant 'to indulge in illicit sexual affairs'. But here it is almost certainly also an allusion to Joan Larke, the mother of Wolsey's two illegitimate children.

197   Proverbial (Whiting G 389).

204–19   Though this evidently refers to *some* of the bishops it seems likely it is aimed principally at Wolsey, who, because he had digestive trouble, had obtained licence to eat meat during Lent (see *L & P* III, 634, 647). Compare *Why Come Ye Nat to Courte?* 219–23, 1081–5, and notes. Lines 213–19, however, seem to refer to sexual improprieties also. There may be a pun on *stued* meaning (1) cooked, (2) from the stews, and *wodicocke*, here, from the context, seems to indicate both the bird and the female pudendum.

205   lenton season] lente so myche *H*.

206   cranes] pranes *H*.

208   Thus pyke ne shrympes ne crevis *H*.

214   To ete eythyr pygge or gose *H*.

216   After this line *H* has 'To knowe whate ys a clocke'. Compare Whiting O 16.

220–23   'And how, when you ordain priests within the area of your dioceses, as around Passion Sunday . . .' *Sicientes* is from the opening of the mass for this day: *Omnes sitientes, venite ad aquas*, 'Ho, every one that thirsteth, come ye to the waters' (Isaiah lv 1). This was not one of the 'four times' specifically set down for ordinations, but if he were prevented at other times a bishop might use this occasion (see H.S. Bennett in *Studies Presented to Sir Hilary Jenkinson*, 1957, pp. 20–21).

220   And when they geve ordyrs *H*.

223–7   'Some are inadequate, some not wise enough, some not at all intelligent, some greatly negligent, some with no sense at all.' For complaints about the inadequate training that priests received, see P. Hughes, *The Reformation in England*, 1950, I, pp. 50–51.

230   *Dominus vobiscum*: 'The lord be with you', a salutation by the priest to the congregation. Skelton thinks that priests are often so badly educated that a phrase such as this is about all many of them know. Compare 281, where the ignorant priest is called *dominus vobiscum*. See also *Ware the Hauke* 286.

235   nor] Ave nor *H*.

240   small] lewde *H*.

242–4   *not H*.

246–9   'Of such vagabonds all the world speaks: how some sing greatly rejoicing at every tavern . . .'. *letabundus* is the opening word of the sequence for Christmas. It inspired various hymns; the best known is probably that attributed to St Bernard of Clairvaux '*Letabundus exultet fidelis chorus* . . .', but there are several English versions (see C.F. Brown, *Religious Lyrics of the Fifteenth Century*, No. 77, and Lydgate's *Minor Poems* II No. 13). It was also the basis of parodic secular love songs. (See '*Letabundus rediit* . . .' in Helen Waddell's *Medieval Latin Lyrics*, 1929, pp. 214–17.) But if Skelton has anything specific in mind here it may be the Anglo-Norman drinking song imitating the *Letabundus* (see A. Jeanroy and A. Langfors, *Chansons Satiriques et Bachiques du XIII e Siècle*, Paris 1921, p. 78).

250   *hake and make*: 'a loafer and his mate'. A proverbial phrase (See Whiting H 38).

252   sory] seke *H*.

253   *the good wyfe*: Perhaps a reference to the church (*mater ecclesia*) if R.S. Kinsman's conjecture is right (see *HLQ* XXVI, 1963, 304); but the copyist of *H* who wrote 'every good wyfe' here obviously understood it otherwise.

255–7   'With these or those who stay in towns there is a wife or a maid servant.' There are frequent complaints about the lechery of the clergy. See, for example, Simon Fish's *Supplication of the Beggars* (1529), ed. F.J. Furnivall, EETS ES 13, 1871, p. 6:

> Ye, and what do they more? Truely nothing but applie theym silves, by all the sleyghtes they may, to have to do with every mannes wife, every mannes daughter, and every mannes mayde, that cukkoldrie and baudrie shulde reigne over all among your subjectes . . .

258–9   *Jacke and Gylla* appears to have been a catch phrase meaning 'everybody' (see Whiting J 2); compare line 29, 'Thei weyl assaylle boythe Iacke &

gylle', from *Friars, Ministri Malorum* in Robbins, *Historical Poems* No. 67. *Petronylla* was a name sometimes applied to a priest's concubine, as in *Piers Plowman* B V 160.

266 juste] fyrste *H*.

277 Some scantlye rede *H*.

282 Jacke] Tom *K M*; see Whiting J 1. According to a late-medieval anecdote: 'Jacke a Throme and Jone Brest Bale; these men seyd in the bibull that an ill drynker is impossibul heven for to wynne; for God luffus nodur hors nor mare, but mere men that in the cuppe con stare...' (T. Wright and J.O. Halliwell, *Reliquae Antiquiae*, 1843, I, 84). *Jacke-a-Thrum* seems here to be the typical drunken, illiterate priest. Compare also *Agenst Garnesche* iii 204, *Magnyfycence* 1427, *Garlande of Laurell* 209.

289 sylver] money *H*.

294 For Peter's curse of Simon Magus see Acts viii 18–24.

297 hermoniake] herman jake *H*. As H.L.R. Edwards pointed out (*TLS* 24 October 1936, 863) *hermoniake* almost certainly means 'Armenian'; compare *The Canterbury Tales* VIII 790. As priests the Armenians had a bad reputation, yet were accepted in the Church, so Skelton's lines probably mean '... for a simoniac is no worse than an Armenian...'.

298–300 Based on a proverb (see Whiting C 220).

306 dare] can *H*.

307–20 Compare Cavendish, *Life of Wolsey*, pp. 23, 52:

'...And than mounted vppon a newe Mewle very richely trapped wt a foote clothe & trapper of Crymmesyn veluett vppon veluett pirld wt gold and ffrynged abought wt a depe frynge of gold very costly his stirropes of silver and gylt the bosses & chekes of his brydell of the same...'

See also *Why Come Ye Nat to Courte?*, *Decastichon* 8 and *Apostrophe*.

312 Rychely and warme wrappyd *H*.

315 mares] morowes *K M*. The phrase 'white as morning milk' was proverbial (see Whiting M 548).

317 begared] be gloryd *H*.

322 *Jacke of the Nocke*: The more usual form is 'Jacke at Noke', as at line 855, which means literally 'Jack at the oak' and is a name for everyman.

323 yoke] choke *H*.

324 sommons] somners *H*.

325 excommunycacyons] extermynacions *H*.

327–8 Compare Giustiniani, *Despatches* II 315: 'Cardinal Wolsey is very anxious for the Signory to send him one hundred Damascene carpets, for which he has asked several times...' Sixty of these were inventoried 24 October 1521.

329 farly] fearfull *K*.

331–2 not *H*.

336–8 And say utterly /That a butterflye/ Was a wethercocke *H*.

345 princeps] prynces *K M*, prinopes *H*. *princeps aquilonis*: 'the prince of the north', i.e. the Devil whose dwelling was in the north, according to Isaiah xiv 13. But the phrase appears to be based on Ezekiel xxxii 30. See also *The Canterbury Tales* III 1413, and *Piers Plowman* C II 111–20. As Archbishop of York Wolsey had his seat in the north.

348–61 Perhaps these lines allude to Wolsey's forced loans of June 1522 to June 1523. Compare *Why Come Ye Nat to Courte?* 50–54, 900–932.

349 monys] mornys *H*.

362   tollage] tollyng *H.*

362–73   'You give monks pain through taxes and tolls in order to get hold of an old cottage that is then consigned to a college, given a charter of madness devoted to the cause of foolishness rather than to service...' The *Tenures* of the judge, Sir Thomas Lyttelton (1422–81), were probably written in about 1480 and were printed soon afterwards. *Service de socage* was here defined as 'where the tenaunt holdeth of hys lorde his tenauncye by certaine service of all maner of service so that the service be not knightes service'.

365   commytted] unnethe *H.*

367–73   *not H.*

374–86   'Religious men are content to turn back forever and forsake their choir and wander through the market place and take a sum for services against the rule of their order, whether of the black monks (Dominicans), or of the Austin canons, or of the Cistercians or of the Friars of the Holy Cross, and sing from place to place like apostates.'

377–9   *not H.*

380   regulam] *presepta H.*

381–6   *not H.*

387–428   In this passage Skelton is referring to the suppression of nunneries in 1521–2, in all probability Higham and Lillechurch in Kent and Bromhall in Berkshire. The possessions of this last which were seized included the church of St Margaret, the churchyard, a grange, a mansion, a manor and a water mill (*L & P* III, 2630).

390   nowe] nonne *H.*

391   *not H.*

393   Sare] Sybylle *H.*

397   fucke sayles] flucke sayles *G.* 1. a type of sail; 2. a dress which falls in folds, but perhaps here the nun's wimple.

398   ventayles: 1. part of the vizor of the helmet which had vents in; 2. here perhaps the starched linen frame of the nun's headdress.

399–400   *not H.*

402   the faute] *not K M.*

403   you prelates] your presepte *H.*

406–11   Compare *Rede Me and Be Nott Wrothe*, p. 113:

I am sure thou hast hearde spoken
What monasteries he hath broken
With out their fownders consentis.
He subverteth churches and chappells
Takynge awaye bokis and bells
With chalesces and vestmentis.
He plucketh downe the costly leades
That it maye rayne on saynctis heades
Not sparynge god or oure Ladye.

414   redes] rede *G K M.*

416   talkes] talke *G K M.* tytyvylles: 'tattlers'. Originally, Titivillus was a devil supposed to collect words mumbled or missed out of the service by the priest. But later the word came to have a more general application indicating anyone with evil propensities. Compare *Magnyfycence* 1267.

417   How that he brekes the deths wylles *H.*

419   Based on a proverb (compare Whiting A 4).

420   Your worke they sey ys veraye straunge *H.*

421-8   One of the primary duties of monks was to say prayers for their found-
ers and their benefactors whose names were listed on the prayer rolls (*bedde
roules*), and also *dyriges*, prayers for all dead Christians' souls. Skelton says that
since monasteries are being suppressed prayers for their founders and benefac-
tors will be discontinued; hence the souls of these people, whose bodies *lye there
rotten* in the ground, may not be released from purgatory.

427-8   not *H.*

429-32   Turks, Saracens and Jews were the traditional enemies of Christen-
dom. At this time the Turks were a particular threat in the Mediterranean: Bel-
grade fell to them in 1521 and Rhodes shortly afterwards. In 1517 the Lateran
Council had sanctioned a crusade and in 1518 some attempt by the princes of
Europe was made to organize one, but quarrels about the election of the new
Emperor effectively ruined all the plans.

430   false] hole *H.*

431-58   not *H.*

434   rescue] rescite *M.*

440   *lanternes of lyght*: This phrase, which occurs again at 694, was commonly
applied to priests and bishops. Compare John Colet's convocation sermon:
   'Preests and bysshops are the light of the worlde. For unto them sayde our
   Saviour: "You are the lythte of the worlde."' (*A Life of John Colet*, ed. J.H.
   Lupton, 1909, p. 294.)

442-7   '... Drowned in delights, in glory and wealth, in O, wondrous hon-
our, in the glory and splendour of the shining spear, living too little chastely.'
The phrase *splendore fulgurantes haste* is from Habakkuk iii 11, though the Vul-
gate reads *fulgurantis*. In that passage it applies to the terrible power of God;
perhaps Skelton applies it ironically to the bishops because they have power yet
their wicked lives leave them unworthy of veneration. (See also Nahum iii 3.)

448   See line 483 and compare Whiting M 476. In Thomas Churchyard's
Tragedy of Cardinal Wolsey the same phrase is similarly used:
   My sauce was sour, though meat before was sweet,
   Now Wolsey lacked both cunning, wit and spreet.
(Cavendish's *Life of Wolsey*, 1887, p. 278.)

449   'After glory, praise.' In the Roman liturgy *Gloria tibi domine* is followed by
Laus tibi Christi and the reference may be to this; or alternatively to the opening
of the Palm Sunday processional hymn *Gloria laus et honor*.

457-8   Proverbial (Whiting C 96).

458   yche do] eche other *K M.*

459   *per assimile*: 'in the same way'.

460   *L* begins.

463   Note well what to saye *L. Nota*: 'Note'.

464   not *L.*

465   Yf yt please the not onely *L.*

467   *Tholome*: Ptolemy, the second-century astronomer and mathematician who
wrote the *Tetrabiblos*, four books which expounded the way in which human life
was controlled by the stars.

468-75   The *fatall fall for one* is a hope on Skelton's part that Wolsey will be
disgraced. Clearly the copyist of *L*, who wrote after line 478 'The profecy of
Skelton 1529', used his knowledge of subsequent events to make these lines
appear prophetic. According to *L & P* III, 1142 (26 January 1521) one

Thomas Gyldon had said that Wolsey would have 'the shamefullest fall that ever had chanced in England' within two years. Gyldon though attributed the prophecy to a brewer named Flude. Perhaps Skelton knew of this and alludes to it here. The references to the zodiacal signs of Aries and Scorpio do not seem to have a precise relevance, unless, as suggested by Williams (p. 211), the mention of Scorpio and a *fatall fall* was prompted by a memory of the story of Phaeton in Chaucer's *House of Fame* 948.

469 In a Signe called arriotte *L*.

470 a degre] *a dextre H*; *ad dextram L*.

472 *not H L*.

474 shall sytte] syttys nowe *L*.

476 whett on] whetten *G*.

478 have none] alon *H L*. *L* follows this with 'The profecy of Skelton 1529' and thus concludes.

479–556 *not H*.

501 see] *Dyce's emendation*, fee *G K M*.

519–27 'Some try to settle conclusively the problem of predestination; and some perversely interpret apostasy, and the foreknowledge of divine being, and the personality of Christ in his manhood.' These questions and others, mentioned at 517–18 and 536–9, were of the kind that interested the Lollards at this time (see A.G. Dickens, *The English Reformation*, 1964, p. 22), and it may be that Skelton has Lollards particularly in mind here. Two of his points – that the standard of learning among Lollards was not high (515–18) and that the movement was popular with women (532) – occur also in anti-Lollard verse of the fifteenth century (see Scattergood, pp. 249–50).

521 resydevacyon] *Dyce's emendation*, resdenacyon *G K M*.

539 By] But *K M*.

540–45 The ideas and books of Martin Luther (1483–1546) were just beginning to be known in England at this time (see A.G. Dickens, *The English Reformation*, 1964, p. 68).

549–53 John Wycliffe (1329–84), in a series of books written mainly in the last seven years of his life, denied the real presence of Christ at the Eucharist, papal and priestly authority, the necessity for Church endowment, the validity of auricular confession, and the use of pilgrimages, indulgences and images. John Hus (1369–1415), who was excommunicated in 1409, based his ideas on Wycliffe's. The doctrines of Arius (died 336) and Pelagius (died 420) were not particularly relevant at this time. Perhaps Skelton includes these notable heretics only to show how seriously he regarded the threat of Luther.

557 Some sey holy chyrche have to mykell *H*.

558–9 *not H*.

559 in materyalytes] him in maierialites *M*.

560–63 Som sey they have tryalytes
  And some sey they bryng pluralities
  And qualifie qualites
  And also tot cotte *H*.

564 commune] talke *H*; sottes] scottes *M*.

565–70 *not H*.

573 *not H*.

583 *solde and bought*: A common phrase usually meaning 'betrayed' but here also bearing its literal meaning. See Whiting B 637.

590   not *H*.

596   They caste then up your bokes *H*.

604   *kynge and kayser*: A proverbial phrase (Whiting K 46).

611   howe ye] that they *H*.

612   Perhaps an allusion to the fall of Edward Stafford, third Duke of Buckingham, in May 1521. See also lines 1011–19, *Why Come Ye Nat to Courte?* 1–28, 874–87, and notes, *Speke Parott* 489.

617   avaunce] avayle *H*.

618   another] a new *H*.

619–23   Compare the story told by Richard Pace, the king's secretary, in his *De Fructu* (1517), about the gentleman who wore his hunting horn even at dinner. In a discussion about the training of children he is said to have maintained that he would rather see his son hang than that he should study letters: 'It better becomes the sons of gentlemen to blow the horn properly, to hunt with skill, to teach and manage the falcon. Truly, the study of letters should be left to the sons of yokels' (Jervis Wegg, *Richard Pace*, 1932, p. 46).

622   Lepe over] Kepe unnethe *H*.

626–31   Compare Pollard, *Wolsey*, p. 76: 'In May of that year (1516) the earl of Northumberland was examined before the king in the Star Chamber and sent to the Fleet; the marquis of Dorset, the earl of Surrey and Lord Abergavenny were put out of the council chamber, and with Lord Hastings, Sir Edward Guilford, Sir Richard Sacheverell and others were indicted in the king's bench and also called before the Star Chamber for keeping retainers. Sir William Bulmer was sent to the Tower for preferring to serve the duke of Buckingham rather than the king . . .' It is probably events such as these which Skelton has in mind.

Lines 627–8 seem to mean 'lords must crouch and kneel before you as if broken on the wheel'; that is, as a torture. The copyist of *H* has 'be on' for 'over' and clearly has in mind Fortune's wheel.

628   crouche] couch *M*.

629   Compare *The Bowge of Courte* 357, and see note to 344–71.

639–40   'from the land of Zabulon, the land of Nephthalim', Matthew iv 15, and also mentioned in Isaiah ix 1–2.

644–7   Compare *Why Come Ye Nat to Courte?* 543–64, the story of Abdalonimus, which Skelton seems to have in mind here.

649   ye] *Dyce's emendation*, thy *G*, they *K M H*.

655   gnawe] grawe *G*.

657   Loggyng in fayre strawe *H*.

660   All] Alas *K M*.

662   Many one have but wynde *G K M*.

664   This and the following four lines are based on I Corinthians x 12: *Itaque qui se existimat stare, videat ne cadet*: 'Wherefore let him that thinketh he standeth take heed lest he fall.'

668   fall] false *K*.

670   Compare Whiting D 218.

675–6   'And have open ears and be little attentive.' Based on Vulgate Isaiah xlii 20.

677   And your coursers betrapped *G K M*.

679–82   'For Master Servile, and Doctor Yes-Man, and I fawn–you fawn, with I lie–you lie . . .'

683–6   The line order in *K* is as follows: 685, 683, 684, 686; in *M*: 683, 685,

684, 686.

686 male doth wrye: Compare *Phyllyp Sparowe* 700 and *Why Come Ye Nat to Courte?* 78 and note. wrye] wryte *K M*.

688 ye prelates] yow so *H*.

693 com forthe] conforte *G K M*.

696 autentyke] attentyke *K*, antentike *M*.

698–9 not H.

702 intoxicate] intoxicall *G*, intrixicate *H*.

713 As] And *G K M*.

718–19 'as it is a certain thing contained in Magna Carta'. *Magna Carta*, Chapters 1, 63, both guarantee that the English Church shall be free and have its liberties. The freedom intended was from royal interference in clerical matters.

720–57 In this passage on the friars some of the references are precise and some seem arbitrary. If *mayster Damyan*, *frere Frederyk* or *frere Hugulinus* refer specifically it is not apparent to whom. On the other hand, *Dominyk*, *Augustinus* and *Carmellus* suggest the Dominicans, the Augustinian friars and the Carmelites. The *frere gray* refers to a member of the Franciscan order. Lines 746–7 refer to the convent of Observant Friars at Greenwich, the charter of which was granted by Edward IV and confirmed in 1486 by Henry VII. These friars were a reformed branch of the Franciscans, and were highly favoured by Henry VII, but under Henry VIII, in 1534, were among the first orders to be suppressed. A Franciscan establishment at *Babvell besyde Bery* (Babwell) was settled in 1257. (See Edwart Hutton, *The Franciscans in England, 1224–1538*, 1926, pp. 72–3, 289–90.)

720 mayster] *not H*.

727 yet] ys *H*.

754 be] *not K*.

756 clerkely] clerely *H*.

758 Men say
But your auctoryte *G K M*.

759 see] fee *M*.

760 your] your hye *H*.

762 not H.

769 This shuld be now more weyed *H*.

774 not H.

775 That wolde reherse these wordes agayn *H*.

776 thousande (2nd)] *not H*.

777 blother] bloder *GK*, blondyr *H*.

777–9 Compare *Rede Me and Be Nott Wrothe*, p. 73, on the preaching of friars:
Their preachynge is not scripture
But fables of their coniecture
And mens ymaginacions.
They brynge in olde wyves tales
Both of Englonde Fraunce and Wales
Which they call holy narracions.
And to theym scripture they apply
Pervertynge it most shamfully
After their owne opinions.
Wherwith the people beynge fedde

In to manyfolde errours are ledde
And wretched supersticions.

See also *Jack Upland* 233–6.

778 Welchmans hose: This phrase appears again in the *Garlande of Laurell* 1239. Dyce (II 289) in a note gives other examples of its occurrence and suggests it is analogous to the phrase 'like a shipman's hose' indicating pliability. For an earlier occurrence than any Dyce gives see John Hardyng's lines of 1457:

The lawe is lyke vnto a Walshmannes hose
To eche mannes legge that shapen is and mete...

(Ed. C.L. Kingsford, *EHR* XXVII, 1912, p. 749.) See also Whiting W 196.

782 broke] boke *H*.

787–8 'Either analogically or else categorically.'

789 in divynyte] dyngnite *H*.

792–3 *not H*.

795–800 'But the possessor of a doctorate with a seal attached to it, too little learned, a master having taken his doctor's degree at Broadgate's Hall, Oxford, Doctor Simpleton and bachelored bachelor...' But a pun may be intended on *Bullatus* which can also mean 'inflated'.

798 *not H*.

801 Proverbial (Whiting M 731).

803 cappe] cuppe *H*.

806 Robyn] a *H*. According to Whiting R 158 the phrase is proverbial.

809 Waltham's calf was proverbial for its stupidity; according to the proverb it ran nine miles to suck a bull (Whiting W 29).

813 *saynt Hyllary*: St Hilary of Poitiers (*c.*300–367), the famous theologian.

814–19 'He cannot get by in logic or scholastic debate, neither syllogize, nor make contracted syllogisms in which one of the premisses is suppressed, nor does he know his logical refutations, nor the ten categories of assertion formulated by Aristotle...'

816 sylogysare] foly *silogizare H*.

817 enthymemare] Dyce's emendation, *emptymeniare G K M H*.

818 elenkes] *eloquens G K M*.

820 melle] medyll *H*.

824 And wyll newyn *H*.

826–7 Temple Bar was the gate leading out of the City of London where Fleet Street and the Strand meet. The *seven sterres* may either refer to the Pleiades or to the Great Bear, or the planets, or even to the seven stars of Revelation i 16, 20. The association here may be arbitrary. If it is not, it may be that Skelton is implying that some clerics do not realize how far things of the world (such as Temple Bar) are from celestial things (the seven stars), because they are so badly trained in theology.

830–31 'Always protesting that I am not attacking.'

834–5 'As limiters within their district will absolve people from sins and charge them for this service.' A *limyter* was a friar licensed to beg on behalf of his convent within a certain specified district.

838–47 Compare *The Canterbury Tales* III 1746–53:

'Yif us a busshel whete, malt, or reye,
A Goddes kechyl, or a trype of chese,
Or elles what yow lyst, we may nat cheese;

A Goddes halfpeny, or a masse peny,
Or yif us of youre brawn, if ye have eny;
A dagon of youre blanket, leeve dame,
Oure suster deere – lo! heere I write youre name –
Bacon or beef, or swich thyng as ye fynde.'

Also *Mum and the Sothsegger* M 440–45, *Pierce the Ploughman's Crede* 595–602.

842–3 H transposes the rhyme words.

850–53 A common enough charge in anti-mendicant satire; compare *The Orders of Cain* (1382) 37–40:

Thei dele with purses, pynnes, & knyves,
With gyrdles, gloves for wenches and wyves –
Bot ever bacward the husbond thryves
Ther thei are haunted till.

And also lines 45–72 (ed. Robbins, *Historical Poems* No. 65). Line 850 is proverbial (Whiting T 378).

853 fraude] faude *G*, fawte *H*.

854–9 Another common charge; see *The Orders of Cain* 121–4:

Thai travele yerne & bysily,
To brynge doun the clergye
Thai speken therof ay vilany
& therof thai done wrong.

Also *Jack Upland* 244–56.

859 open tyde] open tyme *KM*, Estertyde *H*.

863 Proverbial (Whiting N 51).

864 A translation of Vulgate Hebrews xi 37, *Circuierunt in melotis*, 'they wandered about in sheepskins and goatskins'. melottes] flockes *H*.

866 wyl] wyll take *H*.

868 of] if *M*.

871 'But deliver us from evil. Amen.' The final clause of the *pater noster*.

872–6 The Clementines constituted the seventh and last section of the papal Decretals, so called because they were issued by Clement V, who was pope between 1305 and 1316. The Clementines are divided into five books and the passage referred to here begins *Dudum a Bonifacio Papa octavo praedecessore nostro &c* (*lib*. III *tit*. vii *cap*. ii). It deals with the licensing of friars for the purposes of hearing confession, imposing penances and giving absolution, functions usually performed by the *sacerdotes*.

873 they] not *K M*.

875 shryve] shewe *H*.

877–8 A ballad called 'The Friar in the Well' is the source of this allusion. It tells how a friar tried to seduce a maid, but she told him that she was afraid of the pains of hell. He assured her he could sing her soul out of hell. Instead of submitting she tricks him into falling in a well, and tells him he ought to be able to sing himself out of there. She eventually helps him to get out and sends him away sopping wet. See F.J. Child, *English and Scottish Popular Ballads*, 1884–98, V, pp. 100–103.

879 Christen Cloute and *frere Fabian* (881) appear to be arbitrary names suggested by alliteration.

880–82 An allusion to the exordium prefacing Clementine *lib*. V *tit*. xi *cap*. i: '*Exivi de paradiso...*' ('I went out of paradise...'). This Clementine deals with the lax conduct of the friars and urges them to observe again their former ideals.

884 'About this we seek advice.'

885–6 'And they go through the world singing masses for the dead.' *Diryge* and *Placebo* refer to the matins and vespers Offices for the Dead. Compare *Select English Works of John Wyclif*, ed. T. Arnold, 1869–71, III, p. 374; *Jack Upland* 220–25; and *Pierce the Ploughman's Crede* 468–71, on the way in which friars gained money by singing masses for the dead.

890 Suche maner of subiecions *H*.

893 affections] afflictions *K*.

894 sadde] the sayd *K M*.

895 cases] cawsys *H*.

898 sowe] save *G*.

901 ambycyon] and ambycyon *K M*.

904 glum] mume *H*.

905 not *H*. The line is proverbial (see Whiting N 172).

907 Compare Tilley P 378. The meaning here is 'with flattering'. *Placebo* comes originally from the Vulgate Psalm cxiv 9, *Placebo Domino in regione vivorum*.

912 Worshypfully] worshyp *G K M*.

922 them] they *H*.

923 Compare Tilley A 136.

934–9 These lines are reminiscent of medieval attacks on the splendour of friaries: see, for example, *Jack Upland* 168–76, 182–6; *Pierce the Ploughman's Crede* 159ff., on a Dominican convent; *Friars, Ministri Malorum* 33–6. But the target in these lines is probably Wolsey's palaces at Hampton Court and York Place (compare *Why Come Ye Nat to Courte?* 408–10).

938 Stretchynge] So recchyng *H*.

940–68 These lines fairly clearly refer to the sumptuous tapestries with which Wolsey adorned his palaces, notably Hampton Court. He possessed many sets of hangings (see *L & P* IV, pp. 2763–4), but from their descriptions here and from the word *tryumphes* (956) it seems that Skelton had in mind tapestries from the series based on Petrarch's *Trionfi*. The list of his household effects indicates that Wolsey owned three sets of 'triumphs': one bought from the executors of the estate of Bishop Thomas Ruthall who died in February 1523; one set on 'counterfeit arras lined with canvas, perhaps from Spain'; and one bought from Richard Gresham in 1525. Three pieces from the Ruthall set still remain at Hampton Court, and two of these correspond closely to those described by Skelton. Lines 956–63 seem to describe the triumph of Renown: the car of Fame is drawn by elephants and Caesar and Pompey appear in the picture. In the triumph of Death the car of Chastity is drawn by unicorns on which ride naked boys (lines 964–7). On the implication of these descriptions for the date of the poem, see J. Berdan, *PMLA* XXXIX 1914, 499–516 and W. Nelson, *PMLA* LI, 1936, 377–98.

946 Howe god Cupyde shakyd *H*.

948 *shote a crowe*: Kinsman (p. 191) suggests 'to shoot clumsily' and refers to Ascham's *Toxophilus* ii 141: 'Another cowereth down, and layeth out his buttocks, as though he should shoot a crowe.' Perhaps it simply means 'to shoot from a crouching position'.

949 *tyrly tyrlowe*: Kinsman (p. 191) suggests this is 'the refrain of a comic song', which it certainly seems to be in *Elynour Rummynge* 292. Here, however, it is more likely to refer to the female genitalia (see E. Partridge, *Dictionary of Slang and Unconventional English*, 4th edition, 1950, under 'tirly whirly').

951   lege moy] lege de moy *K M*. Evidently some kind of dance (compare *Elynour Rummynge* 586–7), perhaps a corruption of 'le jeu de mai'.

984   tellynge] yellyng *H*.

985   *not H.*

986–7   These lines are based upon a proverb (Tilley S 601). But R.S. Kinsman (*HLQ* XXIV, 1963, 309) takes them to apply to March 1520 when Katherine of Aragon summoned her own council and set out a critique of Wolsey's policies.

987   quenes] commyn *H*.

989   kynge] gyng *K*.

995   *not H.*

996   Proverbial (Whiting C 641).

998–1000   'To be the friend of kings and to rule everyone else is also to weigh yourself down.' *amicare* and *gravare* are presumably infinitives, but *dominor* is strictly a deponent verb and should not have this infinitive form.

998   *Cum*] *Sum G K M.*

1005   reporte] *not K M*, dothe reporte *H*.

1007   ye] we *K*.

1009–10   *H transposes.*

1019   rest] roste *H*. The reading in *H* alludes to the proverb in Whiting R 152.

1026   herke] harte *H*.

1030   *our sovereygne lorde*: Henry VIII.

1035   *your presydent*: Wolsey. 'The *Acta Consilii* from 1516 to 1527 make it perfectly clear that Wolsey was in fact, if not in name, "president" of the council' (W.H. Dunham, *EHR* LIX, 1944, 204).

1036   Nor to expresse] Not to prese *H*.

1037   ...] *left blank in G*, george gascone *H*, your assentacion *M*, your consentacyon *K*. The inclusion of the name *George Gascone* rests entirely on *H*, though the fact that *G* leaves a blank here might be taken to indicate that a name is omitted, as was sometimes the case in political verse. The readings of the other editions – *your assentacion* and *your consentacyon* – do not make very elegant sense and appear to be attempts by later editors to fill out the line with a rhyme. My feeling is that the name was not intended by Skelton to appear, for he says in lines 1111–12:

> ...no man have I named.
> Wherfore shulde I be blamed?

An informed contemporary (though apparently not the copyist of *H* who gets it wrong) would have been able to supply the name of Sir William Gascoigne (1468 –1551), a prominent courtier and Wolsey's treasurer at this time (see *L & P* III, 3458). Kinsman suggests that the copyist may have confused Gascoigne with George Cavendish, who entered the Cardinal's employ in 1522.

1043   *his substytute*: Probably Thomas Ruthall, Bishop of Durham and Keeper of the Privy Seal, is meant. Giustiniani in his *Despatches* (I 260) said that Ruthall 'sang treble to Wolsey's bass' and also that he 'seemed to be acquainted with all his operations' (II 119).

1046   Permytted] Permed *G*, Now *H*.

1052   But they will tell *veritatem H*.

1065–8   'But now you should know and thoroughly attend, in your convocation, to this question of praemunire.' See also line 108 and note.

1067   not *H*.

1071   sure and] *not H*.

1077   olde] as for old *H*.

1093   have] hath *G*.

1095–106   A fairly typical formula in medieval protest verse; see, for example, *Mum and the Sothsegger M* 505, Hoccleve's *Regement of Princes* 1541–2, Barclay's *Eclogue* I 659–69.

1096   I escrye] of the clargy *M*.

1103   rebellynge] in raylyng *H*.

1107   use] cawse *H*; despytynge] despysyng *K M*; dysputyng *H*.

1109   To] Do *H*.

1114   gramed] greved *G K M H*. Dyce's emendation provides a good rhyme. See *Magnyfycence* 1839 for an occurrence of this word.

1130   ydeottes] idolles *H*.

1138   not *G*.

1142   But yet they wolde have no blame *H*.

1143   not *H*.

1148   Whyche ys nothyng avaylyng *H*.

1150–226   These lines may be assumed to be spoken by those prelates who re-fuse to give up their secular interests, and who also attempt to silence criticism. But from the similarity of this speech to *Why Come Ye Nat to Courte?* 425–53, 602–10, it seems that he sometimes has Wolsey specifically in mind.

1150   taunt] daunt *K M*, teche *H*.

1153   losell] pollshorne *H*.

1155   *Syr Gye of Gaunt*: Compare *Agenst Garnesche* iii 70. Kinsman interprets it as 'High and mighty Lollard' because the city of Ghent had earlier been noto-rious for its religious dissenters. Dyce (II 184–5) refers to the well-known story of Guy of Alost (a town about thirteen miles from Ghent) who, after his death, returned to haunt his wife.

1157   Deuyas] Denyas *G*, Devias *H*, dyvers *M*. Compare 'Agaynste a Comely Coystrowne' 55. Probably a combination 'deuce' + 'ace' which was a low throw at dice. Hence perhaps meaning 'worthless'.

1159   matters] medlyng *H*.

1161   losell] lorell *H*.

1163   counsell] prevy councell *H*.

1165–72   Like *Why Come Ye Nat to Courte?* 425–33, these lines refer to the four principal London prisons, the Tower of London, the Fleet, the Marshalsea and the King's Bench. *Lytell Ease* was a very small cell in the Tower in which political prisoners were sometimes kept, but was also used more generally to re-fer to any small, uncomfortable cell.

1173   vyllayne] polshorne *H*.

1175   *fee symplenes*: 'Unrestricted possession of lands', perhaps an allusion to Wolsey's acquisition of property (see Pollard, *Wolsey*, pp. 320–27). fee] fre *K M*.

1178   mercyles] graceles *H*.

1179   insaciate] incessant *H*.

1182   *Poules Crosse*: A pulpit cross on the north side of St Paul's Churchyard from which sermons were preached on Sunday mornings.

1184   *Saynt Mary Spytell*: The Hospital of St Mary of Bethlehem in Bishops-gate.

1185   shyttell] whystell *K M*. Compare *Why Come Ye Nat to Courte?* 354.

1186   *Austen Fryars*: The church of the Austin Friars in Broad Street.

1188   *Saynt Thomas of Akers*: The Hospital of St Thomas of Acre in Cheapside.

1189   carpe] clacke *H*.

1190   wyll rule] ren *H*.

1199   Be hyt ryghte as a ramse horne *H*. The line is proverbial (Whiting R 27).

1201   not *H*.

1206   Isaias] *Dyce's emendation*, Ezechyes *G K M*, Isay was *H*. According to Jewish tradition Isaiah was sawn in half at the orders of Manasseh (for whom see II Kings xxi). The 'Ezechyes' of the editions is perhaps the result of confusion with Hezekiah (II Kings xviii–xx), father of Manasseh. A supposed allusion to Isaiah's death appears in Hebrews xi 37. In fact lines 1205–10 seem to be based loosely on this verse.

1207   was] Ozeas *H*.

1209   *holy Jeremy*: Jeremiah, who according to tradition was stoned to death in Egypt. See Hebrews xi 37 again.

1212   rule] rayle *H*.

1216   our] your *K M*.

1219   Cyvyll] wyll *H*.

1220   Divynyte] Divine *M*, Domynicke *H*; Dryvyll] oryll *H*.

1221   rough] not *H*.

1222–4   Perhaps proverbial (compare Tilley D 267, 268).

1224   And let them take there reste *H*.

1225   Proverbial (Whiting N 194).

1229   Seduces] Adusayes *H*. The Sadducees, the priestly aristocratic party of Judaism, who denied the resurrection of the body (see Matthew xxii 23, Acts iv 1–2).

1230   not *H*; sad] sayd *K M*.

1231   Whiche] Wyttes *H*.

1237–9   Perhaps Skelton is simply anticipating criticism, for there is no certain evidence to indicate that attempts were made to suppress *Collyn Clout*. There is a story told by Francis Thynne that his father, William, in whose house 'the moste part' of the poem was composed, 'was callyd in questione by the Bisshoppes, and heaved at by Cardinal Wolseye, his olde enyme, for manye causes, but mostly for that [his] father had furthered Skelton to publishe his "Collen Cloute" against the Cardinall' (*Animadversions*, ed F.J. Furnivall, E E T S O S, 1865, p. 10). Line 1238 is proverbial (Whiting H 458).

1241   scrolles] not *H*.

1247   not *H*.

1251–65   The nautical metaphor for closing a poem is conventional: see E.R. Curtius, *European Literature and the Latin Middle Ages*, translated by W.R. Trask, 1953, pp. 128–30, for examples from classical times onwards. See also Hawes's *Pastyme of Pleasure* 4487ff. and Spenser's *Faerie Queene* VI 12 1–9. Conventional too is the closing prayer, especially in protest verse, which looks to God to set things to rights; see, for example, Robbins, *Historical Poems* No. 17, line 7, No. 48, lines 189–90, No. 50, lines 111–12, No. 61, lines 25–30.

1257   Compare *Speke Parott* 397, and see Whiting C 339.

1259   stere] pere *K M*.

Amen] not *M*. After this *H* has 'Quod Collyn Clowte'.

1266–8   'In an unfinished work (i.e. the style is unpolished), in a work completely finished (i.e. no more is to be added) and in a work more than finished (i.e. it is a work of a greater than usual sort).' But these lines are enigmatic, and meant to be so.

1268 After this *H* has 'qd Sceltonyus Lawreatus'.

Epilogue

1–11 Not G K M. 'Colin Clout, "Although to the multitude my songs are foolishly contemptible, yet they are rare inspirations to the cultivated who are inspired by the divine breath of the sublime spirit. Whence, it concerns me much less, although the envious tongue is prepared to injure me, because, although I sing rustic songs, nevertheless, I shall be sung and celebrated everywhere while the famous English race still remains. At one time the laurel crown of honour, the queen of realms, and the glory of kings; alas, how feeble it grows, how it wastes away, how sluggishly it becomes inert. Ah, how shameful! Ah, how deplorable! I can expound no more of these things here because of sighing and tears; I pray that the rewards may justify the pain."'

1 mea] Dyce's emendation, *mori H.*

2 pneumata sunt] Kinsman's emendation, *puevinate sunt H.*

3 Pneumatis altisoni] Edwards's emendation, *Pue vinatis altisem H; flamine flatis]* Dyce's emendation, *flamina faltis H.*

10 Vetor may be a mistake for *veto.*

XX WHY COME YE NAT TO COURTE?

This poem may be dated from internal evidence. The reference in 641–5 to the fact that it was sixteen years since Wolsey was chaplain to Sir Richard Nafnan must indicate a date before January 1523. John Meautis (784–840) was formally replaced on 15 March 1523, but may have fallen from favour earlier. If 933 alludes to Thomas Spring of Lavenham the poem must predate June 1523, when he died. But it is possible to be a little more precise. The numeral 'xxxiiii' of the Apostrophe means that, in Skelton's own private calendar, it was thirty-four years since he entered the royal service in October or November 1488. Thus the poem was probably written some time in 1522. Several passages (50–54, 900–914, Apostrophe 2–4) seem to allude to the enforced loans of June and August 1522. Lines 125–52 refer to the treaty between the English and the Scots of September 1522, and 153–68 to the Earl of Surrey's raids in France between 30 August and 14 October 1522. The poem must also postdate 28 October 1522 since it alludes to Sir John Munday as Mayor of London (908). Moreover, Wolsey was suffering from eye trouble (533–5, 1169) in late October and November 1522 (*L & P* III, 2661, 2684). A date of November 1522 for the completion of the poem would fit well enough with these facts.

However, it was almost certainly composed over a few months, for the earlier parts of the poem refer to earlier events than the later parts. It is even possible that parts were circulated before the whole thing was published. The 'Creed' (1–28) appears separately in the various editions of *Certayne Bokes* and in Marshe's *Workes* (1568). Moreover, the copyist of Bodleian M S Rawlinson C813 evidently had access to a version which consisted of lines 1–30, 841–1217, and the Invective, forming a fairly coherent attack on Wolsey. If the poem were composed in parts the breaks would probably have come at lines 30, 232, 398, 840 and 1217.

The text here is based on Kele's edition of c.1545 (K), collated with the editions of Toy (c.1553) (T), Kitson (c.1560) (Kit), and Marshe's edition of Skelton's *Workes* (1568) (M). Also used are the fragmentary version in Bodleian MS Rawlinson C813, ff. 36r–43v (R) and the separate versions of the 'Creed' (C). K is the earliest and best complete text, but has a few slips which are corrected in the later editions. In all editions there are inaccuracies in the Latin and Dyce's emendations are extensively accepted. The readings of R are frequently highly individual and sometimes badly garbled. Yet this text is valuable in that it alone indicates the break between the poem's ending and the beginning of the appended Invective.

The lineation in this edition differs a little from that of Dyce. Line 31, which Dyce took to be the title of the poem, seems to me to be the first question of the interlocutor and is counted as a line. So too are the single words of 40 and 49. The Invective, Epitome, Decastichon and Apostrophe are numbered separately.

Title: M has, following the title, 'The relucent mirror for all Prelats and Presidents, as well spirituall as temporall, sadly to loke upon, devised in English by Skelton.'

1–28 It is difficult to know how precise these lines are meant to be. It seems they are a generalized indictment of the nobility (3–14) and a warning that 'A noble man may fall/And his honour appall' (22–3) unless Skelton's poem is heeded. As such they recall typical 'abuses of the age poems' (see Robbins, *Historical Poems* Nos. 49, 55–58, 62–63). Compare also Skelton's version of Poggio's preface to his translation of Diodorus Siculus:

'For where-as exersise of doctryne is surrendred, ne where ther is no
discretyve ne difference bytwene wysedom & follye, ne where vertue kepeth
no residence, where no respecte of studye is hadde, thenne of necessite this
sequele ensieweth: that there vyce must have domynyon, wysedom &
quyckenes of reason is leyde to slepe, pryncely honour & glorye of realmes falle
vnto decaye, and so fynally all shameful confusion muste ocupye the rowme.'
(p. 2)

If they have a more precise reference it may be that 22–3 allude to the execution of Edward Stafford, third Duke of Buckingham, in May 1521; he apparently had most of the shortcomings mentioned in 3–14 (see Brewer, *The Reign of Henry VIII*, 1884, I, pp. 375–404). These lines are unlikely to refer to Wolsey, since 3, 5–7 and 10 are contrary to the usual impression Skelton gives of him.

1 of this] *not* R.

9 lyght] lyght of R.

15–16 not R.

25 you] hym R. The line is proverbial (Whiting G 7).

27–8 not K R. But K has *etc* after 26.

29–30 not C. 'About these things the famous bard of whom a thousand speak.' Repeated at the end of the poem.

30 mille] *in ille* T Kit M.

31–840 not R.

32–48 Except for the single word line 40, this passage is arranged in four quatrains rhyming *abab*, the rhyme on *-age* being maintained throughout. Furthermore, in each of the lines ending in *-age* there is a medial rhyme on the same syllable. The emphasis on 'age' enforced thus through the metre, as a reason why one should not come to court, applies well enough to Skelton, who was about sixty at the time. But it may also have a more general application; compare

Pace's letter to Wolsey on 24 July 1521: 'As old men decay greatly, the King wishes young men to be acquainted with his affairs' (*L & P* III, 1437).

34–5 'Because age cannot behave wantonly, nor kiss her sweet one sweetly', and, developing the sexual image, *corage* (38) means both 'bravery' and 'desire'.

40–42 'But, alas, the old wise man thus foolishly decays', or, taking *sage overage* to be a French phrase like *graunt domage* (45), 'But, alas, wise policy so foolishly disappears'.

42 So] To *T Kit M*.

44 reconed] recovered *T Kit M*.

45 a] *not Kit M. graunt domage*: 'great shame'.

50–54 Perhaps an allusion to Wolsey's forced loans of 1522. Compare lines 900–932.

61 some] *not T Kit M*.

63 'that troubles begin to increase'; compare *Magnyfycence* 744.

66–7 Evidently the refrain or the opening of a popular song, since lost. Compare *The Bowge of Courte* 360 and *A Devoute Trentale* 63.

77 The] They *K T Kit M. countrynge at Cales*: An allusion to the costly but fruitless negotiations for peace in 1521. Compare Palsgrave's 1529 charge against Wolsey:

> 'We triumphed at our countering at Calais, to the great impoverishing of the noblemen of England, and prodigal dispending of the king's treasure, as well in the sumptuous building made there only to that use, and not to endure, as in mummeries, banquets, jousts and tourneys.' (*L & P* IV, p. 2560)

78 males] wales *K T Kit M*. Dyce's emendation to *males* is justified in view of *Collyn Clout* 686 and *Phyllyp Sparowe* 700. The meaning of the phrase is usually 'things go badly', but here it seems to be literal 'pinched our purses'.

79 *Chefe counselour*: Wolsey.

84 Proverbial (Whiting C 334).

86–7 These lines, rather than 89, seem to be the end of the old song. Compare the *Garlande of Laurell* 1395–6. Eleanor P. Hammond suggests that 'Mocke hath lost her sho' may mean 'lost her virtue' (*English Verse between Chaucer and Surrey*, 1927, p. 524).

89 do (2nd)] *not Kit M*.

90 'As straight as a ram's horn', i.e. crooked. Proverbial (Whiting R 27).

91–2 Marks to the right of *worn* and *shorn* suggest final *es* inadequately printed.

95–8 *Javell* and *Havell* are terms of uncertain origin used for 'rogue' or 'rascal' by Skelton; *Favell* and *Harvy Hafter* are the 'flatterer' and 'purse-stealer' of *The Bowge of Courte* 134ff.; *Cole Crafter* suggests a 'sneak' or 'trickster' and *Jack Travell* a 'base-born labourer'.

101 cravynge] cravyne *K*.

108–12 'Reason and skill may as well perform meaningless tasks for all the good it will do.' 110 and 112 are proverbial; compare Tilley S 12 and Whiting S 782.

114 *hathe the strokes*: 'rules', 'wields authority'. Compare Cavendish's *Life of Wolsey*: '... the Cardinal bare the stroke ...' (p. 146).

120 Compare Whiting H 120, a proverb which suggests the departure of good judgement.

121–2 Perhaps Skelton is here being deliberately obscure in the way in which Pallas says he can be (*Garlande of Laurell* 100–104); but R.S. Kinsman has identified the *buck*, the *fox* and the *gray* with, respectively, Edward Stafford, third

Duke of Buckingham, Richard Foxe, Bishop of Winchester, and Thomas Grey, Marquis of Dorset (*PQ* XXIX, 1950, 61–4). For earlier political verses which pun on animal names see Robbins, *Historical Poems* Nos. 75, 84, 87, 89, 90.

125–52 These lines refer to the truce, of which Skelton disapproved, made between England and Scotland at Carlisle in September 1522.

127 shot: 1. ammunition; 2. money.

128 tot quot: Literally the dispensation to hold innumerable benefices, but here perhaps perhaps 'reward'..

131 lylse wulse: A poor, coarse sort of wool, and a pun on Wolsey's name.

132 'a bitter sweet work'.

133 his] hes *K*. Compare *A Devoute Trentale* 79 and note.

139 'From Bamborough (Northumberland) to Bootham Bar (York)'; for other pairs of places see 145, 147, 149.

142 levell suse: perhaps 'levy sous', i.e. 'collect in the tax money', another reference to the forced loans of 1522; or, more likely, a reference to the game *level-coil* (lever le cul), more politely called *level-sice* (lever l'assise). This rough, noisy game, formerly played at Christmas, was one in which each player in turn was driven out of his seat and replaced by another. So perhaps the line means 'Get up! Move on!' and refers to the breaking off of the campaign against the Scots in September 1522.

143 lent] sent *M*.

145 into] to *T Kit M*.

148 Proverbial (Whiting F 345).

153–68 Thomas Howard, second Earl of Surrey (1473–1554), led the attack on Morlaix (Brittany) in July 1522, then commanded the army which left Calais on 30 August to raid Artois and Picardy. He returned to Calais on 14 October with considerable booty.

166 urcheons] heons *Kit M*.

169–83 Skelton suspects Wolsey of betraying the English cause for money received from France. He certainly had a yearly pension of 12,000 crowns in recompense for his surrender of the bishopric of Tournai in 1518. He may also at this time have been receiving money from Louise of Savoy, mother of Francis I, who in 1525 paid him 100,000 crowns for making peace between England and France (see Pollard, *Wolsey*, p. 148).

172 'I fear we are betrayed'; proverbial (Whiting B 637).

176 They] Thy *K*.

188 Star Chamber, the public court at Westminster which maintained law and order. Wolsey, as Lord Chancellor, presided over it.

197 Proverbial (Whiting R 155). The phrase connoted civility extorted by fear.

201 Proverbial (Whiting R 152).

206 Philargerya] *Philargera K*. 'Avarice'.

209–12 Asmodeus was a demon who promoted sexual licence (see Tobit iii 8); *Dalyda*: 'Delilah' (Judges xvi 4–31) but here used as a term for 'harlot'. A letter, calendared under 1522, probably addressed to Wolsey, advises 'to use nothing but "bele yane frese" and wash his legs once a month with good herbs to bring down the humours' (*L & P* III, Appendix No. 38); so the *membres* (210) referred to may be his legs. Skelton here, and at 1166–201, implies that Wolsey had syphilis, but there is no conclusive evidence of this, and his various illnesses may otherwise be explained. But see *L & P* IV, p. 6075.

216 Castrimergia: 'Gluttony'.

219–23 Because he was afflicted with digestive trouble Wolsey had obtained licence to eat meat during Lent from Leo X in 1520 (*L & P* III, 634, 647). Perhaps Skelton alludes to this, or, more likely, to events in 1522 when, to 'appease' the people and 'lessen the stigma attaching to his name', Wolsey:

'. . . arranged for preachers at Paul's Cross to announce that it would be permissible for all and sundry to consume milk, cheese and eggs during the Lenten period.'

(Polydore Vergil, *Anglica Historia*, pp. 293–4.) See also *Collyn Clout* 204–19.

224   Literally 'He stabs and he rubs', but 225 makes it clear that a sexual connotation is intended. Compare 2 *Henry IV*, II iv 229–30.

234   that] the *Kit M*.

238   According to John Stow's *Survey of London* II 55, there was a stewhouse of this name in Southwark.

240–44   Compare Tilley Q 5: 'Gup, quean, gup'; and also 'The auncient acquaintance' 15–18 and *Elynour Rummynge* 386–95 where women are referred to as mares and fillies and addressed with 'Gup' and 'jayst'.

243   Proverbial (Whiting C 333).

247–53   Soldiers from these shires had gone north to meet the Scots in September 1522. In a letter to Wolsey, George Talbot, fourth Earl of Shrewsbury, said that he 'has promised them the customary wages, as they grudged to set forward without money' (*L & P* III, 2524).

254–5   Perhaps Skelton is remembering that a contingent of Lancashire and Cheshire soldiers, under Sir Edmund Howard, had fled from the Scots at Flodden in 1513.

260   they] the *K*.

265   Proverbial (Whiting S 822).

267   Huntley-bank is a hill near Melrose (Roxburghshire) and famous in literature as the place where Thomas of Ercledoune met a fairy queen (See *The Romance and Prophecies of Thomas of Ercledoune*, ed. J.A. Murray, EETS OS 61 1875). Frequently mentioned by Skelton (*Agaynst the Scottes* 149, *Howe the Douty Duke of Albany* 19) in connection with Scotland, but never with much precision.

268–71   In 1314 Edward II and the English army were disastrously defeated by the Scots under Robert Bruce at Bannockburn, near Stirling. This, and earlier defeats, effectively lost the control over Scotland that Edward I had achieved.

271   all his] al that his *T Kit M*.

272–84   Thomas Lord Dacre, Warden of the West March, who had signed the truce with the Scots (see lines 125–52), had written to Wolsey on 12 September 1522 that his soldiers 'came forward with the worst will that ever did men' (Brewer, *The Reign of Henry VIII*, I, p. 535). The truce had been signed by Dacre without authority, but Wolsey excused it to Henry VIII as a *felix culpa* (281–2) because the English position in the West March was not strong (*L & P* III, 2537).

286   *Lord Rose*: Thomas Manners, Baron Roos, the unpopular and ineffectual Warden of the East and Middle Marches from April to October 1522.

289   Proverbial (Whiting H 295).

290–91   Henry Percy, fifth Earl of Northumberland, who refused the Wardenship of the Marches vacated by Roos. Of this Edward Hall writes:

'For refusing of this office therle of Northumberland was not regarded of his owne tenauntes whiche disdained hym and his bloud, and muche lamented his foly, and al men estemed hym without hart or love of honour and chivalry.' (*Henry VIII*, I, p. 277)

296   at] a *Kit M*.

297–8 Wolsey was the son of an Ipswich butcher, a fact Skelton alludes to again in 494.

300–313 In order to maintain the King's authority, and his own, Wolsey was particularly harsh in his dealings with the aristocracy in Star Chamber (see Hall, *Henry VIII*, I, p. 52).

306 brynges] brynge *K T Kit M*.

312 maketh them] make *T Kit M*.

314–45 Both the Court of Common Pleas (319) and the court of the King's Bench (320) were situated in Westminster Hall (325). In each of these courts judges presided (314) and lawyers (316) pleaded the cases. In the Chancery (326) Wolsey, as Lord Chancellor, presided, though he was not a trained lawyer. In this court there is no pleading as such by lawyers, but the Lord Chancellor judged cases on the basis of submissions by plaintiff and defendant and the evidence of witnesses.

338 'In the court of the Exchequer he threatens them', but also 'In the chess game he puts them in check'. The puns arise because historically the Exchequer dealt with revenue cases and took its name from the table, covered like a chessboard with a squared cloth, on which revenue was calculated by means of counters (see *O E D exchequer* sb 1 2).

345 must] *not M*.

346–55 James V, king of Scotland (1513–42), was only nine years old at this time (348–9) and there does indeed seem to have been a plan to bring him to England (*L & P* III, 2476, 2728).

349 stalworthy] tall worthy *Kit M*.

350 There] Her *Kit M*.

357 John Stewart, Duke of Albany (1481–1536), Regent in Scotland during the minority of James V, who had negotiated the truce of September 1522 with Lord Dacre (see lines 125–52). Skelton evidently thinks that either side is likely to break the truce; certainly Wolsey never took it very seriously: '...the abstinence concluded by the Lord Dacre...does not bind the King, but he is at liberty to make war on the Scots whenever he thinks proper' (*L & P* III, 2537).

370–76 Burgundian and Spanish soldiers, on behalf of the Emperor Charles V, fought alongside the English in France. There is no record of any event corresponding to 372–3, but the alliance was not a happy one (*L & P* III, 2551, 2568, 2592, 2612, 2632).

377 *Mutrell*: Montreuil, near Agincourt.

380 *graunde counsell*: The King's Council met in Star Chamber, a gathering of the most powerful men of the realm. But since the King hardly ever attended it was virtually subject to Wolsey.

383–4 'For fear lest the Cardinal take offence.' 384 is proverbial (Whiting P 141).

386 *by the harde arse*: Dyce (II 360) quotes a line from the *Interlude of the I I I I Elementes*: 'I smot of his legge by the harde arse.' But here the phrase appears not to be literal but an oath meaning something like 'utterly'. There is a pun on *arse* and 'axe'. Compare *Ralph Roister Doister* I i 40.

387–95 An obscure passage which Dyce (II 360) took to refer to Wolsey. But, so far as is known, Wolsey never wore a beard (391) and *our syre* (389) may indicate Henry VIII, who did. In 1519 he and Francis I, as a gesture of their good will to each other, promised to grow their beards, but Henry VIII shaved his off at the 'great instance' of Queen Katherine (*L & P* III, 514).

408–10 Hampton Court, begun in 1515, and York Place, Westminster, were two sumptuous palaces belonging to Wolsey.

415 Compare Cavendish: 'All Ambassitors of fforrayn potentates ware allway dispeched by hys discression to whome they had all wayes accesse for ther dispeche' (*Life of Wolsey*, p. 25).

420 *lawe tancrete*: Canon law as interpreted by Tancredus (*c.*1183–1235) in his *Ordo Judicarium*.

421 'according to theory of precedent'. abstract] obstract *K*.

425–33 The lines refer to four of the principal London prisons – the Fleet, the Tower of London, the Marshalsea and the King's Bench. Compare Palsgrave's charges of 1529 against Wolsey: 'We have Towered [and] Fleeted . . . a great number of the noblemen of England, and many of them for light causes' (*L & P* IV, p. 2561).

430 'without any other remedy'.

443 'that all is worthless' proverbial (Whiting N 195).

447 *in gre*: 'with good will'.

451 By] But *M*.

462 and] an *K*.

463 supersticyous] See Cavendish's *Life of Wolsey*, pp. 127–9, 151–2, for examples.

466 into] in *M*; *Acidiam*] Acisiam *K W Kit M*. Dyce emended to *a caeciam* (blindness) and referred to line 475. Edwards's emendation to *Acidiam* (sloth) is almost certainly right, however, particularly in view of a similar collocation with the people of Sodom and Gomorrah in *Piers Plowman* B XXV 75–6 (p. 220).

475–7 'From blindness of heart . . . deliver us, O lord', a quotation from the Litany.

478 *Amalecke*: Amalek, an Old Testament villain (see Genesis xxxvi 12; Exodus xvii 8–16; Numbers xxiv 20; Deuteronomy xxv 17–19 and so on) alluded to elsewhere by Skelton (*Speke Parott* 118, *Agaynst the Scottes* 116).

479 a Mamelek] Amamelek *K T Kit M*. Dyce's emendation is convincing because appropriate to the context. Mamelukes were the descendants of enfranchised slaves who seized the throne of Egypt in 1254; hence persons, like Wolsey, who rose from obscure origins to positions of power.

489 the] they be *Kit M*.

491 *base progeny*: Wolsey's illegitimate children, Dorothy Clansey and Thomas Winter.

493 *sank royall*: 'royal blood'.

508–12 Skelton's low estimate of Wolsey's academic ability is unjustified. Wolsey was educated at Magdalen College, Oxford, where he took degrees of B.A. and M.A. and was elected to a fellowship.

521–3 Haly Aben Raghel, an eleventh-century Arabian astrologer; *royall Ptholomy*, a second-century Arabian astronomer Ptolemy frequently confused, as here, with members of the Ptolemaic dynasty of pre-Christian times; Albumasar, a ninth-century Arab astrologer frequently read in the Middle Ages. Compare *Phyllyp Sparowe* 501–5 and *Speke Parott* 134.

528–9 'in the faculty of literary culture as defined by Marcus Tullius Cicero'.

533–5 Proverbial (see Tilley E 240); but a reference also to Wolsey's bad eye (see 1169).

543–64 An extended allusion to the story of Abdalonimus, a poor man, to whom Alexander gave the kingdom of Sidon.

572   cotyd] noted *Kit M*.

574-7   These lines imply that Wolsey is guilty of all seven of the Deadly Sins.

582-4   Evidently proverbial, though these lines have not been closely paralleled. For the friend/foe collocation see Whiting F 635, F 652.

597   As Dyce says (II 362), *Mahounde* (Mahomet) is not a character in any of the early miracle plays, though he is mentioned and sworn by. The ruler who characteristically 'dothe revyle and brall' in these plays is Herod. Compare, for example, *Towneley Plays* XVI 8off. Perhaps in 602-10 here Skelton has in mind the way in which Herod addresses his knights:

> ffy, losels and lyars! lurdans ilkon!
> Tratoures and well wars! knafys, but knyghtys none. (XVI, 163-4)

Interestingly, in this play the Messenger refers to Mahomet as Herod's cousin (54).

616   *gentell Jacke Breche*: Perhaps an invented name for an upstart, based on the proverb 'Jack would be a gentleman . . .' (Whiting J 9).

625-38   Wolsey's inaccessibility was notorious. Compare Giustiniani, *Despatches* II 315: '. . . no one obtains audience from him unless at the third or fourth attempt . . . he adopts this fashion with all the lords and barons of England . . .'

641-5   An allusion to the fact that Wolsey was chaplain to Sir Richard Nafnan until the latter's death in January 1507.

657   wonders] wonderous *Kit M*.

663-5   Compare *L & P* II, 2733: '. . . the Cardinall and the Duke of Suffolk, which the King hath brought up of nought, do rule him in all things even as they list; whether it be by necromancy, witchcraft or policy, no man knoweth'.

668   And] *not M. mad kote*: Proverbial (Whiting C 421).

669-71   Compare the lines from *Rede Me and Be Nott Wrothe*, an anti-Wolsey satire of 1528:

> His power he doth so extende
> That the kyngis letters to rende
> He will not forbeare in his rage.

(Ed. E. Arber, *English Reprints*, IV, 105.)

674-6   Compare Giustiniani, *Despatches* II 314: 'This cardinal is the person who rules both the king and the entire kingdom.'

679   wottith] wot *T Kit M*.

687-707   The story appears in Petrarch's *Epistolae de Rebus Familiaribus* I iii.

706   *Acon*: Aix la Chapelle.

713   practique] practyve *K*.

718-41   Robert Gaguin (1433-1501), whom Skelton mentions again in the *Garlande of Laurell* 374-5, had earlier been involved in a literary quarrel with Skelton (see H.L.R. Edwards, *MLR* XXXII, 1937, 430-34). By this time the quarrel appears to have been forgotten, for Skelton refers, without animosity, to the story of Cardinal Jean Balue (?1421-91) which appeared in Gaguin's *Compendium super Francorum Gestis* (1497). Skelton seems, however, to have used another source as well (for Gaguin does not mention Balue's chancellorship) and, moreover, one that was not very accurate for Balue was not executed (740) but ended his days prosperously in Italy.

756-9   Proverbial (Whiting M 735).

772-9   A passage alluding to Wolsey's low birth: the falcon is traditionally an aristocratic bird and the crow an upstart; similarly the mastiff is always associ-

ated with churls and the greyhound with the aristocracy. Compare Tilley M 743:
'The mastiff never loves the greyhound.'

784–840 This passage, referring to John Meautis, French Secretary to Henry
VIII, is obscure. In 822 Skelton admits he had not told all. It is certain that
Meautis lost his job and was replaced by Brian Tuke (*L & P* III, 2894), but the
reason for this is not known. Skelton in 832–3 strongly hints that he is dead, but
794 says he is not.

801   Dymingis Dale: Dimins Dale, Derbyshire, mentioned in the interlude *Ther-
sytes* as a haunt of witches:

And all other wytches that walke in dymminges dale.

(Ed. J.S. Farmer, *Six Anonymous Plays*, 1905, p. 220.)

802   Portyngale: Portugal.

804   'Beyond Sarmatia', a phrase from the opening of Juvenal's second satire.
Ovid was banished to this area and uses the phrase *Inter Sauromotas* twice (*Tristia*
III iii 6, V i 74). The Sarmatians lived between the Vistula and the Don. The
association between the Devil and the north was traditional, based on Isaiah xiv
13–14. As Archbishop of York, Wolsey had his seat in the north.

819   prothonotory] prothonetory *K.*

824   larger] large *M.*

841   *R resumes.*

846   *not R.*

853   flatery] flatteryng *R.*

856   Sym Sly] Symonye *R.*

858   best] *not R.*

859   best] most *R.*

861   Welthfull] Welthe full of felycyte *R.* Compare *Magnyfycence* 23.

871   outcry] dowte cry *R.*

874–87   These lines are obscure, perhaps deliberately so. Several activities are
alluded to: '*trey duse ase*' (3, 2, 1), '*ase in the face*' (1) and '*synke quater trey*' (5,
4, 3) are throws on the dice, and *tall man* is a slang term for a loaded dice. Lines
881–2 refer to dancing, and this is perhaps picked up in 888, if this line refers to
that dance called the 'hay' or 'heydeguies' (compare *Against Venemous Tongues* 46).
Lines 883–4 refer to tennis, since a *chase* is the second impact on the floor of a
ball which an opponent has not returned. The *chase* of line 872 seems to refer to
hunting. Since these are all courtly activities it may simply be that Skelton is
saying that the court wastes its time on games and sports while more important
things are allowed to deteriorate.

However, in fifteenth-century verse political questions are sometimes alluded
to in terms of tennis and dicing (see Scattergood, pp. 51–3, 359–60) and it may
be that Skelton intended these lines to be more specific. If so, perhaps this is
another allusion to the execution of Edward Stafford, third Duke of Bucking-
ham, in May 1521 (see lines 1–28, 121–2 and notes). He frequently played dice
and tennis with Henry VIII, sometimes for money (*L & P* III, 499); his high
social position may be alluded to in 886; and his badge in 889. Furthermore, the
hunting image in 872 may recall the similar reference to the *buck* in 122. But
such an interpretation must be tentative.

881–2   'Some remain at the level of society to which they were born.' Compare
Diodorus Siculus I 359 28–33.

883   me] well *R.*

886   tall] toll *R*.

887   He rode not but he ran *R*.

889   no] a *R*. Compare the proverb 'All his geese are swans' (Tilley G 369).

891   *not R*.

892–3   Datan, Abiram his brother and Korah questioned the authority of Moses and Aaron and were swallowed up into the earth (Numbers xvi 1–33). They were not 'of the tribe of Dan', as Skelton says, but this may have been included because the tribe was especially associated with wickedness (Genesis xlix 17).

892   they cursed] the course *R*.

895   'openly and secretly'.

896   *not R*. Balak was the king of Moab and Balaam a holy man whom he summoned to curse Israel (Numbers xxii–xxiv, Revelation ii 14).

897–8   Emperor Charles V was Grand Master of the Order of the Golden Fleece. He had visited London in 1522 and a welcoming pageant had depicted Jason and the Golden Fleece. His mother Juana, Duchess of Burgundy, was Flemish.

899   See yn Iaphether same *R*. The line seems to refer to the sons of Noah – Shem, Japheth and Ham (Genesis vi 10) – though the spelling Cam for Ham is unusual. It is, however, presumably what Skelton intended; see *Phyllyp Sparowe* 244.

900–914   These lines refer to the forced loans of 1522, which impoverished the wealthier citizens of London and the nobility:

'The kyng about this very tyme sent to the citie of London to borrow xx M poundes, whiche sore chafed the citizens, but the somme was promised, and for the payment the Mayer sent for none but for men of substaunce. Howbeit the craftes sold much of their plate.' (Hall, *Henry VIII*, I, p. 258)

907   Sir John Munday, a goldsmith, became Mayor of London on 28 October 1522.

910   Myght] Most *R*.

912   Pychers and pouchers *R*.

915   now] *not R*.

917   *Syr Trestram*: Tristram was one of King Arthur's knights, but here the name indicates anyone of noble rank.

918–19   Buckram and canvas are hard-wearing fabrics. *Cane* refers to Caen in Normandy, whence the English imported much canvas in the sixteenth century.

920   *not R*.

924   onyons] unyons *R*. Compare 371. *R*'s reading merely emphasizes the pun on *onyons*, meaning both 'onions' and 'unions'.

926   Cate] *not R*.

929   this] *not R*.

931   'be happy and do not cause trouble', a proverb (see Tilley L 92). But also an obsolete game of cards (see *OED laugh* v 1d).

933–52   These lines almost certainly refer to Thomas Spring (1456–1523), the wealthy cloth merchant of Lavenham (Suffolk). The particularly large amount Spring had to pay (944) seems to suggest that the passage refers to the forced loan demanded in August 1522, though 946–7 seem to refer to earlier demands, probably from the same year.

941   'because it is not enough'.

942   Proverbial (Whiting T 406).

947 An] And *K*.

950–53 *sprynge*: A multiple pun on 1. the proper name Spring; 2. young growth on a tree or a young tree; 3. a well.

952 nat ever flowe] never over flowe *R*.

955 of] *not T Kit M*. 'through the straits of Gilbraltar'.

956 *gybbet of Baldock*: This alludes to two stories, each with some relevance to Wolsey. In Esther vii 9, Haman, the ambitious politician and traitor, was hanged at Shushan (the ancient capital of Elam), of which the old name was Baldak. Also, the medieval outlaw, Jack-o-Legs, was first blinded then hanged by the townsmen of Baldock (Hertfordshire) whom he had robbed (see H.C. Andrews, *N & Q* CLXXXII, 1942, 231). For another reference see *Speke Parott* 73.

958 realmys] realme *M*. Perhaps this line refers to the Nine Worthies.

965 so] *not R*.

974 We nedyd never to feyre *R*.

977–80 Compare *Rede me, and be nott wrothe*:

> Yf he be as thou hast here sayde
> I wene the devils will be afrayde
> To have hym as a companion.

(Ed. E. Arber, *English Reprints*, IV, 105.)

981 fyer] fyrye *R*.

985 hell] all *R*.

987 *not R*.

988 And] And make *R*.

989 potestate] prostrate *R*.

991 Lucyfer] Lucyfers *K*.

998 *not R*.

999–1007 A complicated passage involving various puns, but based on Wolsey's love of his gardens at Hampton Court and York Place, a feature of which were the *herbers* (arbours), where he used to like to say his evening prayers. So the *peason* which grow profusely are, in one sense, flowers (presumably some variety of sweet-pea). But Skelton also implies that dicing and whoring went on in these gardens. *Folam* refers to 'Fulhams', a cant word for loaded dice, and, in one sense, this is the *game* that they *play*. In another sense, however, *game* means 'sexual delight' and *play* 'to indulge in sexual activity', so perhaps *ranke* applies not only to flowers but to the *lady bryght and shene*, in which case it may mean: 1. 'lustful or licentious', 2. 'numerous'. Compare Cavendish, *Life of Wolsey*, 'ther wanted no dames or damselles meate or apte to daunce wt the maskers or to garnysshe the place for the tyme wt other goodly disportes' (p. 25).

1008 dystrectyon] dyscrecyon *M R*.

1011 They can have no protectyon *K T Kit M*. The reading from *R*, adopted here, emphasizes what seems to be a shift to another subject, namely, Wolsey's control over those who have authority under his patronage (*protectyon*).

1015 his] him *T Kit M*.

1020 Careles] Marcyles *R*.

1022 bendyd] wendyd *R*.

1023 *not R*.

1026 tatterd] taxed *R*.

1032–3 *not R*.

1034 in] muche *R*.

1036   dolowre] dullness *R*.

1037   Englande] To Englande *R*.

1040   *not R*.

1043   *not R*.

1046   Lo] Soo *R*.

1053   named] name *M*.

1054   ofte] the *R*.

1059   flytynge] fiting *Kit M*.

1066–8   See Exodus v; but Skelton may also have in mind the raging Pharaoh of the miracle plays (see *The Towneley Plays* VIII 223–7).

1067   sore] *not R*.

1069   The wordis of God he lett *R*.

1077   *his wyfe*: Perhaps an allusion to Joan Larke, Wolsey's uncanonical wife and mother of his two children; or perhaps *wyfe* is to be taken in its generalized sense 'woman'.

1080   him] he *R*.

1081–5   See 219–23 and note. Compare also the charge against Wolsey in *Rede me, and be nott wrothe*:

> *Wat.*   Whatt abstinence useth he to take?
>
> *Jef.*   In Lent all fysshe he doth forsake
>   Fedde with partriges and plovers.
>
> *Wat.*   He leadeth then a Lutheran's lyfe?
>
> *Jef.*   O naye for he hath no wyfe
>   But whoares that be his lovers.

(Ed. E. Arber, *English Reprints*, IV, 57–8.)

1083   wyll] doeth *R*.

1084   *not R*.

1086   *not R*.

1087   for] *not Kit M*.

1088   The devyll wold swete *R*.

1089–90   Perhaps an allusion to sanctuary breaking, which Wolsey was accused of encouraging (see *L & P* IV, pp. 2550, 2557).

1097–100   From December 1521 until 1529 Wolsey held the rich abbacy of St Albans *in commendam* (i.e. he took its revenues until a proper incumbent could be provided). This was against the wishes of the monks, against normal practice, and against the decrees of the Fifth Lateran Council (1512–17).

1101–2   Under the strenght of the greate seale
           Thys now he dothe meale *R*.

1102   'on his authority as chancellor'.

1103   *not R*. Wolsey had obtained the office of *legatus a latere* from Leo X in May 1518. This sort of legate was the Pope's representative and answerable to him. Skelton is hinting that to hold this position was inconsistent with being also Lord Chancellor, who was answerable to the King.

1106   of] *not M*.

1108   first] *not R*.

1108–16   Compare Hall, *Henry VIII*, I, p. 167: 'under colour of reformacion he (i.e. Wolsey) gat muche treasure, and nothyng was reformed, but came to more mischief'.

1114   *not R*.

1115   gracelesse] ungratyous *R*.

1117–26   In his capacity as Archbishop of York Wolsey was subordinate to William Warham, Archbishop of Canterbury from 1503 to 1532. But his power as legate enabled him, in certain things, to have authority. As early as 1519 Warham complained about Wolsey's interference in his affairs (see *L & P* III 98, 127).

1127   And now he makethe dyrectyon *R.*

1129   great] brode *R.*

1135   He juggeth hymselfe equypolent *R.*

1139   apostyll] wholly apostle *R.*

1143   According to early Christian tradition, Peter was the first bishop of Antioch.

1147   St Dunstan (*c*.924–98), Archbishop of Canterbury, was chief adviser and close friend of King Edgar of Wessex.

1148   to We] to mee *T Kit M*; we *R.*

1153   'Behold a mighty priest', the opening of the lesson from the Confessor Bishop Mass.

1154   hed: 1. control; 2. behead.

1154–6   Compare Lindsay's *Ane Satyre of the Thrie Estaits* 3217–220:

Sum sayis ane king is cum amang vs,
  That purposis to head and hang vs:
  Thair is na grace gif he may fang vs
    Bot on an pin.

1161   *causa sanguinis*: 'a case which may result in a death sentence', on which cases the clergy traditionally did not sit in judgement.

1164   Perhaps a reference to Lamentations iii 1.

1165   The flayle] *not R.*

1166   Sirus] tyrus *R. Naman Sirus* refers to Naaman the Syrian (II Kings v), who was a leper. Since syphilis, which Skelton hints that Wolsey has, was frequently at this time confused with leprosy the comparison is a pointed one. See J.J. Abraham, *British Journal of Surgery* XXXII, 1944, 234–5.

1169–74   See lines 209–12, 533–5 and notes.

1169   afore] before *Kit M R.*

1170   wene that] say *R.*

1172   they] the *K.*

1173–4   By ther craft and surgerye
        He ys in *manus domini R.*

1174   'It is the hand of the Lord.'

1175   *Antiochus* was the proud and boastful king of the Syrians who was struck down by a loathsome and incurable disease (II Maccabees ix).

1177   *not R.*

1179   That] *not R.*

1181   nowe] *not R.*

1183   trust] harte *R.*

1184   *Balthasor*: Balthasar de Guercis, physician to Katherine of Aragon.

1185   was] *not R.*

1190–93   These lines must refer to the 'Domingo' who is recorded as the recipient of money he won from the king at gambling in *The Privy Purse Expenses of King Henry the Eight*, ed. Sir H. Nicolas, 1827, pp. 17, 32, 33, etc.

1194   nose] pose *M.*

1195   puskylde] pusky *R*; pose] nose *Kit.*

1196 gummys] gynnys R. Perhaps this refers to the Arabian 'gum acacia', a soothing medicine.

1202 aske] make R.

1203 suggestyon] subjectyon R.

1212 glorious] gromys R.

1216–17 All editions read thus and continue without a break into the Invective. After 1215 R has '*finis*' and '*contra quendam doctorem suum calumpniatorem, quia difficile est naturam scribere*'. As they stand in the text these lines are taken from Juvenal's *Satire* i 30, 'because it is difficult not to write satire'.

Heading not K T Kit M. 'Against a certain doctor, his calumniator.' To whom these lines refer is not known. Presumably it was someone who had criticized Skelton for his attack on Wolsey. *furred hode* (19) could indicate either academic or religious dress, but if *decretorum* (9) is accepted it would seem the man was a doctor of canon law. William Lyly has been suggested, but his main achievements were in grammar, not law, and he had no degree, which the calumniator seems to have had (6).

4   escape] be R.

5   shall] *not* R.

9   *decretorum*] *diricum* K T Kit M.

10 From Juvenal's *Satire* viii 140–41:
omne animi vitium tanto conspectius in se
crimen habet, quanto maior qui peccat habetur
('the more distinguished the criminal's name, the more marked the guiltiness of the sin in his soul').

15 horyble] dyshonorable R.

16 any] yn any R.

17 nere] nott R.

19 your] a R.

20 ye (1st)] *not* R.

27 And espetyally to make a lye R.

29 'For soap is not cinnamon.' It is difficult to be sure to what this cryptic line refers. Williams (p. 233) may be right when he suggests that Skelton is alluding to God's instructions to Moses for the consecration of priests in Exodus xxx, which mentions both washing (verses 18–21) and anointing with oil made from, amongst other things, *sweet cinnamon* (23). Skelton may be saying that no matter how much Wolsey may wash himself with soap to cure his diseases, that does not make him fit to be a priest.

30 'But about the absent nothing but good', a slightly altered version of the common saying *de mortuis nil nisi bonum* ('about the dead nothing except good').

34 After this line R. has *finis* and concludes.

Epitome: 'Here follows the epitome about the diseased Thomas, and also about the obscene Polyphemus etc. Next about the very fine dissimulator Pandulph, the great legate, formerly so much feared as a prelate, now stretched out like Naaman the Syrian, now living in solitude, oppressed by the Neapolitan disease, laid low under plaster poultices, pierced by the surgeon's iron instrument, relieved by nothing, nor made better by any medicine, his servants left to servitude, for which infamy may be borne. But a greater madness is evident. If only, therefore, that profligate, that bad Cretan lord, more aptly called disgusting, a mad fanatic, would keep away from the brothel. So the skilful

prosodian asserts. This sort of composition does not need examination in hundredfold speech, or in the *Centimetrum* of the honoured grammarian Maurus.'
Poliphemo: Polyphemus (aptly compared with Wolsey because of his one eye), who imprisoned Ulysses.

2   Pandulphum: Pandulph, the papal legate sent by Innocent III to King John to settle the dispute about the archbishopric of Canterbury.

4   elongatum] *longatum M.*

12   Quo] *quod M.*

16   The Cretans had a bad reputation (Epistle to Titus i 12–16).

22   eget] *egit K T Kit M.*

24–7   A reference to Maurus Servius Honoratus, who wrote a book called *Centimetrum*.

Decastichon: 'A virulent ten lines about a mitred Lycaon of the sea etc. Oh, alas, behold a wolf from the sea and a most wicked bear, a butcher's bull-calf, a wretched British peasant, a bloated bull-calf like Oreb, or Zalmunna or Zeeb, a thistle, a harsh Aʾaph and a reprobate Datan, a flattering Achitophel to the king, among the British the complete sinner for Thomas confounds churches everywhere; this is not the holy Thomas, but Golias with a hard heart who rides a mule. Satan, I implore you, may his fundament excrete, discharging pitch. I pray, read this cautious poem; nothing is more cruel than a wretch who reaches a high position.'

galeratum: 'wearing a priest's cap', therefore 'mitred' in Wolsey's case.

Licaonta marinum: Lycaon was transformed into a wolf because he sacrificed human flesh to Zeus. See also *Speke Parott* 289, where Wolsey is also compared to this man. Skelton is playing on *Licaonta marinum* and *maris lupus* (1) and the Cardinal's name: 'wolf-sea' and 'Wolsey'.

3   Oreb . . . Salmane . . . Zeb: Midianites who fought against Gideon (Judges vii and viii 5, Psalm lxxxiii 11).

4   Asaphque: Possibly a reference to Henry Standish, Bishop of St Asaph from 1518, but more likely mentioned simply because Psalm lxxxiii, alluded to in the previous line, is designated a song 'of Asaph'.

5   Acchitiphel: King David's councillor who advised Absalom to revolt (II Samuel xv–xvii).

7   sacer iste Thomas: Thomas Becket, martyred at Canterbury in 1170. *Goleas*: a name commonly given to educated Latin authors of the twelfth and thirteenth centuries who wrote somewhat ribald verse; perhaps applied to Wolsey because goliards were often renegade clerics, or perhaps because the word designates gluttony (Latin *gula*).

8   cacet] *caret T Kit M.*

10   quum surget in altum] *not M.* Skelton's line is a slightly altered version of Claudian's '*Asperius nihil est humili cum surgit in altum*' (*In Eutropium* I 181), where it relates to a eunuch chamberlain who, in 399, claimed the consulship.

Apostrophe: 'Apostrophe to the citizens of London, (while the ass with a golden mitre spurs on a mule) on encountering a little ass etc. See, the ass rouses the mule, a marvellous sight, with his heels. O citizens, oppose your little ass who rules the realm and the king, who governs your estates, your wealth, your money, your treasures, by plundering. Jestingly, but without deceit, he (the poet) has related the paradox of the ass with the golden mitre.'

ad] *an K T Kit M.*

aselli] *Dyce's emendation, aguile K T Kit M.*

1   mulum] multum T Kit M.
2–4   Perhaps an allusion to the forced loans of 1522.

XXI   GARLANDE OF LAURELL

The question of date presents many difficulties. Dyce and subsequent scholars based their estimates on the date of Fakes's edition, the astrological opening (1–7), and the reference to Janus and the new year (1514–18), and took it that the poem was composed at the beginning of 1523. The ladies to whom the lyrics were addressed (836–1085) were identified accordingly as Countess Elizabeth Stafford Howard, wife of Thomas Howard, Earl of Surrey and the third Duke of Norfolk (who died in 1554) and others. Stahlman and Gingerich, however, basing their conclusions on 1–7, suggested May 1495 as the most likely date for the original version of the poem (*Solar and Planetary Longitudes for the Years −2500–+2000 by Ten Day Intervals*, Wisconsin 1963). M.J. Tucker, accepting this, found that 1495 was the only time the Howards were definitely residing at Sheriff Hutton Castle, Yorkshire, where, according to its headings, the poem was written (*ELN IV*, 1967, 254–9). Furthermore, he showed that the Countess of Surrey referred to was probably Elizabeth Tylney Howard, wife of Thomas Howard, Earl of Surrey and Duke of Norfolk, who died in 1524. Most of the other ladies to whom lyrics were addressed he identifies with her relatives or acquaintances (*RQ XXII*, 1969, 333–45).

But though 1495 appears to be an important date in connection with the poem, parts of it were obviously written at other times. If the recipient of lines 906–25 is to be identified with the daughter of Henry Wentworth and Anne Say (see note) the lyric must have been composed before 22 October 1494, when she married John Seymour. Similarly, if lines 1004–37 are indeed addressed to Margaret, wife of John Hussey, they must have been written before 4 August 1492, by which date she was dead. Lines 1261–366 appear to be a reply to Barclay's attack on *Phyllyp Sparowe*, so they must post-date 1509, and at least one of the works mentioned in lines 1170–504 (*Collyn Clout* 1234) dates from as late as the 1520s.

In the present state of our knowledge it looks as if Skelton began seriously to assemble the poem in 1495, using some lyrics he had composed earlier. Subsequently, he added to it and printed the whole thing in 1523. The original occasion for the poem may have been a celebration at Sheriff Hutton Castle among the friends of the Duchess of Norfolk of Skelton's laureation – a distinction conferred on him for pre-eminence in rhetoric by the University of Oxford in 1488, by Louvain in 1492 and by Cambridge in 1493.

'In one respect the *Garlande of Laurell* stands without a parallel: the history of literature affords no second example of a poet having deliberately written sixteen hundred lines in honour of himself' (Dyce I xlix). Nor are the literary affinities of the poem obvious. A.S. Cook pointed out (*MLR XI*, 1916, 7–14) that several passages of the poem are similar to parts of Chaucer's *House of Fame*, and E. Schulte draws attention to similarities with Petrarch's *Triumph of Fame* (*La Poesia di John Skelton*, Naples 1963, 170–201). But in neither case are the correspondences close enough to suggest direct borrowing.

This poem was printed by Richard Fakes on 3 October 1523 (*F*) and again by Marshe in 1568 (*M*). A depleted version also appears in BL MS Cotton Vitellius E x ff. 208r–225v (*C*). *F* provides the earliest and best text, but is deficient in places. Various lines are omitted: 337–43, 407–13, 662, and the second envoy 1587–602. Some lines are transposed – 1434–5, 1448–9 – and there are various mistakes on individual words. The Latin lines on the laurel and the three versions of the 'abuses of the age', which are appended to the poem in *F*, but which occur separately in *M*, are here included but with separate lineation.

Title: The Crowne of Lawrell *M*.

Eterno . . . Adonis] *not M C*. 'While the stars shine remaining in everlasting day, and while the seas swell, this our laurel shall be green: our famous name shall be echoed to the skies, and everywhere Skelton shall be remembered as another Adonis.'

Adonis: A beautiful youth beloved of Venus, mortally wounded by a boar. The anemone was supposed to have sprung from his blood.

6 plenarly] plenary *F M*.

9 Proverbial (Whiting F 305, F 317).

10 On] One *F*.

11 Proverbial (Whiting F 523).

22–3 The Forest of Galtres, which surrounded Sheriff Hutton Castle, was described by Camden as 'swampy' in places (*Britannia*, ed. Gough, iii 20). The reading 'wose' is established by reference to *Diodorus Siculus* page 18 line 17 and other occurrences of the tag 'myry wose' (see the note of Salter and Edwards on page 397). *F* reads 'mose'.

26 tell] telle now *C*.

27 well] *not C*.

28 purpose] proces *C*.

35 not tell] not wele tell *C*.

43 that] it *C*.

48 *Pallas*: Otherwise Athena, or Minerva to the Romans. She was the daughter of Zeus and Metis and the wisest and most powerful of goddesses.

53 scyence] sciences *M*. The *scyence sevyn* refers to the seven liberal arts of medieval curricula: a *trivium* of Grammar, Logic and Rhetoric, and a *quadrivium* of Arithmetic, Music, Geometry and Astronomy.

54 leven] lene *F C*.

58 a] in *C*.

60 he his tyme] his tyme he *C*.

68 they were the] the were they *F*.

70 grete] a *M*.

74 Elyconis] Elycoms *F*. Properly Helicon was a range of mountains in Boeotia, sacred to Apollo and the Muses. The celebrated fountains of the Muses, Aganippe and Hippocrene, were there.

79 that] for that *C*.

81 Perhaps an earlier form of Tilley R 141: 'Rivers need a spring.'

83–7 Compare *Collyn Clout* 15–37.

83 publisshe] pullishe *C*.

85 so] *not C*.

93 Ovid (43 BC–AD 17) was banished by Caesar Augustus to Tomi, on the Euxine, near the mouth of the Danube, ostensibly for the licentiousness of his *Ars Amatoria*.

95 Juvenal (*c.*55–*c.*140) was banished in about 93 by Domitian, perhaps to Syrene in Upper Egypt, precisely why is not known. Tradition, based on *Satire* vii 90–92, has it that it was because of an attack on the ballet dancer and actor Paris, Domitian's favourite.

96   certayne envectyfys] that he enveiyd *C*.

97   on] upon *M*. The line is based on a proverb (Whiting G 7).

99–105   Compare *Why Come Ye Nat to Courte?* 121–2 for an example of this sort of writing. For verses which pun on animal names see Robbins, *Historical Poems* Nos. 75, 84, 87, 89, 90.

106   ther] that *C*.

107   conjecture] convecture *F*.

123–9   The references to Aristotle (384–322 BC), Plato (*c*.429–347 BC) and Diogenes the Cynic philosopher (*c*.400–*c*.325 BC) are clear enough. But the Cato referred to may be either Marcus Porcius Cato (243–149 BC), whose *De Re Rustica* has survived, or, more likely, Skelton may have in mind Dionysius Cato, the supposed author of the popular collection of maxims known as the *Distichs*, written probably in the third or fourth centuries.

126   that] *not C*.

130ff.   In 330 BC Aeschines (*c*.397–*c*.322 BC) accused Ctesiphon of proposing that Demosthenes (384–322 BC) should be rewarded for his services to Athens with a golden crown. In reply Demosthenes delivered his famous oration *On the Crown* which defeated Aeschines, who withdrew from Athens to Asia Minor and established a school of eloquence at Rhodes.

131   That] Whiche *C*.

132   by] through *M*.

134   my good syster] goode my sister *C*.

143   barrid] debarrid *C*.

149   it] it is *C*.

151–4   '...whose written attack was very effective in provoking Demosthenes to set out brilliantly his skilful argument, from which Aeschines could not escape'.

161   For] Sithe *C*.

162ff.   This refers to Jerome's *Epistle to Paulinus*, prefixed to the Vulgate, which begins, '*Frater Ambrosius*...'. It contains the story of how Aeschines used to praise the skill of Demosthenes to his pupils.

171   But a grete parte yet] Bot yit a grete parte *C*.

180   ye do] tyme ye *C*.

181   For] *not C*.

184   pyke] kit *C*.

185   the] their *M*.

188   lidderons] lidderous *F*.

189   some] and sum *C*.

196   they ryde and rinne] ryde they and ryn they *C*.

197   ye shall] shall ye *C*.

200   but] but a *C*.

201   be out] be set out *MC*.

205–10   Compare *Collyn Clout* 28–32. For *Jacke a thrummis bybille* compare *Magnyfycence* 1427 and *Collyn Clout* 282 and note.

207   well fynde] fynde wele *C*.

209   hym] *not C*.

213   '...but I brought forward as my excuse your kind forbearance...'

215   good] *not C*.

224   be] be be *F*.

235   *Eolus*: In Homer, Aeolus was the ruler of the Aeolian islands to whom Zeus had given dominion over the winds. Compare Chaucer's *House of Fame* 1571ff. that] whiche *C*.

237   a] the *C*.

239   wyll] dare *C*.

242   you] *not C*.

246–720   *not C*.

272   *Orpheus*: This mythical figure was regarded by the Greeks as the most celebrated of poets who lived before Homer. He was the son of Oeagrus and Calliope and lived in Thrace. Apollo presented him with a lyre and the Muses taught him how to play so well that the wild beasts and the rocks and trees upon Olympus moved from their places to follow the sound of his music.

273   *Amphion*: On a lyre he had received from Hermes Amphion played with such magic skill that stones moved of their own accord to form a defensive wall for Thebes. *Archady*: Arcadia, a country in the middle of Peloponnesus, whose inhabitants were famed as musicians.

287–322   Based, at times very closely, on the story of Phoebus and Daphne from Ovid's *Metamorphoses* i 452–567. Among his various attributes Phoebus was god of the sun (hence 289) and of medicine (hence 310–15). Daphne resisted Phoebus because Cupid had struck her with the leaden dart which expels love (290).

295   murnynge] murmynge *F*.

296   'O thoughtfull herte': Compare Lydgate's *Life of Our Lady* i: 'O thoughtfull herte, plunged in distresse', and *Dyvers Balettys and Dyties Solacyous* iii 10.

302   his] this *M*.

303   *Diana*, the goddess of chastity.

304   'O merciless lady, your star is unfavourable.'

314   gresse] gras *F*.

326   Declamacyons] declynacyons *F. olde Quintiliane with his Declamacyons*: Marcus Fabius Quintilianus (first century AD) was almost certainly not the author of the 164 declamations which go under his name, though the 145 *declamationes minores* bear some relation to parts of his *De Institutione Oratoria*.

327   Theocritus (*c*.300–*c*.260 BC) was chiefly famous for his *Idylls*, which are descriptions of rural life.

328   iconomicar] iconomucar *FM*. The work Skelton has in mind here is Hesiod's *Works and Days*, which amongst other things contains economic precepts.

329   *Homerus*: Homer, the ninth-century BC Greek epic poet.

330–32   Marcus Tullius Cicero (106–43 BC), the most famous of Roman orators, as consul in 63 BC was instrumental in crushing a plot led by Lucius Sergius Catalina (d. 62 BC). Caius Sallustius Crispus (86–?34 BC), the historian, wrote an account of this conspiracy, and also the history of the Roman war against Jugurtha, king of Numidia.

334   *Bacchus*: In Roman mythology the god of wine.

335   flotis] droppes *F*. In lines 349, 356, 363, 370, 377, 384, both *F* and *M* read *dropis* (in various spellings). Here, and at 342, *M* reads *flotis*, which I take to be the better reading: it provides a fuller rhyme with *throtis*; and is a more forceful and difficult word.

337–43   *not F*.

337 Lucan: Marcus Anneus Lucanus (39–65). *Stacius*: Publius Papinius Statius (*c.*45–*c.*96) wrote, amongst other heroic poems, the unfinished *Achilleis*.
338 Percius: Aulus Persius Flaccus (34–62), the author of six satires.
339 Virgill the Mantuan: Publius Vergilius Maro (70–19 BC), author of the *Aeneid*, was born near Mantua.
344–6 Titus Livius (59 BC–AD 17) wrote a *History of Rome* in 142 books, divided into *decades* of ten books each by early scribes.
347 Enyus: Quintus Ennius (239–169 BC), whose most important work, now lost, was an epic called *Annales*, a history of Rome from the earliest times to his own day.
351 Aulus Gellius (*c.*130–*c.*180) was a grammarian who also wrote the *Noctes Atticae*, a set of extracts from Greek and Roman writers.
352 Quintus Horatius Flaccus (65–8 BC) wrote an *Art of Poetry* which Skelton seems to have in mind here. But to call it 'new poetry' looks like the result of confusion between it and the *Nova Poetria* of Geoffrey of Vinsauf (fl. 1210).
353 Mayster Terence: Publius Terentius Afer (*c.*190–*c.*159 BC), the comic poet and dramatist.
354 full] *not M. Plautus*: Titus Maccius Plautus (*c.*254–*c.*184 BC), author of some twenty plays, and the most famous comic dramatist of Rome.
358 with] wit *F. Senek*: Lucius Anneus Seneca (3 BC–AD 65), author of ten tragedies, with various other works of a stoical temper.
359 Boyce: Boethius, a Roman statesman and author, first favoured then imprisoned and put to death by Theodoric the Ostrogoth in 524. While in prison he wrote his *De Consolatione Philosophiae*, one of the most influential books of the Middle Ages.
360–61 A reference to the *Elegiarum Liber* of Maximianus, six poems lamenting the evils of old age and recalling the exploits of his youth. Line 361 seems to allude to his encounter, in *Elegy* v, with a young girl.
365 Apparently a reference to the encyclopaedic works of Giovanni Boccaccio (1313–75), such as *De Genealogia Deorum, De Casibus Virorum Illustrium* and *De Claris Mulieribus*.
366 Cursius] Cursus *F*.
366–7 Quintus Curtius Rufus, the first-century writer of a history of Alexander the Great in ten books, two of which are lost.
367–8 In about 400 Macrobius wrote a commentary on Cicero's *Somnium Scipionis*, originally Chapter VI of his *De Republica*. In Macrobius's version the work was widely known in the Middle Ages.
372–3 A reference to the *Facetiae* of the Florentine humanist, Poggio Bracciolini, which were well known in England at this time.
374–5 Robert Gaguin (1433–1501), author of the *Compendium super Francorum Gestis* (1497), whom Skelton had earlier written against according to line 1187 (see H.L.R. Edwards, *MLR* XXXII, 1937, 430–34). See also *Why Come Ye Nat to Courte?* 718–41 and note.
379 Plutarke: Plutarchus, the first-century biographer and philosopher, author of the *Parallel Lives* of Greeks and Romans. *Petrarke*: Francesco Petrarca (1304–74).
380 Lucilius: Caius Lucilius (died *c*. 102 BC), a satirist. *Valerius Maximus*: The first-century author of the collection of historical anecdotes called *De Factis Dictisque Memorabilibus Libri IX*.

381   Vincent of Beauvais, thirteenth-century author of the *Speculum Maius*, first printed in 1473.

382   Sextus Aurelius Propertius (b. 50 BC), the Roman elegiac poet, and, apparently, Pisander, a Greek poet mentioned by Macrobius, *Saturnalia Convivia* v 2.

386ff.   To refer together to Gower, Chaucer and Lydgate as the founders of English poetry was, at this time, a commonplace. See *Phyllyp Sparowe* 784–812.

389   ennewed] a meude *F*.

404   ye] *not F*.

405   *Brutus Albion*: According to medieval tradition Brutus, the descendant of Aeneas, was the founder of Britain.

Poeta Skelton . . . 413] not F.

Mayster Chaucer to Skelton] Maister Chaucher Lawreat poete to Skelton *M*.

421–2   To praise Chaucer for his *pullisshyd eloquence* was common among poets of the fifteenth and early sixteenth centuries. See J.A. Burrow, ed., *Geoffrey Chaucer: A Critical Anthology*, 1969, pp. 41–6.

443   tofore] before *M*.

446   sore] so sore *M*.

451   wyl to hym] to hym will *M*.

457   far] *not F*.

462   worde] worlde *M*. So also at lines 486 and 716. The form in *F* is not a mistake, but simply the less usual spelling.

473   the] the rokky *M*.

492   a] *not M*.

493   *Poyle*: Apulia. *Trace*: Thrace.

497   *the mayne lande*: According to Eleanor Hammond 'probably the Almayne land, Germany' (p. 515).

501   Proverbial (Whiting E 45).

504   *fals quarter*: A soreness on the inside of a horse's hoof (see Dyce II 312).

514   *v portis*: The Cinque Ports – Dover, Sandwich, Romney, Hastings, Hythe.

530   I then] than I *M*.

533–6   Compare *The Canterbury Tales* I 1491 ff. Titan is the sun, since Helios, the sun god, was descended from Hyperion and Thia, who were Titans.

541   *port salu*: 'a safe port'. For the ship image compare *Collyn Clout* 1251–5 and note.

542   Ye] The *F*.

545   that] so *M*.

553   Caspian] Gaspian *F*. Perhaps by *hillis Caspian* Skelton has in mind the Caucasus Mountains.

563–5   Compare Dante's words to Virgil in *Inferno* xi 13–15: '*alcun compenso/ . . . trova, che il tempo non passi / Perduto*' ('some compensation . . . find so that the time is not wasted').

567   Proverbial (Tilley W 777).

575   thos] these *M*.

590   *a lybbard*: The heraldic beast in the English royal arms.

596–601   These lines are the despair of editors. A marginal note '*Cacosinthicon ex industria*' indicates they are 'something ill put together'. 597–8 are based on Juvenal's *Satire* viii 129–30, and 601 on Virgil's *Eclogue* v 16. The lines may be translated as follows:

'You bear things to be feared beyond measure, the very thunderbolts of
Jupiter. With curved talons he is as ready to go to various dangerous places as
was Celaeno the harpy to get treasure from Phoebus. Arms, plague,
lamentation, gall, force, fraud, a barbarous world! You wander a thousand
ways to seek for yourself the strife of Mars. Let the wild nard give place to the
scorned and thorny rose-tree.'

Hammond (pp. 515–16) suggests that the subject of these lines is Industry and
that Skelton is 'alluding to his own industrious use of letters as a weapon of
attack'. But since these lines come from the English heraldic beast perhaps the
subject of them is England. See *A Lawde and Prayse* 27 for the rose as a symbol
of England.

607 haskardis] hastardis *F*.

610 Proverbial; see Tilley C 460, 'Let them that be acold blow at the coal', and
also *Why Come Ye Nat to Courte?* 84.

613 wyll] well *M*. *Powle hatchettis*: 'Soldiers who use pole-axes'. Compare 'My
darlyng dere . . .' 28 and note.

620 Proverbial (Whiting S 580).

623 Compare the gunfire in Dunbar's *Golden Targe* 238 which ends his vision.

629 to-jaggid] to lagged *M*.

632 Compare Whiting H 113 and H 116, and also S 100.

636 *Pers Prater*: 'Peter the talker'.

641 Compare *Phyllyp Sparowe* 409. The doterell is a kind of plover, so named
because it foolishly allows itself to be caught.

642 Compare *Collyn Clout* 416 and note.

662 *not F.*

667–70 The phoenix was supposed to be a unique mythical bird which lived
for five or six hundred years in the Arabian desert, after which it burnt itself to
ashes and arose young again to live through another cycle of years.

670 *the swete olyve* was, according to classical tradition, the thing most useful to
men. In the reign of Cecrops, Pallas Athene and Poseidon contended for the
possession of Athens. The gods agreed to give the city to whoever produced the
gift most useful to men. Poseidon produced the horse, Pallas the olive. The *M*
reading 'rancour' for *cancour* at 672 may be the result of a typographical mistake,
but is more likely to be due to the traditional association of the olive with peace
based on Genesis viii 11.

675 *Saby*: Henderson emends to 'Araby'. But probably Sheba (I Kings x,
Psalm lxxii 10) or possibly Seba (Psalm lxxii 10, Isaiah xliii 3) is meant.

677 *Zepherus*: Zephyrus, the personification of the west wind.

678 and] *not F.*

680 With] Wit *F*. *Pierides by name*: The Muses were so named from Pieria, in
south-east Macedonia, supposedly their birth-place.

681 Testalis] Testalus *F*. *Phillis and Testalis*: Perhaps Skelton derived these
names from Mantuan's *Eclogue* iv 176, 'Thestylis et Phyllis, Galatea, Neaera,
Lycoris', or from Alexander Barclay's *Eclogue* ii 385–6.

685 *Flora*: The Roman goddess of flowers and spring.

687 *Cintheus*: Cynthus was a mountain in Delos, the supposed birth-place of
Apollo, who was for this reason called Cynthius.

688–704 Based on *Aeneid* i 740ff.:

> *Cithara crinitus Iopas*
> *Personat aurata, docuit quae maximus Atlas.*
> *Hic canit errantem lunam, solisque labores;*
> *Unde hominum genus, et pecudes; unde imber, et ignes:*
> *Arcturum, pluviasque Hyadas, geminosque Triones;*
> *Quid tantum Oceano properent se tinguere soles*
> *Hiberni, vel quae tardis mora noctibus obstet.*

'The long-haired Iopas, who had been taught by the great Atlas, performed on the lyre adorned with gold. He sang of the wandering moon, and the labours of the sun; the origin of men and beasts, rain and fire; of Arcturus and the rainy Hyades, and of the two Bears; why the suns of winter hasten so fast to dip themselves into the Ocean, and what holds back the nights and makes them slow.'

Iopas was the Carthaginian poet who sang before Aeneas. *Atlas*, because he had supported the other Titans, was condemned by Zeus to bear heaven on his head and hands. The other references are to star constellations of the northern sky: the Great Bear, the Little Bear and the Pleiades, or Seven Sisters (though these last are not identical with Virgil's 'Hyades' – a group of five stars in Taurus).

699   Trions] Troons *F*. Properly the Latin word *Triones* meant 'ploughing oxen', but it was frequently used (as by Virgil above) to refer to the constellation of the Wain, i.e. the Great Bear and the Little Bear, which were compared to a wagon with oxen yoked to it.

705   and] and in *M*.

706   it] in *M*.

715   *Jupiter*: In Roman mythology the highest and most powerful of the gods, the ruler of heaven.

741   fals mesuris out] owght fals mesuris *C*.

Interpolata . . . 751: 'An interpolated satire on the poet's adversary, which demands an industrious interpreter. At first glance a sort of threepenny driver, second a sort of slave: hunting gnats, he sends sidelong glances from his little eyes, look, he grasps, grabs, seizes winged flies. Whatever Maia cherishes, or Jupiter, or whatever cold things Saturn cherishes, or the Sun, or Mars, or Venus or the chilly Moon, if you should chance to put it into words or commit it to writing, immediately his heart begins to sweat with silent guilt. For this reason he rushes into the flames, he urges on this one and that, arousing them, he eggs them on to strife, however he kindles vain fires, muttering in silence; let Codrus rupture himself.'

Some phrases in these lines are based on or taken whole from classical authors. *Tressis agasonis* is based on '*tressis agaso*' of Persius, *Satire* v 76; *tacita sudant praecordia culpa* is from Juvenal, *Satire* i 167; *Labra movens tacitus* is based on '*Labra moves tacitus*' of Persius, *Satire* v 184; and *rumpantur ut ilia Codro* is from Virgil, *Ecologue* vii 26. Codrus was a poet hostile to Virgil. Davus is the name of a slave in Plautus and Terence.

Maia, the eldest and most beautiful of the Pleiades, was the mother of Hermes (Mercury). The allusion in 745–6 is to the seven 'planets' of the solar system, other than Earth, known at this time; and also to the seven fundamental metals of alchemy, as the marginal note indicates: '*Nota Alchimiam et 7 metalla*'.

The numbers which follow these Latin lines refer, by a simple code, to the name of Skelton's enemy. The numbers below five refer to the vowels in their order of occurrence in the alphabet; the other numbers refer to the letters of the alphabet in the order of occurrence, taking *i/j* as one letter. This gives ROGERUS STATHUM (see Henry Bradley, *Academy*, 1 August 1896). The Roger Statham to whom these lines refer has not been satisfactorily identified. M.J. Tucker (*RQ* XXII, 1969, 339–40) conjectures that Skelton may have been, at some time, in love with Gertrude Anstey (see lines 1038–42), who rejected him in favour of Roger Statham. Hence Skelton's ill temper in these Latin lines.

Interpolata . . . adversarium] not *C*.

744   *appetit*]   *Dyce's emendation, opetit F M C*.

754   and]   if *M*.

755   were to stande in his lyght]   is to stop up his sight *C*.

761   set men a feightynge]   stir men to brawlyng *C*; syt] set *F*.

766   forth]   *not C*.

767   a]   *not F*.

769   *Cowntes of Surrey*: Identified by Dyce, on the assumption that the poem was written in 1523, as Elizabeth Howard, née Stafford, who died in 1558, wife of Thomas Howard II, Earl of Surrey and later Duke of Norfolk. M.J. Tucker, however, probably rightly, identifies her with Elizabeth Howard, née Tulney, who died in 1497, wife of Thomas Howard I, Earl of Surrey and Duke of Norfolk, who died in 1524 (*ELN* IV, 1967, 254–9).

771   a beve]   above *F*.

795   ther]   the *C*.

797   whyte]   whyght as *C*. For the proverb *whyte as mylke* see Whiting M 545.

800   whyte]   whyght blak *C*.

801   *broken warkis*: Eleanor Hammond suggests that this may be a phrase like 'broken ground' and refer to raised surfaces in heavy embroidery (p. 518).

804   byrdis in bowris]   bothe birddis and bowres *C*.

819   *your proces after there degre*: Occupation's instructions to Skelton here prepare for the particularly decorous way in which the eleven lyrics to ladies are organized. Assuming the identifications of M.J. Tucker (*RQ* XXII, 1969, 333–45) to be right, it will be seen that the persons highest in rank and most closely related to Elizabeth Tylney Howard, Countess of Surrey, are praised in rhyme-royal stanzas, the noblest of verse forms and fittest for important subjects (see R.H. Robbins, *Secular Lyrics of the XIVth and XVth Centuries*, 1954, xlvii-li). The other seven ladies, less high in social rank and not immediately related to the Countess, are treated in a variety of other forms.

answeryth]   *not C*.

824   *Mynerve*: The Roman goddess, equivalent to Pallas Athene in Greek mythology, of wisdom and knowledge; hence 825.

826   *Mercury* is invoked here because he was traditionally the god of eloquence.

830   and]   *not C*.

842   *formar date*: Perhaps 'highest quality'.

843–4   A reference to Polynices, son of Oedipus and Jocasta, and to his wife Argia, discussed in Boccaccio's *De Claris Mulieribus*, Chapter 27.

845–6   For Rebekah see Genesis xxiv 15ff.

850–51   For Pamphila and her weaving see Pliny's *Naturalis Historia* xi, 26, and Boccaccio's *De Claris Mulieribus*, Chapter 42.

852 Thamar is Timarete, daughter of Mycon the painter, mentioned in Pliny's *Naturalis Historia* xxxv 40, and also in Boccaccio's *De Claris Mulieribus*, Chapter 54.

857–8 Cyrus, founder of the Persian empire, in 529 BC marched against the Massagetae but was defeated and Tomyris, their queen, cut off his head and threw it into a bag filled with human blood so that, she said, he might sate himself. See *De Claris Mulieribus*, Chapter 47.

859 Agrippina was the daughter of Marcus Vipsanius Agrippa and wife of Germanicus; she was noted for her virtue and heroism, particularly because she accompanied her husband on his military campaigns; see *De Claris Mulieribus*, Chapter 88.

860 perfight] profight *F*.

Lady Elisabeth Howarde: According to Dyce 'the third daughter of the second Duke of Norfolk by his second wife, Agnes Tylney' (II 321); but Tucker (*RQ* XXII, 1969, 335) is probably right in taking her to be the daughter of Thomas Howard I, Earl of Surrey and Duke of Norfolk, and his wife Elizabeth Tylney Howard. She married Thomas Boleyn in about 1500.

865 Aryna is probably Irene, mentioned by Pliny in *Naturalis Historia* xxxv 40 (along with Timarete), and by Boccaccio in *De Claris Mulieribus*, Chapter 57.

866 and (1st)] *not C.*

871–3 Polyxena was the daughter of Hecuba and Priam; Troilus, her brother, loved Cressida; Pandarus was their go-between. Chaucer calls Criseyde the fairest lady in Troy (*Troilus* I 99–105).

Lady Mirriell Howarde was Muriel, daughter of Thomas Howard I and Elizabeth Tylney Howard and sister of Lady Elizabeth Howard. In or before 1500 she marked John Grey Viscount Lisle, and in 1504, after her first husband's death, Thomas Knyvett.

879 to do you] do her *C.*

883 The enbuddid blossoms of] Enbuddid blossome withe *C.*

884 With lillis] The lylly *C.*

885–9 Acontius, a youth from Ceos, came to Delos to celebrate the festival of Diana. In the temple of the goddess he saw and fell in love with Cydippe. To win her he threw an apple on which was written 'I swear by the sanctuary of Diana to marry Acontius', which words, when she read them aloud, were taken by Diana as a vow (Ovid's *Heroides* xx).

887 how] *not C.*

Lady Anne Dakers of the Sowth was the daughter of Elizabeth Tylney by her first husband, Sir Humphrey Bourchier, and so half-sister to the ladies Elizabeth and Muriel Howard. In about 1492 she married Thomas Ferrys, Lord Dacre of the South.

892–6 Zeuxis, who flourished *c.*424–380 BC, was among the most famous of Greek painters. His portrait of Helen of Troy was painted for the city of Croton. Apelles, who lived in the fourth century BC, was the only painter whom Alexander the Great would allow to take his portrait.

899–901 Penelope was the virtuous wife of Ulysses who, despite being wooed by importunate suitors, remained faithful to her husband while he was at the siege of Troy. Deianira was the wife of Hercules, the unwitting cause of his death when she presented him with the poisoned shirt given to her by the centaur Nessus.

Margery Wentworthe is probably not the daughter of Sir Richard Wentworth, as Dyce supposed (II 322), but the daughter of Henry Wentworth and Anne Say, who was half-sister to Elizabeth Tylney Howard, Countess of Surrey. Margery married John Seymour on 22 October 1494 (see Tucker, *RQ* XXII, 1969, 336).

906 margerain: marjoram. Not only does this provide a pun with the lady's name, but the properties of the herb, its prettiness and its usefulness, also match her virtues.

909 maydenhede] maydenhode *F*.

Margaret Tylney: According to J.G. Tilney Basset, *TLS* 11 November 1944, 547, the wife of Sir Philip Tylney of Shelley, Suffolk. Dyce (II 322) and Tucker (*RQ* XXII, 1969, 337) are probably right in identifying her as a sister-in-law of Thomas Howard I after 1497.

933–4 The story of Canace's love for her brother Machareus is found in Ovid's *Heroides* xi. It is retold by Gower, *Confessio Amantis* III 143–360, and alluded to by Chaucer, *The Canterbury Tales* II 77–80.

935 iwus] iwys *F M*.

940 Phedra became the wife of Theseus after he had deserted her sister Ariadne on Naxos. The story appears in Chaucer's *Legend of Good Women* 1896–2227.

947–8 A play on the name Margaret and 'marguerite' meaning 'pearl'.

949 Lodesterre] Lede sterre *F*.

Jane Blenner-Haiset: According to Tucker (*RQ* XXII, 1969, 337), 'Jane was probably the wife of Ralph Blennerhasset, and grandmother to Thomas Blennerhasset, Howard's executor. She died in 1501 at the age of ninety-seven.'

967 The courte of fame *C*.

972 Laodomi: Laodamia followed her husband Protesilaus to Hades. Chaucer instanced her as an example of 'trouthe' in love, *Legend of Good Women*, G 221.

Isabell Pennell: Identified by Tucker with the daughter of John Paynell, who was alive in 1492, the husband of Margaret Tylney who was probably the sister of Philip Tylney (*RQ* XXII, 1969, 337–8).

977 rosabell is apparently a word invented by Skelton from the Latin *rosa bella*, 'beautiful rose'.

985 your] her *C*.

993 I make you sure] I yow assure *C*.

Margaret Hussey was probably the daughter of Simon Blount of Mangotsfield and wife of John Hussey, son of Sir William Hussey. She died shortly before 4 August 1492 (see Tucker, *RQ* XXII, 1969, 338–89).

1004–5 A play on the lady's name and on 'margaret', meaning 'daisy', the *mydsomer flowre*.

1006–7 Perhaps 'Of high breeding like the falcon or the hawk which towers high in the air', or perhaps in 1006 Skelton has in mind the 'Falcon gentle', the female and young of the goshawk. See Whiting F 26.

1025 fayre] the fayre *C. Isaphill*: Hypsipyle, daughter of Thoas, king of Lemnos, saved her father when the women of Lemnos killed all the men on the island. She bore Jason twin sons but was deserted by him and was forced by the laws of Lemnos to send them away. She left the island herself in search of them and her father and endured captivity and slavery. See Boccaccio, *De Claris Mulieribus*, Chapter 15.

1028 Cassaunder: Cassandra, daughter of Priam, king of Troy, who long before the siege had predicted its events. According to Boccaccio's *De Claris Mulieribus*, Chapter 33, her father and brothers beat her for her unfavourable prophecies but she refused to withdraw them. Perhaps this is the steadfastness that Skelton has in mind.

1032   that] than *C*.

1035   This] The *C*.

  Geretrude Statham: Identified by Edwards as Gertrude Statham, née Anstey, wife of Roger Statham (pp. 31, 302). For Roger Statham see lines 742–51 and note. They married in 1482.

1038–40   Perhaps based on *Religious Lyrics of the XV Century*, ed. C.F. Brown, No. 9, lines 10–12.

1048   *Dame Pasiphe*: Pasiphae was the wife of Minos, King of Crete, and mother of Ariadne and Phaedra. Her liaison with a bull produced the Minotaur. Dyce (II 324–5) adduces evidence to show that she was highly regarded by some Renaissance writers.

  Isabell Knyght: 'Isabel Knyght may well be the wife of Leonard Knyght of South Duffield, York, one of the justices of the assize for York city and the northern counties in 1492 and also one of the commissioners of gaol delivery for York city in 1489' (Tucker, *RQ* XXII, 1969, 340).

1070   womanly] maydenly *C*.

1076–81   Galatea was a sea nymph who loved the river god Acis. See Virgil's *Eclogues* i and iii.

1083   you] *not C*.

1096   *maister Newton*: This man has not been identified. He is presumably someone in the household of the Duke and Duchess of Norfolk whose duties consisted of scrivening, illuminating or painting.

1097   of] with *F*.

1102   me curteisly] kurteisly me *C*.

1106   All other besyde were counterfete] All thos that they ware were counter-fettis *C*.

1116   thought] thouhht *F*.

1118   amonge them no worde] not a worde amonge them *C*.

1119   wolde to me] to me wold *C*.

1123   you] *not M*.

1125   by the] thorow *C*.

1126   triumphe] promocioun *C*.

1132   To all that to] To all tho that *F*.

1135   for to] for me to *C*.

1142   – end] *not C*.

1143   *Caliope*: Calliope, the muse of epic poetry.

1149   boke] bokes *F*.

1167   *aurum musicum*: 'mosaic gold', bronze powder used by painters. all] *not M*.

1172   *In primis*: 'In the first place.' *The Boke of Honorous Estate* is now lost, but presumably it was a work on the subject of government like *Royall Demenaunce* (1174) and *Soveraynte a noble pamphelet* (1191), also lost. (See Nelson, p 49.)

1173   *the Boke how Men Shulde Fle Synne* is also now lost but was presumably a moral tract.

1175   *the Boke to Speke Well or be Styll* is now lost but may have been a version of Albertanus de Brescia's (fl. 1246) *Tractatus de Doctrina Dicendi et Tacendi*, which was very popular.

1176   to] do *F*. *Lerne You to Dye* is again lost, but is presumably an 'ars moriendi'. Caxton published two, in 1490 and 1491.

1177 This interlude is lost unless it is the fragmentary piece called *Good Order*, printed by Rastell in 1533 (see G.L. Frost and R. Nash, *SP* XLI, 1944, 483–91).

1178 *Boke of the Rosiar*: Dyce (I ix) suggests that Skelton may have had in mind his *Lawde and Prayse Made for Our Sovereigne Lord the Kyng*, which opens:

The Rose both White and Rede

In one Rose now dothe grow . . .

Prince Arturis Creacyoun is now lost but was presumably a work celebrating Prince Arthur's assumption of the title Prince of Wales in 1489. Nelson points out that Bernardus Andreas composed his *De Arturi Principis Creatione* for the occasion (p. 54).

1179 *The False Fayth* is now lost. Perhaps it was an attack on heretics of the sort found in *Collyn Clout* 486–592.

1180 *Diologgis of Ymagynacyoun*: Edwards points out that this 'was probably taken from a French prose work entitled *Imaginacion de vraye noblesse*. A copy of it, written out by Poulet, the royal librarian, was presented to Henry VII in 1496: perhaps the king took a fancy to it and asked Skelton to turn it into English for his son' (p. 58). It is now BL MS Royal 19 C viii.

1181 Automedon] *Dyce's emendation* Antomedon *FMC*. The reference is to Ovid's *Art of Love*, which Skelton may have translated.

Curribus Automedon lentisque erat aptus habenis,

Tiphys in Haemonia puppe magister erat:

Me Venus artifem tenero praefecit Amori;

Tiphys et Automedon dicar Amoris ego. (I, 5–8).

'For pliant reins and the driving of chariots Automedon

was well fitted; Tiphys steered the Thessalonian ship:

Venus has made me master of the gentle art of love.

I shall be named the Tiphys and Automedon of love.'

Automedon was the charioteer of Achilles and Tiphys was helmsman of the Argo.

1182 *New Gramer*: Now lost but presumably a Latin grammar written in English.

1183 A reference to *The Bowge of Courte* (see p. 46).

1184 *Achademios*: Perhaps a lost comedy written when Skelton obtained his Laureateship at Oxford, *c*.1488.

1185 A translation, now lost, of Cicero's *Epistolae ad Familiares*.

1186 *Good Advysement*, now lost, but presumably the piece mentioned in *Replycacion* 360–61.

1187 *Recule ageinst Gaguyne*: Poems now lost, but presumably those which Skelton wrote against Gaguin in 1489. See 374–5 and note, and also *Why Come Ye Nat to Courte?* 718–41 and note.

1188 *the Popingay*: Presumably *Speke Parott* (see p. 230), though the description does not fit it very well.

1192 Skelton's morality *Magnyfycence* (see p. 140).

1198 Margery Maystres] maistres Margery *M*. A reference to *Manerly Margery Mylk and Ale* (see p. 35), which uses equestrian imagery of the kind found in the lines which follow; but only one poem, not 'many', is now extant on this subject.

1200 I] ye *F*.

1210 Compare the refrain 'It may wele ryme, but it accordith nought' of Lydgate's 'Ryme Without Accord' (*Minor Poems* II No. 65), which consists of a list of contraries and impossibilities like 1211.

1212–18   Though Skelton says that these verses make things apparent (*Patet per versus*) they are extremely obscure, and line 1216 is, to me, untranslatable. Perhaps the rest means: 'In this way this boy is born; in this way the husband was deprived of the bedrights of the wife; the progeny is descended from the blood of Delos; hence I praise him more, because the boy will be another Apollo. If you ask of what kind? Such a most chaste harlot...'. John Norton-Smith (*Essays in Criticism* XXIII, 1973, 62) suggests that these lines refer to Skelton who regards himself as born of his own verses. The phrase *fro Wanflete to Walis* is proverbial, according to Whiting W 8. Wainfleet is in Lincolnshire.

Et reliqua ... tractatibus: 'And other books of homilies from various treatises.'

1221   *Of Mannes Lyfe the Peregrynacioun* is now lost but was a translation of Guillaume de Deguileville's *Pélerinage de La Vie Humaine*.

1223   *Tratyse of the Triumphis of the Rede Rose* is now lost, but it must have been something similar to Bernardus Andreas's *Les Douze Triomphes*. A marginal gloss mentions *bellum Cornubiense, quod in campestribus et in parentioribus vastisque solitudinibus prope Grenewiche gestum est* ('the Cornish war which was fought on the wide and lonely wastes of moor near Greenwich') in 1497, an account of which Skelton's treatise may have included.

1229   *Speculum Principis*: 'The prince's mirror', a Latin homily on the duty of a ruler written on 28 August 1501, while Skelton was Prince Henry's tutor ('*creauncer*', 1226); printed by F.M. Salter, *Speculum* IX, 1934, 25–37.

1233–4   For *The Tunnyng of Elynour Rummyng* see p. 214; and for *Collyn Clout* p. 246. Dyce (II 329) points out that John Ive was a heretic in the reign of Edward IV, and that *joforth* is an exclamation used in driving horses. If there were poems on these subjects they are now lost.

1237   Proverbial (compare Whiting W 231).

1239   *Walshemannys hoos*: Compare *Collyn Clout* 778 and see note.

1241–2   Unless the poem referred to here is 'Womanhod, wanton, ye want' on p. 40, which is addressed to 'Mastres Anne', it has been lost. The verse beginning 'Masteres Anne' in Cambridge University Trinity College MS R 3. 17, Flyleaf 1, attributed to Skelton by F. Brie, *Archiv* XXXVIII, 1919, 226–8, does not seem to be his.

1245   *The Balade ... of the Mustarde Tarte*: Now lost, but see Edwards, p. 51, for a speculation about the kind of poem it was.

1247–53   For Skelton's poem against Adam Uddersall, a manorial bailiff of Diss, see p. 109.

1248   *Dormiat in pace*: 'May he rest in peace' and for the second half of the line compare Whiting D 353.

1254–60   Skelton's *Phyllyp Sparowe* (see p. 71).

1261–375   These lines repeat *Phyllyp Sparowe* 1268–382; for explanatory notes see the notes to that passage.

1315   powre] bowre *M*.

1344   Of] And *M*.

1353   myselfe] me selfe *F*.

1365   *petiit*] *peciit F*.

1367   that] as *M*.

1370   than] and *F*.

1376   and the] a *F*; of the] *not F*. A similar line appears in *Against Venemous*

Tongues 4, and in *Agenst Garnesche* ii 2, which may be the item referred to here.

1377 Murnyng] murmyng *F*. Dyce (II 330) quotes part of a nonsensical song in Ravenscroft's *Pammelia* (1609), No. 31, which has a refrain 'Why weepst thou maple roote'. Perhaps Skelton wrote a poem, now lost, which had a similar refrain. See also R.L. Greene, *Early English Carols*, 1935, No. 473.

1381–2 Another lost work. The notion that Moses was horned derived from the Vulgate version of Exodus xxxiv 29, '*Cumque descenderet Moyses de monte Sinai . . . ignorabat quod cornuta esset facies ex consortio sermonis Domini.*'

1382 scornis] stormis *F*.

1383 Another lost work. *Joyows Garde* was Lancelot's castle, which Malory says was sometimes considered to be at Bamborough and sometimes at Alnwick (*Works*, ed. E. Vinaver, iii 1257).

1384–6 Another lost work, probably comic.

1387 *Castell Aungell*: R.S. Kinsman, *John Skelton: Canon and Census*, p. 25, suggests this may have been a pageant based on Ovid's *Amores* I ix. But the actual Castle Sant'Angelo was refurbished by Pope Boniface IX in 1398 (see John Capgrave's *Chronicle of England*, ed. F.C. Hingeston, Rolls Series i, 1868, p. 268).

1390–98 Another lost work; perhaps a collection of erotic lyrics.

1396 *Mok there loste her sho*: Compare *Why Come Ye Nat to Courte?* 86–7 and note.

1400 his limbis] her lambis *F*, her lambe is *M*. If Henderson's suggestion, here followed, is right the reference is to Ixion, king of the Lapiths, who, because of his ingratitude and treachery towards Zeus, was bound by Hermes to an ever-revolving wheel. If the *F* or *M* reading is accepted the reference is perhaps to Hesione, Priam's sister, who was taken prisoner by Telamon and the Greeks on the expedition against Troy in which Laomedon, Priam's father, was killed. The work, whatever its subject, seems to be lost.

1404–10 The words printed in italics appear in *FM*. They add little to the sense of the stanza and seem to be included only to give it a second rhyme scheme. For another reference to the planting of the olive see 670 and note. The work referred to in this stanza is not extant. 1410 is proverbial (compare Whiting B 613).

1405 it there where] yet wher *M*.

1406 hit] it *M*.

1411 *Epitomis of the Myller and his joly Make*: Another work now lost, perhaps a verse tale of a miller with a wanton wife something like the tale told by Chaucer's Reeve (*The Canterbury Tales* I 3921–4324).

1416 Swaffhamm] Swasshamm *FM*. The line refers either to Swaffham, Norfolk, or Swaffham Prior or Swaffham Bulbeck, Cambridgeshire, and Soham, Cambridgeshire.

1418–20 Poems with the titles *Wofully Arayd* and *Vexilla Regis* were accepted by Dyce (I 141, 144) as Skelton's. Poems on these subjects were fairly common, but none of the extant productions seems to be by Skelton and it must be assumed that his versions have been lost (see Pollet, pp. 259–60, for a discussion). If *Shamefully Betrayd* refers to a separate poem, it is lost.

1421 *Sacris Solempniis*: Dyce (II 332) considers that his lost work is probably not a version of the hymn beginning '*Sacris solemniis juncta sint gaudia . . .*'.

1425–6 Four of the great physicians of antiquity: Galen (*c*.130–200), Dioscorides Pedacius (second century), Hippocrates (*c*.460–357 BC) were all Greeks; Avicenna (980–1037) was an Arab.

1428   *Albumasar* was an Arabian astronomer (805–85).

1430   Evidently proverbial (compare Whiting R 19).

1432   Proverbial (Whiting S 830).

1433   Proverbial (Whiting D 434).

1434–5   *F transposes.*

1434   The line is proverbial (compare Whiting D 199).

1435   Proverbial (Whiting S 697).

1438   Proverbial (Whiting C 108).

1439–45   According to Tilley C 52 and Whiting C 30, this stanza is based on a weather proverb. For the *Frenshe proverbe olde* see Le Roux de Lincy, *Le Livre des Proverbes Français*, 1842, I, 64–5. *Marione Clarione* is presumably the heroine of this lost work.

1443   a colde colde] a colde *M*; *F* adds 'anglice a cokwolde'.

1448–9   *F M transpose.*

1451   a] *not M*; ungracyous] ungraryous *F*. This line and the next are based on a proverb (see Whiting C 206).

1455   *Mary Gipcy*: St Mary Egyptiaca, who, after a youth of wantonness, spent forty-seven years in the wilderness as an ascetic.

1456–60   'What I have written, I have written; your wife is like a vine, you will have her in your charge, guard her as best you know how, according to Luke, etc. . . .'. Based on phrases from the Vulgate John xix 22; Psalms cxxviii 3; and perhaps Luke i 13 or Luke xx 35.

1461   *the Bonehoms of Ashrige besyde Barkamstede*: The College of the Bonhommes at Ashridge completed in 1285, founded by Edmund, Earl of Cornwall, in honour of the blood of Christ. The poem on this is lost.

1465   were] where *F*.

1467   distichon] distincyon *F*.

1468–9   'The ash-tree on the ridge flourishes and grows green without a brook, there is not another like it under heaven without a living stream.'

1468   rivo] viro *F*.

1470   *The Nacyoun of Folys*: Dyce (II 334) suggested that this referred to *The Boke of Three Fooles* included by Marshe in his 1568 edition of Skelton's poems. Henderson suggests the lyric beginning:

>Of all nacyons under the hevyn,
>   These frantyke foolys I hate most of all . . . (p. 36)

Alternatively, perhaps some lost verses on Barclay's *Shyp of Folys* (1509).

1471   *Apollo that whirllid up his chare*: Another lost work, evidently a controversial one, of which Skelton was not particularly proud, judging from 1480. The lines:

>Appollo whirleth up his chaar so hye
>Til that the god Mercurius hous, the slye . . .

begin the third part of Chaucer's *Squire's Tale* (*The Canterbury Tales* V 671–2), at which point the Franklin interrupts the tale.

1472   snurre] surt *F*.

1489   scrape] scarpe *M*.

1490   *ragman rollis*: Originally a set of rolls on which is recorded the homage paid to Edward I by the Scots in 1296; but here simply a set of records with seals attached.

1493 redde] rede *F*.

1495–7 All these works are now lost. 1496 may refer to a translation of Ovid's
Heroides or parts of it; 1497 paraphrases Virgil's *Eclogue* iii 78 and may refer to
a lost translation.

1498 Diodorus Siculus . . . my translacyon: Diodorus Siculus's *Historical Library*
was written in Greek in the first century BC. Poggio Bracciolini translated it into
Latin at some time before 1449. Skelton's translation of the Latin is preserved in
Corpus Christi College, Cambridge MS 357, and is edited by F.M. Salter and
H.L.R. Edwards (EETS OS 233, 1956).

1507 the noyse went to Rome: Compare Chaucer, *The House of Fame* 1927–30.

1511 dreme] slepe *M*.

1515 Janus: The Roman god of the new year, and, in fact, of all beginnings,
usually represented with two faces looking different ways.

1519–32 'Do you wish your mind to be skilful? In that case, pay attention to
your mind; let it be like that of Janus which looks back and forward. Skelton
speaks to his book. Go, shining light of the Britons, and celebrate, our songs,
your worthy British Catullus! Say, Skelton was your Adonis; say, Skelton was
your Homer. Though barbarous, you now compete in an equal race with Latin
verse. And though for the most part it is made up of British words our Thalia
appears not too rude, nor is my Calliope too uncultured. Nor should you be
sorry to suffer the intrigues of malice, nor to endure the attacks of a mad dog;
for Virgil himself bore similar threats; nor was Ovid's muse spared them.' Thalia
was the muse of comedy, Calliope of epic poetry.

1520 sit] sis *M*.

  alloquitar] alloquin *F*.

1553 then] that *M*.

1554 Ye] You *M*.

1579 they]·thy *F*.

  Ad serenissimam . . . 1602] not *F*.

  Ad serenissimam . . . 1593: 'To his most serene majesty the King, also with the
Lord Cardinal, most honoured legate *a latere*, etc. Go, book, and bow down
before the famous king, Henry VIII, and worship him, repeating the rewards
of his praise. And in the same way, you should greet with reverence the Lord
Cardinal legate *a latere*, and beg him to remember the prebend he promised to
commit to me, and give me cause to hope for the pledge of his favour. Be-
tween hope and dread.'

  This envoy marks a sudden shift in Skelton's attitude towards Cardinal
Wolsey, whom he had criticized severely in previous poems. Compare the
second envoy to *Howe the Douty Duke of Albany* (p. 359) for similar senti-
ments.

  ADMONET . . . 13: 'Skelton advises all trees to give place to the green laurel
after its kind. The ash tree in the woods, the rowan in the high hills, the
poplar by the streams, the fir, the widest spreading beech, the pliant willow,
the plane, the thick productive fig-tree, the acorn-bearing oak, the pear, the
winter oak, the tall pine, the resinous balsam, the wild olive, Minerva's olive,
the juniper, the boxtree, the mastic tree with tough points, the grapebearing
vine most pleasing to lord Bacchus, the holm oak and the barren wild vine
hated by farmers, the frankincense exuding fragrance for the soft Sabeans,
likewise the famous myrrh scenting the Arabians, and you, O frail hazels, the

humble tamarisks, and you, O fragrant cedars, you myrtles also, all kinds of
tree, give place to the green laurel.'
Admonet . . . suum] *Admonitio Skeltonis ut omnes Arbores viridi laureo concedant
M*.

1   ornus] *orni F*.
The Laurelle] not *F*.

EN PARLEMENT A PARIS . . . *end*: These lines bear very little relation to the
rest of the poem. They are simply three versions of the conventional 'abuses of
the age', a popular topic in medieval protest verse. See Robbins, *Historical
Poems* Nos. 55–63, and Scattergood, pp. 299–306.

5   absunt] *abiunt F*; *munera*] *numera FM*.
5   takith] *bidythe M*.
6   over the] *ever M*.
A grant tort Foy dort] not *M*.

XXII   A COUPLET ON WOLSEY'S DISSOLUTION OF THE CONVOCATION AT ST PAUL'S

The couplet is preserved in Edward Halle's *Union of the Two Noble and Illustre
Famelies of Lancastre and York* (1548) sig. TTt 2v, and prefaced by the following:
    'And in this season, the Cardinal (i.e. Wolsey) by his power legantine,
    dissolved the Convocacion at Paules, called by the Archebishop of Cantorbury
    (i.e. Warham), and called hym and all the clergie, to his convocacion to
    Westminster, which was never seen before in Englande, wherof master
    Skelton a mery Poet wrote . . .'
The events referred to took place in late April 1523, and the couplet is likely
to have been contemporary. The title has been editorially supplied.

1   In medieval art St Paul was traditionally depicted carrying the sword of his
martyrdom.
2   Peter: Westminster Abbey is dedicated to St Peter; but there may also here
be an allusion to Wolsey's use of his power as papal legate, for St Peter was tradi-
tionally supposed to be the first pope. Compare *Why Come Ye Nat to Courte?* 117–
52. *hath shaven thy beard*: 'has overcome you'; proverbial (Whiting B 119). But
apt too because in medieval art St Paul was often represented as bald but
bearded.

XXIII   HOWE THE DOUTY DUKE OF ALBANY

In early November 1523 John Stewart, Duke of Albany, with a large army of
Scots and Frenchmen, crossed the English border and besieged the castle of Wark
(Northumberland). After an artillery barrage for two days, 'At 3 p.m. on Mon-
day, the Tweed being too high to ford, Albany sent 2,000 Frenchmen (compare
43) in boats to assault the place. They entered the base court, and were kept
back for an hour and a half by Sir Wm Lizle (38) captaine of the castle and 100
men. At length they gained the inner ward, but were immediately attacked by
Lizle, and driven out of both the inner and outer wards, and ten persons slain'
(*L & P* III, 3506). '. . . 22 more died that night and 160 were sore hurt' (*L & P*
III, 3512). After this reverse, and fearing that the flooding river might cut off
their retreat, Albany pulled back his army to the monastery of Eccles, six miles

from Wark. Then, when he heard that Thomas Howard, Earl of Surrey, Lord Admiral of England, was close with an army (54ff.), he retreated to Edinburgh. Albany left Scotland for France on 20 May 1524 and never returned. Since the events with which this poem is concerned were 'tidinges newe' (3) it must have been written shortly after 3 November 1523.

The text is taken from Marshe's edition of Skelton's *Workes* (1568) (*M*).

4–5 Proverbial (compare Whiting G 399).

12 Proverbial (compare Whiting B 139).

19 Huntley banke: A hill near Melrose (Roxburghshire). Compare *Agaynst the Scottes* 149, *Against Dundas* 58, *Why Come Ye Nat to Courte?* 267 and note.

20 Lowdyan: Lothian. Compare *Speke Parott* 72, *Agaynst the Scottes* 59.

21 Locryan: Loch Ryan, a bay in Wigtonshire, near the Rinns of Galloway (23). Compare *Agaynst the Scottes* 61, 109.

24 'Dunbar, Dundee'. Compare *Agaynst the Scottes* 121, *Agaynst Dundas* 60.

37 Compare *Elynour Rummynge* 168.

63–4 St Cuthbert's banner was supposed to have originated at the time of the Battle of Neville's Cross (1347) when St Cuthbert (*c*.635–87), patron saint of Durham, appeared to John Fossour, prior of the abbey, in a dream and instructed him to take the holy corporax cloth, which St Cuthbert had used to set on the chalice at Mass, and to put it on a spear point like a banner. Its presence at the battlefield was supposed to have helped the English to victory and to have protected the monks of the abbey against the Scots. The cloth was then placed in the centre of a banner 'which was never caryed or shewed at any battell, but, by the especiall grace of God Almightie and the mediacione of holie Saint Cuthbert, it browghte home the victorie' (*Rites of Durham*, Surtees Society, XV, 1842, p. 23). However, a banner or standard of St Cuthbert existed earlier: it is mentioned under 1098 by Fordun (*Scotichronicon* i 278) and in 1296 and subsequently with increasing frequency (see *Archaeologia Aeliana*, Second Series, ii, 1858, pp. 51–65 for details). At Flodden (1513) the banner was carried in the English front line, at which battle fought the same Lord Thomas Howard, who, as Earl of Surrey, put Albany to flight in 1523.

The banner was considered by the English both as a reminder of past victories and as a token of future success: Surrey mentions it at least three times in his correspondence (*L & P* III, 3481, 3482, 3506). Skelton's reference here to 'the auncient manner' probably is meant to recall past victorious engagements against the Scots when the English crown and clergy found themselves with identical interests. The reference to Wolsey (*my Lorde Cardynall* 60) is apt because technically he would have had possession of St Cuthbert's banner is his capacity as Bishop of Durham; he would also have had the banner of St William of York (d. 1153) because he was Archbishop of York.

65–71 According to Surrey, Albany's performance at Wark and subsequently was 'shameful' and 'cowardly' (*L & P* III, 3507), an opinion shared by some of his men who said at his withdrawal: ' "By God's blood, we will never serve you more, nor never will wear your badges again" and tore them off their breasts and threw them to the ground saying "Would to God we were all sworn English" ' (*L & P* III, 3512). In Surrey's opinion 'His estimation in Scotland is gone forever' (ibid.). According to Holinshed the Scots thought that 'the duke returned with honar' (V, 498–9).

88–98 Were the young James V to have died without issue, Albany would have succeeded to the Scottish throne. The English frequently said that the Duke's patriotism was merely a cloak for his ambitions (*L & P* III, 3224, 3271).

102–6   The contacts between Albany and Francis I were close: Albany spent most of his time at the French court and organized his policies in accord with those of Francis, who had promised (and given) the Scots help in this campaign (see *L & P* III, 3057, 3118).

117, 125   Perhaps a reference to the rumours circulated deliberately by Albany that he would not come to Scotland:

'But when he heard that the Navy lay in wayte to fight with him, he durst not aventure, but sate styll. And when he heard there was no capitaines of name on the borders of England toward Scotland, he devised by policie that all his shippes should be removed to the haven of Brest, and sayd himself and caused it to be noysed that he would not saile into Scotland that yere. So ranne the voice al the wastes of Normandy and Britaigne, and so passed tyll the end of Septembre.

'The kyng of England was enformed by such as knew none other, that the duke of Albany had broken his jorney, and would not pass that yere into Scotland. Wherfore the kyng of England in the middest of September caused his shippes to be layd up in havens tyl the next spryng. The Duke of Albany beyng therof advertised boldly then tooke his shippes and shipped his people...' (Hall's *Chronicle*, pp. 644–5).

126   *Unhaply ured*: Compare *Magnyfycence* 6, *Replycacion* 95, 405.

131   *Gabione*: Gibeon, whose inhabitants, through deceit (*falshod* 128), effected a league with Joshua (Joshua ix 3–17). See also *Agenst Garnesche* ii 15. Perhaps Joshua's curse (ix 23) on the Gibeonites, which condemned them to perpetual servitude for their deceit, suggested in 136–44.

159   the] thy *M*. Compare *Magnyfycence* 303; and *Against Dundas* 28.

161   Proverbial (Whiting F 344).

165   Proverbial (Whiting M 608).

183   Proverbial (Whiting B 230).

192–6   Hamilcar Barca (d. 229/8 BC) and his sons Hannibal (247–183/2 BC) and Hasdrubal (d. 207 BC) were Carthaginian generals who fought long and bitterly against the Romans and their allies.

209   Proverbial (Whiting B 105).

226   Based on the proverbial phrase 'make and mar' (Whiting M 24).

254–71   Heiserman (p. 278) quotes a song from Peter Langtoft's *Chronicle* which he implies is the basis of 255:

Tprut! Scot riveling
In unseli timing
Crope thu out of cage.

But the whole passage seems to refer more generally to Albany's pavilion or tent.

281   hors] *Dyce's emendation*, fors *M*.

287   *Sir Topias*: The reference to Chaucer's burlesque knight is appropriate since he, like Albany, 'drow abak ful faste' and 'faire escapeth' when confronted by an enemy (*The Canterbury Tales* VII 827–32).

288   *Bas*: Presumably the Bass Rock in the Firth of Forth.

290   las] *Dyce's emendation*, as *M*.

292–3   'I curse your Scottish ears, teeth and neck.'

296–7   Compare *Agenst Garnesche* iii 186 and note, and *Speke Parott* 89.

309   *lyon white*: Surrey, whose badge this was. Compare *Agaynst the Scottes* 135.

346 pounde] pouned *M*.

351 *par case*: 'by chance'.

355 'Though I fashion you this harness . . .'

357 save] sava *M*. 'save your grace'.

373 *our friar*: A play on Francis I's name and the order of Franciscan friars; *cordylar* (375) meaning Franciscan friar (because they wore knotted cords about their waists) continues the joke.

382 An imitation of Scottish dialect, as in *Why Come Ye Nat to Courte?* 126.

398 fayctes] faytes *M*.

418 *overage*: Perhaps 'excessive rage' or, taking the word as French *ouvrage*, 'work' or 'piece of work'. Compare *Why Come Ye Nat to Courte?* 41 and note.

430–43 The first three heroes mentioned in this list are the subjects of proverbs: 'As strong as Hercules' (Whiting H 358); 'As wise as Soloman' (Whiting S 460); 'As fair as Absolon' (Whiting A 18). But Hector is proverbial for his hardiness and strength (Whiting H 317, 318), not his loyalty. *Scipiades* is Scipio Africanus (236–184/3 BC), the Roman general who had to his credit victories over Hasdrubal (in 208 BC) and Hannibal (in 202 BC). *Ptholome* refers probably to Ptolemy I (*c*.367/6–283/2 BC), the Macedonian king of Egypt. *Duke Josue*: Joshua. *Machube*: Judas Maccabaeus.

449 frugalite] fragalite *M*.

476 'And you do to him great wrong.'

487–8 *M transposes*.

506 *Sainct George to borowe*: 'with St George as my surety', the invocation of the patron saint of England is apt in such a particular context.

511 worlde] worlds *M*.

531 *an ammas gray*: An ecclesiastical hood or hooded cape usually lined with grey fur. Wolsey had promised Skelton a prebend.

Je foy . . . grace: 'I trust completely in his good grace.'

XXIV   A REPLYCACION AGAYNST CERTAYNE YONG SCOLERS
ABJURED OF LATE

Though it is nowhere explicitly stated it is fairly clear that this poem refers to two Cambridge scholars – Thomas Arthur and Thomas Bilney – who, on the feast of the Conception of the Virgin Mary (8 December 1527), carried symbolic faggots at Paul's Cross as a token of their renunciation of heresy. Skelton's statement that they preached '. . . howe it was idolatry to offre to ymages of our blessed Lady, or to pray and go on pylgrimages, or to make oblacions to any ymages of sayntes in churches or els where . . .' reflects the accusations made against Arthur and Bilney in their trial before Bishop Tunstall (see J. Gairdner, *Lollardy and the Reformation*, 1908, I, p. 393). Arthur abjured without argument, but Bilney, though he did penance, was never made to admit that he was guilty of heresy. Lines 176–96 of Skelton's poem appear to doubt the seriousness of (presumably) Bilney's abjuration. And lines 393–6 were prophetic. After he was released from prison and allowed back to Cambridge, Bilney, late in 1528, began to preach again in and around Norwich. He was arrested, tried, and, in 1531, burnt at the stake as a relapsed heretic.

Nelson draws attention to similarities between Skelton's poem and Sir Thomas More's *Dialogue concerning Heresies* (published 1529, but probably written in 1528), the first part of which deals with Bilney and his errors. Since his dedica-

tion makes it clear that Skelton wrote at Wolsey's suggestion and More at Tun-
stall's it may be, as Nelson says, '. . . that the *Dialogue* and the *Replicacion* form
part of an officially inspired concerted attempt to destroy the heretical movement
in England with the weapon of eloquence' (p. 216).
    The text is taken from Pynson's print of *c*.1528 (*P*).

Honorificatissimo . . . felicitatur, etc.: 'To the most honourable, most mighty,
and by far the most reverend father in Christ and lord, Lord Thomas, in the
title of St Cecilia priest of the holy Roman church, the most worthy cardinal,
legate of the apostolic see, the most illustrious legate *a latere etc.* the laureate
Skelton, royal orator, makes known his most humble obeisance with all the
reverence due to such a magnificent and worthy prince among priests, and the
most equitable dispenser of every justice, and, moreover, the most excellent
patron of the present little work *etc.* to whose most auspicious regard, under
the memorable seal of glorious immortality, this little book is commended.'
Thomas Wolsey was elected cardinal on the title of St Caecilia trans Tiberim in
1515, and was made legate *a latere* in 1518.
orator regius] ora. reg. *P*.
Argumentum . . . rege indulto: 'The Argument. Our wish is to cut back the too
thick and too sterile vines which the vineyard of the Lord of Hosts does not
allow to spread more freely any further. With the privilege granted by the
king.'
orator regius] ora. reg. *P*.
Ad almam . . . eram: 'To the dear university of Cambridge. A consolatory utter-
ance. O Cambridge, kind parent, why do you weep? Albeit that your little
sons will turn out degenerate, but, O kind mother, you shall not be disparaged
through their idleness and ignorance. Perhaps all those descendants which
your breast cherished are not noble. Nevertheless, you shall be mighty in
nourishing wisdom, full of the glory of knowledge for as long as the pole stars
shine. And now be strong, cherish me, for indeed I was once one of your dear
pupils.'
    Pallas was the Greek goddess of wisdom; Minerva her Roman counterpart.
    Cambridge was, at this time, the intellectual stronghold of the English refor-
mers. Bilney was at Trinity Hall, and Arthur had been, but left for St John's.
A Latin sidenote to this passage says that 'Skelton the Laureate poet first suck-
ed the breast of learning at Cambridge'. There are several references to stu-
dents called Skelton in the records, but none which indisputably refer to the
poet. The most likely is that which refers to 'Dominus Skelton questionist'
(i.e., about to take his B.A.), dated 18 March 1480.
enbolned] enbolmed *P*.
8–9   Compare *Stow's Survey of London*, ed. C.L. Kingsford, 1908, I, 239, '. . .
then the three Cranes Lane, so called not onely of a signe of three Cranes at a
Taverne door, but rather of three strong Cranes of Timber placed on the Vintrie
wharf by the Thames side, to crane up wines there . . .'. This London inn is
referred to as a meeting place for 'pretenders to wit' in Ben Jonson's *Bartholomew
Fair* I i 33. The reformers, however, seem to have met more often at the White
Horse Inn in Cambridge (see J.B. Mullinger, *History of the University of Cam-
bridge*, 1873, I, p. 572).
    Ergo . . . pro primo: 'Therefore, perhaps not following on what has gone before,
    but, nevertheless, an argument, it must be noted in the first place that nothing
    may be in excess. So much for the first part.'

maister Porphiris problemes: Porphyry (232/3–*c*.305) was a polymathic scholar and philosopher, one of whose works (now lost) attacked Christianity. He was said to be the greatest enemy Christianity had, and a copy of his book was publicly burnt by Theodosius in 388.

23 convent] content *P*. *Dyce's emendation based on the evidence of 'convenio' in the Latin sidenote*. The word must mean 'summon before a tribunal'.

35 Proverbial (Whiting H 116).

69–71 'Either through the equivocal, or the unequivocal, or thus or not so.'

99–103 '... how to syllogize, it is not from the particular, nor from negatives, if you wish to conclude properly, etc., in a case such as this...'

104 *corde tenus*: 'in your heart'.

105 *verbo tenus*: 'in your name'.

107 'You were then downcast.' Proverbial (Whiting H 295).

110 'To reply adequately.'

111 '... so much confounded'.

113 your] you *P*. The line is proverbial (Whiting C 641) and means 'to have an unexpected fall'.

115 *Harpocrates*: A Latin sidenote reads: 'Harpocrates, with his finger pressed to his lips, warned one to become silent in the temple of Isis.' The Roman god Harpocrates was supposed to be the same as Orus among the Egyptians. He was the god of silence and the Romans put his statues at the entrance of their temples to indicate that the mysteries of religion and philosophy ought not to be revealed to the people.

127–8 '... concerning apparent and non-existent things'.

140–50 A Latin sidenote to this passage calls it an 'obscure sarcasm'. Nelson (pp. 217–19) supposed it referred to the fact that Wolsey had given Bilney, whom he had questioned earlier, money to finance his studies.

152 Proverbial (Whiting B 348).

157 Proverbial (Whiting T 465). A Latin sidenote quotes Vulgate Matthew vii 20.

163 Jovinian was a fourth-century heretic monk who denied, amongst other things, the virginity of Mary, opposed some forms of asceticism and thought that all sins, and the punishments for them, were equal.

166 John Wycliffe's (1329–84) works were known to the sixteenth-century reformers, and used by them. Perhaps he is mentioned here because he denied the efficacy of pilgrimages and the worship of images as Arthur and Bilney were said to have done. See also 269–70.

167 Martin Luther (1483–1546) had been excommunicated in 1520, and in this same year some of his books were publicly burnt in Cambridge.

172–3 'You stumble among riddles and among paradigms.'

212 *muse*: In hunting a hole or gap in a fence through which the game is driven.

217 *rechatyng* refers to the blowing of a 'recheat', a series of notes sounded on a hunting horn to call hounds together; *chatyng* may be a nonce word formed from this. But perhaps Skelton had in mind 'chatting', in anticipation of *pratyng* (218).

234–5 'You are wicked logicians and much worse at introducing studies...'

244 *ye have eaten a flye*: According to the Lollard author of *The Lanterne of Light* (ed. L.M. Swinburn, EETS OS 151, 1917, p. 11) this was a frequent jibe against heretics: 'Thus prelatis & freris in this daies ben traveilid with this synne agen the Holi Goost & schamfulli sclaundren her symple britheren that casten yvel maners from her soule or prechen the gospel to Cristis entent to turne the peple to vertuouse lyvyng. Thei seien this man hath eten a fliye that gyveth him lore of Goddis lawe. This is more foule to eete a flie than to be a god and chare [i.e., drive off] thise fliyes. Thus han they brought her malice aboute to sclaundir for Lollardis that speken of God.' Compare also 252. Whiting (F 349) says that the phrase is proverbial.

275–9 Gregory the Great (*c.*540–604), Ambrose (?340–97), Jerome (*c.*340/342–420), Augustine of Hippo (354–430) and Thomas Aquinas (*c.*1225/1227–74) were five of the most notable theologians of the medieval church. All were saints and doctors of the church. All had, at one time or another, preached or written against heresy.

281–8 latria is the worship which is due to God alone; *hyperdulia* the worship due to the Virgin Mary; *dulia* the worship due to saints.

Tantum pro secundo: 'So much for the second part.'

Peroratio . . . argumentum est: 'A peroration against certain hypothetical heretics lately abjured. Listen, men of Ishmael, I do not say Israel, listen, I say, men of Midian, of Askalon, of Ammon, of Gibeon, listen to the words which I will speak. The gospels are food for the elect; but because you are not of the race of the good, you who give instruction in the categories of evil spirits, therefore also the rest of your problems, schemes and dilemmas shall be anathema. It is an inescapable argument.'

catechisatis] *caterisatis P*, which Henderson translates as 'make improper use of'. I cannot find an occurrence of this word in Latin. Dyce suggested ? *catarrhizatis*.

Ishmael, the son of Abraham, was '. . . a wild man; his hand will be against every man, and every man's hand against him' (Genesis xvi 12). The Midianites frequently appear as the enemies of Israel, principally in Judges vi 1–8. Askalon was one of the five principal cities of the Philistines (Judges xiv 19). The Ammonites frequently joined with others in opposition to the Israelites (Deuteronomy xxiii 3–4, Judges iii 13, II Samuel x 1–19). For the treachery of the Gibeonites see Joshua ix 3–27.

314–42 Skelton's defence of divine poetry rests on the authority of Jerome, whose letter to Paulinus (325) prefaces the Vulgate Bible. In one paragraph of this letter Jerome compares the psalms of David with the lyrics of classical writers. Skelton first quotes his authority verbatim, then renders Jerome's Latin into English in two rhyme-royal stanzas.

Simonides (*c.*556–468 BC), Pindar (518–438 BC) and Alcaeus (born *c.*620 BC) were all Greek lyric poets. Quintus Horatius Flaccus (65–8 BC) and Gaius Valerius Catullus (?84–?54 BC) were two of the best-known writers of Latin lyrics. For an account of the obscure, but frequently praised, Aulus Septimius Serenus, and texts of those of his poems which have survived, see *Poetae Minores Latini*, ed. J.C. Wernsdorf, 1780, II, 247–92.

323 This] Thus *P*.

Simonides] *Siphonides P*.

331 Symonides] *Symphonides P*.

360–61 the Boke of Good Advertysement is one of Skelton's lost works, presumably on 'hevenly inspyracion/In laureate creacyon' (372–3). Mentioned again in the *Garlande of Laurell* 1186.

375–8 The Latin sidenote quotes Ovid's *Fasti* vi 5–6.

385–8 A Latin sidenote refers to Vulgate Psalm liv 2.

Dixi . . . exaltare cornu: 'I said to the wicked, do not persist in wickedness, and to the evil-doers lift not up the horn.' Vulgate Psalm lxxiv 5.

Tantum pro tertio: 'So much for the third part.'

De raritate . . . coluere poetas: 'The epitome of Skelton, the laureate poet, is about the rarity of poets and about the infinite abundance of gymnosophists, philosophers, theologians and the rest of the learned sort. Infinite and innumerable are the sophists, infinite and innumerable are the logicians, innumerable are the philosophers and theologians, infinite the doctors and innumerable the masters; but poets are few and rare. Thus, everything that is rare is precious. Therefore, I think that poets, before all others, are filled with divine inspiration. Plato prophesies thus, and thus Socrates; thus the great Macedonian, thus Caesar, the greatest of Roman heroes, always honoured famous poets.'

For a similar defence of poets see Cicero's *De Oratore* I iii and Boccaccio's *De Genealogia Deorum Gentilum* XIV vii; and for a discussion of the concept see Fish, p. 32.

The gymnosophists were a sect of hermits who disregarded the decencies of life. Plato (*c*.429–347 BC) and Socrates (469–399 BC) were two of the most famous Greek philosophers. The 'great Macedonian' is Alexander (356–323 BC) who, with Julius Caesar (100–44 BC), were the greatest war leaders of antiquity.

Skeltonidis Laureati] Skel. L. P.

Appendix
A Descriptive List of Latin Poems not Included in this Edition

1. *Epigramma ad tanti principis maiestatem in sua puerice* (*c*.1494). Twenty lines of elegiacs. F.M. Salter, *Speculum* ix, 1934, 36–7.

2. *'Diligo rusti* [*cul*] *um cum porta* [*t D*] *is duo qu* [*in*] *tum . . .'* (*c*.1506). An untitled elegiac couplet. Dyce I 174.

3. *Lamentatio Urbis Norwicen* (shortly after 25 April 1507). Ten lines of elegiacs. Dyce I 174; Henderson, pp. 432–3.

4. *Ad serenissimam iam nunc suam maiestatem regiam . . . palinodium* (1509). Twelve hexameters. F.M. Salter, *Speculum* ix, 1934, 37.

5. *'I, liber, et propera, regem tu pronus adora . . .'* (the holographic dedication to the manuscript of *Chronique de Rains, c.*1512). Ten hexameters. Dyce I 147; Henderson, p. 432. But preceded by two complete hexameters and part of a third not given in modern editions:

Quamvis annosa est, apice et sulcata vetusto
Pagina trita, tamen fremit horrida praelia Martis
Digna legi.

This is followed by 'Skelton loyall'.

6. *Eulogium pro suorum temporum conditione* (shortly after April 1512). Thirty-six lines of elegiacs, followed by four lines of elegiacs. Dyce I 179–80; Henderson, pp. 435–6.

7. *Henrici Septimi . . . epitaphium* (lines 1–24 completed 29 November 1512; lines 25–8 added after the Battle of Flodden in September 1513). Twenty-four lines of elegiacs, followed by four lines of elegiacs. Dyce I 178–9; Henderson, pp. 434–5.

8. *Chorus de Dys contra Gallos* (between 22 and 28 August 1513). Sixteen lines of elegiacs. Dyce I 191; Henderson, p. 437.

9. *Chorus de Dys contra Scottos* (between 9 and 22 September 1513). Twenty lines of elegiacs. Dyce I 190; Henderson, pp. 436–7.

10. *Elegia in serenissimae principis et domine, domine Margarete* (16 August 1516). Twenty lines of elegiacs, followed by two lines of elegiacs, followed by a couplet. Dyce I 195–6; Henderson, pp. 437–8.

11. *In Bedel quondam Belial incarnatum, devotum epitaphiam* (1518). Fourteen lines of elegiacs, followed by four short rhyming lines, followed by two lines of elegiacs, followed by two rhyming couplets. Dyce I 175–6; Henderson, p. 433.

Glossary

This selective glossary explains only words whose meaning departs from that of modern English, or whose form within the poems is likely to cause difficulties of recognition. When the same word bears more than one meaning the meanings are normally listed in the chronological order in which they occur in the poems. When more than one spelling of a word appears the variants are normally arranged in alphabetical order. Difficult phrases are listed under the word in them most likely to cause difficulty. Though there is inevitably some overlap, words and phrases explained in the Notes are not normally listed in the Glossary. The following abbreviations are used:

adj	adjective	*past*	past tense
adv	adverb	*phr*	phrase
comp	comparative	*pl*	plural
excl	exclamation	*pres*	present, present tense
gen	genitive	*s, sing*	singular
imp	imperative	*subj*	subjunctive
inf	infinitive	*superl*	superlative
int	interjection	*trans*	transitive
intrans	intransitive	*v*	verb
n	noun	*vbl*	verbal
part	participle		

abandune   *inf* subjugate XVI 1459
abate   *inf* beat down, destroy XIX 973; *abated past part* XX 162
ab(b)rogate   *inf* abolish, cancel XVIII 317, XIX 707
abjecte   *adj* wretched XXIV 240
abjections   *n pl* degradations, humiliations XIX 890
abjectyd   *past part* cast out XVI 2484
abolete   *adj* obsolete XX 713
abrogate   *see* ab(b)rogate
abusion, abusyo(u)n   *n* injurious language XV 56; heresy XXIV 14; perversion of the truth or the law XX 456; *abusions, abusyons pl* VII 1347, XXI 1340
abusyd   *past part* deceived VI 5
abyde   *inf* endure, withstand XVI 1879, XXIII 187
abylement, abylyment   *n* array, attire XVI 2059, 2405, XXI 44; *habillimentis, habylementes pl* VII 1180, XXI 851
accompte   *inf* tell, give a verbal account XVI 2421
ac(c)orde   *inf* coexist harmoniously IX 12; suit XI 3
accustome   *n* habit XXI 64
acomberyd   *past part* burdened XVI 2215

acorde *see* ac(c)orde

adaunted, adauntid *past part* subdued VII 1310, XXI 1303

adres(se) *inf* apply, prepare XII 89, XVI 1549; *adresse imp* XVI 2497

advertence *n* care, attention XVI 42, 1333, 1635

advertysment *n* instruction XVI 196; observation XXI 808

advertysyng *pres part* advising, warning IV ii 39

advysed, avysid *1 s past* looked about, observed XXI 386; *as I me advysed* as I came to myself XXI 36; *avysed past part* determined XVI 774

advysement *n* consideration XVI 2406, XXI 807

adyment *n* adamant XXI 306

affeccyon, affection *n* tendency, inclination XVI 1470, XXIV 190

af(f)orce, aforse *inf* attempt, undertake V 17, XXI 817; exert oneself XVI 2483

affray *inf* disturb XVI 2493; *afrayd(e) past part* VII 1283, XVI 362, XXI 1276

affyaunce *n* trust XVI 2501

affyaunsynge *pres part* pledging XXI 555

affynite, affynyte *n* following, retinue V 139, XX 835, XXIV 266; *of one affy-nyte* unanimously XIX 497

aforse *see* af(f)orce

after-clappes *n pl* unexpected blows, unfortunate consequences XXIII 278

after-dele *n phr* disadvantage XVIII 463

agaspe *inf* gasp for life XVI 1508

agerdows *adj* bitter-sweet XXI 1250

alayd *past part* put down XXIII 496

alcumyn *n* a mixed metal, mainly of brass, which imitated gold XX 907

alderbest *adv* perfectly XX 1188

ale-joust *n* a large pot with handles used for ale XVII 192

allectuary, (e)lectuary *n* a medicine consisting usually of something powdered mixed with honey, jam or syrup IV iii 8, XVI 2355, XXIV prose; *allectyues pl* XXI heading

allygate *inf* cite, bring forward as evidence XIX 1162

almesse *n pl* alms XVI 1344

aloes, alowes *n pl* a bitter purgative procured from the juice of plants of the genus *liliaceae aloinae* XII 81; at XVI 2354 perhaps used figuratively to mean bitter experiences

alowde, alowed *past part* approved of XV 40, XVI 533, 1247

alys *n pl* paths XXI 654

amense *n pl* reparation XVI 9

ammas, amysse *n* in ecclesiastical dress a square of linen worn over the neck and shoulders VII 560, XXIII 531

amounte *3 pl pres* make up, comprise XXI 346

amysse *see* ammas

amyte *n* friendship XX 374

animosite *n* courage XXIII 448

antetyme *n* text for a sermon XVI 359

aparte *adv* openly, evidently XIX 729

apase *adv* swiftly XVIII 413

apay(e)d *adj* pleased (usually used in phrases) V 298, XV 72, XVI 2402, XX 731 apayere, appare *inf* deteriorate, diminish, grow worse XIII i 19, XIX 191; *appayre 3 s pres* XVIII 166

apostataas *n pl* apostates; those who abandon or renounce their faith or religious order XIX 386

apostrofacyon *n* in rhetoric, an exclamatory direct, personal address VI 30

appall *inf* weaken XX 23; *appalle 2 pl pres* XIX 611

apparayle *n* rigging of a ship V 38

appare, appayre *see* apayere

apparently *adv* clearly XXI 170

apply *inf* try VII 780; wield XX 1104

appose *inf* dispute XVI 1425; *apposed past part* questioned XIX 265

apposelle *n* question XXI 141

aquyte *inf* pay for, recompense XXI 550, 1062

ar *adv* before XIII ii 11

arace, arayse *n* a rich tapestry fabric from Arras XIX 942, XXI 475

aray *n* order of battle XIII ii 33; *a shrewd aray* a sorry state of affairs XVII 163; *of aray* especially arranged for festivities XXI 539

arecte, arrect *1 s pres* entrust, offer, raise up XVI 94, XXI 55; *arrectinge, ar(r)ectyng pres part* XXI 1, 410, 824; *arrectyd past part* made up IV iii 8, *erectyd* XVI 2482

arerage *n* arrears XX 48

ascry, askry *inf* shout, exclaim, cry out against, denounce, VII 903, XIII v 66, XXIII 73; discover VII 1358, XXI 1351; *escrye 1 s pres* XIX 1096; *ascrye 3 pl pres* XIX 335

askrye *n* loud cry, noise XX 870

assay *3 pl pres* try XIX 125; *asayde past part* XXI 775

assayes *n pl* trials; *at all assayes* for all purposes XVI 428, 2275

assoyle *inf* absolve from sin XIX 875

assurded *3 s past* broke out XXI 302

assystence *n* presence XVI 2373

astate *n* high rank XXI 54, XXIII 461; *estates pl* people of high rank XXI 45

astroloby *n* astrolabe, an astronomical instrument used for taking altitudes XVIII 135

aswage *inf* become less violent XX 37

atame *inf* subdue XV 60; *attamed past part* XXIV 61

athrust *adj* thirsty XVII 254

attayne *inf* extend as far as XI 54

attaynted, attayntyd, atteintid *past part* condemned XVIII 343, XXI 611; infected XVIII 363, XIX 900; struck with fear XX 158, XXIII 29, 493

attemperaunce *n* moderation XVI 189

auncyente *n* antiquity VII 767

aureat *adj* highly decorated, making use of stylized poetical vocabulary I 128

autentyke *adj* of authority, entitled to obedience or respect XIX 696

ava(y)le *inf* accomplish a purpose, help VII 1117, XVI 2249, XIX 1

avauns *n pl* boasts XXIII 323

avaunt *int* Away! Begone! XIX 1155, 1156, 1157

avowed *past part* acknowledge as one's own XV 41

awayte *n* ambush; *layde awayte* spied upon V 468

axes, axys *n* ague, fever IV iii 9, XXI 315

ayle *inf* be affected by XVI 2365

ba   *see* basse

babyl(le)s   *n pl* baubles XVIII 428, XXIV 175

ba(i)le   *n* torment (usually of hell), trouble I 81, III iii 46, XVI 744, 2070, XXI 376; set of dice V 389; *bales pl* troubles XX 63

baile   *imp* deliver blows; a call to combatants to engage in fighting XIII ii 31

balas   *n* delicate rose-red variety of the spinel ruby XVIII 367; *balassis pl* XXI 1166

balke   *n* beam of wood XVII 615

ballyvis   *n pl* bailiffs XXI 514

bane   *n* death XXIII 284; *banes pl* XI 65, XII 173

banne   *inf* curse XVI 2238; *ban 3 pl pres* XX 891

baratows   *adj* contentious XXI 673

barbellis   *n pl* barbels; large European freshwater fishes so named from the fleshy filaments which hang down from their mouths (*barbus vulgaris*) XXI 661

barbican   *n* the outer defence of a city or castle, especially a double tower erected over a gate or bridge XXI 1397

barbyd   *past part* as if wearing a nun's barb, a piece of white plaited linen worn over or under the chin XVI 987

bare   *adj* destitute XVII 109

bare . . . in hande   *v phr* lay to one's charge, accuse XVI 352

barlyhood   *n* fit of drunkenness, or of ill-humour brought on by drinking XVII 372

barme   *n* froth that forms on the top of fermenting malt liquors XVII 455

barnacle   *n* species of wild goose (*anas leucopsis*) VII 450

barrid   *past part* excluded from consideration XXI 143

basked   *past part* bathed XXIV prose

basnet   *n* usually a helmet with a visor, but at XIII i 23 evidently some sort of cap

basse   *inf* kiss XVI 1560, XX 35; *ba, bas imp* IV i 8, XIII v 43, XVII 227; *bassed 1 s past* XVI 2069; *bassyd past part* XIII iii 62

bastyng   *n* anything sewn on; lining or trimming XIII iii 200

bate   *inf* set on a dog to bite and to worry XXI 27; *bayteth 3 s pres* attacks XX 307; *baytyd past part* XVI 1961

bate   *n* discord, dissent XIX 913

batowe   *n* kind of low boot XVI 755

baud, bawde   *n* go-between, procurer VII 721, XIII v 73

baudeth   *3 s pres* dirties XVII 90

baudrie   *n* lewdness in speech or writing, foul language XXIV 48

bawde   *see* baud

bawdias, bawdyas   *n* rogue XIII v 76, XXI 639

bawdry   *n* finery XIII v 40

bawme   *n* balm XVI 2347; *bawmys pl* XXI 674

bayarde   *n* a bay-coloured horse, originally the magic one given by Charlemagne to Rinaldo XIII iii 101; *bayardys gen sing* III i 8

bayned   *past part* ? boned XXIV prose

bayte, beyght   *n* allurement, temptation, trap XVI 442, 1568; XXIII 110

bayteth, baytyd   *see* bate

bechrewde   *see* beshrowe

becke   *n* beak XVI 1000

becked *adj* beaked XVI 927

bedawyd *past part* made a fool of XIII iii 182

bedell *n* officer who makes a proclamation VII 980

bede roule *n phr* prayer roll; a list of persons to be especially prayed for VII 242; *bede rolles, bede roules pl* VII 12, XIX 422

bedleme *n* lunatic (literally, an inmate of London's Bethlehem Hospital) XX 655

befo(u)le *1 s pres* make a fool of XVI 876, 1045, 1805

begared *past part* faced, adorned XIX 317

beknave *inf* call a knave XIII i 9, v 107; *beknavyd past part* VI 310

beks *3 s pres* makes a mute signal or significant gesture, usually by nodding the head XX 339

belapped *past part* enveloped XIX 310

bely-joye *n* appetite, pleasure in food XVIII 492

belymmed *past part* disfigured V 289

bemole *n* softened B; in music notation B flat VII 534

bende *n* group XVI 818

bended *past part* grouped XX 1023

besene *adj* appearing; *the most rychely besene* of the most rich appearance XXI 483; *well besene* of attractive appearance XXI 1076; *wonderly besene* strangely attired V 283

beshrowe *inf* curse XVI 563; *beshrew, beshrowe 1 s pres* XVI 1105, XVII 503; *beshrewe imp* II 1; *all bechrewde, all beshrewde past part phr* thoroughly corrupt, depraved III iv 28, XIII v 86, XVIII 516, XIX 91

bestad(de) *past part* beset XXI 830, XXIII 364

bet *past part* inlaid XXI 41

bete *past part* assailed VII 930

betell *n* ? club XVI 755

betrapped *past part* furnished with trappings XIX 309

be tyme *adv* quickly XVI 1117

beve *n* bevy; a group of women XXI 771

bewreye *inf* expose a person by betraying his secrets V 223

birdbolt *n* blunt-headed arrow used for shooting birds XXI 1380

birrall *n* beryl XXI 467

blased *past part* burnt XXIV 294

blasy *inf* proclaim XIII v 32

blaynes *n pl* blisters XVI 1901

ble *n* complexion, colour XIII i 36, XVII 218, XXI 1412

blenkardis *n pl* persons lacking intellectual perceptiveness XXI 610

blennes *3 s pres* mixes XVII 201

blere...eye *3 pl pres* deceive XIX 684; *bleryd 3 s past* IV i 28; *blerde past part* ? blinded XVI 354

blinkerd *adj* lacking in intellectual perceptiveness IV i 24

blommer *n* ? uproar, ? confusion XVII 407

blo(o) *adj* blackish-blue, leaden-coloured XVI 2054, XXI 1399

blother *1 s pres* talk nonsense, babble XVI 1037; *3 s pres* XIX 66; *3 pl pres* XIX 777

blow *inf* flourish IX 4

blowboll *n* drunkard IV i 24

blowe *1 s pres* ? puff, ? pant, ? be breathless XVI 1037; *1 pl pres* XVII 291.

blunder   *i s pres* cause confusion XVI 1037
blunderyng   *vbl n* confusion XVI 460
blurre   *n* ? blister, ? swelling, ? smear XVI 1179
blysse   *inf* thrash XVI 2182; *blyst past part* XVI 1622
blyssyng   *vbl n* blessing XVIII 516
bobbe   *inf* strike V 259
bolte   *n* arrow XVI 294
bonet   *n* small sail XV 32
bonne, bonny   *n* pretty creature XVI 990, XVII 227
borde   *n* table XIII ii 10, XX 190; *bordes pl* ship's sides, planks VII 248
borde   *n* jest XX 785, XXIII 319
boryall   *adj* northern XXI 261
boskage   *n* thickets XX 53
botchment   *n* make-weight XVI 1113
bote   *3 s past* bit VII 305
bote   *n* boot XIII ii 5
bote   *n* remedy XVI 2070, XXI 376
boteles   *adj* without remedy III iii 46
botell   *n* bundle of hay or straw XVIII 147
botowme   *n* clew on which to wind thread, or a skein or ball of thread XXI 799
bottell   *n* leather container for holding liquids XVII 402, XIX 650
bottes   *n pl* worms; a disease caused by parasitical worms or maggots XI 63,
   XII 171
bottons   *n pl* ? buds of flowers, ? raised knobs XXI 803
bougets   *see* bowget
bounce   *n* thump VI 86
bo(u)nde   *adj* owing allegiance XI 36, XII 127
bourne   *adj* burnished XXI 41
bow   *inf* obey VI 74
bowget   *n* bag, purse, wallet XVI 2232; *bougets pl* VII 752
bowsy   *adj* affected by drinking XVII 17
boystors   *adj* rough XXI 20
brablyng   *vbl n* chattering VII 461
brace   *inf* bluster, assume a defiant attitude XII 33, XVI 1330, 1890; *bracyd
   past part* XVI 2221
brace   *inf* embrace, clasp XVI 1560; *brased past part* VII 1195
bracers   *n pl* blusterers XXI 189
brake   *n* position of powerlessness, a trap (properly, a wooden frame used for
   holding steady the feet of a horse while it is being shod) XI 61, XII 158,
   XVII 325; an instrument of torture XVI 2187, XX 983
brake   *inf* break from restraint XVI 2085
brall, brawle   *inf* revile XX 596; contend in an unseemly fashion XVI 1722,
   XXI 786
brased   *see* brace
brast   *inf* burst XVI 2160, 2562
braules   *n pl* brawlers XXIII 218
brayde   *n* sudden movement; *at a brayde* suddenly V 181, VII 485
breke   *n* breeches XVII 452
bremely, brymly   *adv* roughly, ruggedly XIII i 25, XVI 1245, XXIV 221
bremis   *n pl* breams; freshwater fish (*abramis brama*) distinguished by their
   silvery-yellowish colour and high arched back XXI 661

brende, brent *see* bryne

bresyth *see* brose

brevely *adv* briefly XXI 1092, XXIII 82

brevyate *inf* abbreviate XVI 2338

broisiours *n pl* bruises, wounds XXI 673

broke *inf* digest XVII 212

brose *inf* crush, break XX 983; *bresyth 3 s pres* IV ii 31; *broisid 3 s past* XXI 625

brothell *n* wretch, worthless person XVI 2106; *brothells pl* XIII v 73

brow-auntleres *n phr* cuckold's horns XVIII 488

brute *n* saying XXIV 156

bruted, brutid *past part* talked about, famous XIX 487, XXI 155, 405

brybaunce *n* ? plundering, ? swindling XVI 1503

brybery, bryboury *n* pilfering XVI 1226, 1354, XXI 183, 614

brymly *see* bremely

brym(me) *adj* rough, rugged XII 161, XVI 1502

bryne *inf* burn XXIII 152; *brende, brent past part* VII 1327, XXIV 89, 295

bucolycall *adj* pastoral XXI 327

budge furre *n phr* lamb's skin fur XVI 1057

bukram *n* kind of coarse linen or cloth stiffened with gum or paste XX 918

bullyfant *n* ? bull elephant XVII 520

bullyons *n pl* knobs or bosses of metal XXI 1165

bushment *n* ambush I 81

buske *inf* prepare, busy oneself, hurry XIII i 41; *buskt 3 pl past* I 81; *buskyd past part* XII 149

buskyn *n* half-boot XVI 755, 853

bussheth *3 s pres* grows thick like a bush XVI 835

buttes *n pl* marks set up for archery practice XVI 294

buttyng *n* term of endearment XIII v 43

by *inf* buy XVI 1082; *3 pl pres* ? experience, ? acquire XVI 10

bybyll *inf* drink XVII 550

bydene *adv* indeed, all together XIX 954

byl(l)(e) *n* document XVI 1667, invective 33; petition, legal plea XIX 97; *bylles pl* letters, messages VII 683

byllys *n pl* swords XI 26

bynde *1 s pres* strain, brace, tighten up (like a strung bow or wound-up harquebus) XIII iii 160

byrle *inf* draw or pour out drink XVII 269

byse *adj or n* darkish grey or dull blue XXI 1158

bytter *n* bittern XVI 1837

cabagyd *past part* grown to a head like the horns of a deer XVIII 488

cacademonyall *adj* consisting of bad angels XX 810

cache *inf* ? catch, ? run away, ? lie low XVI 1495

calcydony *n* chalcedony; a crypto-crystalline sub-species of quartz XXI 587

call *n* summons; *make...to the call* train to be obedient to the summons (a metaphor from falconry) XVI 1573

callet *n* lewd woman, scold XVII 462; *calettes pl* XVII 347

calodemonyall *adj* consisting of good angels XX 809

calstocke *n* cabbage stalk XX 355

camamell *n* camomile (*anthemis nobilis*), a creeping herb XXI 978 cam(m)o(c)ke   *n* crooked piece of wood XIII i 30, XX 117

camously   *adv* concavely XVII 28

can   *1 s pres* know, know how to XVI 424; *canest 2 s pres* XVI 1143; *cond past part* learnt XVIII 143

cankard(e), cankerd   *adj* corrupted, infected, ill-tempered XVI 757, 758, XX 335, XXIII 361

canonically   *adv* in accordance with canon law XXIV prose

cantell   *n* thick slice XVII 429

captacyons   *n pl* attempts to acquire (by address or art) XXI 815

carbuckyls   *n pl* protuberant inflammations of the skin XVI 1902

carectes, carectis   *n pl* letters, magical signs XX 697, XXI 585

carefull   *adj* full of grief IV v 6, XVI 2049, XXI 1255, XXIV 15

carke   *3 pl pres* are burdened with care XIX 120

carle   *n* churl XVI 1820; *carles, carlys gen sing* XVI 288, 998; *karlis pl* I 34

carlyng   *n* old woman, witch XVIII 205

carlyshe   *adj* churlish VII 282

carp   *inf* recite, sing III i 13; *carpe 3 pl pres* find fault, criticize XIX 547, 1189

case   *n* costume XVI 1046

casseth   *3 s pres* dismisses from service V 117

cast   *inf* vomit XVI 1726, 2161; *imp* XVI 1614; *past part* aborted XX 85; *cast up* forsake XIX 386; abandoned XX 140

cast(e)   *n* throw at dice V 390; ? throw, ? stroke of fortune XXI 1401; stratagem XXIII 101

castyng   *vbl n* in embroidery the making of knots on the ends of threads XXI 802

casuall   *adj* precarious, fickle XVI 2511

casuelte, caswelte   *n* accident, chance, chance occurrence XIII v 121, XX 747, XXI 1406

catell   *n* livestock XVI 1135

caudell   *n* caudle; a warm drink usually of thin gruel mixed with wine or ale, sweetened and spiced XVI 1614 (or perhaps the cup or bowl it was served in; compare XVI 1728); *cawdels pl* XVI 2008

causes   *n pl* matters of interest, legal actions XIX 107, 1196

cavell   *n* low fellow XVI 2190

cawdels   *see* caudell

cawry-mawry   *n* coarse material XVII 150

cayser   *n* emperor XVI 797

caytyfe   *n* wretch XVI 1950, 1954

Centaures   *n pl* fabulous creatures with the heads, arms and trunks of men joined to the bodies and legs of horses VII 1294

chace, chase   *n* hunting; *fre chace* free range XVI 1329; spot (technically in tennis, the second impact on the floor of a ball an opponent has failed to return) VI 62, XX 883

chaf(f)er, chaffre   *n* merchandise V 54, XVI 450, XVIII 129

chare   *inf* turn aside IX 22

chares   *n pl* chariots XIX 961

charge   *n* heed XVI 296, 2081

chase   *see* chace

chaunce   *n* misfortune XXI 1255

checke   *n* taunt, rebuke XVI 297; *have a checke* meet with an unfavourable turn of events XIX 165; *Tyborne checke* hanging XVI 910

checke   *3 pl pres* quarrel XVI 1362; *checked past part* struck XVI 951; *cheked at the fyst* refused to be obedient (a hawking metaphor) XX 735

chepe   *n* bargain, price; *best chepe* lowest priced II 24

chere   *n* countenance, expression, face I 176, XVII 14, XIX 395, XXI 697, 1515; *royall chere* high living XVIII 399

chermed   *past part* bewitched V 340

cheryssheth   *3 s pres* favours V 117; *cheryshed, 3 s past* caressed IV i 9

chevynge   *vbl n* outcome XVII 186

chevysaunce   *n* profit V 100; loan XVI 2236

chowgh   *n* chough, one of the smaller members of the crow family VII 448

chydder   *1 s pres* shudder XVI 1817

chyll   *1 s pres* shall XVII 1

chyncherde   *n* miser XVI 2492

ciromancy   *n* palmistry XVIII 138

clap   *n* blow VI 89, XII 169; *clappys pl* IV ii 32

clappyth   *3 s pres* plays, strikes (a musical instrument) III i 36

clarioner   *n* trumpeter XXI 233

clarke   *n* educated man, clergyman XVI 480, XVIII 119

clatering   *vbl n* tattling XV 74

clat(t)er   *inf* babble, talk in a garrulous or noisy way XXI 1195, XXIV 159; *clatters 3 s pres* XIX 23; *clatter 3 pl pres* XIX 547

clawes   *n* clause; a single passage usually of a larger discourse XXIV 38

clepe   *inf* embrace XVI 1802

clobbyd, clubbed   *adj* shaped like a club XVI 1494, XVII 422

clokys   *n pl* claws, clutches XVI 1874

cloth of astate   *n phr* canopy XXI 484

clout   *n* cloth containing a certain number of pins XVII 564; *clowtes pl* clothes XVI 1211

cloute   *inf* patch up XX 527; *clout 2 pl pres* XXIV 222

clubbed   *see* clobbyd

clyfte   *n* the cleft between the buttocks XVI 2176

clyttreth   *3 s pres* chatters XIX 23

coarte   *inf* constrain XV 45; *coarted past part* XX 441

cobbill   *inf* cobble, mend XX 527; *cobble 2 pl pres* XXIV 222

cocking   *vbl n* fighting XXIII 299

cockly   *adj* wrinkled XX 288

coe   *n* jackdaw VII 468

cognisaunce, conusaunce   *n* armorial device, badge IV ii 34, XV 22

coke stole   *see* co(o)ke stole

cok wat   *n* cuckold; but sometimes used as a more general term of abuse XV 15; *cok wattes, cokwoldes pl* V 173, XXI 186; *play cocke wat* ? play the fool XVI 1191

colation   *n* treatise XX 717

colerage   *n* ? the plant water-pepper (*polygonum hydropiper*) or arses smart (*culrage*); ? piles; ? an elision of choler + rage XIX 363

cole rake   *n phr* instrument for raking out cinders XX 982

coloppe   *n* a piece of meat XVI 2272

columbyn(e) n the flower columbine (*aquilegia vulgaris*) VII 1052, XXI 913, 982, 1448

colyaunder n coriander XXI 1026

comberaunce n distress XVI 715

comberyd, combred *past part* distressed XVI 2325, 2539, XIX 177

comerous *adj* troublesome V 294

commoditis *n pl* useful things XXI 1500

commune *3 pl pres* talk, speak XIX 564; *commaunde 3 s past* V 198; *comonynge pres part* XVI 1688

commyth *3 s pres* becomes, is fitting XIII v 107

comon n discourse, talk XVI 1539

compas *1 s pres* wonder at XVIII 411; *compast past part* contrived XXIII 102

compendyously *adv* concisely XIX 768

competent *adj* sufficient XXI 1082

compound *inf* settle a debt XVII 597

comprehendynge *pres part?* summing up, ? recognizing XVI 2511

comprise *inf* bear in mind XXIII 529; *comprisid past part* put together XXI 180

comyne hall *n phr* properly, a hall in which a corporation or guild meets, but at VII 646–7 *knyght/Of the comyne hall* means cuckold

conceyte, consayte n conception of a subject, notion XVI 60, 191, 2421, XXI 814; wit XVI 678, XXI 16; good opinion, favour XVI 951, XX 541; exaggerated sense of one's own worth V 302, 310; fancy XVI 961

conceyved *past part* understood VII 1064

cond *see* can

condicyons, condityons, condycyons *n pl* qualities VII 1351, XX 572; manners, personal characteristics XVI 2219

condyssende *inf* agree XVI 39; *condiscendyng pres part* XXI 1132; *condiscendid, condyscended past part* XX 1023, XXI 232

confecture n literary composition XXI 110; *confectures pl* mixtures of ingredients usually made up into a drug or conserve XII 82

confeterd, confetryd, confettred *past part* confederated, joined I 26, V 527, XXIV 54

conflewence n flocking together of persons XX 413

confuted, confutid *past part* proved to be in error XIX 488, XXI 157

confyrmable *adj* ready to conform, amenable XVI 2407

congruence n *of very congruence* as is totally fitting XXI 52

conjecte *inf* guess, form an opinion XVIII 327; *conject 1 s pres* XXI 735

conjuracions *n pl* incantations XVIII 514

conjure *1 sing pres* appeal to, constrain by an oath VII 1290, XXI 1283

conny n rabbit XVII 245, but at XVII 225 a term of endearment

con(n)yng(e), cunnyng *adj* learned, skilful V 445, XVIII 134, 392

con(n)yng(e), konnyng n learning V 63, 450, XXI 140, 886, 898, 905, 1235, XXIV prose

conquinate *3 pl pres* defile, pollute XIX 703

consequently *adv* subsequently XXIV 315

consyderacyons *n pl* meditations XXI 1422

consystory n diocesan or provincial court XX 817

contemplacyo(u)n n meditation XXI 1219, but at XVI 1633 perhaps 'petition' controlle, controule *inf* challenge, find fault with, reprove VI 3, XIII iii 89, XV 22, XX 674; *controld(e) past part* VI 96, XV 9

controlleynge *vbl n* reproving XIII iii 39

contynewe *n* contents XVI 2421

conusaunce *see* cognisaunce

convayd, conveyed *past part* ? arranged, ? accompanied VII 1066; conducted XX 783

co(n)venable *adj* suitable III iii heading, XXI 712, 821

conventuall *adj* of or belonging to a religious convent XX 808

convenyent *adj* suitable XVI 173, 219

convenyently *adv* suitably VII 1069

conveyauns *n* skilful or cunning management or artifice XXI 1238

conveyed *see* convayd

conyng(e) *see* con(n)yng(e)

co(o)ke stole *n phr* cucking stook XIII ii 38, XVIII 481

coost *n through every coost* through every region XIX 203

coost *inf* approach V 431

copborde *see* cupboard

copy(e)hold(e) *n* tenure of lands 'at the will of the lord according to the custom of the manor' XI 35, XII 126

corage *see* co(u)rage

cordyall *n* a medicine, food or drink which stimulates the heart XII 82, XXI 131

cornys *n phr newe ale in cornys* ale drawn off the malt XVI 772

corporas *n* the square of cloth on which is set the host and chalice during Mass VI 63

coryed *past part* drubbed XVI 1622

coryously, curyously *adv* elaborately, intricately XXI 658, 853

costious *adj* costly XXI 570

cote *n* tunic V 358

coted, cotyd *past part* referred to XIX 755; marked XX 572

coughe *inf coughe me a dawe* make a fool of me XVI 1060; *coughe me a foole* XVI 1064

countenaunce *n* continence XVI 47

counter *n* imitation coin of inferior metal XVI 1171

countrynge *vbl n* improvisation below plainsong VII 468, XXI 705; meeting XX 77

countyr *2 pl pres* sing a part accompanying plainsong XIII ii 11; *cowntred 3 sing past* III i heading

co(u)rage *n* desire XVII 11; sexual desire IV ii 7, XIX 973; vigour VII 545; confidence VII 1154, XVI 47; bravery VII 1309

course *n* custom, practice XVI 213

coursers *n pl* horses such as a jouster might ride on, chargers VII 1314

coverture *n* shelter XVIII 9

cowche quale *n phr* ? a game in which one couches or flattens oneself like a quail in covert; *play cowche quale* lie low XVIII 426

cowchyd *past part* set down XVI 1276

cowntred *see* countyr

coye, koy *adj* distant, disdainful V 288, XVI 1583; *make it koy(e)* behave haughtily XVI 1246, XVII 586

coystrowne   *n* kitchen boy III i title, XXIII 171
cra(c)k(e)   *n* loud talk, boast XX 256, XXIII 68; *crackes, crackis pl* XXI 189
   XXIII 350
cra(c)k(e)   *inf* boast, speak out loudly V 168, XII 32, XVI 775, 812, 875,
   1513, XX 977, XXIII 307; *crake 2 pl pres* XIX 602, *cracked 3 s past* VI 50
crakar   *n* boaster XIII iii 110; *crakers pl* XIX 1189, XX 274
crakynge   *vbl n* loud speech, boasting XX 1073
craftely   *adv* skilfully XXI 366
crafters   *n pl* crafty persons XVI 2656
crafty   *adj* skilful, ingenious XVI 1532
crag   *n* neck XXIII 293
crake, craked   *see* cra(c)k(e)
crase   *inf* break XXI 1209; *crased past part* broken to pieces VII 1105
craw   *n* the crop of birds or insects *cast(e)…craw(es)* vomit XIII iii 155,
   XVII 489
creauncer, creaunser   *n* tutor XIII v 102, XXI 1226
credence   *n* credentials XVI 2441
credensynge   *vbl n* believing XX 442
creke   *inf* ? make a (croaking) sound IX 33; *creketh 3 s pres* XIX 19
cribbis   *n pl* baskets XXI 640
crokenebbed   *past part* with a hooked nose or beak XVII 427
cronell   *n* circlet for the head, wreath, garland XXI 288, 776
croppy   *n* throat, stomach XVII 561
croppyd   *past part* having the top cut off XVI 47; shaven XIX 677
crose   *n* crosier, the pastoral staff or crook of a bishop XIX 292
crosse, crowche   *n* the 'cross' on a coin; the coin itself V 364, 398, XIX 929
crosse rowe   *n phr* alphabet XV 18
crowche   *see* crosse
crownes   *n pl* coins; four crowns made up one pound sterling XX 171
cruyse   *n* cruse, a small vessel for liquids XVI 2166
cue   *n* half a farthing, a trifling amount XVI 36; *kues pl* XX 235
cule   *n* buttocks XX 133
cunnyng   *see* con(n)yng(e)
cupboard, copborde   *n* service of plate or a set of vessels displayed on a side-
   board XX 901, 914
cure   *n* the spiritual charge of parishioners VI 4, XIX 102; *busy cure* diligence
   V 221; *under cure* under authority XX 284
curyously   *see* coryously
custrell   *n* servant, base fellow XVI 485
cut   *n kepe…cut* know one's place VII 118, 119
cyatyca   *n* sciatica XVI 1956
cyrcumstance   *n* circumlocution XVI 637, ceremony XXIV 394

dagged, daggid   *adj* slashed XXI 630; bemired XVII 123
daggeswane   *n* coarse coverlet of rough material XVI 2169; but *dagswayne* at
   XXIII 172 is apparently a term of reproach
dagmatista   *n* dogmatist XIX 550
dalyaunce, delyaunce   *n* leisurely talk VII 1095, XVI 237, 1524
dant   *n* loose woman XVII 515
dare   *inf* cower XVI 1342; *dared 3 sing past* XXIII 271
darke   *adj* obscure, difficult VII 801

dased, dasid   *see* dasyng

dastarde   *n* dullard, base coward XVI 2193; *dastardis, dastardys pl* XVI 1486, XXI 190

dasyng   *pres part* staring stupidly XXI 641; *dased, dasid past part* dazzled XX 181; stupefied XXI 734

daucock(e)   *n* simpleton, fool XIX 1160, XX Invective 34, *daucockes, dawcokkis pl* XXI 618, XXIII 380

daw(e)   *n* simpleton V 437, VI 8, 129, XVI 1207, 1379; *dawys gen sing* XVIII 467; *dawes, dawis, dawys pl* XVI 1242, XX 264, 1061, XXIII 478, XXIV 39, 124; *to free of the dawe* too much fooling XVI 2090

dawpate   *n* simpleton XIII iii 94

daynnously   *adv* disdainfully V 82

day-wach   *n phr* duties performed during the day IV ii 30

debarre   *inf* contravene XVI 60

decacorde   *adj* having ten strings XXIV 340

decke   *imp* cover XVI 749; *decte 2 pl past* XXIII 280; *decked past part* covered with abuse XX 611

decollacyon   *n* beheading VI 100

decrees   *n pl* edicts or laws of an ecclesiastical council settling some point of doctrine or discipline VI 131

decretall   *n* papal edict establishing points of ecclesiastical doctrine and law XX 1157; *decretals pl* VI 131

decte   *see* decke

defacid   *past part* ugly, unseemly XXI 1581

defoyle   *inf* foul XXIII 383; *defoyled past part* XVII 373

degre   *n* social rank VII 55, XII 52; *in degre* kindly XVI 1521

delated   *past part* amplified XXIV prose

dell   *n* piece; *every dell* all XVI 1275

delyaunce   *see* dalyance

demeane   *inf* supervise VII 553; *demene imp* behave XXI 1534

demenaunce   *n* behaviour IV iii 6, XVI 1419

demensy   *n* madness XX 682

demeryttes   *n pl* blameworthy acts XXIV 14

demye   *n* short, close-fitting garment V 359

denominacyons   *n pl* names XXI 581

departed   *past part* separated VII 329

deprave   *inf* vilify, disparage, desecrate VII 1274, XIV 43, XIX 513, 1132, XXI 1267; *2 pl pres* XXIII 191; *depravyd 2 pl past* VI 308

derayne batayle   *v phr* vindicate one's right by battle XXI 1563–4; *felde derayne* XXIII 243

derogate   *inf* disparage XIX 706

derogacyo(u)n   *n* disparagement, detraction VII 1277, XXI 218, 1270

dese   *n* table; *hye dese* upper table XVII 175

desolate   *adj* comfortless, wretched XI 24

despensyth with   *3 s pres* excuses XX 682

desteynyd   *past part* dishonoured I 148

devyse   *inf* plan V 424

devyse   *n* advise VII 100; arrangement XVI 2075; *devisis pl* compositions XXI 1494

deynte   *n* pleasure V 150, 338

dictes   *n pl* sayings XVIII 41

diffuse, dyffuse   *adj* difficult VII 768, 806, XXI 111, 338

disable   *inf* disparage XXIV 26

discomfect   *past part* defeated, overthrown XII 84

discommende   *inf* find fault with VII 1270

discorage   *inf* dishearten XXIV 356

discured, discurid   *see* dyscure

discust, dyscust   *past part* determined, decided I 40, XX 751, XXI 881; realized III iii 4

dissuasyve   *n* exhortation against something XXI 151

doddy patis   *n pl* blockheads XX 652

domage   *n* injury XXIII 468

dome   *n* judgement VII 147, XXI 1505

donne, donny, dyne   *adj* dark coloured, gloomy III iii 45, XVI 989, XVII 400

donnyshe   *adj* darkish XVI 1095

dosen broune   *n phr* ? a full dozen, ? a throw at dice V 393

doted   *3 s past* spoke or acted foolishly XIX 757

doterell, doteryll   *n* dotterel, a species of plover; now a very rare summer visitor in Britain VII 409, XVI 1175; *dasyng after dotrellis* ? staring like simpletons XXI 641

dottage   *n* folly XIX 366, XX 43; *dottages pl* XXIV 272

doutted   *adj* feared I 109

douwsypere   *n* powerful lord; the *douzepeers* were originally the twelve peers or paladins of Charlemagne, said to be attached to his person, as being the best of knights XX 639

dow   *n* pigeon VI 72

dowche   *adj* soft, sweet XVIII 29

drabbes   *n pl* slatterns XVII 139

draffe   *n* brewer's grains XVII 171

drane   *n* drone XXIII 164 *dranes pl* XII 172

drawttys   *n pl* moves in chess III iii 31

dres(s)(e)   *inf* prepare, array, equip VII 1346, XVI 1391, XIX 975, XXIII 399; exert oneself XXI 122; *dresses 3 s pres* VII 1170; *dreste 1 s past* V 33; *dreste past part* ornamented XVIII 368

drevyll, dryvyll   *n* drudge, foul person V 337, XIII iii 26

dribbis   *3 pl pres* drivel, dribble XXI 641

drift, dryfte   *n* scheme XVI 1731, XXI 757

dronny   *inf* proceed sluggishly or indolently XVII 230

dropsy   *n* morbid accumulation of watery fluid in the serous cavities or the connective tissues of the body XVII 481

dryvyll   *see* drevyll

dud   *adj* coarse, ragged XIII iii 46

dumpe   *n* fit of melancholy, gloominess or dullness XXI 15, *dumpis pl* XXI 734; *dumpys pl* slow pieces of music written in memory of someone dead III i 47

dun   *n* quasi-proper name for a horse of a dull greyish brown colour III i 10

dure   *inf* last VII 723

dyetyd   *past part* fed in a particular way XVIII 3

dyffuse   *see* diffuse

dykes   *n pl* ditches XIX 622

dyne   *see* donne
dynge   *inf* strike XVI 2183, XXIII 210
dynt   *n* blow XVI 1486, 1878, 1879; *dyntes, dyntys pl* IV iii 30, XVI 1798
dyrection   *n* instruction XXIV 390
dyriges   *n pl* prayers for the souls of the dead XIX 425
dysavaylynge   *pres part* damaging XIX 1104
dyscharge   *inf* exonerate, relieve of an obligation VII 1360
dyscrease   *n* decrease XVI 2521
dyscry   *3 s pres* discover by observation XVI 1356
dyscryve   *inf* examine XVI 2370; *dyscryved past part* discoveied XVI 535
dyscure   *inf* disclose, reveal IV v 7, V 219; betray V 18; *discured, discurid past part* XXI 731, XXIII 128, XIV 92
dyscust   *see* discust
dyser, dysour   *n* jester, professional fool XVI 1176, XXI 635; *dysers pl* ? dice players XXI 608
dysgysed   *past part* dressed in fashionable or newfangled clothes V 351; having behaved in an inappropriate way VI 22, XIX 580; adorned in an unusual way XXI 38
dyvendop   *n* dabchick or little grebe VII 452

elacyon   *n* pride XX 482, XXIV prose
elate   *adj* proud XX 1177
elect(e)   *adj* choice I 11, VII 773, XVI 1533, XXI 76
electuary   *see* allectuary
elenkes   *n* a logical refutation XIX 818, XXIV 126
ellumynynge   *vbl n* embellishment I 128
embesy   *inf* occupy XXI 66; *enbesid past part* XXI 805
emblomed   *past part* covered with flowers VII 1038
embosyd, enbosed   *past part* exhausted by running XXI 24; foaming at the mouth XXIII 477
enbawmed   *past part* endued with balmy fragrance XVI 1557
enbesid   *see* embesy
enblased   *past part* adorned with heraldic devices, but referring in XX 179 to the devices on coins
enbolned   *past part* puffed up XXIV prose
enbosed, enbosid   *past part* embossed, sumptuously decorated XXI 467, XXIII 324; *see also* embosyd
enbraid   *inf* fasten together XXI 789; *embraudred past part* XV 39
enbrased   *past part* clasped XXIV prose
enbudded, enbuddid   *past part* covered (with buds) XVI 1554, XXI 883
enbulyoned   *past part* studded, richly decorated XXI 478
enbybe   *inf* moisten XII 79; *enbybed, enbybid past part* XXI 682, taken in, absorbed VII 872
encankryd   *past part* consumed, corrupted XVIII 362
encraumpysshed   *past part* restricted XXI 16
encrisped   *past part* curled XXI 289
endarkyd   *past part* darkened XXI 645
endiyd   *past part* dyed, coloured I 117
enduce   *inf* adduce, bring forward for consideration as examples or as evidence XXI 94, 1135; *enduced past part* given rise to XXIV 236
endude   *past part* supplied with XXI 1044

endude, endued   *past part* digested (of a hawk) VI 78, XIX 215
endure, indeuer   *inf* remain, dwell XVI 247, 248, 2569
endyght, endyte   *inf* write, compose VII 152, 861, XXI 1017
energiall   *adj* operative, efficacious XXIV 368
enfatuate   *adj* besotted XVIII 384
enfayntyd   *past part* made faint XVIII 391
enferre   *inf* adduce, bring forward XVI 59
enflamed   *past part* burnt XXIV 16
enflorid   *past part* embellished with flowers XXI 1160
engendred   *past part* born VII 1329, XXI 1322
engladid   *past part* made glad XXI 536
englasid   *past part* furnished with flowers XXI 479
engolerid   *past part* having galleries XXI 460
engrapid   *past part* covered with grapes XXI 656
engrosed, engrosid, engrosyd, ingrosed   *past part* enriched, thickened, plumped up XXI 41, 335ff.; written out in large letters, made plain XVI 2438; collected together XXI 1502; swollen XXIII 325
enhached, enhachyde   *past part* figured, engraved VII 1078, XXI 40
enhardid   *past part* hardened XXI 306
enharpid   *past part* ? hooked I 125
enlosenged   *past part* decorated with figures shaped like lozenges XXI 469
enmyxyd   *past part* mingled XVI 2516
ennew   *inf* revive, make fresh VII 1032; *enneude, ennewde, ennewed, enuwyd past part* VII 775, 1002, XXI 389, 985, XXIII 420
enplement   *n* ? place, ? arrival at a goal XXI 402
enportured   *past part* depicted VII 1154
enprowed   *past part* put to advantageous use VII 793
enrailed   *past part* bordered, enclosed XXI 656
enroll   *inf* set down in a register, copy out VI 210; *enrold(e), inrolde past part* VII 787, 1258, X 9, XII 39, XVIII 291, XXI 938
ensaymed   *past part* cleansed or cleaned of superfluous fat VI 79
ensembyll   *adv* together XVIII 423
ensew   *inf* follow XX 62
ensorbyd   *past part* ? swallowed up XVI 2561
ensowkid   *past part* soaked XXI 23
entachid   *past part* ? crowded XXI 470
entendyng   *pres part* stretching towards XXI 1131
ententifly   *adv* diligently, carefully XXI 962
enterement   *n* burial VII 1281, XXI 1274
enterlased   *past part* connected intricately, involved XXIV prose
enterpryse   *inf* attempt VII 856; *enterprysed, enterprysyd past part* ventured to suggest XIX 581; experimented XXI 388
entrusar   *n* intruder XXIII 227
envawtyd   *past part* arched over XXI 476
envayned   *adj* veined IV iii 17
enverdurid, enverduryd   *past part* made green IV iii 13, XXI 666
envyrowne   *adv* around XXI 489
envyve   *inf* enliven, freshen XXI 872; *envyved, envyvid past part* XVI 1551, XXI 1161
epylogacyon   *n make epylogacyon* sum up conclusively XIX 519

equipolens *n* equality of power XX 1134

erectyd *see* arecte

erkith *3 s pres* wearies, annoys XXI 1491

erste *adv* soonest XVIII 370

escrye *see* ascry

estates *see* astate

etermynable *adj* without end I 199

excede *inf* go beyond the bounds of propriety XVI 217

exhibycion *n* an endowment given to a student in a school, college or university XXIV 143

experte *adj* experienced XI 8

exployte *inf* achieve the expulsion of XVIII 307

expres *adv* clearly, plainly I 21, VI 232

expres(se) *adj* clear, plain IV iii 39, VII 1151

expresse *inf* put into words, expound XVIII 386

extort *past part* extortionate IX 28

eyndye, inde *adj* indigo XVI 1553, XVIII 368

eyre *n ear* XVI 712

eysell *n* vinegar XIX 454

fables *n pl* lies XVI 717

face *inf* assume a bold or threatening attitude IX 39, XII 33, XVI 1330, 1601; face out XXIV 196; *2 pl sing* XIX 602; *facyd past part* XVI 2217, 2220

facers *n pl* swaggerers XXI 189

faces *n pl bere no faces* lack boldness XIX 896

facion *n out of facion* disordered, disorganized XX 1041

facyd *see* face

faine, fayne *adj* glad IX 42, X 17, XVI 784, XVIII 188

faitours *see* faytour

falowe *n* arable land XVII 87;; *fallows pl* fields XXI Epilogue 6

fals quarter *n phr* soreness on the inside of a horse's hoof XXI 504

falyre *n* devotee, follower XVII 229

fange, fonge *inf* obtain XIX 1197; seize XX 1156

fantasticall *adj* perversely or irrationally imagined XXIV prose

fantasy *n* wilfulness, caprice XX 187

farle, farly *adj* strange, marvellous XVI 923, 1160, XXIII 303; dreadful XIX 329

fat *n* vat XVI 1319

faute *n* fault XV 25

favell *n* duplicity, flattery XVI 727

favour *n* beauty VII 1048

fawchyn *inf* cut with a sword XVI 2189

fawconer, fouconer *n* falconer VI 43, 81

fayctes *n pl* deeds XXIII 398

fayn *adv* gladly III i 40

fayne *inf* sing with due regard to the 'accidentals' of the score III i 53; invent a story V 135, XXIV 353; pretend VII 695; *fayned past part* deceitful XX 365; *see also* faine

faynted *past part* made afraid XX 157

faynynge *vbl n* pretence V 465

faytour *n* cheat, impostor XXIII 494 *faitours, faytors pl* I 172, XV 27

fe(e)   *n* service I 185; possessions, money XVI 1967
feed   *past part* given payment, bribed VI 151
fee symplenes   *n phr* unrestricted possession XIX 1175
feffyd   *past part* enfeoffed, given up entirely XVI 1536
fel, fell(e)   *adj* cruel, angry XIII i 15, XIII v 65, XV 79, XX 279, 650, 1167, XXIII 6
felashyp   *n a felashyp assaye* join in a part-song V 254
feld(e)fare   *n* fieldfare, a large member of the thrush family VII 412, XVI 1838
fele   *inf* test out, discover 760
fell   *n* skin III iii 18
fell(e)   *see* fel
fenaunce   *n* ransom, redemption I 195
fenestrall   *n* window-frame, lattice XXI 1387
ferre   *adj* far XVI 337
fet   *n* neatly attired woman XVII 52
fet   *inf* fetch VI 107, XVI 64; *fet(te) past part* fetched, obtained XI 65, XVII 334
fete   *adj* neat, comely XVIII 18
fetewse   *adj* handsome V 370
flagra(u)nt   *adj* fragrant XXI 671, 978
flappe   *inf* strike suddenly XVI 1507
fle(c)kyd   *adj* of variegated colour VII 397, XVIII 204
flery   *inf* smile obsequiously in a flattering way XVI 738, XXIII 135; *fleriing pres part* XIII v 152
flesshe-flye   *n phr* fly which lays its eggs in dead flesh XVII 509
flete   *inf* ? drift aimlessly, ? overflow XVI 1080; *2 pl pres subj* float XVI 254
flingande   *pres part* violent XXIII 317
flocket   *n* loose garment with large sleeves XVII 53
flod(d)e   *n* flood VII 71, 268; river VII 1334, XXI 1327
florisshyng   *vbl n* adding elaborately curved lines to that which is set down XXI 802
flotes, flotis   *n pl* flowings, drops XXI 335 *ff.*
floure   *inf* froth XVII 206
flusshe   *n* hand consisting of cards all of one suit XVIII 430
flycke   *n* flitch or side of bacon XIX 844
flyp-flap   *n* hanging piece of cloth XVII 508
flyt(te)   *inf* deviate XVI 2466; depart XIX 994, XX 634; *1 pl pres* XVI 2478
flytynge   *vbl n* wrangling, complaining XX 1059
fode   *inf* beguile XVI 1698
fode   *n* deceiver, flatterer II 10
foggy   *adj* bloated XVII 483
foisty, fusty   *adj* stale-smelling, mouldy XIII v 76, XXI 639
folabilite   *n* folly XV 43
follest   *adj* foulest
fond(e)   *adj* foolish VI 43, XII 5, XIII iii 191, XIII v 171, XVI 742, 1096, XXI 741, XXIII 383
fondnesse   *n* foolishness XVI 1866
fonge   *see* fange
fon(ne)   *n* fool VII 128, XIII iii 30, XVI 863, 1185
fonne, fonny   *adj* foolish XVI 877, XVII 229

fonnysshe   *adj* foolish XVI 650

fopped   *2 pl past* acted like fools XXIV 120

forborne   *past part* parted XVI 220

forcastyng   *vbl n* planning beforehand XVIII 463

force, fors   *n no force, no . . . fors* no matter V 334, XVI 1752, XXIII 282; *I ne force* I do not care XXI 731

for-drede   *adj* very frightened VII 667

foretop(pe)   *n* the fore part of the top of the head, or the hair thereon XVI 1514, XIX 531, XXI 1333

forfende   *1 s pres* forbid, prevent XVI 2456; *3 sing pres subj* XVI 1114

forge   *inf* pretend XVI 1613

forme foote   *n phr* forefoot XXI 595

fors   *see* force

forseth, forsyth   *3 s pres* cares XVI 254; matters XVI 1150; *forsede 3 pl past* I 84

fose   *n* house leek XX 288

fotys   *2 s pres* walk XVI 765; *fotyth 3 s pres* treads a measure in a dance XVI 1331; *fotid 3 s past* XXI 686

fouconer   *see* fawconer

foundacyons   *n pl* institutions (monasteries, colleges, hospitals) founded by endowments; the endowments by which such institutions are founded XIX 415

founde   *past part* maintained XXIV 147

foy   *n* faith XXIII 436

foynes   *3 s pres* thrusts, pokes XX 224

frame   *inf* succeed XVI 1838; *it frames* it turns out, it profits XXIV 11

franesy, frenes(s)y(s)   *n* madness, frenzy XVI 1932, XVIII 47, XX 186, XXIV prose

franty(c)ke   *adj* mad, insane VI 43, 249, XIII v 118, XVI 1294, 1300, XVIII 46, XX 186, XXIV 299

fraunchys   *n* legal immunity III iii 26

fray   *n* fear, terror VII 228, XXIII 242; assault, attack V 501, XI 44, XXIII 35; quarrel XVI 808, 932; *frays pl* XVI 814, XXI 182

fray   *inf* frighten XIII v 171, XX 154; *fraye 3 pl pres* attack V 446

frayne   *inf* ask XX 400

freat, frete   *inf* consume, eat away VII 58, 482; *frete past part* VII 931

freers   *n pl* friars XVI 487

freke   *n* man (often a derogatory term) XVI 657, 1160; XXIII 303

frenes(s)y(s)   *see* franesy

frenetykes   *n pl* madmen XXIV 400

frese   *n* coarse, woollen cloth XIII iii 46

fresshe   *adj* new, (of clothes or ornaments) gay, unsullied by use VII 1180, XVI 460; elegant XXI 1499

fresshe   *adv* gaily XXI 39

fret   *past part* adorned VII 1048, XXI 485

frete   *see* freat

friscajoly   *adj* sportive XXIV prose

frompill   *inf* frumple, wrinkle II 16

froslynges   *n pl* things nipped or stunted by the frost XVII 460

frounce   *inf* cause someone to become wrinkled XVI 1514; *frownsid past part* XXI 1333

frounce   *n* illness producing soreness round a hawk's mouth VI 85
frowarde   *adj* adverse XVI 2560, XXI 1450
frowardes   *n pl* awkward words VII 779
frubyssher   *n* one who removes rust, who polishes or burnishes XVI 1063
frygges   *3 s pres* rubs XVII 178, XX 224
frytthy   *adj* woody XXI 22
fucke sayles   *n phr* fore sail; a dress which falls in folds; a wimple XIX 397
fume   *n* passion, zeal XX 423
fumously   *adv* passionately XVI 2497
fumygacion   *n* the action of generating odorous smoke or flames XX 699
furdrers of love   *n phr* pimps, pandars XXI 609
furnysshe   *inf* provide for XVI 1391
fustiane   *adj* worthless, sorry, pretentious XXI 1206
fusty   *see* foisty
fuyson   *n* abundance I 131
fyer drake   *n phr* fiery dragon XX 981
fyest   *n* foul smell, stink XVII 343
fyle   *3 pl pres* smooth, polish XIX 850
fylythe   *3 s pres* defiles, dirties XIII iii 198
fynde   *n* devil VII 283, XXIII 156, 251
fysgygge   *n* flighty woman, gadabout XVII 538
fysnamy   *n* physiognomy XIII ii 25
fytte   *n* unpleasant experience XIX 329

gabyll   *n* cable XXI 833
gadde   *?n* or *?v* ? fool, simpleton ? rush about madly XVI 1301
gaglynge   *adj* cackling VII 447
gall   *n* bile; any very bitter substance XVIII 153, XIX 454
gall   *n* sore or irritating place XVI 1232, XX 25, XXI 97; *galles pl* VII 473
gambaudynge   *vbl n* capering XX 73
gambawdis   *n pl* pranks VI 65; acrobats XXI 608
gambone   *n* ham, the bottom part of a flitch of bacon XVII 327
gamut   *n* the lowest tone in the hexachordal scale; the whole hexachordal system III i 13
gan   *n* ? gander XX 888
gane   *inf* gape, yawn XIII ii 15
gant   *see* ga(u)nt(e)
gape   *3 pl pres* crave XIX 85
gar   *see* gar(re)
garded   *past part* ornamented, trimmed or faced as with braid or lace V 356, 508
gardevyaunce   *n* chest for valuables XVI 2231
garnisshed, garnysshed   *past part* decorated, equipped XXI 39, 387
gargone   *n* gorgon XIII v 1; *gargons gen sing* XIII ii 29
garlantes   *n pl* garlands XIX 963
gar(re)   *inf* cause XVI 1514, 1835, *garde 3 pl past* XVI 1508, 2067
gase   *n* thing or person that is looked at XXI 1206
gaspe   *inf* ? desire earnestly, ? catch the breath with astonishment XVI 2067; *gaspe 3 pl pres* XIX 85
gasy   *inf* gaze, look proudly XIII v 29
gate   *n* way, road XVI 946
gaude   *n* jest, trick XVI 1829

gaudry   *n* trickery XIII v 39

gaudy   *adj* deceitful, full of trickery XIII ii 36

gaunce   *adj* gaunt VII 444

ga(u)nt(e)   *n* bird; ? great crested grebe XVII 516; but evidently a gander at VII 447

gaure   *1 pl pres* stare XVI 2247

gelt   *n* money XVII 610

generacion   *n* birth, family XIV 52

genet   *n* originally a light horseman, but in English usually applied to a small horse. At XVII 392 contemptuously applied to a woman

gentle, gentyll, jantyll, jentill, jentyll   *adj* noble VII 325, 1251, XIII v 67, 69, 70, XVI 212, XXI 1006

gere   *n* apparel XIII i 26; matters, stuff (usually in a depreciatory sense) XVIII 394

gerfawcon, jerfawcon   *n* gyrfalcon, a large falcon VII 557

gery   *adj* changeable VI 66

geson   *adj* barren, producing scantily XIII iii 129, XX 1000

gest   *n* tale, story XVII 622

gest(e)   *n* guest, fellow XVI 703, 1096, XX 1212

get   *see* jet

gewgaw, guygaw   *n* trifle, unimportant thing VI 157, XVI 1013, XVIII 481; *gygawis pl* XX 1063

giggishe   *adj* flighty, wanton XXI 1206

glaymy   *adj* slimy, sticky XIII iii 168

glayre   *n* beaten egg whites used as a medical adhesive; anything viscid or slimy XVII 25

gle   *inf* squint, close one eye, cast a sidelong glance XVI 2067

gle   *n* music XXI 278

glede   *n* fire, glowing embers XIII i 37

glede   *n* kite (*milvus regalis*) but applied locally to other birds of prey XVI 1047, but perhaps used contemptuously of a falcon

glent   *adj* glowing XVI 980

glent   *n* ? fall, ? glancing blow XVI 1668

glint   *adj* slippery XXI 572

glome, glum   *n* sullen glance V 80, XXI 1117

glommynge   *vbl n* scowling XIX 83

glose   *inf* deceive, blandish I 41, XXI 760, 910; *gloseth 3 s pres* XIX 25

glose   *n* gloss, marginal comment and interpretation XVI 1427, XIX 779

glosynge   *vbl n* deceit, pretence XIX 356

glowtonn   *n* needle used in embroidery XXI 795

glum   *see* glome

gnar   *n* snarl XX 300

gomys   *n pl* gums XIII i 12

goostly   *adv* spiritually XIX 742

gorbelyd   *adj* having a protuberant belly XIII ii title

gore   *n* wedge-shaped panel of material forming part of a skirt VII 346

gowndy   *adj* bleary XVII 34

gramatolys   *n pl* smatterers XVIII 318

grame   *inf* be angry XVI 1839; *gramed past part* XIX 1114

gratyfyed   *past part* bestowed, freely given XIX 715

gravin, gravyd   *past part* engraved IV iii 48, XXI 587

grayle   *n* the gradual or antiphon sung between the Epistle and the Gospel at Mass VII 441

gre   *n in* gre kindly, willingly XVI 1979, XXI 1487

gree   *inf* agree, be in harmony XXI 275; *greyth 3 s pres* is suitable XII 52

gressop   *n* grasshopper VII 137; *gressoppes pl* XXI 1158

greuyned   *past part* having a granular or coarse texture XVII 32

grey   *n* badger XXI 101

greyth   *see* gree

groinynge   *vbl n* grunting, growling XIII ii 2

grone   *inf* (of a male deer) utter its cry at rutting time XXI 1408

grope   *inf* investigate, pry into XVI 600, 725, XXI 617; rummage, get into XVI 2231, XXI 832; understand XVI 2377

grosely   *adv* thickly XXI 645

grossolitis   *n pl* chrysolites (gems of a green or yellow colour) XXI 466

grote   *n* coin of small value; sixty made up one pound sterling XVI 1193, 1206; *grotes pl* XVI 337, XIX 160. At XVI 384 perhaps this meaning or perhaps meaning hulled or crushed grain

grouchyng   *adj* grumbling, complaining, cherishing resentment XX 80

grounde   *inf* establish XIX 724

grownde   *n* foundation, basis XX 780, XXI 866, XXIII 81; ground-work XXI 41

groynis   *3 pl pres* grunt XV 4; *groynyd past part* XVIII 441

grudge   *inf* grumble, complain XIX 64; *grugyd 3 pl past* XX 252; *grugyd past part* XVIII 441

gryll   *adj* harsh, cruel XVII 6

grypes   *n pl* griffins VII 307

gumbed   *adj* with conspicuous gums XVII 40

gup   *excl* Go on! (usually a word applied to horses) II 6, XIV 1, XX 240

guygaw   *see* gewgaw

gyb   *n* usually a familiar name for a tom-cat (see VII 27) but at XVII 99 applied contemptuously to an old woman

gygawis   *see* gewgaw

gyll   *n* woman (contemptuous) XVII 4

gyn   *n* contrivance VI 93; instrument of torture, the rack, but metaphorically, pain at XVI 2255

gyrne   *2 pl pres* show the teeth in a snarl or grimace XIII i 12; *girned 3 pl past* XXI 265

gyse   *n* fashion, manner, practice VII 1251, XVI 408, 453, 809, 813 XXI 121

gytes   *n pl* dresses, gowns XVII 68

habarion   *n* coat of mail XIII v 34

habillimentis, habylementes   *see* abylement

haburdashe   *n* petty merchandise XVI 1279

hach   *n* bottom half of a divided door IV ii 33

hafte   *inf* ? cheat, ? rob V 521

hafter   *n* cheat, fraud XVI 257; *hafters pl* XVI 2456

haftynge   *vbl n* deceiving, fraud XIII iii 38, XVI 697, 1678

hagge   *n* usually a repulsive old woman of vicious nature, but at XIX 52 a term of opprobrium applied to males

hailid   *past part* dragged XXI 622

hake   *n* loafer, idler XIX 250

hallows   *n pl* shrines or relics of saints XXI Epilogue 7

halow   *inf* consecrate VII 405

halow   *inf* shout at dogs in order to urge them on VI 110

halse   *inf* embrace about the neck XVI 1801; *halsyd 3 s past* IV i 18

halt(e)   *inf* limp XVI 1906, 2273; halted *3 s past* XVII 493

halter   *n* hangman's rope XVI 1911

haltynge   *vbl n* limping, lameness XVI 449

hampar   *imp* strike, beat VI 332

handy dandy   *adv* in rapid alternation (as in the children's game in which a small object is shaken between the hands of one of the players) XVIII 171

hap(pe)   *n* luck I 61, XII 168, XVI 2049, XXI 628

happe   *inf* chance, fortune XIX 88; *happid 3 s past* XXI 643; *happed past part* XVI 1984; *so mote I hoppy* if I may have good luck XVII 560

happe   *inf* cover XVI 2037; *happed past part* XVI 2018

happely   *adv* perchance XX 60, 367

harde   *adj* tough, obdurate XV 3

hardely, herdely   *adv* confidently IV i 4; certainly, assuredly VII 272; firmly XVI 151; by all means XVI 1352; truly XVI 2087

hardy   *adj* bold, courageous XVI 1479, XX 328; *hardy on his hede* boldly, presumptuously XIX 1023

hardy dardy   *n phr* rash daring XVIII 457

harnnes   *n* armour XXI 1556

harolde   *n* herald XI 8; *haroldes pl* XIII v 71

harow   *inf* despoil VII 1291, XXI 1284

harre   *n* hinge of a door or gate; *out of harre* out of joint XVI 912, 2095

harres   *n* a group of loose women XIII v 77

hart rote   *see* hert rote

harum   *n* hare (with a pseudo-Latin termination) VI 104

hasarde   *n* game of chance played with dice V 393

haserdynge   *vbl n* gambling (usually with dice) XX 1193

haskardis   *n pl* low fellows XXI 607; *hastarddis* I 24 is perhaps an erroneous form of this word

hastyve   *adj* hasty XXI 1133

haute, hawte   *adj* proud, haughty V 284, XIII ii 26, XVI 824, XIX 71, XX 880; high of pitch in music III i 23; high, elevated of literary style VII 812; high of academic standard XV 24

havell   *n* low fellow, rascal XX 607

hawe   *n* fruit of the hawthorn; thing of small value XVI 2089, XVIII 478

hawtly   *adv* proudly, arrogantly XXI 1117

hay   *n* country dance, the 'heydeguies', XIII v 170, perhaps referred to also at XV 46 and distantly at XX 888

haylynge   *vbl n* greeting XIX 1149

hayne   *n* low-born rustic V 327

haynyarde   *n* mean wretch, niggard XVI 1725

he(a)le   *n* health, well-being XVI 313, XX 771

hecke   *n* gate XXIII 155

hed   *inf* behead XX 1154; *hedyd past part* XX 740

hedellis   *n pl* heddles, cords sustaining the warp of a loom XXI 791

hekell   *n* comb for flax or hemp XVII 295

hente   *1 s past* grasped V 530

herber   *n* arbour XXI 652
herelace   *n* hairband XVII 145
hermoniake   *n* Armenian XIX 297
hernest   *adj* ornamented XVII 280
hert rote   *n phr* bottom of the heart VII 1148; *swete hart rote* dear one XX 667
herynge   *vbl n* audience, hearing XXI 1217
heyre parent   *n phr* heir apparent XVI 507
hight   *see* hyght
Hipocentaures, Hippocentauris   *n pl* fabulous creatures, half men half horses
    VII 1296, XXI 1289
hob(b)y   *n* hobby, a small falcon VII 567, XVI 1342
hobby   *inf* to hunt with a hobby XVI 1564
hoddypeke, huddypeke   *n* simpleton, fool XVI 1161, XX 329, XXIII 301
hoddy poule   *n phr* blockhead, fool XX 673
hoder moder, hugger mugger   *adv phr* secretly XVI 387, XIX 69
hofte   *n* head XVI 749
hogeous   *adj* huge VI 48
hokes   *n pl* rascals, rogues XVI 1374
holde   *n* refuge, stronghold XVI 1581; secure position XVI 2549 *holdes pl* XX
    167; possession XXI 292
holde   *1 s pres* derive a title from X 13
holde   *1 s pres* bet, wager XVI 1193
holde up   *v phr* leave alone V 188
homager   *n* one who owes homage or fealty XI 30
hoppy   *see* happe
hore   *adj* grey, greyish-white VII 1338
horne keke   *n* garfish or hornfish (*Belone vulgaris*), so called from its long pro-
    jecting beak XXIII 304
horson   *n* whore's son, a term of contempt or sometimes coarse jocularity XVI
    517, 1616, 1618; *horsons pl* XX 602
houres   *n pl* prayers or offices appointed to be said at seven stated times of the
    day XIX 241
hovyr-wachyd   *past part* stayed up late too often at night XIII iii 179
howgye   *adj* huge XVIII 494
howst   *imp* hush, be quiet
hoyning   *pres part* grunting XV 4
hucke   *3 pl pres* haggle, bargain XVI 2121
huckels   *n pl* hips, haunches XVII 45
huddypeke   *see* hoddypeke
hudge   *adj* huge XXI 102
hugger mugger   *see* hoder moder
huke   *n* cape or cloak with a hood XVII 56
humlery, home   *excl* exclamation of impatience or dissent V 467
hyche   *inf* move jerkily, hobble XVII 401
hyght   *1 s pres* am called XVI 164; *hight, hyght 3 s pres* VII 253, 1225, XV 73,
    XVI 165, XXI 753; *hyghte 3 s past* V 294; *hight past part* IX 15; *hyght (trans)*
    1 s pres assure XXI 643
hyght   *n of hyght* proudly, in high fashion XVI 962
hystoriall   *adj* historical I 9

iconomicar *n* economist, writer on husbandry XXI 328

ierarchy, yerarchy *n* hierarchy I 211, XX 185

impechment *n* impediment XVI 1418

importe *inf* provide, bring VII 216

imprynted *past part* impressed on the mind XIX 761

incleryd *past part* made bright and clear XVI 2524

inconvenyently *adv* inappropriately XXIII 189

inde *see* eyndye

indeuer *see* endure

industry *n* skill, dexterity, ingenuity XXIV 370

indyfferente *adj* impartial V 535

inevytably *adv* in a manner so as not to be avoided XXIV prose

inferrid *past part* introduced XXI 141

inflammacion *n* the action of exciting or provoking fervour XXIV 379

influence *n* inflowing, infusion of divine power I 157

ingrosed *see* engrosed

inhateth *3 s pres* ? hates inwardly or intensely XVI 2430

inpurtured *past part* portrayed, delineated XVI 1552

inrolde *see* enroll

intentyfe *adj* diligent, heedful XXI 942

intoxicate *inf* corrupt morally or spiritually XIX 702

inwyt *adj* inward, secret XVI 1356

ipostacis *n* hypostasis, underlying substance XIX 526

irous *adj* angry, irascible XX 1167

isagogicall *adj* introductory XX 717

jackenapes *n* monkey XVI 2098

jacounce *n* jacinth XVIII 366

jaggynge *pres part* the fashionable slashing of garments XVI 2097

jangelers *n pl* chatterers XXI 566

jangelyng(e) *adj* chattering XVI 258, XXI 1262, XXIV 37

jangelynge *vbl n* chattering XVI 262

jangle *inf* chatter, speak angrily XVI 565, XIX 330; *2 pl pres* XXIV 264

jantyll *see* gentle

jape *inf* jest, make sport, enjoy oneself V 290, XXI 361; *imp* III i 50; *japed past part* deceived II 19

japes *n pl* tricks XVI 558, 1133, 1846

jaspe *n* ? jasper XIII ii 17 (Dyce II 182 suggests 'wasp')

javell *n* brawler, rascal, rogue XVI 2191, 2211, XIX 600, XX 608

ja(y)st exclamation applied to horses IV ii 18, XIII iii 13, XX 242

jelof(f)er *n* gillyflower; usually the clove-scented pink (*dianthus caryophyllus*) is meant, but also sometimes the wallflower or the stock VII 1053, XXI 983, 1392, 1446

jentill, jentyll *see* gentle

jentylnes *n* nobility XIII v 70

jerfawcon *see* gerfawcon

jet *inf* strut III i 43, XVI 465, XVII 51; *jettes 2 s pres* XVI 962; *jet 2 pl pres* XIII ii 17; *jettynge pres part* XVI 2097

jet, get *n* style, fashion (usually derogatory) XVI 453, 877, XXI 1193

jetter *n* strutting, fashionable gallant XVI 796

jetty   *n* the projecting part of a wharf, the overhanging upper storey of a building XVII 38
jo   *n* darling, sweetheart XII 91
journey   *inf* ? travel, ? engage in a military expedition V 408

kalkyns   *n pl* the turned-down ends of a horseshoe IV ii 23
karlis   *see* carle
keke   *inf* kick XVII 450; *kyketh 3 s pres* IV ii 23
ken   *inf (trans)* teach, instruct XVI 88, XXI 825, 1428 *imp* VII 970; *(intrans) 3 pl pres* know XIX 1053
keteryng   *n* marauder XXIII 248; *keterynges pl* XII 83
klycked   *adj klycked gate* gate with a latch V 371
knackynge   *pres part knackynge ernyst* downright earnest XVI 33
knak   *inf* sing merrily, descant III i 17
knakkes   *n pl* ingenious contrivances, toys, trinkets XVIII 292
knappishe   *adj* testy, rudely abrupt or perverse XXIII 475
knavate   *n* evil man VIII 65
knokylbonyarde   *n* clumsy oaf XVI 480
knowledge   *inf* acknowledge XXIV 207
konnyng   *see* con(n)yng(e)
kote   *n* coot XX 668
kownnage   *n* coining XXI 611
koy(e)   *see* coye
kybe   *n* chapped or ulcerated chilblain, especially on the heel XVII 493
kyby   *adj* chapped, ulcerated XXI 502
kyketh   *see* keke
kynd(e)   *n* nature I 34, VII 388, XVI 1285
kyrtell   *n* gown VII 1194, skirt XVII 70, 419
kyry   *n* the *kyrie eleison*, the short petition used in the Mass XIX 753
kythyd   *past part* made yourself known as XIII i 8

lacke   *n* blame XVI 720, 2533; disgrace XXIII 45, 53
lacrymable   *adj* expressive of mourning III iii heading
lakyn   *n by lakyn* by Our Lady, an oath XVI 338, 506
lampatrams   *n gen sing* ? lamprey's (a term of abuse applied to a woman) XVII 506
lanners   *n pl* lanner falcons VII 565
lap   *imp* wrap XVI 2011; *lapped past part* XVI 1985, 2331
larg(e)   *n a larg(e) and a long(e)* in early musical notation the longest note III i 49, XIII v 3
large   *adj* unrestrained XVI 37, uncontrolled XVI 295
large   *n* ? liberality, ? freedom XVI 180
laud(e), lawde   *n* praise VII 720, 871, XIII v 74; panegyric poem IX title
laude   *inf* praise XXIII 403
lawe   *adj* low XVI 188
lay   *n* law (especially religious law), faith XXIV 171
lay   *inf* present, put forward XXI 1136, but at XVI 2173 ? beat, ? strike
lay(e)   *n* song VII 394, 702
lay fee   *n phr* laity XXIV 267
layne   *inf* conceal, hide V 311
lazars   *n pl* lepers XVI 1904
le   *n* lea XVI 2068

leche   *n* physician XVII 447

lecture   *n* text XXI 109

ledder, lidder, lydder, lyddyr, lyther   *adj* wicked, base, rascally VII 908, XIII v 146, XV 30, XVI 200, 1231; treacherous, false XXIV 234; sluggish, ill XVI 2038; used as *n* meaning 'wicked men' at XVI 1266

legacy   *n* position and power as papal legate XX 1103

lege   *inf* declare an oath V 412

lege de moy, lege moy   *n* a sort of basse-danse XVII 587, XIX 951

lemman(n)   *n* sweetheart, mistress V 401, XIII v 42

leneth...on   *3 s pres* provides with XVII 131

lere   *inf* find out, learn XVI 1268; *lyerd past part* XVIII 504

lering   *n* glancing askance or stealthily XV 67

let   *inf (trans)* prevent, hinder VII 1199, XX 1069 restrain XVI 45; *(intrans)* desist, refrain, delay VI 106, XVI 2072

leude, lewde   *adj* unlearned, unskilful, ignorant V 173, XIII v 85; vile V 457, XXIII 336

leudly, lewdly(e)   *adv* inelegantly XIII iii 42; ignorantly XVIII 294; in an evil way XXIV prose

leven   *inf* trust for support, rely on XXI 54

lever   *comp adj* rather, more willingly XVI 2040, XIX 909

lewdnesse   *n* ignorance XXI 786

le(y)re   *n* face, complexion, cheeks VII 1034, XIII ii 5, XVI 1555, XVII 12

leysshe   *n* leash, set of three dogs XVI 586

lidder   *see* ledder

lidd(e)rons, lydderyns   *n pl* rogues, rascals XV 29, XVI 1919, XXI 188

liddyrnes   *n* sloth XXI 733

limyters   *n pl* friars licensed to beg on behalf of convents within a certain specified district XIX 834

lode stare   *n phr* pole star, guiding light VII 1226

lollardy   *adj* heretical XXIV 204

lome   *n* loom XX 130

longe   *n* lungs VII 918

lorell   *n* worthless person, rogue XIII iii 14, XIII v 85

losell, losyll   *n* scoundrel XVI 200, 1824, 1880, 1886, XIX 1153, 1161, XX 610; *losel(le)s pl* VI 138, XVIII 513, XIX 574, XXI 188, XXIII 459

loselry   *n* scurrilous behaviour XX 664

loure, lowre   *inf* frown XX 428, XXIII 58; look dejected or frightened XVIII 426, XIX 1168

loute, lowte   *inf* bow down XVI 1500, 1623, 1779; *lowttede 3 pl past* I 45

luge   *n* place of confinement, prison XVI 2334

luggard   *n* sluggard IV i 25

lugges   *n pl* ears XXIII 292

luggyng   *vbl n* violent pulling, especially against an animal VII 1316, XXI 1309

lumbryth   *3 s pres* make a rumbling noise III i 29; *lumber 3 pl pres* XIX 95

lurdayne, lurde(y)n(e)   *n* sluggard, loafer, vagabond XVI 418, 1722, 1824, 1887, 2112, XIX 1168, XXIII 336

lure   *n* apparatus usually made of feathers and leather with which a falconer attracts his bird to come to hand XX 283; that which allures or entices XXI 992; *make to the lure* catch, bring to hand VII 1100, XVI 17

luske   *n* idle or lazy fellow XIII i 24

lydder, lyddyr   *see* ledder
lyerd   *see* lere
lyght   *adj* wanton, unchaste VII 645; easily persuaded, fickle XVI 740
lyghtly   *adv* easily, readily XVI 228
lylse wulse   *n phr* linsey-wolsey; a poor, coarse sort of wool XX 131
lyme rodde   *n phr* rod smeared with bird lime XVI 1815
lynde   *n* lime tree; *lyghte as lynde* nimbly V 231
lynkes   *n pl* links of sausage or black pudding XVII 443
lyppers   *n pl* lepers XVI 1904
lyst   *n* desire, wish VI 83, XII iii 5
lyst   *1 s pres* wish, please XVI 1394; *3 s pres* VII 193, 1044, XII 42, XVI 133,
   164, XVIII 67; *list 3 pl pres* XV 31; it is pleasing (impersonal) XX 428
lyste   *n* strip of cloth V 356; stripe of colour XVI 1200
lythe   *imp* listen XIII v 86
lyther   *see* ledder
lytherly   *adv* wickedly XVI 723
lytterkture   *n* learning, knowledge of letters V 449

maddynge   *vbl n* foolish behaviour XVI 285
make   *n* husband VII 732; consort, companion XVIII 234, XIX 250
make   *inf* compose poetry XIII iii 93, XXI 112, XXIV 399
maker   *n* poet XIII iii 108, XVIII 161
makyng   *vbl n* poetic composition XIII iii 7
malapertly   *adv* presumptuously XX 675
malarde   *n* mallard; the male of the wild duck (*Anas boscas*) XVI 926
male   *n* purse, wallet, bag V 138, XIII iii 8, XVI 2232; *males pl* XX 78; *made
   the male to wryng* caused suffering VII 700; *the male dothe wrye* things go badly
   XIX 686
male uryd   *adj* ill-fortuned XII 111
mal(t)apert(e), malypert   *adj* presumptuous, impudent III i 45, XI 7, XII 97,
   XIII ii 4, XIII v 147, XVI 1362
mam(m)ockes   *n pl* scraps, shreds, broken or torn pieces XVI 2009, XIX 652
man   *3 pl pres* must XVI 1500
mande   *past part* provided with men or followers XVI 436
mantycare, mantycore   *n* a fabulous creature, having a man's face, goat's eyes, a
   lion's body, a scorpion's tail, and a serpent's voice XIII ii 4, XIII iii 165
mare   *n* melancholy XVI 1325, XVII 110
marees   *n* marsh VII 69
marefoles   *n pl* young female horses, but at XX 244 applied derogatively to
   women
margerain   *n* marjoram XXI 906
marke   *n pl* a sum of money worth 13s 4d
marlyons   *n pl* merlins, small swift falcons VII 565
marm(e)set, marmoset(e), mermoset   *n* small monkey; grotesque figure XIII ii
   39, XIII iii 13, 172, XVI 457, 1132
marmoll   *n* ulcerous sore XVI 1906
martynet   *n* martin VII 407
mase   *n* club XVI 1494
mase   *n* madness XXI 1208
mase   *1 s pres* confuse XVI 742

mased, masid, masyd, maysyd *adj* confused, bewildered, mad V 83, VI 331, XVI 1506, 1144, XXI 266, 632 XXIV 293

mashfat, masshefat *n* vat or tub in which the brewer's malt was mixed with hot water XVI 1319, XVII 190

masked, maskyd *past part* enmeshed, entangled XVI 30, 458

mastris *see* maystery

mated *past part* checkmated, defeated XX 161

matens, matyns *n pl* properly the prayers said at the midnight office XIX 406, but occasionally those said at daybreak and followed immediately by lauds; more generally, morning prayers XIX 238, 1158

mater *see* ma(t)ter

materyalytes *n pl* questions or arguments relating to matter as opposed to form XIX 559

matriculate, matryculate *past part* registered in an official list, enrolled VII 288, XXI 1281, XXIV 357

ma(t)ter *n* substance or subject of a piece of writing V 537, XVIII 201; *matters* *pl* subjects of contention or dispute XIX 94

matyns *see* matens

maumet *see* mawme(n)t(t)

maunchet *n* small loaf of white bread III i 11

mavys *n* song thrush VII 424

maw(e) *n* stomach VI 57, XIX 656

mawme(n)t(t), maumet *n* Mahomet; an idol or false god, sometimes used as a term of abuse XIII iii 170, XVIII 402, XX 1070, XXIII 257

mayn(n)y *n* group I 46, XX 244, 295

mayntenance *n* support, urging XXI 1133

maynteyne *inf* back up by argument or force XXI 170

maysterfest *adj* bound to a master XVI 2549

maystery *n* skill, achievement XVI 150; *mastris, maystryes pl* tricks, feats XVI 1190, 1716, XXI 383

maysyd *see* mased

mekyll, mykkylle *adj* much XIII v 153, XVI 430

mell(e) *inf* concern oneself with, have dealings with, interfere, meddle III iii 24, XIII v 94, XVI 1497, XIX 162, 211, 428, 820, 1015, XX 378; *melles, mellis, mellys 3 s pres* XVIII 328, XIX 415, XX 961; *mell imp* XXIII 146; *mellynge pres part* XIX 985

mellyng *vbl n* contention, interference XXIII 298

melottes *n pl* garments made of skins worn by monks and friars XIX 864

memory *n* written record XVI 1447; memorial XXI 860

mene *n* intermediate part of a polyphonic musical composition III i 27, XVI 380, 1463; mediator, go-between V 93; stratagem, plan V 308

mengith *3 s pres* mingles XXI 345

merciall, mercyall *adj* martial XXI 236, 347, 1298, XXIII 397, 430

merely *adv* prettily XXI 1382

meritory *adj* deserved XXI 429

mermoset *see* marm(e)set

mery *adj* agreeable XVI 380

mes(s)e *n* portion, serving of food XVI 1756, company of people XVI 996

mesure *n* in music, the proper time relation between one note and the next III i 25, XVI 380 met   *n* measure XVII 333

mew   *n* place in which hawks were kept; *in the mew* in confinement XVI 35

mew   *inf* cover, hide XX 61; *mewed past part* cooped up XX 222

mewte   *inf* mew (of a cat) XVIII 24

miseracyon, myseracion   *n* mercy, compassion XX 1044, XXIV 375

mislyng   *vbl n* drizzle XXI 698

mockys(s)h(e), mokkysh(e)   *adj* scornful, skittish XIII ii 12, XIII iii 172, XIX 180, XXIV 216

moght   *n* moth XVI 1200

molde   *n* earth XVI 1505

molle   *n* mole XVIII 413

molys   *n pl* blemishes XX 246

mommynge, mummynge   *vbl n* inarticulate murmuring XIX 83; performance, representation XVII 620; *make . . . a mummynge* treat with levity or contempt XXI 200

mood(e)   *n* state of mind or feeling, usually angry VII 1158, XII 135, XX 579; *mevyd all in moode* angered V 317; *pyketh mood* grows angry XIII iii 21

morell(e)   *n* dark-coloured horse or the name of such a horse III i 11, XIII iii 13

motynge   *vbl n* debate, argument XIX 1073

motyve   *n* proposition XXI 114

mountenaunce   *n* duration XX 361

mow   *n* grimace XIII v 50

mowte   *1 pl past* might XXI 425

mowynge   *pres part* grimacing XVI 2098

moyles   *n pl* mules XIX 319

mullyng   *n* term of endearment XVII 224

mummynge   *see* mommynge

munpynnys   *n pl* teeth XXIII 293

murnyng(e)   *vbl n* complaining XXI 295, 1377

mur(re)   *n* catarrh VII 419, XVI 2259

murrioun, murryon   *n* Moor XIII i 22, XIII iii 170

muscull   *n* mussell (the shell of which is frequently scabbed) XVII 556

muse   *n* gap in a fence through which game runs for relief when hunted XXI 1384, XXIV 212

muses   *n pl* songs XXIV 338

muskette   *n* musket, the male of the sparrowhawk VII 567

musse   *n* mouth VII 362, XVIII 266

muster   *1 s pres* show myself XVI 736

mutyd   *3 s past* dunged VI 62

myght, myte   *n* mite, very small amount XX 677, XXIII 165

mykkylle   *see* mekyll

mynyon   *n* favourite XVIII 19

myschefe   *n* suicide XVI 2338

myscheved   *past part* ruined XVI 2332

myscreantys   *n pl* unbelievers VI 214

mysdempte   *3 s past* thought ill of, suspected V 137

myseracion   *see* miseracyon

mysproude   *adj* wrongly proud, arrogant V 453

mysteriall   *adj* mysterious, mystical XXIV 366

mysuryd   *adj* unlucky I 118

myswrought   *past part* done badly XXIV 184

myte   *see* myght

myt(e)yng   *n* small amount XIII iii 115; diminutive creature (a term of endearment) XVII 224

napery   *n* household linen XVII 532

narde   *n* spikenard XVI 2345

narrow   *n* (an) arrow XVIII 74

narrowe   *adj* close to one's financial limits XVII 297

nebbis   *n pl* nose, snout (of an animal) XVIII 424

neder   *adj* lower XX 1200

negarshyp   *n* miserliness XVI 2493

neven   *inf* mention XIX 824

newter   *n* neutral thing XX 905

next(e)   *superl adj* nearest XX 260, XXI 252

nobbes   *n* darling (term of endearment) XVII 225

noble   *n* former gold coin, first minted by Edward III; three nobles made up one pound sterling XVI 2125; *nobles pl* XX 922

nody polle   *n phr* fool, simpleton XIII iii 88; *nodypollys, noddy polles pl* XVIII 318, foolish heads XIX 1243

noll(e)   *n* head XIII iii 90; top of the head V 259; *nolles pl* XIX 232, 1242

nones, nonys   *n for the nones, nonys* on that occasion VII 211, XXI 267

noppe   *n* nap, the rough layer of projecting threads on the surface of a textile fabric requiring to be smoothed by shearing XVI 448

noppy   *adj* heady, strong XVII 102, 557

noughty   *adj* worthless XVII 460; dissolute XXI 188

nyce, nyse   *adj* foolish II 2, VII 173, 1132, XVIII 128, XX 760, XXIV 130; extravagant, flaunting in dress XVI 459; affectedly coy XVI 477

nye   *adv* thoroughly XX 966

nyfyls   *n pl* trifles XVI 1142

nyse   *see* nyce

nysot   *n* affectedly coy woman XVI 1228

nysyte   *n* affected coyness XVI 478

obliqui, obloquy   *n* abuse, detraction XVIII 363, XXI 1559

occupy   *inf* use, employ XVI 425, 472; *3 s pres* XX 245; *occupyed 3 s past* XVI 2129; *occupied, occupyed past part* I 73, XVI 428, 705, 2131, XVI 144; busy XVI 1019

oder   *adj* other XVI 386

odly   *adv* singularly, remarkably XVI 533, 1605

olyfa(u)nt   *n* elephant XIII iii 171, XVII 519; *olyfauntes pl* XIX 962

on-flote   *adj* free from money troubles V 488

onlyve   *adj* alive VII 728

Onocentaures, Onocentauris   *n pl* fabulous creatures, half men half asses VII 1295, XXI 1288

open tyde   *n phr* time when no fasts are imposed XIX 854

optayne   *inf* succeed, prosper VII 697, XVI 1792

or   *adv* ever XVI 515

orbicular   *n* circuit XXI 4

ordynall   *n* ordinal, a book setting out the order of the services of the church VII 555

orgulyous *adj* insolent XXIV prose
ornacy *n* ornateness XVI 1531
ouche *n* brooch VII 686
outface *inf* put out of countenahce, overbear XX 623 *imp* V 315
outray(e) *inf* vanquish VII 87, XXI 156
overbrace *inf* overbear through swaggering IX 37
overse *2 s pres* fail to perceive the truth about something, err, forget oneself XX Invective 7; *2 pl pres* XXIV 285
overthw(h)art, overwharte, ovyrthwarthe *adj* perverse, unfavourable, cross IV v 5, XII 36, XIII v 136, XVI 562, XX 1181, XXI 307
overthwartes *n pl* perverse objections XII 37 (p. 120)
overthwartyd *3 s past* acted in opposition VI 230; *overthwarted past part* overthrown XIX 371
overwharte, ovyrthwarthe *see* overthw(h)art
owle flyght *n phr* twilight XVI 671, XXIII 312

pachchyd *past part* collected together in a hasty fashion XIII iii 178
packe *inf* leave, take oneself off XVI 1774
packinge *vbl n* conspiracy I 71
packis *n pl* persons of worthless character XXI 188
paja(u)ntes, pajaunttis *n pl* tricks XIII iii 190, XIII v 37; public displays XVIII 480
pall, paule *n* fine rich cloth, often velvet XIX 310, XXI 474; *paules pl* XIX 941
paltoke *n* doublet or short coat, but at XIII ii 6 it appears to be worn on the head
palyard(e) *n* beggar, knave XVIII 433, XXIII 167
pange *inf* pain VII 44; *panged past part* XVI 1734
parbrake *inf* vomit XXIII 322
parcel(l)(e) *n* part, portion XIII v 97, XVI 55
parcyall *adj* biased XIX 1075
parcyallyte *n* bias XIX 1193
parde, perde *int* truly, verily VII 171, XXI 1236
paregall *adj* fully equal I 134
parker *n* park-keeper XXI 1386
parvertyd *past part* disordered VI 229
pas *inf* excel VII 151
passynge *adj* surpassing XXI 841
passynge *adv* surpassingly XXI 589
pastaunce *n* recreation IV ii 4, VII 1096
pate *n* head XIII ii 6, XIII v 89, XVI 876; *pates pl* XIX 1152, 1245
patlet *n* woman's collar or ruff XVI 2074
patters *3 s pres* mumbles one's prayers in a rapid or mechanical way XIX 22
paule *see* pall
paves, pavys *n* large shield covering the body I 48, IX 46, XVIII 203
pawtenar *n* bag, scrip VI 44
pay *n* pleasure, satisfaction VII 395
paynty *inf* ? pant XVII 584
pe(a)son *n pl* peas XIII iii 127, XIX 212, XX 999
pecke *n* measure of capacity for dry goods, a quarter of a bushel XVI 384, 385, XVII 275

pek　*n* dolt, silly creature VII 409; *pekes pl* XIX 262

peke　*inf* peer, pry XVI 658

pekysh　*adj* stupid VI 225

pelfry　*n* ? spoil, ? plunder, ? trash XIII iii 178

pencyon　*n* payment XIX 452

pendugim　*n* ? penguin XVIII 205; *pendugims pl* XVIII 415

pensell　*n* artist's paint brush made of hair gathered into a quill XXI 1097

peradvertaunce　*n* thorough carefulness XVI 2472

percase　*adv* perhaps XII 38 (p. 120), XX 874

perde　*see* parde

perdurable　*adj* everlasting XVIII 186

perihermeniall　*adj* pertaining to interpretation XXIV prose

perke　*n* perch XIII iii 157

perplexyte　*n* distress XVI 1461

persuacyon　*n* inducement XXI 34

perte　*adj* saucy, forward V 71

pert(e)ly　*adv* saucily XIII v 48, XVI 305

peson　*see* pe(a)son

phronessys　*n* understanding XVIII 47

piggesnye, pyggys-ny　*n* literally 'pig's eye', a flower (perhaps the trillium) at III iv 20, but at II 17 used as a term of endearment

pip(p)lyng　*pres part* blowing with a gentle sound XXI 676, XXIV prose

pirlyng　*pres part* twisting, winding or spinning threads into a cord XXI 796

plane　*n* flat tool resembling a plasterer's trowel XVII 49

playn(e)　*adj* clean, empty of writing VI 222; *In playn felde and battayle* in regular open battle XXIII 205

plenar(e)ly　*adv* fully, completely V 216, XVI 207, XXI 6

plete　*inf* plead, argue a case XVI 2035, XX 324

pletynge　*vbl n* pleading, legal argument XX 318

plummet　*n* pencil of lead usually used for ruling lines XXI 1097

plumpe　*n* mass, cluster XXI 258

pocky　*adj* pustular, infected XX 246, 1170, 1195

poddynge prycke　*n phr* skewer that fastened the pudding bag XVI 2122

podynges, puddynges　*n pl* the stomach of an animal (usually a sheep or a pig) stuffed with a mixture of seasonings and boiled XVI 1128, XVII 443

pohen　*n* peahen, female of the peacock III iv 13

poke　*n* bag, small sack V 179

poll　*n* head; *poll by poll* one after another VI 211

pollaxis　*n pl* halberts or the like, carried by the bodyguard of a king or great personage XVIII 517

poll(e)yng(e)　*vbl n* plundering, extortion, robbery XIII iii 38, 190, XVI 1753, XVIII 495, XIX 360, XX 100

polytyke　*adj* (of poems) skilfully contrived III i heading

pomaunder　*n* mixture of aromatic substances, usually made into a ball, to be carried about with one as a safeguard against infection XXI 1027

pomped　*past part* ostentatiously arrayed XVI 2012

ponder　*n* weight XVI 118

popagay, popigay, popyngay　*n* parrot; when applied to persons it connotes vanity II 3, VII 421, XVIII 14, 106 pope holy, popholy *adj* hypocritically pious, sanctimonious XVI 467, XXIV 247, prose

popped *3 pl past* stated suddenly or unexpectedly XXIV 121

poppyng(e) *adj* ? chattering XVI 232, XX 264, XXIV 39

popyngay *see* popagay

porisshly *adv* in the manner of a person with weak sight XXI 626; blindly XXIV 121

port(e) *n* bearing, behaviour III iv 5, IV ii 6, XIII ii 3, XVI 1540, XXI 43, 866, XXIII 473; reputation XVI 163, 1471

port(e) salu(e) *n phr* safe port XIX 1260, XXI 541

portis *n pl* gateways XXI 580

portlye *adj* imposing, extravagant XVIII 460

port-sale *n phr* public sale XVII 103

pose *n* cold in the head XVI 825, 2259, XVII 365, XX 1195

postell, postyll *inf* write comments on XVIII 393, XIX 753

posty *n* power VII 1332, XXI 1325

potecary *n* apothecary XVI 2351

potell-pycher *n phr* pitcher of about half a gallon capacity XVII 402

potenciall, potencyall *adj* powerful XX 591, XXI 348

potestate *n* ruler XX 989

potestolate *n* power-worshipper XX 988

pounsed *past part* ornamented by cutting eyelet holes, figures and so on in cloth V 508

poynt(e) *inf* fix, appoint III i 41; equip XIII iii 191; *poynted past part* appointed XXI 420; dressed XVI 961

poynte *inf* ? penetrate the secrets of, ? inform on XVI 726; *poynt imp* note, direct one's attention towards XVIII 220, XXI 136

prane *n* prawn XVI 1489, XXIII 163; *pranes, pranys pl* XVI 1243, XIX 208

prankes *3 s pres* struts XIV 57; *pranked past part* decked out in a showy manner XVII 69

prankyng *vbl n* prancing, strutting XIII i 19

prankys *n pl* tricks, frolics XII 150

pranys *see* prane

prate *inf* talk in a not very useful or concise way V 373, XII 32, XVI 305, 1403, 2124 XXI 613, XXIV prose; *prates 3 s pres* XIV 57, XIX 1153; *prate 2 pl pres subj* XIII ii 7; *prated past part* XVI 746

praty(e) *adj* pretty II 8, III iv 20, XVIII 20, 236; clever XVI 501, 688, 1731; *praty space* considerable length of time V 198; *pratyer comp adj* more skilful XVI 2225

pratyng(e) *vbl n* offensive chattering XVI 2173, XVIII 464, XX 76, XXIV 39, 218

pray *n* plunder IV i 13; food III i 45

prease *inf* hurry XIX 1039; *pressyd 2 pl past* XIII v 48

pre(a)se, prece *n* crowd, company V 44, XVI 995, XVII 174, XXI 239, 455, 958; *put . . . in prese* applied themselves, hurried XXI 794

precely *adv* ? particularly, ? briefly XVI 2553

predicamentes *n pl* the ten categories devised by Aristotle, classifying the ways in which assertions may be made about a subject XIX 819

predyall *adj* belonging to a farm XIX 930

predycacion *n* preaching XXIV 206

pregnacy   *n* productiveness, inventiveness XXIV 371
preketh   *3 s pres* goads, incites XIX 20
prendergest   *n* ? person of haughty bearing III i 6
preordinate   *adj* predestined XXI 1232
prepensed   *past part* premeditated XXIV prose (twice)
preposycyon   *n* proposition, a logical form of statement or assertion XIX 977
preposytour   *n* scholar assigned by the master to supervise the rest XVI 1941
prescrypcyons   *n pl* rights XIX 112
pressyd   *see* prease
prest(e)   *adj* quick, brisk VI 71, VII 264; ready XXI 790; neat VII 127, XVI 844
prestys   *n pl* forced loans, especially to a sovereign in an emergency XIX 350
presydent   *n* one who governs or presides XVI 2082; president or head of the king's council XIX 1042
pretence   *n* claim; the putting forward of a claim XXI 817, 1124; intention, purpose XVI 738
pretende   *inf* attempt XIX 1127; *pretended 3 s past* claimed XX 1110; *pretendynge pres part* portending XIX 472
pretory   *n* palace, court XXI 477
preventid   *past part* anticipated XXI 428
prevye   *adj* secret XVIII 512
prevyly   *adv* secretly XIX 1041
prevynge   *n* success; *yll prevynge* ill success VII 185
preye   *inf* rob, plunder V 437; *preyeth 3 s pres* XIX 20
primordiall   *adj* earliest XIII v 105
primordyall   *n* origin, starting point XX 489
probate   *n* test, proof XVI 4, XXI 368
probleme   *n* difficult question, topic proposed for discussion XVI 2505; *pl* XVIII 344
proces(se), prosses   *n* story, narrative VI 231, VII 735, XII 90, XIII v 157, XVI 2510, XVIII 389, XX 536; account XXI 1099; treatise XXIV prose (twice)
professed   *past part* having taken religious vows XX 1121
promotyve   *adj* having the quality of promoting XXI 117
pronge   *n* ? prank, ? trick XVI 501; *at a pronge* ? under pressure XIX 1194
prop(e)   *n* pole VII 1341, XXI 1334
proper, propir, propre, propyr   *adj* pretty, handsome VII 127, XVIII 20, 235, XXI 1447; falsely attractive XVI 442
properly   *adv* attractively VII 1171, XVI 1331; truly XIX 874; with propriety XVI 1337
properte   *n* essential or distinctive talent or attribute XVIII 30
prosecute   *inf* continue XXIV 158
prosses   *see* proces(se)
prothonatory   *n* chief clerk or chief recorder of a court XXI 432
provincyall, provyncyall   *adj* of or pertaining to an ecclesiastical province XIX 221, XX 1158
provincyals   *n pl* documents issued by the head of an ecclesiastical province VI 133
provision   *n* preparation XVIII 454, XXI 757
provynciall   *n* head of an ecclesiastical province XVIII 53

pry *inf* look about for VII 134; *pryeth 3 s pres* III i 45, XX 20

prycke *1 s pres* spur on, incite XVI 2084; *prickyd past part* pointed XIII v 132

prycke-me-denty *n phr* someone affectedly over-precise in bearing or behaviour XVII 581

prycke song *n phr* descant on a plain song written or pricked down III i 48

pryk *inf* ? to be in pain, ? vomit XIII iii 157

prymates *n pl* ecclesiastical superiors, archbishops XIX 1151

prymes *n pl* prayers said at the first canonical hour of the day, 6 a.m. or sunrise XIX 241

psautry *n* psaltery, an ancient and medieval stringed instrument, resembling the dulcimer but played by plucking the strings with the fingers or a plectrum XXIV 340

puaunt *adj* stinking XXIII 120

puauntely *adv* stinkingly XIII iii 143

puddynges *see* podynges

pultre *n* poultry; any domesticated bird XVI 1135

pultrowne *n* mean-spirited wretch XXIII 170

punyete *adj* sharp-tasting XVII 435

pursevantis *n pl* suitors XXI 492

purveance *n* provision XVI 880

pusant *adj* mighty XXI 50

puscull *n* pustule XVII 555

puskylde *adj* pustular XX 1195

py(e) *n* magpie VII 397; term of abuse usually applied to a wily or to a chattering or saucy person IV ii 34, XI 10

pyggys-ny *see* piggesnye

pyke *2 pl pres* choose XIX 208; *pyked past part* XX 1106

pyke *inf* depart, be off XVI 946

pykes *n* ? pickaxe, ? pitchfork XIII iii 72

pykynge *vbl n* pilfering V 236

pylche *n* outer garment made of skin dressed with the hair XVII 398

pylery *n* pillory XVI 356

pyll *inf* peel XX 109, 265; strip of wealth XX 453; *pylde, pyllyd past part* bald, bare XIII iii 68, XIII v 89, 117; mangy XVI 1054, 1055

pyllyng *vbl n* stripping bare, plundering XVIII 495

pyllyon *n* priest's hat XIX 803

pynche *inf* be miserly XVI 384; *pynche curtesy* be over-punctilious, stand on ceremony XVIII 395

pynchyng *vbl n* parsimony XVIII 493

pystell *n* letter, epistle VII 425, XVI 649, XIX 237, XXIV 325; *pystels pl* XXIV 219

pystyllers *n pl* readers of the epistle VI 121

qualytes *n pl* (in law) the ways in which things are possessed or enjoyed XIX 560

quatrivials *n pl* subjects of the quadrivium (i.e. arithmetic, geometry, astronomy, music) XX 514

queed *n* evil VIII 4

quell *inf* kill III iii 23

quere *n* choir, group of singers I 155, VII 553

queresters, querysters *n pl* choristers VI 122, VII 564

quest *inf* (of hunting dogs) break out into a peculiar bark at the sight of game, give tongue XXI 1409

quibyble *n* ? pipe, ? whistle XXIII 389

quight, quyte *inf* repay XV 74; give XVI 1877; *quyte imp* acquit XVI 688

quikly, quyck(e)ly *adv* in a living fashion VII 1121, XVI 1551, XXI 592, 1161; vigorously XVI 1549

quycke, quike *adj* alive VII 205; pungent XIII iii 78, XVII 431

quysshon *n* cushion XIX 996; *quosshons pl* XXIV 113

rachchyd *past part* tortured XIII iii 180

rage *inf* be angry; behave wantonly XX 33

railes *see* rayle

railles *n pl* ? strapwork, ? marginal ornamentation in manuscripts XXI 1157

raist *2 s pres* afflict XXI 317

rammyshe *adj* rank XIII iii 166; wild XVI 1807

ranke *adj* coarse, gross XI 64, XVI 1266; corrupted XVI 2269, XVII 540; wanton XX 1001; proud XXIII 18, 382

rankis *3 s pres* rages, wrangles XIV 56

rappes *n pl* blows XXIII 277

rase *inf* erase, scrape out XXI 72, 1490; *rasid 3 s past* XXI 137; *raysed* cut into VII 1148; *rasyd past part* XXI 1582, lacerated IV v 1

ratches *n pl* hunting dogs XVI 586

rate *n* standard of conduct or action, style; *after the rate* in proportion XVIII 143; *after the funeral rate* in the style of a funeral poem XXI 1286

rate *inf* chide, scold XIII iii 95; *ratyd 3 s past* XVI 1481

rather *comp adv* earlier XVI 1313

ravener *n* plunderer XVI 2191

rawe *adj* crude, inexperienced XIX 94, XX 1107

ray *n* dance XIII v 170, XXIV 169

ray(e) *n* array XVIII 421, XXIII 22

rayle *n* land rail or corncrake (*crex crex*) XIX 869, 870

rayle *inf* jest at, revile V 368, XV 30, XIX 5, XXIII 478; complain VII 396; *1 s pres* XIII v 137; *railes 3 s pres* XIV 9; *rayle, rayll 2 pl pres* III iv 4, XIII iii 130; *imp* XIV 63; *raylyng(e) pres part* XIX 536, XXIV 268

raylyng(e) *vbl n* reviling, abuse XIII v 136, XIX 1147 (but here possibly it means 'fencing')

raynes *n* fine linen cloth made at Rennes in Brittany XIX 374

rebawde, rybawde *n* worthless fellow, rogue XIII v 79, 106; *reba(w)d(i)s pl* XX 604, XXI 607

reboke *inf* belch V 180

reboyled *past part* caused to boil up XXIV prose

rechate *inf* blow a 'recheat', a series of notes on a horn to call hounds together XVI 2152

rechatyng *vbl n* the blowing of a 'recheat' XXIV 217

recheles(se), retchlesse *adj* careless, heedless, irresponsible XVI 2133, XIX 1176, XX 72, 1019, XXI 1393; perhaps adverbial at III iv 4, XVIII 387

reckys *3 s pres* cares XVI 1167

reclame *imp* (a falconry term) call back to the hand, tame, subdue XIII v 106; *reclaymed past part* VI 80, VII 1125, XVIII 260

reconusaunce *n* acknowledgement XXI 838

reconynge *vbl n* calculation XX 760

recorde *n* witness, testimony XVI 114, 309

recounfortyd *3 s past* comforted XXI 359

recrayed *adj* false, cowardly XX 606, XXIII 115, 495, XXIV prose, 45

recule *n* literary compilation XVIII 227, XXI 1390

reculed *3 s past* retreated XXIII 52

rede *1 s pres* advise XVI 998, 2184, 2185, XXI 1598; *redes 3 s pres* XIX 414

redlesse, rydlesse *adj* devoid of counsel XVI 2417, 2051

redouted *past part* feared I 43

reflaring *adj* odorous XXI 977

reflayre *n* scent VII 524

reformacion, refformation *n* correction XXI 145, 411

refrayne *inf* restrain, hold back XX 37, 690; question XVI 2478; *refrayned past part* XVIII 259

regestary *n* registrar XXI 522

regester *n* registrar XXI 1141

regiment *n* rule, government XVIII 437

regraciatory *n* thanks XXI 431

rehayted *past part* ? scolded, ? rebuked XVI 1658

rehers(s)(e) *inf* recite, repeat V 245, VI 246, XXI 706; cite XVI 1490; *rehersyd past part* written about at length VI 199

rejagged *adj* torn XX 605

relacions *n pl* narrations XXIV 108

rele *n* rotary instrument on which thread is wound after it is spun XVII 295

relucent *adj* bright, shining IV iii 21, VII 1159, XIV 46, XVI 1556, XX 1038, XXI 950, XXIV 332

reme *n* realm XII 156

remorde *inf* rebuke, find fault with XIII v 101, XVIII 370, XXI 86; *3 pl pres* XII title (p. 120), XIX 981; *remordyng(e) pres part* XII 11 (p. 120), XX 1058, XXIV prose; *remorded past part* XXIV 23

remorders *n pl* critics XVIII 369

remordes *n pl* rebukes XVIII 298

remorrs, remorse *n* regretful memory IV iii 29; scruple XIII ii 18

remotes *n pl* out of the way places XIX 867

renayenge *vbl n* contradicting XX 193

renome *n* renown V 15

rent *n* income XVI 1667

reny *inf* recant XXIV 87; *renyyd 3 pl past* refused I 78

repa(y)re *inf* make one's way VII 344, XII 42; return XVI 2394; *repayrid 3 pl past* XXI 392

repete *n* recital XXI 1390

replicacion, replycacion *n* answer XVIII 282, XXIV title

replycable *adj* that which may be replied to XXIV 303

reporte *n* commendation XVI 1541

reporte *1 s pres* cite as an authority XVI 280

reprobitante *adj* ? considered worthless XVIII 442

repugnaunce *n* contradiction XXI 221

repyne *3 pl pres* complain XIX 873

reserved, reservyd *past part* kept back XVI 1643, XXI 171; given back XXI 409; retained in someone's service XVI 1702; made exceptions of XXI 1190 responsyve   *adj* answering XXIV prose

resseyte   *n* the Receipt of the Exchequer; the place at which monies were received on behalf of the crown XVIII 341

rest   *n* ? means of stopping a horse; ? wrest, an implement for tuning stringed instruments XVI 136

resty   *adj* rancid XVII 328

resydevacyon   *n* backsliding, apostasy XIX 521

retayne   *inf (trans)* keep in one's retinue or service X 19; *(intrans)* be attached as a retainer XVI 668; *retaynyd past part* XVI 763

retrogradant   *adj* going backward (in apparent motion) in the zodiac XXI 3

revynge   *vbl n* robbing, plundering XX 102

rew(e)   *inf* be sorry, have pity VII 336, 676, XVI 2104, XX 60; *rewed past part* VII 42

rewth(e), r(o)uthe   *n* sorrow, distress I 102, XVI 2051, XIX 343, XX 841

rochis   *n pl* roaches, small freshwater fishes (*leuciscus rutilus*) of the carp family XXI 661

rocke   *n* distaff XVII 296

rocket   *n* outer garment; smock, cloak or mantle XVII 54; *rotchettes pl* XIX 314

rode   *n* cross of Christ VI 178, XVI 1139

rode   *n* sheltered anchorage XVIII 284; *at rode* at anchor V 39, XIX 1255

rolleth   *3 s pres* enrols, makes entries XX 194

rome   *see* ro(w)me

rosabell   *n* beautiful rose XXI 977

rosary   *n* rose tree XXI 979; rose garden IX 27

rosers   *n pl* rose bushes XXI 656

rost(e)   *n* roast XVI 804, 805

rotchettes   *see* rocket

roufled   *past part* set in disarray or confusion XVIII 168

rough, rowte   *inf* clear the throat XIX 1221, XX 341; *what revell route* let revelry roar V 368

rounde   *adv* quickly V 396, XXIII 82, 348

rounde   *2 pl pres* cut the hair short round the head XIX 673

rounde, rowne   *inf* whisper V 513, XVI 1645; *rounded 3 s past* V 526; *rownyd 3 pl past* XXI 250

rounses, rounsis   *n pl* horses for riding VII 1314, XXI 1307

ro(u)sty   *3 pl past* roast VII 1333, XXI 1326

rout   *inf* snore XVII 232; *rowtyth 3 s pres* IV i 20

rout(e), rowte   *n* gathering, company usually of a disordered or riotous sort XVI 848, 992, XVII 362, XIX 1082, XXI 240

routh, row(e), rowth   *adj* rough IV i 15, X 64, XIII i 23, XIII iii 124, XXI 803

routhe   *see* rewth(e)

rowlis   *n pl* rolls, records XXI 192

ro(w)me   *n* place, office, appointment XVI 1328, XX 498, XXI 116

rowne, rownyd   *see* rounde

rowte   *see* rout(e)

rowth   *see* routh

rowtyth   *see* rout

royals   *n pl* gold coins formerly current in England, first issued by Edward IV in 1465; two royals made up one pound sterling XX 921

royle   *n* lout XXIII 270

ruddes, ruddys, rudyes   *n* pink or red parts of the face, complexion IV iii 16, VII 1035, XVI 1551

rule   *n* lines drawn on paper for the writing of music III i 22

ruly   *adj* woeful XVIII 114

rulye   *adv* woefully XVIII 401

rune   *inf* ? chant, ? devise XIII v 170

russet   *adj* made of coarse homespun woollen cloth formerly used for the dress of peasants XVII 54; perhaps at XIX 865 the cloth itself

russhe   *inf* swagger XVI 847; *russheth 3 s pres* ? moves, ? rustles (as it moves) XVI 837; ? dashes about XVI 1317

rusty   *adj* old, worn out VII 914; of neglected appearance V 345; surly, uncivil XVI 758; (of style) old-fashioned, inelegant VII 777, XIX 56

ruthe   *see* rewth(e)

rutter   *n* gallant XVI 752; *rutters pl* XVI 1287

rutterkyn   *n* young gallant XVI 747

ruttyngly   *adv* in a manner befitting a gallant XVI 838

ryat, ryot(t)   *n* dissipation, extravagance III iv 4, XVIII 101, 387

rybawde   *see* rebawde

rybskyn   *n* leather apron worn by women while 'rubbing' flax XVII 299

rybybe   *n* properly a rebeck, a three-stringed bowed instrument, but at XVII 492 a contemptuous term for an old woman

rydlesse   *see* redlesse

rynde   *n* bark of a tree XXI 21

ryot(t)   *see* ryat

sacerdotes   *n pl* priests XIX 874

sacke   *n* class of white wines formerly imported from Spain and the Canaries XIX 541

sacre   *n* saker falcon (*falco sacer*) VII 561

sacrynge   *vbl n* consecration of the elements of the Eucharist; the elements of the Eucharist themselves XIX 1028

sad(d)(e)   *adj* serious V 420, VII 1097, IX 54; wise XIII v 117, XVI 16, XXI 1575, XXIV 390

sadly   *adv* seriously XXIV 359; wisely XVI 1940

sadnesse   *n* seriousness XVI 468, 2475

sallowe   *adj* of a brownish yellow colour XVII 321

salt   *n* salt-cellar XVII 247

sampler   *see* sa(u)mpler

sank   *n* blood XX 493, XXI 1463

sattiray   *n* satirist XXI 340

sa(u)mpler   *n* piece of canvas already embroidered or to be embroidered upon as an example of the sewer's skill VII 210, XXI 789

sautes   *see* sawte

saw(e)   *n* discourse XVI 71; body of knowledge XIX 732, XX 511; *sawes, sawis pl* sayings, maxims XX 1062, XXIV 122

sawe   *inf* sow, plant XVI 187

sawte   *n* assault, attack XVI 1581, XXI 1398; *sautes pl* XVI 2329

sayne   *past part* called; *sad sayne* truly called XIX 1230 scalles *n pl* scaly or scabby disease of the skin, especially of the scalp XXIII 219

scallyd *past part* scurvy, scabby XIII v 116

scape *inf* escape XVI 1776, XX Invective 5

scape thryfte *n phr* spendthrift prodigality XVI 761

scarce *adj* niggardly XX 5

scath *n* harm, damage VII 619

scole *n* teaching, a particular method or discipline XV 24; *scoles, scolys, skoles* VI 248, XVI 1216, 1264, XXIV 144, 298

scot *n* reckoning XVII 281

scrupulus *adj* hesitant, over-meticulous XXI 726

scruteny *n* vote in one's favour XXI 782

scut *n* hare XXI 632

scutis, scutus *n pl* French coins worth about 4 shillings XX 170, 171

season *n* time; *mene season* interim, meantime XVI 1688; ? relish, ? meaning XXI 108

seasyd *past part* put in legal possession of XVI 1536

sedeane *n* subdean, an ecclesiastical official in rank immediately below a dean and acting as his deputy VII 552

see-boorde *n phr* ? bulwark, ? side of a ship, ? plank to cover up the porthole V 112

sekernes, sykernesse *n* security, certainty XVI 2028, XXI 1597

sely *adj* simple, foolish XIX 77; defenceless XIX 389, 576

semblaunt *n* appearance, demeanour VII 936, XVI after 1206

semewe *n* seamew, the common gull VII 458

semynge *adj* fitting XVI 1546

semyth *3 s pres* is fitting XIII v 89

sence *imp* perfume with odours from burning incense XII 62

sene *adj* decorated, furnished XIX 955

sennet *n* sevennight, week XVII 394

sentence, sentens *n* meaning VI 227, 247, VII 807, XVIII 92, XXIII 519

sere *imp* burn, brand XVI 360

serpentins *n pl* cannons XIII iii 159

serviture *n* servant X 20

servyceabyll *adj* ready to do service XVIII 247

seryously *adv* one after another XXI 581

sew(e) *inf* make a petition III iii 37, VII 1075

seygnyoryte *n* authority XIX 925

seymy *adj* greasy XIII iii 169

seynty *n* saint XVII 582

shap *n* the female sexual organs XVII 507

shavynge *vbl n* stripping clean of possessions and money XX 100

shayle *inf* blunder, go wrong III iv 19, XVIII 83; *shayles 2 s pres* XIX 599; *shayle 2 pl pres* XXIV 172

shene *adj* beautiful XX 1004

shent *past part* disgraced, ruined XII 124

shone *n pl* shoes XVII 98

shorne *past part* tonsured XXIV 81

shot *n* ammunition; payment XX 127; *shote forthe his shot* utter his words XIX 751

shoure, shower   *n* copious falling of missiles or blows XII 133, XXIII 241
showell   *n* shovel XX 560
shrewde, shrewed   *adj* wicked XIX 358, XX 269
shrewdenes   *n* wickedness, evil XVI 735
shrewdly, shroudly, shurewlye   *adv* wickedly XIX 414, XX 621, XXI 620;
   harshly, severely XX 92; badly XVIII 445, XXI 1210; woundingly, sharply
   XVI 1277
shrewe, shrow   *1 s pres* curse XIII v 127, XXIII 292
shrewes   *n pl* rogues, villains V 525
shroudly   *see* shrewdly
shrow   *see* shrewe
shrowde   *n* concealment, cover XVI 532
shurewlye   *see* shrewdly
shurvy   *adj* ? squalid, ? scurfy XIII iii 132
shyderyd   *past part* splintered, shattered III iii 13
shyfte   *imp* make an effort to accomplish something V 99
shyfte   *n* means, way of proceeding XVI 1443
shyll   *inf* shell XX 111
shypborde   *n* side of the ship V 530
shyre   *adv* sheerly, utterly XVI 1303
shytell, shyttel-cocke   *n* shuttlecock XIX 1185, XX 354
sinodals, synodalles   *n pl* decisions made by ecclesiastical assemblies VI 132,
   XIX 716
sith(e), syth   *adv* since XIII i 1, XVI 282, 303, 1790, XXI 318
sittynge, syttynge   *adj* fitting, suitable XI 66, XII 174, XVI 176, XXI 77
skan   *inf* analyse the metrical composition of verse V 245
skelpe   *inf* strike XVI 2180, 2181
skewed   *adj* irregularly marked in colour XVII 142
skoles   *see* scole
skommer   *n* shallow ladle or sieve XVI 408
skyes   *n pl* clouds XXIV 165
skyll   *n* reason *it shall not (gretely) skyll* it will not (much) matter XVI 1596,
   2138, XX Invective 32
skyr(e)galyard, skyrgaliarde, squyergalyarde   *n* wild and dissolute young man
   XI 11, XII 101, XVIII 433, XXIII 168
skyt   *adj* hasty, unruly XII 101
slaiis   *n pl* weaver's reeds XXI 791
slaty   *adj* stony XVII 258
slo(o)   *inf* kill I 27, 35, 63, 154, XVI 2326, 2330
slufferd   *2 s past* gobbled up noisily XIII iii 32
slyd(d)er   *adj* slippery XVI 1816, XVII 258
slyght   *n* stratagem XVI 1308
smacke   *n* flavour XIX 540
smaragd   *n* emerald IV iii 21; *smaragdis pl* XXI 480
smat(t)er   *inf* talk ignorantly or superficially XVI 1257, XX 714, XXI 1194;
   smatters 3 s pres XIX 24; *smatterynge pres part* XVI 2095
smery   *adj* dirty, grimy VI 331, XIII v 58
snappar, snapper   *inf* stumble, trip III i 4, VI 142, XXIV 274
snuf   *inf* snuffle, draw air through the nostrils XXI 1472
snurre   *inf* snort XXI 1472
snyte   *n* snipe VII 412, XVI 1840

solacious, solacyous *adj* pleasant, delightful IV i heading, VII 791, XXI heading, 683

solacyusly *adv* for comfort XVI 2367

solas *n* pleasure, comfort XXI 655

solayne, solen, soleyne *adj* unsociable, morose, sullen III i 51, V 187, XVIII 304, 326

solfe *inf* sing a tune using the *sol-fa* syllables VII 415; *solfyth 3 s pres* III i 23

somdele *adv* somewhat X 16

sonde *n* that which is sent, usually a present or a message XVI 2360

soppy *inf* imbibe XVII 558

soppys *n pl* pieces of bread steeped in wine, ale or the like; things of small value XVI 2233

sorte *n* company or collection of people or things I 212, XVI 1373, XXI 868, XXIII 445, 475, XXIV 65

sorte *2 pl pres* arrange XIII iii 19; *sorted, sortyd past part* associated VII 1287, XXI 1280

sottes, sottys *n pl* stupid people XII 5, 30, XIX 564, XX 263, XXIV 65

sounde *n* swoon, faint VII 35

sowe *n* ingot, large oblong mass of solidified metal XVII 72

sowse *n* sauce XIII iii 32

sowter *n* shoemaker XVI 1825; *sowtters pl* III iii 87

space *n* interval between lines of a musical staff III i 22

sparred *past part* shut securely VI 91

sparys *2 s pres* refrain from VI 280

spattyl *n* spittle VII 358

spayre *n* opening or slit in a gown VII 345

speculacyon *n* contemplation, consideration or profound study of a subject XIX 970

spede *n* success, prosperity I 61, XXI 1596, XXIII 32, XXIV 386

spede, speed *inf* succeed, prosper XI 57, XII 154, XVI 1664; *sped(de) past part* skilled, successful III i 34, VII 754, XVI 556, 722, 1571, XXIV prose

spell *inf* expel, drive out XVI 619

spelles *3 s pres* talks XIX 414

spence *n* expense, expenditure XVI 2125; separate room in which victuals and liquor are kept XVII 598

spere *n* stripling XIII iii 41, XVI 937

splay *inf* display XIII ii 30

sprede *2 pl pres* unfold in display, as a peacock does its plumage III iv 13

spycke *n* piece of fat meat or bacon XVII 335

spyll *inf* destroy XVI 1478, 2139; *spylt past part* I 106

spyndels *n pl* rounded pieces of wood used for twisting wool and flax fibres into thread III i 34

spynke *n* finch, usually a chaffinch VII 407

squyergalyarde *see* skyr(e)galyard

stable *inf* establish, put on a firm basis XX 536

stale *n* bait, lure XVII 324

stalkynge *pres part* walking with stiff, high, measured steps VII 1244

stare *n* starling XVIII 207

stark(e) *adv* thoroughly, utterly I 50, XVIII 126, XXIV 56

starke *adj* clumsy, lacking suppleness XVI 481; thorough, complete XXIII 169; severe XVI 1208 start(e)   *inf* flinch, draw back XVI 768; spring open XVI 2229; *sterte 3 s past* moved suddenly V 502, XXI 282

state   *n* person of standing or importance XVI 945

stede   *n* place VII 1352, IX 3, XIII iii 69, XVI 680, XX 786, XXI 1345; *standeth in no stede* does no good XIX 35

steke   *n* stick XIII iii 79

stellyfye   *inf* set among the stars XXI 963

stepe   *adj* (of eyes) staring, brilliant VII 1014

sterte   *see* starte

sterve   *inf* destroy XXIII 251

stevyn   *n* voice XIII v 144

stewys, stuse   *n* brothel V 400, XVI 1225

stobburne   *adj* hard XVI 1494

stole   *n* stole, ecclesiastical vestment consisting of a narrow strip of cloth worn over the shoulders and hanging down in front XVI 359

stole   *n* stool XIX 30

stoppell   *n* stopper XVII 404, XIX 651

stormy   ? *adv* ? stormily XVI 2017

stoule   *n* frame on which to work embroidery or tapestry XXI 790

stounde, stownde   *n* short time, moment VII 34, XX 626, XXIII 344

stout(ty), stowte, stowty   *adj* strong XIII i 10, XXI 1509, XXIII 78; proud XVI 932

stow(e)   *excl* call used by falconers to bring down the hawk XVI 917, 967

stowre   *adj* obstinate, hardy XII 12

stowte   *adv* proudly XX 340; *see also* stout(ty)

stowty   *see* stout(ty)

straught   *adj* bereft of one's wits XV 27

straunge   *adj* distant, unencouraging XXI 444

strawry   *adj* ? like straw in colour or texture XVII 149

strayned   *3 s past* squeezed VII 1122

strayte   *adv* tightly XVI 852

strayte, streyte   *adv* straightaway XVI 399, 1592

streitly   *adv* tightly XX 1155

streynes   *n pl* lines, threads XVI 1553

streyte   *see* strayte

stubbed   *past part* short and thick, stumpy XVII 422

stuse   *see* stewys

stut   *inf* stutter XVII 339

stycke   *3 pl pres* hesitate XVI 2121

stynt   *inf* stop XVI 2188; *stynteth 3 s pres* XVI 367

styth   *n* anvil VI 332

suete   *n* suit, petition XIX 1031

suffrage   *n* intercessory prayers, assistance, support XVIII 195

sunnyng   *vbl n be out a sunnyng* be idle in the sunshine, like something of no worth or use XXI 201

supplement   *n* ? that which is provided to supply a deficiency, ? addition XXI 415

suppl(y)e   *inf* pray, beg XVI 797, XVIII 33; *supply imp* XVIII 359; *suppleyng pres part* XXI 1478; *supplyed 3 s past* XXI 49; *supplyed past part* ? entreated, ? provided XVI 1663

supportacyon   *n* assistance XXI 1577

supposicyon   *n* (in scholastic logic) something held to be true and taken as the basis for argument XVIII 197

supprisid, supprysed   *past part* taken unawares, overwhelmed I 145, XVI 1529, XXI 537

surcudant   *adj* arrogant XXIV prose

surfetous   *adj* immoderate IV iii 20

surffillyng   *vbl n* embroidering XXI 803

surfled   *past part* embroidered XIX 218

surmysed   *past part* alleged XIX 582, XXIV 209

surpluse   *n* remainder XVI 71

suspecte   *n* suspicion IV iii 20

sute   *n* train, suite XXIV 168

suter   *n* ? tenant with a duty to attend the court of his lord, ? one with a duty of service to his lord, ? petitioner XII 123; *suters pl* XI 31

suyng   *vbl n* petitioning XXI 253

swap   *3 pl pres* strike the ground noisily XVI 765

swart(e)   *adj* dark in colour VII 911, XVII 321, XXI 1399

swynged   *3 s past* drank violently XVII 568

swynkers   *n pl* workers XVII 115

syar, syer   *n* lord XVI 1473, XX 987

syb   *adj* related XVII 100

syde   *adj* ample V 440; extensive VII 475

syght   *inf* cite XII 53

syke   *adj* such XVI 1090, 1833

sykernesse   *see* sekernes

sylt   *n* mud XXI 23

symoniake   *n* one who practises simony XIX 296

symony   *n* act or practice of buying or selling ecclesiastical preferments, benefices or emoluments XIX 299

symper-the-cocket   *n* affected simpering manner XVII 55

synamum   *n* cinnamon XVIII 185

synodalles   *see* sinodals

syppet   *n* little sip XVII 367

syse   *n* measure XVI 845

syth   *see* sith(e)

syttynge   *see* sittynge

taber(te)s   *n pl* upper garments, sleeveless or with short sleeves, open at the sides XIX 316, XXI 395

tabull   *n* ? writing tablet, ? notebook VI 222; *tables* tablets VII 150

tacke   *n holde . . . tacke* keep at bay, be a match for XVI 2084

talwood   *n* wood for fuel, cut to a prescribed length XX 82

tangyd   *past part* given point XVI 2234

tante   *inf* taunt, quarrel verbally XIII ii 37

tappett   *n* wall hanging, table-cover, carpet XIII v 75, XVI 1233; *tappettis pl* XXI 474, 787

tappyster   *n* woman who drew ale to be served in a public house XVI 420

tarsell gentyll   *n phr* male peregrine falcon VII 558

taumpinnis   *n pl* disk-shaped or cylindrical pieces of wood made to fit the bore of muzzle-loading guns, rammed between the charge and the missile to act as a wad XXI 642 tavellis, tavellys   *n pl* bobbins on which thread was wound III i 34, XXI 791

tawle   *adj* brave, bold XVI 821

tayle   *n* tally XVII 616

tayle, tayll   *n* female sexual organs V 369, XVI 1346

teder   *adj* the other (of two) V 484

te(e)ne   *n* anger I 24, VII 742

tegges, teggys   *n pl* yearling sheep; but at XIII i 31 and XVII 151 applied contemptuously to women

tele   *n* teal (*Anas crecca*), a small member of the duck family VII 454

tende   *inf* attend XVI 790, 1018

tene   *see* te(e)ne

tenter-hokys   *n pl* hooks or bent nails by which cloth is fixed to the wooden frame or 'tenter' on which it is stretched after milling XVI 1001

terestre   *adj* earthly XVI 2559

termes, termys   *n pl* manner of expressing oneself, way of speaking VII 776, 801, XIII iii 96

tetrycall   *adj* harsh, bitter XXIV prose

tetter   *n* disease of the skin, eczema XVI 543

tewly sylk   *n phr* dark red silk XXI 798

thee   *inf* prosper XVI 635, 862; *3 s pres subj* XVI 515

theke   *1 s pres* cover a roof XVI 1026

theologisacion   *n* the act of theologizing XXIV prose

thewde   *adj* educated in manners and morals XIII v 147, XX 331

thought   *n* anxiety II 26, XVI 287, 1969

thoughtfull   *adj* anxious IV iii 10, XVI 2050

threstyl   *n* throstle, song-thrush VII 460

throte bole   *n phr* protuberance of the throat, Adam's apple XVI 2315

throw   *n* instant, moment XIII v 122

thrust   *n* thirst XVII 303

thurifycation   *n* burning of incense VII 522

thwartid   *3 s past* opposed, contradicted XXI 1039; *thwartyng pres part* XX 200

timorous   *adj* terrifying, terrible XXI 260

tirikkis, tirykis   *n pl* theorics; theoretical statements or notions XVIII 137; mechanical device theoretically representing or explaining astronomical phenomena XXI 1517

titivyllis, tytyvylles   *n pl* tattlers, chatterers XIX 416, XXI 642

to-fret   *past part* consumed, eaten away XXI 1450

toies, toyes   *n pl* tricks, antics XV 33, XVI 1137

token   *n* female sexual organs XVII 497

told(e)   *past part* valued VII 785; calculated XV 8

tole   *n* pen XIII iii 118

tollage   *n* exaction of tolls, levies, impositions XIX 362

tolman   *n* penman, writer XIV 40

to-mangle   *inf* break into pieces XIX 333

to-myryd   *adj* very befouled XIII ii 12

tonge   *n* piece, perhaps the uvula XVI 2314

tonnell   *n* cask or barrel for ale or wine XVII 403

tonnysh   *adj* corpulent, enormously fat XVII 99

to(o)te   *inf* peer, peep, pry VII 411, 1146, XVIII 10; *toteth 3 s pres* VII 422

to to   *adv* overmuch XVI 872

tot quot *n phr* licence to hold innumerable benefices XX 128; *tot quottes pl* XIX 563

totynge *vbl n* prying XIX 1074

touche *inf* depict, illustrate V 11; *towchid, towchyd past part* XXI 143, 592, 1161

towchis *n pl* qualities XXI 764

towe *n* fibre of flax prepared for spinning XVII 287

toyle *n* net set so as to enclose a space into which game is driven XXIII 269

trace *n* ? part of the harness of a draught animal XXIII 913; *out of trace* disordered XVI 913

trace *inf* make one's way, walk XVI 692; *trasid past part* ornamented XXI 395

tradiccyon *n* ? betrayal IV ii 10

tramynge *vbl n* trifling efforts XVI 2234

trasid *see* trace

tratlande, tratlyng *adj* prattling XII 6, XXIII title

tratlers *n pl* tattlers, idle talkers XV 63

tratlynge *vbl n* idle talk XII 2

tratyse *n* treatise XXI 1228

travarse *n* dispute, opposition XX 388

traves *n* screen, curtain V 58

trayne *n* deceit, trickery I 86, XX 363; trap, bait XXIII 369

traytory, treytory *n* treachery I 151, XXIII 100

tre(a)de *inf* (of birds) tread, copulate VII 512, 600

trentale, trentall *n* set of thirty requiem masses VIII heading, 70

trete *inf* negotiate XVIII 424; deal with, write about XX 1087, XXIV 281; *trete 3 pl pres* XVIII 137

treytory *see* traytory

tried, tryde *past part* demonstrated XX 707; proved XVI 2192; tested XVI 2449, XX 1013

trivials *n pl* subjects belonging to the *trivium* (i.e. grammar, rhetoric, logic) XX 515

trold *past part* rolled together XVIII 168

trompe *see* trumpythe

trowe *inf* think, believe, consider XXIII 25; *trowe(e) 1 s pres* V 313, VII 156, XIII v 154, XVI 74, 309, 589, XX 953, XXIV 285; *trowed 3 s past* V 72; *trowyd 2 pl past* XII 107

trowle *n* trull, prostitute XIII v 36

trumpet *n* trumpeter XXI 235

trumpythe *3 s pres* ? makes a trumpeting sound, ? wins with a trump at cards XVIII 432; *trompe imp* sound trumpets XX 205

trusse *inf* go packing, be gone XVI 1774; *trussed* dressed compactly V 505; compactly framed V 410

tryalytes *n pl* holding of three ecclesiastical benefices at once XIX 562

trybyll *n* treble, the highest part of a harmonized musical composition III i 24

trym *adj* finely dressed XIX 641

trymme *inf* ? have sexual intercourse with XVI 1346; *trym 1 s pres* arrange, prepare XXIII 355; *trymmyth 3 s pres* elaborates III i 26

trym-tram *n phr* trifling ornament of dress XVII 76; trifle, worthless thing XVIII 128

trymynge *vbl n* trifling efforts XVI 2234

trysyd *past part* snatched, carried off XIII v 36

tumrell *n* cart so constructed that its body tilts backwards to empty out its load; often a dung-cart XIII v 93

tunnyng(e) *vbl n* storing of liquor in barrels XVII title, 130

turkis *n pl* turquoises XXI 466

turney *inf* fight in a tournament XIII ii 37; *tyrnyd 3 s past* XIII i 4

twybyll *n* axe with two cutting edges XIII iii 72

twynk(l)yng *pres part* tinkling XIX 491, XXI 687

tyd *n* short while XIII v 162; *tydes pl* times VII 507

tyned *adj* having sharp points XVI 727

typpet *n* long, narrow piece of cloth, worn as a scarf or part of the headdress; fur or woollen garment covering the shoulders XVII 366

tyrly tyrlowe *n phr* female sexual organs XIX 949

tyrnyd *see* turney

tyryd *3 s past* (of birds of prey) tore with the beak VI 60

tyse *inf* entice XXIV 132

tysyke *n* phthisic, phthisis; wasting disease, usually pulmonary consumption XVI 555

tytmose *n* tit; bird of the family *Paridae* VII 458

tytters *n pl* ? rags XVII 126

tytyvylles *see* titivyllis

umanyte *n* polite literature XXI 818

umblis *n pl* numbles; certain of the edible inward parts of a deer XXI 1240

umwhyle *adv* sometimes XIII ii 11

unassured *past part* not certain or sure XXIV 93

unbrased *past part* with the fastenings of clothes undone XVII 134, 320

unbrent *past part* unburnt XXIV 22

uncouthes *n pl* strange things XIX 1052

undermynde *inf* undermine XX 437

underset *past part* propped up XVI 454

unfayned *adv* sincerely XVIII 255, XX 1209

unhap(pe)ly *adv* unfortunately, disastrously XVI 6, XXIII 126, XXIV 405

unhappy *adj* mischievous, troublesome XV 55, XVI 1374, 2337

unkindly *adv* unnaturally I 47

unlased, unlast *past part* with the fastenings of clothes undone XVII 133, 320

unlust *n* repulsiveness XVII 148

unlusty *adj* repulsive VII 915

unlykynge *adj* in poor condition, unpleasant XVI 1958

unmete *adj* unsuitable XX 33; unseemly XXIV 49

unneth *adv* scarcely, barely V 275, VII 37, 1124, XIX 80

unpullyshyt *adj* unpolished, unadorned I 127

unsowndy *adj* unhealthy, diseased XVII 35

untayde *past part* untied, loose XV 37

unthriftes *n pl* prodigals XV 26

untrust *past part* unbound, loose XVII 147

untwynde *3 s past* destroyed VII 284; *past part* XIX 662, XXI 1445

urcheons *n pl* hedgehogs XX 166

ure *n* fortune, luck XIX 1001

ured, uryd *past part* ? disposed, ? fortuned, ? accustomed XVI 6, XXIII 126, XXIV 95, 405 utter   *adv* out of the way, further off XVI 753, XVII 535

vagys   *n pl* pranks, tricks XVI 1942
vale   *inf* lower XV 32
varry   *inf* quarrel, contend XXIII 341
vaunte-parler   *n phr* ? boaster XVIII 433
vawte   *n* vault XXI 476
vayleth   *3 s pres* is of value, succeeds XX 104
velyarde   *n* old man, dotard XVI 1878
ventayles   *n pl* properly the whole movable part of a helmet, but at XIX 398
   the starched linen frame of a nun's headdress
verduris   *n pl* shades of green XXI 776
vergesse   *n* verjuice; the acid juice of green or unripe grapes, crab apples or
   other sour fruit XVI 1756
versynge boxe   *n phr* ? dicing box V 232
vertibilite   *n* inconstancy XV 42
vertue   *n* strengthening, sustaining or healing properties XVII 451
vice   *n* ? voice I 80
vovell   *n* astronomical instrument, consisting of one or more movable circles
   surrounded by other graduated or figured circles, used to ascertain the rising
   and setting of the sun and moon, the state of the tides and so on XVIII 135,
   XXI 1517
voyde   *inf* avoid, evade XVI 297
vyse, wyse   *1 s pres* advise XIII iii 121, XXIV 297
vyser   *n* fool's mask 1177

wachyng   *see* wa(t)chyng(e)
wake   *inf (trans)* stir up, arouse VII 668; *(intrans)* sit up late for pleasure or
   revelry V 382
walter   *inf* totter, tumble XVI 1910
wambleth   *3 s pres* (of the stomach) is afflicted with nausea XVI 1617
wamblynge   *vbl n* feeling of nausea XVI 1620
wane   *adj* lacking, deficient XX 920
wanhope   *n* despair XVI 2337, 2340
wan(ne)   *adj* dark in colour IV i 15, VII 61, XX 890, XXI 1399
warde   *n* ? wardrobe XIII iii 53
warely   *adv* ? in a warlike manner, ? watchfully XIX 331
warke   *n* account VII 642; business XVI 483; trouble XVI 361, 1094
warke   *inf* be in a state of agitation XVI 1563; *3 pl pres* perform VII 799
warne   *inf* prevent, restrain XVI 1809
warre   *comp adj* worse XVI 914
wary   *inf* fight XIII iii 75; defend by force XIX 154
wary   *inf* curse XVI 2238
wa(t)chyng(e)   *vbl n* staying awake, revelling at night V 352, XVIII 512
water-lag   *n phr* water-lugger, one who sold water from house to house; at
   XVIII 86 a term of abuse
wather-hen   *n phr* moorhen VII 453
wawes   *n pl* waves XIX 1253
wed   *n to wed* pawned, pledged XVI 2167
wedge   *n* tapering metal tool for splitting wood XVII 294
wel(e)away(e)   *excl* alas! XI 20, XXIV 78
weltyth   *3 s pres* sets in a confused state, overturns XVI 1363

wene *inf* think, believe XIX 1121; *1 s pres* V 303, 357, VII 637; *2 pl pres* XVI 259; *wende 1 s past* V 320

weryed *past part* ? satiated, ? choked XVI 1568

werynge *vbl n* taste XIX 210

wesa(u)nt *n* throat, gullet XVII 517, XIX 1154

wete, wote, wyt *inf* know, be aware of V 466, VII 198, XVI 22, 1654; *wote 1 s pres* V 349, XIII v 143, XVI 50, 247, 1033; *wotest 2 s pres* XVI 1092; *wot(e), wottyth 3 s pres* VII 168, XIX 17, 232; *wot(t)e 2 pl pres* XV 12, XXIV 46; *wotteth 3 pl pres* XIX 234; *wist, wyste 1 s past* XV 9, XVI 1029; *wyst 3 s past* III i 33

wetewoldis *n pl* men who are aware of and complaisant about the infidelity of their wives XXI 187

wetynge *vbl n* knowledge, information V 278

wharrowe *n* small flywheel or pulley on the spindle of a spinning wheel XVII 298

wheled *past part* marked with ridge-like injuries XX 1185

whett *imp* sharpen XIX 476

whey-wormed *adj* covered with pimples from which a whey-like substance exudes XVII 553

whipling *vbl n* ? piping noise, ? feeble whistling XX 350

whitte, whyt(te) *n* small amount, jot XVI 1006, XIX 516, XX 1017, XXI 1099

whym-wham *n phr* trifling ornament of dress XVII 75

whynarde *n* short sword V 363

whynnymeg *n* ? instant XVIII 71

whypslovens *n* ? slovenly people who deserve whipping XIII ii 38

whyste *adj* hushed XXI 267

whytyng, wyteyng *n* properly a small white fish XIII iii 116; but at XVII 223 a term of endearment

widders *n pl* withers, the highest point (between the shoulder blades) of the back of a horse IV ii 25

wins, wynche *inf* kick skittishly V 411, XIII ii 4, XVI 2023, XIX 181; *wynsyth 3 s pres* IV ii 22; *wynshed 3 s past* XXI 1201

wirry, wyrry *inf* seize by the throat, bite IX 26, XX 299

wist *see* wete

withholde *inf* guard XV 6; *withhold(e) past part* guarded by, in the charge of VII 1302, XXI 1295

withsay *inf* contradict, oppose XVIII 402

wod(d)e, wo(o)d(e) *adj* fierce, turbulent, mad I 100, VII 1157, 1335, XVI 2561, XIX 1253, XX 578, XXI 1328

woke *n* week XVI 1682

wonders *adj* wondrous XVI 89

wonne *inf* live, dwell XVI 900, 1311; *wonneth, wonnys 3 s pres* XVI 22, 624; *wonne 1 pl pres* XVI 624; *wonnynge pres part* XIX 141

wonnynge *vbl n* house, dwelling XVII 94

wo(o)d(e) *see* wod(d)e

worde *n* world XXI 462

wordly *adj* worldly XXI 486, 716

worldly *adv* publicly XXIV 62

worrowyd *3 s past* bit VII 29

wortes *n pl* vegetables XVI 1128

worth   *n in worth* at its true value III i 68; in good part VII 817, XVI 1439
worthe   *3 s pres subj wo worthe the* may evil come to you XVI 2103
wose   *n* mud, ooze XXI 23
wot(e), wotest, wot(t)e, wotteth   *see* wete
wrake   *n* disaster, ruin XVI 2086
wrastynge   *adj* contentious, arbitrary XVI 1608
wraw   *adj* angry XIII ii 40
wreke   *2 pl pres* exercise, given vent to XIX 1091; *wroken past part* revenged
   XVII 498, XIX 598; ? satiated, ? gratified XVI 1566
wrench(e)   *n* quick pull or jerk XX 321; trickery IV ii 25; *wrenchis pl* tricks
   XXI 1207
wrest   *inf* contend III i 47; tune by twisting the pins of a musical instrument
   XIX 490; *wrestyd past part* afflicted XVI 2274
wretchokes   *n pl* puny birds, the smallest of the brood XVII 465
wringe, wrynge   *inf* struggle violently I 82, XVI 2196; *wryngeth 3 s pres* afflict,
   hurt XVI 2047, XX 321; *wronge past part* pained VII 919
wroken   *see* wreke
wrote   *inf* uproot by turning over the soil IX 27; *wrotes 3 pl pres* XV 4
wroth(e)   *adj* angry, offended XVI 606, 1748, XX 1132
wrothsome   *adj* bad tempered XVI 2293
wrygges   *3 s pres* wags, wriggles XVII 177
wrythen   *past part* twisted, circled XVII 73
wrythyng   *vbl n* twisting, turning XVI 136
wrythynge   *adj* capricious XVI 1608
wygges   *3 s pres* moves from side to side, wiggles XVII 137
wyght   *n* creature, man (usually derogatory) XXIII 232
wyl   *adv* well XIII v 97
wylles   *n pl* sexual desires VII 681
wymble   *n* gimlet, a sort of boring tool XVII 526
wynche, wynshed, wynsyth   *see* wins
wynde   *n* breath XVI 1403
wyrry   *see* wirry
wyst(e)   *see* wete
wyte   *inf* blame XVI 2304
wyteyng   *see* whytyng

xall   *1 s pres* shall XIII v 158, 180; *xalte 2 s pres* XIII v 17; *xall 3 s pres* XIII
   iii 122, 139, 176, v 22; *xulde 1 s past* XIII iii 34, v 154, 166; *xulddst, xuldyst*
   2 s past XIII iii 175, 180; *xulde 2 pl past* XIII iii 119, v 57
yane   *inf* yawn XVII 331
yarke   *inf* lash XVI 484
yawde   *past part* hewed, cut down XIX 1204
ydder   *n* udder XVI 1814
yede   *3 s past* went VI 55
yerarchy   *see* ierarchy
yerne   *inf* (of hounds) give tongue XXI 1409
ylke   *adj* each XXIII 155
ylle hayle   *n phr* misfortune XVI 2248
yonkerkyns   *n pl* young men XXIV prose
ypocras, ypocrus   *n* cordial drink made of wine and spices XIX 456, XX 218